CHINA TODAY: AVIATION INDUSTRY

The China Aviation Industry Press

1989, Beijing

China Today :   Aviation Industry
English Edition

Editorial Board

Published by China Aviation Industry Press
Printed by Beijing Xinhua Printing House

CONTENTS

Part Five

Preface

More than thirty years have passed since the Chinese socialist revolution and socialist construction started. Great changes have taken place in all aspects and achievements in every field have attracted worldwide attention in these thirty and more years. "China Today", a series of books, will faithfully record this period of history and sum up the experience in each field, not only reflecting the development and progress since the founding of the People's Republic of China but also depicting failures and setbacks in our progress. This will undoubtedly benefits our on—going construction of socialist material and spiritual civilization. They will help the world to get an all round understanding of China. They will also be a precious wealth to our posterity. That is why I am so pleased that the book of "China Today: Aviation Industry", one of the series of books of "China Today" is published.

To set up a strong aviation industry is a long cherished wish by the Chinese people of different nationalities. Early in this century, at the dawn of man's flight, quite a number of Chinese with high ideals studied abroad, seeking scientific truth and advanced technology, including the science of flying as well as aircraft design and manufacturing in the hope that they could return home and serve their country in strengthening its defence and resisting foreign aggression and save the nation from peril. But in a semi—feudal, semi—colonial country like old China, these beautiful aspirations were only dreams. A strong aviation industry can only be materialized when the people come to power and become the masters of their own fates. Such time had at last come. Soon after the founding of the People's Republic of China, the Chinese Communist Party and the people's government put the problem of creating a strong aviation industry atop of its agenda. Chairman Mao Zedong and Premier Zhou Enlai were deeply concerned with and personally involved in the construction of the aviation industry. The guiding principle for aircraft industry development, which was "from repair to copy production and then from copy production to design and manufacturing", was established by the Premier himself. Historical practice has proved that the guiding principle was correct. It closely combined scientific methodology with revolutionary spirit, learning foreign advanced technology with adhering to self—reliance. Under this guiding principle, the aviation industry had grown from small to large, from low level to higher level. The thirty and more years had seen one after another major achievements in the Chinese aviation industry.

In its early days, the People's Republic had a very poor foundation to start with. There was the Korean War externally and everything to do internally. Under the extremely difficult financial situation, the Party and the Government resolutely concentrated its man—power and financial resources on aviation industry which had been given the highest priority. Two strategic steps were taken: to train technical personnel from the beginning and to base the aviation industry on domestic materials, which was not an easy task. I was working at that time with the State Council and the State Economic Commission and was deeply aware that the technically complicated aviation industry must be based on the development of the national economy and must be strongly supported by basic industries, so that it could be well established and vigorously develop. The State Economic Commission made great efforts to organize and coordinate the support to the aviation industry by basic industries. Especially in the early 1960s, when the Soviet Union broke off the contract and withdrew its experts, special measures were taken in time to solve the problem of domestic material supply. These policies and measures taken by the Party's Central Committee and the State Council turned out a complete success. The Chinese aviation industry developed quickly into a burgeoning industry of considerable scale. It produced batches of aircraft to arm the Chinese Air Force and Navy and to equip the Chinese airlines. It also boosted the technical progress of the Chinese raw and processed material industry and machine building, and provided favourable conditions for the start of the Chinese rocket and missile industry.

The Chinese aviation industry has entered into a new stage of development after more than thirty years of unremitting efforts, especially after the Third Plenary Session of the Eleventh Central Committee of the Communist Party of China, when policies of bringing order out of chaos, rectification, reform and opening to the world were adopted. The Chinese aviation industry has become an industrial system with a relatively complete range of categories and a more solid foundation. China is a large country with a vast territory. Its socialist modernization construction, centred around economic construction is vigorously developing. The State and the society have an urgent demand for civil aircraft. Civil aviation is tending to big increase. The development of civil aircraft has now been emphasized by the State and positive policy measures have been taken accordingly. It is expected that the Chinese aviation industry will in the near future produce one after another good civil aircraft to serve the country's socialist modernization construction and its international exchanges while military aircraft is being developed. The path of the Chinese aviation industry in more than thirty years was not all smooth sailing. It was tortuous rather. This part of the history needs to be systematically studied and summed up. I should say that with its detailed faithful record, "China Today: Aviation Industry" has done something in this respect. Predicting the future by reviewing the past, we sum up our past to reveal and usher in our future. We cherish what we have achieved and what we have learned from our success. We will not forget our lessons and failures and we will not neglect our shortness and existing problems. In the new era of building socialism with Chinese characteristics, all comrades in aviation industry should stand on a higher plane and see further ahead. We have to face the world. We have to face the future. We must have faith in and rely on our own strength, conscientiously learn from foreign experience and their advanced technology, continuously carry on the spirit of plain living and hard struggle, quietly put our shoulders to the wheel and keep forging ahead to make the aviation industry contribute more to China's modernization construction.

Bo Yibo

September 15, 1987

Introduction

1. Aviation and Aviation Industry

Aviation is an art or practice of operating vehicles by human being to fly in the atmosphere of the earth. The general term used to describe these vehicles is aircraft. Those which are lifted by air static buoyancy, such as the balloons and airships, are deemed as lighter−than−air aircraft, whereas those which are lifted by aerodynamic force, for example, airplanes, helicopters and gliders, are regarded as heavier−than−air aircraft, and it is the latter ones that are widely used and fast developed in our days.

China is a country with an ancient civilization in the world. In their struggle against nature, the ancient Chinese people had dreams of flying in the sky and walking on the clouds and with wind, which formed all kinds of fairy tales of flying men, passing from generation to generation. Chinese classics "Era of Kings and Emperors" and "Canon of Mountains and Sea" recorded the stories of flying carts. Lie Zi walking with wind was written in "Happy Excursions−Zhuang Zi" and the story of Chang'e flying to the moon in "Huai Nan Zi" and "Records of Spirits". All of these classics depicted dreams of the ancient Chinese people to fly in the sky.

The attempt at flying vehicles by the Chinese people has a long history. It could be traced back to the ancient times. The classic "Lu Wen − Mo Zi" told us that during the "Spring and Autumn period" (770−−476 B.C.) the famous craftman Gong Shuban made a magpie from bamboo and wood and made it fly to sky. Classic "Wai Chu Zuo Shang − Han Fei Zi" wrote about a flying wooden eagle made by Mo Di, founder of Mohism (468−−376 B.C.). The famous scientist of Eastern Han dynasty, Zhang Heng (A.D. 78−−139) made a wooden bird which could fly several kilometers according to the classic "History of the Later Han Dynasty −Zhang Heng Biograghy". All the above mentioned tales were about making flying vehicles after flying birds. The classic "History of Han Dynasty − Wang Mang Biography" recorded that in the sixth year of Tian Feng period of New Dynasty (A.D. 19) a man was witnessed flying dozens of meters with two huge bird wings and feathers all over his body, even on his head. That was believed the earliest recorded flying and gliding experiment by physical force of human being. Kite, the earliest practical flying apparatus in the world, was invented in China two thousand years ago. Kites once used by Han Xin during the war of Gaixia between states Chu and Han in 202 B.C., were recorded in "Xi Deng Yao Wen" written by Zhaoxin of Tang dynasty. In the Southern and Northern Dynasties (A.D. 420−−589) kites were already used for military liaison purpose. The "Records of the Chen Dynasty—History as a Mirror" written by Si Maguang of the Song dynasty said that in the tenth year of Tian Bao period, Northen Qi Dynasty (A.D. 559), a man glided downwards from a high place for a certain distance by a kite. The appearance of kite reflected the idea that things could be lifted off the ground by aerodynamic force, which was a leap in practicing and understanding of the aerodynamic principles. Meanwhile it also reflected that apart from the flying method of ornithopters like birds and insects with movable wings the flying could also be realized with fixed wings which could produce both the pulling force and the lift. This understanding was a great enlightenment to the later invention of the aircraft. Lots of aviation forerunners in the world learned a great deal from the kite during the course of exploring aircraft invention. In the classic "Master who Embraces Simplicity — Neipian — Zayin" written by Ge Hong of Eastern Jin dynasty (A.D. 284—364) the author stated that the flying birds were supported by ascending air, which was an important discovery of the flight principle of birds. During the Five dynasties (A.D. 907—960) some one made a lantern which was supported by a bamboo frame and covered by paper with pine resin burning in the bottom tray. It served as a military signal at night when it was lifted into the air. This kind of pine—resin lantern, also called Kong Ming Lantern, was a kind of primitive hot—air balloon. The principle of trotting horse lamp at that time was basically the same as that of the present day gas turbine. The bamboo dragon—fly invented by the ancient Chinese could be lifted by the horizontal spinning of a twisted bamboo strip, realizing the earliest mechanical flying. This bamboo dragon—fly was called "Chinese Gyro" by European scholars then and became the origin of the present day lifting propeller. These brilliant achievements in aviation of the ancient Chinese together with the inventions in aviation of other ancient civilized countries had great influence and revelation to the later generations in their study and invention of aircraft.

The modern aviation started after the Industrial Revolution of the western countries in the 18th century. In 1783, the hot—air and hydrogen balloons were lifted into the air in France one after another. In 1852, the first powered flight by man was realized with an airship which was powered by a steam engine in France. In 1903, the beginning of the 20th century, the Wright brothers (Wilbur Wright and Orville Wright), two Americans, built an aircraft with a piston engine and a propeller. It successfully made the first continuous, powered, controlled and manned flight in history. This was an epoch—making creation and opened a new era in aviation history.

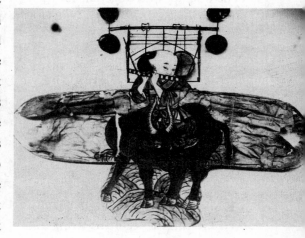

Fig. 1 A Chinese kite

Soon after the appearance of the aircraft, all governments and people in the world paid great attention to it due to its broad potential applications. The two World Wars in the 20th century and the social requirement became the great incentive to the development of aviation. The fast development of science and technology and social productivity in the 20th century provided a good foundation to the development of aviation. During the First World War, to defeat their enemy, countries involved in the War produced reconnaissance aircraft, pursuit aircraft, (later called fighter plane or intercepter plane) bomber and attack aircraft one after another. More and more aircraft had been put into the War. Their total reached more than 180,000 planes. Great progress had been made in aircraft structure and power plant and the aircraft design, manufacture and flight had been clearly divided. Aviation industry which undertook the development and manufacture of aircraft experienced fast development and became a large scale and newly developed industry. Aviation then reached the stage far beyond the scope of individual activity, and came into the shape of an organized collective cause. Some countries established aviation science and research institutes in succession. The close combination of theoretic study with design and manufacture helped upgrade the aircraft with each passing day. During the 1920s and 1930s, aircraft changed from biplane to monoplane, from wooden structure to metal structure, from open cockpit to enclosed cockpit and from fixed landing gears to retractable landing gears. The aircraft ceiling had increased twice and speed 2 to 4 times, while engine power 5 times. Right after the First World War, civil aviation was flourishing. The aviation industry was pushed into a new phase of its development by the Second World War. The Air Force became an important armed Service with its great influence to the overall situation of the War. The total number of aircraft put into the War reached an enormous scale. Aircraft performance was greatly improved, hence the heavy and long range bombers like "Air Fortress" and "Super Air Fortress" came into being. The total production of aircraft in all countries in 1944 was up to 230,000, which exceeded the sum of aircraft production of all countries during the First World War. Aviation industry became a great industry and aeronautical science and technology made a great progress. After the Second World War the initial achievements in jet technology, supersonic aerodynamics, structural mechanics, thermodynamics and material science, etc., occurred during the War were further improved and utilized. Piston engines were gradually replaced by jet engines and the aircraft broke through the "Sound Barrier" and "Thermal Barrier", flying speed reached 2 to 3 times of the sound speed, which meant that mankind had entered the supersonic jet flying era. With the worldwide revolution in new technology and the utilization of microelectronic technology, computer, new material, new process method and new aviation scientific and research achievements, the aircraft had changed a great deal. Not only the traditional military aircraft and helicopters of all kinds have been improved in their capabilities of communication, navigation, active control, electronic countermeasure, manoeuvrability, target acquisition, identification and tracking, automatic fire control and all weather operation, but also appeared many kinds of special mission aircraft like airborne warning aircraft, electronic countermeasure aircraft and RPV, as well as various missiles which can be carried by aircraft to attack targets. At the same time the civil aircraft had been greatly improved in its safety, comfort and cost effectiveness. A variety of wide body inter—continental jet airliners and cargo planes had been produced. The ancient Chinese people once dreamed: "At daybreak from the land of Plane — trees grey, I came to Paradise ere close of Day" and wished to fly several thousand kilometers in a day. Now the speed of aircraft is even far beyond that wonderful imagination and the immense space above the earth has been magically shortened.

Experience of more than eighty years development reveals the fact that the aviation industry is a typically knowledge intensive and technology intensive industry, which unceasingly applies the achievements of basic sciences of aerodynamics, aerothermal mechanics, structural mechanics, aeroelasticity and technological scientific achievements of metallurgy, polymer chemistry, electronics, jet propulsion, automatic control and processing technology. Aviation industry also needs support from lots of other industries concerned like metallurgy, chemistry, petroleum, machinery, electronic, textile and construction material. The aero product—aircraft, therefore, is the crystalization of modern science and technology and is widely regarded as "the flower of industry", which in turn pushes forward all relevant science and industries.

Nowadays, the development speed of aviation and the advancement of aircraft have become an important mark for judging a country's national defence capability and economic strength. In modern three dimensional wars, the military aircraft not only undertake important missions of obtainning air superiority, ground attack, interdiction of battle field and air transportation, but also surprise attack before break out of a war. Aircraft, therefore, is an important factor in deciding progress and termination of wars. Strategically, long range bombers carrying nuclear bombs together with nuclear missiles form the nuclear deterrent power, which is an important means to threaten peace and to stop wars as well. In the field of civil aviation aircraft provides human society with a fast, economic, safe and comfortable transportation means, which facilitates people's living, improves working efficiency of the whole society, quickens the development of backward areas and expands the exchange of visits of countries all over the world. In the field of industrial and agricultural production, aircraft provides services of various kinds and is widely used for geographical survey, natural resources investigation, earth measuring, land planning, off—shore oil exploration, aerial hoisting, ambulance and liaison, seeds sowing and fertilizer applying, weeding and insect killing, forest fire prevention and environment protection, which creates far reaching influence to the revolution of traditional production method, while in the economy and trade fields, aircraft is a product of high value and consumes relatively less material and energy. The industrially developed countries, therefore, always consider aircraft as an important product for exportation. The aviation industry is regarded as a strategic and high technology industry and plays an important role in the national defence and economy and every industrially developed country and some developing countries pay great attention to its development. The importance of aviation industry is also emphasized in the Chinese socialist modernization. The Chinese aviation industry is striving to provide the best products and technology for the modernizations of industry, agriculture, national defence and science and technology.

2. Aircraft Repair and Manufacture in Old China

The present day aviation in China started at the end of Qing dynasty. After the Opium War in 1840, China was open to foreign countries of the West, which brought in modern aviation knowledge as well. There were lots of articles and pictures introducing hydrogen balloons, airships and aircraft since the second half of the 19th century to the beginning of the 20th century. In 1887, Hua Hengfang, a mathematical lecturer of Tianjin Army School, designed and manufactured a balloon with 1.66 meters diameter. The balloon was filled with self–made hydrogen and successfully flew into the air. This was the first hydrogen balloon made in China. The Qing government appointed Liu Zuocheng and Li Baojun, both of whom returned from Japan, to set up a factory in Nanyuan, southern suburb of Beijing to manufacture aircraft in 1910. The first aircraft was witnessed in April of the following year, but was crashed during a flight test due to engine failure. This was the very beginning of modern aircraft manufacture in China.

In the revolutionary cause of overthrowing the Qing dynasty, Dr. Sun Yatsen clearly saw that the aircraft would become a new type of military weapon and be greatly helpful to the nation's revolution. He, therefore, called overseas Chinese youths to learn skills of flying and technologies of manufacturing, and to organize companies for manufacturing aircraft in order to establish Chinese aircraft manufacturing industry after the success of the revolution. He later even put forward the idea of "saving the nation with aviation". Soon after the success of the Revolution in 1911, the first Air Force of the revolutionary military government was established and lots of people who devoted their lives to aviation wasted no time in seizing the opportunity to work for the motherland. Feng Ru, a patriotic overseas Chinese and a noted aircraft designer and flyer at the beginning of this century, successfully designed and manufactured aircraft by himself in the United States. He and his assistant came back to China in 1911 with two aircraft he made and he was appointed the Air Force leader of Guangdong military government. Unfortunately he died in 1912 in an air crash and was buried in Huanghuagang Martyrs' Graves. In remembering him the Nationalist government erected a monument with a written inscription honouring him as "China's great pioneer in aviation". Tan Gen who lived in the United States was one of the earliest designers and manufacturers of water–based airplanes in the world. He produced a ship–body type water–based airplane in 1910 and won the first prize in the international aircraft competition held in Chicago. This water–based airplane also created world flying altitude record of water–based airplanes in the Philippines. He was then invited to come back to China in 1915 to set up Guangdong Aviation School. Yang Xianyi, who joined the Chinese Revolutionary League in his youth and graduated from an aviation college in the United States. He established an aircraft company himself. Dr. Sun Yatsen Called him back to China in 1918 to take part in the war against the warlords. He was appointed Chief of the relief air force of Guangdong army to Fujian province, and later appointed Director of Aviation Bureau of Guangdong Revolutionary Government and Director of aircraft repair factory in 1922. Under his supervision a two-seater biplane reconnaissance-trainer was produced in 1923 and was named "Rosamonde" (after the student name of Song Qingling) by Dr. Sun Yatsen. Huang Guangrei successfully flew the aircraft with Song Qingling onboard in July 1923. In order to encourage the development of aviation cause, Dr. Sun Yatsen wrote a scroll of "Aspiration Soaring Sky High" for Yang Xianyi, who was unfortunately died in an explosion when he was testing a mine.

Fig. 2   Dr. Sun Yatsen and Song Qingling with Rosamonde-Ⅰ

After the founding of the Republic of China, Beiyang government established an aviation school with an aircraft repair factory in Nanyuan of Beijing in 1913 and later established another aircraft repair factory in Qinghe, Beijing. Pan Shizhong, Director of Nanyuan Aircraft Repair Factory and Li Ruyang, a flying instructor, designed and manufactured an aircraft respectively in 1914. Pan's aircraft was named "Gun Vehicle" with engine fitted at rear of the aircraft and gun in the front. In the turmoil of wars between warlords, aircraft was deemed the symbol of power and the weapon for fighting Chinese civil wars. Each individual force hurried to buy aircraft from abroad, forming aviation fleet and establishing aviation school or flying training institute. The number of aircraft posessed and purchased increased with each passing day. Some provinces established aircraft repair factories one after another, among which the fairly formal ones were: The Naval Aircraft Engineering Department and the Dashatou Aircraft Repairing Factory. The Naval Aircraft Engineering Department was established in Mawei of Fujian province in 1918 by the Navy Department of Beiyang government, it was dedicated to the manufacture of water—based airplanes and a total of 15 different types of aircraft were studied and developed using indigenous wood and paint for navy training, reconnaissance and bombing, but none of them was put into mass production. After it was moved to Shanghai and merged in to the Jiangnan Shipbuilding Institute, this factory designed and manufactured a folded wing reconnaissance aircraft for " Nin Hai" Cruiser and manufactured several land—based aircraft. The Dashatou Aircraft Repairing Factory was established in 1920, where the "Rosamonde" aircraft was built and about another ten types of trainers, pursuit planes and bombers all named "Goat City" were produced from 1928 to 1934.

Following the break of the first cooperation between the Kuomintang and the Chinese Communist Party, the Kuomintang government established aircraft repair factories in Hangzhou, Shanghai, Nanjing and Wuchang. These factories were in different sizes and capabilities, some of which could produce aircraft by copying and repairing aircraft parts and the others could only carry out parts repair and replacement. After the January 28 Incident of 1932 in Shanghai the cry of rescuing China by developing aviation was ever louder. In 1934 and 1935 the Kuomintang government, by using foreign investment, material, equipment and technology, set up three factories which were basically for copy production and assembly of aircraft. One of them, called Central Hangzhou Aircraft Factory, was run as a joint venture with the United Continental Inc. of the United States. The factory with a staff of 1,700 was moved to Leiyong, Yunnan province during the War of Resistance Against Japanese Invasion, and it repaired, assembled and copied about 300 U.S. aircraft in eight years. In 1942, the Japanese heavy bombing near the frontier of Yunnan forced the factory to move, but all equipment and facilities were destroyed. The Central Nanchang Aircraft Factory was another one which was set up jointly with four Italian companies for licence production of Italian aircraft. It was destroyed by Japanese bombing after it produced some aircraft in 1937. It was re—set up in Nanchuan, Sichuan province, and was renamed as the Air Force No.2 Aircraft Factory in 1939. In addition to the copy production of some Russian pursuit planes and basic gliders it also successfully designed and manufactured transports Zhong Yun—1 and Zhong Yun—2, but none of them was put into batch production. There was another one which was called Shaoguan Aircraft Factory run jointly with the Curtis Wright Inc. of the United States. After the break of the War of Resistance Against Japanese Invasion the factory was also forced to move to Kunming and to Guiyang and renamed as the Air Force No.1 Aircraft Factory, where the American and Russian pursuit planes and American basic and advanced trainers were copy—manufactured. The Air Force No.3 Aircraft Factory was set up in Chengdu, which was dedicated to training technical personnel for aircraft design and manufacture. An engine manufacture factory producing American piston engines was set up in Dading of Guizhou. Both of the Air Force No.3 Aircraft Manufacturing Factory and the engine manufacture factory were later moved to Taiwan. In addition tens of thousands of parachutes of various types were made by Hangzhou Parachute Factory.

Training aviation engineering personnel in old China started at the end of the Qing dynasty and the beginning of the Republic of China, when a small number of Chinese students were studying aviation technology abroad. More and more students went abroad to study aviation after the 1930s, by the 1940s the total reached about one thousand. Among them there were some best ones such as Wang Zhu who was the aircraft designer at Boeing Company of the United States in the early days of the Company and later returned to China to develop Chinese aviation industry; Qian Xuesen, co-inventor of Karman-Tsien Formula used in the aerodynamic design of high subsonic aircraft, and Wu Zhonghua, the inventer of the theory of three dimensional flow for machines with blades. China stressed on the training of pilots initially and the earliest pilot training school was established in 1918 in Mawei, Fujian province, which was called Naval Aircraft and Submarine School. Starting from the 1930s, many colleges in China began to set up aviation courses and the Beiyang University, Central University, Qinghua University, Jiaotong University, Zhejiang University, Xiamen University, Yunnan University, Sichuan University and Northwest Polytechnic College all set up departments of aviation engineering one after another. Aviation and mechanical major was set up in Central Industrial College and Qinghua University even educated some graduates in aviation engineering. According to incomplete statistics the total number of undergraduates who graduated from the aviation engineering in all Chinese universities was about one thousand by the end of 1949.

Kuomintang government virtually paid no attention to science and research of aviation and only relied on one or two universities to do some development. Low speed wind tunnels were built in the 1930s by the Central University and the Aviation Research Institute of Qinghua University. Although a larger wind tunnel was built in Nanchang in 1939, it was destroyed by Japanese invaders in the following year. During the War of Resistance Against Japanese Invasion the Aviation Research Institute of Qinghua University was moved to Kunming and continued their scientific research with a small wind tunnel there. In 1939 Aviation Committee of Kuomintang government established an aviation institute in Chengdu, which was expanded to an aviation research centre in 1941. It constructed two single-flow, wooden structure and open test section wind tunnels. Technical personnel under the very difficult conditions concentrated on the development and trial production of aviation materials and created aircraft skin of "Bamboo Layer" instead of metal, with which tens of thousands of drop tanks were produced. The research centre also designed and trial-manufactured wooden Trainer-1 and bamboo and wood composite structured Trainer-2 and Trainer-3.

There were some aviation societies in old China. China Aviation Engineering Society was formed in 1934 with Qian Changzuo as its Chairman and, in 1947 Aviation Engineers Society was formed in Nanjing. These societies only had limited number of members, did not last very long and did not conduct any academic activities.

Looking back over 40 years of the history of old China starting from producing aircraft in Beijing's Nanyuan factory in 1910 by the Qing dynasty to the year of 1949 it can be seen that the old China had never established an independent aviation industry. The reasons of the saying are follows: first, the aircraft, both military and civil, used in old China were mostly bought from abroad; second, China did not have basic industry to support the aircraft development. Even if a small number of aircraft were produced, it was only limited to airframe production and assembly due to the fact that important components, airborne equipment and finished parts such as engine, metal propeller, landing gear, instruments and important raw materials were not available in China and had to rely on foreign suppliers; third, aviation research and test facilities were too simple, lacking fundamental ways and means of research and test. Old China, therefore, was not capable of research, design and test for high performance aircraft; and fourth, old China was corrupt in politics and with frequent wars. Although there were certain number of people experienced and educated in aviation engineering, their talent could not be fully utilized under that conditions. In one word, old China had only a very weak foundation for manufacturing aero products and was dominated by the imperialists, by whom China was turned into a market place for selling their commodities. This was the inevitable result after China was turned into a semi-feudal and semi-colonial society. Because the years of bombing by the Japanese during the War of Resistance caused frequent moves of the factories, and the destruction by the Kuomintang in the War of Liberation, aviation factories and their facilities were destroyed and the already weakened foundation of aviation was almost vanished. Old China only left us a limited number of professional persons.

3. Preparation for Establishing New China's Aviation Industry

Even before the founding of new China the Chinese communists had paid great attention to the role of aviation in the revolutionary cause and actively carried out preparations for new China's aviation cause under severe conditions. As early as in 1924 the Chinese Communist Party, cooperated with Kuomintang headed by Dr. Sun Yatsen and supported by the Soviet government, set up the Huangpu Military Academy and a military aircraft school and some students were sent to study aviation in the Soviet Union. After the failure of the Great Revolution, the Central Committee of the Chinese Communist Party decided to transfer Chang Qiankun, Wang Bi and Tang Duo who were already in the Soviet Union, to the Soviet Rookovsky Air Force College for further study.

During the War of Resistance Against Japanese Invasion, 44 cadres were selected by the Central Committee of the Chinese Communist Party to learn flying and maintenance in Xinjiang Aviation Team, where an aviation training class was also set up to train more aviation personnel. A mechanical engineering school (aviation school) was set up in Yan'an in 1941, and it was called the engineering team of the Military and Political University of Resistance Against Japan when it was merged with the university where personnel were trained and gathered for the development of aviation cause.

After the surrender of Japan, Yan'an Aviation Team of the Military Commission of CCCPC, together with aviation cadres coming from all other places, went to Northeast China with the armed forces to take over Japanese aviation facilities and equipment. An aviation station belonging to Shanxi—Chahar—Hebei provinces was set up in September 1945 in Zhangjiakou to take over from the Japanese forces the airport and aviation equipment and to train personnel. An Air Force team of the Northeast Democratic United Forces was established in December of the same year and in March 1946 an Aviation School of the Northeast Democratic United Forces was set up, where a group of cadres who studied aviation in Xinjiang and in the Soviet Union together with insurrectionary air force personnel of Kuomintang and the Japanese aviation technical personnel who stayed in China, were gathered. The school educated more than 500 aviation personnel in different professions. In the school a repair factory, a mechanical factory and a material factory were set up and a number of aircraft and engines left over by the Japanese were repaired. In November 1948 the Maintenance Department of the Northeast Aviation School was stationed in Shenyang. They took over factories and warehouses of Kuomintang Air Force. These factories together with the original 3 ones of the Northeast Aviation School were reorganized into 6 factories and one equipment and material warehouse.

The take—over working group of the aviation school went down to the south with the armed forces in 1949 and took over in succession the Nanyuan airport and its repair factory in Beijing, the airport and an aircraft component manufacture factory in Nanjing, the Shanghai airport and the Supply Command of the Kuomintang Air Force and air force airports and repair factories in south—central, northwest and southwest areas in China. All senior engineers and technical persons inside China then were organized by the East China Military Region and based on these people the East China Aviation Engineering Research Department was established. More over, the aviation sections of the East China and Northwest Military Regions mobilized students who just graduated from the Departments of Aviation Engineering at Shanghai Jiaotong University, Nanjing Central University and Northwest Polytechnic College to take part in the aviation construction in China. The above mentioned activities and preparations had laid a good foundation in persons and material for establishing the new China's Air Force and aviation industry.

This book will describe in five parts the founding and development of China's aviation industry after the founding of the People's Republic of China. Part one will introduce the founding and development of new China's aviation industry; Part two will describe the development of aircraft; Part three will introduce the development of aero engines, airborne equipment and missiles; Part four will describe development of aviation science and technical research and Part five will describe aeronautical education, capital construction, management system, quality control, employees' education in ideology and style of working, trade, scientific and technical exchanges and finally the Chinese Society of Aeronautics.

PART ONE

Under the leadership of the Communist Party of China and the people's government, on the "poor and blank" basis, aviation industry of the P.R. China has established a combined system of research, development and manufacture as well as education of aircraft, aero engine, airborne equipment and missile through efforts of more than 30 years. China's aviation industry has already become an important part of the national economy with the support of the relevant industries. New China's aviation industry had experienced arduous struggle and setbacks and gained progress continuously.

Chapter Ⅰ The Founding and Initial Development of New China's Aviation Industry

(1951 — 1960)

The founding of the great People's Republic of China on October 1, 1949 not only ushered in a new era of development of China's history, but also opened up a limitless bright future for establishing and developing China's aviation industry. The Chinese people who experienced endless bullying and humiliation by imperialists understood that a strong economy and national defence should be established in order not to be bullied again and to stand in the forest of world nations. Immediately after the founding of new China, the Chinese Communist Party and the central people's government took a long term view and paid great attention to the establishment of aviation industry, rendering strong support to it since it was deemed as an important pillar for the economic development and the national defence enhancement. Ten years from 1951 to 1960 were the years of the rise of new China's aviation industry, during which aviation industry adopted policy of adhering self-reliance; the Soviet technology was actively introduced; material and technical basis were constructed in large scale and the training of staff was strengthened with great efforts. The industry started trial production and normal production of aircraft in a planned and step by step way; transition period from aircraft repairing to manufacturing and then to aircraft design was successfully accomplished, which realized the high speed of aviation establishment and initial development. Although the "big leap forward" in the later half of the 1950s had brought some setbacks, aviation achievement in the initial stage of establishment was yet enormous and, rich experience was accumulated as well. This was a glorious page worth recording in the development history of China's aviation industry.

Section 1 Emerging from Flames of the Korean War

Chairman Mao Zedong, in September 1949, solemnly proclaimed to the world that "the Chinese people has stood up" at the first plenary meeting of the Chinese People's Political Consultative Committee and he also expressed that "our people's armed forces must be kept and developed. We will not only have a powerful army, but also a strong air force and navy." At the beginning of the founding of new China, construction of air force and navy was among the important issues subject to discussion by the government leaders. As early as in January 1949, the Political Bureau of the Central Committee of the Chinese Communist Party pointed out, in the resolution of "Present situation and the Party's task in 1949," that "in 1949 and 1950 we should try to organize an operational air force." In March 1949, Aviation Bureau of the Military Commission of the Communist Party of China (hereinafter called Military

Commission of CCCPC) was set up and, the Military Commission announced the forming of the air force leadership of the People's Liberation Army on November 11, 1949.

At the same time of setting up PLA Air Force, PLA took over and checked up aviation personnel and equipment left over by the Kuomintang in succession during their triumphant march forward. By the end of October 1949, the total number of people taken over was 2,312, among them 100 persons had engineering background. There were also 113 aircraft, 1,278 aero engines and 40,910 tons of other aviation equipment and materials, 40 airports and 12 factories. But most of those aircraft, airports and factories were damaged in the war or in the retreat of the Kuomintang.

When the War of Liberation was still continuing in 1949, the Kuomintang aircraft harassed the front lines and frequently bombed the liberated cities, which forced PLA to use aircraft fighting back. Though the aircraft taken over from the Kuomintang were very old, people yet cherished them and did the best to repair them for further use. Right after the liberation of Shenyang in November 1948 and even before the war flames were completely vanished, the Military Control Commission put out announcements of recruiting the scattered workers and five small repair factories were very quickly restored, where 26 aircraft were repaired in just more than half a year. When Beijing was liberated in March 1949, PLA immediately took the control of Nanyuan Aircraft Repairing Factory and all types of aviation equipment, wasting no time in carrying out repair of fighters, trainers and transporters. This factory was visited by Zhu De, Commander in Chief of the PLA, in September 1949. Repair of transporters organized at high speed was also practiced in Shanghai after it was liberated in June 1949. Aircraft used by PLA during the initial stage of the PLA Air Force were repaired by those people overcoming difficulties of lacking professional skill, equipment and materials. They even risked bombing and shooting by the Kuomintang aircraft. On the ceremony of proclaiming the founding of the People's Republic of China, October 1, 1949, the People's Air Force had 17 aircraft of bombers, fighters, transporters and trainers flying over Tiananmen to accept the inspection of the state leaders and the people.

Just relying on repairing a small number of aircraft could not meet the requirement for a large number of aircraft by the Air Force and the solutions were to set up an aviation industry to produce aircraft in large quantity. According to the instruction of the CCCPC, Liu Yialou, the Air Force Commander, Chang Qiankun and Wang Bi, Deputy Air Force Commanders, carried out investigations and wrote a report to the Central Committee in February 1950, suggesting to set up aviation factories, to train aviation personnel, and to form a leading organization of aviation industry and research institutions. The Ministry of Heavy Industry set up a preparatory team of aviation and automobile industries in March 1950 and appointed Vice Minister Liu Ding the team leader, to start the preparation of establishing new China's aviation industry.

June 25, 1950 saw the break—out of the Korean War and, China's Northeast area was invaded by the U.S. with large number of aircraft soon after. Chinese national security was severely threatened. At that crucial moment the CCCPC and Chairman Mao Zedong made the decision of sending Chinese people's voluntary army and air force to join the Korean War. The urgent requirement of the War greatly pushed the establishment of China's aviation industry.

The newly formed Chinese People's Voluntary Air Force in the Korean War fought bravely against the enemy's large formation of aircraft, effectively supported the friendly army. The Chinese People's Voluntary Air Force won a major victory in protecting rear important targets and transportation lines. The Chinese and Koreans also suffered certain losses for these achievements. The War not only brought urgent and heavy tasks of aircraft repairing, but also of buying new aircraft. In order to support the front line, the Chinese General Organization of Aiding Korea initiated the movement of donating aircraft and cannons for the War. People all over China economized on food and clothing, and donated their savings worth 3,152 aircraft. This action showed the desire of the people to strengthen the fighting capabilities of their Air Force. The progress of the War indicated that speeding up the establishment of aviation industry and producing aircraft by ourselves to reinforce the People's Air Force brooked no delay.

In December 1950, Premier Zhou Enlai called meetings in succession to discuss the issue of construction of the Chinese aviation industry. Meetings were taken part in by Nie Rongzhen, Acting Chief of Staff of PLA, Liu Yialou, Air Force Commander, He Changgong, Acting Minister of the Ministry of Heavy Industry, Shen Hong of Finance and Economy Commission of the Central People's Government (hereinafter called the Central Finance and economy Commission) and Duan Zijun of the Ministry of Heavy Industry. In conclusion, Premier Zhou Enlai pointed out: Construction of China's aviation industry should be carried out according to the Chinese practical situation. Our case was that we had air force first and we were fighting in Korea, which made large number of fighters need to be repaired urgently. Our country had a land of 9.6 million square kilometers and 5 to 6 hundred million people. We could not just rely on buying foreign aircraft and only carrying out repair by ourselves. The construction road, therefore, of China's aviation industry should be conducting repair first, manufacture afterwards and then the design. The principle was to develop it from small scale to large scale. It had to be pointed out that when a repair factory was designed certain consideration should be given to the planning and arrangement of turning it into a manufacture factory in the future. Meanwhile, negotiations should be carried out with the Soviets about their assistance for the construction of our aviation industry. Premier Zhou's conclusion pointed out the road of China's aviation development.

According to Premier Zhou Enlai's instruction and plan, a delegation headed by He Changgong with Shen Hong and Duan Zijun as its members left China for the Soviet Union in January 1951 to negotiate for their assistance to the construction of China's aviation industry. Just before the departure of the delegation, Chen Yun, Chairman of the Central Finance and Economy Commission, said to He Changgong wittily: "When you are on the plane I'll be on horseback right away" (i.e. to prepare the material condition for establishing aviation industry).

The Soviet Union paid great attention to this negotiation and assigned 7 people headed by the Foreign Minister Vishinsky to specially handle this matter. The negotiation was quite smooth and very soon agreements were reached on matters of the Soviet assistance to China to reconstruct its aircraft repair factories and then to gradually expand them into complete aircraft manufacture factories and of sending specialists and advicers to China. After the approval of Zhou Enlai, Premier of P.R. China and Stalin, President of the Council of Ministers of U.S.S.R., two governments, in October 1951, formally signed "Agreement of U.S.S.R. rendering technical assistance to P.R.C. in organizing repair of aircraft and engine and organizing aircraft factories." This timely assistance by the Soviet Union at the time when P.R.C. was just founded and was suffering from tight blockade by western countries played an important role in the fast establishment and development of China's aviation industry.

After tense and adequate consultations and preparation, the Military Commission of CCCPC and the Government Administration Council on 17 April 1951 promulgated "Decision on the construction of aviation industry," pointing out:

1. The present task of the construction of China's aviation industry is to fully ensure the repair of all aircraft used by the Chinese Air Force and then gradually to develop towards manufacture;

2. The principle of unified management of aviation industry at the present stage must be adopted and, the manufacture and repair could be divided when the aviation industry developed to the stage of concentrating forces on aircraft manufacturing. It is, therefore, decided that all air force factories including personnel, equipment, finance and material, buildings and plant sites should be transfered to the Bureau of Aviation Industry;

3. After these factories taken over by the Bureau of Aviation Industry, they should begin to undertake the tasks of repairing Air Force aircraft and of providing spare parts on the basis of economic accounting;

4. The Bureau of Aviation Industry and Air Force Headquarters should set up inspection and acceptance organizations respectively in order to improve product quality;

5. In the light of strengthening the leadership of the aviation industry construction, it is decided that the Management Commission of Aviation Industry should be set up, which would be under the leadership of the Military Commission of CCCPC. It is decided that Nie Rongzhen, Li Fuchun, Liu Yialou, He Changgong, Duan Zijun and Ma Wen were members of the Management Committee with Nie Rongzhen as its Chairman and Li Fuchun as Vice Chairman.

The CCCPC on 18 April 1951 telegraphed all organizations of the Party, the government and the military in every large administrative area saying: to suit the Air Force construction, the Ministry of Heavy Industry set up the Bureau of Aviation Industry, according to the decision of the Central Committee, to be solely responsible for all kinds of repairs of aircraft; Duan Zijun was appointed Director of the Bureau. It also pointed out: Aviation industry was a kind of new work with "high technology and political nature", "great assistance should be given and timely supervision and guidence should be rendered". The Government Administration Council, in July 1951, appointed He Changgong Acting Minister of the Ministry of Heavy Industry, concurrently Director of the Bureau and Duan Zijun, Chen Yimin and Chen Ping Deputy Directors. Handing over repair factories from the Air Force to the Ministry of Heavy Industry according to the decision of the Central Committee had been completed in September 1951, when the Bureau of Aviation Industry had taken over 16 factories from the Air Force and 2 factories from the Bureau of Weaponry Industry and had owned 18 factories in total with about ten thousands people. The aviation industry expected by the people of the whole country and the People's Army had at last come into being in the lap of new China.

The major task of the aviation industry after its forming was to meet the requirement of the Korean War and to ensure the repairing of air force aircraft. An aircraft repairing train (mobile factory) was rented from the Soviet Union and it arrived in Shenyang in early May 1951. And the Soviet advicers, specialists and large number of aviation equipment arrived in China in succession soon after. The Aviation Bureau immediately organized Chinese technical personnel and workers to learn seriously from the Soviets to gradually master repairing technology of aircraft on one hand and, carried out adjustment and reconstruction of factories taken over from other units with the assistance of the Soviet experts on the other hand. According to Premier Zhou Enlai's instruction "When the repair factory is designed certain considerations should be given to the arrangement and planning for transferring it to manufacture factory in the future," He Changgong and Duan Zijun accepted suggestions of the Soviet experts after their investigation and worked out a plan of realizing manufacture of complete aircraft within 3 to 5 years, which was reported to the CCCPC in August 1951. Zhu De, Commander of PLA, wrote instruction on the report saying: "go ahead as it is planned." Meanwhile, Nie Rongzhen and Li Fuchun also wrote a report to Chairman Mao Zedong and the Central Secretariat, proposing the construction policy of aviation industry and principle of production scale and site selection etc. The report also proposed the following work divisions: the Shenyang Aircraft Factory and the Shenyang Aero Engine Factory for repair of jet fighters; the Harbin Aircraft Factory and the Harbin Aero Engine Factory for repair of bombers and the Nanchang Aircraft Factory and the Zhuzhou Aero Engine Factory for repair of piston type trainers. The expansion of these factories was also described in the report. Having had the report checked by Liu Shaoqi, Zhou Enlai and Chen Yun, Chairman Mao Zedong wrote the instruction "Act accordingly" on August 21, 1951. Afterwards, the aviation industry began its intensive work of adjusting factories and factory reconstruction and expansion, concentrating about 80% of personnel and 70% of equipment of the industry to the above mentioned 6 factories. Meanwhile, construction of factories, reinforcement of workers and technical personnel were carried out actively in accordance with repairing task and the requirement of gradually transferring from repair to manufacture. By the end of 1952, aviation industry was adjusted into 13 factories (including 2 factories taken over from Civil Aviation Bureau) and set up primarily one Capital Construction Design Institute and 12 schools. The number of employees increased to 30,000; metal cutting machines increased to 2,020 and factory floor areas enlarged to 160,000 square meters. The 6 major factories were all equipped up to the standard of large scale repair factories.

Factories were in severe short of process technical documents, raw materials and finished parts needed for the repair work at that time. Factory had no way but to carry out the work according to the Soviet experts' demonstration and oral instructions. Damaged aircraft were repaired by every possible means. People were determined to accomplish the task day and night, even without having meals, as long as it was required by the Korean War. People worked very hard indeed and the numbers of aircraft and engines repaired increased rapidly. Aircraft and engines repaired were 70 and 336 in 1951, 284 and 2,027 in 1952 and 475 and 1,626 in 1953 respectively. 16 types of fighters, attack aircraft, bombers, trainers and transporters and 10 types of piston and jet engines were repaired. The newly established aviation industry actively supported the Korean War and laid a necessary foundation for the smooth carrying out of large scale construction in the First Five-year Plan.

Section 2   Building the First Batch of Backbone Enterprises

The aviation industry worked out the practical target and detailed plan of transition from repair to manufacture while organizing repair of aircraft urgently needed by the front line. In December 1951, Premier Zhou Enlai himself presided over a meeting discussing the plan and the decision was made at the meeting. The aviation industry was requested to implement a plan of trial production of the Soviet Yak-18 primary trainer and MiG-15bis jet fighter and then the batch production of them within 3 to 5 years. Several meetings were held to discuss plans and arrangement of construction of aviation industry by leaders of the Central Committee, Zhou Enlai, Chen Yun, Nie Rongzhen and Li Fuchun in spring and summer of 1952. Li Fuchun stressed that prerequisites needed for the transition from repair to manufacture should be created actively. He said the prerequisites would include: complete set of technical documentation, complete technical facility, necessary production area, ensured supply of raw material and the development of cooperation between relevant industries. Chen Yun pointed out: aircraft factory was, strictly speaking, the precision machine manufacture factory. The objective law of development was from backwardness to advanced stage and from simpleness to complexity. Haste would do no good. Aircraft was built with parts and components and good foundation should be laid for producing them, otherwise the progress would be slower instead of quicker. More haste, less speed. He repeatedly stressed that there could be no principle mistake to put the construction of aviation industry on top priority. Nie Rongzhen presided over a meeting of the Military Commission of CCCPC in May 1951 and worked out a "Resolution on the construction of aviation industry," which spelt out plans of major tasks during the stage of initial construction. In July 1951, Premier Zhou checked out the more than one year's work of aviation industry, during which he reiterated the development policy, the principle and the capital construction plan of aviation industry and made further arrangement for constructing a light bomber aircraft factory. In order to strengthen the leadership of national defence and aviation industry, the CCCPC and the central people's government in August decided to set up the Second Ministry of Machine Building, i.e. the Ministry of Defence Industry, Zhao Erlu was appointed the Minister and Concurrently Director of the Bureau of Aviation Industry, Wang Xiping, First Deputy Director and Secretary of the Sub-Party Committee of the Bureau of Aviation Industry. All those series of major decisions and careful planning formed construction outline of aviation industry in the First Five-year Plan, which paved the way for marching towards manufacture from repair.

Repair and manufacture are in two different levels in terms of technology and management. The former is to perform routine repair according to different regulations and requirements of depot maintenance, field maintenance and organizational maintenance and conduct trouble shooting to aircraft (including engine and airborne equipment). Only the depot maintenance takes place in a special repair factory. Each aircraft has different problems, therefore, the corrective actions should be different. The latter is to precisely organize workers and technical persons to coordinately carry out high quality mass production of parts, assemblies, final assembly and test according to the approved technical drawings, documents, equipment and tools. Transition of high standard manufacturing from low level to high level manufacture is a qualitative leap of aviation industry. Aviation industry would not be able to meet the requirement of development until large scale capital construction is carried out, repair factory is modified into aircraft manufacture factory and new factories are constructed according to the need of the formation of a complete system.

The China and the Soviet governments signed an agreement in May 1953 to assist China by USSR in 143 major projects (later increased to 156 projects), among which 13 projects were for aviation industry, including aircraft factory, aero engine factory and airborne equipment factory. These projects formed the first batch of backbone enterprises of aviation industry and were the key projects for large scale construction in the First Five-year Plan of aviation industry.

The construction of the 13 projects was carried out according to their different priorities so that the schedule of aircraft manufacture could be ensured and the investment effectiveness could be brought into play as soon as possible. The Nanchang Aircraft Factory (producing piston trainers) was first constructed in 1953, then the Zhuzhou Aero Engine Factory (producing piston engines), the Shenyang Aircraft Factory (manufacturing jet fighters) and the Shenyang Aero Engine Factory (manufacturing jet engines) were constructed. Except the Shenyang Aero Engine Factory was newly built with the support of old factories, the others were reconstructed and expanded on the basis of repair factories. After construction of these aircraft and engine factories, construction focus was shifted to the necessary accessory factories starting from 1956. Those accessory factories were: the Xi'an Aircraft Accessory Factory and Engine Accessory Factory, the Xinping Aviation Electronic Factory and Wheel Brake Accessory Factory and the Baoji Aviation Instrument Factory in Shaanxi Province.

All the above mentioned factories were equipped with advanced technology and good equipment, being China's high precision machining enterprises. The government paid special attention to the construction of these due to heavy investment and great difficulties. Capital construction investment of aviation was adequately ensured during the period of First Five-year Plan and complete sets of equipment were basically bought from the Soviet Union. The whole country, from the Central Government to local governments, were all concerned about the construction of aviation industry, offering full support at any time. As for those urgently needed equipment that could not be bought from abroad, the aviation industry was given special permission by Bo Yibo, Vice Chairman of Finance and Economic Commission of the Central People's Government, to select in the state warehouse. The Shenyang Aero Engine Factory picked 553 equipment at one time. Shao Shiping, Governor of Jiangxi Province and Jiao Ruoyu, Party Secretary of Shenyang City organized construction of aviation factories in their own places by themselves. Shao Shiping was also the Chief of Construction Committee of the Nanchang Aircraft Factory, while Jiao Ruoyu called meetings many times to check, supervise and coordinate construction schedule. For instance, in order to ensure the construction schedule of a runway for aircraft flight test in the Shenyang Aircraft Factory, the Shenyang municipalities had cut one third of its work amount of that year's city construction. The leaders' care and support at each level from the Central Committee to local governments were the fundamental guarantee for the smooth progress of construction of aviation industry.

Advantages were fully utilized during the construction of these backbone enterprises. Most of the factories were located in large and middle size cities; geological and hydrological conditions were known; transportation was convenient; products to be manufactured were defined and drawings and technical documentation were approved, which helped the practice of construction and production at the same time of design. Once the construction of the part of the factory was finished that part was checked and accepted for the production and the same principle was adopted for installing equipment. Civil engineering and installation of almost all large plants were carried out in crisscross with production and, construction force had close cooperation with factory leaders, technical persons and workers, working day and night. Construction cycle was effectively shortened thanks to the method of the old bringing up the new, i.e. old factory took full responsibility for the construction of a new one, which improved the investment results and speeded up the forming of production capability.

The most typical factory constructed among them was the Shenyang Aero Engine Factory, which was built on the basis of a nearby old repair factory. In order to realize construction while carrying out production, the factory adopted the method of "One Director for two factories", i.e. Director of the old factory was also the director of the new factory, for the unified management and, so was the Chief Engineer and Managers of every functional department. Each new functional department, therefore, was bred and fostered from the relevant department of the old factory and then divided into two after its ripeness. The old factory started trial production of parts and components of jet engine at the same time of constructing the new factory. Once the construction of a workshop of the new factory was finished, the workers, together with their equipment and new products moved to the new one, so that the immediate trial production could be carried out in the new workshop. This practice of carrying out construction in crisscross with production gained time and efficiency. The total investment of this new factory was 210 million RMB with 230,000 square meters production area, 2,000 equipment and 13,000 employees. It only took one and half years from construction to production and the date of finishing construction was the date of acceptance of the trial produced new jet engine, which was one year ahead of the original plan and which realized high speed of constructing China's first jet engine factory and trial production of new engines.

Fig. 3   A bird's–eye view of the Shenyang Aero Engine Factory

This was not only the case with aircraft and engine factories, but also with the construction of airborne equipment factories. For example, Shenyang and Baoji Aviation Instrument Factories, Shaanxi Xinping Aviation Electrical Factory and Xi'an Aircraft Accessory Factory were all bred and derived from old factories in Shenyang, Tianjin, Taiyuan and Xinxiang. This practice played an important role in mitigating the obvious situation of airborne equipment lagging behind aircraft and engine at that time.

Besides, inviting a complete range of Soviet experts to assist China in designing and constructing aviation factories was also an important factor for the fast construction of the first batch of aviation factories. There were lots of advantages in so doing compared with the method of conducting design drawing abroad and bringing the design back for the construction. This method greatly reduced circulating time for site surveying, document collection and drawing, design, and facilitated issuing design documents in batches, and helped solve problems on the spot, hence the construction time was greatly shortened by more than one year. The most important of all was that the Chinese had the opportunity to learn from the Soviet experts a complete range of professional knowledge and skill "On Job". The capital construction design force of China's aviation industry were almost capable of working independently at the end of the First Five-year Plan. Starting from January 1958, design work of capital construction was changed from the system of the Soviet experts responsibility to the system of the Soviet consultation.

Fig. 4   Mao Zedong visiting Shenyang Aircraft Factory

Construction of the aviation industry achieved fruitful result during the First Five-year Plan thanks to the concern and correct policy of the government and the marching forward of the construction of national economy. The five years witnessed construction of 42 organizations and enterprises with more than 8 projects each year, among which there were 17 factories, 19 schools and 4 warehouses. The capital construction plan originally scheduled for five years was completed one year ahead of time. Among the 13 state key projects constructed, 8 projects were completed one to one and half years ahead of time and 4 were completed on schedule. Quality of all the completed projects were all up to "Good" condition after acceptance by the state. Immediately after completion of the factories, production was started, and the utilization of fixed assets investment reached 82.7%. By the end of 1957, aviation industry possessed 3.55 million square meters construction area, 11,160 sets of metal cutting equipment — 5.5 times of that in 1952, and 100,000 employees — 3.3 times of that in 1952. All of these greatly changed the material and technical foundation of the aviation industry, i.e. from a small business only capable of repairing aircraft to a newly emerged industry capable of mass production of piston trainers and jet fighters, being an important high standard precision machine building business in the country. This was a great achievement in the economic construction at the initial stage of the founding of new China.

Section 3   Gathering and Training Qualified Personnel

Aviation industry is a kind of high know—how and technology intensive industry, which could not be moved forward without setting up organizations with a wide scope of qualified personnel, including aviation scientists, professors, designers, engineers, directors, managers and technical workers, etc. Qualified personnel were badly needed at the initial stage of establishing the aviation industry. There were only about 500 technical persons of different professions, far from the number needed at the end of 1951. Chen Yun, Chairman of the Central Finance and Economy Commission, pointed out at a meeting held in April 1952 that of all conditions needed for producing aircraft, the most difficult ones were the problems of technical personnel and raw material. With regard to this problem, the government adopted important measures of organizing qualified persons in China while setting up schools with every effort, the so called walking with two legs, which quickly formed and strengthened the force of aviation industry.

The Communist Party of China took great care to win over and search for aviation technical personnel even on the eve of the founding of new China. Before the liberation of Shanghai in 1949, Wang Yuqi and other 40 high and middle level technical persons of the Kuomintang air force agreed to stay in the mainland thanks to the efforts and work by Li Yangqun, the underground Party member of the Communist Party of China. Right after the liberation of Shanghai in May 1949, the City Military Control Committee made announcement in news papers of recruiting aviation professional personnel. Vice Chairman of the Military Commission of CCCPC Zhou Enlai instructed at once: "Assemble these aviation technical persons first and their work will be assigned later." According to this instruction, the Aviation Department of the East—China Military Region assembled aviation technical persons who studied and were trained abroad and had returned to China and a research laboratory of East—China Aviation Engineering was set up. In August 1949 and with regard to the uprising of personnel of the two aviation companies of China Air and Central Air of China (hereinafter called " Two Aviation Cos.") who were staying in Hong Kong, Vice Chairman Zhou Enlai instructed: "To mobilize staff and workers of the 'Two Aviation Cos.' to revolt together and stop inciting individual aircraft defection," "The most important thing is to win over the people."

About one hundred aviation professional personnel, most of them were the Kuomintang high and middle level technical personnel who refused to be forced to go to Taiwan, were transferred into the Bureau of Aviation Industry not long after its establishment. Uprising personnel of the "Two Aviation Cos." and overseas students and aviation professional personnel who returned to motherland from abroad with hardships were dearly cherished by the government. Proper arrangement was made according to their professions and lots of them were appointed to important positions with the development of aviation cause. Xu Shunshou, Huang Zhiqian, Wu Daguan and Yu Guangyu who studied in the U.K. and U.S.A. were appointed to be responsible for setting up the first aircraft design department and engine design department; Lu Xiaopeng, who studied in England, was appointed designer of aircraft and later led the design work of China's first generation attack aircraft; Zan Ling who came back from the USA was appointed to set up first Chinese Aero Instrument Design Department; Rong Ke who studied in England and was a specialist in casting was appointed Vice Director of Aviation Material Research Institute and Shen Yuan, who studied earlier in England and was a member of the Royal Aeronautical Society, was appointed Vice President of BIAA (Beijing Institute of Aeronautics and Astronautics). The government assigned about one hundred students who just graduated from universities to work in aviation industry from 1951 to 1953. With the help of engineering personnel of the old generation, the new comers and the old generation formed a combined team of technical backbone during the initial stage of the aviation industry. They made important contributions to the development of production, research and development, construction and education of China's aviation industry.

To strengthen the leadership of aviation industry, many intelligent and capable people were transferred to work in the industry by the government. Lots of leaders who experienced the rigorous trials of revolutionary wars and stood severe tests went to work in aviation industry from all parts of China. Two days after the Chinese delegation went to the Soviet Union to negotiate for their assistance to the Chinese aviation industry in January 1951, Premier Zhou Enlai sent a telegram to the North-east Bureau of the Central Committee of Communist Party of China, saying that chief leaders and key members in the management of the Jian Xin Company (a military enterprise) in Dalian were to be sent to organize the Bureau of Aviation Industry in the Second Ministry of Machine Building which was established in 1952. The leading members of the Bureau of Aviation Industry were Wang Xiping, Duan Zijun, Wang Bi, You Jiang, Fan Ming, Chen Yimin, Xu Changyu, Chen Shaozhong, Fang Zhiyuan and Li Zhaoxiang. These people were transferred to the Bureau from Jian Xin Company, South-central Military Region and the Air Force. They were given the responsibility to make transition of the aviation industry from repair and overhaul to manufacture and hence laid a good foundation for the development of the industry.

The Party and the government paid great attention to the leadership of the aircraft and engine factories. All the chief executives were appointed directly by the Central Committee of the Chinese Communist Party. Selected leaders were not only politically reliable and capable, but also well educated, young and promising. Gao Fangqi and Mo Wenxiang, Director and Party Secretary of the first model factory in the early 1950s, were appointed directors of the Shenyang Aircraft Factory and Engine Factory respectively. Managers with educational background like Niu Yinguan, Wu Jizhou, Yang Cheng, Zou Wenxuan, Tang Qinxun and Xu Xizan were also appointed Director, Party Secretary and Chief Engineer of the major factories. In the period before and after the First Five-year Plan, many executives were transfered to aviation industry from Party organizations, administrative departments and army units by the government. Fairly large groups of people were transfered into the industry in 1954, more than 70 cadres at prefecture and divisional level, about 200 cadres at county and regiment level came to factories handed over from the Air Force and civil aviation industry. These cadres forcefully strengthened the leadership at each level of the aviation industry. Some of them, like Xong Yian, Yu Hui, Ma Zhen, Lu Hongan, Zhou Hongen, Diao Junshou, Su Zhi and Li Zhongyuan were assigned to important leading posts then.

The government also showed deep concern to the transfer of technical workers. Premier Zhou Enlai instructed personally to Li Fuchun, Vice Chairman of the Central Finance and Economy Commission to transfer 2,500 technical workers to the industry from the Bureau of Weaponry Industry and automobile assembly factories. In March 1952, with the instruction of the State Council, more than one thousand technical people were transfered to work in aviation industry from departments of railway, transportation and communication in North-east, North-China, South-west and East-China and in Tianjin. The instruction required that among those people the model workers had to occupy 2%, hence most of the workers transfered to the industry were with high political consciousness, hard working and with superior skills.

Those leaders, technical persons, workers and students, who came to work in the aviation industry from all parts of China, were honoured to have the opportunity of taking part in the construction of new China's aviation industry. They left their familiar work for completely new posts at one order, some of them went to the freezing Shenyang and Harbin from the big southen city of Shanghai and the rich area of Zhejiang. Although they were not accustomed to northern food and climate, none of them complained. They threw themselves in the hard struggle of establishing aviation industry, their common target.

Collecting people and forming a labour force did not mean a capability of accomplishing the task because lots of those people were unfamiliar with the repair and manufacture of aircraft. The best and quickest effective method of solving the problem was to make good use of the Soviet assistance, to invite Soviet experts to China and to send people out for training. There were totally about 847 Soviet experts and advicers being invited to China by the Chinese government. Lots of those invited people were with rich experience and excellent skill. They were friendly and worked actively. Each of them was assigned 3 to 10 Chinese people as their students, who were requested to reach the standard of doing the work by themselves when the experts left. At the same time, 353 cadres, technical persons and workers were sent to study in U.S.S.R. Large number of good students were also selected from universities and colleges and sent to the Soviet Union and other east European countries for further study. The above mentioned measures were just taken to cope with the urgent need. Aviation industry needed large number of qualified personnel and the only solution was to set up more universities to train more people. According to the instructions of Premier Zhou Enlai that we should be determined to set up our own aviation universities, the aviation industry treated the constructions of universities and production facilities with equal importance.

The three aviation universities of new China were established in 1952. The aviation majors of the existed universities in China were adjusted primarily in 1951 and in October the following year, with the general adjustment of universities in China, the aviation universities were further adjusted by the government. The BIAA was formed by combining Aviation Institute of Qinghua University and aviation departments of Sichuan University and Beijing Polytechnic College; the East—China Institute of Aviation, later called Xi'an Aviation Institute when it was moved to Xi'an in 1956, was established by a merger of aviation departments of the former Central University, Jiaotong University and Zhejiang University; The Xi'an Aviation Institute was merged with Northwest Polytechnic in 1957 and formed the present NPU (North—west Polytechnic University). 1952 also saw the establishment of Nanjing Aviation Industrial School, which later was upgraded to NAI (Nanjing Aeronautical Institute) in 1956.

Meanwhile, the secondary technical schools and the skilled workers training schools were set up in large numbers by the Bureau of Aviation Industry. There were about 8 secondary technical schools and 11 skilled workers training schools being set up during the First Five—year Plan period. Those schools were built up from nothing and under very difficult conditions. Students learned and carried on the tradition of hard struggle of the Yan'an Military and Political University of Resistance Against Japan. Old houses were used for their classrooms in day time and for bedrooms at night. Teaching facilities were self made and classes started while schools were still in construction. The first year students were already at grade three when the construction work of school was nearly completed in 1954. Thousands of students graduated from these colleges and universities by the end of the First Five—year Plan, among them were 96 graduate students, 1,980 university undergraduates, 2,137 college students, 5,558 secondary technical school graduates and 26,144 students of skilled workers training schools. This technical force had met the urgent demand of the development of aviation industry. While students were educated in these schools experiences of running schools were accumulated simultaneously. Chairman Mao highly praised the Kunming Aviation Industrial School and Xi'an Aviation School at a Supreme State Conference in 1957 and at a Nanning Conference of the Central Committee of the Communist Party of China in 1958, asking people to learn from their hard working spirit as well as their experiences of running schools.

Training staff and workers was another important way of improving their quality. After the

First Five-year Plan and under the slogan of " Learning from the Soviet experts" and " Marching forward to science", an atmosphere of learning business, techniques, foreign language and political theory were created among the leading members, technicians as well as workers of the aviation industry. Here and there early in the morning, one could see people reading and studying in offices, factories or institutes. Every one was busy in the day time at his work, while in the evening workers and staff members including directors and Party Secretaries of factories all went to classrooms . By the year of 1956, 7 spare time colleges and 7 spare time technical schools were run by aviation industry. Total number of students in those schools reached 21,000 which was one quarter of the total number of staff and workers of the industry. Short term training classes in factories and institutes were sprung up like mushrooms. Besides, about one thousand cadres were released from their work to learn technology. Young cadres with less education background were sent to study in the Workers and Peasants Accelerated Middle School, while the leading members with good education background were sent directly to special classes of BIAA which speeded up the technical training of cadres.

More and more graduates were assigned to aviation industry continuously thanks to the fast development of education. The educational and technological quality of the working force was greatly improved. By the end of 1957, technical personnel of the whole industry reached 15,000, that was 14.3% of the total number of workers compared with 500 in 1952. Technical school graduates and workers who were specially trained with aviation technology occupied half of the total number of employees in most factories. This industrial working force of the first generation of the aviation industry formed after the founding of new China not only ensured the smooth transition from repair to manufacture, but also was the backbones in the development of aviation industry all the time. Aviation colleges and universities also educated large number of graduates for space industry, People's Air Force, shipbuilding industry and other sectors of national economy, making contributions to the establishment and development of these newly established organizations.

Section 4 Completing Transition from Repair to Manufacture

The purpose of constructing factories and assembling and training personnel was after all to realize the development target of the aviation industry from repair to manufacture. Approved by the government, the detailed tasks of aircraft manufacture in the First Five-year Plan of aviation industry were: to successfully produce Yak-18 Primary Trainer with a Chinese name of CJ-5 and its M-11 engine by the third quarter of 1955; and to successfully manufacture MiG-15bis jet fighter and its engine VK-1A by the end of 1957. In October 1954, the fighter and engine types were changed to more advanced MiG-17F and VK-1F with Chinese names of J-5 and WP5 respectively.

There were only a few people who had the experience of aircraft repair and overhaul among the working force of aviation industry at the beginning of First Five—year Plan, most people were new to the aviation industry and some of them even had not seen the aircraft. Some automobile repair workers were working on the aircraft assembly line, some watch repairers and tin smiths were working as fitters and instrumentation workers. It obviously was not an easy task for such a young and inexperienced working force to produce in three to five years two types of aircraft, especially newly appeared jet fighters.

Pioneers of new China's aviation industry were dauntless and their only wish was to let the aircraft manufactured by themselves fly in the sky at the earliest date. The Secretary of the Party Committee of Jiangxi Province said: "Jiangxi is an old revolutionary base. And Nanchang is the place where the first bullet was shot in August 1 military uprising to seize power. The first aircraft of new China must also be manufactured here in Nanchang." His remarks truly expressed the desire of workers of Nanchang Aircraft Factory and the wish and enthusiasm of all workers and people of aviation industry to manufacture the aircraft as soon as possible.

This strong feeling of honour and the strong sense of master's responsibility turned into the spirit of hard working and diligent study. Workers and staff made their efforts in learning technology, striving to reach the target of manufacturing aircraft by climbing up the ladder of repair.

Since 1953, the aircraft sent back for repair by the Air Force were damaged ever more. Repair work load and the type and number of parts for replacement were increasing rapidly, which would not be fulfilled if just relying on the normal way of repair. The stored spare parts were limited, the ordered parts from abroad could not be supplied on time and some parts could not be supplied from abroad because production of them was stopped. To let the repair and manufacture move forward each other, the Bureau of Aviation Industry promptly put forward the policy of "while meeting the requirement of repair, taking into consideration the technical development and actively developing new products," and quickly organized enterprises to enlarge the manufacturing scope of components to meet the requirement of repair, which accelerated the growth of manufacture factory.

The types of new trial produced parts in each factory increased quickly after implementing the above mentioned policy. Shenyang Aero Engine Factory only produced 767 parts in 1952, but rapidly increased to 1,574 in 1953, 2,720 in 1954 and 3,353 in 1955. 44 percent of RD—20 engine parts and 55.6 percent of RD—45 engine parts could be manufactured in our factories. Before the manufacture was carried out in full swing, Zhuzhou Aero Engine Factory had trial—produced 60% of complete M—11 engine parts. The period of manufacturing large number of parts to meet demands of repair was the period of employees to learn and master the complete complicated manufacturing techniques of machining, heat process, test, assembly and inspection.

Management skill was quickly improved due to the extension of scope of part manufac—turing. Production of important and complicated parts must be carried out strictly according to the manufacturing specification and production tooling should be produced. Actual production should not be allowed prior to the trial production and certification. It was obvious that the management method for the repair was no longer suitable and the management system must be reformed according to the requirement of formal manufacture factory. Therefore, the Director's responsibility system and Chief Engineer's production technical responsibility systems including metallurgy, process, design, power supply and production were established in each factory. To ensure product quality, a complete organization of management was set up, planning and production technical management were strengthened and the incoming material inspection and finished part inspection were more strictly controlled. Eventually, a good foundation of scientific management was laid for the transition from repair to manufacture.

During this period, each factory, according to the plan and work division for developing new product, adopted the method of "dividing work in accordance with profession and with workers fixed to it," technical persons were fixed to their professions and workers to the job and operation, so that every one was working with clear aims to improve their skills. To let the employees adapt themselves to the modern large scale production, and get rid of the habit of repair, it was stipulated that production could not be started until a complete and correct manufacturing process was established and worker was certified for the operation. This greatly improved the quality of technicians and workers.

Because attention was paid to the correlation between repair and manufacture at an early stage, after three years repair work conditions for manufacturing were technically prepared and management improved and people trained. As the Chinese saying goes: where water flows, a channel is formed. The year of 1954 was the turning point of aviation industry from repair to manufacture, which was fully proved by the successful trial production of the primary trainer CJ—5 in the Nanchang Aircraft Factory.

The factory started to repair the Yak—18 aircraft early in 1951 and, the aircraft assembly and test techniques were grasped during the repair period. In 1952, the factory started to expand the scope of repair, and to produce spare parts and to get themselves familiarized with the techniques of producing aircraft parts and assemblies. 1953 was the year of more active preparation for the transition from repair to manufacture. The factory set up the goal of mastering manufacturing techniques of Yak—18 parts and components which could be interchanged and matched on the aircraft. 44 main assemblies of outer wings, flaps, empennages and landing gears etc. were manufactured according to the repair documentation and sample parts. These parts were assembled on one aircraft for test and checkout and good result was witnessed after the aircraft underwent 50 sorties and 78 hours of flying. The method of using lofting, templates and master parts was adopted for the manufacture of aircraft parts from the second half of 1952. With this method correct aircraft configuration, and interchangeability and matching of parts could be ensured, hence the first and most important step was taken towards the manufacture of a complete aircraft. In early 1954 when the factory was formally set to trial produce the primary trainer CJ—5, 235 aircraft had already been repaired. People in the Nanchang Aircraft Factory made all aircraft parts with the only exception of control system.

After the visit to the factory by Minister Zhao Erlu of the Second Ministry of Machine Building at the end of 1953, he believed that the conditions for manufacturing complete aircraft ahead of schedule was matured. An order was issued to the factory after the approval of the State Council, by which the time for formal successful trial production of primary trainer CJ—5 was changed from the third quarter of 1955 to an earlier time of the third quarter of 1954.

After the order had reached the factory, the people of the factory were mobilized immediately and the trial production was carried out day and night. The first aircraft successfully completed its test flight on July 11, 1954. The State Certification Committee arrived at the conclusion: The performance of the primary trainer CJ—5 manufactured by the Nanchang Aircraft Factory met the requirement of the specification and it could be used by the Air Force as a trainer aircraft. On August 26, the Defence Minister Peng Dehuai approved the batch production of the aircraft. Only more than half a year was used from trial production to batch production. The power—plant of the aircraft M—11 engine was also trial—produced successfully by the Zhuzhou Aero Engine Factory in August of the same year.

Fig. 5   Celebration for the successful manufacture of CJ—5 primary trainer

The success in manufacturing CJ—5 Aircraft marked a good start for aircraft manufacture in new China. The Chinese aviation industry had entered a new stage. To celebrate this achievement, Chairman Mao Zedong signed two letters of praise and encouragement to the Nanchang Aircraft Factory and Zhuzhou Aero Engine Factory on August 1 and August 10 of 1954 respectively. In his letter of praise and encouragement to the Nanchang Aircraft Factory, Chairman Mao Zedong said: "Your report of July 26 had been received. Congratulations to the successful trial production of the first Yak—18 aircraft. This is a good start in establishing both aircraft industry and strengthening the national defence of China. I hope the factory will continue their efforts to further master technology and improve quality under the guidance of the Soviet experts and ensure the fulfilment of regular production task."

Zhu De, Commander in Chief of PLA, also wrote words of encouragement to the Nanchang Aircraft Factory saying: "Carry on the enthusiasm and creativeness of the working class; strengthen national defence and defend the motherland."

When the aircraft of CJ—5 primary trainer was batch produced in Nanchang in 1955, the trial production of J—5 and its engine was carried out in full swing in the Shenyang Aircraft Factory. J—5 aircraft was a high subsonic jet fighter in service with the Soviet Air Force in the early 1950s, which was one of the advanced jet fighters in the world at that time. Manufacture of this type of aircraft was much more complicated than that of CJ—5 primary trainer.

The Shenyang Aircraft Factory had repaired 534 jet fighters from 1951 to 1953 and also manufactured more than 140 major items of aircraft wings, front and rear fuselages and empennage. The factory had basically mastered the manufacturing technology of MiG type aircraft.

The trial production of J—5 started in February 1955. Final assembly, sub—assembly, component assembly and parts manufacture were carried out in parallel in the factory using Soviet supplied subassemblies, assemblies and raw materials. In more than a half year, workers and engineers of each profession were tempered effectively in technology, production and management. Trial production time was shortened and the quality of trial production was ensured. With this situation, Vice Premier Bo Yibo, on November 30, 1955, reported to Premier Zhou Enlai, and suggested that the time of successful trial production of aircraft could be changed from originally the end of 1957 to the time before National Day of 1956. The aircraft with all Chinese made parts came to the final assembly shop in February 1956, just as it was predicted. Test flight of the first aircraft was witnessed on July 19 and finished on August 2. The State Certification Committee announced on September 8: "MiG—17 jet aircraft has been successfully manufactured in the Shenyang Aircraft Factory and the aircraft can be manufactured in batches for the service of the Air Force and Navy." This was one year and five months ahead of the state specified schedule. WP5 jet engine trial manufactured in the Shenyang Aero Engine Factory passed acceptance test in June of the same year. On September 9, the "People's Daily" proclaimed to the world on the front page the successful manufacture of new type jet aircraft. The Central Committee of the Communist Party of China and the State Council sent special telegraph of congratulations on September 10, 1956. On the same day, Marshal Nie Rongzhen, Vice Chairman of the National Defence Committee and Vice Premier of the State Council went to Shenyang and took part in the celebration.

Nearly 40 years of arduous research and exploration had passed from the birth of the first aircraft in the world at the turn of the century to the appearance of jet aircraft in the beginning of the 1940s. In the mid 1950s there were only a few industrially developed countries in the world that could manufacture jet fighters. New China's aviation industry was established in

1951 with the assistance of the Soviet Union on a very weak foundation. Piston trainer was manufactured in 1954, soon after, the jet fighter was manufactured in 1956, which marked China's entering into a jet era and put China among the few countries in the world that could produce jet aircraft. This achievement only took five years and such a fast development was undoubtedly astonishing.

After the successful trial manufacture of two types of aircraft, the Nanchang Aircraft Factory trial manufactured Russian An-2 multi-purpose small transport in only one and a half years without let up. This aircraft was later named Y-5, which was approved for production by the Military Product Certification Committee of the State Council in March 1985. It became the first civil aircraft in China.

Fig. 6   Nie Rongzhen cutting ribbon for the flight demonstration of J-5

During the period of the First Five-year Plan, trainers, jet fighters and transports were trial manufactured in China one after another, and were put into batch production and released for service. This was really a historical break through in the development history of China's aviation. Why such great achievement could be gained during such a short period of five and six years? The main reasons were: the Communist Party of China and the Chinese People's Government attached great importance to it, giving special support on manpower, material and finance and, organized all relevant industries to cooperate; correct policy of transition from repair to manufacture and a stable realistic plan were formulated; adherence to the policy of self-reliance and simultaneously actively striving for technical assistance and detailed guidance from the Soviet experts; production construction and personnel training at the same time; particularly bringing the cadres' and workers' enthusiasm and creativeness into full play, truely reflecting the close combination of high political enthusiasm with practical and realistic scientific attitude. In the final analysis, this achievement fully reflected the superiority of the socialist system, which recorded a glorious page in the aviation history of new China.

Achievement of aviation industry gained during the First Five-year Plan were highly praised by the government. Old generation proletariat revolutionists Mao Zedong, Liu Shaoqi, Zhou Enlai, Zhu De, Chen Yun, Deng Xiaoping, Li Fuchun, Peng Dehuai, Nie Rongzhen, Ye Jianying and Xu Teli all paid visits to the two aviation exhibitions held in 1956 and 1958 respectively and visited aviation factories, universities and schools, ardently expecting the aviation industry where the best of all industries were assembled, to catch up with the advanced level of the world at an earliest possible time.

Fig. 7   Liu Shaoqi, Deng Xiaoping and Yang Shangkun visiting the Shenyang Aero Engine Factory

Section 5   Attempt at Aircraft Design

Another objective of China's aviation industry was to establish aviation scientific research institution and to develop and design aircraft on its own. Although the aircraft it produced at that time was fairly advanced, it would lag behind, if China's own R&D were not carried out and its personnel not sufficiently trained. The Bureau of Aviation Industry therefore, called for a special meeting in May 1955 to discuss problems of development and design, and the guiding principle of carrying on scientific development, production and personnel education simultaneously was defined and a proposal was made to the Ministry of Defence to set up aviation research and development institutions immediately in order to change the backward status of research and development. In the report of "The development status and future task of aviation industry" to Chairman Mao Zedong by Director Wang Xiping of the Bureau of Aviation Industry in May 1956, the grave situation of research and development lagging behind production was further analysed and the practical measures of conducting work immediately using the existing conditions were proposed. During this period of time, state leaders in charge of defence science and technology and leaders of aviation industrial departments paid several visits to the Soviet Union, negotiating for their assistance to China in setting up a complete set of research and development organizations. Apart from setting up research and development organizations closely associated with material, process and test flight, no agreements were signed on other matters, which further aroused determination of the Chinese people to establish aviation research and development institutions independently.

In 1956, the Central Committee of the Communist Party of China and Chairman Mao Zedong called for a "march towards the modern science". A 12 year−development−plan of China's science and technology was worked out under the guidance of Zhou Enlai, Chen Yi, Li Fuchun and Nie Rongzhen, mastering and developing the jet technology for catching up with the world advanced level was ranked one of the five major programmes. This greatly inspired and pushed forward the work of setting up research and development institutions. According to the spirit of the Central Committee, aviation industry began to put the development of scientific research and product design in the important position during the Second Five−year Plan. Three catagories were divided for the establishment of aviation research and development in the initial stage:

1. A group of excellent engineers and technicians were assembled within the industry around 1956 to establish an aero material research institute, an aero manufacturing technology research institute and aeronautical science and technology information research institute which were urgently needed for production, research and development.

2. Since production already started before research and development in the Chinese aviation industry, there had existed already backbone engineers and production floor area, equipment and test facilities. All these advantages had been used for the setting up of design and research departments and institutes. Design departments of aircraft, aero engine, aero instrumentation and parachute were established in aviation factories in Shenyang, Nanchang, Nanjing and Beijing. These design departments were later developed into design and research institutes gradually.

3. Design and research institutes of flight test, aerodynamics, aircraft accessory and avionics were established in Shaanxi and Shenyang respectively around 1958. At the same time, aviation scientific research departments were set up in BIAA , NPU and NAI; product design departments were also set up in some factories.

Through several years' efforts, aviation industry already possessed 6 research institutes, 3 product design institutes, 19 research and design departments or offices in factories and colleges, about ten thousand employees and several thousand research and design personnel by the end of 1960. Thus, the embryonic form of aeronautical scientific research and design institutes was bred in the cause of production development.

Technical cadres transfered to work in scientific research and design institutes all devoted to their work and most of them were the first class technical persons in aviation industry at that time. They went to their posts with lofty aspirations and great ideals of developing aviation scientific research of the motherland. Some of them applied for the permission to leave their offices in government departments or leading posts for the first line design and scientific research work; some of them left their families for the far away work site, living singlely and having meals collectively. They worked hard and arduously for construction of test facilities, for design of new products and the scientific research work. They were the first generation of pioneers of aeronautical scientific research work and made praiseworthy achievements.

Fig. 8   Test section of FL−1 wind tunnel

Aerodynamic research and test facilities must be provided for the design of aircraft. China only had a few small wind tunnels for teaching purpose, which could not meet the requirement of aircraft design then. The government, hence, decided to build a transonic and supersonic wind tunnel in Shenyang, which was a copy of the Soviet AT−1 wind tunnel, named FL−1. The test section area of the wind tunnel was 0.6m x 0.6m, and an air supply system with 8 atmospheric pressure and a complete system of automatic control, measuring and video recording equipment was included. Construction of the wind tunnel was undertaken by the Shenyang

Aircraft Factory, starting in September 1958. Great difficulty was involved in the construction in view of the technical level of China at that time. In order to build the wind tunnel soon, the relevant departments, Liaoning Province and Shenyang City organized a large scale cooperation. The welding of the air storage tank required high standard, about 100 best welders, therefore, were assembled from 29 units in Shenyang and Beijing. The work was finished with good quality in six hard-working months. Construction, testing and acceptance of the wind tunnel were all completed by March 1960, and the quality of which was up to the requirement. This was the first wind tunnel for industrial test, built mainly by our own efforts in China. For many years, this wind tunnel had played an active role in scientific research tests of aerospace industries.

Scientific research and design people deeply felt that they had been entrusted with ardent expectations from the motherland and the people. Warm support was rendered from the Air Force. Air Force Commander Liu Yalou once said at a meeting to leading cadres of aircraft and engine factories in March 1958: "There are a lot of young people in aviation factories. They must have enthusiasm and be bold to design; factories should try to manufacture them; our Air Force will support them and fly the aircraft you turned out." An upsurge of aircraft design and manufacturing was unfolded immediately and, two types of aircraft—Primary Trainer CJ—6 and jet fighter trainer JJ—1 were successfully designed.

Fig. 9   Ye Jianying and Liu Yalou watching flight demonstration by JJ—1 aircraft

JJ—1 jet fighter trainer was the first aircraft designed and manufactured by China itself. It was designed by a group of young people in design department of the Shenyang Aircraft Factory headed by Chief Designer Xu Shunshou, Deputy Chief Designers, Huang Zhiqian and Ye Zhengda. Its power plant, PF—1A jet engine was designed under the leadership of Wu Daguan, Director of design department, and designer Yu Guangyu of the Shenyang Aero Engine Factory. Design preparation work started in 1956. Xu Shunshou suggested "To read 300 Tang dynasty poems and do not stick ourselves to just one MiG theory," asking young designers who had no practical experience then to collect various kinds of aircraft information and select only the best for our own use. He reminded, at the same time, that our design should not fall into MiG aircraft pattern. Our aircraft were not to be the copy of MiG Aircraft. Bifurcated inlets was boldly adopted, not following MiG tradition of nose air intake arrangement. Initial design was soon finished after very hard work. The state approved trial manufacture in April 1958 after a consultation in the Soviet Union, check up by government departments and the Air Force and some design modifications. In July of the same year, the final assembly of the aircraft was finished. When the aircraft was ready for test flight, the whole factory was just as happy as celebrating a grand festival. People beat drums and gongs, standing in lines at both sides of the road to accompany the aircraft to the flight test station. The first test flight was piloted successfully by the shooting practice hero Yu Zhenwu. Ye Jianying, Vice Chairman of the Military Commission of CCCPC, and Air Force Commander Liu Yalou went to Shenyang from Beijing personally to take part in the celebration meeting. The aircraft afterwards also flew to Beijing for a flight demonstration.

Fig. 10   A welcome to the return of the test pilot of JJ—1

The first aircraft designed by China itself was the jet aircraft, which reflected the high standard. Design and manufacture were basically successful as proved by the initial flight test. It was regretful that this type of aircraft had not been put into batch production because of a change of the Air Force flight training system. However, it opened up the road of aircraft design in new China. primary trainer CJ—6, Q—5 series attack aircraft and J—8 series fighter were designed by this design department which later developed into design institute, on the basis of JJ—1. Therefore, the flying of this aircraft was worthy commemorating, which had been talked about widely even today.

The Chinese designed primary trainer CJ—6 was the successor of primary trainer CJ—5, developed as a trainer to link up JJ—1 in the training system. The aircraft was designed starting from the later half of 1957 by design department of the Shenyang Aircraft Factory. When the initial design was finished in May 1958, the design was continued in the Nanchang Aircraft Factory and also manufactured there. Test of the first aircraft was made in August and later went to Beijing to join the flight demonstration. Test flight was finished in December 1960. In 1961, its engine was changed to the Chinese—made piston engine HS6 from the original Czechoslovakian engine. Piston engine HS6 was certified by the state and released for batch production. This was the first aircraft designed and batch produced by China. About 1,796 such aircraft were manufactured by the end of 1986, and they were in service with the Air Force, the Navy air force and aviation schools as well as the Chinese civil aviation and friendly countries. The aircraft was awarded National Gold Medal for Quality in 1979 due to its good performance and high quality.

Fig. 11   Organizers, designers and test pilots of primary trainer CJ—6

Section 6   Setbacks in Flourishing Development

The successful transition from repair to manufacture and the completion of the First Five—year Plan ahead of time tempered the working force, and gave them more confidence to construct aviation industry in a better way. From 1957 to 1960, the production of the aviation industry saw a rapid and flourishing development. This was mainly reflected in the following aspects: production of Chinese made aircraft was increasing rapidly; more and more types of aircraft were produced; missile production capability began to be established; civil production was developed very fast and capital construction had been extended to the inland. A Chinese aviation industry began to take shape.

With support from basic industries, aviation industry organized batch production of J—5, CJ—5 and Y—5 immediately after the trial production of these three types of aircraft. 17 aircraft of the J—5 were manufactured in the same year of their trial production (1956), 142 aircraft in 1957 and 429 in 1958. Production of Primary Trainer CJ—5 and Y—5 was doubled in succession. Aviation industry delivered to the Air Force 1,086 aircraft by 1960, among which 767 were fighters, 278 trainers and 41 transporters. Hence, the aircraft supply source of the Chinese Air Force and the Navy air force had started an important strategic change from mainly depending on imported aircraft to mainly depending on the Chinese made aircraft. From then on, the Chinese aviation industry had become a powerful backing to the Chinese Air Force. The Chinese made J—5 aircraft quickly became one of the main weapons of the people's Air Force, which was quickly sent to the front line air base in Fujian to join the fight against Kuomintang aircraft invading the Mainland. 216 aircraft were also provided to China's civil aviation by the aviation industry during this period of time, among which 199 were transport aircraft and 17 trainers. Y—5 aircraft was very soon operated on domestic short distance routes and services were provided to agriculture, forestry, animal husbandry and fishery. Aviation industry had provided more than 1,300 aircraft to constructions of national defence and economy in just 6 years since the first aircraft was in the air in new China. Such a big progress was not possible in old China.

At the same time of increasing aircraft production, more types of aircraft were actively developed. Starting from the Second Five—year Plan, trial manufacture of MiG—19 supersonic jet fighter and Mi—4 multi—purpose helicopter was carried out by aviation industry according to design drawings and technical documents supplied by the Soviet Union. These two aircraft were designated as J—6 and Z—5 respectively. The Shenyang Aircraft Factory and Shenyang Aero Engine Factory began the trial manufacture of MiG—19P all weather intercepter and its engine in the first half of 1958. Except the design drawings of aircraft and engine which were provided by the Soviet Union, the preparation of process documents and manufacture of production tooling were all accomplished by themselves. The first trial produced aircraft lifted into the air at the end of the year and batch production of it started the following year. According to the urgent need of the Air Force, the factory developed a derivative MiG-19C on the basis of MiG-19P fighter in 1959 and its test flight was undertaken in the same year. At the same time, MiG-19P and MiG-19M fighters and their engines were manufactured in the Nanchang Aircraft Factory and Zhuzhou Aero Engine Factory. Test flight of the jet aircraft in 1959 demonstrated the turning point of these two factories from piston type product to jet type product. Mi-4 helicopter and its engine were trial produced by the Harbin Aircraft Factory and Harbin Engine Factory. The aircraft lifted into the air in 1958 and batch production started in 1959. Airborne equipment was also witnessed fruitful progress simultaneously. 49 kinds of instruments, 89 kinds of accessories and 152 electric products were already trial produced in 1958.

By 1959, two types of fighters, one type of trainer, small transport and helicopter were already trial manufactured by the Chinese aviation industry; the Chinese designed JJ-1 and Primary Trainer CJ-6 had also flown. There appeared a prosperous scene of production and trial manufacture of aircraft and engines of more types. But people also understood that all aircraft produced were small size aircraft and efforts should be made to manufacture larger aircraft with greater take-off weight, especially bomber aircraft, which was put in the development program by Premier Zhou Enlai in the initial stage of the aviation industry construction. Great concern was also shown by Defence Minister Peng Dehuai. When the First Five-year Plan was completed ahead of schedule in 1956, the aviation industry began to prepare for the construction of bomber aircraft factory. In 1957, agreement was reached with the Soviet Union regarding introducing Russian manufacturing technology of Tu-16 Bomber. But the newly built bomber aircraft factory lagged behind its schedule because of the change of construction site. To fill in the gaps in China's bomber aircraft, Harbin Aircraft and Engine Factories actively undertook preparations for Tu-16 trial production. Sample aircraft, drawings and part of technical documents were introduced at the beginning of 1959. The first Tu-16 aircraft assembled with Soviet made parts and components was flight tested before National Day (October 1) of 1959, which provided a good and effective practice for the later trial manufacture. This bomber was designated H-6.

The Chinese aviation industry concentrated on the development of aircraft and simultaneously considered trial production and regular production of missiles during this period of time. The missile development was included in China's 12 years science and technology development plan formulated in 1956. In April 1956, Premier Zhou Enlai presided over a special meeting to discuss China's missile development. Development of missiles and rockets in industrially developed countries was progressing very fast. More over, there was a popular opinion in favour of missile instead of aircraft. There were three opinions to the issue of handling development relations between aircraft and missile in China: some held to carry out development and trial production of missiles in China with every efforts; others insisted on the simultaneous development of aircraft and missile and still others said missile development first in first five years and then came back to aircraft development again. After repeated discussions and demonstrations by well-known aviation experts of Qian Xuesen, Wang Bi, Xu Changyu, Shen Yuan, Gao Fangqi and Ren Xingmin, the second opinion was endorsed. It was held that both aircraft and missiles had their strong points and weak points; it was not correct to bias against any of them. The theory was further proved by the long coast line of China in terms of national defence. In consideration of transportation, agriculture, forestry, measuring, exploration and ambulance, aircraft played even bigger role and was in urgent need. In the national scientific development plan, therefore, jet propulsion and rocket technology were listed as important development projects. The Fifth Research Institute of the Ministry of Defence, a rocket and missile research institute was established in October 1956 (hereinafter called the Fifth Institute). One aircraft factory was assigned to the Fifth Institute to be reformed as a missile trial production base according to the unified plan. Since missile and aircraft were similar in technical process, trial production of missile was started within aviation industry. Air to air, surface to surface , surface to air and sea defence missiles were trial produced in 1958 while facilities were constructed. By 1959, trial production lines of tactical missiles and rocket engines were basically set up in Shenyang and Nanchang; trial production work was proceeded in full swing in the associated missile design institutes. Cooperative relationship was established between lots of aviation factories and missile trial production factories. This was the beginning of China's missile industry.

With the increasing development of manufacturing capability of the aviation industry, the combined production of military product and civil product had become major subject for discussion. Chairman Mao Zedong mentioned the production of military product and the civil product as well at the Supreme Meeting of State Council at the beginning of 1956. He also pointed out: " to learn two sets of skills, i.e. the skill of producing civil products in military industry, and the skill of producing military product in civil industry. This is a good method and we must do it in this way" when he was at a briefing about the Second Five-year Plan in April. To implement this instruction, civil production management organization was set up by the Second Ministry of Machine Building; plans and measures of civil production were formulated under the leadership of Vice Minister Liu Ding. A meeting on civil production was held at the beginning of 1958 by the Bureau of Aviation Industry and, the policy of "production of both military and civil products simultaneously on the basis of ensuring the fulfilment of military production and gradually raising the level of technology" was adopted. Many civil products like metal cutting machine tools, generators, steam turbines, automobiles, tractors and motorbikes were manufactured that year. The value of civil product in the total value of production of the whole industry was increasing extensively, which was more than 40% in 1960. Civil product manufacture showed initial success, reflecting the great technical superiority and production potential of the aviation industry, which could serve the national economy widely.

Large quantities of new aviation factories were constructed one after another to meet requirements of production development and increased variety of aircraft. Construction plan at this time had some changes compared with previous one. In his " Report on the Second

Five-year Plan for developing the national economy", Premier Zhou Enlai pointed out: "In order to reasonably distribute the production force in China, promote economy development in all areas and to let our arrangement of industry suit our natural resources and national defence conditions, some new industrial bases must be constructed in inland of the country in a planned way." With this principle, the stress of aviation industry construction during the Second Five-year Plan period was shifted to inland, except a few airborne equipment factories built in coastal area. Main factories for manufacturing aircraft and engines were specially constructed in inland. To speed up the construction, the method of letting the old coastal factory contract to build the new inland factory with fixed investment was used. By the year of 1960, a set of aircraft and engine factories were established both in Chengdu and in Xi'an; aviation instrument factory, electric factory, electric motor factory and accessory factory were set up in Lanzhou, Beijing and Changchun. Some old factories were also reconstructed and expanded including Harbin Aircraft and Harbin Aero Engine factories, and Nanjing Aero Hydraulic Accessory Factory. After this period of construction, the scope of aviation industry was further expanded; aviation industrial bases were established in south-west and north-west inland areas, starting to change the situation that main aviation factories were situated in the coastal areas.

The initial stage of the aviation industry construction in the Second Five-year Plan was coincided with the country-wide movement of the "big leap forward". That movement brought heavy setbacks and losses to the flurishing development. Seeking more and fast, exaggerating subjective role without counting practical possibility prevailed in aviation industry. Arrogance and overanxiety for quick result were developed under the situation of "big leap forward", stressing the method of "trial production at a fast pace". A lot of serious quality problems happened due to careless large scale process changes, blindly reducing the use of necessary tools and fixtures and standard parts and the cancellation of many approved procedures and inspection operations. There was not a single qualified aircraft or engine of the J-6 and Z-5 aircraft delivered from 1958 to 1960.

The unpractical high design target was set for the new aircraft. Although the East Wind 107 fighter whose design was started in 1958 already had high target performance, another development programme East Wind 113 fighter had even higher performance target. It was designed by a military engineering institute and was put into trial production too almost at the same time. It was hoped to break the "thermal barrier" and reach 25,000 m service ceiling and Mach 2.5 maximum speed in level flight, without sufficient necessary development and test facilities and technical base. The development of East Wind 107 was later stopped in order to concentrate on East Wind 113, but the latter had to be cancelled too because it was too far from reality.

There were also a lot of problems in capital construction. Under the slogan of "Two for Three, One for Two" (i.e. three-dollar things done with two dollars and two-dollar things done by one dollar), too many projects but with overlow standard and overhigh construction speed were constructed. Consequently, 1.02 million square meters floor area buildings, about

70% of the total construction area built by 25 construction units from 1958 to 1960, were reconstructed or repaired later due to their inferior quality. More over, more than 50 large projects were constructed simultaneously with long construction cycle and less investment effect. There was not a single newly built factory up to the final acceptance standard until 1962.

Those problems concerning product quality, new aircraft development and capital construction were all closely linked with negligence of scientific management. At that time, scientific management was devalued as taboos and commandments fettering productivity. Therefore, each factory or agency of construction and scientific research had to reshuffle its management organizations, cadres and technical persons were ordered to leave their posts, reasonable regulations and rules and strict technical responsibilities were cancelled, which made a mess of the technical foundation of production and scientific research. Because the quality inspection system under an unified leadership was neglected as the typical case of "one man leadership system", quality management was greatly weakened. The two important pillar—process regulations and quality supervision with which the product quality was ensured during the First Five—year Plan period had been vanished almost completely.

During the "big leap forward", leaders of the Ministry of Defence Industry and the Bureau of Aviation Industry were somewhat hot—minded and, hence, some unpractical practices like "doubling the output value" and "the fast trial production" were initiated, bringing negative effect to the production of enterprises. However, the quality of aviation product was after all the issue of high sensitivity and great importance and the alertness could not but be aroused by the weakened management and inferior quality of products. With the support of Minister Zhao Erlu, the Bureau of Aviation Industry held meetings in succession starting from early 1959 in Nanchang, Harbin and Xi'an to lower temperature and improve quality of products, stressing that quality first was the unshakable policy of aviation industry and the effective management organizations and regulations and rules were requested to be restored. To stop the tendency of getting worse in quality, Minister Zhao Erlu wrote twice to enterprises and called one telephone meeting. He also said sincerely to leading cadres: "Product quality should be regarded as the most important thing even at the last minute of our life if we are determined to work in aviation industry for all our lives." But it was a pity that those "temperature lowering" measures had not been implemented due to the nationwide struggle "against right deviation". Further efforts were made by the Minister at the beginning of 1960, who personally went to Shenyang to check product quality in aviation factories, requesting factories to reestablish quality assurance system and to support the movement of delivering finished articles without defects. Leaders of the Bureau of Aviation Industry such as Wang Xiping, Jiang You and Xu Changyu later headed groups respectively to Shenyang and Harbin factories to guide the reestablishment of quality control system.

The Central Committee of the Communist Party of China and the State Council were soon alarmed by the inferior quality of military products. The Defence Industry Commission of the Military Commission of CCCPC and the Secretariat of the Central Committee of the

Communist Party of China issued circulars and held telephone meetings in August and September of 1960 about the detailed arrangement of reestablishing quality control system. To strengthen the defence industry, decision was made by the government in September to re—seperate military production from civil production which had been merged into the Ministry of Machine Building and, the Third Ministry of Machine Building was formed to take care of the management of defence industry, with Zhang Liankui as the Minister and Xue Shaoqing as the Vice Minister and Director of the Bureau of Aviation Industry. The unprecedented large scale meeting of leaders at three levels of the defence industry was held by the Defence Industry Commission in December 1960, which greatly accelerated the reestablishment of quality control system currently implemented in aviation industry. After the meeting, all factories unfolded more detailed work regarding reestablishment of quality control system. But under that historical situation, the wrong "Left" guiding thought could not be corrected. "Self—criticism" was practiced at each level, a number of leading cadres were hurt and enthusiasm and creativeness of technical personnel were dampened. Incorrect criticism to civil production affected the implementation of the principle of combining military production with civil production for a long time.

Three years of "big leap forward" had brought heavy losses to aviation industry. But after all, it was only a small portion of 10 years of initial establishment and in the first 7 years fast development and great achievement were made. Some creative and fundamental achievements were made evidently in some fields even during the three years of "big leap forward". By 1960, China's aviation industry had become a newly established business. Fighters, trainers, helicopters and small transports were being manufactured in batches. New designs were on the drawing boards and foundation for the later development had been laid.

Chapter II   Establishing A Complete System of Aviation Industry

(1961 — 1976)

China's aviation industry entered into the stage of independent construction and development with her own efforts after the withdrawal of experts and unilateral breach of contracts by the Soviet government in July 1960. With the purpose of carrying out self—reliant R&D and manufacturing new type of aircraft, scientific research institutes were systematically set up, which completely solved the problems of the supply of domestic airborne equipment and materials; and fairly complete set of production capabilities were constructed and the so—called third line (inland) construction was started. By the mid—1970s, was established a rather complete system of aviation industry which experienced the prosperity in the early stage of the 1960s as a result of the policy of " Adjustment, Consolidation, Replenishment and Improvement." It also saw unprecedented heavy destruction caused by 10 years long "great cultural revolution". Old generation of proletariat revolutionists like, Zhou Enlai, Ye Jianying and Deng Xiaoping showed deep concern to aviation industry even during the "great cultural revolution", encouraging people to strive forward continuously to eliminate interferences.

Section 1   Prosperity Brought by Adjustment and Reorganization

Aviation industry suffered very much at the end of the 1950s and the beginning of the 1960s as a grave consequence of the "big leap forward". The breach of contracts by the Soviet Union and three years of natural disasters had added to the difficulties of the aviation industry on its road of development.

In winter 1960, the Central Committee of the Communist Party of China and the State Council decided to implement policy of " Adjustment, Consolidation, Replenishment and Improvement" and, a series of policies and measures were worked out. To implement the above mentioned four words policy and to act in the spirit of the three level cadres' meeting of the defence industry and to centre the work on improving product quality, an enterprise reorganization in aviation industry was carried out. But the problem of the over extended "battle line" of aviation industry caused by the "big leap forward" was not solved; arrangement of trial production and batch production was far beyond the practical possibility; and capital construction projects were still too many to handle.

In July and August 1961, a defence industry working meeting was held in Beidaihe presided over by He Long, Nie Rongzhen and Luo Ruiqing. The meeting was concentrated on the discussion of implementing the four words policy comprehensively and shortening production construction lines. Premier Zhou Enlai delivered a speech at the meeting, pointing out that the policy of current plan—adjustment was to "withdraw completely from some projects; allow for unforeseen circumstances; focus on adjustment and fight battles of annihilation." Aviation industry was also requested to compress its "battle line" and the plan must be worked out on the basis of the minimum possibility in order to carry out thorough adjustment, project consolidation and to advance steadily. Adjustment of aviation industry was discussed at special meetings presided over by Luo Ruiqing. It was decided that aviation industry should concentrate on the production of spare parts with some development of new aircraft within two to three years to solve the problem of low rate of operations of the Air Force due to the lack of spare parts. New aircraft work was focused on quality improvement of J—6 and Z—5 and the type approval production of Primary Trainer CJ—6. The work on other more than ten types of new aircraft were either slowed down or stopped; working line of missile development was also shortened; capital construction within two years was only to ensure two aircraft factories and two engine factories in Chengdu and Xi'an and the reconditioning of several electrical and instrumentation factories in Lanzhou, all other large and middle size projects were stopped or slowed down. As for the design of aircraft, it was stressed to respect science and to go step by step. The design could only be started on the basis of the information and technology of the MiG—21. In this way the correct relationship was developed between development of new aircraft, batch production of aircraft and manufacture of spare parts and between aircraft and missiles. This drastic measure of withdrawing completely helped aviation industry truely return to the road of development.

The country was suffering economical difficulties then. In 1961, the newly appointed Minister of Defence Industry Ministry, Sun Zhiyuan, during the period of implementing Beidaihe Meeting, did painstaking ideological work, he wrote articles himself, introducing experience of hard working of Yumen oil workers and asking people in defence industry to learn from their spirit of working hard without wasting time, to actively plunge into work centered on ensuring quality of products. He also had many heart—to—heart talks with enterprise leading cadres, hence those cadres were relieved of their ideological pressure and their creativeness was motivated. The masses were united, working day and night and leaders shared weal and woe with workers. A new picture appeared in aviation industry.

All factories and military products were strictly checked according to requirement of quality first and quality standard details were worked out during the adjustment of quality activity. Technical documentation, raw materials, finished parts, equipment, tools and fixtures were checked page by page and piece by piece; sections, workshops and factories were checked and approved one by one according to standard. Principle of detail analysis with each different product and seeking truth from fact were insisted during the standardization activity. As for those aircraft trial manufactured not according to original drawings and documents and with severe problems, complete set of original drawings and documents were reproduced, complete set of good quality tools and fixtures and master parts were manufactured and trial production was reorganized. A transition method was allowed to be used to ensure the quality of the aircraft getting better with each batch. Those aircraft that could not be delivered due to partial quality problems were overhauled according to the best quality requirement. All those measures ensured the development of quality adjustment on the right road. At the same time, all factories earnestly implement " State Industrial Enterprise Management Regulations (draft)" , i.e. "Seventy Rules of Industry" promulgated by the Central Committee of the Communist Party of China; responsibility system of leaders at all levels and all regulations were strictly practiced; enterprise management was systematically restored and adjusted through out China.

Fig. 12   Zhou Enlai shaking hands and talking with workers and cadres of the Harbin Aircraft Factory

The Central Committee of the Communist Party of China and the State Council showed great concern to the adjustment and reorganization of the aviation industry and encouragement and guidance were rendered. When the Shenyang Aero Engine Factory and the Tianjin Aero Electrical Factory won the first battle of reaching the standard of good quality in May 1962, the Defence Industry Commission of the Military Commission of CCCPC circulated a notice of commendation, and bonuses were awarded. Premier Zhou Enlai, with numerous state affairs to handle every day, paid a visit to the Shenyang Aircraft Factory in June 1962, called a meeting with leading cadres of aviation factories in Shenyang area, focused on the discussions of "linkup" between old and new aircraft and the supply of indigenous raw materials in China; cadres were encouraged to learn techniques. Premier Zhou later paid three visits to the Harbin Aircraft Factory in 1962, 1963 and 1966 respectively. He asked about the quality of Z-5 helicopter, and discussed with cadres and workers. He told the factory to "make best use of time", "make a good showing" and "feel proud and elated"; to manufacture more helicopters to support national construction and friendly countries.

The Z—5 and J—6 aircraft passed state certification successively in September and December 1963 respectively, successfully reached the standard of good quality, hence batch produced. Aircraft and engine newly manufactured were fitted with best quality parts in China and 352 airborne equipment were all of good quality. Technical cruxes like buffeting with the MiG—19 prototype and vibration with Mi—4 helicopter respectively were also tackled one after the ano—ther, which reflected the capability of China's aviation industry of manufacturing more complicated aircraft independently. In December that year the Military Commission of CCCPC sent a telegram of congratulations regarding the high standard of quality of these two aircraft, saying: "This is a symbol showing that China's aviation industry is turning for the better all—round."

The high standard of quality also accelerated the coordinated development of the complete aircraft as well as spare parts. From 1961 to 1963, aviation industry produced more than ten thousand items with 85.8 million pieces of spare parts for 15 types of aircraft and 13 types of engines, and 778 units of spare engines, which changed the situation that the Air Force and the Navy air force stopped flying and overhauling due to lack of spare parts in a certain period of time. Some spare parts originally supplied from abroad were now supplied by domestic sources.

When the activity of letting product reach high quality standard was organized, engineering quality of capital construction was rechecked with great efforts as well. All bad quality projects were repaired and strengthened and, constructions of two sets of aircraft and engine factories in Chengdu and Xi'an and two airborne equipment factories in Lanzhou were all finished and production started by the end of 1963. At the same time, some factories which were urgently needed to fill the blanks in a complete production system were newly built or expanded, concentrating on the expansion and reconditioning of old factories plus the taking over of several local civil factories to ensure development and production of missiles and aircraft. The newly increased assets in 1963 was 106% of that year's plan, creating the best investment effect of aviation industry since 1958.

The negative influence caused by the "big leap forward" in aviation industry was basically eliminated through adjustment and reorganization from 1961 to 1963. Production and management of aviation industry were on the right direction; quality of product and capital construction was being improved; economic situation was turning for the better and the whole industry began to make profit.

In September 1963, the government decided to establish the Ministry of Aviation Industry (it was designated as the Third Ministry of Machine Building), and Sun Zhiyuan was appointed the Minister and Liu Ding, Wu Yongfeng and Duan Zijun Vice Ministers. A leading cadres meeting of enterprises of aviation industry was held and presided over by newly formed Ministry leadership in early 1964. At that meeting, situation was analysed comprehensively and achievements during the three years of implementing the four words policy were affirmed. But it was pointed out that the achievements were just a beginning which could only be regarded as one step in the cause of climbing to the top; status of aviation industry was far behind the need of constructions of national defence and economy. The meeting discussed the plan of future construction and development, established the strategic objective from copy – production to design and development, decided to continue to implement the four words policy in 1964 and 1965 and to create conditions and lay good foundation for the long term development by working in a down–to–earth way according to the requirement of "constructing the Chinese People's Air Force to meet the requirement of national economic development and unceasingly provide modernized aviation technical equipment." After the meeting, the Minister and Vice Ministers headed cadres in the ministry to each enterprise and institute to explain the decisions to all cadres and workers, organized joint battles of trial production of new aircraft and batch

Fig. 13   He Long and Sun Zhiyuan in the Shenyang Aircraft Factory

production of a variety of aircraft and unfolded the movement of learning from Daqing and learning from models. The broad workers and staff had clear target ahead of them and actively plunged themselves into production construction. From 1964 to 1966, before the breaking out of the "great cultural revolution", the whole industry had developed in a healthy way with everything in good order.

In the meantime, development of new missiles and aircraft had got exciting progress:

"PL-1" air to air missile, "Red Flag-1" ground to air missile, "SY-1" ground to ship missile and rocket engine for ground to ground missile were all successfully trial manufactured and batch produced consecutively in 1963, 1964 and 1966, which ended the history of having no missiles in China. When the heroic people's army were equipped with missiles, it was just like a tiger that had got wings, and became a stronger peace keeping force. Having realized high quality production of J-6, all weather high subsonic fighter J-5A and two times of sound speed, high altitude high speed fighter J-7 were successfully trial produced in 1964 and 1966 respectively; the attack aircraft Q-5 whose design was started by China itself in 1958 had reached preliminary design certification and was put into batch production in 1965; light jet bomber H-5 was flight tested in 1965 as well. Successful development of all those aircraft and missiles reflected the strong will of workers and staff of aviation industry to develop new aircraft themselves and their ever increasing technical capability.

Batch productions of high quality aircraft and missiles were carried out successfully as well. Output of J-6 aircraft and "Red Flag-1" missile increased rapidly and their annual production jumped to a new level in 1965. During three years from 1963 to 1965, 1,055 various kind of high quality aircraft, 3,081 engines were produced and delivered; and missiles were batch produced as well, which greatly improved the armed forces equipment and strengthened the capability of national defence. The total industrial output value of the industry in 1965 was 1.6 times that of 1960. All kinds of economic and technical norms reached the best level ever since the establishment of aviation industry until 1966. This was really a new upsurge in the development of aviation industry.

Section 2   Aeronautical Material and Equipment Based on Indigenous Sources

The contract of supplying materials and equipment to China was turned down by the Soviet Union at the beginning of the 1960s. But domestic aero products were continuously delivered, just because the guideline had been set up earlier that most of the aeronautical materials and equipment should gradually be supplied by indigenous sources. So that the Chinese aviation industry could cope with the situation caused by the sudden change of the Soviet attitude.

Aeronautical materials and equipment, in aviation industry, generally refer to the materials, elements and parts and finished parts used for the manufacture of aircraft (including flying vehicle), aero engine and airborne equipment. Modern aircraft is a kind of product with intensive technology and complicated structure, which needs a variety of materials and equipment. J-5 aircraft, for instance, needed 7,652 items of different types of materials and equipment and 12,319 items for J-6 aircraft. These aeronautical materials and equipment, different from ordinary industrial materials and equipment, are required to work repeatly for many times under conditions of high temperature, low temperature, high stress,heavy corrosion with minimum size and weight. Because aircraft can not be stopped for repair and replacement during flight, requirements regarding strength, stiffness, high and low temperature performance, anti—corrosion and fracture toughness of aeronautical materials and equipment are very harsh. The supply of indigenous aeronautical materials and equipment reflects the level of science and technology of a nation, and the development status of its base industries, and its economic strength.

In the initial stage, new China's aviation industry was based on the very weak foundation of industries, which could manufacture and supply only ordinary steel, brass and red copper and, there was almost a blank of special aeronautical materials; it was completely out of question to supply precision bearing, rubber products, acrylic plastic sheet, large castings and forgings and aluminium materials for aviation use. Although those materials and equipment could be imported from the Soviet Union, but that could not last forever. Chen Yun once pointed out in 1952 that one of the most difficult problems to be solved for the aircraft industry from repair to manufacture was the indigenous material supply. Li Fuchun also pointed out that the supply of raw materials and coordination with other industries were important factors to decide the development speed of the aviation industry. The government, under their leadership, had arranged production bases of the manufacture of indigenous aviation materials and equipment while the plan of basic industries construction was formulated.

Fig. 14   Chen Yun and other leaders of the Central Committee with
the cadres of the Harbin Aircraft Factory

Under the unified government planning and directly organized by industries of metallurgy, chemical, machine building and textile, a number of enterprises with fairly good equipment and strong technical force through out China were picked up to undertake trial production of aeronautical materials and equipment and, were guaranteed as key projects by the government for replenishment and expansion. Chen Yun personally led Wang Heshou, Minister of the Ministry of Metallurgical Industry, to Fushun and Shenyang to solve problems of superalloy trial production for use in aero engine. Up to 1955, Fushun Steel works was replenished as the first production base of aero superalloy in China; Shenyang Fourth and Fifth Rubber Factories were emerged as aeronautical rubber products production base; Shenyang No.3 Rubber Factory and Tianjin Paint Factory were reconditioned as production bases of aircraft tyre and aeronautical paint respectively; in Jinxi Chemical Factory a workshop of aeronautical acrylic plastic sheet was constructed; Shanghai Textile Industry Bureau organized relevent factories, and on the basis of the Shanghai Chemical Fibre Factory, to form a complete production line as a production base of special textile materials for making China's high speed parachutes.

At the same time of reconditioning and expanding old factories, the government also focused on the construction of a number of large enterprises to undertake aeronautical materials and equipment production as their main task, such as the Harbin Aluminium Machining Factory, Harbin Bearing Factory and Angang No.2 Cold Drawing Seamless Steel Tube Factory. At the end of the First Five-year Plan and with the completion of these factories, supplying status of aeronautical material and equipment changed rapidly. For instance, after the Harbin Aluminium Machining Factory started its production, proportion of China's own aluminium alloys needed by aviation industry jumped from 2.1% in 1955 to more than 90%; 93% of tubes needed by aviation industry was supplied when production in the Angang No.2 Cold Drawing Steel Tube Factory started. The indigenous raw materials for batch produced primary trainer CJ-5 and its piston engine and J-5 aircraft and its WP5 engine were up to 98%, 96%, 81% and 78% respectively.

The smooth start of supplying aeronautical materials and equipment from indigenous sources was first of all due to the hard work of material and equipment production organizations. People of those organizations thought it was their responsibility to develop and supply indigenous aeronautical materials and equipment and to early terminate the reliance on import. They worked by every possible means to fulfil the task and simultaneously were supported by cooperation of production and application departments. A special organization in charge of development of materials and equipment was set up by the Bureau of Aviation Industry, and a number of university graduates and interpreters, and quite a number of senior engineers, were assembled to translate the standards of the Soviet aeronautical materials and equipment and technical documentation or to provide technical data by analysing finished parts stripped from aircraft. When the first type of superalloy was trial produced, the Ministry of Metallurgy together with the Bureau of Aviation Industry organized Fushun Steel Works, the Aeronautical Materials Research Institute, the Steel and Iron Research Institute and Shenyang Aero Engine Factory to work cooperatively like in a relay race, which greatly accelerated the progress of trial production.

With the performance improvement of newly developed aircraft around 1960, high requirement was put forward on materials. Compared with J—5 aircraft, working temperature of turbine blade of engines for J—6 and J—7 aircraft increased from 750 ℃ to 800 ℃ and 900 ℃ respectively; working temperature of the burner liner and the turbine disc also greatly increased. A superalloy with better composition had to be developed because the original superalloy was no longer suitable. Other materials and equipment had similar problems. It was just at that time that the Soviet Union broke off the supply contract. Hence, the task of paramount importance at that time was to ensure the supply of aeronautical materials and equipment.

In 1960, the Secretariat of the CCCPC and the Military Commission of CCCPC held meetings separately and it was decided to organize forces all over the country to solve the problem of indigenous aeronautical materials and equipment. A series of urgent measures were taken and attention was paid by Li Fuchun, He Long, Bo Yibo, Nie Rongzhen and Luo Rui— qing. Vice Premier Bo Yibo went to the Fushun Steel Works personally to discuss and arrange production of aeronautical superalloy. He also instructed the Ministry of Metallurgy to urgently issue a special task order with 104 as its code name on December 29, 1960 to 10 large steel works such as the Anshan Steel Works and the Fushun Steel Works etc. In 1961, in order to solve critical materials needed for the production of J—6 aircraft, another special task order with the code name of 105 was again issued by the Ministry of Metallurgy after approval by the State Council. A nation wide special profession group of aeronautical materials was set up in 1963. Assembled more than 20 noted experts including Li Xun, director of the Metal Research Institute of Academy of Sciences. They worked together formulating plans for indigenous aeronautical materials supply.

In order to break through critical points of superalloy material, the Ministry of Metallurgy had set up vacuum furnaces and electroslag furnaces in the Fushun Steel Works, Qiqihare Steel Works, Dayie Steel Works, Shanghai No.5 Steel Works and Chongqing 102 factory; construction of Gansu nickel mines was speeded up and Shanghai refinery factory where metal nickel purifying was done was replenished. Shen Hong, Vice Minister of The First Ministry of Machine Building and a noted mechanical engineering expert, was appointed to be specially in charge of the manufacture of the cold rolling machine for superalloys. Xie Beiyi, member of the National Economic Commission called a series of meetings to see the progress and solve existing problems. To coordinate the work of the Steel and Iron Research Institute, Aeronautic Material Research Institute, Metal Research Institute of the Chinese Academy of Sciences, Fushun Steel Works and Shenyang Aero Engine Factory in tackling difficulties, a coordination group was set up consisting of Liu Bole, Director of Steel Bureau of the Metallurgy Ministry, Fang Zhiyuan, deputy Director of the Bureau of Aviation Industry, Wu Fengqiao, director of Steel Institute and Wei Zhuye, director of Aeronautical Material Research Institute. Through more than four years efforts, chemical compositions of superalloy newly developed and methods of smelting, rolling and die forging were at last grasped. And the material performance was better than that of the imported material.

Up to 1965, not only the 104 special task was accomplished well on time, but also the good foundation of trial production of superalloy needed by aviation industry was laid.

In order to tackle the "hard bone" of aviation special bearings of about one thousand types, discussions were held among the Defense Industry Office of the State Council. The First Ministry of Machine Building and the Ministry of Metallurgy and a decision was made to list the two military bearing workshops in Harbin and Luoyang as key projects which were constructed ahead of schedule; technical forces were organized all over the country to tackle key technical problems. After ten years of hard work aviation bearings at last came to the stage of being supplied completely in China. At the same time, metallurgical and mechanical organizations constructed bases in Maanshan in Anhui Province, Deyang and Chongqing in Sichuan Province, solved manufacturing problems of large steel forging and rolling. The Great Wall Steel Works was built later in South-west China as one of the special steel supplying bases. In the 1960s, cooperated with the Air Force and the Ministry of Aviation Industry, Yumen and Daqing oil fields of the Ministry of Oil Industry successfully trial produced various kinds of aviation fuel and oil with Chinese crude oil, hence, the days of aviation industry relying on "imported fuel and oil" were gone forever.

Another important factor of the indigenous supply of aeronautical materials and equipment was to carry out scientific research on the basis of domestic resources to form a series of aeronautical materials with Chinese characteristics. Since the mid-1950s, Aeronautical Material Research Institute worked coordinately with departments of metallurgy, chemical, machinery, petroleum and light industries as well as Chinese Academy of Sciences and universities concerned to undertake trial production while doing test and research, and successfully trial produced and manufactured in succession series of sealing materials, gold based alloys, superalloys, high strength aluminium alloys, synthetic rubber and orientated acrylic plastic sheet for aircraft canopy, etc. Compared with the similar alloy of the Soviet Union and the United States, the high strength aluminium alloy developed jointly by scientific research department of Metallurgical Ministry and Aeronautical Material Research Institute had unique advantages in improving its characteristics of anti stress corrosion and anti crack elongation. The iron-and-nickel base superalloy, non-nickel structural steel and cast titanium alloys etc. developed during that period of time all were original achievements. The achievements in the iron-and nickel-base material fully utilized rich Chinese resources and reduced importation of expensive nickel element. The utilization of non-nickel structural steel and titanium alloy saved the weight of aircraft and engine and improved the process performance.

The great effect and far-reaching significance of the government's decision on having aeronautical materials and equipment supplied by indigenous sources became clearer and clearer in production practice. The batch produced J-6 aircraft and Z-5 helicopter needed 12,319 items and 9,019 items of materials respectively, of which 20% could not be supplied domestically in 1960, but could be fully supplied in China by 1965. The more important thing was that starting from the mid—1960s China had already established development and production bases of aeronautical materials with fairly complete professions and types. These bases consisted jointly of departments of aviation industry and Chinese Academy of Sciences and universities, basically possessed the capability of supplying aeronautical material and equipment needed for research and development of new aircraft independently. For example, 4,461 items of materials needed for H—6 aircraft were all supplied in China by 756 factories and institutes; integral panels, high temperature glass, fluorine plastic high pressure hose and metal hose, were better than all that were used by previous aircraft. Materials and equipment needed for Spey engine introduced from England and Z—8 helicopter later in the latter half of the 1970s were better than those previously used. Their technical standard was higher, they were basically supplied and developed in China except only a few. Aeronautical materials and equipment supplied by indigenous sources was really a great achievement of new China.

Section 3   Setting Up the Chinese Aeronautical Establishment

Scientific research is the base and precursor of the development of modern aviation industry and also a decisive constituent part in establishing an independent system of aviation industry. In order to respond to Chairman Mao Zhedong's call for marching towards science in the mid—1950s, aviation industry began to set up scientific research institutes with the support of Minister Zhao Erlu. But construction scale at that time was fairly small, mainly aimed at solving science and technical problems incured during trial production. The situation of scientific research and design lagging behind production and development was revealed gradually with the passing time. Fully relying on China's own efforts to solve problems of development and manufacture was required after the foreign aid was stopped in 1960. Therefore, strengthening construction of scientific organizations became even more important, under which situation the CAE was set up and, its construction could be divided into three stages from the beginning of the 1960s to the 1970s:

— Stage One: Setting up of the Chinese Aeronautical Establishment and a number of science institutes and product design institutes in the beginning of the 1960s.

The Military Commission of CCCPC, on December 27, 1960, issued "Circular of setting up three establishments of aeronautics, naval vessels and military electronics" , pointing out: to assemble associated scientific research forces, to speed up development of scientific technical research work of China's national defence and to strengthen the power of armed forces, the Central Committee of the Communist Party of China approved on December 20, 1960 the setting up of an Aeronautical Establishment, a Naval Vessel Establishment and an Electronics Establishment by relevant scientific research organizations of the Defence Industry and Machine Building Industry.

To implement the Circular of the Military Commission and the decision of the Central

Committee, starting from January 1961, aeronautical scientific research organizations were adjusted, and the Ministry of Defence's Sixth Establishment (the Chinese Aeronautical Establishment) was set up with Tang Yanjie as President, Wang Zhengqian political commissar, Han Gusan, Wang Li, Xu Lixing and Cao Danhui Vice Presidents. The Establishment was consisted of 7,600 people, from 11 organizations of the Bureau of Aviation Industry, the Air Force, the Harbin Military Engineering Academy and the headquarters of No.22 Army Garrison Division, among them were 6,961 people and 4,498 units of equipment from aviation industry . The following scientific research institutes were subordinate to the Establishment: institutes of aeronautical material, aeronautical manufacturing technology, aeronautical science and technology information, flight, flight automatic control, aeronautical weapons and accessories etc; the Shenyang Aircraft Design Institute, Aero Engine Design Institute and Aerodynamics Institute; Shanghai Aeronautical Measuring Equipment factory, and other product design organizations set up in factories, metrology institute set up at later stage, aeronautical precision machinery institute and aeronautical standardization institute, all of which formed the initial scientific research capability.

Not long after the setting up of the Aeronautical Establishment, the CCCPC promulgated in June 1961 "Proposals of 14 rules for the present work of natural scientific research institutes (draft)" (simplified as "14 rules"). Premier Zhou Enlai later made a " Report on the issue of intellectuals" at the national scientific & technical work meeting and on the Forum of national drama, opera and children drama writing. The Premier said that most intellectuals were a part of the working class. According to that spirit, the Establishment seriously carried out the work of adjustment and reorganization to eliminate chaos

Fig. 15　Tang Yanjie, President of the CAE (Second from right) in the Aeronautical Material Research Institute

and turmoil due to the "big leap forward". Intellectuals in all scientific research units had their "caps removed" i.e. their caps of "Bourgeois intellectuals" removed, and they were crowned by the announcement that they were a part of the labouring people. They were encouraged to have different schools and opinions in free discussion and free competition; military ranks, technical and professional titles were awarded to them according to regulations and rules. At the same

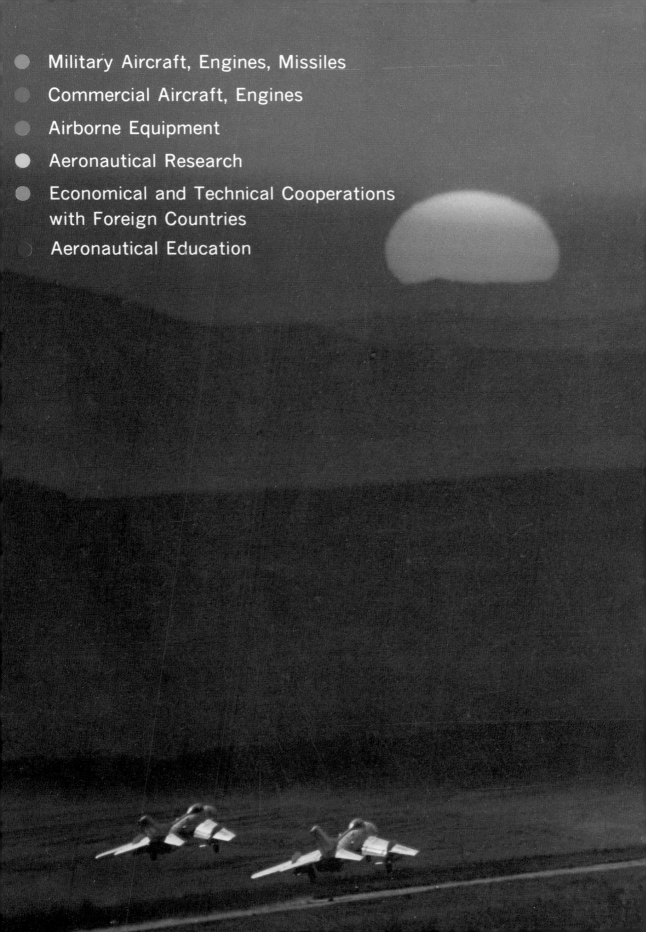

- Military Aircraft, Engines, Missiles
- Commercial Aircraft, Engines
- Airborne Equipment
- Aeronautical Research
- Economical and Technical Cooperations with Foreign Countries
- Aeronautical Education

Military Aircraft, Engines, Missiles

3. J-8II fighter

2. J-8II in the air

4. People who took part in the development of J-8II:
Wen Junfeng (left to right), Gu Songfen, Qu Xueren, Wang Ang, Guan De

5. J-8 II Cockpit
   instrument panel

6. WS6 engine

7. J-8 II in landing

8. J-8 fleet

9. Final assembly line of J-8 I

10. WP7A engine

11. J-8 aircraft fatigue test

12. Citation awarded for J-8 aircraft

13. Office building of the Shenyang Aircraft Company

证 书

获奖项目：歼八（白天型，全天候型）飞机
获奖单位：航空工业部沈阳飞机制造公司等
奖励等级：特等
奖励日期：一九八五年
证 书 号：85-K G3-T-009-2

为表彰在促进科学技术
进步工作中做出重大贡献，
特颁发此证书，以资鼓励。

国家科学技术进步奖
评审委员会

14. Citation certificate for J-8

15. Entrance gate to the Shenyang Aircraft Company

China's aviation industry takes off in the world.

China's aviation industry reached an important milestone on March 11 when Boeing received the first vertical fin made in China for the Boeing 737.

The largest 737 component manufactured outside Boeing, the vertical fin must be built to exacting standards.

In meeting those requiremen[ts] people of Xian Aircraft Comp[any] proved they can work to qual[ity] that few companies anywhere [in the] world can match.

Plans call for China to deliver fins to Boeing each month un[til]

about 200 fins in all.
Demand is high because the Boeing 737
is the most popular commercial airliner
in history. More than 2,000 have been
sold to 140 airlines around the world.

Boeing is honored to be a part of
China's emergence as a contributing

member of the worldwide commercial
aviation industry.

BOEING

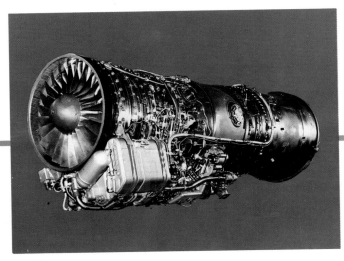

16. WP13 engine for J-7Ⅲ fighter

17. People who took part in the development of J-7Ⅲ: Song Wencong (left to right), Yu Mingwen, Xie Ming, Li Xiangjun

18. J-7Ⅲ supersonic fighter

19. J-7M fleet

20. J-7M with air to air missiles

21. J-7 II fighters in flying

22. J-7 II engine running at night

23. J-7 II fighter production line

24. J-7 II fleet

25. JJ-7 trainer

26. JJ-7 trainer taking-off

27. JJ-7 maiden flight ceremony

28. JJ-5s in formation flight

29. Guizhou Aircraft Factory
    at night

30. H-6D bomber taking-off

31. H-6D bomber

time, it was pointed out that "to serve science and technology" and "to serve scientific research workers" were the concrete reflection of serving the people, and best efforts were made to create better conditions of work and study for scientific research personnel. All those measures made most intellectuals feel warm and hence initiated their creativeness of achieving good results in their scientific research.

According to requirements of the 14 rules, the Establishment defined the objective, task, equipment and personnel for each institute (or factory), formulated a complete set of regulations of science and technology, working procedures of science and development, new product trial production regulations and temporary regulations of aeronautical institutes and clearly specified that scientific research work was the centre of all work in the Establishment and institutes, no less than five sixth of the working time in a week should be guaranteed for scientific research work and the political work and logistics should ensure the smooth progress of R&D.

Guiding thought and working policy of research and design work were corrected during this time by the Establishment regarding the unpractical requirements of aircraft design incured in the "big leap forward". Premier Zhou Enlai, in June 1962, pointed out at the cadres meeting of defense industry in North—east China: "research in the most advanced branches of science should be performed in order and advanced step by step." Chief of the General Staff Luo Rui—qing also instructed: "A thorough study of the MiG—21 aircraft will not waste time, it will help the Sixth Establishment (i.e. CAE) achieve good results earlier instead. The general policy and the only way of the development for the Establishment's scientific research work is to design aircraft through copy manufacturing." The Establishment carefully organized the "study". Reverse designs of key products were done during copy manufacturing, which trained technical personnel, improved design skill and accelerated the design progress of new aircraft.

After three years efforts, fairly regular scientific research working procedures were set up in each aeronautical scientific research organization and all kinds of research and professional work began to advance onto the right track by the end of 1963.

—Stage two: Construction of scientific research and test facilities was enhanced in the mid and late 1960s.

With the change from copy manufacture to design, a variety of test technology and test facilities for mathematical and physical simulation tests and engineering tests of various kinds were needed for new aircraft design and old aircraft improvement. Practice told people that design of advanced aircraft could not be realized without these test technology and equipment. Construction of scientific research and test conditions, therefore, became an important issue for discussion.

After the merger of MAI and CAE in 1964, Minister Sun Zhiyuan repeatedly stressed the priority for the development of aviation scientific research and that scientific research and test facilities should be constructed even if at the cost of several sets of factories. The MAI very soon decided that construction of scientific research and test facilities should be regarded as a strategic task of the development of aviation industry and that it should be planned with the highest priority during the Third Five—year Plan period. Construction of Aerodynamic Institute, Aero Engine Institute and Aircraft Structural Strength Research Institute were started in inland at the beginning of 1965 and simultaneously the construction of Flight Research Institute were speeded up. The above four scientific research and test bases were fairly large with technical complexity. They had been undertaken as key projects. Aircraft Structural Strength Research Institute could accommodate 120 tons static test of a complete aircraft in 120 tons. Test plant of this Institute was formally delivered for use in the mid—1960s, which was replenished with test facilities, and became a fairly complete test base of aircraft static and fatigue tests. High Altitude Simulating Test Facility of Aero Engine Research Institute was a very large project, the first stage of which was finished in the late 1970s with a nation wide cooperation. Plus engine component test rigs and equipment of various kinds, the Institute basically possessed a complete test facilities for engine research. Flight Research Institute was a comprehensive flight research and test centre and its flight research personnel had rich practical experience and good theoretical foundation. They formed a complete set of professionals through their research practices. Low speed wind tunnel, transonic wind tunnel and supersonic wind tunnel of different types and velocities were constructed in succession in inland Aerodynamics Research Institute, which formed China's Aerodynamic Test Establishment later. With wind tunnels of different types belonging to the MAI in Harbin, Shenyang, Beijing, Xi'an and Nanjing, China had then a series of wind tunnels of different sizes and velocities.

Test base of Shenyang Aero Engine Design Institute was established at that time as well. The construction of scientific research and test facilities by other research institute and design institute according to their requirements and possibilities was also flourishing. Factories and universities all set up their scientific research and process research organizations. Because of their variety of types and kinds, airborne equipment were mainly developed by design organizations in factories, where best technical forces were assembled to carry out the work.

— Stage three: Filling gaps, strengthening weak points and striving for a complete aeronautical scientific research system in the late 1960s and beginning of the 1970s.

In order to carry out the design of large aircraft, to unfold the research and application of electronic technology and computer technology in aviation industry, and to fill the gap of ejection seat a number of research and design institutes were built newly or replenished in succession during this period of time. The newly built or replenished institutes included five aircraft design institutes of helicopter, seaplane, large aircraft, fighter (second set) and trunk airliner; the Zhuzhou Aero Engine Design Institute and four airborne equipment institutes of survival aids, airborne radar, avionics and aerial fire control and, the institute of airborne computer technology. Considering aviation industry as a whole, it had not only some institutes with application research as their main tasks but still carrying out some basic research, but also some product design institutes with development of new products as their main tasks and some basic technology research institutes of metrology, standard and information. The combination of professional research institute, design institute, factory design department and process research departments, and university scientific research institutes formed the framework of aeronautical scientific research system.

Section 4　Systematization and Inland Construction of China's Aviation Industry

Old China almost had no production capability for airborne equipment. Due to the fact that the complexity and importance of airborne equipment were not fully understood and the country was in short of money and technology during the initial stage of new China's aviation industry, the issue of constructing airborne equipment factories at the same time with aircraft and engine factories had not been brought for discussion during China's first negotiation with the Soviet Union on their assistance to China's aviation industry in 1951. When this problem was realized later, 5 airborne equipment factories were listed in the First Five–year Plan projects constructed with the Soviet assistance in 1953. But some of these projects were located in coastal area and due to strategic considerations were moved to inland not long after they started production, which delayed the advancement of factory construction. That was happened at the time when China's aviation industry was in the transition period from repair to manufacture. Very heavy task of aircraft repair was there, and completion of production task was greatly affected due to frequent shortage of instrumentation and special equipment, which could not be provided by the Soviet Union. Though some local state–run factories and private factories were replenished and reconditioned to meet the urgent need, production capability was after all limited, far from meeting the needs of the development of aircraft and engine. In manufacturing, the critical technology needed for the manufacture could not be tempered since the repair of airborne equipment at that time was mainly limited to inspection and simple parts manufacturing. And this also increased the difficulty of the transition for airborne equipment from repair to manufacture.

To change this situation, the Bureau of Aviation Industry decided to turn their attention to the construction of airborne equipment factories after completion of six aircraft and engine factories construction in June 1955. At the same time, the original special equipment workshops in aircraft and engine factories were reconstructed and expanded into factories although they still trial produced some accessories for aircraft and engines. Measures were also adopted to accelerate training of technical personnel for airborne equipment factories. By this way, 11 airborne equipment factories of instrumentation, accessory and electrical systems etc. were constructed or almost constructed at the end of the First Five–year Plan, and they batch produced 80% of 245 items of airborne equipment needed by J–5 aircraft and its engines; a number of precision and complicated products, such as fuel pumps, gyros and micro motors were trial produced too. Hence, the problem of auxiliaries and accessories production not in proportion to aircraft and aero engines production was alleviated. With the increase of aircraft types, the complexity of airborne equipment was increasingly higher and the proportion of their manufacturing hours in that of aircraft and engine was rising rapidly. But the construction projects listed in the Second Five—year Plan were far from meeting the actual requirement, lacking lots of disciplines, and this made the problem of airborne equipment not matching with the development of aircraft and engine outstanding again.

Bearing this in mind, aviation industry actively practiced " filling gaps and setting up complete set of systems" during the three years of adjustment after 1960. Apart from constructing new factories, some local factories and abandoned schools were replenished and reconditioned, hence, a number of factories of aeronautical instrumentation, electrical system and accessory, including armament factory, propeller factory, high altitude cockpit equipment factory, oxygen instruments factory, aeronautical magneto factory, filter screen factory and high altitude compensating suit factory etc., which filled up gaps of many disciplines in China and basically formed a fairly complete set of balanced system of aircraft, engine and airborne equipment. Product design departments were set up by factories one after another. There were 832 items of good quality airborne equipment trial produced and manufactured within two years of 1961 and 1962. At the same time, factories of airborne radar, communication, navigation, electronics, optical equipment and airborne weaponry were newly built or reconditioned by industries of machinery, electronics and weaponry according to the state unified plan. Construction of these complete set of airborne equipment factories created good conditions for the development of aircraft, engine and missile.

At the beginning of 1964, Minister Sun Zhiyuan requested the industry to realize the strategic objective of "five aircraft, three missiles" within two years (five aircraft: J—6, Z—5, Y—5, J—5A and Primary Trainer CJ—6; three missiles: ground to air, air to air and ship to air), which was a forcefull impetus to the improvement of a balanced system of aviation industry. To reach this objective, the shortage of 60 items of airborne equipment became the bottle neck of batch production of aircraft and missile of various types. Chen Shaozhong, Director of the Airborne Equipment Bureau led people to the factories to provide guidance on the spot and quickly solved these critical problems. Except a few items not yet certified, airborne equipment needed by batch produced aircraft of different types were manufactured and provided in China by the second half of 1965. Airborne equipment, therefore, had entered into a new stage of independent system gradually.

At the same time of constructing complete production system, inland construction was carried out with great efforts by aviation industry in view of national defence and industrial distribution as a whole.

Inland construction of aviation industry started as early as in the First Five—year Plan period and was developed in the Second Five—year Plan and three years of adjustment. At the Working Meeting of the CCCPC in May and the Meeting of the Central Secretariat in August 1964, Chairman Mao Zedong proposed to divide China into one, two and three lines; factories in the first line should be moved and the third line should be strengthened as a rear base in case of war; factories should be divided into two parts and quickly move one part to inland.

Afterwards, inland construction of aviation industry was carried out in large scale. At the beginning of 1965, the Ministry of Aviation Industry made the decision to thoroughly stop and slow down first and second line construction projects and move enterprises situated in large cities in the first and second line to the third line in a planned way according to the requirement of adjusting the first line and concentrating on the third line in the "Guide lines for defence industry in 1965" approved by the CCCPC. All the first and second lines enterprises worked out plans of moving to the inland. In the same year of making the decision, the moving of 6 airborne equipment and avionics factories making lamps, parachutes and engine accessories in coastal area was completed and, another 9 factories and 3 institutes started their construction in third line as well.

At that time, workers and staff of aviation industry were very enthusiastic on the construction of the third line. After dividing factories into two parts with moving tasks, preparation management for new factory construction started intense work immediately, some of them departed their relatives and friends for the third line even without bringing their belongings. About two thousand workers and staff of aviation factories in Shanghai, Tianjin and Beijing moved to Guizhou by orders, with equipment completely moved and installed for production within less than half a year.

Large scale third line construction started in the late 1960s, focussing on the construction of a complete set of Guizhou bases, and auxiliary factories and institutes were also constructed in North-west, South-central and South-west areas. The 1970s saw the construction focus on aircraft factories in Shaanxi, Jiangxi and Hubei Provinces. Most of these construction projects were located in poor and remote mountainous areas. The hardships were imaginable when the large scale construction project was to be carried out in mountainous areas near the Hanjiang River and Guizhou mountainous areas of "the place without three consecutive fine days and three yards of flat ground". But in order to prepare for a sudden war and for the development of aviation industry, workers and staff in the third line cooperated with construction engineering army and civilian people with great enthusiasm. They dined and slept in the open area, repaired bridges and roads, crossed mountains and rivers to find out water source; they suffered great difficulties during construction of factories. After their hard struggle and efforts, a number of factories were at last constructed, equipment installed and associated living facilities set up in these remote barren mountainous areas of the third line.

Some plants were even built in the large mountain tunnels formed billions of years ago. Outstanding achievements were witnessed on the third line construction through people's hard and arduous struggle.

Third line investment of aviation industry during the Third Five-year Plan period was 93.4% of its total investment, 83.2% during Fourth Five-year Plan period. Large number of factory plants were constructed in the third line during those ten years. A group of enterprises and administrative organizations including aircraft and engine factories, accessory factories, special factories and design institute, warehouse, hospitals and schools were set up in the remote strategic Guizhou area and mountainous area in south Shaanxi Province. Up to that time China's aviation industry not only had possessed good production systems of aircraft, engine and airborne equipment in North—east, North—China and East—China areas, but also established a complete set of production capability of manufacturing fighters, bombers, transports and helicopters in South—central, South—west and North—west areas. A great change of distribution of aviation industry had taken place.

Marching into the third line, aviation industry had brought water, electricity, transportation, school, department stores and modern information of economy, technology and culture to remote areas, supported remote area construction and hence, accelerated the change of situation in those industrially and economically weak areas.

It is obvious that the "leftist" influence and lash of "great cultural revolution" had created a lot of problems in the construction of aviation industry in the third line. But the hard work and great efforts of the workers and staff for the construction of the third line in creating a material foundation for the development of aviation industry is everlasting.

Section 5   From Copy Production to Independent Design and Development

Development of China's aviation industry can be divided into the following stages: repair stage — before the successful manufacture of the Primary Trainer CJ—5 in 1954; copy production stage — in the late 1950s; attempting independent design of aircraft in the late 1950s and early 1960s and the new stage of independent development after the Soviet Union broke off the contract.

Independent design and development of new types of aircraft were carried out fairly smoothly during the early 1960s, but were hindered during the "great cultural revolution", detail work in this period included: partial design in connection with copy production, reference design, improvement and modification and independent design.

1. Copy Production Was Carried out in Combination with Partial Design

The newly developed aircraft in this period were: the high altitude high speed fighter J—7, light jet bomber H—5 and the medium range jet bomber H—6. They were not manufactured by pure copying, but with some improvement and / or partial design.

When the trial production of H—5 started in the Harbin Aircraft Factory in 1963, the only technical documentation available was the document of old and incomplete design drawings for overhauling Il—28 aircraft provided by the Soviet Union. The factory carried out repeated tests and computations on aircraft strength and aerodynamic performance; test flight was carried out by Air Force aircraft and gained plenty of data. 13,637 pieces of improvement and supplementary drawings, 40% of the total, for the complete aircraft were created; major modifications were carried out on aircraft wing structure, tail section structure, front cover and feeding guide rail; WP5A engine was used instead of WP5; more than 60 types of domestically supplied products like turret etc. were fitted on the aircraft. All these helped improve the workability and tactical performance of this type of aircraft. During the manufacture, all process documents were prepared by the factory and more than ten thousand sets of tools and fixtures were designed and manufactured. After three years hard work, this aircraft was successfully trial produced at last in 1967 and the stable batch production followed soon.

Fig. 16   Li Xiannian in the Harbin Aircraft Factory

Development of other aircraft such as H-6 was carried out almost at the same time of that of H-5 bomber. That was the first time for China to manufacture medium range jet bomber with 75 tons take-off weight. The Number of parts, the complexity of structure, and the technical difficulty and engineering work of this aircraft all exceeded that of any other previous aircraft. When it was trial produced in 1964, the factory only had the incomplete Soviet Tu-16 aircraft technical documents. Xi'an Aircraft and Engine factories fully relied on their own efforts to make up strength calculation documents and their design documents were more than 15,400 pieces; they successfully modified its fuselage, vertical tail, nose landing gear and fuel drain system and prepared all process sheets by themselves. During installation of assembly jigs, new technology of optical telescope and micrometer rods were first used to overcome matching and coordination difficulty of large aircraft trial production and successfully broke through the thermal and cold manufacturing difficulties of large wing sliding rail, aluminium alloy beam, main landing gear and armor plate etc.. High risk and more difficult test like fuel dump at high altitude was also conducted during trial production.

In the process of aircraft trial production, the Special Commission of the Central

Committee issued an order to modify an original type of H−6 for the mission of transporting and delivering atomic bomb, which should be arranged simultaneously with the trial production of H−6 and, materials and equipment needed were to be produced in China as an urgent task. The modified H−6 aircraft successfully fulfilled the mission of delivering atomic bomb test first ever in China on May 14, 1965, which won telegrams from the CCCPC and the State Council. Premier Zhou Enlai met and dined in the Great Hall of the People with the persons and representatives of relevant organizations who had rendered great service, including representatives of the Ministry of Aviation Industry and Xi'an Aircraft Factory.

Successful development of H−5 and H−6 bomber aircraft indicated that in the field of aircraft design and manufacture, China's aviation science and technology had entered into a new stage — a big step towards independent aircraft design and development; Chinese aviation scientific and technical people not only concentrated on learning and simulating but also had capability of understanding, appraising and improving, which was undoubtedly a kind of practical effective exercise for future independent development.

Fig. 17   Deng Xiaoping and Li Fuchun visiting the Xi'an Aircraft Factory

2. Carrying out Reference Design to Develop New Types of Aircraft

Through analysis, test, research and calculation of the existing sample aircraft and then to carry out reverse design to obtain systematic data and reliable conclusion and then on that basis design and development of new types of aircraft was started, which was one of the methods adopted in China for the development of new aircraft. Medium and short range passenger plane Y−7 and medium range transport Y−8 were developed in this way.

In October 1966, Premier Zhou Enlai and vice Chairman Ye Jianying approved to develop Y−7 passenger plane. Soon after, a design team of more than 300 people was formed, which consisted of mainly people from the Xi'an Aircraft Factory and Aircraft Design Institute plus people from the Nanchang and Harbin Aircraft Factory, Aeronautical Material Research Institute and Manufacturing Technology Research Institute. Various kinds of necessary data were obtained on the basis of actual measuring and analysis and lots of tests, with which complete set of drawings, technical conditions, test and calculation reports and manufacturing process documents were designed and prepared; complete production tooling and fixtures were designed and manufactured and, various new technology and process were adopted. Consequently this 50−seat Y−7 passenger plane successfully flew in December 1970.

Flying of Y−7 aircraft filled the blank of medium size transport aircraft and also trained a technical team of design, process and manufacture working coordinately. It was also this team that continued to work with the Air Force No.1 Institute and NPU, they formed an even stronger force for the development of Y−8 aircraft, a transport with about 60 tons of takeoff weight, in October 1969. Its first test flight took place in December 1974 after 5 years efforts. By then the Xi'an Aircraft Factory and Aircraft Design Institute had successfully developed three aircraft — H−6, Y−7 and Y−8, which helped China's aviation industry enter into the field of developing large and medium size aircraft, one more step towards developing new types of aircraft independently.

3. Undertaking Improvement and Modification, Developing More Types and Enlarging Applications

Derivation and modification were performed on the basis of the existing types of aircraft to improve structure and performance, prolong life and derive new types in order to meet the requirement of more applications, which was widely used in the world due to less investment, less risk and cost effectiveness.

During the initial development stage, aviation industry concentrated its efforts on copy manufacture. Modifications and derivations were started no sooner than the beginning of the 1960s, when the Harbin Aero Engine Factory had difficulties to provide many different types of engines for many different aircraft under repair. They started with the derivation and modification of the original Z−5 power plant — a piston engine HS7 as a sample engine; a modified piston engine HS8 was developed in 1963, which was certified by the Aero Products Certification Commission. This new type of engine could be used on the Soviet Tu−2 bomber, Il−12, Il−14 transport aircraft and U.S. C−46 transport, realized " one engine for four applications". About one hundred imported old aircraft, which had been grounded due to lack of engines, were rescued. The aircraft high altitude performance was also improved by using this engine. It met the requirement of flying to Tibet.

Derivations and modifications in other field were performed in succession as well. The day time fighter J—5 aircraft was modified successfully to J—5A in 1964; J—5, H—5 and J—6 were modified to JJ—5 trainer, HJ—5 bomber trainer and JJ—6 in 1966, 1972 and 1973 respectively; modification of bomber reconnaissance aircraft HZ—5, and JZ—6 were also carried out. Modifications of these aircraft were realized by overcoming defects of the original design, and fitting more advanced equipment for various needs. These modified aircraft had achieved very good results in practice. The outstanding achievements further encouraged people and pushed forward the work of modification and derivation.

Fig. 18   Zhu De with leading cadres of the Shenyang Aircraft Factory

4. Designing New Types of Aircraft

Since the 1960s China successfully designed a supersonic attack aircraft Q—5 and high altitude high speed fighter J—8.

Although JJ—1 aircraft and its engine designed in the late 1950s and the Primary Trainer CJ—6 in the 1960s were certified for batch production, the design work at that time was in the initial stage with little experience. The smooth copy production of several types of aircraft had given people a false impression that the design of aircraft and engine was not that complicated. People had no personal experience to the fact that design should be based on the previous accumulated research and technical base. This lack of understanding of the design law plus the prevailing atmosphere of the "big leap forward" caused people to put undue emphasis on what is new, neglecting practical possibility. It was just under this situation that the unpractical, too high target of design performance of the East Wind 113 came out. Design of the Q—5 aircraft also started in the late 1950s and was more or less influenced by that situation.

The development of Q—5 aircraft was done in the Nanchang Aircraft Factory and its chief designer was Lu Xiaopeng. When the design started in August 1958, its design concept was defined of good low altitude performances, manoeuvrability, surprise attack and ground attack according to the Air Force requirement. After 20 months hard and arduous work, the prototype aircraft was trial produced in May 1960. When the whole country entered in the stage of adjustment in 1961, the Q—5 faced the problem of being "abandoned". The factory decided to continue the work by "making use of every bit of time", which won the support from the Air Force, the MAI and the CAE. The first aircraft was flight tested in June 1965. After design certification its small batch trial production started at the end of the year. Further modifications were carried out from 1968 to 1969 to get rid of the problems found out by the Air Force. After those modifications, the aircraft was praised by pilots and was deemed as a fairly good attack aircraft. At the end of 1969, the government approved its batch production. Ten years of hard work filled the blank of China's supersonic jet attack aircraft. This was a good aircraft successfully designed by China. Having tempered in activities of the design of the primary trainer CJ—6 and Q—5 aircraft, the Nanchang Aircraft Factory had formed a capable and powerful aircraft design team, which was a far reaching achievement than the successful design of one or two types of aircraft.

At the same time of developing the Q—5 aircraft, design of another aircraft was also started. When the CAE was set up in 1961, it was stressed to draw lessons from the failures of the East Wind 113 and thoroughly study MiG—21, i.e. J—7, step by step and to design a new type of aircraft with better performance, i.e. the J—8 fighter according to the requirement of the Military Commission of CCCPC. Design of this new type of aircraft was taken place in the Shenyang Aircraft Design Institute with Huang Zhiqian, and later, Gu Songfen as its chief designer. Based on the copy production experience of the J—7, designers had fully understood all characteristics of this aircraft and they also studied and analysed documents of foreign fighters obtained, therefore, a comprehensive understanding of design principle, specification, standard, material and process of supersonic fighter at Mach 2 level was gained. Designers had basically mastered methods of design, calculation and test of high altitude, high speed fighter. On this basis, the fighting objective was defined and specification of the new fighter J—8 was worked out according to the Air Force requirement. After the objective was defined, four large scale investigations in Air Force were made, and more than 6,000 pieces of suggestions were collected and, 73 items with 11,000 times of wind tunnel tests and 500 items of various kinds of structure and system tests were performed specially for the J—8 aircraft. The design philosophy did not stress on "all new", but on the right selection of new technologies that were available through efforts. On the critical issue of power plant selection, aircraft designers did not stick to the planned high performance engine, but adopted WP7A engine, the thrust of which could be increased after modification. This decision helped the smooth development of the aircraft. The J—8 high altitude high speed fighter design was finished in 1966 and the first flight of the J—8 aircraft was made in July 1969. It was really not easy to send the new aircraft into the sky during the years of the "great cultural revolution". The J—8 development group still continued their work in the great turmoil and disorder. The flying of J—8 aircraft marked a new era of China's aviation industry.

During the 16 years from 1961 to 1976, 7 new types of aircraft, 7 types of engine, 4 types of missiles and one type of special aircraft had been successfully developed and certified for production; 6 types of aircraft, 7 types of engines and 3 types of missiles had been improved and modified for production. 13 types of aircraft, 14 types of engines, 7 types of missiles and 1 type of special aircraft were provided, which enabled the Air Force and CAAC to have a variety of aviation equipment. Compared with what were possessed before 1960, now their equipment included not only trainers, fighters, transports, but also helicopters, attack aircraft, bombers and pilotless aircraft. Aircraft weight was also increased gradually from below 10 tons to 25 tons take off weight of the H—5, and 75 tons of H—6. The heavier aircraft Y—10 transport with 102 tons was under development as well. Fighter's performance was developed from subsonic in the 1950s to supersonic and then to two times of the speed of sound, from day type to all weather type. Engines and airborne equipment for all types of aircraft were designed and manufactured by China. China's aviation industry already had the capability of supplying a variety of aviation equipment.

Section 6   Destruction and Anti—Destruction During the Period of the "great cultural revolution"

Under the guidance of the policy of self—reliance and hard struggle, aviation industry had made progress in establishing a complete set of systems, by efforts of all workers and staff and with the impetus of nation wide war preparation from the early 1960s to the mid—1970s. But during this period, the work also suffered heavy destruction caused by the "great cultural revolution". Because Wu Faxian, a member of the Lin Biao counter revolutionary clique, had his hands in the aviation industry personally, aviation industry was turned into a "disastrous area" during that turmoil period.

After the "January Storm" in 1967, top management of the MAI and factories and administrative organizations had all been forced to "give away the power" and been "smashed" due to the influence of "Down with everything and civil war all over China" initiated by Lin Biao and Jiang Qing, etc. A large number of injustice cases, false cases and wrong cases were created and, a large number of best leading cadres, scientific technology experts and labour models were suppressed and maltreated even to death. Creativeness of broad cadres and masses was heavily dampened. Management organizations in many units were "cut by one strike" and management regulations were "blown away with wind". Production and development was brought into the status of anarchism or semi—anarchism. But just under that condition, Wu Faxian and his like forced people to work with high targets and issued confusion orders, which created grave problems of product quality. Large number of aircraft, engines and missiles could not be delivered but were kept in warehouse because of quality problems, enterprises run heavily into debt and the whole industry was on the brink of bankruptcy. Under the influence from the "left", the normal order of scientific research and new aircraft development in aviation industry was no more and the order of working on new types of aircraft was issued at will. There were as more as 27 different types of aircraft ordered to develop just in one year of 1971. The long range bomber, large transport and vertical take off and landing aircraft etc. were requested to be developed within two to three years without having a simple three view drawing. As for the aircraft performance, it was fixed in the morning but changed in the afternoon and in the situation of "raising level gradually, but never having it certified". Consequently, scientific research investment and technical force were too widely dispersed, which caused delay of development cycles. For instance, J—7 was successfully developed as early as in 1966, but it was looked down upon and modification stopped. Several ups and downs of the aircraft caused 10 years delay. Development cycles for the J—8, Y—7 and Y—8 aircraft were more than 10 years each without giving certificate for production. Some other types of aircraft had to be stopped in halfway. It was calculated that during the "great cultural revolution" development of more than 30 types of aircraft was stopped, large amount of development investment paid for nothing; as for the cost of time, it could never be compensated.

Because of the destruction and interference of Lin Biao counter revolutionary clique, capital construction was carried out blindly without planning and feasibility study. The policy of "going into the mountains, being dispersed and entering into tunnels" i.e. plants should be constructed near mountains, dispersed and inside tunnels. The investment was not only wasted, but it also left over many outstanding problems which could not be solved for a long time. Construction projects of aviation industry in 1971 were more than 100 with 28 projects stopped later, which caused a loss of about one billion yuan. Among the 46 newly constructed projects from 1969 to 1971, about 36 projects were started without product documents, primary design and approval. Some factories were constructed without having done hydrogeological surveying, some plants were built on slopes subject to landslide, which had to be stopped by investing tens of million yuan after the production had been started; some aircraft research and design institutes were constructed in the romote valley where no railway and no flat land for construc—ting runways for flight test, which had to be reconstructed again by investing tens of million yuan. Especially in the third line (inland) construction the method of locating plant in caves or tunnels was emphasized. The plants were inlayed and buried underground and it was required that they should be like villages and native farm houses in a "Melon vine style" and locations of bases, factories and institutes were scattered. Even some small factories had to be constructed along a valley of 10 to 20 kilometers long. This arrangement not only wasted lots of man power, finance and material, but also created great difficulties for production and livelihood. Some of those projects had to be adjusted and reconstructed later with huge investment and some of them could hardly be corrected.

The " great cultural revolution" had brought aviation education to the brink of disintegration; colleges and universities of high education had to "stop classes to carry out revolution"; secondary technical schools and skilled workers schools were all forced to turn into factories and, workers' spare time education was abandoned completely. Termination of training qualified personnel caused shortage of aviation professional personnel and the educational and technical standard of employees was generally dropped.

Workers and staff of the aviation industry were greatly worried and concerned about heavy destruction caused by the "great cultural revolution". Proletarian revolutionists Zhou Enlai, Ye Jianying and Deng Xiaoping showed special concern about the condition of the aviation industry. When the quality problem started to alarm people, Premier Zhou Enlai timely called Vice Premier Li Fuchun, Yu Qiuli, leading cadres of Defence Industry Office of the State Council and MAI for meetings to discuss it specially in April 1969. At that time leaders of the Military Control Committee of the MAI tried to stall the Premier's call for the restoration of inspection system with a vague answer, saying that it could only be restored gradually. On hearing this, Premier Zhou Enlai severely criticized him immediately by saying: "What is a gradual restoration? How can you say in this way, how can you use this wording? It can not be a gradual restoration, but it should be restored right away." He also stressed: "Some people want to smash all systems. This is an ultra—left ideological trend." What a force of justice! What an awe—inspiring righteousness!

At the same time, Premier Zhou Enlai also entrusted Ye Jianying, the newly appointed Vice Chairman in charge of daily affairs of the Military Commission of CCCPC, to organize meetings of discussion on aviation product quality. When he was debriefed about the meeting, the Premier delivered an important speech, clearly pointing out: "Lin Biao anti—Party clique should be criticized, anarchism and ultra—left ideological trend should be criticized; the number one in the management of each organization should pay attention to product quality personally" and "to improve general quality by working hard at foreign aid products; to bring up other products by working at J—6; to push national defence industry and civil industry by working on aviation industry." According to the spirit of Premier Zhou Enlai's speech, measures for solving quality, problem and changing the backwardness of aviation industry were worked out. Soon after, the CCCPC adjusted top management of the MAI and rehabilitated posts of ministry and bureau leaders who had been forced to leave their posts before. In March 1972, Li Jitai was appointed Minister of the Ministry, Air Force leadership in the MAI had been removed and the MAI was put under the direct leadership of the State Council again. Special documents were issued by the State Council and Military Commission of CCCPC, which emphasized to thoroughly change the situation of poor quality, incomplete systems and insufficient spare parts existed in the national defence industry and aviation industry. Product quality adjustment was carried out widely in all units of aviation industry starting in 1972, which was in essence an actual action of resisting and criticizing the leftest ideological trend, restoring and reorganizing enterprises. It is also worth mentioning that in order to introduce foreign technology and accelerate China's development, Premier Zhou Enlai and Vice Chairman Ye Jianying strongly supported aviation industry to introduce "Spey" engine technology from England by firmly removing "leftest" interference under very difficult conditions in the period of the "great cultural revolution". The introduction of "Spey" engine at that time not just played an important role in improving technology of China's aero engine, but more importantly, it broke through China's long term closed—door policy and technological blockade by the west, which had a far—reaching significance.

When Vice Premier Deng Xiaoping was entrusted to take care of daily affairs of the CCCPC in 1975, he immediately waged a tit—for—tat struggle against Jiang Qing counter revolutionary clique. At a enlarged meeting of the Military Commission of CCCPC presided over by him, Deng Xiaoping put forward proposals of recorganizing Army and defence industry. The Chengdu Aircraft Factory, Aero Engine Factory and Aero Instrumentation Factory attended a key enterprises report meeting approved by the State Council and the Military Commission of CCCPC in March 1975. The meeting was aimed at solving situation problems of those long time disordered organizations. Deng Xiaoping, Ye Jianying, Li Xiannian and Wang Zhen all went to the meeting and delivered important speeches, sternly criticizing ultra left ideological trend and anarchism, requesting those enterprises to get rid of paralysed status within a certain time. Drastic measures of reorganizing the management of each factory was soon adopted. Entrusted by Premier Zhou Enlai and Vice Premier Deng Xiaoping, Vice Chairman Ye Jianying presided over a report meeting on defence industry and military equipment in May, at which the need for rectification of military equipment and production of defence industry was re—confirmed. Deng Xiaoping pointed out specially: we must make our existing defence factories capable of producing products. Situations in some key factories are not good because bad persons are in power, like Chengdu Aircraft Factory. This must be solved in due time and the situation must be quickly changed. The employees of the aviation industry who were in the arduous struggle were undoubtedly greatly encouraged by his remarks. Having approved by the CCCPC, the key enterprises meeting of defence industry was held again in July and August of 1975, at which Deng Xiaoping mentioned further: three things should be tackled in solving problems of defence enterprises. First, a powerful management must be set up; Second, quality should be put in the first place and third, the livelihood of the masses must be taken care of. Responsibility systems of Chief Engineer and Chief Accountant must be set up to guarantee normal order of enterprises. Employees of aviation industry were energized by this meeting. By the end of 1975, most of enterprises had fulfilled their tasks fairly well; the whole industry had made up its deficits; good progress of development of new type aircraft and capital construction was achieved and a number of factories had their product quality passed approval and acceptance. The year of 1975 was the best year of fulfilling the task by aviation industry during the period of "ten years turmoil". It was a pity that this good scene did not last long. The upward trend of the situation brought up by reorganization was soon stopped by "fighting against right trend of reversing verdict". Aviation Industry, like other industries in China, was again caught in disorder.

But no matter what kind of setbacks and relapses happened, most of employees of aviation industry were still loyal to their work and stayed in their posts. A large number of veteran cadres continued their work in spite of being framed and humiliated. Broad cadres and masses of aviation industry had experienced rigorous trials during the "great cultural revolution" and pushed forward aviation industry in the struggle against destruction. No doubt, aviation industry would have made greater achievements if there was no "great cultural revolution".

Chapter III   Stepping into a New Period of Development
(1977 — 1986)

The Central Committee of the Communist Party of China smashed Jiang Qing counter revolutionary clique (the gang of four) at one blow in 1976, which cleared the biggest obstacle on the road of socialist China and helped aviation industry take a favourable turn. After the Third Plenary Session of the Eleventh Congress of the Central Committee of the Communist Party of China, the focus of the Party's work shifted to the construction of socialist modernization. Soon the policies of "reorganization, reform, adjustment and improvement" and opening to the outside world, vitalizing domestic economy were implemented in the construction of national economy. Aviation industry, therefore, had stepped into a new period of development and begun the exploration of constructing aviation industry with Chinese characteristics.

According to the spirit of the Third Plenary Session of the Eleventh Central Committee of the Communist Party of China and the National Science Convention, the Ministry of Aviation Industry in 1979, in the light of requirement of the government, put forward the policy of "scientific research going ahead of the rest", "quality first" and "working according to economic law", with the objective of "producing one generation, developing one generation and exploring one generation" and simultaneously started to reform the industry's foreign trade system. In 1980, the system of contracting business responsibility, with profit contracting as its main content, was adopted between the government and the Ministry of Aviation Industry, and between the Ministry and its enterprises. This policy gave more power to enterprises in making their own decisions. The development program was adjusted and compressed according to the guiding principle of "doing things according to one's capability and getting things done" in 1981. At the beginning of 1982, the Ministry of Aviation Industry put forward further the task of "four transforms" and "three breakthroughs". "Four transforms" were: transforming the purely military production structure to the combined military and civil production structure; transforming copy production to independent design and development; transforming the supply of products for domestic application mainly to the combination of supply for both domestic and foreign use and transforming the method of pure administrative management to the method of economic management as well. The "three breakthroughs" were: breakthrough in the development of new type of aircraft, breakthrough in civil production and breakthrough in export. The implementation of these general and specific policies and tasks played a guiding role in changing the face of the aviation industry.

The Twelveth National Congress of the Communist Party of China called for "creating an overall new aspect of the socialist modernization construction" in 1982. The "Decision on reforming economic system" was worked out at the Third Plenary Session of the Twelveth

Congress of the Communist Party of China in 1984. The Military Commission of CCCPC made a decision in 1985 based on the change of international situation, that defence construction should be subject to economic construction. Under the guidance of these important policies, adjustment and reform of aviation industry were deepening gradually. From 1983 to 1986, the Ministry of Aviation Industry put forward the plan for creating a new aspect gradually and issued regulations to give more power to enterprises in making their own decisions, and defined the objective of "accelerating replacement of aircraft, manufacturing more civil products and improving economic results" and the requirement of setting up combined military and civil products enterprises. New progress was made by the industry in scientific research, production, adjustment of product structure, reform of management system and improvement of economic result etc.

The Central Committee of the Communist Party of China and the State Council made a decision in 1987 to reform the defence industry system, i.e. to bring it into the management channel of the entire national economy. According to this decision, the Ministry of Aviation Industry, summed up the work in the previous period, and further defined two major tasks for the strategic change. First, development policy changed from previous combination of military and civil productions with military production as the main task to the combination of military and civil with civil production as main task. Second, economic pattern changed from product economy to the planned commodity economy. The development policy of the aviation industry was that: its production should be a combination of military and civil production, with civil production as its main task; aeronautical production as its base, with diversified business; scientific research should go in advance; quality first; and facing the world and joining in group competition. The general line of the system reform was also formulated, which was that the production of aeronautical products should be carried out according to a central plan, while civil production be open and cross—cooperation was encouraged to form group organization; administration to be simplified to energize enterprises and the functions of the Ministry should be changed to purely governmental (no more business management).

Section 1 Reorganizing Enterprises in an All—round Way and Laying a Better Foundation for the Future

During the "great cultural revolution", aviation industry had been heavily damaged, enterprise management was brought into chaos and product quality was greatly worse. It was, therefore, an urgent task for the aviation industry to rectify and reorganize enterprises in an all—round way and to improve production and technology etc. after smashing the "gang of four". On the 5th December 1977, the Central Committee of the Communist Party of China decided to appoint Lu Dong as the Minister and Secretary of the Party Group of the Ministry of Aviation Industry and, the leading body of the Ministry was soon reshuffled. On the 6th December, Deng Xiaoping met with Lu Dong and other newly appointed leaders of ministries of defence industry, asking them to expose and criticize the "gang of four", to reorganize leading bodies at each level, to make great efforts on product quality in connection with actual task and to raise management and science and technology level. The aviation industry started work of reorganizing enterprises in an all-round way in accordance with the above requirement, which was divided broadly into two stages: First stage was from 1978 to 1981 centred on the overall inspection of product quality and the reorganization. Second stage was the acceleration of overall reorganization and improvement of enterprise management in connection with economic system reform since 1982.

In 1978, the whole industry concentrated on deepening the exposure and criticism of the "gang of four", checking faction systems of the "gang of four", rehabilitated a large number of fabricated, false cases, completely reorganized leading bodies of enterprises and administrative organizations, implemented the policy of intellectuals and restored production order. Some large and backbone enterprises which were spoiled by group and faction elements had quickly changed their situation after reorganization. Shenyang Aero Engine Factory once achieved good results of quality reorganization under direct concern of Premier Zhou Enlai in 1972 and 1973. But group and faction elements in the factory stirred up troubles and threw the factory into chaos, causing serious product quality problem. During four years with them in power, 48 severe quality accidents had happened and more than half of 4,400 engines produced had been returned to factory for repair because of bad quality. People said with grief and hatred: "factory will not have a single quiet day without eliminating those group and faction forces." After smashing the "gang of four", the original Party Committee Secretary Wu Xia was transfered back again to be in charge of the factory work after approval of the Central Committee of the Communist Party of China. After more than one year's work of reorganization, the bad persons were removed from their power, production and management orders were restored and the new atmosphere of happiness was felt by everybody, quality improved and production fulfilled on schedule, which helped the factory enter into the rank of advanced enterprises both in the city and the province. Similar situations were occurred in Chengdu Aircraft Factory and Nanchang Aircraft Factory etc. The whole industry had enjoyed political unity and stability.

An overall product quality inspection was carried out to check and analyse the outstanding quality problems and hidden troubles so as to give workers and staff further understanding of the extreme importance of aviation product quality and to switch the production onto the right track of quality first. Cadres and masses of the industry earnestly summed up their historic experiences and lessons of flight accidents and quality problems which caused batches of products returned to the factory for repair. The sense of 100% responsibility for aviation products was fostered. At the same time, quality problems in the process of product design, manufacture and field service was carefully checked and analysed. The 110 problems voiced by the Air Force in the service were dealt with one by one technically on the spot. Upgrading of quality of products and parts were unfolded within enterprises. In order to lay a good foundation for product quality and to reorganize and restore management system destroyed in the ten years turmoil, chief engineer technical management system was matured, centralized product quality inspection system was re-established, production management system was strengthened and especially the fundamental work of technical quality management was enhanced. In the course of reorganizing disciplines, employees were educated to understand that "even the smallest negligence in manufacturing aircraft can lead to severe accident", therefore the working discipline of strictly observing regulations, working style of being scrupulous about every detail and keeping improving to quality were firmly established. High standard and strict requirement were insisted on for tight quality control. A lot of factories launched mass activities of "good quality and four satisfactions", every worker was required to produce good quality product so that the operator, inspector, leader and the customer would be all satisfied.

Good result was achieved thanks to these reorganizations. Enterprise management was recovered gradually and product quality was greatly improved. Compared with 1978, in 1979, the average acceptance ratio of flight test was raised from 79.1% to 94.2%, engine first test bed acceptance ratio raised from 58.7% to 78.4% and airborne equipment first fixed time inspection acceptance ratio raised from 85.3% to 93.8%. The whole industry had put an end to the passive state of affairs of not fulfilling the state plan in continuously five years due to bad quality and completely accomplished the state plan in 1979.

During the two years of 1980 and 1981, the industry's main task was still the reorganization, on the basis of enhancing achievement of overall quality inspection. Reorganization was also implemented in scientific research institutes and product design institutes. Some technical specialists with strong management capability were promoted to leading posts, five sixth working time in a week were ensured for technical work and logistics was improved. The Ministry of Aviation Industry had promulgated management methods in fundamental research and application research, institute regulations (for trial implementation), working regulations of project engineers (for trial implementation), science and technology achievement management provisional regulations and provisional methods of technology transfer, which led scientific research management gradually to standardization.

From 1982 to 1985, overall reorganization aimed at accelerating product replacement and improving product quality with the objective of raising economic result were launched in enterprises of aviation industry according to "Decision on staging overall reorganization in state run industrial enterprises" promulgated by the Central Committee of the Communist Party of China and the State Council in January 1982. The Ministry of Aviation Industry had set up an enterprise reorganization leading group headed by Vice Minister Wang Qigong to implement even larger scale and more comprehensive reorganization. The outstanding characteristics of this stage was the close combination of reorganization with reformation.

According to the requirement of the Central Committee, cadres should be revolutionized, younger, knowledgeable and professional, aviation industry reorganized leading bodies at each level in 1980. In September 1981, the Central Committee of the Communist Party of China and the State Council appointed Mo Wenxiang the Minister and Party Group Secretary of the

Ministry of Aviation Industry instead of Lu Dong, and reorganized the leading body of the Ministry. This reorganization was accelerated in a much quicker pace after 1982. By 1985, the average age of managers and directors in aviation enterprises and administrative organizations dropped to 46.2 years from 53.1 years in 1981, cadres with high educational background increased to 72.2% from 20.5%. 70% enterprises tried director responsibility system in production management and administration management in succession.

A new development of quality management during the reformation was to extend quality control from the course of production to the course of product development and product support with special stress on the development of new aircraft. This development was achieved first of all due to good foundation of quality reorganization in production. Because of the fact that when the whole industry's working stress shifted to the development of new type of aircraft, a lot of quality problems occurred due to poor quality management. The typical example was the first J−8 all weather aircraft in June 1980. Because its hydraulic system had not been tested as a complete system and the breakoff of hydraulic pipe due to resonance on test bed, fuel leakage was happened and the aircraft was burned. In order to learn from this lesson, the first quality working meeting of new types of aircraft of aviation industry was held in Shenyang Aircraft Factory in October that year, presided over by Vice Ministers Duan Zijun and Wang Qigong. The meeting decided to put stress of quality work on the new types of aircraft. "Quality management regulations in developing new types of aircraft and missile" and "Quality management regulations of new product of airborne equipments" were formulated soon after to eliminate severe accident during the course of development and ensure the safety flight of new types of aircraft of J−7Ⅲ, J−8Ⅱ, JJ−7 and Z−8. At the same time, product support of aircraft was strengthened, maintenance personnel were trained for customers, spare parts provided. As for new aircraft which were already in batch production, the aircraft was taken as "dragon head" leading all the associated organizations in creating good quality products. Enterprise also implemented reorganization of planning, accounting and labour management according to the requirement of cost−effectiveness, hence the enterprise management fundamental work of original record, metrology, norms and statistics etc. was further strengthened and economic accounting was implemented.

Enterprise reorganization during this stage was closely connected with the reform of economic system. The centre of the work was to simplify the administration and giving more power to enterprises by the Ministry of Aviation Industry, the purpose of which was to energize enterprises and solve the problem of enterprise eating from the "big pot" of the country and workers eating from the "big pot" of the enterprise. Aviation industry started to implement "enterprise profit contracting", "Administrative unit expenses contracting" and "Scientific research fund contracting" in succession, starting from 1980. When the profit contracting norm was completed by an enterprise with surplus, the 40% of the surplus could be kept by the enterprise, the same for institutions. After 1982, aviation industry speeded up changing structure from single military production to the combination of military production with civil production and actively and steadily pushed forward the management system reform. In 1984, greater power was given to enterprises for making self decisions in 10 aspects like planning, finance, labour, distribution, supply and sale and foreign trade etc.. Necessary reform was also implemented within each enterprise, which mainly included establishing and improving economic responsibility aimed at contracting, dividing into smaller accounting unit, establishing internal accounting centre, strengthening product sale and turning the enterprise from pure production type to a type of scientific research, production and business combined.

During the enterprise overall reorganization and reform, political, technical and professional training of leading cadres and workers was carried out. There were 222 directors and deputy directors in aviation industry joined and passed national unified examination of training class from 1983 to 1985; 33,731 middle level cadres, 11,627 scientific and technological cadres and 60,537 professional management cadres of enterprises had been trained. All young workers finished supplementary classes of culture and technology and political training as well off their jobs. Hence, the political, cultural and technical quality of the workers had been improved.

Through this period of large scale reorganization in an all-round way, solid foundation had been laid for the good quality batch production, and the quality control in developing new aircraft began to set up. From 1979 to the end of 1986, aviation industry had 10 items such as the primary trainer CJ-6 etc. being awarded National Gold Medal for quality, 45 products being awarded silver medal and 374 products being awarded prize for excellent products by the Ministry of Aviation Industry. Because of the stable product quality, improved enterprise management standard and the initiative of personnel, production in aviation industry still witnessed an increase even with decreased work load of the military products which was controlled under a central plan. Compared with that in 1978, in 1986 the total output value of the industry increased 73.8%, profit and tax increased by 1.52 times and the average labour productivity of aviation industry increased 28.4%.

Section 2　Insisting on Scientific Research Going Ahead of Others and Speeding Up the Development of New Generation Aircraft

After smashing the "gang of four", aviation industry immediately began to strengthen scientific research and speed up the work of developing new generation aircraft. This was the central task for aviation industry in the new period.

1.　Carrying on Scientific Research in Advance, Strengthening Aeronautical Scientific Research and Education

Because of fierce arms race and commercial competition in the world from the 1960s to the 1970s, the industrially developed countries of the United States, the Soviet Union, the United

Kingdom and France used large investment, manpower and material to strengthen their aeronautical scientific research and developed many new types of high performance military and civil aircraft for the armed forces and civil aviation market, causing fast development of aeronautical technology and active international aircraft trade. But just during that period of time, China's aviation industry suffered severe destruction from the "great cultural revolution". China lagged behind in scientific research, slowed down the development of new generation aircraft leaving the Air Force a shortage of main force equipments. By 1976, the J−6 aircraft had already been manufactured for 16 years, but still could not be replaced by J−7 aircraft. The Y−5 civil aircraft had been there for 20 years without any new generation for replacement and the development of a new generation transport aircraft had not been certified for production over a long period of time. The gap between China's aviation industry and the advanced aviation industry in the world had become greater.

The Central Committee of the Communist Party of China, the State Council and the Military Commission of CCCPC all showed great concern to the situation of China's aviation industry. Not long after the downfall of the "gang of four", state leaders like Deng Xiaoping, Ye Jianying, Luo Ruiqing and Wang Zhen heard reports several times and gave their instructions. In October 1977, Deng Xiaoping delivered an important speech concerning the development of defence industry, pointing out that scientific research in defence industry should be unified, both scientific research and production should be subject to strategic requirement, plan should be worked out and manpower should be concentrated on tackling problems one by one. He also pointed out that the present fighter fleet should be mainly the J−7. A certain time should be fixed to transfer production capability to the production of J−7 aircraft, then concentrate on the development of one generation after another for replacement. At the National Science Convention in March 1978, Deng Xiaoping put forward the correct thesis that science and technology were productive forces and confirmed the position and role of scientific research in economic construction. Having heard reports twice from the Minister of Aviation Industry Deng Xiaoping stressed: science and technology were great productive forces, which was more the case with aviation industry. The key point is to work out a plan and take measures to set the strategic objective of aircraft replacement by new generation and try every effort to put qualified personnel in important positions. These instructions provided correct guiding policy for the development of aviation industry in the new period.

In order to act in the spirit of the National Science Convention and to meet the requirement of Deng Xiaoping's speech, the Ministry of Aviation Industry held a working meeting on aviation science and technology in Tianjin in July 1978. The meeting summed up historical experience of aviation industry, mainly discussed the special important role of aviation scientific research in the development of aviation industry and clearly defined the task of speeding up the design and development of a new generation aircraft and the policy of scientific research going ahead of the rest. The meeting put the stress on correct handling of five relations: i.e. the relation between scientific research and production, adhering to scientific research going ahead of production and eliminating wrong thinking of "production is more important than scientific research"; the relation between project development and advanced research which provides technical base for project development, there was no way of "cooking without rice"; the relation between aircraft, engine and airborne equipment, more attention should be paid to strengthening weak link of engine, taking care of airborne equipment development, especially electronics equipment to improve general performance of aircraft; the relation between present and future, wasting no time in solving the present issue and simultaneously taking a broad and long-term view for the future; the relation between learning from abroad and self creation, breaking through the isolation of the country and actively introducing foreign advanced technology on the basis of self-reliance to raise the starting point of development of aviation science and technology. At the meeting the objective of aircraft development was planned "to produce a generation, to develop a generation and to explore a generation". This meeting was important in the new period of development of aviation industry, after which the strategic change started in aviation industry i.e. stress shifted from production to scientific research and development of new generation aircraft.

The shortcoming of this meeting was the overestimation of the capability of our national strength and the planned task was too much and with a too high speed. According to the policy of the Central Committee in 1981 regarding reorganizing national economy, the whole industry clarified the guiding policy of "acting according to our capability and doing something feasible", and reorganized and compressed those tasks that were beyond the national strength and the capability of aviation industry primarily planned in Tianjin meeting, making the objective and task more practical.

The biggest change in scientific research work during this period was that the advanced research was strengthened. The direction and task of the advanced research were assessed and planned and, adjusted and supplemented in practice. The task could be divided into two parts: one was the new technology needed by the development of new generation aircraft and, the other was the critical technology needed by the future advanced aircraft in the 1990s, including advanced aircraft aerodynamic distribution, high thrust / weight ratio engine, active control technology, inertial navigation technology, diffraction optical head up display and fire control technology, electronic flight instrument system (EFIS), environment control, application of electronic computer, composite material and new type of aeronautical material etc. It was also confirmed that 30% of aeronautical scientific research expenditure should be used for advanced research and the rest 70% for project development so that the previous practice of advanced research being subject to project development and no expenses for advanced research had been changed.

Scientific research is to explore the unknowns. Once it is guided by correct line and supported by good environment, people's talents will be brought into full play and scientific research achievements will spring up continuously. The harvest period of aeronautical scientific research was after the Third Plenary Session of the Eleventh Congress of the Central

Committee, CPC. Until 1986, aviation industry had 287 items of achievements which won National Science Convention prize for major scientific achievement, 68 items of science and technology achievements were awarded national prize for science invention, 53 items were awarded national prize for scientific and technology progress, 152 items were awarded prize for major scientific and technological breakthrough in defense industry and 1,377 items were awarded prize of science and technology achievement of the Ministry of Aviation Industry. There were also 4 items of achievements being awarded gold medal at Geneva Invention Exhibition, 2 items were awarded gold plated medal and 4 items were awarded silver medal. All these achievements were gradually used in aircraft development and production, and some of the achievements also found applications in other industries. The use of CAD / CAM greatly shortened the development time of J-8Ⅱ aircraft; achievement of advanced research in fracture fatigue raised aircraft design standard; research results in finite element by Zhou Tianxiao raised alternating induction method from experience level to scientific theoretical level which could be applied to strain analysis of aeronautical structure, mechanics and nuclear engineering; Gao Ge, a post graduate of Beijing Institute of Aeronautics and Astronautics invented "barchan dune flame holder", putting forward the new standard of stabilization and fast computation method for calculating eddying numerical value. When this was used on WP6A engine, the engine performance was effectively improved, bringing China into the front line in this field of technology in the world. This achievement was awarded first class national prize for science invention and the inventor was entitled ph. D..Hu Yaobang and Zhao Ziyang met with him and his teacher on February 4, 1985. It only took 4 years from starting research to the theoretical breakthrough, then to the practical application, which could be hardly realized before the Third Plenary Session of the Eleventh Congress of CCCPC.

In order to provide solid material foundation for implementing the policy of conducting advanced research, the construction of scientific research test facilities were greatly enhanced in the new period. The method of combining independent design with the introduction of foreign equipment was adopted. First, major institutes, design offices and universities and colleges, were further equipped with large quantity of test and measuring equipments. These equipments included real time data acquisition

Fig. 19   Gao Ge discussing with Professor Ning Huang

and processing system for handling flight test data, loading data processing system for structural strength test, simulation test system for fire−control system, material constant static pressure test equipment, micro−wave anechoic chamber and thermal fatigue test control data processing system, and aerodynamic and aeroengine test equipments, etc. Then forces were concentrated on continuously constructing large test facilities including aeroengine altitude simulation test bed (first stage construction finished, second stage started), standard ground rocket sled and wheel brake inertia test rig etc. Construction investment for research and test facilities during this period was increased greatly and work was done in a down−to−earth manner, therefore the result was better. The real−time data acquisition and processing system for flight test shortened the time for preparing flight test, reduced test flight sorties and improved cost effectiveness of flight test. After the completion of the first phase construction of the altitude test facility for aeroengines, a simulated certification test of a turbojet engine inlet distortion with 65 kN (6,600 kg) thrust was done in 1985. The test was finished with complete success, which marked that the use of the altitude test facility had reached a new level. The wheel brake inertia test rig started service in 1985. It not only carried out tyre and brake tests for the Chinese customers, but also undertook tests of large aircraft tyres for foreign companies and is entitled to issue the worldwide recognized quality certificate.

Construction of aviation education was also stressed at the same time of enhancing construction of scientific research. Since 1978, the number of universities and colleges of aviation industry increased to 6 from 3, two post graduate institutes, three secondary technical schools were set up by the industry and 28 workers universities and 45 skilled workers schools were established by enterprises and administrative organizations, formulating a multi−level education system of aviation industry. From 1979 to 1986, there were 22,252 university and college graduates, 1,254 post graduates, 600 students returned from abroad, 4,555 professional college graduates, 31,000 skilled workers school graduates, 2,523 secondary technical school graduates and a large number of workers who had experienced different kinds of short term training. These graduates not only eased the short term need for qualified personnel, but also prepared a back force for the future development of aviation industry.

2.　**Paying Close Attention to New Generation Aircraft Development, Speeding Up the Design and Development of New Generation Aircraft**

The purpose of enhancing scientific research and educating qualified personnel was to speed up the design and development of new generation aircraft. In early 1978, the State Council and the Military Commission of CCCPC asked the defence industry to put scientific research ahead of production and to devote major efforts to developing new equipments. The principal policy of aviation equipments was to improve the air force's territory air defence capability centered on strategic points defence and to improve support capability to land and sea battles. According to this requirement, aviation industry learned lessons from history, especially the lesson of developing too many types of new aircraft at the same time, reviewed the speech by

Vice Chairman Ye Jianying delivered at the aviation report meeting in 1972, i.e. "aircraft development should be realistic, attention should be paid to continuity, i.e.: one generation after another, because a son is nowhere if there is no father."

In March 1983, Yang Shangkun, Vice Chairman of the Military Commission of CCCPC and deputy Secretary—General Yu Qiuli, Yang Dezhi, Zhang Aiping and Hong Xuezhi delivered important speeches regarding development of modern equipments at a working meeting of the Commission of Defence Science, Technology and Industry. They pointed out that efforts should be made to develop and improve the aviation industry and that new weaponry must be developed step by step, according to the actual capability and scientific procedures. Zhang Aiping required: "to contract the battle line, concentrate on key points, pay more attention to scientific research and to speed up the development of new generation aircraft," and "to recondition tooling, improve manufacturing process, raise quality and reduce cost." According to the above instructions, aviation industry rearranged its types of aircraft into three generations in the order of importance.

Fig. 20   Wang Zhen shaking hands with pilot Lu Mindong who had just flew J—8

The first echolen, i.e. the generation being produced included J—7, J—8 (day light and all—weather types), Y—7, Y—8 and Q—5Ⅰ aircraft. All these types of aircraft had been developed for quite a long period of time, the only problem was that some critical technical problems and auxiliary or accessory problems still remained. Only when the best manpower being concentrated on tackling them and having them certified for production, could the new generation of equipment be used to equip the military services. J—7 Ⅰ aircraft was not loved by the Air Force because its ejection life saving system unit was not safe. The Chengdu Aircraft Factory improved and successfully developed a zero height, low speed, safe and reliable ejection life saving unit. With this new ejection seat and a new engine of bigger thrust the aircraft became J—7Ⅱ, which was certified and released for production in 1979. As for the J—8 day light aircraft, Shenyang Aircraft Factory, after making great efforts on it, solved the long outstanding problems of engine shut—down in the air and high temperature on the rear fuselage, hence ended its 13 years development and had its design certification in 1979 as well. After the pilot flew J—8 aircraft and completed the flight program, he said with excitement: "we welcome the aircraft designed by ourselves. We love it, this is the way to reinforce our air force." After entering into the 1970s and 1980s, J—7Ⅱ and J—8 have been batch manufactured and were the major new types of aircraft to equip the Air Force and the Navy. During this period, Q—5 Ⅰ and its modified types of ⅠA, Ⅱ and Ⅲ were simultaneously certified in 1983 and 1985 respectively. Because technical difficulties of Q—5 series aircraft and J—8 day light and all—weather aircraft were solved and because of their success, these two types of aircraft had been awarded The State special—class prize for science and technology progress.

The second echolen, i.e. the generation of aircraft under development, was mainly J—8Ⅱ aircraft with better performance. J—8Ⅱ aircraft was technically more difficult. It was the aircraft for the late 1980s and the early 1990s. The participants in the project included aviation industry and more than ten other relative industries with the aviation industry in charge of system engineering. A system of chief designer, administrative manager, chief accountant and quality control was set up. And the contracting system of development expenses was implemented. In the course of development, the achievement of advanced research had been utilized promptly and technical reconditioning had been carried out to those factories and institutes which shared the task. Engineers, technicians, leaders and skilled workers worked very hard to speed up the development of J—8Ⅱ aircraft and they ensured the development program to complete on schedule with good quality. The first flight took place on June 12 1984. It only took three years and one month from the go—ahead to the first flight. The factory only spent 17 months for the trial manufacture and final assembly, which was much shorter than that for J—7 and J—8 prototype aircraft. About 115 newly designed or improved airborne equipments needed by the aircraft were all delivered on schedule, which reflected that the technical and management level in developing the advanced aircraft had been greatly raised.

The third echolen, i.e. the generation of aircraft being explored, was mainly to unfold advanced research and development in sophisticated aircraft for the 1990s and the year of 2000.

Major efforts were also made on improvement and modification of aviation products while the above mentioned development of the three different generations were carried out. New technology and equipment could be used on aircraft through modification and improvement, which was an effective method not only for improving aircraft performance, extending application and elongating service life, but also was one of the effective ways to develop new aircraft.

The period from 1979 to 1986 was one of the most fruitful periods in the history of the Chinese aviation industry. During these eight years, 5 types of new aircraft and 2 special purpose aircraft had been certified for production, 15 different types of aircraft had been modified, improved and retrofitted, and 7 types of super—light aircraft had been developed. Development of aero—engines also witnessed outstanding progress with 3 types of engines newly developed and 7 types improved and modified. There were four series of WP6, WP7, WP13 and WJ5 engines available. Turbo shaft engine had also been successfully developed and been used in operation. There were about one thousand new products of airborne equipment being certified for production or fitted on aircraft. In the field of missile, 2 types were newly developed and 3 types were successfully improved. Among these successfully developed new types of aircraft, some were the results of continued work from previous development and some were developed completely fresh, both of which were much better either in variety or in performance.

Fig. 21   Zhang Aiping writing inscription for Chengdu Aircraft Factory

A number of certified batch manufactured aircraft had been delivered to the People's Air Force, Naval air force and CAAC, among which fighter aircraft included J−7Ⅱ, J−8 (day light and all weather type), Q−5Ⅰ and missile bomber; transports included Y−12Ⅰ, Y−12Ⅱ, Y−7, Y−7−100 and Y−8, from small to large with different tonnages; and Z−9 multi−purpose helicopter.

The new types of aircraft filled some blanks in aircraft types, for instance, RPV5 unmanned reconnaissance aircraft, H−6 electronic counter−countermeasure aircraft, Y−8 sea patrol aircraft, high manoeuvrability target drone, super—light aircraft and small RPV. Exported aircraft also increased in variety. Some high performance aircraft like J—7Ⅲ, J—8Ⅱ, Z—8 large helicopter and JJ—7 trainer etc. had been developed and flight tested one after another.

Production of new aircraft also changed the structure of aircraft production and the percentage of new aircraft increased rapidly. In the Sixth Five—year Plan period (1981—1985), 75% of the batch produced 20 types of aircraft were newly developed and certified, or modified and improved. The percentage of production of new aircraft in the total production in 1985 was up to 66%.

During a large scale military exercise in north China by PLA in September 1981, the Air Force undertook tasks of air superiority, air reconnaissance, ground support, air supply, rescue, occupying key position by parachuting, air mining and electronic countermeasures. The Air Force used 114 batches of aircraft with 838 sorties. All those fighters, attack aircraft, bombers, transport aircraft and helicopters were manufactured in China. Each fleet finished its mission by arriving punctually, shooting and bombing accurately, landing accurately, in good cooperation and safety, reflecting very strong fighting capability. In the military parade celebrating the 35 anniversary of the National Day in 1984, formation flight of 94 aircraft of fighters, attack aircraft, bombers and trainers precisely passed over Tiananmen to receive inspection by the State leaders and masses.

Fig. 22   Zhao Ziyang and other state leaders meeting with specialists from the
Ministry of Aviation Industry

These excellent aircraft embodied the sweat and blood of the workers and staff of the aviation industry. Designers, engineers, specialists, professors and workers who took part in these aircraft design and manufacturing all worked very hard and devoted their every effort to the work and to the motherland. But those people were unknown to the public because of security reasons in the defence industry. The government highly praised contributions made by those people and 20 representatives of those seldom known people from the Ministry of Aviation Industry and the Ministry of Weaponry Industry were received by the State leaders Zhao Ziyang, Yang Shangkun, Hu Qili, Li Peng and Fang Yi on January 24 1986. Among the 20 specialists 10 of them were specialists from aviation industry. They were Lu Xiaopeng——aircraft designer, Gu Songfen——aircraft designer, Zhou Yaohe——professor of North—west Polytechnic University and a Casting specialist, Zhang Qishan——professor of Bei—jing Institute of Aeronautics and Astronautics and inventer of the telemetry system of array separation, Lu Qingfeng——RPV designer, Cai Yunjin——aeroengine compressor specialist, Yang Yanshen——aero accessory specialist, Liu Xiashi——finite element specialist, Zhou Tianxiao——finite element specialist and Xu Peilin——aircraft designer. In his speech during the meeting, Premier Zhao Ziyang praised all workers and staff of defence industry for their great contributions and pointed out that great development had been achieved and good foundation of China's defence industry had already been laid, and a good team of science and technology workers had been established, but with more potential to be tapped. He asked the defence industry to make greater contributions to the four modernizations of the whole country. This would not affect the modernization of our national defence but on the contrary this would further ensure it, enterprises would be more flourishing and working forces would be more vigorous. The state leaders' remarks showed clearly the direction of further progress of the defence industry and aviation industry.

Section 3　Combining Military and Civil Production and Developing Civil Products

Aviation Industry should combine military production with civil production. After the Second World War, aviation industry of the developed countries had completed their transition very quickly from war time to peace time and their civil aircraft turnover occupied a large proportion in total civil sales. In the late 1950s civil production of China's aviation industry once had fairly quick development thanks to the implementation of Chairman Mao Zedong's instruction: "Pay attention to learning both military and civil production technologies." After 1961, civil production was affected by the idea that military industry should be based on the assumption of fighting wars earlier and on a large scale, and should be prepared for those wars. The influence of the "left" ideology was another factor. Civil production once was criticized as " not the professional work" , which greatly hurt the workers and staff. Hence the aviation industry had mainly military production during the past 20 years. In 1978, the total civil production value of the industry only was 6.5% of the total production value and the ratio of military aircraft to civil aircraft was 95:5; more than half surplus production capability had not been utilized and the economic result of the industry was not good. This industrial structure of aviation industry had lasted until the Third Plenary Session of the Eleventh Congress of the

Communist Party of China when a series of policies and instructions concerning the combination of military and civil production were stressed.

Civil production of aviation industry had thus ended a period of tortuous road and regained vitality and began to develop.

1. Transformation from Military − Civil Combination Centred on Military Production to Military − Civil Combination Centred on Civil Production

In the new period of development, there was a distance to go in implementing the policy of military − civil combination.

The main task of aviation industry from 1979 to 1981 was to implement the policy of "military − civil combination, peace − war combination, taking the military production as its main task and supporting the military production with civil production" proposed by the Military Commission of CCCPC. The industry was required to "find more rice for cooking", to develop civil production for "feeding the industry itself" because the industry could no more feed itself due to a sharp decrease of military order. Civil production had gained fast increase due to the adoption of profit contracting and the policy of encouraging civil production. The proportion of civil production value in the total production value of the whole industry increased to 26% in 1981. The characteristic of this period was that civil production had started and the military − civil combination was still centered on military production.

During the period from 1982 to 1984, Deng Xiaoping, Chairman of the Military Commission of CCCPC once pointed out: "Every Ministry of defence industry must go all out for research and production of civil products apart from fulfilling the task of military research and production," and Premier Zhao Ziyang also pointed out: "defence industrial enterprises should be a military − civil combination system." According to these instructions and requirements, the Ministry of Aviation Industry first of all clarified its guiding ideology: practicing military − civil combination was not only a short term measure to solve the problem of feeding workers and the staff by using the surplus capability, but also was a long − term plan to contribute to the four modernizations. After clarified the ideology, the overall adjustment on production capability, organizations, science and technology forces and investment direction was implemented, enabling the change of product structure of aviation industry from single military product structure to that of military − civil combination. A number of mainstay civil products had been developed and about a dozen civil production lines were established with lots of products sold well domestically and some already entered into international market. Characteristics of this period was the great change from serving only the national defence to serving the development of civil aviation as well as the national defence, and serving technical renovation in other departments of the national economy and enriching market and export.

After 1985, the Central Committee of the Communist Party of China decided that the national defence construction should be subject to the economic construction according to the change of international situation. And in 1986 the Central Committee of the Communist Party of China and the State Council decided to put the Ministry of Aviation Industry under the direct leadership of the State Council. These decisions and ·plannings had further guided the change of product structure of aviation industry — from "military — civil combination centred on military production" in the war preparing period to "military — civil combination centered on civil production to suit the construction need in peace time — completely discarded the thinking of development just on military production. Civil products development in multi—channel and multi—direction were carried out afterwards, enabling the proportion of its production value in the total production value of the industry rising rapidly to 40.1% in 1985 and 61.2% in 1986. The civil product service covered every area of the national economy and 29 provinces, cities and autonomous regions, except Taiwan province.

2. Developing Civil Aircraft

In implementing military — civil combination, no matter whether "centered on military production" in the past or was "centered on civil production" later, aviation industry had always insisted on aviation as its profession, making best use of its advantages, putting the development of civil aircraft in the first place in an attempt to provide Chinese civil airlines with Chinese made aircraft.

Transports with different payloads had been developed in China as early as in the 1970s, including Y—11 with 8 seats and 940 kg payload, Y—7 with 50 seats and 4.7 tons payloads, Y—8 medium sized transport with 20 tons payloads and Y—10 mid—range jet passenger plane with 150—seats and 21.4 tons payload. These aircraft all had been flight tested. After successful maiden flight, Y—10 flew to cities of Beijing, Hefei, Harbin, Urumqi, Guangzhou, Kunming, Chengdu and Lhasa respectively, which reflected the continuous increase of China's civil aircraft development capability. But because of the stress on development of fighter aircraft at that time, development of civil aircraft was slowed down. Except for the Y—11 which had been certified and batch produced in 1977, all other types of civil aircraft were not batch produced and operated, therefore all aircraft operated on both trunk lines and branch lines in China were bought from abroad. Encouraged by the spirit of the Third Plenary Session of the Eleventh Congress of the Central Committee, the Ministry of Aviation Industry began to work on the development of civil aircraft in order to change the situation of civil aircraft. The work was first concentrated on tackling difficult technical problems and flight test of the already developed types of aircraft — Y—11 and Y—12. Simultaneously the manufacturing of Z—9 helicopter introduced from abroad was also started. Then the Y—11 aircraft agricultural service team was set up in May 1980 in Harbin Aircraft Factory to provide services for agriculture, forestry, animal husbandry, mining and wild life resources surveying after the approval of the State Council and the Military Commission of CCCPC. This was the first time in China's aviation industry to organize a professional team using Chinese designed and manufactured aircraft for direct business.

To support China's own aircraft to enter into operations on domestic air routes, Deng

Xiaoping pointed out in October 1981 in his speech at the enlarged politburo meeting of the Central Committee of the Communist Party of China: "Chinese made aircraft should be considered on domestic air routes operation." On January 2 1982, the State Council working meeting presided over by Premier Zhao Ziyang defined that using Chinese made civil aircraft operating on domestic air routes would be one of the government policies in accordance with the above proposal by Deng Xiaoping. This decision was the new starting point for the development of China's civil aircraft. To implement this policy, Duan Junyi and Zhao Jianmin, members of the Central Advisory Commission, put forward detailed proposals again in May 1985 to the State Council, which gained active support immediately from Premier Zhao Ziyang, Vice Premiers Wan Li and Li Peng and State Councillor Gu Mu.

Under the guidance of the correct policy and with concern and support of State leaders, China's civil aircraft manufacture had since enjoyed an unprecedented good situation on the foundation of the previous work. During the 7 years since 1980, all together 8 types of 202 transports and helicopters had been manufactured, among which 6 types were been put into production in this period. After its type certification in February 1980, Y−8 was released for production and delivered for service consecutively with the first successful flight to Lhasa on May 19 1984. It successfully transported cargo for the 20th anniversary celebration of the founding of Tibet autonomous region in September 1985. Y−8 aircraft has been widely used in China for cargo transportation nowadays. As soon as it had passed technical approval in December 1984, Y−12 I aircraft was immediately put into service for geographical exploration in Hebei and Inner Mongolia. The Y−12 II aircraft modified according to international civil airworthiness regulations had passed technical evaluation at the end of 1985. Having been awarded CAAC airworthiness certificate, Y−12 II is now entering into the international market. Z−9 commercial helicopter made its maiden flight in 1982 and it was soon batch produced and delivered to the Air Force, airlines and China's Ocean Helicopter Service Company. Y−7, the commuter plane, was type certified and batch produced in July 1982 and been delivered for operational test at the beginning of 1984. The newly developed large multi−purpose helicopter Z−8 made its successful maiden flight in December 1985. The 150−seats MD−82 large trunk line passenger plane, jointly manufactured by Shanghai Aviation Industry Company and the McDonnell Douglas Company of U.S., had its first aircraft riveted in Shanghai in April 1986, which made its first flight in July 1987.

The bright future of military − civil combination of China's aviation industry relies on the vigorous development of commercial aircraft and, the development of the Chinese made civil aircraft depends largely on flight safety, which drew people's attention especially at the time when disastrous accidents occurred with passenger planes in some technically advanced countries. The Ministry of Aviation Industry regarded the issue of safety and reliability of Chinese made aircraft as an outstanding task. A great deal of careful work had been done with the active support and cooperation of CAAC. Y−7 aircraft acted as a demonstrator and pioneer in opening domestic airline service by Chinese made passenger planes, which had been tested by long time trial use with safety and reliability.

With modified WJ5A−I engine, and the equivalent power increased from 1,875 kW (2,550 hp) to 2,132 kW (2,900 hp), i.e. an increase of 13.7%, the Y−7 aircraft could take−off and transport 20 tons full load in hot and high areas with a better take−off and climb performance than that of similar aircraft bought from abroad and operating on domestic lines.

To further test the safety of the aircraft, a "single engine take−off and landing flight test" — with one of the two engines shut down was performed in April 1982 in Tianjin. This kind of flight test was risky. The flight test team was headed by He Wenzhi, Vice Minister of the Ministry of Aviation Industry and joined by leading members from CAAC fleet No.8 and Xi'an Aircraft Factory. This flight test, the first ever done in China, had ended with great success, which demonstrated that in case of one engine being damaged or lost control, the Y−7 aircraft could still be able to perform full load take−off and landing with the other engine. Because of the success of this record breaking test, 49 people of the test team including Zhang Yun, Cheng Yuanyong and Zhang Qinliang had been cited and received by Vice Premiers Geng Biao and Zhang Aiping.

The Y−7 aircraft had flown to 28 provinces, cities and autonomous regions to test its suitability in different environment conditions and airports. When it was type certified in July 1982, Y−7 had already flown 3,665 sorties, 1,656 hours and 700,000 kilometers, once again created a safety record.

Starting from early 1984, the batch produced aircraft had been delivered to Shanghai and Wuhan aviation administrations for cargo transport. The aircraft has since been shuttling between cities of Shanghai, Wuhan, Hefei, Zhengzhou, Jinan, Dalian, Fuzhou and Xiamen. It accumulated more than 1,000 flying hours of cargo transportation in the last two years, withstood complicated climatic tests of thunderstorm, icing and high temperature and long time flight far away from maintenance base. These actual facts demonstrated that the Y−7 aircraft was fully up to the standard for passenger transportation, therefore the CAAC Wuhan Administration pioneered in putting the Y−7 into airline service in November 1985.

In the process of trial use of Y−7 by CAAC, the Ministry of Aviation Industry continued work on its modification. Its communication, navigation, radar equipment and cabin facility were modified with advanced technology and equipment in 1985. The wing was modified with the addition of winglets to improve its safety and comfort. The aircraft was renamed Y7−100.

When the Chinese made commercial aircraft of Y7−100, Y−12 II , Y−8 and Z−9 with complete new look flew in Beijing for demonstration at the end of 1985 and beginning of 1986, people from all walks of life paid their great attention to it. On November 22 1985, Vice Premier Wan Li and Secretary of the Secretariat of the Central Committee of the Communist Party of China Hao Jianxiu visited the aircraft, and on December 1 1985, Vice Premiers Li Peng, Yao Yilin and Secretary of the Secretariat of the Central Committee of the Communist Party of China Hu Qili visited the aircraft and took a flight aboard Y7−100. Vice Premier Li Peng also presided over a State Council Meeting on Civil Aviation held on the spot of the demonstration.

He declared at the meeting that the purpose of the meeting was only one — to support Chinese made civil aircraft. He also pointed out that the Chinese made aircraft must be of good quality to ensure "safety, comfort and economy".

The first large scale Chinese made civil aircraft exhibition was held in Beijing's capital airport in April 1986, which attracted more than 20,000 people from all walks of life, such as the Central Committee of the Communist Party of China, the Advisory Commission of CCCPC, the State Council, the Military Commission of CCCPC, Standing Committee of the National People's Congress, the Commission of Defence Science, Technology and Industry, the Air Force and Navy. More than 1,000 people took a flight of the aircraft, their speeches and remarks brimmed over with concern, love and expectations. Member of the Advisory Commission of the Central Committee of the Communist Party of China Yang Xianzhen on his wheelchair flew the Y-8 aircraft at his high age of 90 and said excitedly: "I am very pleased on board of our own aircraft and I am feeling very well." A veteran pilot who flew the aircraft for many years praised the advanced equipment and comfort of the modified Y7-100 aircraft and, a man who named himself "a man who wanted to fly all his life" had written on a visitors' book with warmth: "Excellent! Excellent! Excellent! At last I have seen the aircraft made by ourselves," "the Chinese people should love and support with every effort China's aircraft manufacturing industry and China's aviation cause. China's aircraft should fly to the world!"

Fig. 23   Li Peng, Hu Qili and Yao Yilin at the State Council Civil Aviation Meeting

"The fragrance of the plum blossom came from bitterness and the cold". Having confirmed the flight safety, CAAC held a grand inauguration for the formal passenger operation of Y-7 aircraft in Hefei, Anhui Province on 29 April 1986. When the first anniversary of the inauguration was celebrated on 29 April 1987, there already had 18 Y−7 aircraft flying on 5 routes of Hefei, Shenyang, Wuhan, Xi'an and Huhhot with more than 18,400 flying hours and over 24,000 sorties in one year, maintaining safety flying record. The operation of Y−7 aircraft for passenger service by Chinese airlines had since ended the history of using all foreign aircraft on China's main regional airlines and turned out a new page in China's civil aviation history.

3.   Serving the Technical Renovation of the National Economy and Serving the Market

China's aviation industry also gave full play to its advantages to speed up transplanting military technology into civil production and to provide services for the technical renovation of the national economy and to serve the market.

Aviation Industry had provided more than 400 items of special equipment, instrument and production lines for technical renovations of 28 industries, i.e.: energy, transportation, light industry, food industry, textile, construction, chemistry, metallurgy, medicine and environment protection and, provided more than 3,000 items of several thousand hundreds of spares for imported large equipment of oil industry, chemistry, chemical fibre, metallurgical equipment and heavy duty trucks, saving large amount of foreign currency for the country.

Providing service to the country's development of energy was an important direction of civil production development of aviation industry. The industrial gas turbine power generating sets derived from aeroengine are now already operating in oil field for power generating, heat supplying and water injection, which have advantages of light weight and high thermal efficiency and could burn natural gas and oil field gas for combined supply of heat and electricity. It is convenient to transport and very useful for oil field development. A power generating set provided by Shenyang Aero Engine Factory generating electricity with oil field gas in Daqing Oil Field generated 26,980,000 watt−hours of electricity and supplied 75,000 tons of steam in one year's operation, with which the investment could be recovered within two years, demonstrating the cost effectiveness of this energy installation. When the refrigeration turbine was used for the recovery of oil field gas — light hydrogen carbon gas — by the Aero' Accessory Research Institute, the previous burned away oil field gas has been recovered. There are 30 units being supplied and each unit can recover more than 100,000 tons of light hydrogen carbon gas annually, valued RMB 70,000,000 yuan. Premier Zhao Ziyang showed special interest in this project and instructed associated departments to "Support this matter which is another achievement of transplanting military industrial technology into civil production."

Successful facts proved that transplanting military technology into civil production had broadened the application scope of the industry's technical advantage and superiority. Shenyang Aero Engine Design Institute helped two chemical fibre factories in Dandong and Hangzhou successfully manufacture China's first viscous auto−screen filtering machine and viscous long threat pressing and washing machine by using its high temperature and anti−corrosion technologies for aero engine development, thus enabling China's viscous filtration technology jumped from the level of the 1940s to the level of 1970s. In co—operation with the Ministry of Urban and Rural Construction and Environment Protection, the Ministry of Aviation Industry used aero hydraulic technology to develop hydraulic pump, hydraulic motor and hydraulic valve for construction machinery. Their main technical performance reached the level of similar products abroad in the 1980s and some of the performance even surpassed that of foreign products. These products had increased the number of Chinese made parts on the hydraulic excavator from 89% to 95%. The coal mine safety monitoring system developed by using precision measuring and electronic integrating technology of the aviation industry was the first of its kind ever developed in China to provide more safety to coal industry.

Another important aspect of aviation industry in implementing the policy of military — civil combination, was to insist on developing such civil products that requires similar technology to make and sell well in the market. Civil production is now developing very fast, which had already reached more than 3,000 kinds of products. Some of the civil products had already been channelled into the State industrial management. The whole industry had established 60 production lines for batch production of mainstay civil products in 1986, including textile and light industry machines, medical equipments, automobiles, motorbikes, bicycles, washing machines and refrigerators. The quality of these civil products had been improved gradually and in the eight years from 1979 to 1986, two items of civil products had been awarded National Gold Medal, 18 items had been awarded Silver Medal and 162 items had been awarded the Quality Prize of the Ministry of Aviation Industry.

4. Opening to the Outside World and Developing International Technology and Economical Exchange

As a kind of technology condensed industry, aviation industry can be quickly developed only when it participates in international exchanges and cooperations. After the Third Plenary Session of the Eleventh Congress of the Communist Party of China, the government affirmed the policy of opening to outside world as a long term national policy and the speeding up construction of socialist modernization as a strategic measure. Hence, China's aviation industry had ended its self—isolation from outside world for about 20 years and the exchange and cooperation with foreign countries had entered into a new stage of development.

Approved by the State Council, the Ministry of Aviation Industry set up China National Aero—Technology Import and Export Corporation (hereinafter called CATIC) in early 1979. This Corporation undertakes detailed work of technical, economical exchanges and cooperations between the Chinese aviation industry and foreign companies under the guidance of the government policies and laws. Compared with the 1950s, technical introduction and cooperation in the new period had changed from single pattern to multi — forms with a variety of contents, which provided adequate room for selecting what was needed. The government also authorized CATIC to organize foreign trade and export its own products to the world market and to absorb foreign investment.

In order to obtain first hand material of foreign countries, and correctly implement the policy of opening to the outside world, Lu Dong, the Minister of the Ministry of Aviation Industry and Vice Ministers Duan Zijun, Chen Shaozhong and Xu Changyu headed a Chinese Delegation of Aviation Industry consisted of more than 20 specialists of various professions and visited the United Kingdom, France and the Federal Republic of Germany in November 1978. During their 52 days surveying, they visited 4 universities, 9 institutes and 32 factories, which was the first important visit by China's aviation industry since the implementation of the policy of opening to the outside world. Since then China's aviation industry began marching to the world and sending delegations of various kinds on visits and survey in foreign countries. After investigations and study in foreign countries, China's aviation industry had formulated concrete plans of opening to the outside world.

Fig. 24   Lu Dong, Duan Zijun, Chen Shaozhong and Xu Changyu surveying in Western Europe

The work of opening to outside world of aviation industry in the new historic period mainly concentrated on the following two aspects:

1.   Cooperations with Multi-Nations

In the early 1980s the British aviation industry held a large exhibition of new technology and new products in Shanghai. The Ministry of Aviation Industry actively sponsored the exhibition and actively staged activities of technical exchanges. Minister Lu Dong also had discussions with the British Defence Secretary Mr. Pimm who came specially to cut the ribben for the exhibition on the future cooperation of aviation industry between the two countries. Consequently the decision was made to set up a representative office in the U.K. by China National Aero-Technology Import and Export Corporation to strengthen the cooperation in aviation industry between China and the U.K. In that year, CATIC signed contracts with two British avionics companies for buying British airborne avionics equipment for modifying Chinese J-7 aircraft. Soon after, a contract was signed with the French Aerospatiale for buying manufacturing licence of the high speed and medium size helicopter Dauphin (later named Z-9 in China).

In addition to the establishment of technical cooperation with Britain and France, China's aviation industry had established technical cooperative relations with the Federal Republic of Germany, Sweden, U.S.A., Japan, Italy and Hong Kong area and, trade relations with East European countries and U.S.S.R. had also been developed. More than 50 countries and regions in the world had established relations with China's aviation industry.

During this period the Chinese aviation industry also introduced American airborne radio and navigation equipment to modify its sea patrol plane and small transport. In cooperation with Hong Kong Aircraft Co. its passenger plane was modified and, attack aircraft was modified in cooperation with Aeritalia in Italy.

All the above cooperations were fruitful and the modified aircraft had their performance improved and their scope of service widened with some of the aircraft even exported to other countries.

Apart from introducing airborne equipment, China's aviation industry also introduced large electronic computers, test aircraft, control and measuring instruments, test facilities and machine tools from industrial countries in the world to improve its research and test capability.

At the same time of introducing advanced products and technology from foreign countries, the Chinese Aeronautical Establishment also cooperated with foreign aeronautical science and research organizations. CAE signed a "special agreement of cooperation in the field of civil aviation research" with German DFVLR in accordance with the agreement on science and technology cooperation between governments of China and the Federal Republic of Germany in April 1980. Similar agreements were signed later with FFA, NASA and the French ONERA. Cooperative relations had also been established with aeronautical scientific research institutions in Italy, Belgium and Romania. Cooperation forms included joint research, co-sponsoring academic symposium, exchanging specialists and documentation. By the end of 1986, about 140 Chinese aeronautical scientific research personnel and specialists had been sent to those countries for short visits or study and about 87 foreign specialists came to China for scientific and technological activities. The cooperation covered many important areas like aerodynamics, aircraft structural strength, aero engine research and aeronautical materials etc. Effective cooperations produced fruitful results. Achievement of the research program on aircraft ground resonance test technology conducted jointly by China and the Federal Republic of Germany satisfied the need in aircraft flutter analysis and power response computation.

New development had also been witnessed in introducing foreign knowledge and know—how. One of its forms was to seek technical consultation from foreign countries, such as from the British Vickers Limited Co. on the design of exhaust cooler of China's engine altitude test facility and from the U.S. Lockheed Co. on the issue of airworthiness of Y—12 aircraft. Another form was to send people directly to foreign countries to study, to be trained or to work. From 1978 to 1986, aviation industry had sent 949 students abroad and 110 engineers to work in aircraft and engine companies in 12 countries; about 235 specialists from 12 countries were invited to China for lectures and technical seminars and 545 Chinese people from the industry participated 240 international academic symposiums in the world.

Fig. 25   Mo Wenxiang leading a delegation surveying American aviation industry

Introduction of foreign advanced technology through multi—channels in a variety of forms and the international cooperation in science and technology enabled China's aviation industry to have more opportunities to absorb advantages from many companies in the world, to learn new technology and speed up its development.

2.   Actively Organizing Export of Aviation Products

China's aviation industry began to export its products to foreign countries from the end of the 1950s. But at that time products were exported as free aid. During the 20 years from the 1950s to 1970s, China had provided several thousand aircraft to 17 developing countries free of charge. Since the making of aircraft consumes large amount of investment and China itself is a developing country, China could not afford to provide assistance free of charge for long. Therefore when the policy of opening to outside world was implemented in January 1979, the Chinese government decided to change the free assistance into paid trade. The first formal contract for exporting aircraft was signed in that year, which marked the beginning of a new stage in foreign trade of aviation product.

Export of aircraft, engine and their spare parts is the focal point for export in China's aviation industry. China's aircraft has good basic performance. They are priced comparatively low on the international market, and can be conditionally retrofitted according to customer's requirement, therefore China's aircraft are loved by their customers. Starting from 1980, large number of J—6 and J—7 aircraft have been exported; J—7M fighter and Q—5Ⅲ attack aircraft which have been modified with advanced electronic equipment introduced from abroad also enjoy a good sale.

From 1979 to 1986, China had exported to more than ten countries several hundred aircraft and engines, including both military aircraft and Y—12Ⅱ passenger aircraft, spares for aircraft, engines, ground equipment and associated aircraft tools. About one thousand maintenance people from customers have been trained and 70 specialist teams have been sent out to customers' countries for after sale service. It was really not easy to obtain such an encouraging result at the starting stage of China's aircraft export amongest so many strong competitors in the severe competition on international aircraft market.

While exporting aircraft, engines and spare parts China's aviation industry also exported major machined components for aircraft and engines under subcontracts to aircraft and engine manufacturers in U.S.A., Canada, France, England and Italy. Those components were manufactured according to international advanced standard with good and reliable quality and been praised by customers.

The export of non—aero products was actively organized at the same time of developing export of aviation products. Aviation industry is a sophisticated machinery industry and it can provide a variety of civil mechanical and electrical products to both domestic and foreign markets after its adjustment of military — civil production structure. Export of civil mechanical and electrical products started in the early 1980s, which included measuring tools, cutting tools, aggregate fixtures, forgings, castings and precision machine tools. When the western countries were using NC machines in large scale, developing flexible manufacturing systems and worrying about the long lead time in manufacturing special fixtures which could not meet the requirement of new systems, China's aviation industry sent its aggregate fixtures to the international flexible manufacturing systems conference held in London, 1983 as well as the Birmingham International Machine Tools and Tools Exhibition, 1984 in England, which drew people's attention and won their welcome. The exported measuring and cutting tools meet international standard with good performance and quality and have won good reputation. Carl Zeiss Co. of the Federal Republic of Germany bought a batch of quartz glass ball from China's Aviation Precision Machinery Research Institute as its process measuring datum after a long time comprehensive checking and inspection, believing it reached the high precision standard in every aspect. Having checked the quality of large size granite tables (2.2 x 1.4 m) manufactured by China's Aviation Pneumatic Tools Factory and confirmed that the accuracy was up to grade "0", the Zeiss Co. ordered 50 pieces as major components of its precision three—axis measuring machines it is selling to the world.

Export of China's aviation industry is now in the ascendant. At the working meeting of aviation foreign trade held in August 1986 presided over by Vice Minister Jiang Xiesheng, the issue of opening to the outside world was discussed as one of the strategic tasks for the development of aviation industry and experience was summed up to accelerate the progress of foreign trade. In September 1986, China's aviation industry participated the Farnborough International Air Show in England for the first time with models and photographs of 11 types of aircraft and missiles, reflecting economical and technical capabilities of China's aviation industry. It aroused visitors' great interest. The British Foreign secretary Sir Geoffrey Howe visited the Chinese stand at the Show. Chinese aircraft had won praises from aviation specialists of other countries who were shocked to see so many aircraft and missiles first shown by China. Some visitors voiced their doubt about the actual aircraft J—8 Ⅱ being manufactured in China just by seeing its model until they had watched a video tape of J—8 Ⅱ flying, they couldn't help praise it with their thumbs up.

1986 saw the 35 anniversary of the founding of the aviation industry of new China. During the past 35 years, China's aviation industry experienced tortuous road, overcame difficulties and reaped achievements attracting worldwide attention under the leadership of the Chinese Communist Party.

A large scale aviation industrial system with fairly complete categories, military — civil combination and scientific research— production— education combination have been established on the weak foundation of old China.

Fig. 26 Wang Qigong and Jiang Xiesheng visiting Beijing International Gas Turbine Exhibition

Aviation industry's total number of employees in 1986 was 27.8 times as many as that in 1952, metal cutting machine tools 28 times and construction area 35 times as much as that in 1952; the accumulated investment was 146 times, industrial total production value 63.7 times and profit 13.7 times as much as that in 1952. China's aviation industry has become a newly established technology condensed industry with a strong foundation in the Chinese national economy, and a powerful aviation industry in the world.

In the last 35 years. China's aviation industrial organizations had developed and manufactured more than 12,000 aircraft of 55 types in 25 categories of fighters, bombers, attack aircraft, transports, helicopters, trainers and special purpose aircraft as well as many types of super—light aircraft. China's aviation industry has become a powerful backing of the People's Air Force and one of the sources of supplying aircraft to China's civil aviation organizations. China has assisted the third world developing countries with Chinese made aircraft to strengthen their national defence capabilities.

China's aviation industry has set up 35 independent scientific research institutes, product design institutes, manufacturing process research institutes and material research institutes and, most of the 116 enterprises have established their own product design departments and manufacture process research departments as well as a number of large establishment for aviation scientific research and test. Aviation engineers and technicians occupy 13.7% of the total number of the people of the industry, one third of which are working on scientific research and product design. China has already developed and manufactured a variety of military and civil aircraft and the capability of developing modern advanced aircraft is increasing. Professional scientific research and technical renovation have been performed widely with lots of fruitful scientific and technological results, some of which even reached the world advanced level. China's aviation industry is now an industry with scientific research as its guide.

China's aviation industry has primarily established a production structure of military – civil combination. The total production value of civil production shares more than 60% of the total production value of the industry. Scientific technology and civil product provided by aviation industry are serving the development of civil aviation, technical renovation of the national economy, the light industry market and export.

China's aviation industry was developed on the steady growth of the national economy and gradual improvement of the nation's industrial base. It enjoyed great support from relevent organizations of metallurgy, chemistry, construction material, machinery and electronics and in turn it promoted the development of these organizations in a certain degree. Raw materials and associated products required by aircraft manufacturing in China can be supplied from indigenous sources and, the ratio of Chinese made components for imported advanced equipments are increasing gradually. China has already established scientific research and production bases of raw materials and mechanical and electronic products.

China's aviation industry has already changed its self contained nature to the nature of opening to outside world. It has established cross—profession contacts with 28 institutes in many provinces and cities at multi—levels and in a variety of forms domestically and trade and scientific technological cooperative relations with 50 countries and regions the world over. Export of China's aviation products is expanding daily with good reputation.

Through 35 years of arduous experience and a great deal of practices of scientific research, production and construction, China's aviation industry has trained a contingent of managers, engineers and workers with good ideology, good working style and excellent professional knowledge. This contingent has accumulated both positive and negative experiences and wholeheartedly supported the line and policy adopted since the Third Plenary Session of the Eleventh Congress of the Communist Party of China. With the strong desire to develop the Chinese aviation industry for the motherland, every one in the contingent works hard with carefulness, modesty and selfless spirit to climb the technological peak of the aviation industry. This contingent is forming a shock force in the construction of the national four modernizations, and the development of China's aviation industry has surely a bright future!

PART TWO

An airplane is a heavier—than—air aircraft flying in the atmosphere, driven by the thrust of a power plant and supported by the lift of fixed wing(s). Aircraft, other than balloons and airships, are generally called airplanes, but in this book the word aircraft has the same meaning as the word airplane.

It has been only 80 years and more since the appearance of the first airplane in the world, but the structure and performance of airplanes have been greatly improved, their applications widely expanded and the variety of airplanes increased with each passing day. Military aircraft include fighters, intercepters, fighter—bombers, bombers, attack aircraft, military transports, anti—submarine aircraft, reconnaissance aircraft, early—warning aircraft, electronic counter—measure aircraft and tanker airplanes; and in the area of civil airplanes there are passenger airplanes, cargo airplanes, executive airplanes, agriculture airplanes, sport airplanes, air ambulance airplanes and other special airplanes. The helicopters are increasingly showing their unusual functions in satisfying various military and civil needs. The development of the aircraft has become an important sign representing the development levels of science, technology, national economy and defence of a modern nation.

The creation of the aviation industry in new China began in 1951, starting with aircraft repair. The success in manufacturing its first aircraft——a primary trainer in 1954 and the licence production of jet fighters, small transports and helicopters in the following years symbolized the completion of the transition from aircraft repair to manufacture. The second transition, from licence production to development, began in the late 1950s and early 1960s and since then several fighters, attack aircraft, bombers, trainers and transports have been designed, manufactured, improved and modified. Since the beginning of the 1980s, a new prospect has appeared, characterized with strengthened R&D, active introduction of the foreign technology, the shorter cycle of replacement of aircraft in service and expansion of export trade. During the 35 years from 1951 to 1986, a total of 11 aircraft manufacture factories and 6 aircraft design institutes plus several factory—owned aircraft design institutes were set up and with the support and cooperation of organizations concerned 12,000 aircraft in 25 types and 55 versions including fighters, bombers, attack aircraft, helicopters, transports, trainers and pilotless vehicles were produced. These aircraft have been used to equip the Chinese Air Force, the Navy and the airlines, to assist 17 developing countries and exported to nearly a dozen countries. The fast growth and enormous progress of the Chinese aviation industry has been the focus of attention of the world aviation industry.

Chapter Ⅳ   Development of Trainers and Fighters

Section 1   Appearance and Development of Primary Trainers

Trainers are the aircraft used for training pilots. There are either tandem seats in fore and aft cockpits, or two side—by—side seats in a single cockpit, inter—connected dual controls and two sets of instruments for use by an instructor and a trainee. Generally the trainers are divided into 4 classes, i.e the primary trainer, the basic trainer, the advanced trainer and the fighter—trainer.

During its growth the Chinese aviation industry has consistently felt its duty to develop quality aircraft to satisfy the needs of the military services and airlines in their operation and training. Importance has also been attached to the development of trainers while various other aircraft were developed and produced. The first aircraft marking the transition from aircraft repair to manufacture was a primary trainer indeed. Afterwards the fighter—trainers and bom ber— trainers were also successively developed. By 1986 a total of 4,056 trainers in various types, approximately one third of the total aircraft made in China, were produced. With these trainers the military needs in training have been basically met and large quantities of superior pilots have been trained. Some trainers have also been sent to other countries to assist training their pilots.

1.   Appearance of the CJ—5 Primary Trainer

A primary trainer is used for training potential trainees to master primary flying techniques because of its low speed, good controllability and stability. These factors make the task of learning simpler.

The CJ—5, manufactured by Nanchang Aircraft Factory, was a licence production of the Soviet primary trainer Yak—18 developed in 1946. It had a frame type fuselage, a wing with one rectangular center panel and two tapered outer panels and a tailwheel type landing gear. A piston engine drove a wooden propeller. The flying instruments, engine instruments, a transceiver, a directional gyro and an interior communication system, etc. were installed to enable the trainees to learn the operational skills of the aircraft after they had finished the primary training programme.

In accordance with the First Five—year Plan of the aviation industry approved by the government, the trial production of the CJ—5 was to be completed in September, 1955. But it was decided to cut this by 1 year as the Chinese Air Force was in urgent need of a primary trainer and the Nanchang Aircraft Factory had already mastered aircraft repair techniques, and techniques for manufacture of parts and components for 5 types of aircraft including the Yak—18. After the assignment of this task the factory proceeded rapidly under the instruction of some Soviet experts and the organization of chief engineer Li Shaoan and chief technologist Gao Yongshou. First CJ—5 was delivered to the flight test station in June for flight test on June 30 and second full size airframe began its static destructive test on May 12.

Aircraft static destructive tests were totally new to the factory at that time and this was the first of its kind ever carried out even in China. There were no Soviet experts for consultation. A project engineer, Zhang Azhou who studied in the United Kingdom and had just returned to China, was put in charge of the test. Zhang Azhou asked all his staff members to study all available Soviet data on static testing and made careful preparation for the test. Under his orderly command load applying, instrument reading and data measuring and recording were carried out as planned. When the load was increased to 105——110 per cent of the ultimate load, a sudden thundering sound came out and the airframe broke at the front spar of outer wing panel. This was a proof that the strength of airframe was in conformity with design criteria and this first destructive static test of a full size airframe was a complete success. Later on the static tests were also successively carried out in 57 design cases on 14 major components, e.g. central wing panel, aileron and fuselage, showing that their strength was in compliance with design criteria. All static tests of CJ—5 had been thus completed and the strength of the aircraft was proven. Zhang Azhou made an outstanding contribution to the static test programme and, therefore, was awarded a special—class merit.

The first flight of the first aircraft made in new China, the CJ—5, took place on July 3, 1954. Piloted by Duan Xianglu, the aircraft had a successful flight and made a safe landing. On July 20 the State Flight Test Commission came to the conclusion that the performance of CJ—5 was in conformity with its specification and therefore it was agreed that the aircraft should be put into mass production and be delivered to the Air Force for use in training. A celebration of the successful production of the first CJ—5 was held at the factory on July 26. Zhao Erlu, minister of the Second Ministry of Machine Building, Shao Shiping, the governer of Jiangxi province, Duan Zijun, deputy head of the Aircraft Industry Bureau, and other leaders from the Air Force came to the celebration. Three CJ—5s made a flight demonstration. A telegram reporting the success to Chairman Mao Zedong from all staff and workers of the Nanchang Aircraft Factory was passed during the celebration.

After the mass production of CJ—5 was approved in August a total of 379 CJ—5s were produced from 1954 to 1958 and delivered to the Air Force, the Navy air force and CAAC. The CJ—5 made a great contribution to the training of pilots in the early days of new China.

2. Independent Development of CJ—6 Primary Trainer

Further progress in the pilot training of the Air Force raised a requirement for a primary trainer with tricycle landing gear and better performance than that of the CJ—5. By that time the Yak—18A, a derivative of the Yak—18 with tricycle landing gear had been developed in the

Soviet Union and its drawings delivered to China. Xu Shunshou, project chief designer of the Aircraft Design Department in the Shenyang Aircraft Factory, concluded after his analysis that the performance of the Yak—18A was not advanced enough and its structure of steel tube frame was not suitable in China where aluminum material was in mass production. Therefore, he suggested

Fig.27　CJ—5 primary trainer aircraft

developing a more advanced primary trainer to suit the conditions in China. His suggestion was accepted. The design work began soon after designers' visits to Air Force bases where they made investigations and interviewed pilots. Lin Jiahua and Cheng Bushi took the responsibility of general layout design. From later part of 1957 to May 1958 the conceptual definition study, general layout design, wind tunnel test, performance analysis and preliminary design of the structure and systems were successively completed. A mockup in 1:1 scale was manufactured in the Shenyang Aircraft Factory. According to the general configuration the CJ—6 was evidently better than the CJ—5 in its performance, especially in flight speed, rate of climb, controllability and pilot's vision. It was decided by the Aircraft Industry Bureau in May, 1958 to transfer the development of the CJ—6 to the Nanchang Aircraft Factory. An Aircraft Design Department was established in the Nanchang Aircraft Factory and more than 20 designers including Tu Jida and Lin Jiahua were sent to assist the Nanchang factory by the Shenyang Aircraft Design Department. The upper authorities appointed Gao Zhenning project chief engineer and Tu Jida and Lin Jiahua deputy project chief engineers. Due to the joint efforts of the two design departments a complete set of drawings in 5,177 standard pages were released in a short period of time.

Immediately after the release of these drawings, workers, with a sense of pride in manufacturing an aircraft designed by their own people established new records one after another: the sub—assembly by riveting took only two weeks to finish and the final assembly only 7 days and nights.

The static test of a full size CJ—6 airframe and drop test of its landing gear showed its compliance with design criteria.

First flight of the CJ—6 by test pilots Lu Maofan and He Yinxi took place on August 27, 1958. In September two CJ—6s were ferried to Beijing and made a flight demonstration there to the leaders of the Military Commission of CCCPC.

A severe technical problem was found during the first flight. The engine and propeller made in Czechoslovakia did not match each other so that the CJ—6 could not fly at high speed. In

August 1959 project chief designer Ye Xulun proposed to retrofit the CJ−6 with Soviet A−14P engine and F530D35 propeller. His proposal was accepted and a retrofitted CJ−6 began its flight test by two pilots including Huang Zhaolian on July 18, 1960.

Huang Zhaolian was a test pilot for the CJ−5 national certification programme. He had flown many airplanes made in Germany, Japan, Italy, the United Kingdom, the United States of America, France and the Soviet Union with a total of 5,000 flying hours. During the flight test he undertook the most difficult and dangerous tasks—spin. Spin is a kind of unintentional motion occurring when the angle of attack is beyond the critical angle of attack, in which the center of gravity of the aircraft descends rapidly along a steep helical line while rotating about its three axes. This is an unusual flight condition which will end in a crash if the aircraft can not be recovered from the spin. The primary trainer is required to have good spin characteristics so that a trainee may practice the spin and to learn how to recover.

The answer to the question of whether the CJ−6 could recover from a spin was unknown because the spin test were not conducted in a vertical wind tunnel. Although the technical people had carefully carried out a theoretical analysis and some emergent safeguards against accidents such as the installation of an anti−spin chute had been adopted, the risk involved in the flight test still existed. Huang Zhaolian made a detailed theoretical analysis of the spin and practiced recovery actions repeatedly before actual flight until he was confident of a successful flight. At nine o'clock in the morning on November 16, 1960 he started his spin flight test. He made a check of stall, then tried the spin from half circle to three circles. Every time he recovered successfully and so fulfilled the task of spin flight.

In 1961 the CJ−6 was redesigned in the Nanchang Aircraft Factory and another prototype aircraft was produced for certification in an attempt to overcome the following four major deficiencies found in its flight test: temperature too low at engine cylinder heads, poor heat dissipation of oil system, unwanted right yaw and unbalanced fuel consumption between right and left fuel tanks. The flight test of the new prototype aircraft was completed on October 15. A total of 1,800 takeoff−and−landings and 612 flying hours were accumulated. The Military Products Certification Commission of the State Council certificated the CJ−6 and approved its mass production on January 5, 1962.

In 1963 the HS6 piston engine and the propeller used on the CJ−6 were successfully produced. Since then all aircraft parts, components and accessories have been made in China.

An uprated engine HS6A was certificated in December,1965. A derivative of the CJ−6 with the HS6A engine was designated as CJ−6A.

The development of the CJ−6 took four and a half years, a rather short period for an aircraft developed on our own. The reasons for this short development period were the unsophisticated nature of the CJ−6 itself, its practical and realistic design philosophy and moderate aircraft performance requirements. The CJ−6 had its own distinguishing features in aerodynamic layout, i.e. emphasis on controllability and safety. In performance it was as advanced as similar aircraft in the world. Domestic airborne equipment were chosen as much as possible for use in the aircraft. This maximum use of what was available in China made it possible to concentrate on the improvement of the performance of the new aircraft.

Various difficulties were encountered and many setbacks suffered in the development of the CJ—6. Its development was almost stranded in its early stage of development because of improper selection of the engine. In addition it met strong competition from the Yak—18A. With support from higher authorities, the leading cadres and scientific workers at the Nanchang Aircraft Factory kept on with the development. They overcame all difficulties one after another, worked steadily and made solid and uninterrupted progress. At last they succeeded.

From 1964 to 1966 ten CJ—6Bs with armament mounted were retrofitted at the Nanchang Aircraft Factory.

The CJ—6 was awarded a National Gold Medal in 1979. A total of 1,796 CJ—6s in all versions were produced from the beginning of production to 1986. It has not only made great contribution in training tens of thousands of pilots in China, it has also been flown by many countries around the world.

Section 2   Success in Manufacturing Jet Fighters

Fighter is a military aircraft used to destroy either enemy aircraft or other airborne weapons. It can also be called a pursuit airplane. Its purposes are to fight enemy fighters for air superiority and to intercept intruding enemy bombers, and to attack aircraft and missiles. In addition it can also carry certain ground attack weapons to attack ground targets. Since the first appearance during the First World War, it has been developed rapidly. Since the Second World War it has experienced several evolutionary stages, i.e. subsonic flight, transonic flight, Mach 2 flight and high manoeuvrability flight. After the founding of the aircraft industry in China, the policy in the field of military aircraft was to put more stress on the development of fighters. In the past 30 years its R&D and production facilities have been constructed both in coastal area and inland. Ninteen versions of 4 types of fighters, i.e. J—5, J—6, J—7 and J—8, have been developed and thousands of them produced by 1986. The Chinese Air Force and Navy air force have built "a Great Wall in the sky" with these domestic fighters for the defence of our territorial air space and waters.

The development of Chinese fighters began when the aviation industry started its transition from repair to manufacture. The decision to produce jet fighter J—5 was made in October, 1954, soon after the first flight of the first aircraft made in new China.

The J—5 fighter was a licence production of a Soviet high subsonic fighter MiG—17F. The MiG—17F was mainly used to fight for air superiority, to air defence, and to close air support. Its design began in 1948 and its flight test in 1949. Its delivery to the Soviet services began in 1951 and production was completed in 1958. It was powered by one centrifugal—flow turbo—jet engine with an afterburner. The engine air entered through a pitot type intake in the aircraft nose. Maximum speed was 1,145 km / h, service ceiling 16,600 m, maximum range with auxiliary tanks 2,020 km and maximum endurance 3 hours. It used a sweptback wing and was one of the most advanced jet fighters in the world at that time.

The Chinese aviation industry began its fighter production with the J—5. This was a difficult point at which to start. The J—5 had 253,550 parts in 14,719 varieties and 228 vendor—furnished—equipment. Its manufacturing techniques were far more complicated than those of the primary trainers. To produce the aircraft in a short period of time was a severe test to the young Chinese aviation industry.

The manufacture of the J—5 was carried out in the Shenyang Aircraft Factory which was constructed as one of 156 major engineering projects assisted by the Soviet Union in the First Five—year Plan. In order to speed up production the factory decided to carry out aircraft production and personnel training while the factory was in construction.

The prototype production of the J—5 aircraft started in early 1955. The Soviet Union supplied a complete set of drawings, technical documents, manufacturing processes and most of the tooling. They also supplied 2 example aircraft, 15 complete kits, forgings and raw materials for 10 aircraft, vendor—furnished—equipment for 8 aircraft and standard parts for 15 aircraft. In order to reduce prototype aircraft manufacturing time and master manufacturing techniques as soon as possible, the factory accepted Soviet experts' proposal—to divide the work into four phases and to carry out all work in parallel and crisscross. During the first phase five aircraft would be assembled with Soviet—furnished—components for the purpose of learning final assembly techniques. During the second phase, the components for four aircraft would be assembled with Soviet—furnished—sub—assemblies, then proceed to initial assembly and final assembly for a complete aircraft. Stress was put on learning initial assembly techniques. In the third phase the sub—assemblies for four aircraft would be assembled with Soviet—furnished—parts and then the initial assembly and final assembly would be completed. Stress in this phase was put on mastering riveting assembly techniques. In the fourth phase the parts would first be produced with Soviet and domestic raw materials and then the aircraft would be assembled. All manufacturing techniques had to be mastered in this phase.

The later practice showed the obvious advantages of the Soviet proposal. The factory started prototype production on April 8, 1955 and the final assembly of the first aircraft with parts all made in China was completed on July 13, 1956. On July 26 a full size airframe passed its static test, in which 129 load cases were tested and the airframe showed that it met the requirements. The flight test was completed on August 2 and showed that both the aircraft performance and quality were up to standard.

Fig. 28   The flight of the J—5

On September 8 the State Acceptance Committee declared the success of the manufacture of the J–5 aircraft and gave permission for mass production and delivery to the military services.

On September 10 a grand celebration for the successful trial production of the jet fighter was held at the Shenyang Aircraft Factory. Marshal Nie Rongzhen, vice chairman of the National Defence Committee, accompanied by Zhao Erlu, minister of the Second Ministry of Machine Building came to the ceremony, and cut the ribbon for the first J–5 fighter (China 0101). The director test pilot Wu Keming, who shut down two enemy aircraft in Korean War, flew the aircraft and performed a brilliant demonstration. The good performance of the domestic aircraft won the acclamation of all the people who watched the flight. On the same day the Central Committee of the Chinese Communist Party and the State Council sent a congratulatory telegram to the staff and workers of the factory and encouraged all the staff and workers in the aviation industry to "make persistent efforts to further improve the aviation industry's state of the art, to ensure the quality of the aero–products and to obtain the experience of mass production."

Fig.29   Peng Zhen receives test pilot Wu Keming

On National Day of the year 1956, four J–5s produced by the Shenyang Aircraft Factory flew over the Tian An Men Square for a review. Chairman Mao Zedong happily told the foreign friends on the Tian An Men rostrum: "Our own aircraft just flew over."

Four hundred and eighty one days (approximately 1 year and 4 months) had past from the preparation of the prototype production to the completion of the flight test programme. The reasons for the comparatively speedy development were: the correct leadership of the Chinese

Communist Party and more particularly the arrangements and instructions on the aircraft production made by Zhou Enlai, Chen Yun, Li Fuchun and Nie Rongzhen; the strong support from various regions and ministries all over the country; the technical assistance from the Soviet experts and the hard struggle of the aviation industry constructors. The following factors played their important roles in the aircraft development in the area of administration and coordination:

1. A correct policy for the transition from repair to manufacture was made. Repair formed a technical basis for manufacture. During the repair of thousands of aircraft, more emphasis was placed on manufacturing replacement parts and in the end manufacturing techniques were mastered.

2. The division of the prototype production into four phases and the parallel and crisscross performance of the four phases gave the programme impetus. This approach conformed to real Chinese conditions and, therefore, it not only cut down the prototype production period, ensured the quality of products and accelerated the establishment of various managerial systems, but also enabled engineers in different disciplines and workers in different types of work to practice in parallel and to master manufacturing techniques rapidly. There were many workers trained in this way in different types of the work and they became skilled. The number of workers trained by the Shenyang Aircraft Factory and skilled in prototype production reached 4,994, 80 per cent of the total production workers by early 1956.

3. The licence production of engines, airborne equipment and raw materials was carried out in advance or in parallel. It was the basis for the rapid success of prototype production and for the early commencement of the mass production of J—5 aircraft. The WP5 engines were available when the airframe of J—5 was completed. The vendor—furnished—equipment and accessories made in China for the J—5s had reached 48.3 per cent by 1957.

After successful prototype production, the J—5 was rapidly put into steady mass production. A total of 767 J—5s were produced from 1956 to 1959. They were delivered to equip the People's Air Force and Navy air force and to strengthen the national defence force. The heroic People's Air Force flew the domestic J—5 aircraft to defend the sacred territorial air space of our country. They shot down several intruder aircraft. In 1958 alone 2 F—84Gs, 6 F—86s and 1 aircraft equipped with Sidewinder air—to—air missiles were shot down in the coastal area of Fujian province. In 1957 the Navy air force J—5 shot down 1 RB—57 high altitude Reconnaissance airplane and in 1967 an Air Force J—5 shot down 1 F—4B. Thus the combat examples of using inferior equipment to defeat superior equipment in combat were set up.

The successes in prototype production and mass production of J—5 fighter and its delivery to the military services in large quantities helped the Chinese aviation industry leap forward into a jet age. China had become one of the few countries in the world, which had mastered jet technology and had written a splendid page in its history of fighter development.

Section 3 Manufacture of Supersonic Fighters

The pioneers of China's young aviation industry, after their successes in the prototype production of the J−5, immediately turned their eyes to the next target — the supersonic fighter.

At that time the "Sound Barrier" had just been broken and only a few countries such as the United States of America and the Soviet Union, etc. could develop the supersonic aircraft. The so−called "Sound Barrier" is a phenomenon occurring when the speed of an aircraft approachs the speed of sound, in which the aircraft drag drastically rises, lift drops, violent buffeting occurs and the aircraft becomes unstable and even uncontrollable, resulting in damage. The Sound Barrier was broken using two main improvements. One was the use of a turbojet engine which was lighter in weight and higher in power and efficiency at supersonic speed than the piston engine. The other was wing modification, reducing aircraft drag at supersonic speed by use of a sweptback wing, reducing wing thickness and using an area ruled①aircraft shape. The USA first broke through the "Sound Barrier" with its X−1 rocket research aircraft on October 14, 1947. The Soviet MiG−19 and American F−100 supersonic fighters were successively developed in 1953, and since then supersonic aircraft began its operational services.

The original design of the J−6 supersonic fighter built by the Shenyang Aircraft Factory in March, 1958 was the aforementioned Soviet MiG−19.

The development of the MiG−19 was begun in the Soviet Union in 1951. It reached the speed of sound in flight test at the end of 1952. Significant improvements were incorporated thereafter. In September 1953 M1.4 was reached in flight test. Flight test was completed at the end of 1954 and the delivery to the military services began in mid−1955. It used a nose intake, 2 turbojet engines, a high sweptback and tapered wing and movable tailplane. Maximum speed was 1,452 km / h, service ceiling 17,500 m and maximum range 2,200 km.

The first version produced at the Shenyang Aircraft Factory was the MiG−19P, all−weather fighter. What was different from the production of the J−5 was that all the technical documents for the manufacturing were prepared and all the production tooling was designed and manufactured by the Shenyang Aircraft Factory itself except the design drawings which were provided by the Soviet Union. The Chinese made MiG−19P flew for its first time by test pilot Wang Youhuai on December 17, 1958 and it was certificated for mass production by the State Certification Committee in April, 1959. The military services needed a large number of the front−line fighter MiG−19s at that time, therefore the Shenyang Aircraft Factory produced a

---

① Area rule is the relationship between zero lift wave drag of an aircraft at transonic or supersonic speed and the distribution of aircraft cross areas along its longitudinal axis. Design to area rule reduces the aircraft wave drag at transonic and supersonic speed and therefore, improves the aircraft performance.

derivative of MiG—19P designated as J—6 on the basis of the Soviet supplied example aircraft. Pilot Wu Keming flew the J—6 for the first time on September 30, 1959.

At that time the aviation industry was under the influence of the "big leap forward" in 1958. Many good rules and regulations were put aside, necessary organizations were disbanded, and unhealthy tendency of neglecting quality while pursuing quantity appeared. In the end a large number of finished aircraft could not be delivered to the military services because of inferior production quality and all the J—6s produced in that year had to be improved in three years.

The Shenyang Aircraft Factory began its prototype production of the J—6 in 1961 for the second time. The methods used in the initial prototype production were not repeated. A complete set of drawings and technical documents of the Soviet MiG—19C were copied and the production tooling and master tooling were rebuilt. Based on a proposal by Wang Qigong, vice general secretary of the party in the factory, Luo Shida, vice chief technician of the factory drafted a document "Standards for Operation" which set up 10 standards to be conformed to in the second prototype production period of the J—6. Lu Gang, director of the factory, formally issued orders to put into practice "Standards for Operation" in prototype production, so that it began on the right lines. A J—6 was at last successfully built with high quality domestic parts in December, 1963 and the design of the J—6 was certificated for mass production by the State Certification Committee.

The Nanchang Aircraft Factory was the second factory to be assigned the task of licence production of the MiG—19P and the MiG—19PM. Thus it was planned to convert the propeller aircraft factory into a jet aircraft factory. In September after receiving the drawings and technical documents supplied by the Shenyang Aircraft Factory, the Nanchang Aircraft Factory immediately set up a Prototype Production Committee and 7 professional groups. Relevant workshops also set up prototype

Fig. 30　The J—6 fighter

production groups to assist in organizing the programme. All the staff and workers of the factory worked very hard and created conditions needed for the production of jet fighters. At last, with the cooperation of relevant organizations, the MiG—19P was successfully produced in Nanchang. This prototype aircraft piloted by Wang Youhuai flew for the first time on September 28, 1959. On November 28, it was certificated by the State Certification Committee. A total of 7 aircraft were produced. Licence production of the MiG—19M, a front—line intercepter carrying missiles began in March 1959 based on the drawings and technical documents supplied by the Soviet Union. Five MiG—19PM were assembled with the Soviet kits. Thereafter the Nanchang Aircraft Factory built 19 aircraft on their own. The Nanchang Aircraft Factory mastered the production techniques of jet aircraft through the licence production of these two versions of the MiG—19. They also laid the foundation for the development of their own jet fighter.

The J—6 fighter was an aircraft successfully produced under licence and then put into mass production by the Chinese aviation industry. Through the life cycle of the aircraft (prototype production, mass production, delivery and operation) the aviation industry completely mastered manufacturing techniques and gained managerial experience, thus improving work in both these fields.

Aircraft production differs from general machinery production in forging, casting, welding, machining, metal sheet forming and assembling. Moreover, the interchangeability and assembly techniques in aircraft production are unusually complicated. Through the licence production of the J—5 and J—6 a transition from the pure imitation of Soviet manufacturing techniques to the ability to apply and develop these techniques at will was achieved. After learning the three methods of assembly, i.e. lofting and template, master tooling and reference holes, the Chinese developed their own qualified master tooling and all production tooling. New equipment such as the jig assembly machine and optical instruments were widely used and a complete set of technical methods for solving interchangeability problems was established. Significant progress in other manufacturing techniques such as welding, casting and heat treatment had also been made. In a word, manufacturing techniques in the aviation industry had been improved comprehensively.

Management in aircraft industry has its own peculiarity as well. Beginning with licence production of the J—5 the Shenyang Aircraft Factory studied Soviet experience in management and set up its own series of production management systems. For example:

—Aircraft manufacturing activities were organized in accordance with work sharing by workshops, manufacturing schedules, master tooling manufacturing schedules, assembly diagrams, assembly cycles and part kits in order to ensure the timely supply of parts and components to the aircraft production.

—All the parts and sub—assemblies were divided into different groups according to their manufacturing schedules and their assembly orders. The parts and sub—assemblies in the same group were manufactured at the same time. If a group of parts and sub—assemlies took a longer period of time to manufacture or they were to be used on the assembly line first, they were manufactured first and vice versa. In this way no parts would be manufactured too early and kept on the shelf or manufactured too late thus delaying the assembly.

—In order to ensure the quality strict quality control was carried out from the incoming raw materials, through finished parts, assemblies, tests and even to flight test.

Due to the aforementioned systems the production of the J—6 was stable and the quality good enough for mass production, so the industry progressed from the old fashioned production techniques to modern large scale production.

After the J−6 was put into mass production and delivered to the military services, another supersonic fighter, the J−7 with M 2.0 maximum speed was manufactured based on the Soviet MiG−21.

The design of the MiG−21 started in the Soviet Union in 1953. It flew for the first time in 1955 and delivery to the military services began in 1958. This high altitude, high speed fighter came in more than 20 versions and in development, performance, quality, emergency escape systems, armaments, avionics and engine,etc. were greatly improved. Production lasted 25 years.

According to a licence agreement signed in 1961 between the Chinese and the Soviet governments, the Soviet Union transferred to China the licence to produce the MiG−21F−13 fighter and its engine, and supply a complete set of technical data for production, complete aircraft and engine kits, some vendor−furnished−equipment and raw materials not available in China. But, some technical data was not received by China and this caused difficulties in prototype production.

The Defence Industry Office of the State Council made a quick decision and instructed the newly established CAE and its Shenyang Aircraft Design Institute to carry out a "thorough technical study" of the MiG−21. The prototype production of the J−7, the Chinese version of the MiG−21, started in the Shenyang Aircraft Factory in early 1964. The static test was completed in November, 1965. The result of the flight test conformed to the design requirement. On January 17, 1966 the J−7 piloted by pilot Ge Wenrong flew for the first time and 12 sorties and 29 takeoffs had been flown by the end of April. The J−7 was good in stability and controllability. All systems operated normally . The maximum speed reached M 2.02. The main tactical and technical performance conformed to the operational requirement. The J−7 was certificated for production in June, 1967. The prototype production of the J−7 took only 2 years and 4 months, one year ahead of the original plan.

A couple of major problems in manufacturing techniques were solved one after another by the engineers during the prototype production of the J−7, such as the forming of titanium alloy parts, the Chemical milling of integral panels, manufacture of an integral radome, assembly of an integral fuel tank and manufacture of non−metallic honeycomb cone.

In 1964 and 1965 the MAI decided to transfer J−7 production to the Chengdu Aircraft Factory and the newly−established Guizhou Aircraft Production Base with the support of the Shenyang Aircraft Factory. Therefore, three aircraft factories were constructing the J−7 at the same time.

The J−6, J−7 and their derivatives were the main aircraft produced by the aviation industry to equip the military services. The heroic People's Air Force and Naval air force flew these domestic fighters and scored one victory after another in defencing the teritorial air and sea of our motherland. The pilots of the Naval air force and Air Force shot down two intruding high altitude reconnaissance aircraft RF−101s with J−6s in 1964 and 1965. One F−104C fighter—bomber was shot down by a Naval air force J—6 in 1965. In 1967 Air Force J—6s shot down 2 intruding A—6 attack aircraft. From 1964 through 1971 a total of 14 enemy aircraft including 8 pilotless aircraft were shot down by Air Force J—6s and J—7s shot down 6 pilotless aircraft and more than 300 high altitude reconnaissance and psychological warfare balloons. From 1965 through 1968 the Navy air force shot down a total of 7 enemy aircraft with domestic fighters. All these victories discouraged intruders.

Section 4   Modification and Development of Fighters

The evolution of Chinese fighters started from licence production of the Soviet MiG series fighters. This approach raised the technical level of the Chinese aviation industry and thus shortened aircraft development cycles. The purpose of technology imports is to strengthen self—reliance and to design our own high performance aircraft. To realize this purpose the principle "to follow accurately and to advance step by step" must be observed and the procedure of "import, investigation, improvement and innovation" or "writing regular script first and cursive hand second" must be followed. This practice shows that continuously improving and updating fighters based on need and capability and proceeding from the easiest and simplest modifications to the hardest and most complicated ones is an effective way to progress and to develop aircraft on our own.

Since the founding of New China a total of 13 versions have been successfully derived from 3 fighter types produced under licence.

1.   Modification and Development of the J—5

There were two main derivatives of the J—5, i.e. the J—5A, JJ—5.

a. J—5A

This aircraft was based on the Soviet all—weather intercepter MiG—17PF. It differed from the basic J—5 by the addition of a radar, a bigger and longer forward fuselage section and relocation of systems and components in the fuselage. Fifty per cent of the parts in the J—5A were new.

J—5A prototype production was assigned to the Chengdu Aircraft Factory by the MAI in May, 1961. The Shenyang Aircraft Factory sent a professional team consisting of technical people in different disciplings to Chengdu to help with the J—5A prototype production, specifically production preparation, parts manufacturing, assembly and flight test. They also provided a set of master tooling and production tooling for the J—5. The assistance sped up prototype production. A complete set of drawings for production was completed by the Chengdu Aircraft Factory in September 1962, component manufacture started in March, 1963, and final assembly in June, 1964. The full size static test was completed in September of the same year.

—118—

The first flight of the J—5A prototype (02) took place on November 11, 1964 at Yanliang airfield, Xi'an. It flew for 30 minutes and all systems operated normally. All flight tests were completed by the end of November and the aircraft operational and tactical performance was approved. It was certificated for mass production by the Military Products Certification Commission in December. Prototype production took 3 years and 3 months.

The J—5A was put into mass production in 1965. The delivery of this all weather fighter provided the military services with a new weapon which could counter the enemy aggression at night.

b. JJ—5

In the early 1960s a large number of fighters produced by the aviation industry were delivered to the military services, but the trainers used were still the UMiG—15 imported from the Soviet Union in the early days. The performance of this trainer could no longer meet the needs of training. Therefore, the Air Force required a new jet trainer urgently. The MAI decided in early 1965 to

Fig. 31   The J—5A fighter

develop a fighter—trainer JJ—5 based on the J—5A in the Chengdu Aircraft Factory.

The JJ—5 was in a tandem configuration with a fuselage slightly longer than the J—5A. The equipment and the shape of the nose cowling and tail cowling were changed. One 23—1 gun was retained. The power plant was a WP5D centrifugal—flow jet engine.

The JJ—5 flew for the first time on May 8, 1966. Its performance was certified by the State Certification Group and it was certificated for mass production at the end of the year. A total of 1,061 JJ—5s had been produced by the end of 1986.

Operation in the military services showed that the overall performance of the JJ—5 was better than that of the UMiG—15. The JJ—5 could be used not only in flight training but also in combat training such as dog fight and ground attack. An Air Force Aerobatic Team flew a number of demonstrations with the JJ—5s for distinquished foreign guests. On National Day of 1984 . 8 JJ—5s painted in red and guided by a

Fig. 32   The JJ—5 fighter—trainer

H—6 flew over Tian An Men Square trailing coloured smoke.

2. Modification and Development of the J—6

After its delivery the J—6 fighter was modified several times based on the Air Force's operational requirements. The main derivatives were JZ—6, JJ—6, J—6Ⅲ and J—6A.

a. The JZ—6 Reconnaissance Version

Because of military services' urgent need for a supersonic reconnaissance aircraft the Shenyang Aircraft Factory began to modify the J—6 as a reconnaissance aircraft JZ—6 in 1966. This medium and low altitude day and night reconnaissance version was put into small—scale production in 1967. Two J—6s were modified as a high altitude day time reconnaissance aircraft in 1971 and one was modified to perform missions both at high altitude and medium—low altitude in 1975.

In January 1976 the State Council and the Military Commission of CCCPC approved the operational requirement for the JZ—6 reconnaissance aircraft and the MAI formally assigned the task of development to the Shenyang Aircraft Factory. The JZ—6 took pictures with an optical camera in day time and an infrared scanning camera at night.

One J—6 was modified as a demonstrator aircraft to meet the requirement of design certification. Beginning in April 1976, the certification of bays used for high altitude and medium—low altitude reconnaissance, and static test of forward fuselage and camera bays were carried out. These tests showed that they met design requirements. The design certification was approved by the Aero Products Certification Committee.

b. The JJ—6 Fighter—trainer

The J—6 was put into mass production and delivered to the military services after 1963. Very soon it became the mainstay of the Air Force's attack capability. The military services urgently needed a type of trainer which was similar to the J—6 in performance in order to train pilots for J—6s. In October 1966 the MAI approved a design proposal for a derivative called the JJ—6, which was made jointly by the Shenyang Aircraft Factory and the Shenyang Aircraft Design Institute. The prototype production began soon after approval. The design drawings were released in 1967 and the first flight happened on November 6, 1970. It was certificated for production in December 1973. A total of 634 JJ—6s were produced by the end of 1986.

The JJ—6 was the first supersonic jet fighter—trainer in China. The main modifications were: the two—pilot cockpit instead of single pilot one, a slight longer fuselage, one gun instead of three; disc brakes on the main landing gear, new compass, beacon, interphone and cockpit blinds for blind flying.

c. The J—6Ⅲ

In order to increase the maximum speed of the J—6 at medium altitude the Shenyang Aircraft Factory began to develop a derivative called the J—6Ⅲ in 1969. The main modifications were: an uprated WP6A engine; a shorter wing span; increased chord length and consequently larger flaps and ailerons; addition of an adjustable shock cone in the center of the nose intake and a single hydraulic system instead dual. The first J—6Ⅲ flew on August 6 of the same year. Its initial flight test showed that the J—6Ⅲ was more manoeuvrable, faster in climbing and turning and faster than the basic J—6. But it also had severe problems. The design had not been evaluated by sufficient ground and flight tests, and it was put into mass production before certification. Hundreds of J—6Ⅲs had to be returned to the factory because of oversensitivity of controls and missing rivets inside the intake. Dual hydraulic systems were restored. This took four years and heavy losses were incurred.

The lessons learned by the J—6Ⅲ derivation were profound. They told that violating objective laws and scientific procedures would bring in punishment.

d. The J—6A

The J—6A was an all—weather derivative of the basic J—6 developed by the Guizhou Aircraft Factory. Its main improvements were: the addition of an all—weather radar and "pili" 2 air—to—air missiles, installation of a rocket ejection escape system, relocation of the drag chute bay to a position above the tail cover; adoption of disk brakes on main landing gear, dual engine starting systems, and the addition of a tail warning system.

The development of the J—6A began in 1974 and its certification was completed in November 1976. It was certificated for small—scale production and for delivery to equip the military services in 1977.

3. Modification and Development of the J—7

A number of improved versions of the J—7 were introduced by the Chengdu Aircraft Factory based on military services' operations. They were the J—7Ⅰ, J—7Ⅱ, J—7Ⅲ, J—7A, J—7B and J—7M. Among them the J—7Ⅱ, J—7M and J—7Ⅲ were the three most important versions.

a. The J—7Ⅱ

The Chengdu Aircraft Factory began to develop the J—7Ⅱ based on the J—7Ⅰ in 1975 for further improvement in performance. Its main improvements over its predecessor were:

(1) Canopy ejection was replaced by open rocket ejection and, therefore, the safe ejection was possible even at low altitude and low flying speed.

The ejection escape system was used in an emergency to safely eject a pilot from the aircraft cockpit. On the basic J—7 aircraft the canopy was automatically engaged to the seat at the beginning of ejection and separated from the seat after ejection. It was prone to failure because of the complicated structure and release mechanism. Open ejection was used on the J—7Ⅱ, by which the canopy would be jettisoned prior to the ejection of the seat. An aft—hinged canopy was designed for this escape system and it suited the physical size of the Chinese pilots. A rocket pack was incorporated into the new Type Ⅱ rocket eject seat to increase the ejection height and safe separation was ensured by the addition of a seat / pilot separation system. Safe escape at low altitude and at 250—850 km / h IAS could be performed. Design was certificated in 1979 and it first succeeded abroad in 1984. By the end of 1985 the Air Force used the ejection system 5 times and each time was successful. In 1985 Type Ⅱ rocket ejection seat won a National Gold

Medal of Quality.

(2) Relocation of the drag chute bay improved aircraft landing performance and shortened the landing run. With this improvement the aircraft could deploy its drag chute when the aircraft height above the ground was less than 1 meter and the landing run was reduced to less than 800 m.

(3) A 720 liters center line auxiliary fuel tank was carried to increase aircraft range.

(4) The engine was changed to a WP7B. Aircraft performance was improved by the increased thrust.

A J—7 II with these four improvements was flown by test pilot Yu Mingwen for the first time on December 30, 1978. Design was certificated in September 1979. A First Class Prize for Major Technology Improvement was awarded by the Defence Industry Office of the State Council in 1980. The J—7 II s were used not only to update Chinese Air Force's equipment but also for export. Thirty five J—7 II s in seven groups flew over Tian An Men Square with other types of aircraft in a grand military parade held in Beijing on National Day, October 1, 1984.

b. The J—7M

After 1979 the Chengdu Aircraft Company (former Chengdu Aircraft Factory) developed three export versions: the J—7A, J—7B and J—7M on the basis of foreign customers' requirements with imported airborne equipment. Among them the J—7M was the most successful version.

J—7M, the latest version of the export aircraft, was based on the J—7B. The most important improvements incorporated in the J—7M were to the avionics and fire control systems.Imported equipment was used for this . The others were the use of a bird—proof windshield, the addition of two store carriers under the wing, the strengthening of the landing gear and eight other improvements. Amongst the advantages of the J—7M were the head—up display, high precision and fast speed firing and ground attack capabilities, long distance radar with counter—countermeasures capability and an advanced communication transceiver. Moreover, the life of the aircraft, engine and vendor—furnished—equipment and components were extended. The J—7M was significantly improved over the J—7B in its overall performance so that it became one of the most advanced high speed high altitude light fighters in contemporary China.

The development of the J—7M began in 1981 and Tu Jida was appointed chief designer.

In order to test the weapon system and performance of the J—7M, several flight tests were carried out at the Flight Research Institute. In—flight target practice was performed abroad. Air—to—air and air—to—ground weapon capabilities and dog fighting were tested in 40 sorties and 18 accumulated flying hours. Target practice scores were good. In December 1984 the MAI certificated the design of the J—7M and by the end of 1985 all aircraft ordered by foreign customers had been delivered on time.

The successful development of the J—7M shows that it is feasible to import advanced foreign airborne equipment to improve the performance of domestic aircraft and thus to

32. H-6 bomber fleet

33. H-6 bomber in
formation flight

34. H-5 light bomber
final assembly line

35. SH-5 water based bomber
back to its base

36. SH-5 water based bomber

37. Q-5 attack aircraft

38. Q-5 aircraft night flying operation

39. Q-5 aircraft final assembly line

40. Q-5 aircraft in a foreign country

41. Q-5 aircraft flying over Qiantang Bridge

42. Citation for Q-5 aircraft

43. Citation certificate
    for Q-5 aircraft

44. WP6A engine flame tube

45. Z-8 large helicopter

46. Z-8 first flight

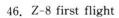

47. Z-9 marine operation

48. Z-9 in assembly shop

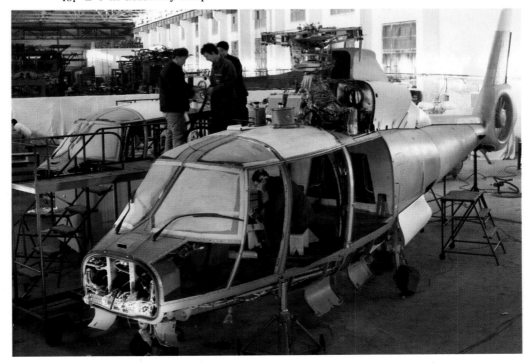

A-5M, sino-italian joint venture

A-5M, 中意合营

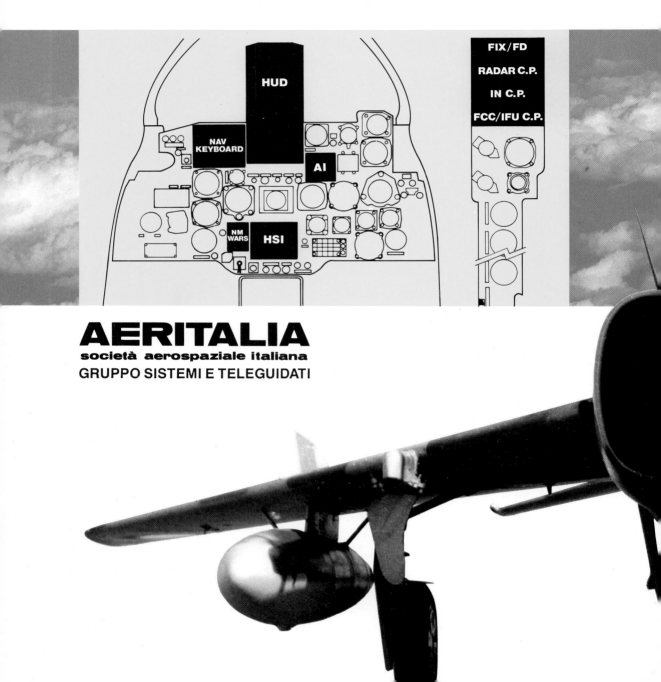

HUD

NAV KEYBOARD

AI

NM WARS

HSI

FIX/FD

RADAR C.P.

IN C.P.

FCC/IFU C.P.

AERITALIA
società aerospaziale italiana
GRUPPO SISTEMI E TELEGUIDATI

Now, flights have proven that the state
of the art Nav/Attack System integrated on-board
has significantly increased the A-5 performance.

CATIC

CHINA NATIONAL AEROTECHNOLOGY
IMPORT - EXPORT CORPORATION

49. Z-5 air mining

50. Light helicopter Yan'an-II

51. CJ-6 primary trainer fleet

52. The medal for CJ-6

53. The medal certificate for CJ-6

54. A high altitude reconnaissance drone
    carried under an aircraft wing

55. Parachuted target

56. Changkong I highly
    maneuverable target in
    test base

57. An RPV launched from a ship

58. An RPV launched from ground

59. A fighter with air to air missiles

60. Air to air missiles to be carried by a fighter aircraft

61. An air to air missile is launched

62. A ship to ship missile is launched

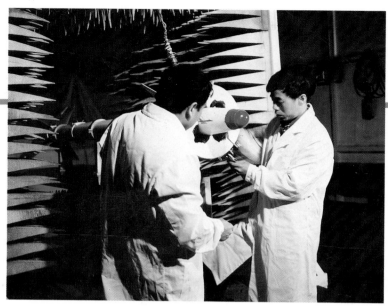

63. An air to air missile in microwave anechoic chamber

64. Final assembly line of a coastal defence missile

promote exports.

　　c. The J—7Ⅲ

　　The J—7Ⅲ is a high—medium altitude, high speed all—weather fighter and it can operate by day or night. Many modifications were introduced into the J—7Ⅲ. Compared with the J—7Ⅱ, 80 per cent of components and 43 per cent of vendor—furnished—equipment were different. 37 new materials and 190 new vendor—furnished—items were used. The main improvements were: incorporation of an all—weather radar and an advanced fire control system, increased capabitilies in carrying missiles and rockets, a new engine WP13, improved ejection system, additional fuel tanks and changes in structure and geometry.

　　Development was jointly undertaken by the Chengdu Aircraft Design Institute, the Chengdu Aircraft Company and the Guizhou Aircraft Company. The Chengdu Aircraft Design Institute was responsible for design, the Chengdu Aircraft Company for the manufacture of the fuselage, final assembly and flight test, and the Guizhou Aircraft Company for the manufacture of the wing and main landing gear. The development programme was managed by system engineering. Development was led by Gao Zhenning, vice Minister of MAI, and Song Wencong was appointed chief designer. An Management Office for the programme was set up in April, 1983 and Xie Ming was appointed its director. During the prototype production the staff of the office worked on the spot, directing and providing services and, so a matrix managerial system was formed to facilitate development.

　　The design of the J—7Ⅲ began in 1981 and component manufacture in 1982. Final assembly began after the mating of the fuselage and the wing for the first J—7Ⅲ in December 1983.

　　During final assembly the Chengdu Aircraft company was the mainstay and the vendors cooperated closely. The Chengdu Aircraft Design Institute sent more than 100 designers to the factory to follow production and to solve various problems. The leading cadres also worked on site. With the hard work of hundreds of final assembly workers and engineers excellent quality and high effciency were achieved. The final assembly of the first J—7Ⅲ took only 30 days and nights and was completed on February 6, 1984.

　　An unexpected accident happened during a period of intense work. An urgent report came from the ejection system test range in Henan province on March 23, saying that the rocket sled had turned over when a rocket ejection seat was undergoing a ground test, the fuselage and the rocket sled were destroyed and the test had to be terminated. In view of the fact that

Fig. 33　Full size airframe vibration test of the J—7Ⅲ

the rocket ejection test was a major test which had to be completed prior to the first flight of the newly developed aircraft, the Management Office immediately decided to build another fuselage test section and rocket sled and to carry out the test from the beginning. The Chengdu Aircraft Company built a new fuselage test section in 9 days and the Hubei Escape System Research Institute built a new sled in 7 days. The test was resumed at the test range on April 9 and was successfully completed in 6 days, the shortest period of time that this kind of test had ever been carried out. It saved time and ensured the smooth development of the J-7Ⅲ.

On April 6 the full-scale static test was successfully performed and on April 26 test pilot Yu Mingwen flew the J-7Ⅲ for its first time. There were no occurrences of sideslip, and the systems all operated normally. The flight programme was completed by the end of December, 1984.

The success of the J-7Ⅲ development programme was a crystallization of the hard work and wisdom of the workers, engineers and cadres who worked for the programme. The practices of the system engineering management and the matrix management system, and the wide applications of new technology, new manufacturing techniques, new vendor-furnished-equipment and new materials marked a new phase in the design and production of Chinese fighters. It was the first time since the founding of the aircraft industry to construct the prototype aircraft by two factories in different places, Chengdu and Guizhou. The experience was obtained in sharing and cooperating on the prototype production.

d. The JJ-7

Since the beginning of 1980s the J-6s in the military services have been gradually replaced by J-7s and J-8s. The supersonic aerodynamic layouts of these two generations, J-7 and J-8, are significantly different from their predecessors. The JJ-5s and JJ-6s were no longer considered to be the most suitable trainers to train pilots for J-7s and J-8s because the conversion period was too long and even unsafe. Therefore, the MAI made a decision to develop a new trainer—JJ-7.

The design of JJ-7 was derived from J-7Ⅱ by the Guizhou Aircraft Design Institute and the Guizhou Aircraft Company. Its conceptual definition study began in 1979 and the main operational requirement was issued in 1981. All the design drawings were completed by the design institute in 1983 and the factory started the prototype production immediately after the release of drawings. The full size static test was completed on June 12, 1985. On July 5 test pilot Yan Xiufu flew the domestic JJ-7 for its first time over the Guizhou plateau and landed safely after all flight test subjects had been completed.

The JJ-7 differed from the J-7Ⅱ by addition of an aft cockpit, relocating the pitot tube to the upper right of the nose, ensuring the ejection escape safety of two pilots in emergency with a sequenced ejection system, additions of a "failure simulation system" and an interphone and adoption of red cockpit lighting. Approximate 40 per cent of the drawings were changed. The JJ-7 could not only perform all the day time training subjects of the J-7 in fair or adverse weather but also the most training subjects of the J-8. In addition it also had certain air combat and ground attack capabilities.

In order to enhance the leadership to the design and the prototype production, the MAI set up a Chief Designer System and an On—site Directing Office of the JJ—7 and appointed Yu Xiuming chief designer and Tang Wenbing chief director. The administrative system cooperated closely with the Chief Designer System to take charge of the necessary vendor— furnished— equipment and accessories, coordination, quality and schedule based on the development plan, and ensured the smooth development. The staff and workers overcame many difficulties caused by insufficient infrastructure, know—how and budget, worked meticulously in their designing, testing and manufacturing and tackled many key technical problems. It was very hot when the ejection test of an escape system was carrying on in Henan province in the middle of June, 1984. But all the people of the test team from the Guizhou Aircraft Company, the Guizhou Aircraft Design Institute and the Hubei Escape System Research Institute worked in open air, completed the seat ejection tests at high, medium and low speeds and obtained satisfactory test results. It was bitterly cold when the Guizhou Aircraft Company was carrying on a dorsal fuel tank pressurization test. The test site was also in open air. During the test the empty fuel tank had to be placed in the water at the depth of 1.3 m and then pressurized and carefully checked. The test had to be repeated a number of times. In order to find every minor leakage Wang Jianchang, a tester and a Party member, stayed in the cold water for dozens of minutes to perform detailed checks in every test. It was so cold that his lips turned purple. When his leader bought him some liquor and ask him to drink to warm his body, he answered: "I don't drink liquor and I don't feel cold either. Doing test is my job and my duty too." It was because the hard work of these heroic and moving unknown heros like Wang Jianchang that the triumphant birth of the JJ—7 in Guizhou plateau was seen.

The J—7 series aircraft are rather successful among all the derivative fighters. A number of versions with different features and applications have been derived step by step from a single basic aircraft. This achievement is a natural result of the fact that the scientific people have mastered the laws and peculiarity of the modifications to a basic aircraft through their enormous practice and exploration. The laws and peculiarity of the aircraft modification and derivation can be concluded as follows:

(1) The aircraft modification and derivation is different both from the licence production in that the partial development is incorporated and the development of a new aircraft in that only partial innovation is incorporated. The peculiarity of the aircraft modification and derivation determine that the designers have to first have a thorough understanding of the basic aircraft design and of aircraft structures and systems then find out the weak points of the basic aircraft by analysing the operators' inputs while investigating the objectives of the modification and derivation and at last determine the new technology to be used.

(2) The technology to be used for the modification has to be tested and proven by a number of ground tests and flight test. Therefore, the infrastructure and the test team must be expanded and strengthened from time to time to ensure the smooth carrying out of the tests.

(3) The retrofitting of an aircraft must be accompanied by the synchronized development,

certification and problem solving in other related areas, e.g. engine and airborne equipment, otherwise any delay or failure in these related areas will adversely affect the whole retrofitting programme.

With the renewal of Chinese fighters further modification and derivation based on an advanced existing fighter will soon be carried out.

Section 5   Initiation of Independent Fighter Development

The ability to develop advanced aircraft is an important indication of aviation industry's state of the art of a country. An independent and self—reliance aviation industry system must be set up in China on a solid basis of the science and technology if the Chinese nation wants to live on the planet with other nations in the world and the Chinese aviation industry wants to penetrate into the world market. Since the early date of the Chinese aviation industry, to build up the ability of aircraft development has been one of its goals. In 1956, immediately after the success of prototype production of the jet fighter, the aircraft design organizations were set up to carry out the development work and the aeronautical R& D. In the 20 years and more thereafter, Chinese scientific workers in the aviation industry have made continuous efforts and have obtained important achievements in the areas of R& D, design and production of the fighters.

1.   First Try in Aircraft Development

In September 1956 first aircraft design organization of Chinese aviation industry, the Shenyang Aircraft Design Department, was established. It was located in the Shenyang Aircraft Factory. Xu Shunshou was appointed the director designer, and Huang Zhiqian and Ye Zhengda vice director designers. Before they came back to China they had studied the aeronautical enginee— ring in the United States of America,

Fig. 34   The JJ—1 trainer

the United Kingdom and the Soviet Union respectively. They led a design team with an average age of 22. Only 3 per cent of the team members were experienced engineers who had designed aircraft before. Most of the others just graduated from the universities and colleges. It was from such a starting point that they began to march towards the goals of the aircraft development.

The Shenyang Aircraft Design Department chose the JJ—1, a subsonic jet fighter—trainer, as the first aircraft to develop. This was because the military services needed such a trainer to train their pilots and the design department needed it to temper its design team. Through the development of a trainer the designers could enrich their knowledge, accumulate their experience and prepare themselves for the development of a fighter.

The design of the JJ−1 started in October 1956. It had two tandem cockpits, two intakes at sides of the fuselage, a centrifugal−flow turbojet engine, a low set tapered wing and a tricycle type landing gear. The hydraulic system, fuel system, control system, pneumatic system, electric system, instruments, and transceiver, etc. required by a subsonic fighter were installed in the aircraft. The main systems could be controlled by both pilots.

Pilot Yu Zhenwu flew the JJ−1 for its first time on July 26, 1958. On August 4 Ye Jianying, Vice Chairman of the Military Commission of CCCPC and Liu Yalou, Commander of the Air Force came to Shenyang to attend a ceremony for celebrating the success of JJ−1's first flight.

Part of the flight test subjects were done below 3,000 m from July to October, 1958 and it showed that the performance was basically in conformity with the design specification. The development cycle of the JJ−1 was two years shorter than that of the similar aircraft made in Japan and Czechoslovakia and the performance was better. But later on the Air Force changed its flying training system from three levels (primary trainer—JJ−1—UMiG−15) to two levels (primary trainer—UMiG−15) and, therefore, the development of the JJ−1 was terminated.

Through the development of the JJ−1 a development work procedure which was in the order of conceptual definition study, the sketch design, the preliminary design, the review of mockup, the detailed design and the prototype production was set up, the Chinese first generation designers were trained and the data in design, analysis and test were accumulated.

The development programmes of the East Wind 107 fighter and the East Wind 113 high speed fighter began in 1958. But both of them came to a premature end.

The East Wind 107 was a supersonic all−weather fighter designed by the Shenyang Aircraft Design Department. Its operational requirements called for maximum speed of M 1.8 and service ceiling of 20,000 m. It used two engines. The design began in 1958 and the prototype production in May, 1959. In June,1959 the design was significantly modified. Its development was terminated in November of the same year in order to concentrate on the development of the East Wind 113 fighter.

The East Wind 113 was a high altitude and high speed fighter developed by the Military Engineering Academy in Harbin. Its operational requirements called for maximum speed of M 2.5 and service ceiling of 25,000 m. Its design began at the end of 1958 and part of the aircraft parts were manufactured in 1960. Because of the undue operational requirements the materials, vendor−furnished−equipment and components, armament and engine, etc., had to be developed from scratch so that they could not be available in a short period of time. The design speed of the aircraft was so high that the aircraft had to pass the "heat barrier". But at that time the heat related problems such as aerodynamic heating and thermal stress had not been solved either in theory or in test and the necessary infrastructure had not been constructed either, therefore the

East Wind 113 fighter had to be terminated.

2. Investigation to MiG—21

The world aviation history shows that no country in the world has been always smooth in its aircraft development and the failures are sometimes hard to avoid. The important thing is to be able to draw lessons from the failures and to use it as reference for later work. The problem which caused the termination of the East Wind 113 aircraft was found in later days and it was the shaky foundation of the aircraft development. At that time the necessary R&D and design institutes, as well as the infrastructure, had not been set up and the design team itself lacked experience and necessary knowledge. In order to solve these two problems some transonic and supersonic wind tunnels were constructed and a Flight Research Institute was set up in the late 1950s and CAE was set up in 1961. A number of new professional design institutes for design of aircraft, aeroengines, instruments, electrical equipment, accessories and weapons were also successively set up in addition to a number of new research institutes for the applied research of aerodynamics, structure stress analysis, escape system, optical machinery and automatic control, etc. Among them was the Shenyang Aircraft Design Institute which gathered many technical people who had worked on the aircraft design in different disciplines and was divided into 13 design sections,e.g. the general layout section, aerodynamics section and structure stress analysis section, 3 laboratories and 1 factory responsible for manufacturing test equipment. All these work were an organizational and technical preparation for the later development of fighters.

Meanwhile the work on improving quality of the design team personnel was also carried out. The aircraft designers were organized to systematically study the Soviet MiG—21 fighter.

In May 1962 an instruction to arrange the study of the MiG—21 was jointly issued by CAE and MAI. Tang Yanjie, President of CAE, went to the Shenyang Aircraft Design Institute a couple of times to explain the far—reaching signsficance and to mobilize the technical and design personnel to work on a solid technical basis and to lay a solid foundation for the development of advanced fighters.

The first step of studying the MiG—21 was to find out key issues in the manufacturing techniques including its key technical problems and the key materials used. The second step was to understand its design philosophy, design methods and technical features through the licence production and some necessary tests. The design team personnel were requested to know not only "what" but also "why". During the study of the MiG—21 the Shenyang Aircraft Design Institute performed 39 tasks, e.g. verification of the Aircraft Stress Analysis, the Stress Analysis of the Nose Cone, the Wing Stress and Rigidity Analysis, the Aircraft Combat Performance Analysis and the verification of the Aerodynamic Characteristics, 3,300 runs in 27 subjects of the high speed and low speed wind tunnel tests and 64 kinds of test including intake test, aircraft resonance test, ground ejection test of the ejection seat and flight test. By these analyses and tests the design data were supplemented and verified, the Soviet design method was studied and mastered and the experience was accumulated.

The another way which was used to temper the design team and to improve its quality was to investigate and analyze the western aircraft so that the design art other than the Soviet's could be learned. A total of 5 fighters and high altitude reconnaissance aircraft were systematically analyzed and studied by the Shenyang Aircraft Design Institute. In the end some papers on the technology of these aircraft which could be used as a reference were prepared and partial drawings were drawn.

The later practice proved that the decision about the investigation to the MiG—21 in the 3 years period was right. It gave designers a chance to study and to practice. It gave the manufacture people a chance to familiarise and to master the manufacturing techniques for the prototype production. "Sharpenning an axe would not delay the firewood cutting". The investigation to the MiG—21 naturally made a preparation for the later development of fighters.

3. Development of a High Altitude and High Speed Fighter J—8

After several years of careful preparation and deliberation the development of a new high altitude and high speed fighter was unveiled in the aircraft industry. In May 1964 the CAE proposed at a meeting to develop a fighter with better performance on the basis of Soviet MiG—21 fighter. The work on the conceptual definition was commenced in October of the same year. At a meeting on investigation of the conceptual definition the Shenyang Aircraft Design Institute put forward two design options. One was a single engine design which required an all new high thrust engine to be developed. The other was a twin engine design which required a new derivative of a proven engine to be developed. The latter was finally accepted at a meeting convened by Tang Yanjie, President of the CAE. This was a right selection because there existed already certain technical bases. This design selection became the prerequisite of the success in the development of the J—8. Luo Ruiqing, chief of General Staff approved the development programme and its operational requirement on May 17, 1965. The fighter was designated as J—8 and the major tasks of the development were undertaken by the Shenyang Aircraft Design Institute and the Shenyang Aircraft Factory.

The State leaders showed their deep concern for the development of the J—8. On August 14, 1965 when vice premier He Long was hearing a report on the development status of the J—8, he pointed out: "The J—8 must be successfully developed at an early date." Marshal Nie Rongzhen expounded several issues which had to be taken into consideration in the design of the new fighter in his letter dated August 18 to vice chief of General Staff Zhang Aiping, and these issues played an important role in the development of the J—8.

In the design concept of the J—8 the stresses were put on the service ceiling, speed, range, rate of climb and fire power, etc. The deficiencies of the J—7 were made up one by one on the J—8, therefore the performance of the J—8 was improved as follows:

   a. Maximum flight speed   M 2.2;
   b. Absolute ceiling   >20,000 m;
   c. Maximum rate of climb   200 m / sec;

d. Basic range   1,500 km;

   Maximum range   2,000 km;

e. Duration of combat at 19,000 m altitude was specified;

f. An improved aerial gun and air—to—air missiles were installed; and

g. A radar with longer search distance was installed.

The aerodynamic configuration of the J—8 featured a nose intake, a high sweptback, low aspect ratio and thin delta wing, a low set tailplane and two ventral fins. Two WP7A engines were chosen as its power plant. The aircraft thrust to weight ratio reached 0.89, which was better than that of the J—7.

The design of the J—8 was in full swing in September 1965. Its technical work was led by Ye Zhenda and coordinated by a Chief Designer Office headed by Wang Nanshou after the chief designer Huang Zhiqian unfortunatly died in an airliner crash abroad in May of the year. In December a wooden mockup of the J—8 was reviewed. In March 1966 the designers went to the factory and started their on site design with the assistance of workers and manufacture engineers. A complete set of drawings was released for the production at the end of 1966 and the production documents in early 1967. The factory began the prototype production immediately after they had received these drawings and documents.

Vice chief designer Gu Songfen and his design staff investigated several alternative aerodynamic layouts and conducted a great number of wind tunnel tests. One layout was finally selected and many major technical problems, e.g. the supersonic direction stability, the choices of the locations for the tailplane and the vertical fin and the pressure center of the aircraft, were successively solved.

During the on site design a way of three—in—one combination was adopted, by which 570 and more designers including Wang Nanshou, 80 and more experienced workers including Chen Ayu and Wang Ahui and 30 and more manufacture engineers were combined into a single team for investigation to the designs and drawings. In this phase the manufacture engineers from the factory made 2,330 and more suggestions. Out of them 1,660 were accepted and 40 significantly improved the workability of the design in the manufacturing. One example was an innovative proposal to delete the pads underneath the wing main spar, which was realized by the designers after they tested a wing main spar of the MiG—21 fighter with the help from the manufacture engineers and workers. This innovation changed the traditional structure of the MiG aircraft and saved 4 kg in weight on the J—8.

One difficulty in J—8 development was the design of the bullet feed and ejection system of the aerial gun. The system should ensure the continuous firing in flight. Soviet experts took the design of the system as their patent and, therefore, they kept it secret.

In tackling technical problems of the bullet feed and ejection system, the designers worked together with workers. They run the tests and modified a gun to simulate the firing in flight. 10,000 rounds of dummy bullets in total were fired. They had at last found the laws of the system and succeeded in its design.

The Shenyang Aircraft Factory began their preparation of the J—8 prototype production in the second half of the year 1965. Under the leadership of Gao Fangqi, first vice director and chief engineer, Luo Shida, vice chief technologist, presided over the formulation of a general technological production scheme for the J—8, which had made use of the Soviet and English advanced experience. This scheme used a new technological coordinating method in which the lofting on a transparent plastic sheet was used as a base in combination with the optical instruments,assembly jigs, line drawing and hole drilling stands,partial guages and partial male molds. In later practice the assembly of 114,000 and more parts , 1,200 and more standard parts and 100 and more sub—assemblies, the mating of the fore and aft fuselages and of fuselage and wing and the installment of engines and fuel tanks succeeded almost all in their first times. This new method significantly reduced tooling and sped up the prototype production of the J—8.

While the development of the J—8 was going on smoothly Gao Fangqi died of illness. Then Liu Hongzhi, director of the Shenyang Aircraft Design Institute, was appointed first vice director and chief engineer of the Shenyang Aircraft Factory in charge of the on—site—design and prototype production of the J—8. After Liu Hongzhi was forced to stop his work in November,1966 because of the unfair treatment he received during the " great cultural revolution", a J—8 Development Command headed by Wang Xin, vice director of the factory, was jointly established by the factory and the institute. Afterwards, the people of the factory and the people of the institute cooperated well in a harmonic work atmosphere.

In 1967 under the impact of the " great cultural revolution", especially its " January Windstorm", violence and the "Seizure of Power", the production process in the factory was severely disturbed and manufacturing work on the production lines almost stopped. But most engineers and workers still went to work at the risk of their lives. The development of the J—8 was carried on even in July and August, the months when the severest violence took place. The final assembly of first two J—8s were completed in July,1968.

The J—8 flew for the first time on July 5, 1969. At half past nine o'clock in the morning Cao Lihuai, on site chief director for the flight test and the vice commander of the Air Force, gave the clearance for flight. The pilot Yin Yuhuan flew the J—8 and passed over the airfield twice. As soon as he made a safe landing the people in the field broke into deafening cheers. They hailed the success of the first flight of the first high altitude and high speed fighter designed and produced in China.

From the conceptual definition through its first flight, the stages of general layout, technical design, mockup review, prototype production and static test were experienced and a total of four years and ten months were spent. This speed of development was comparatively high. The follows were considered to be the reasons of the speed:

—The J—8 development programme was launched on a solid technical basis and its moderate operational requirement was in conformity with the actual situation in China. The J—8 design was based on the three years study of the MiG—21 design and on the investigation of foreign aircraft technologies. The selected design configuration for the J—8 was not only advanced but also similar to the previous MiG aircraft which had been put into production in China. In addition it was basically suited to the industry and technology conditions in China.

—Right technical decisions were made. The detailed feasibility study had always been completed before any technical decisions were made. This was true especially to the selections of the engine, the intake configuration and the ejection escape system. The selected engine WP7A was derived from the WP7 but incorporated with a high temperature turbine. Its first batch were successfully produced as early as in 1968 due to the joint efforts of the MAI, the China Academy of Science and the Ministry of Metallurgical Industry. The success with the engine ensured the successful first flight of the J—8.

—Every positive factor and the wisdom of the masses were brought into full play. During the process of prototype production two three—in—one combinations, i.e. the combination of the R&D teams, manufacturers and operators and the combination of leading cadres, workers and engineers, were put into practice. All the people worked in full cooperation and with unity of purpose, so that various technical problems in the development of the J—8 were solved rapidly and satisfactorily.

—Powerful leadership was exercised. The MAI asked all its people to give green lights to the J—8 development programme. All Ministries and provinces in China worked in full cooperation. The relevant departments established a Flight Test Leading Group, the MAI and the CAE set up a Joint Flight Test Command and the Shenyang Aircraft Factory and the Shenyang Aircraft Design Institute set up an On—Site Flight Test Directing Office. They worked on site and helped to solve 23 key technical problems which otherwise would adversely affect the first flight of the J—8. Cao Lihuai played an important role at the critical moment when he was responsible for the flight test of the J—8.

4.   Flight Test and Technical Problems Solving of the J—8

The development of the J—8 suffered seriously from the turmoil caused by the " great cultural revolution". The Flight Test Leading Group and the Joint Flight Test Command were disbanded after the first flight of the J—8. The Chief Designer Office was dismissed as well. The rules and regulations were put aside. Technical cadres like Wang Nanshou, Gu Songfen and Feng Zhongyue were ordered to stop their work one after another. The development work of the J—8 was repeatedly delayed and even stagnated for a time. Under the extremely difficult condition most staff and workers in the aircraft industry still tried their best to protect the J—8 aircraft programme from the fate of a premature end.

Flight test is a key factor in the aircraft development. The performance and the manufacturing quality of a new aircraft, the behavior of the vendor—furnished—equipment and components, the operational and maintainability characteristics of an aircraft, etc., have to be checked in flight. It is an iterative process of problems finding and solving, which will at last lead to a better design. That is why the flight test is a necessary step towards the type certification of a new aircraft.

During the lengthy ten years from 1969 through 1979, the flight test of the J−8 accumulated 1,025 takeoff−and−landings and 663 flying hours at the Flight Test Research Institute and the Flight Test Station of the Shenyang Aircraft Factory. In this phase a series of technical problems were solved.

a. Elimination of transonic and supersonic vibration. In 1969 when the flying speed of the J−8 reached M 0.86, a sudden strong transonic vibration occured, which made the aircraft unable to exceed sound speed. The test pilot Lu Mingdong took vigorous actions to assist the designers in finding the vibration source. He repeatedly tested the phenomenon in flight but did not give a thought to his safety. Gu Songfen himself took part in the high speed wind tunnel model oil flow test and the ground resonance test. At last it was found that the vibration came from a disturbed flow. The problem was basically solved after some corrective actions were taken at that time. But eight years later the phenomenon occured again at transonic speed. Gu Songfen cooperated with pilot Lu Mingdong for a second time. He was lifted into air in a supersonic trainer piloted by Lu Mingdong three times to follow a J−8 aircraft in order to observe and to take picture of the streamlines spectra at the tail of the J−8 fuselage. The air flow separation zone was further ascertained and the real cause of the vibration was found. After local modification to the geometry of the aft fuselage, the flow separation was completely eliminated. .

The supersonic vibration of the J−8 occured at Mach number 1.24. Theoretical analysis and tests showed that the vibration was caused by a power control system. The designers at the shenyang Aircraft Design Institute used an foreign product as a reference and designed a new damping cylinder. The supersonic vibration was eliminated after the damping cylinder was installed on the rudder of the aircraft.

b. Working out a solution to the problem of the overheated aft fuselage. It was discovered in 1970 that the aft fuselage was overheated when the J−8 flew at high altitude and high Mach number. The problem was temporarily solved by using forced cooling. But it was found in 1967 that the drag chute and even the bay of drag chute were damaged by the high temperature in the aft fuselage when the J−8 flew at high Mach number for a longer time. The problem was completely solved by heat insulation, cooling, vibration suppression and local replacement of materials. Afterwards, The unusual phenomenon no longer occured.

c. Solving the problem of in−flight shutdown. Three in−flight shutdown accidents of the J−8 happened before 1976 and the problem was temporarily solved by the addition of a throttle retainer block. Three more in−flight shutdown accidents happened successively in October, 1976. In order to solve the problem, the MAI set up a leading group to coordinate the work. Corrective actions were taken to both the aircraft and the engine so that the problem of in−flight shutdown was completely solved. This achievement won a Second Class Prize of Scientific and Technological Achievement awarded by the MAI.

Test pilots Lu Mingdong, Hua Jun, Wang Ang and flight commander Su Guohua made great contributions in their cooperative work with design engineers during the type certification flight test.

In September 1978, the Shenyang Aircraft Design Institute restored the Chief Designer Office and Gu Songfen was appointed the chief designer.

The Aero Products Certification Commission agreed to freeze the design of the J−8 on December 31, 1979 and the National Military Products Certification Commission formally certificated the design of the J−8 on March 2,1980. Whole ten years were spent from the first flight to design certification. The reasons for the slowness were not only the turmoil caused by the ten years of the "great cultural revolution", but also the lack of knowledge in the law of the development of a new fighter as well as the underestimation of unexpected difficulties in the area of development:

a. The work on the advanced R&D and ground tests were not sufficiently done when the development programme was launched so that some key technical problems could not be solved in advance and, therefore, the possible solutions had to be tried or even to be found out by flight test.

b. Long lead time items such as new engine, new airborne equipment and avionics, new manufacturing techniques and new materials were neither developed in advance, nor in parallel with the J−8 programme. They were not available when they were needed. For instance the design of the J−8 originally required the use of an A.C. electrical system and an all−weather fire control radar but later on it was temporarily changed into a day fighter with D.C. electrical system and a ranger because the A.C. electrical system and the radar was not available and could not be developed in a short period of time. Similar cases also occured to the selection of the aerial gun, rockets and missiles.

c. Lack of experience in the flight test of a new design. Too few prototype aircraft were constructed for and too less money spent on the flight test, therefore the flight test phase was prolonged. At the beginning only one prototype aircraft was available. Its flight test time was too little because of the frequent failures of its engine and equipment. In addition the flight test for adjustment should have been carried out at the Flight Test Station of the Shenyang Aircraft Factory to facilitate the handling of the problems found in the flight test by the factory and the design institute. It should be transferred to the flight certification institute for test only after it had passed the flight test at the factory. But it had not been done in this way and the duration of flight test of the J−8 was thus prolonged.

d. Frequent changes of the technical management system and the administration system, especially in the middle of the development. The control, dispatch and coordination could not exercised effectively, therefore the development schedule of the J−8 was adversely affected.

5. The Development of the J−8I

The J−8I was an all−weather fighter. Compared with the day fighter J−8, it was mainly improved in three areas, i.e. the addition of eleven items in the avionics including the fire control radar, the redesignes of the conopy, pilot seat, oxygen system and combined instrument and the installation of 23—Ⅲ aerial gun, 4 "Pili" (it means thunderbolt in Chinese) —2B air—to—air missiles and 4 rocket packs.

Soon after all the production drawings of the J—8I were released by the Shenyang Aircraft Design Institute in February 1978, the Shenyang Aircraft Company (formerly the Shenyang Aircraft Factory) started the prototype production. The final assembly of the first prototype was completed by May 1980.

A major accident happened on June 25 when the prototype aircraft was carrying out its first engine ground run. The running had barely lasted for twenty minutes, when the engine suddenly broke out into fire. The aircraft was completely burnt. A significant loss and a delay of the development programme were caused.

The later analysis, investigations and tests on the accident showed that the fire was caused by hydraulic fluid which was sprayed on to the engine through a rupture of hydraulic pipe.

In the J—8I design the hydraulic pump was changed to YB—20B. The manufacturer of the pump thought the pump was qualified in view of the fact that its dynamic pressure at the outlet was not higher than the specified value. But it had not been tested with a complete hydraulic system according to the actual aircraft condition. The test carried out after the accident showed that the resonance occured when the pressure pulse frequency of the pump coincided with the natural frequency of the pipe at 0.8 engine rated speed. The resonance caused rapid increase of the pulse pressure inside the pipe and, therefore, the rupture of the pipe.

The lessons given by the accident are profound. It explains once more that science should be taken seriously. In the development of a new aircraft, a complete test specification must be set up, tests must be fully carried out, and the simulations of the systems in ground tests must be as true as possible, otherwise something serious could unexpectedly happen. In order to remove the design deficiencies which had caused accidents, the Shenyang Aircraft Design Institute decided to replace the pump with ZB—34. The Shenyang Aircraft Company organized its all staff and workers to assemble another J—8I aircraft to the best quality and in the shortest time. The finished aircraft was flown into air by pilot Lu Mingdong on April 24, 1981. In October second J—8I was flown. The static destructive test of a full size airframe was conducted in July 1983 and it proved that the design was in conformity with the design criteria.

The J—8I had been flown in three and half years for the tests of performance, avionics including radar and armament system, as well as for the solutions of some difficult technical problems. The flight test programme was completed in November 1984. The 204 radar installed in the aircraft was jointly developed by relevant institutes and factories of the Ministry of Electronics Industry and the MAI. Ninety flight tests carried out after the radar had been instal-led showed that the main performances of the radar were in conformity with the original requirements, or even better.

On July 27, 1985 the Aero Products Certification Commission formally awarded the design certificate to the J—8I. The development period from the beginning of the design to the design certification was only a little more than eight years, far less than that of the basic J—8. This was because the development of the J—8I was carried out in one of the best political and economical periods in China. In addition the technical team had obtained more experience in the past J—8 programme; the leadership of the J—8I flight test was powerful and actions taken by the leaders were effective and a total of four prototypes were used for the flight test. Among the aforementioned reasons the last one was considered as a valuable experience to speed up the development of a new aircraft.

The successful developments of the J—8 and the J—8I marked a new level the Chinese ever reached in developing their own fighters. In October 1985, these two programmes were awarded a Special Class Merit of National Science and Technology Progress Prize by the National Evaluation Committee of the Science and Technology Progress. The main awardees were Gu Songfen, Wang Nanshou, Ye Zhengda, Luo Shida, Zhao Peilin, Fang Wenfu, Lu Mingdong and Zhu Kexin.

6.　Development of Light Fighter J—12

In 1969 based on the analysis of the past local wars in the world the Chinese Air Force proposed to develop a light STOL (short takeoff and landing distance) supersonic fighter with good manoeuvrability, outstanding low and medium altitude performance and good controllability and maintainability. The aircraft designated J—12 was developed by the Nanchang Aircraft Factory. Its design activities were coordinated by Lu Xianpeng, vice director of the factory's aircraft design institute.

Fig. 35　The J—12 fighter

The J—12 was a fighter of different style from the Soviet MiG aircraft and it was a new aircraft designed on our own. It was a single seat aircraft with nose intake and a WP6B turbojet engine. The double—slotted flaps and the leading edge slots were incorporated on the wing. There were auxiliary air inlet doors on each side of the fuselage, which could protect the nose intake from ingestion of dust during takeoff. There were two aerial guns in the aircraft.

The conceptual definition study of the J—12 began in July 1969. Its general configuration was approved in August and the tunnel tests, designs, strength tests, system ground simulation tests and the construction of three prototype aircraft were carried out in the following seventeen months. The first flight of the first prototype took place on December 26, 1970.

On September 10, 1973, Ye Jianying, Li Xiannian, Xu Xiangqian and Nie Rongzhen, etc. watched the flight demonstration of the J—12 at Nanyuan airfield in Beijing. They affirmed the achievements in the development of the aircraft and instructed for further improvement. Afterwards, the Nanchang Aircraft Factory made ten major improvements to the design of the J−12, supplemented some necessary tests and released the updated drawings for the production of the improved aircraft. The first improved J−12 made its first flight in July 1975. By January 1977 it accumulated 135 flyings in 61 hours and 12 minutes. The further development of the J−12 was terminated because of the adjustment of the Air Force acquisition plan. Only six J−12s were produced in all.

The outstanding features of the J−12 were "light, short, and agile." Here the word "light" meant that the J−12 was only 4,500 kg in its normal takeoff weight. Its geometry and maximum cross area was also the smallest of its kind. The word "short" meant that its takeoff and landing run distances were short and both were less than 500 m, the shortest among the aircraft in service in China. The word "agile" meant that the rate of climb, the turn rate, the controllability and the acceleration and deceleration were all better than that of the J−6.

The main shortcomings of the J−12 were its insufficient fire power and engine thrust.

In the structure and production process of the J−12 more new technologies were applied, such as the integral fuel tanks in the central wing section and the fuselage, chemically milled integral skin panel, metal honeycomb skin panel, foamed−sandwich structure, titanium alloy sheet, aluminum alloy landing gear, one−piece windshield, etc. The development of the J−12 had explored a new way and accumulated some experience for the future development of the light fighters in China.

Section 6   March to Higher Level
— Development of J−8 II

After 1970s there was a noticeable change in the world fighters. Very high flying speed and flying altitude were no longer pursued but good manoeuvrability at low and medium altitude and improved avionics, armament and fire control system came into vogue. This was because the practice in the past ten years and many local wars had showed that most air battles between the supersonic fighters were conducted at low and medium altitude and at a speed near the sonic speed and that the dog fight in the air required the fighter to have good manoeuvrability, i.e. good performance in turn rate, acceleration, deceleration and rate of climb. The gun(s) and missiles mounted or carried on a fighter were of equal importance.

Since the early 1980's Chinese aviation industry had closely followed the trend of world fighters, marched to a higher level and began to develop a contemporary fighter J−8 II to meet the Air Force's needs in updating and improving its combat capability.

The J−8 II was developed on the basis of J−8 aircraft but significant improvements were incorporated. The improvements were emphasized on the armament, fire control system, avionics and power plant. The intakes were moved to two sides of the fuselage, therefore the space in the nose could be saved for a big antenna of the radar. Two engines were changed to the uprated WP13As for improvement of the manoeuvrability at low and medium altitude. The hard points were increased for carrying several different weapons so that the J-8 II could have the all-weather interception capability as well as the ground attack capability. The J-8 II had more than 70 per cent modifications over the J-8 and one third of its total vendor-furnished-equipment were replaced.

The operational requirement of the J-8 II was approved by authorities in September 1980. The conceptual definition study was started in April 1981 and then the general configuration was determined. The development tasks were taken by the Shenyang Aircraft Design Institute and the Shenyang Aircraft Company.

The development of the J-8 II was managed with the principles of the system engineering. Under the leadership of the J-8 II chief director He Wenzhi, vice minister of the MAI, the feasibility study of the J-8 II had taken 3 factors into consideration: technology, cost and schedule. Various systems of job responsibility were established: chief designer's responsibility for design art, administration responsibility, cost contractual responsibility, and quality control responsibility. And the management was carried out in four areas: technology, cost, schedule and quality. The chief designer Gu Songfen had an important position in this system engineering management. In the area of technology there were four responsibility levels, i.e. the programme chief designer, system chief designer, director designer and project designer. In this system the divisions of work and responsibility were clearly defined. In the area of administration Tang Qiansan, general manager of the Shenyang Aircraft Company, Guan De, vice general manager and on-site chief director, and Gu Yuanjie, chief engineer, carried out their work effectively. The chief accountant used fixed-price-contract to stimulate the development of the programme. Quality control was carried on throughout the development process. The designs were carefully reviewed for the second time before their drawings were released. With all these efforts, the smooth progress of the aircraft development was ensured and all the sub-systems, work items and even every work procedure in manufacturing were completed as scheduled.

The Shenyang Aircraft Design Institute began its technical and structure designs in 1982, all the drawings were released for production by May 1983. By the end of May 1984, 11,000 wind tunnel tests for 39 test items, 58 structure and system test items and 25 dynamic and static test items were completed.

The Shenyang Aircraft Company began its manufacture of production tooling and aircraft parts in 1983. It only took the company 17 months to send the prototype aircraft into the air. It was only 3 years from the beginning of the development of the WP13A engine by Guizhou Engine Design Institute, Guizhou Engine Company and Chengdu Engine Company to the delivery of the first engine for the prototype aircraft.

The vendor-furnished-equipment and components for the aircraft basically satisfied the aircraft requirements.

On June 12, 1984 the graceful-looking and novelly configured J-8 II was flown for the first time by test pilot Qu Xueren.

In the past 30 years and more China has developed three generations of several types of fighters and now it is striding towards a higher level to develop more advanced fighters. Before the end of this century a new generation of fighters with better performance will be developed to equip the Chinese military services and to make contributions to the modernization of the national defence.

Chapter Ⅴ　Development of Bombers, Attack

Aircraft and Pilotless Aircraft

Section 1　Development of Bombers

Bombers are the aircraft used to bomb forward areas, strategic rear areas and targets at sea. According to their weights, bomb loads and ranges, they can be divided into light bombers (or short range bombers), medium bombers (or medium range bombers) and heavy bombers (or long range bombers). They can also be divided into strategic bombers and tactical bombers according to their operational missions.

The bombers were first used in the First World War. Most of them were retrofitted from reconnaissance aircraft and could carry a small amount of bomb loads. The bombers were widely used during the World War Ⅱ. The four-engine heavy bombers also appeared at that time. The high subsonic jet bombers were developed in 1950s and the supersonic medium range strategic bombers in 1960s . During 1970s the USA and the Soviet Union developed strategic bombers with speed higher than Mach number 2. These supersonic strategic bombers could penetrate into enemy's territorial air in supersonic speed at high altitude or in high subsonic speed at very low altitude.

A policy of active defence was adopted by China in its national air defence so that the light bombers and medium bombers have also been developed while the stress of the aircraft development was placed on the fighters.

After 1950s the Chinese aviation industry planned to develop the bombers step by step. Two enterprises for development and production of bombers (also transports and helicopters) and two design institutes for design of land based and water based bombers were respectively established and the corresponding infrastructure was constructed. The H-5 light bomber and the H-6 medium bomber with its derivatives were produced and the water-based SH-5 was developed on our own. Through all these activities a technical team of bomber development was tempered and a moderate production capacity formed. China had then basically the ability to develop light and medium bombers.

1. Licence Production of High Subsonic Medium Bomber H-6

The development of bombers is an important part of the construction of an independent and self-reliance aviation industry system. As early as in 1956 an agreement of assisting China to construct a medium bomber factory was reached between the Chinese and the Soviet governments. In September 1957 the Soviet government agreed to licence China to produce its medium bomber Tu—16. The prototype production began immediately after a complete set of Soviet furnished Tu—16 technical data arrived in China in February 1959. The process of the licenced production was:

a. The Soviet Union supplied two example aircraft;

b. The Soviet Union supplied China with an aircraft in the form of components for final assembly and flight test by Chinese;

c. The Soviet Union supplied China with a complete kit for assembly by Chinese;

d. The Soviet Union supplied China with blanks and raw materials for parts manufacturing by Chinese; and

e. The aircraft was totally manufactured by China.

The Tu—16 was a high subsonic medium bomber developed in the Soviet Union. Its development was started in 1950. Its first flight was made in 1952 and its delivery in 1955. The aircraft had a slender and streamlined fuselage. Two turbojet engines were mounted. It was an aircraft produced by the Soviet Union in a large quantity. H—6 was a designation for the Chinese manufactured aircraft.

The agreement between China and the Soviet Union put the prototype production of the H—6 on China's agenda. The Bureau of Aviation Industry decided that the task be jointly undertaken by the two factories in Harbin and Xi'an.

The Harbin Aircraft Factory started its technical reform in 1958. During the reform, its covered area was doubled and the number of general machines and large special machines were increased. Immediately after the two Soviet built example aircraft and a complete set of components for one aircraft arrived at the factory in May 1959, the factory began its intense prototype production. When final assembly began the main leading cadres including the director of the factory Lu Gang kept staying on the site of the final assembly to handle the problems encountered. The Shenyang Aircraft Factory sent 200 workers to support the final assembly according to a decision made by the Bureau of Aviation Industry. From June 28 through September 3 it only took 67 days to finish the final assembly of the first aircraft. This Chinese assembled bomber flew for the first time on September 27 and was delivered to the Air Force in December.

Starting from 1958 the Xi'an Aircraft Factory also sped up their construction and a number of industrially experienced leading cadres came to work in the factory. Liu Gang, former vice governor of Pingyuan province and director of the Luoyang Tractor Factory was appointed the director and Sun Zhiduan, former acting director of the Nanchang Aircraft Factory, the chief engineer. The Shenyang Aircraft Factory sent their 1,040 backbone technical and managerial people in all disciplines and 1,697 workers in half year. They played an important role in the construction of the Xi'an Aircraft Factory.

In 1961 the Bureau of Aviation Industry decided to transfer all the work of the H—6 prototype production to the Xi'an Aircraft Factory. The transfer was started in 1962 and completed in 1964.

In order to master the manufacturing techniques the Xi'an Aircraft Factory organized their designers to make up the incomplete data of the H−6 structure analysis by the addition of 15,400 standard pages with the help from relevant organizations. On the other hand, the workers were trained in basic techniques for preparation of H−6 prototype production.

The aircraft transfered for prototype production at that time was H−6A. Its power plant was two WP8s, the fore and aft sections of the fuselage were pressurized for carrying the crew. The aircraft could carry conventional bombs as well as atomic bombs, hydrogen bombs, missiles and torpedoes. The aircraft empty weight was 37,700 kg and the maximum takeoff weight 75,800 kg.

The H−6 was the heavist aircraft China had ever produced. There were a total of 240,000 parts in 50,000 varieties, 360,000 standard materials and 1 million rivets. It needed 150,000kg various raw materials, 25 km cables, 2 km pipes, 1,100 various bearings and 894 vendor−furnished−equipment. Its complexity in technology and heavy work load in production could not be compared by any other aircraft produced in China.

In face of such a magnificent system engineering project, the H−6's prototype production, the Xi'an Aircraft Factory started its careful and well−planned work. A general plan for the prototype production was made in 1963 and the manufacture of the production tooling started in 1964. To ensure the high precision in installment of the assembly jigs was a major technical difficulty. Lu Songshan, vice chief engineer of the factory, successfully solved the problem by combining a Soviet jig assembly machine with an English assembly jig which used an optical telescope and micrometer rods. The installment of fuselage assembly jig which was 23 m in length, 6 m and more in width and 5 m and more in height was completed in 100 days by 8 workers with Lu's method, but it would otherwise took one and half months by more than 60 5th class or above experienced fitters in two shifts with the Soviet method. The efficiency was doubled and the precision improved. The technical people at the Xi'an Aircraft Factory explored some new methods and innovations. The male moulds made of epoxy resin were used to replace the traditional metal ones, the explosive forming was used to produce corrugated sheets and the electrochemical machining was used to drill unusual holes on the landing gears and splines. These innovations were all a complete success.

In October 1966 the Xi'an Aircraft Factory completed the construction of a full size airframe for static test one year ahead of the plan. For H−6's static test there were more items to be tested and its load applying procedures more complicated. A total of 51 test items in 105 test cases had to be tested. The static test for such a huge aircraft could not only rely on the factory alone. Therefore, the Nanchang Aircraft Factory, the NPU and the Aircraft Structure Analysis Research Institute all worked together with the Xi'an Aircraft Factory in the test.

The static test of a full size airframe was carried out at the Aircraft Structure Analysis Research Institute. The B case suspension test was conducted on December 9, 1968. The load was applied to 80 per cent, which proved the conformity with the design requirement and therefore the test was good. The case A suspension destructive test was conducted on December

28 and the failure load was 134.8 per cent, which was in conformity with the design requirement and it proved the qualification of the full size airframe in strength.

Fig. 36   The final assembly of the H—6A

On December 24, 1968 a H—6A piloted by Li Yuanyi air crew lifted off and flew into the air with the roaring of its engines. This was a significant achievement in the history of Chinese aviation industry. A series of performance flight tests showed the reliability of various systems, the normal engine operation, good controllability and stability and the conformity of main performances with the operational requirement.

All the H—6As were delivered to the bomber squadrons of the Air Force and the Navy after they left the production line and they soon became an important combat force in defending our motherland. On National Day of the year 1984 18 H—6As flew over the Tian An Men Square in a formation for review.

2.   Retrofit of H—6 Bomber

Since 1963 the Xi'an Aircraft Factory began to retrofit the H—6 aircraft according to the Services' operational requirements and several improved versions were developed.

a. The Nuclear Weapon Carrier of the H—6

In order to cooperate with the development and test of the atomic bomb the Bureau of Aviation Industry assigned the Xi'an Aircraft Factory a task in 1963 to retrofit a H—6 aircraft assembled by the Harbin Aircraft Factory in 1959 into a nuclear weapon carrier. According to the defined general configuration the bomb carrying and delivering system, heating and heat preservation system, protection system and the temporary test equipment should be retrofitted or incorporated.

Li Xipu, vice director, was in charge of the retrofitting of the carrier aircraft. An office and a retrofitting team were established. Preparation of the retrofitting began in June 1963 and was completed in September 1964. Support and cooperation were received from relevant organizations all over China. Organizations in the chemical industry, machine building industry and textile industry supplied the required materials and equipment.

The retrofitted H−6 carrier was flown for the first time by Li Yuanyi and his air crew on May 14, 1965, and a successful delivery of an atomic bomb was made over the western area in China. Six people of the Li Yuanyi air crew were thus awarded Collective First Class Merit and Li Xipu was invited to an interview with Premier Zhou Enlai and to attend a celebration dinner party in Beijing.

b. Retrofitting H−6A with Second Generation Navigation System

In order to improve the automation of the H−6A's navigation and bombing system and solve the problem that the H−6A could not fly for a long distance with the ground navigation, the development of the second generation automatic navigation and bombing system was unveiled in 1970. The system consisted of 9 vendor−furnished−equipment, i.e. computer, automatic navigator, Doppler Radar, heading and attitude system, autopilot and bombing radar. They were installed in a H−6A and tested in flight in 1975 after they had been developed. In 1980 a H−6A was formally retrofitted, its flight test programme completed in 1981 and the pre−production started in 1982. The retrofitting with the second generation automatic navigation and bombing system had an important effect on increasing the H−6's vitality and improving the Air Force's operational capability.

c. The H−6D Bomber

The H−6D was a derivative of the H−6A. Two air−to−ship missiles were carried under the wing. A fire control system for missile aiming, an automatic navigation and bombing system, a missile heating system and a new radar, etc., were incorporated and some structures were strengthened.

The development task was formally assigned in 1975, the first flight of the prototype aircraft was successfully made on August 29, 1981 and all the telemetry missiles hit the targets in the air firing test on December 6 of the same year. After two years testing and training, an air firing test with actual missiles was carried out at the end of 1983. Four missiles were fired and all hit the targets. The design of the H−6D was certified in December, 1985. The H−6D was a first generation air−to−ship missile carrier aircraft in China. Its flight tests showed that the selected retrofitting concept was correct, the airborne equipment integrated successfully and the aircraft's controllability, stability and various flying parameters were in conformity with the design requirement. The successful development of the H−6D added a new weapon into the Chinese Navy air force's inventory.

In addition, the H−6 aircraft had been successively retrofitted into a flight test bed for testing aero−engines by the Flight Research Institute, a carrier aircraft to carry a high altitude and high speed pilotless drone and a defensive counter—measure aircraft for the military services.

3.   Light Bomber—H—5

The light bomber is a kind of tactical bomber and is used for close air support to the ground troop operations. Its bomb load is small but it is light, manoeuvrable and agile and has some peculiarities which make it irreplaceable by medium bombers. The Chinese built H—5 light bomber is an equivalent of the Il—28 aircraft but with some local improvement in design.

The Il—28 aircraft is a light bomber designed and produced in the Soviet Union. It flew for its first time in 1947 and entered into service in 1950. It was put into production in large quantities and was widely used in 1950s and 1960s because of its simple structure and low price.

The prototype production of the H—5 was different from that of the H—6. It was not a complete licenced production, because a great number of design modifications were incorporated according to the military Services' operational requirements. The design modifications were made possible by the following: China imported a number of Il—28 bombers and a lot of suggestions were made by the military Services based on a long period of operation; the Harbin Aircraft Factory had repaired the Il—28s since the mid—1950s, manufactured main parts and components for the purpose of repairing and, therefore, mastered necessary manufacturing techniques, the factory was expanded and reconstructed on a large—scale for purpose of the H—6's prototype production and had capabilities for manufacturing production tooling, assembling a complete aircraft and then testing it in flight; and finally the factory had experienced prototype productions of the Z—5 helicopter and the H—6 medium bomber.

The H—5 was a light subsonic bomber with a cantilever high set wing. Fourty per cent of the original Il—28 design was modified. Main modifications were:

a. A conventional structure wing was used to replace the wing which was spliced at the central line and, therefore, 110 kg of weight was saved.

b. Major airborne equipment were in common with that of the H—6. One example was use of H—6's tail turret. Of course it introduced corresponding structure changes.

The operational performance was remarkably improved by use of a great number of new airborne equipment: a new radar with significantly increased operational range, a new sight which increased aiming angle and observation angle and hence bombing precision, the new turrent with an electrical control system which was good in the follow—up behavior, an increased ammunition capacity, higher rate of fire and longer effective firing range; and a new and improved friend—or—foe identification.

The Harbin Aircraft Factory initiated their preparation for the trial—production of the H—5 in 1963. They first corrected the drawings used for aircraft repair, and then supplemented with some drawings and data of stress analysis and aerodynamic computation and prepared a complete set of processing documents. The manufacturing of production tooling and aircraft parts began in 1964. Two prototype aircraft were completed in 1966 and one of them was used for static test. The static test was carried out from July to September and it proved that the structure strength was in conformity with the technical requirement. Another prototype flew for its first time on September 25, 1966. The H—5 aircraft was formally put into production in April, 1967.

Hu Xichuan, chief engineer, Qi Zhikun, vice chief engineer, Xiong Wenjie and Li Guangshu who were in charge of the design work, made active contributions to the development of the H—5. Sun Zhaoqing who was in charge of manufacturing techniques and his colleagues made bold innovations in managing manufacturing techniques. They applied some new techniques such as the plastic molds, combined fixtures and explosive forming, etc. so that the product quality was improved and the prototype production was completed in a shorter period of time. With support from various departments and agencies all over the country most of the necessary 3,200 materials and 334 vendor—furnished—equipment could be manufactured in China. The success in partial redesign of the H—5 marked the breaking away from the yoke of pure licenced production in area of bomber technology and the beginning of transition from modification and derivation to independent development.

4. Derivation of the H—5

Several derivatives were developed on the basis of the requirement of the military Services after the H—5 aircraft was certified and put into production.

a. H—5 Nuclear Bomb Carrier

In September 1967 the government assigned a task for retrofitting the H—5 into a nuclear carrier which could be used both for nuclear test and operational missions. A retrofitting group headed by Xia Zhenhua, assistant to chief engineer, and Sun Zhaoqing, chief technologist, was established in the Harbin Aircraft Factory. The task was satisfactorily fulfilled after their intense work in half a year and a H—5 nuclear carrier was successfully used in the nuclear test on December 27, 1968.

b. The HZ—5

This was a photographic reconnaissance aircraft retrofitted from a H—5 prototype aircraft. Its design was started in December 1970 and was certificated in 1977. The main modifications were the addition of 2 large medium—high altitude day and night aerial cameras inside the fuselage bomb bay and wing integral fuel tanks. Compared with the prototype aircraft its range was increased by 47 per cent, combat radius by 50 per cent and endurance by 1 hour and 23 minutes. The success of the HZ—5 filled a gap in the field of short / medium reconnaissance aircraft.

c. The HJ—5

The Harbin Aircraft Factory began to develop the bomber—trainer HJ—5 in the mid—1960s to satisfy the need in training military Services' bomber pilots. The new off the shelf vendor—furnished—equipment and components were selected by the factory. But in order to improve air crew's environment, the air condition system was redesigned to properly heat or cool the cockpit. The HJ–5 prototype production began in May 1967, its first flight took place on December 12, 1970 and its design certification was awarded by the government in April 1972. A total of 186 HJ–5s were produced.

The success of the HJ–5 development closed a gap in the area of the bomber–trainer and ended the history in which the training of bomber pilots depended upon imported foreign trainers.

5.   Development of the Water–based Bomber

The water–based aircraft, especially the ones which can be used in anti–submarine warfare, are needed in China to defend its vast territorial waters. In the late 1960s there were only several Soviet Be–6 water–based aircraft which were going to be phased out. Therefore to develop Chinese own water–based aircraft was an urgent task to the Chinese aviation industry.

The preparation for establishment of a Water–based Aircraft Design Institute began in 1968 and the design concept of the SH–5 was approved by the government in December of the same year. Its development task were jointly undertaken by the Water–based Aircraft Design Institute and the Harbin Aircraft Factory and its design activities were directed by Wang Hongzhang, director of the Water–based Aircraft Design Institute. Three prototype aircraft were constructed in the phase of development.

The SH–5 was a first generation huge water–based anti–submarine bomber developed by China itself. It was powered by 4 WJ5A turbo–propellers and was equiped with advanced navigation aids, bombing radar, magnetic anomaly detector, transceiver, etc. The empty weight was 26,000 kg. The bombs, torpedoes and airborne depth charges could be carried. A remotely controlled turret was incorporated to counter the

Fig. 37   The SH–5 is taxiing on water surface

attacks from enemy aircraft. The SH–5 could attack both surface warships and underwater submarines. In addition it could also be used for tasks such as search and rescue, scientific research and patrol, etc.

The detailed design of the SH–5 was completed in February 1970 and the drawings for production were released from March to October. Afterwards the Harbin Aircraft Factory began the prototype production. A number of advanced manufacturing techniques, e.g. spot–weld bonding, sealing riveting, and chemical milling were used so that the prototype production was sped up.

The final assembly of a full size airframe was completed in October 1971 and the static test programme in August, 1974 at the Aircraft Structure Strength Research Institute. The destructive load for the static destructive test of the full size airframe was 110 per cent, which was in conformity with the design requirement.

The final assembly of a SH-5 used for flight test was completed in December 1973. It was shipped to the flight test site in October 1974. The MAI and Navy Headquarters jointly set up a flight test office to control the SH-5 flight test. From May 1975 to March 1976 the SH-5 carried out 30 hours of taxi test on water surface for 28 subjects of static water tests in addition to four successful pre-flights.

A grand ceremony for the SH-5 first flight was held on April 3, 1976. At 10 o'clock in the morning the SH-5 taxied into the water and took off. The flight lasted 23 minutes. The air crew consisted of 7 pilots including Huang Xinghui, a Navy air force squadron leader.

Another 4 SH-5s were built after the first flight and began their flight tests before November 1984. The flight tests were coordinated by on-site director Yang Shouwen and all four aircraft completed their flight tests on a delta course over Hubei and Hunan Provinces by the end of 1985. During the 18 flying days from November 15 to December 15, 1985 100 per cent aircraft availability and 100 per cent flight test success rate of the flight test in the planned flight subjects were reached so that the fault-free flights were realized. The SH-5s had been delivered to Chinese Navy and the type was awarded a First Class Prize of the National Science and Technology Progress in 1987.

The development of the SH-5 began in the years of the "great cultural revolution". The turmoil of the political situation at that time and lack of experience and necessary infrastructure made the development of the SH-5 extremely difficult. But it still proceeded very well due to the hard work of the leading cadres, engineers and workers. They completed the general layout and technical designs, structure and system designs and wind tunnel and water tank tests for geometry definition in first 18 months and the manufacturing and assembly of parts and sub-assemblies as well as the final assembly of the aircraft in second 18 months. The production cycle of first two SH-5s was 4 years and 10 months. This speed was not slow and it reflected in one aspect that the Chinese aviation industry had already a comparable high technical basis and state of the art for aircraft development.

The Chinese bomber industry has had a considerable development and reached a certain scale. But a big gap between Chinese bomber industry and the world advanced bomber industry still exists. The ability to develop new bombers will be gradually improved in future with further construction of the infrastructure and introduction of foreign advanced technology.

Section 2   Development of Attack Aircraft

The attack aircraft is also called close air support aircraft. Its main task is to attack from low altitude or nap-of-the-earth enemy's tactical surface effective strength and military targets or the targets in depth of a battle field to support directly operations of own ground troops. The aircraft used for ground attack appeared for its first time during the First World War. During the Second World War the Soviet Il−2 and Il−10 attack aircraft played their powerful roles. In the mid−1950s Americans developed their carrier−based attack aircraft A−4, and, afterwards, the A−6, A−7 and A−10 were successively developed. Based on the MiG−23 fighter the Soviet Union derived a fighter−bomber MiG−27 whose main task was the ground attack. The Su−25 attack aircraft which was mainly used for attacking enemy's tanks was developed in the 1980s.

The Chinese attack aircraft were developed on the basis of the fighters. In a battle to liberate the Yijiangshan Island the Air Force, in cooperation with the Navy and the Army, used Soviet Il−10 attack aircraft and they played an important role. The aviation industry developed a supersonic attack aircraft Q−5 to meet the need of the rapidly growing people's Air Force soon after the successful manufacture of subsonic jet fighter. Its preliminary design certification was awarded in 1965, modifications were made in 1968 and it was put into serial production and began the delivery in 1970. A number of derivatives were developed and some were exported.

The development and production practice of supersonic attack aircraft in past 20 years and more, a long period of time, was an important chapter in the history of the Chinese aviation industry. It has provided beneficial experience, lessons and enlightenment to the further development of the aviation industry.

1. Towards a Chinese Design of the Attack Aircraft

The development of the attack aircraft started later than that of the fighter, but it started with a Chinese design since its very beginning. Due to the urgent need of the Chinese Air Force the Shenyang Aircraft Design Department presented a preliminary concept of a supersonic attack aircraft in early 1958. In August of the same year Wang Xiping, director of the Aviation Industry Bureau, and Xu Changyu, vice director of the Bureau convened a technical meeting in Shenyang and decided that the development task of attack aircraft Q−5 should be undertaken by the Nanchang Aircraft Factory. The Nanchang Aircraft Factory immediately sent 10 people and more including Feng Xu, vice chief engineer, and Gao Zhenning, section director, to Shenyang to work on the design of the general layout. Lu Xiaopeng, who was working at the Shenyang Aircraft Design Department at that time, was also named to join the design of the general layout. With the help from the Shenyang Aircraft Factory and the Shenyang Aircraft Design Department the construction of a full size mockup was completed and it was shipped to Beijing in October 1958. Chen Geng, vice chief of the General Staff heard a briefing on the design concept of the aircraft and approved its development.

Based on the Air Force's operational requirement, the visits to the operational troops and the status and trend of the foreign attack aircraft, the designers of the Nanchang Aircraft Factory believed that the main task of the attack aircraft was to support the operations of ground troops and in order to bring its combat effectiveness into full play the attack aircraft had to have good performance in low altitude, powerful armament and fire power, high flying speed and certain capabilities in dog fight and in self-defence, proper range and endurance, good takeoff and landing performance and proper armours in some critical areas.

Based on this design philosophy and with a reference to the J-6 which was being developed at that time the general configuration of the Q-5 was finalized. Its features were as follows:

—The engine air was taken from the inlets on each side of the fuselage, therefore the length of the air-intake was shortened and the efficiency of the inlet air was improved.

—The use of a conic nose improved the pilot's vision, facilitated the horizontal bombing and saved the space for the installment of radar and other avionics.

—A coke-bottle fuselage was designed according to transonic area rule to reduce transonic drag.

—A sweptback wing with bigger area and smaller sweptback angle was chosen to improve its lift characteristics and, hence, turning characteristics.

—A bigger area tailplane was chosen to increase its longitudinal stability.

—A rear hinged and upward open canopy and a bigger and better streamlined dorsal spine were used. The aircraft could carry a number of ground attack weapons and attack ground targets in a number of different ways, etc.

This distinctive general configuration embodied the wisdom and painstaking labour of the Chinese aircraft designers. The preliminary analysis of the configuration showed that the Q-5 would have good performance. The designers selected a high level starting point for the development of the domestic attack aircraft.

2. Transition from Manufacturing Propeller Aircraft to Manufacturing Jet Aircraft at the Nanchang Aircraft Factory

In 1958 the Aviation Industry Bureau decided that the Q-5 should be developed by the Nanchang Aircraft Factory and the factory should perform a transition from manufacturing propeller aircraft to manufacturing jet aircraft in three years. The Nanchang Aircraft Factory was founded in May 1951 and it was one of the eariest factories in New China. From September 1951 to 1958 the factory had repaired successively 1,600 aircraft including Yak-18, Yak-11, La-9, Ula-9 and La-11 and had mastered the repair techniques of propeller aircraft.

In 1953 the Nanchang Aircraft Factory was put on a list of 156 major engineering projects to be assisted by the Soviet Union and began reconstruction and expansion on a large scale. Because the central government paid great attention and the Jiangxi provincial government provided great support to the Nanchang Aircraft Factory, its large factory buildings were rapidly constructed and a shift from aircraft repair to aircraft manufacturing was rapidly carried out. In July 1954 the licenced production of the CJ-5 trainer was succeeded and in March 1958 the production of a general purpose transport Y-5 began.

As a propeller aircraft manufacturer the Nanchang Aircraft Factory began to take shape in 1958, an aircraft design and production team was trained and a set of managerial systems and organizations which could basically meet the requirement of aircraft production were established. But to design and build supersonic jet attack aircraft a further leap in quality was still required.

The transition of the Nanchang Aircraft Factory was realized by the work in two fields. One was to master the design art and manufacturing techniques through the licenced productions of the Soviet MiG—19P and MiG—19PM so that the technical people could know not only "what" but also "why". A road for the development of the Q—5 was thus paved. The other was to replenish necessary infrastructure including factory buildings and equipment. For example, the original runway length was only 1,520 m which could not meet the takeoff and landing requirement of a jet aircraft. The factory organized its cadres and masses to participate in the labour to expand the runway. The expansion was completed in 3 months. Other facilities such as the static test building, stamping workshop and ejection test range of rocket ejection seat were also constructed in short periods of time with the labour forces organized by the factory. Taking into consideration the parallel production of propeller aircraft and jet aircraft, the factory adjusted and reformed the layout of the facilities and production lines to facilitate the prototype production of the new aircraft.

3.   Development History of the Q—5

The design of the Q—5 began during the "big leap forward". Some of our comrades could not keep their brains "cool" under the influence of "Left" ideological trend. Some young designers were in extraordinary zeal but short of knowledge in aircraft development laws. They put forward not only a "left" but also a ridiculously childish slogan: "Work without a letup for one year to fly the aircraft before celebrating National Day". The development of the Q—5 was thus brought on to a rough and bumpy road since its very beginning.

Starting from the end of 1958 the Design Department of the Nanchang Aircraft Factory adjusted its design team and with the help of the teachers and students from NAI a complete set, 15,000 pages and more, of aircraft drawings were released by February 1959. It only took 75 days.

Some problems in the drawings were found immediately after the beginning of the prototype production. Some parts of the design were not matched; some new materials were not available in China; some airborne equipment such as the sight could not be developed in a short period of time and some problems in structure and manufacturing techniques were not solved. Some problems were found in the model when it was tested in a transonic wind tunnel. Therefore, the factory organized its designers to make major corrections to the drawings four times. The corrected 20,000 pages and more drawings and 260 reports on aerodynamic behavior and structure stress analysis were released in May 1960. Through these corrective actions to the drawings the designers not only realized the arduous and complex nature of the aircraft development but also learned a lesson that they should consider the actual conditions and obey the scientific laws in their work.

While the factory was going to set up a leading group for the Q—5 prototype production and to begin the prototype production in an all—round way, it happened that the Chinese national economy encountered a temporary difficulty and the aviation industry had to cut its aircraft development activities and to rectify its product quality. Therefore, a lot of aircraft development programmes were cancelled and among them was the Q—5 programme. In 1961 its prototype production was terminated temporarily, the leading group for the prototype production was dismissed, the production line of the prototype aircraft was dismantled and the Q—5 trial production faced a fate of prematured end.

Lu Xiaopeng, who had been appointed vice director of the Design Department of the Nanchang Aircraft Factory, representing in strong desire the staff and workers submitted written statements one after another to higher authorities for approval of continuing the Q—5 prototype production. The director of the factory Feng Anguo supported his opinion but only obtained a permission to use "bits of time and space available" for the Q—5 development. And only 15 people out of 300 and more of the original prototype production team were left.

It was not easy to develop a brand new aircraft by making use of bits of time. But, compared with the termination, it gave the chance to survive. Lu Xiaopeng and his colleagues felt their grave responsibilities and were determined to try their best to keep the Q—5 programme alive. They utilized the conditions obtained with their efforts and worked very hard. They not only drew drawings, worked on computations and run the tests, but also went to find the workshops where the parts could be manufactured, the vendors which were willing to cooperate, the necessary materials and equipment which they would use or borrow. In addition they had to move the parts from workshop to workshop themselves and to operate the machines with workers. An aged worker Fan Jiebao was a versatile person in production and was proficient in riveting, benchworking and forging, etc. He solved a lot of difficult problems in the prototype production. They moved the people around them with their own actions and all the staff and workers offered help to them. After Xue Shaoqing, Vice Minister of the MAI, and Tang Yanjie, president of the CAE, paid a visit to the factory for a check on the Q—5 development and reported to higher authorities, the development programme of the Q—5 was resumed. Since then the pace of the development was sped up. After using every bit of time for two years, a full size airframe for the static test was miraculously completed.

The last item of the static test—applying load on to a suspended full size airframe was carrying out on October 26, 1963 after 32 load cases had already been tested. When the applied load increased to 85 per cent of the ultimate load, a sudden thundering sound came out and the fuselage unexpectedly broke into fore and aft sections. The test failured. After inspection it was found that a cable of 16 mm in diameter was improperly replaced with 2 cables of 8 mm diameter and the break of the smaller cable caused the damage of the fuselage unexpectedly. The improper replacement of the cable ruined the full size airframe static test.

Facing the two halves of the airframe all the people participating the test very sad. The on site Air Force leaders Cao Lihuai and Chang Qiankun and the president of CAE Tang Yanjie hoped that the comrades in the factory could seriously sum up their experience and draw lessons from the accident but should not be disappointed. Sun Zhiyuan, Minister of the MAI, specifically came to the factory and stood by the damaged airframe to hear 3 hours briefing by Lu Xiaopeng. At a meeting attended by all cadres of the factory on the second day Sun Zhiyuan spoke highly of the painstaking work put by the staff and workers of the factory for the Q—5 development. He announced firmly that the Q—5 aircraft would have its bright future and the development of the Q—5 should be continued. He asked all the participants of the Q—5 development programme to work in a down—to—earth manner, to test carefully and put the work on to a reliable and firm base. The Minister's speech deeply moved every one attending the meeting. They were determined to retrieve the loss by their own careful work. The Air Force submitted a report to Luo Ruiqing, chief of the General Staff, showing their support to the Q—5 programme and the report was approved. The Nanchang Aircraft Factory resumed the suspended full size airframe static test and the test showed that aircraft strength was in conformity with the specification.

Fig. 38   The Q—5 was in a static test

At last came the repayment for the painstaking labour. On June 4, 1965 it was drizzling when the Chinese made Q—5 aircraft piloted by Tuo Fengming lifted off the ground and flew into sky, which declared the success of its first flight. At the end of the same year the Aero Products Certification Committee affirmed the basic structure and performance of the aircraft, at the same time pointed out some shortcomings which had to be improved and awarded its preliminary certification.

Ye Jianying, Vice Chairman of the Military Commission of CCCPC, watched the flying demonstration of the Q—5 in Beijing on March 10, 1966. He said: "This aircraft was designed by ourselves. It is a good aircraft. You have succeeded. Now the problem is how to improve it so that it can better play its role. The task of the improvement is also yours." During the later 2 years a series of improvements to the hydraulic system, wheel brake, fire control system, armament, fuel supply system, etc. were made and some new airborne equipment were incorporated by the Nanchang Aircraft Factory. Two prototype aircraft with these improvements made their first flights in October 1969. Their flight test showed:

Fig. 39   Liu Ding was at a meeting for design certification of the Q—5

—The main deficiencies of the original prototype aircraft were made up and various operational performances were improved;

—The aircraft controllability and manoeuvrability were remarkably improved;

— The aircraft could fly at supersonic speed at medium altitude and at near—sonic speed at low altitude;

— The landing gear could be normally retracted and extended when the flying speed was less than 500 km / h;

—The landing run distance was reduced from 1,312 m to 1,000 m.

— The aircraft pitch down phenomenon occured when the air brakes were extended at high flying speed was eliminated; and

Fig. 40   Chang Qiankun, Vice Commander of the Air Force was having a talk with Lu Xiaopeng by the Q—5 aircraft

—The reliability of the emergent control was improved.

At the end of the same year the government formally approved the serial production of the improved Q—5 prototype aircraft. The ten years and four and half months long prototype production phase was thus ended and the phase of mass production and operation was begun.

A lot of difficulties were encountered and setbacks suffered during the prototype production of the Q—5 and every one of them made the development programme of the new aircraft in imminent danger. Due to the insisted effort of the vast number of technical people, workers and cadres, and the fervent concern and strong support from the leaders of the departments concerned every difficulty was overcome and the Q—5 was kept alive. The Q—5, a new aircraft created by our own effort, had indomitable vitality.

The Q—5 was also a crystallization of Chinese aircraft designers' wisdom. It was being gradually perfected by continuous improvements. The following unique and novel designs of the Q—5 attack aircraft can still be used for reference today:

—The conical nose and the intakes on sides of the fuselage were firstly used on Chinese fighter;

—The transonic area rule was resolutely applied to the fuselage design and it set an example of boldly applying advanced technology;

—The ingeniously constructed canopy and the way of its automatic opening were copied by other newly developed Chinese aircraft; and

—The unique design of the nose wheel which retracted, rotated and laid flat in fuselage set a new approach for landing gear designs of other aircraft.

The lessons given by the Q—5 development was also profound. At the beginning, the Q—5 design was affected by the "big leap forward" and the scientific development procedure could not be followed. The design of structure and systems hastily began before wind tunnel test had been completed. Therefore, the design had to be modified again and again. The preliminary type design was certified when the prototype had only been flight—tested for 25 hours and its hidden problems had not been fully exposed. The flight test conducted prior to the mass production also had similar hasty problems. It was until the early 1980s that this kind of problems were completely solved. These facts of the Q—5 development tell the people that the objective laws must be followed otherwise it can only be "more haste and less speed".

4. Derivation of the Q—5

After the basic Q—5 was successfully developed a number of derivatives, e.g. nuclear weapon carrier, Q—5I, Q—5IA, Q—5Ⅲ, etc., were successively developed in order to satisfy some special needs of the military Services and other operators and to meet the needs for exportation.

a. The Q—5 Nuclear Weapon Carrier

In order to support nuclear test the Nanchang Aircraft Factory completed the manufacture of several nuclear weapon carriers which were derived from the basic Q—5 in 1970. In the thirteenth nuclear test in China on January 7, 1972 the loft bombing of the nuclear bomb was successfully carried out with the Q—5 nuclear weapon carrier.

b. The Q—5I and Q—5IA

Because of its short range the operational application of the Q—5 aircraft was restricted. Gao Zhenning, director of the Design Institute of the Nanchang Aircraft Factory, proposed to develop an extended range Q—5 based on the requirement of military Services in 1976. The derivation tests were carried out in 1977. Five Q-5Is were built and the flight test was carried out at the end of 1980. On October 20, 1981 the National Defence Industry Office of the State Council appointed Lu Xiaopeng chief designer for the Q-5 extended range version. The Aero Products Certification Committee formally approved the type design certification of the Q-5I.

Compared with the basic Q-5, the Q-5I had following main improvements:

(1) The bomb bay was retrofitted into fuel tank bay, the main fuel tank was enlarged and flexible fuel tank was added;

(2) The fuselage carried stores were adjusted so that the bomb load was increased;

(3) The engine was changed into the WP6AⅢ;

(4) The landing gear was modified.

(5) The drag chute bay was moved upward to reduce landing run distance;

(6) The ejection seat was changed into Type I rocket ejection seat and the sea survival aid were added; and

(7) A 50 watt short wave single sideband transceiver was added to meet the communication need for extended range flight.

The Q-5IA had four more improvements, i.e. the installment of an omni-bearing warning and counter-measure equipment, new gun-bomb sight system, use of pressure refuelling system and external stores of rocket pods and a number of types of bombs. Its design was certificated in January 1985.

Various tests were carried out in the development of the Q-5I and Q-5IA so that the derivation had solid basis. Some key technical problems existed on the basic Q-5 were solved, such as the jamming of bullets and link, and the significant measurement error of the pitot tube.

The flight test carried out from August 1979 to October 1983 showed that all the flying performances were in conformity with the operational requirement. Compared with the basic Q-5, the derivatives had the following improvements: increases of 26 per cent in range and 35 per cent in combat radius at low altitude, reduction of 130 m in landing run distance and increase of 500 kg in bomb load. In addition the flying speed, service ceiling, rate of climb and controllability were also improved.

c. The Q-5Ⅲ

The Q-5Ⅲ is a version for export, which was derived from the Q-5I according to customer requirement.

A total of 32 modifications were incorporated. Main modifications were: the addition of store carriages with ejection hooks which were compatible with customer's bombs and missiles, the installment of more advanced avionics, etc.

The Q-5Ⅲ prototype production cycle, starting from signing of the contract in April 1981 and ending with the certification in January 1983, was only 1 year and 10 months. During this period of time the Nanchang Aircraft Factory released 3,949 pages modified drawings (12.4 per cent of total Q-5 drawings), carried out wind tunnel tests and resonance tests, built 570 special production tooling, constructed 3 prototype aircraft and made 101 hours and 37 minutes flight test in 130 takeoff—and—landings which showed all the performances were in conformity with the specified values.

Several dozens of Q—5Ⅲ were delivered to the foreign customer from January 1983 to January 1984 so that the contract was fulfilled. On March 21 of the same year, a mission of the China National Aero Technology Import and Export Corporation (CATIC) attended a ceremony for delivery of the first Q—5Ⅲs. Twelve Q—5Ⅲs flown by the customer's pilots made a brilliant demonstration.

In addition to the aforementioned main derivatives, the Nanchang Aircraft Factory derived another version, Q—5 torpedo attack aircraft in response to the operational demand of the military Services.

Q—5, the Chinese first generation attack aircraft developed independently by China and produced in great numbers, were used to equip Chinese Air Force and Navy and, hence, strengthened the national defence. On National Day 1984 32 Q—5s flew over Tian An Men Square in a formation of every 4 aircraft and displayed the might of our country and our military Services. The achievement of the Q—5 was awarded State Special Class Prize for Science and Technology Progress and main prize—winners were Lu Xiaopeng, Gao Zhenning, Feng Xu, He Yongjun, Yong Zhengqiu, Yang Guoxiang and Chen Yaozu. An aircraft design team was trained and tempered and the ability in developing domestic aircraft was strengthened through the development of the Q—5 attack aircraft.

Section 3 Development of the Pilotless Aircraft

The pilotless aircraft is an aircraft in which there is no pilot and it is flown either by its own onboard programable flight control system or by a remote control system operated by a pilot in a carrier aircraft or on ground. Its controlled long distance flight was realized by use of its onboard autopilot, programable flight control system, remote control and telemetering system, automatic navigation system, automatic landing system, etc. Compared with the manned aircraft it is lighter in weight, smaller in size, lower in production cost and better in stealthiness. It is particularly suitable for high risk missions.

The pilotless aircraft has been developed rapidly since a radio controlled model airplane was used as a drone abroad in the 1930s. The small low altitude and low speed piston—engined drones became operational in the 1940s and the high subsonic and supersonic high performance drones appeared in the 1950s. With the development of microelectronics, navigation and control technologies some countries developed pilotless reconnaissance aircraft after the 1960s. Now the applications of the pilotless aircraft are increasingly expanded. In military area the pilotless aircraft are used in missions of reconnaissance, communication, anti—submarine, electronic counter—measures and ground attack and in civil area they are used in geophysical survey, natural resource exploration, meteorological observation, forest fire—fighting and artificial rainfall; and in R& D area they are used in air sampling proof and advanced technology demonstration.

The investigation to the pilotless aircraft in China began in the late 1950s. The laws of the automatic takeoff and landing for both the An—2 and Il—28 aircraft were basically mastered in 1959. The development of the pilotless aircraft began in second half of the 1960s and now it has grown into 3 series of products, i.e. the Changkong 1 drones, WZ—5 high altitude photographic reconnaissance aircraft and small remotely controlled aircraft D4s. The pilotless aircraft design and research organizations were founded in NAI, BIAA and NPU. These universities have been used as the bases and have the capabilities of design and small scale production. The various types of the pilotless aircraft made in China have basically satisfied the needs of military and civilian applications and have gradually entered into the world market.

1. The Changkong 1 Drone Series

Drone is a kind of pilotless aircraft used as a target for air defence missiles, aeriel guns and anti—aircraft cannons. Drones used in China in 1950s mainly were the soviet built La—17. In 1968 the government formally assigned to the NAI a task of developing Changkong 1 medium—high altitude drone. In 1976 and 1977 the institute successfully developed Changkong 1 and Type 1015B radar parachute drone. The Pilotless Research Department was established in 1977 and it was expanded into a Pilotless Research Institute in 1979. In the institute there were four research sections, i.e. general configuration, stress analysis and systems, radio and electrical system and engine, as well as two workshops. In addition there were a research section of flight control system and a workshop of special equipment which were set in the Department of Automatic Control Engineering at NAI. After 1977 NAI completed the development of Changkong 1 nuclear test sampling aircraft, Changkong 1 low altitude drone and Changkong 1 high manoeuvarable drone. These drones have basically met the needs of target practice for domestic antiaircraft missiles and successfully fulfilled sampling task for nuclear tests.

a. Changkong 1 Medium—High Altitude Drone (CKI)

The Changkong 1 medium—high altitude drone was developed on the technology base of the La—17 drone. The La—17 drone was brought into air by a carrier aircraft and then propelled by its own ramjet engine. Its performance was rather inferior and its operation was not convenient. Some modifications and innovations were incorporated into the design of the Changkong 1 drone. The WP6 engines which were going to be phased out were used to replace the ramjet engines; it took off from a ground running dolly rather than being delivered by a carrier aircraft in air; a domestic autopilot was used; general layout was changed; structure strength and stiffness were improved; new fuel feeding system and control system were designed; new flying trajectory was selected; aircraft electrical network was changed and a standby electrical system for power—off recovery was added; and a radio telemetering system was also added.

The Changkong 1 was a high subsonic drone with conventional aerodynamic

—158—

configuration, rectangular wing, slender and circular cross section fuselage which consisted of streamlined parabolic revolutionary nose and tail and a cylindrical middle section. Underneath the fuselage was suspended an engine pod in which a WP6 engine was installed. A pod was carried at each wing tip. Both tailplane and vertical fin were rectangular surfaces.

The drone automatically run and took off with the help of a takeoff dolly. It climbed at first under programable control system and then under radio remote control. Afterwards it could carry out either level flight or other manoeuvres. It could be guided to land by a remote control system after its mission had been performed. Generally the drone could come into target practice zone three times for every flight. If it had not been shot down in target practice, it could be guided to land and repaired for next use.

The development of the Changkong 1 medium—high altitude drone began in April 1968. A total of 9 prototype drones were flight—tested. The delivery began after its design certification in 1977. The target practice of the military Services showed its satisfactorily performance and conformity with the operational requirement.

b. Changkong 1 Nuclear Sampling Aircraft (CKIA)

The government assigned a task to convert the Changkong 1 drone into a nuclear test sampling aircraft in March 1977.

Sampling for a nuclear test is an important work for the development of nuclear weapons. Before the CKIA was developed the sampling for nuclear test was done by a manned aircraft. This was harmful to pilot. In addition because the cross—cloud—flight could only allowed at a later time, the sample taken would not be fresh enough and, therefore, the evaluation and analysis of the nuclear test would be adversely affected. The scientific people at NAI began the development of the CKIA with sense of serving the national defence and with sense of responsibility to pilot's health. Three sampling aircraft were constructed and a number of tests were carried out in a period of time as short as half a year. Prior to the mission flight a sampling simulation flight chased by a J—6 fighter was made. These tests and flight test showed that the development of the sampling aircraft was a success. On September 17, 1977 one sampling aircraft participated in the cross—cloud—flight sampling of 22nd nuclear test of our country. The aircraft was only 150 km away from center of explosion when the nuclear bomb exploded. It flew according to predefined course and crossed nuclear cloud twice with a door of the sampler opened. It landed in good condition at a designated site about ten minutes later with "fresh sample" in intact sampler.

The NAI supplied a number of sampling aircraft for nuclear test and these aircraft participated in four nuclear tests. Enough samples were obtained and the assigned tasks were successfully fulfilled. Since 1980 they have been exclusively used in nuclear test sampling.

c. Changkong 1 Low Altitude Drone (CKIB)

In order to evaluate and certificate a low altitude antiaircraft missile by target shooting the NAI was requested to develop the Changkong 1 low altitude drone in February 1980. It was an improvement of CKI, the medium—high altitude drone. To meet the need of low altitude flight were incorporated some major modifications, e.g.the use of low thrust "low altitude cruise condition" which was an equivalent of 40 per cent of WP6 rated static thrust, one 160 liters auxiliary fuel tank under each wing for extended range and the adjustment of flight control system.

Successful first flight of the low altitude drone was made on May 18, 1982. It flew for 48 minutes and landed safely. The design was certificated and was approved for small scale production in February 1983. Afterwards, the production drones were successively supplied to meet the need of target practice for domestic low altitude missiles.

d. Changkong 1 High Manoeuvrable Drone (CKIC)

To strengthen the national defence a number of high performance missiles had to be tested and certificated and, therefore, a high manoeuvrable drone which could fly a sharp level turning at low and medium altitudes and at high speed was in urgent need. At that time this kind of drone was not available in China although they were available in a few other countries.

The task assigned to NAI in early 1983 was to develop and produce a high performance and high manoeuvrable drone in one year and a half. The task was tough, required technology complicated and time strictly limited. This meant that no fault was allowed in general design concept and in prototype production and that every pieces of the work had to be carried out in fast speed and high quality and in a systematic fashion. After acceptance of the task the NAI decided to go all out to fulfil the urgent task. A leading group headed by president of NAI, the chief designer system and the administration system were set up. The system engineering management was applied and the contractual system was also applied on trial basis. The development of the drone was thus fully under way in NAI.

Lu Qingfeng, chief designer, and Luo Feng, vice chief designer, directed conceptual definition study and determined that the Changkong 1 low altitude drone would be used as the basis of the new drone. The design team was faced with a key technical problem, the improvements to the power plant, structure, flight control system, fuel supply, electromagnetic compatibility, electrical network and flight trajectory. Among them the most challenging and most critical ones were the improvements of flight control system and fuel supply system.

New flight control system was required to control engine thrust and movements of three control surfaces according to control laws so that sharp turning could be flown in a more constant speed and altitude. This requirement was fulfilled by redesigning autopilot components, and by carrying out of ground centrifugal test and hybrid computer simulation of whole system. To realize coordinated controls for high manoeuvrable turn a high precision load factor transducer was used in an American pilotless aircraft to adjust bank but to keep load factor. But this transducer was not available at that time in China, therefore the designers creatively used other kind of domestic equipment to realize coordinated turn at constant altitude and at load factor of high manoeuvrability.

To ensure normal fuel supply in high manoeuvrability flight a unique fuel supply system was designd which used bleed air from engine compressor to pressurize fuel supply system.

More than 10 key technical problems were tackled by the technical people in the development of the high manoeuvrable drone. Among these technical people was Yao Kaidi, a veteran lecturer in his fifties, who was in charge of the technology of the fuel supply system. He contracted abdominal malignant tumour and had had two operations on his abdominal muscle so that he could not stand for a long time. But during the fuel line system test he came to the laboratory every time and very often worked ten hours and more a day. Although the kerosene smell made him feel dizzy and nauseating, he insisted on staying and working there. He tried hard to contribute to our cause of pilotless aircraft.

The construction of two flight test prototype aircraft was completed in July 1984. The flight test made at a test range in September was a complete success. The load factor of level turn reached 4g. Another eight high manoeuvrable drones were built at NAI by the end of 1984. In the certification test of a high performance missile carried out from February to March in 1985 only four drones were used as targets for five effective missile launches.

The Changkong 1 high manoeuvrable drone has excellent performance as a target to meet a variety of missiles training requirements and it is the one of most advanced drones in the world.

To commend the NAI upon its great contribution to the development of the pilotless aircraft the MAI awarded it a collective merit and Lu Qingfeng and Luo Feng first class merit.

Except five failures in flight test of the medium–high altitude drone the later three derivatives of the Changkong 1 series all succeeded in their first flight test. So far a great number of drones in various versions have been operated and no accident has ever been recorded.

2. High Altitude Photographic Reconnaissance Pilotless Aircraft—WZ–5

Based on the needs of national defence and aeronautical R&D the government assigned a task in 1969 to the BIAA to develop a high altitude photographic reconnaissance pilotless aircraft.

The BIAA is one of the universities and colleges which first carried out R&D in pilotless aircraft field. A pilotless aircraft section was established in 1963 and more than 50 technical people worked there. A systematic investigation and analysis to foreign technology of the pilotless aircraft began one year later and the development of a supersonic drone B–6 in 1965, which was terminated later because short of ramjet engine. But these activities prepared necessary technologies for later development of a high altitude reconnaissance pilotless aircraft WZ–5.

The design concept of the WZ–5 defined a pilotless aircraft which was capable to fly at high altitude and at high subsonic speed and to perform the mission of high altitude photographic reconnaissanse in day time. Its visible light camera could swing left and right about its longitudinal axis so that it could take pictures from five windows. A small size and short life WP11 engine, an automatic control system and radio remote control and telemetering system were installed in the aircraft. No takeoff and landing device such as landing gear was installed so that it had to be carried by a carrier aircraft to a certain altitude and then to be released. It was guided to a predetermined recovering site and recovered by its own parachute after it had performed its mission.

In the development of the advanced high altitude photographic reconnaissance pilotless aircraft the BIAA was responsible to develop airframe, engine and ground radio control station and for final assembly, debugging and flight test. They rapidly gathered all technical staff inside the institute and set up a design team. Yang Weiming was appointed chief designer. More than 1,000 teachers, technical people, workers and students took part in the development. Two pilotless aircraft were built in 1972. In 1976 two more aircraft were built with all the domestic materials.

In addition to a lot of development ground tests a total of seven flight tests were carried out since first successful flight in 1972. The aerial photography was tested in second flight test in 1973 and its result was certified as good by photo reading. The predetermined objectives were realized in a high altitude and medium range development flight test carried out in 1975. The ground test for several engines was up to 100 hours. For test of ground control station four more flight tests over land and sea were carried out. In total one hundred and twenty flights were accumulated. The full size static test and resonance test to verify structure strength of the pilotless aircraft were carried out in October 1972 and these tests proved that they were in conformity with the design requirement. To the airborne equipment more than 10 environmental tests such as high and low temperature test, high altitude test, vibration test and impact test were also successively carried out according to the specification.

A good number of technical people tried their best to develop the advanced pilotless aircraft. The automatic control system was the most critical part of the aircraft and, therefore, a ground−based flight simulation test rig was specifically constructed by the BIAA and the Lanzhou Aero−instrument Factory. Several flight simulation tests of the aircraft were conducted in connection with the simulation test rig supported by a computer. The Doppler radar did not function normally at the outset. To solve the problem the Air Force flew its Trident and Tu−4 aircraft more than 80 hours over various surface features such as land, ocean, mountain, plain and desert and took various actual Doppler spectra to study the effect of frequency interference on the radar. After repeated tests and modifications the radar met the design requirement at last. In the development of the WP11 engine the machining of transonic axial compressor rotor was a challenging problem. At the outset it was built with precision cast steel and only one thirtieth of the products were up to standard. But the problem was solved by the technical people at last. For the design of radio control station there were not any similar stations or information which could be used as a reference. The technical people worked in a creative way and in the end a radio control system, which combined the capabilities of tracking, remote controlling and telemetering in one single system, was successfully developed. The ground control station could be used not only to track, remotely control and telemeter the pilotless aircraft, but also to display by instruments and digital display, and to record on paper tape and to mark automatically on a map the necessary flight information.

The certification test of the WZ−5 was completed in 1978. In the same year the BIAA formally set up a Pilotless Aircraft Design and Research Institute. The institute had sections of general layout, structure, engine, automatic control and radio, workshops of sub−assembly and final assembly and an environmental test laboratory. The type design was certificated by the government in 1980. It began to enter into service in 1981 and since then it has played important role in training and tactical reconnaissance.

The WZ−5 is mainly used for photographic reconnaissance but it can also be used as an air sampling aircraft and drone if the corresponding equipment were fitted. No doubt the successful development of the WZ−5 is a leap in the field of pilotless aircraft technology.

3. Miniature Remotely Piloted Vehicle (RPV)—D4

To meet the requirements of aerial survey to small area but in large scale and aerial physical exploration the NPU began its exploratory study based on a miniature model drone. The conceptual definition study and ground and flight tests of the flying quality, autopilot, high precision navigation, small area but large scale aerial survey and mineral prospect and remote sensing equipment were carried out in a nature of advanced R&D so that the precious firsthand information and data were obtained. The formal development of the miniature RPV D4 began in March 1981. The persons in charge of technical issues were Xue Mingxian, etc. The successful first flight of the D4 was made in February 1982 and its technical certification was awarded in December 1983.

The D4 is a low altitude, low speed miniature pilotless aircraft with wing span of 4.3 m, fuselage length of 3.3 m and maximum takeoff weight of 140 kg. It is the smallest and the lightest Chinese pilotless aircraft. It can carry 28 kg payload of special instruments and equipment. The power plant is a gasoline piston engine developed by the NPU. An engine−driven two rotors generator supplies the electricity to the aircraft control system and special instruments and equipment. The aircraft is flown by an autopilot and is controlled and guided to fly on a predefined course through a radio remote controlling, telemetering and locat-ing system. The action radius is 40 km. It can also flown by a programable control system if high precision of flight path is not required.

The D−4 is of glass fibre reinforced plastic construction. It is launched from a zero−length launcher by a rocket booster which uses solid fuel and is automatically disconnected after takeoff and can be repeatedly utilized. The takeoff process is automatically performed according to the programme. A parachute is used for recovery. The oleo−pneumatic shock absorbers were installed at two sides of the fuselage belly to absorb landing impact. The wing and tailplane can be rapidly dismantled for transportation.

In October 1984, the NPU set up a Pilotless Aircraft Design and Research Institute. Some experimental studies were carried out to extend range of the D4. In addition to the main application in aerial photography now the RPVs have also been used in survey of terrains, cities and towns, railways and rivers, exploration of mines and oil fields, output forecast of forests, agriculture and fishery, water and soil conservation, water regimen observation and archaeological survey. In addition it can also be retrofitted into front line reconnaissance aircraft and electronic—jamming aircraft.

The approach to develop the pilotless aircraft is featured with Chinese characteristics, i.e. all the development activities of the pilotless aircraft have been exclusively carried out in three universities and colleges owned by the MAI. This approach is beneficial in improving teachers' ability in solving pratical problems and in running the universities and colleges both as an education center and as a R&D center to obtain the research achievements and at the same time to train qualified students. The universities and colleges have comparablly complete disciplines, various professional people and capabilities to develop products which are advanced but need less man powers. Therefore, it is appropriate to undertake the task of developing pilotless aircraft by them. The technology development in the field of the pilotless aircraft will be more rapid with the deepening of the worldwide technology revolution. The cause of Chinese pilotless aircraft must further advance and the minimum altitude flying drones and the supersonic drones must be developed in order to better serve our national defence and national economy.

Chapter Ⅵ   Development of Transports, Helicopters and Light Aircraft

Section 1   Development of Transports

Transports are airplanes used for transportation of passengers and cargo. Usually they are divided into two categories: military transports and civil transports. The military transports are used for carrying troops, weapons and other military equipment; the airplanes used for transportation of passengers are called airliners or passenger airplanes and the ones used for transportation of cargo are called air freighters or cargo airplanes. The small transports usually are general purpose airplanes and they can be used for a number of special operations after retrofitting.

The transports have extensive applications in national defence and national economy. Their development have dramatically changed transportation structure and provided people with a fast, convenient, economic, safe and comfortable transportation means. In a modern war the military transports are important tools to improve troop's mobility and adaptability. Therefore the development of transports are greatly emphasized by all countries in the world.

The development of transports in China began in the mid-1950s and a small general purpose airplane was first trial-produced and then put into mass production. The development of a short / medium range airliner and a medium cargo transport began in the 1960s. The development and prototype production of a large airliner began in the 1970s. The 1980s has been a prosperous period in which large, medium and small transports have been parallelly developed and several new types of airplanes have competitively come out. It appeares that the development of transports is in ascendant.

There are six transport manufacturers and two professional design institutes in China. The manufacturers are located in Harbin, Nanchang, Xi'an, Shaanxi, Shanghai and Shijiazhuang and the design institutes in Xi'an and Shanghai. The infrastructure is being gradually perfected. Now the Chinese aviation industry has the ability to independently develop medium / small transports and to cooperate with foreign manufacturers on development of large airliners.

1.   Small General Purpose Transports

Due to the need of domestic airline industry and the actual possibility in production, the aviation industry made a decision of licence production of the An-2 aircraft in October 1956.

The An-2 is a small general purpose transport developed by the Soviet Union. It is good in flying performance and economics, easy to operate and maintain, safe and reliable. It is a conventional biplane with tailwheel type landing gear. A piston engine drives a four blades metal propeller. It can operate from an airstrip.

The Chinese designation of the An–2 is Y–5. Its prototype production was decided to be undertaken by the Nanchang Aircraft Factory. Although the factory had exprience in production of the CJ–5 trainer, it was the first time to build a transport. Prior to the arrival of drawings from the Soviet Union an An–2 transport was borrowed from the Chinese airline for familiarization of its structural and manufacturing features by engineers. They made a plan for prototype production and set up rules for manufacture. After the Soviet drawings arrived at the factory in January 1957, the technical people were organized to study these drawings and documents in Russian. Based on these drawings and their own practice in the prototype production of a new aircraft, engineers in the Nanchang Aircraft Factory prepared themselves 6,960 manufacturing processes and designed and manufactured 3,000 pieces of production tooling. To improve the efficiency in the prototype production they boldly used some new techniques such as a coordination method which used both standard parts and reference holes, and standardization of production tooling designs. It was particularly commendable that the Nanchang Aircraft Factory fulfilled the task of prototype production without expanding its factory floor area and only by addition of seven machines. In October 1957 first Y–5 completed its final assembly and successfully passed static test. On December 7 another Y–5 made its first flight. In March 1958 the Military Products Certification Commission of the State Council certificated Y–5's design for serial production. In May of the same year the Y–5 was exibited at a National Farm Tools Exhibition in Beijing.

The basic Y–5 was a transport. Based on it a number of derivatives were developed in the process of mass production according to user's different requirements. An agricultural version was produced in 1958 according to the Soviet drawings and 229 aircraft were produced. A passenger version was derived in 1959 and 114 aircraft were produced and were used on regional air lines. Afterwards, the versions for training of navigator–bomber, parachuting and aerial photography were successively produced.

A total of 727 Y–5s of all versions were produced by the Nanchang Aircraft Factory from 1958 to 1968. The continued production of the Y–5 was transferred to the Shijiazhuang Aircraft Factory in 1970 and 221 Y–5s were produced there by the end of 1986. In all, 948 Y–5s were turned out.

The Y–5 is the first transport produced in China. It is also a transport which was produced in largest quantity and in the longest period of time. Its various versions played remarkable roles in many areas of national economy. It flew over all the places in our motherland. The Y–5s were also supplied to some countries in Asia and Europe and have been a witness to the exchange between China and foreign countries.

The long lasted production and operation of the Y–5s showed the existance of a broad market for small transport in China. To meet the increasing need of the national economy and to develop a better new aircraft, the aircraft industry began to develop by themselves small general purpose transports in 1970s. In November 1974 the government assigned a task to the Harbin Aircraft Factory to develop a small transport Y—11 and Xiong Wenjie was appointed chief designer. The design drawings were completed in June 1975 and the prototype production began immediately after release of the drawings. The full size airframe static test was passed on December 19, the first flight was made on December 30 and the type design was certificated in 1977.

The Y—11 is a general purpose airplane which is mainly used in agriculture and forestry but as second missions it can also be used for geological exploration, detection of shoals of fish, transportation and rescue. The safety and low altitude performance were emphasized in the design. It can fly at minimum low altitude and features short takeoff and landing run distances. It is powered by two domestic HS6D piston engines, maximum payload is 1,250 kg and an air crew of 8 members can be carried.

In order to serve the economy construction with the Y—11s and to test the aircraft performance in practice it was approved by the government in May 1980 to set up an Air Service Team by the Harbin Aircraft Factory. With the Y—11s the team has provided various professional aviation services. In past several years the Y—11s have flown to more than 10 provinces, e.g. Heilongjiang, Inner Mongolia, Hebei, Anhui, Jiangsu and Guangxi, and provided services such as insects killing, seeds sowing and fertilizer applying for agriculture, forestry and animal husbandry, geological exploration and aerial survey for industries and survey of wild animal resources such as red—crowned cranes and northeast tigers. When Mudanjiang region was suffering a plague of insects in May 1981 several Y—11s were sent to spray pesticide and a kind of worldwide harmful moths were quickly wiped out with a rate of killing over 90 per cent. In 1982 the Y—11s flew to Xinjiang and operated for forest belts and farmlands with good effect. In 1984 the Shihezi Production and Construction Corps in Xinjiang Autonomus Region bought 10 Y—11s and set up an Air Service Detachment to carry out their professional operations. Another Y—11 Air Service Detachment was set up in the same year in the city of Changzhou in Jiangsu Province.

The Harbin Aircraft Factory launched another general purpose aircraft development program—Y—12 after the Y—11 program. The Y—12 was powered by two PT6A—11 turboprops made in Canada and its performance was significantly improved.

The Y—12I was developed to meet the geological sectors' need of high precision and large scale mineral exploration. Lu Kairen was appointed chief designer. The version was designed in accordance with the standards of internationally accepted airworthiness regulations and a system of Designated Engineering Representative (DER) was used in its development. In addition a great number of tests which had never been carried out before in our country were conducted, such as fire—resistant test of the power plant system, climatic test of the fuel system, rain ingestion test of the engine, electromagnetic compatibility test, etc.

Three Y—12Is were produced in first batch. The static test was completed in July 1982 and first flight was made on July 14. To test its operational performance, a geological survey flight was made over the Hebei plain in February 1984. Its low altitude flying was steady and its endurance, rate of climb and fuel consumption, etc., were all in conformity with the requirement. The geological prospecting was carried out over the Inner Mongolia plateau in September of the same year. Over 90 per cent survey routes were qualified and the quality of operation was up to the standard. To this point the Y-12I had completed all flight tests and the accumulated flying hours had reached 724. After the Y-12I was jointly certificated by the MAI and the Ministry of Geology and Mining Industry in December of the same year it began to enter into service.

The Y-12II is a passenger version with 17 seats in the cabin and has two higher rated Canadian PT6A-27 engines. After retrofitting of the interior and the air condition system in Hong Kong from May to August in 1985 cabin noise was reduced, cabin temperature was automatically controlled and fire-retardant materials were used inside the cabin and, therefore, the Y-12II had come up to the standards of international airworthiness regulations. In December of the same year the CAAC awarded Type Certificate to the Y-12II.

2. Filling the Gap of Domestic Commuter Airplane

By the mid-1960s China had adjusted its national economy and began its performance of the Third Five-year Plan. With the development of domestic air transportation, a domestic commuter airplane was thus needed.

At this time the aviation industry had had years of experience in production of small transports, a factory for production of medium bombers had been constructed and a large airliner design institute had also been established. It was the right time to develop a domestic commuter airplane.

In October 1966 Premier Zhou Enlai and Vice Chairman Ye Jianying approved the design concept of the Y-7. After the assignment of the development task a design team was formed, which was composed of three aircraft factories in Xi'an, Nanchang and Chengdu and the Xi'an Aircraft Design Institute. The design team was headed by Li Xipu, vice chief engineer of the Xi'an Aircraft Factory. Xu Shunshou, vice director of the Xi'an Aircraft Design Institute was appointed its deputy leader. One of the ground rules for the design was to utilize domestic materials, vendor-furnished-equipment and components and accessories to the maximum. Designers worked very hard in a strong wish to develop our own civil airplane and finished the design drawings and specifications in March 1968. The prototype production began in October 1969 and the final assembly in early December 1970. The first flight of the Y-7 piloted by Li Benshun air crew took place on December 25.

The Y-7 was composed of 16,963 kinds of parts, 500,000 standard parts in 5,248 kinds, 520 kinds of vendor-furnished-equipment and components, of which 246 kinds were new, and 2,135 kinds of metal materials. A lot of advanced manufacturing techniques were required and among them were integral panel, shot peen forming, titanium alloy forming, aluminium alloy spot-weld bonding, integral fuel tank construction, stretch forming for the orientated acrylic plastic sheet, etc. It was really not easy to solve all the problems related with these advanced manufacturing techniques and to send a commuter airplane into the sky in less than five years.

"It is not easy to reach the stage of flight and even more difficult to be certificated." The Y-7, as a civil passenger airplane with more emphasis on safety, economics, comfortability and operational life, needed more ground and flight tests. But it was in the time of turmoil and it was difficult to carry out all the development activities. That was why the Y-7 could not be certificated for mass production for a long time after its first flight. The Y-7 development was sped up until the normal production order was restored in 1977.

In 1980 in order to solve the problem related to engine starting at high altitude and high temperature the higher rated engines WJ5A-1s were used. The followed flight tests accumulated 1,600 hours. The airfields operated were in 28 provinces and cities and among them were the high altitude airfields, high temperature airfields and unpaved airstrips. These flight tests showed that the aircraft controllability, safety, engine starting behavior at high altitude and high temperature airfields and airworthiness with the passengers onboard were all good and were in conformity with the design requirements.

To be highly responsible for passengers' safety and to ensure the airplane's safe flying in any conditions the Y-7 was tested with one engine inoperative in takeoff and landing. This was a high risky and technically complicated test which had never been carried out in our country. The purpose of the test was to verify the aircraft ability of normal takeoff and landing when one of two engines was damaged or out of control. The flight test was jointly administrated by the MAI and CAAC

Fig.41　Final assembly of the Y-7

on April 4, 1982 at Zhangguizhuang airfield, Tianjin. Commanded by He Wenzhi, Vice Minister of MAI, a six-member air crew including Zhang Yun, captain of the 8th brigade of CAAC, and Cheng Yuanyong, executive captain, successfully carried out single engine takeoff and landings with takeoff weight of 19,200 kg and 21,000 kg and created a first Chinese record. On April 16 Vice Premiers Geng Biao and Zhang Aiping had an interview with the flight test members. The MAI and CAAC awarded merits and prizes to the people who had rendered outstanding services to the Y-7 single engine flight test. Zhang Yun, Cheng Yuanyong and Zhang Qinliang, the leader of the technical group for the Y-7 flight test of Xi'an Aircraft Company, honourably won the first class merits.

In July 1982, the government approved the design certification of the Y-7 for pre—production.

The Y—7 is a monoplane with high set wing and low—mounted tailplane. Two WJ5A—1 turboprop engines are mounted at inboard wings. The cabin normally accommodates 48—52 passengers. In addition there are also a mixed passenger—cargo version and a freighter version. The Y—7 can also be retrofitted for aerial survey and mapping and natural resource exploration.

To further improve the safety, reliability, passenger comfortability and economics, the Xi'an Aircraft Company cooperated with Hong Kong Aircraft Engineering Company (HAECO) in 1985 in refurbishing the Y—7 with foreign advanced technology and equipment. The Y—7 was retrofitted with 30 advanced communication and navigation equipment, winglets, new cabin interior for lowering cabin noise, new three—man flight deck layout instead of original five—man layout, new cabin air conditioning and pressure regulation system and new style pain—ting. It was considerably improved and its airworthiness flight test carried out on long distance air route in our country showed the following improvements: the equipment MTBF was significantly increased; the fuel consumption was reduced by 3—4 percent; the cabin noise level was reduced by 5—6 EPNdB, the passenger uncomfortable feeling caused by the pressure difference was basically eliminated; and the cabin interior was more beautiful and comfortable. Therefore, the Y—7 had more favourable airworthy capability to operate at various regions in China and was awarded a certificate of airworthiness by CAAC on January 23, 1986.

Since the first delivery of a Y—7 to the Shanghai Civil Aviation Bureau in December 1983, a total of 18 Y—7s had been in operation on a number of domestic air routes by April 1987.

3. Development of Medium / Large Transports

The Air Force's transportation troops were successively set up since the founding of new China. But in the following ten years and more the equipment they used mainly were American transports captured during the Liberation War and purchased Soviet transports and they could neither meet the needs of the practical war and training nor the civil transportation and emergency and disaster relief uses. The need for a medium / large transport in national defence and economy was increasingly urgent.

The development of a medium / large transport was an important objective of the aviation industry's Third Five—year Plan. The task of developing medium transport Y—8 was assigned to the Xi'an Aircraft Factory by the MAI in December 1968. The Factory organized a design team of 570 persons in early 1969 and part of them came from other aircraft factories and design institutes. The design team began their intense work immediately.

It took two years and four months to finish the design. A complete set of drawings, specifications and analysis reports were released in February 1972. The parts production and assembly activities began soon afterwards. On December 10, 1974 the final assembly of first Y—8 was completed. Li Jingrui and his air crew flew the Y—8 for its first time on December 25. The flight lasted 26 minutes and the flying altitude was 6,000 m. It exhibited good controllability and normal functions of all the systems.

In 1972 the MAI decided to transfer the Y-8 production to the Shaanxi Aircraft Factory which was located in Shaannan (southern part of the Shaanxi province). The factory was constructed as a transport airplane production base in the "third line" (inland) area since the mid-1960s and had had certain capability of prototype production. On December 29, 1975 a Y-8 built by the Shaanxi Aircraft Factory also made its first flight with the help from the Xi'an Aircraft Factory. The Y-8 full size static test was completed on September 25, 1976 and the type design was formally certificated for serial production in February 1980.

The Y-8 is both a military and a commercial transport powered by 4 WJ6 turboprops. It is of an all-metal structure and a monoplane with a high-set wing. The fore fuselage and tail section are pressurized and the central fuselage is a cargo compartment with a volume of 123.3 cubic meters. The typical payload are as follows: bulk cargos 20,000 kg; containerized cargos 16,000 kg; 96 troops; 58 paratroops; 60 severely wounded and 20 slightly wounded troops and 3 attendants; two "Liberation" brand trucks.

The Y-8 has the advantages of long range, high speed and low fuel consumption. On June 30, 1984 two fully loaded Y-8s successfully flew to Lhasa from Chengdu for its first time and exhibited its capability to withstand the severe plateau weather. On the eve of the 20th anniversary of the founding of the Tibet Autonomous Region in August 1985 the MAI sent 40,000 kg various commodity to Tibet by two Y-8s and it was warmly welcomed by the local government and people.

The safety of the Y-8 experienced a severe test when Xu Guocun and his crew successfully made a flight test with one engine inoperative in May 1985. It proved that the Y-8 could still takeoff and land normally when one of the engines was inoperative or damaged. The success of the flight test marked a breakthrough in flight test with one engine out for a heavy and multi-engines Chinese transport.

The Y-8 is a general purpose transport with a great potential for further development. In 1985 it was retrofitted into a maritime patrol version and a carrier version for Black Hawk helicopter by aircraft designer Xu Peiling and his colleagues. To the maritime patrol version the main changes were the installment of a new radar, new navigation and communication equipment and the addition of optical camera, infrared camera, infrared submarine detector and sonobuoy, etc. Thus it can not only search, reconnoitre and photograph the targets on the water surface or under the water but also rescue the people from perils of the sea. It has successfully performed patrol missions since it was technically certificated for operation in September 1985. The carrier version was specially designed for carrying the Black Hawk helicopter. It can quickly and conveniently transport the helicopters to the border areas. In December 1985, the Y-8 carrier version aircraft successfully transported the Black Hawk into Tibet and made contribution in using the Black Hawk for timely rescue of soldiers and civilians who were trapped in a snow storm in Mote region.

By 1986 a total of 25 Y-8s have been produced and delivered to the military Services and airlines and have become an important force in Chinese air transportation.

The development of a large long range airliner in Shanghai was brewed in early 1970s. On August 21, 1970, the National Planning Commissin, and the Defence Industry Leading Group of the Military Commission of CCCPC appoved in principle the "Report on the Transport Trial Production in Shanghai" which was prepared by the Aviation Industry Leading Group. Since then the project was put into the government plan. After some discussions on the conceptual definition, a general design concept was proposed. On June 27, 1973, the State Council and the Military Commission of CCCPC formally approved a report on development of a large airliner which was jointly prepared by Shanghai municipal government and the National Planning Commission. The development of the Y-10 airliner was thus started in Shanghai.

The Y-10 is a large airliner and is the heavist of the airplanes so far developed in China. The preparation for setting up a design organ in Shanghai was started in September 1970. Both the MAI and the Air Force sent their outstanding designers to the organ which had only 300 people in its early stage and then 800 people when the Aircraft Design Institute was established in 1973. In 1978 the institute was renamed as the Shanghai Aircraft Design and Research Institute. Ma Fengshan was appointed director of the institute.

Due to the close cooperation between the MAI and Shanghai municipality and the hard work of the staff the design drawings of the Y-10 were completed in June 1975. The intense prototype production began immediately in the Shanghai Aircraft Factory and a Y-10 for the static test was made available in September 1976. A full size airframe destructive test was carried out in the Aircraft Structure Strength Research Institute on November 23, 1978. The airframe was broken at predicted place of left wing when the applying load was increased to 100.2 per cent. The test result was in agreement with the theoretical analysis and proved that the aircraft strength was in conformity with the design requirement.

The first flight of the Y-10 took place on September 26, 1980, which was flown by flight test captain Wang Jinda and his air crew.

To test the adaptability to different air routes and airports a Y-10 made ferry flights to a number of airports in the country. Among them were the airports in Beijing, Hefei, Harbin, Urumqi, Guangzhou, Kunming, Chengdu, Lhasa, etc. A total of 121 flights and 167 flying hours were accumulated. The longest non-stop flight distance was 3,600 km, the longest endurance 4 hours and 49 minutes and the highest airport 3,540 m above the sea level. On January 31, 1984 A Y-10 successfully flew to Lhasa from Chengdu for its first time. It was the first airplane which was made in China and flew over the roof of the world and it also proved the Y-10's adaptability to fly in complicated climate over the plateau.

The cabin of the Y-10 can be configured into three classes: tourist class (149 seats), mixed class (124 seats) and economic class (178 seats). The flight deck is designed for five-man layout. It is powered by four Pratt Whitney JT3D-7 turbofan engines. The maximum takeoff weight of the aircraft is 102,000 kg.

There are eight breakthroughs in the Y-10 design:

a. The American Fedral Air Regulation was used as a standard and the Soviet regulation only as a reference so that the past traditional way in which only the soviet regulation was used was changed.

b. A peaky airfoil profile was used in the wing design so that the aircraft had better high speed behavior and the maximum cruise aerodynamic efficiency reached 15.4.

c. The aircraft structure was designed according to the fail—safe and safe—life concepts and the rules and regulations for the detailed design to prevent the structure from fatigue were made according to the aircraft total life of 130,000 hours or of ten years.

d. The largest integral wing fuel tank and pressurized cabin were designed and the problems of fuel leakage and air tightness were solved.

e. A unique control method for control surfaces, in which the control surfaces were brought into motion by tabs, and a general configuration with underwing mounted engine pods were adopted.

f. The largest full scale simulation tests of control system, hydraulic system, fuel system and electrical network were carried out.

g. A great number of new materials, new vendor—furnished—equipment and components and new standards were used. A total of 76 new materials were used, which was 18 per cent of all the materials used. 305 new vendor—furnished—equipment and components were 70 per cent of the total and 164 new standards were 17 per cent of the total.

h. The computer was widely used in the analysis of the general configuration, aerodynamics, stress, structure and system design. More than 50 big application programmes were prepared and among them was an optimization programme for the general configuration parameters.

Two Y—10 prototypes had been built although the development program was terminated because the reasons of market and cost. Precious experience was obtained, which became the technical basis for the later co—production program of the McDonnell Douglas MD—82 airliner between China and the U.S.A..

To meet the airlines' need for a trunk—route airliner the Shanghai Aviation Industrial Company and McDonnell Douglas of the U.S.A signed an agreement for assembly of 25 aircraft with the MD—82 kits in Shanghai for CAAC in April 1985. It was planned that first delivery would take place in second half of the year 1987 and last delivery in 1991.

Fig. 42   The Y—10 is inside a hangar

The MD—82 is a trunk—route airliner with 147 seats. It can operate at high temperature and high altitude regions and is powered by two Pratt & Whitney JT8D-217A turbofans. The riveting of first MD-82 began at the Shanghai Aircraft Factory in April 1986. The first flight of the MD-82 assebmled in Shanghai was made on July 2, 1987 and its delivery to the Shenyang Airline Bureau at the end of July.

Section 2 Development of Helicopters

Helicopter is an aircraft whose lift is generated by engine-driven rotor(s) and whose flight is realized by changing the magnitude and direction of the lift through special transmission system and control system. Generally it has the abilities to fly forward, to ascend and descend vertically, to hover, to autorotate and glide downward and to fly backward and sideward.

The generally acknowledged first manned helicopter in the world appeared in Germany in the 1930s and it was a side-by-side twin-rotor helicopter. So far four generations of the helicopter have been developed since its pratical application in the late 1940s. The first generation helicopter was generally powered with piston engines, it used the rotor blades made of steel and wood and the maximum forward flight speed was about 200 km / h. The second generation helicopter generally used turboshaft engines and metal rotor blades and the maximum forward flight speed was about 250 km / h. The third generation helicopter generally used turboshaft engines and reinforced glassfibre plastic rotor blades and the forward flight speed was 300 km / h. The fourth generation helicopter has been developed since the mid-1970s. It generally uses turboshaft engines. The composite materials and titanium alloys have been widely used in its structure. The forward flight speed usually is higher than 350 km / h. The helicopters have broad applications. In military field they are used for liaison, patrol, logistic support, antisubmarine and mine-sweeping, airmobile assault, ground attack, etc. In commercial field they are used for short haul transportation, rescue and disaster relief, geological exploration, aerial photography, aerial hoisting, aerial erecting of power transmission lines, salvage, scientific survey, etc. Nowadays in military field the antitank armed helicopters and carrier-based helicopters are being competitively developed in the world and in commercial field being developed are the general purpose helicopters which can be used for passengers / cargos transportation, medical air evacuation, fire prevention, agriculture and forestry work and oil field operation.

The Chinese helicopter industry began its career in the late-1950s. It experienced the development steps of licence production, copy design, independent development, acquisition of foreign technology and international cooperation. A total of seven types of light, medium and heavy helicopters have been developed and among them three helicopters, i.e. Z-5, Z-8 and Z-9, have been put into production. In total 588 helicopters have been delivered to the military Services and other operators. In addition they are also used for the foreign aid to other countries.

The road of the Chinese helicopter development was tortuous and there were some failures and setbacks. But a considerable foundation for further development has been laid by the hard work of the staff and workers in the aviation industry, and one helicopter design and research institute and two helicopter factories have been established. In addition there are also helicopter research organs in the China Aerodynamics Research and Development Center, the Flight Research Institute and NAI. A comparable complete helicopter system including R&D, design, production, flight test and education has been formed. The Chinese helicopter industry has had certain abilities in design and production of helicopters, their engines and transmission systems. It has become an important part of the Chinese aviation industry.

1. The Birth of Chinese First Generation Helicopter

In 1956 the Mi—4 helicopter production technique was introduced into China from the Soviet Union and it was decided that the licence production of the Mi—4 with the Chinese designation of Z—5 would be undertaken by the Harbin Aircraft Factory.

The Mi—4 was a single rotor medium helicopter of the world first generation helicopters. Its design began in 1951 in the Soviet Union and its development work successfully completed in 1953. The Harbin Aircraft Factory, after a large scale updating and expansion during the First Five—year Plan and the overhauls to a number of aircraft, had the basic conditions for the aircraft production.

The technical drawings and documents of the Mi—4 helicopter arrived at the factory in early 1958 and the prototype production of the Z—5 was begun while a part of drawings were still being released. The prototype production proceeded very fast. The static test was completed in December of the same year. The first indigenous Z—5 helicopter, piloted by test pilots Qian Guangyou and Liu Xingxiang, flew into the air on December 14, 4 months ahead of the schedule. In December 1959, the Z—5 was certificated for production.

But the prototype production of the Z—5 was adversely affected by the ideological trend of the " big leap forward" . The tendency to concentrate on production speed only and the insufficient selected production tooling caused serious problems in quality. These problems had to be solved and the process of prototype production had to be repeated from scratch in 1960. The updated drawings were released in March 1961 and the construction of 8,000 production tooling were completed in March 1962. On August 20, 1963 first high quality Z—5 made its first flight and on September 21 the Z—5 "passed the evaluation with excellent quality" and was formally accepted and put into mass production by the government.

The rotor is the critical component of the helicopter. The Soviet technical document specified that the blades of the rotor was made of wood and the criteria for the timber selection was very harsh. To find out qualified domestic timbers equivalent to the Soviet ones in characteristics a lot of work was done by the Harbin Aircraft Factory with the help from the Forestry Science Academy of the Forestry Ministry. The tests showed that it would waste astonishingly a lot of pine trees whose skin look like the fish scale to make the blades. Therefore, another timber, dragon spruce, was used instead, and the waste was reduced, but a considerable amount, approximately 20,000—30,000 cubic meters, precious timbers had to be cut down each year. To find suitable dragon spruce, workers had to climb a height of 3,700 m above the sea level and three comrades from the Forest Department of Sichuan province died in this connection.

The costly price of the three lives and enormous natural resource impelled the technical people to march towards another direction—the metal blades.

The advancement in technology is frequently combined with the complexity and difficulty. The metal blade was a major progress in the helicopter technology and it had been invented only for a short time in the world. The development of the metal blade at the Harbin Aircraft Factory began in May 1963. Hu Xichuan, chief engineer, organized the technical people to work on the project. With the help from the factories and institutes concerned they solved a number of technical problems one after another, such as the machining of blade spar, the fabrication and assembly of aluminum honeycomb structure and the making up of special adhesive, designed and produced 84 sets of assembly cramps and some special equipment such as a large autoclave which was 1.7 m in diameter and 11 m in length, and constructed the first metal honeycomb production line in the aviation industry. They completed the spar fatigue test whithin 16 months, in which a total of 570 million vibration cycles was recorded, and obtained very precious test data. A Z—5 equipped with indigenous metal rotor began its 8 days flight test on June 22, 1966 and it was showed by the flight test that the behavior of the metal rotor was better than that of the wooden rotor in all aspects. The metal rotor passed technical evaluation in July 1966 and since then wooden rotors have been completely substituted by metal ones.

The Harbin Aircraft Factory continuously improved its own manufacturing skills in the Z—5 prototype production. The qualified key components, i.e. swashplate, rotor hub and engine exhaust pipe, were manufactured and some critical tests, e.g. landing gear drop test, swashplate life test and thermal stress measurement of exhaust pipe at high temperature, were carried out so that the prototype production of the Z—5 was put on a reliable basis.

The Z—5 was a single four blades rotor helicopter powered by a domestic HS7 piston engine. A two—man flight deck was inside the nose of the fuselage. It could fly in the day and night and under complicated weather conditions. The helicopter was equipped for transportation, airborne landing and rescue. It can carry 11—15 paratroopers, or 1,200—1,550 kg cargos, or 8 noneffectives and 1 attendant. It can carry 1,300 kg sling load in hoisting work.

A total of 545 Z—5s were produced by 1979. Among them 437 were of basic version, 86 of passenger version, 7 of agriculture and forestry version, 13 of rescue version and 2 of aerial survey version. These helicopters played their roles in various fields such as in the national defence and national economy. During the counterattack wars at Zhenbao Island in northeast China, on the southwest border and at the Xisha Islands the Z—5s carried out military transportation missions very well. The Z—5s participated in rescues and disaster reliefs in Henan, Inner Mongolia grass land fires and Xingtai and Tangshan earthquakes. On January 10, 1983 the pilots of the People's Air Force flew the Z—5s to the Yellow River, and used the hovering technique to land on ice surface with single wheel and rescued 58 passengers in distress. In addition the Z—5s also took part in the survey of the halobios and the explosion test of the Chinese first atomic bomb. In a large scale military exercise in North China 35 Z—5s performed their missions. The Z—5s have been also sent to some countries as foreign aid.

Premier Zhou Enlai showed his deep concern to the helicopter development. He issued a number of instructions to the development of the domestic helicopters and for 7 times he was flown in a Z—5 helicopter to carry out his tours in the country, to accompany foreign guests in their visits to China, and to express sympathy and solicitude to the people of disaster areas. A great numbers of staff and workers of the helicopter industry were greatly encouraged and inspired by him.

Fig. 43   Zhou Enlai was flown in a Z—5 helicopter
to Xingtai earthquake disaster area

2. Studying and Exploring Different Types of Helicopters

On the basis of Z—5's licence production the study and exploration to a number of helicopters in different types began after 1965 and 5 types of light, medium and heavy helicopters were developed.

a. The 701 and Yan'an 2 Light Helicopters

The 701 helicopter was designed and produced after a foreign helicopter by the Harbin Aircraft Factory. It was powered by a domestic HS6C piston engine. A semi—rigid rotor with two adhesive blades was used. It had a welded frame fuselage. A ski type landing gear made it possible to land on a snow and ice surface or on a marshland. Its successful first flight was made in January 1970.

The Yan'an 2 is a light helicopter which was designed on the basis of the military Services' requirement. The initial design work was carried out in NPU but was transfered to NAI afterwards. It was powered by a HS6C piston engine which drove a three blades rotor. A tricycle type landing gear was incorporated. The takeoff weight was 1,150 kg, maximum flying speed 192 km / h and range 230 km.

The design of the Yan'an 2 began in 1965, the full scale static test was completed in 1967 and the successful first flight was made in 1975. A total of 3 helicopters were built.

The Yan'an 2 is the only light helicopter developed by universities. A complete development cycle from conceptual definition study through design, production, ground test and flight test was experienced and some key technical problems were solved. The original metal blades were changed into composite material ones in 1983. The measurement of the rotor blade inherent behavior and the analysis and test methods for the blade coupled vibration have reached an advanced level.

b. Medium Helicopter Z−6

Based on the military Services' conversion requirement and to make up Z−5's deficiency, e.g. insufficient power, poor performance at high temperature and high altitude and low payload, the Harbin Aircraft Factory began to develop Z−6 helicopter in 1966. The development work was transfered to a newly founded Helicopter Design and Research Institute in 1968. The Z−6 helicopter is powered by a WZ5 turboshaft engine which is installed at the top of the fuselage. It is a general purpose helicopter but is mainly used for airborne landing. It can also be converted to adapt different mission requirements.

On December 15, 1969 pilot Wang Peiming flew the Z−6 for its first time. Prior to the first flight he simulated the sudden shutdown of the engine and the autorotation for three times to ensure the successful first flight. The simulation not only tempered the pilot but also further verified the theoretical analysis.

In 1970 many provinces made great efforts to develop their own aviation industry. The development and the production of the Z−6 were thus transfered to Jiangsu province and Jiangxi province. A situation was formed in which three provinces with a common syllable "jiang" (i.e. Heilongjiang, Jiangsu and Jiangxi) were involved in the Z−6 program. Jiangsu province organized 7 cities, 6 prefectures and more than 470 factories to coordinately work on the Z−6 program. The Hongzhuang Machinery Factory in Changzhou was responsible for final assembly and a total of 11 Z−6s were successively constructed.

On August 7, 1972 a Z−6 crashed near Gongzhuling, Jilin province and all 6 people onboard including pilot Fu Guifa died in the accident. The accident was caused by the jam of a shaft inside the engine gear box. The disastrous and bloody lessons were learnt from the accident and 11 design improvements to the helicopter and the engine were made afterwards.

Several technical problems, e.g. severe vibration, overtemperature of the oil, over high idle engine power, jam between the rotor and the oil separator and insufficient tail rotor thrust were tackled by the technical people one after another in the development process. In 1977 the State Council and the Military Commission of CCCPC formally issued a design certificate to the Z-6 helicopter.

One significant step from the piston-engined helicopter to the tuboshaft-engined helicopter was taken in the Z-6 program, but unfortunately it was not able to be put into serial production because the improper engine selection and the less safety inherent in a single engine helicopter.

c. Heavy Helicopters Z-7 and Z-8

In the mid-1960s there existed medium helicopters which had been put into mass production and light helicopters which were being developed in the Chinese helicopter field. But the heavy helicopters still did not existed. Based on the needs of war preparation and training, the military Services requested to develop a heavy helicopter which could carry a reinforced platoon of troops. In 1969 the CAE decided that the design task of the heavy helicopter designated as Z-7 would be undertaken by the newly founded Helicopter Design and Research Institute and CAE owned factories and institutes would perform the main development activities.

The Z-7 design concept was to use two WZ5A turboshaft engines driving a six-blade rotor, and new designs of rotor hub and gear box. The remaining parts and components should be as common as possible with the ones in the Z-5 and Z-6. The design targets were as follows: maximum takeoff weight 14,400 kg, payload 3,500 kg, maximum speed 240 km / h, maximum range 350 km and service ceiling 6,000 m.

By May 1975 the manufacturing of 97 per cent of Z-7 parts and sub-assemblies had been completed, two airframes assembled and 90 per cent of vendor-furnished-equipment and components supplied. The full size static test was completed in 1979. But the limited national resource could not support at one time both the Z-7 and Z-8, two heavy helicopter development programmes and the Z-7 programme thus had to be terminated in 1979.

The Z-8 heavy helicopter was designed after a foreign helicopter. The MAI decided that the trial production of the Z-8 would be undertaken by the Jiangxi Helicopter Factory.

The Z-8 was powered by three engines which drove a six metal blades main rotor and a five metal blades tail rotor. Its fuselage was of a water-proof all-metal semi-monocoque structure. Maximum takeoff weight was 13,000 kg. It could be used for transportation, search and rescue, air early warning, anti-submarine and mine sweeping.

The Jiangxi Helicopter Factory began the Z-8 development in 1975. A design team of 150 people was formed and chief engineer Li Zaijian was concurrently appointed chief designer. Six large scale meetings for technological coordination and analysis were convened by the MAI and more than 130 units were mobilized to participate in the development programme. The development activities were performed in a fast speed. With the adjustment of national economy the Z-8 programme was suspended and the performance of many activities of the Z-8 programme were slowed down accordingly in 1979. To ensure the continuance of the Z-8 programme the Jiangxi Helicopter Factory adjusted its products in time and carried out a policy of "supporting the military development programmes with the profit earned in civil production" so that the income from the civil product sales could be used to supplement the limited Z−8 programme budget.

According to premier Zhao Ziyang's instruction the state of the Z−8 programme was positively changed from suspension to immediate performance in June 1984. On September 7 premier Zhao Ziyang visited the Jiangxi Helicopter Factory and watched the final assembly of the Z−8. In October the MAI appointed Su Min chief director of the Z−8 Programme On−site Office and Guo Zehong chief designer and decided that the Helicopter Design and Research Institute to be the unit of chief designer.

On December 11, 1985 a Z−8 slowly lifted off at Lumeng airfield in Jingdezhen, Jiangxi province. It hovered five meters above the ground surface and made 360−degree left and right turns, forward flight, side flight, backward flight and accelerated flight. The first flight ended with a success.

3. Marching Towards the Helicopter Manufacturing Techniques of the Eighties

Since the Third Plenary Session of the Eleventh Central Committee of the Chinese Communist Party the Chinese helicopter development has entered into a new era with the carrying out of the open policy and years of exploration. In this era the policy in the helicopter field is to meet the needs of national economy development, to enhance the foundation and raise the technical level of the helicopter industry considerably, to actively acquire foreign advanced technology and to march towards the helicopter manufacturing techniques of the eighties.

In 1980 China decided to acquire the manufacturing techniques of the French SA365N / NI Dauphin II helicopter and its engine based on a combination of trade with technology transfer, and to manufacture the helicopter under a Chinese designation Z−9. A licence agreement was signed on July 2 between

Fig.44   The Z−8 static test

Chinese CATIC and French companies Aerospatiale and Turbomeca and it was approved by Chinese and French governments on October 10.

The agreement specified that France would transfer its manufacturing rights of the

Dauphin helicopter and its engine to China for assembly of 50 helicopters and 100 engines. The Chinese factory was to assemble the helicopter with parts and components first supplied by France, then partly made in China and at last, by performing the activities divided into 6 phases, totally made in China and to master the advanced helicopter manufacturing techniques.

The Dauphin is a new general purpose helicopter developed by France in the late 1970s. It has advantages of light structure, heavy payload and high performance. Eighty per cent of exposed areas are covered by composite material. The rotor system consists 4 blades made from composite material and a starflex glassfibre / carbonfibre hub. An advanced "fenestron" type of ducted fan tail rotor is used to improve its safety in low altitude flying and landing. The large vertical fin uses an unsymmetrical airfoil so that less power is consumed in high speed cruise. The power plant is two Turbomeca Arriel IC turboshaft engines.

The Z—9 production was decided to be taken place at following places: the airframe would be produced at Harbin Aircraft Factory, the engines at the Zhuzhou Aero—engine Company, the transmission system at the Harbin Engine Factory and the hubs and the tail rotor blades at Baoding Propeller Factory.

From Z—5 to Z—9 the manufacturing technique has qualitatively advanced from the state of the art of the fifties to the one of the eighties. Accordingly the factories and institutes concerned, such as the Harbin Aircraft Factory, have been technically reformed. In the area of machining the high precision general purpose and special purpose machines have been added. As to the welding, equipment have been supplemented for electron beam welding, friction butt welding and metal skin welding. In the area of heat treatment the equipment for vacum heat treatment and controlled atmosphere heat treatment have been added and some new techniques such as the aluminium—chronium metallzing, shot peen,etc. have been mastered. In the area of surface treatment new production lines have been set up and the qualities of water and chemicals have been upgraded. In the area of composite materials the modern factory buildings including the ones in which the air conditioners can be automatically controlled have been constructed. In other areas such as the measurement, inspection and test, high precision equipment have also been added and new methods used. According to the French Aerospatiale rule the critical aircraft components can be installed on to the aircraft for flight only after they have been certificated by fatigue test, therefore, several factories have set up fatigue test facilities. To test key components such as the rotor and the gear box, the dynamic balancing test rigs and functional test rigs have also been set up.

To improve the technical quality of the staff and workers involved in the helicopter production technical training has been carried out in all factories concerned. As an example the Harbin Aircraft Factory alone has run 25 training courses and has trained more than 1,200 person—times. More than 100 persons have been to France either for training or for technical visit.

In the Z—9 trial production the technical people and workers were organized to begin with the study of technical data and to carry out their activities step by step according to the scientific procedures so that the difficulties caused by the frequent changes to the design drawings by French and the late supplies of the French components were overcome, the qualified helicopters were produced and the small scale production capability was formed. A total of 31 Z−9s had been produced by the end of 1986 and they had been delivered to the Air Force, Navy, CAAC and the Chinese Ocean Helicopter company. They have begun to play their roles in the military Services' training, the exploitation of offshore oilfields and the general aviation services.

Since the production of first generation helicopter Z−5, a total of 6 types have been developed but four of them did not go into production. The reasons for that were many−sided, such as the adverse affect of the "great cultural revolution", the mistakes in the work such as the insufficient systematic study to the domestic and foreign markets and hastily launching and cancelling of development programmes, and the ignorance to the special laws of the helicopter development. The helicopter is different from conventional aircraft and has its own specialities: its flight speed is lower but the performed flight states are much more complicated; it requires less structural strength but its requirement to the dynamic components is much more severe. To proceed steadily in the helicopter field the necessary specific infrastructures must be constructed and advanced R&D must also be carried out.

The development of the helicopter depends upon market demand. With the growth of national economy the prospects of the Chinese helicopter industry will be brilliant. The foreseen direction of the helicopter development is to improve the reliability, maintainability and availability on the technology basis of the conventional rotor aircraft and to develop various derivative helicopters which will use same lift system, same power plant system and approximately same airframes and will be in same class but will have different uses to satisfy different needs in various geographical environments and climatic conditions.

Section 3   Development of Light Aircraft

The word "aircraft" is a common name of all the vehicles which can perform the controllable flight in the atmosphere. The Chinese aviation industry has not only developed and produced various kinds and types of airplanes and helicopters but also studied and developed some light aircraft including mainly the microlight aircraft, hot balloons, airships, etc.

1.   The Rising of Microlight Aircraft

The microlight aircraft is an aircraft between the modern light airplane and the powered hang glider and it first rose in the United States of America in the mid−1970s. A simple hang glider was installed with a small size piston engine and later with landing gear, elevator and aileron etc.. The earliest microlight aircraft thus came into being. At the beginning it was mainly used for personal sport and recreational activities but it has gradually evolved into a vehicle which can be used for a variety of purposes.

The development of the microlight aircraft in China began with the parasol aircraft. In the mid—1970s the Shenyang Aircraft Factory and Shenyang Air Sports School developed multi—seat and single seat parasol aircraft respectively and several flight tests were made. In June 1979 Hu Jizhong, an engineer, and some other people at BIAA developed a microlight parasol aircraft designated as Mifeng (Honeybee)—1. It was a radio remotely controlled aircraft and its flying weight was 100 kg. Its flight test was made at Tongxian airfield, Beijing. In 1982 Hu Jizhong and his colleagues began to develop a single seat Microlight aircraft Mifeng—2. The design was defined on the basis of abundant wind tunnel tests, and static test and flight test were carried out after the aircraft was made available, therefore, good flying quality was resulted.

The Mifeng—3 was a two—seat microlight aircraft developed on the basis of the Mifeng—2. Its first flight was made in July 1983. It could carry a payload of 70—100 kg after removal of aft seat.

Since 1982 a series of microlight and light aircraft have been successively developed at the Shijiazhuang Aircraft Factory. They are the microlight aircraft of single seat Qingting (dragonfly)—5, side—by—side two—seat Qingting—5A and tandem—seat Qingting—5B and the light aircraft of single seat Qingting—6 and two—seat Qingting—6A. The wind tunnel test, static test and performance flight test were carried out during their development and, therefore, the aircraft performance conformed to the design target. All the Qingting versions aforementioned were technically certificated.

The Chinese Water—based Aircraft Design and Researth Institute also developed an agricultural aircraft A1 and it successfully flew for its first time in May 1984.

Except the Qingting—6 which was of an aluminium alloy riveting structure, the others were generally the same in their structures. They were either high—wing monoplanes or biplanes with the tapered tailplanes, open or partly—inclosed cockpits, main frames of metal tubes, Dacron covered wings and tails, the engines mounted at a place behind and above the cockpit and the pusher propellers.

The purpose to develop the microlight aircraft in China was to serve the development of national economy, therefore it was decided in the design concept selection that the aircraft had to be in compliance with the national conditions in China and to be an aircraft which should be a simple and general purpose aircraft and could be bought and operated by agricultural, forest, animal husbandry and other units themselves. The operational tests had been carried out during the development and good result achieved.

On August 13, 1983 a Mifeng—3 carried out an ultra—low—density pesticide spray test on the Northen Suburb Farm, Beijing and the purpose of the spray was to protect the rice against locusts. The aircraft was equipped with a Type 3WQ—1 sprayer and 60 kg liquid pesticide was carried. The effective spraying width was bigger than 30 m, the pesticide of 150—200 millilitres per mu was sprayed and the killing rate of the locusts reached 92 per cent. From October 13 to November 4 of the same year another pesticide spray test to kill pine moths was carried out on a forestry farm in Lishui county, Jiangsu province. The forestry farm was located in a hilly land with complicated topography of hills and valleys and the Mifeng—3 was able to follow the terrain in its operation. The effective spray width was 20—30 m, the flying speed in its operation 20 m / sec, the operation area 6,000 mus and the killing rate over 90 per cent.

In the development of the microlight aircraft the international cooperation has been seeked and the foreign advanced technology acquired. So far the Q2 and AD—100 aircraft have been produced.

The Q2 was designed by the Quickie Aircraft Corporation of the U.S.A. and was manufactured and assembled by the Shanghai Aircraft Factory. It had a unique structure and looked like a dolphin. It was an aircraft of canard configuration. The foreplane was mounted low on forward fuselage and in front of the wing. Almost all the airframe was made of reinforced glassfibre plastic. The assembly of first Q2 aircraft was completed in June 1983 and the flight test was made by a fully authorized designated test pilot. The flight test proved that main aircraft performances and quality were in compliance with the American standard.

The AD—100 was a single—seat microlight aircraft co—developed by NAI and an American company,the Adaso,Inc. All the design and development work were undertaken by NAI. It was of a canard configuration with a fully enclosed cockpit and the airframe was made of glassfibre sandwich structure. An onboard parachute could be deployed to ensure safe landing of both the aircraft and the pilot in an emergency. The successful flight test of the AD—100 aircraft was taken place at Tushan airfield, Nanjing on August 20, 1985. The aircraft can be easily dismantled for transportation and reassembled for flight. Being dismantled, the whole aircraft could be put into a special trailer which can be towed either by a car or by a mini bus.

To the rise of the microlight aircraft development in China a great deal of attention was paid by the people concerned in China and in foreign countries. During the Guangzhou Export Commodities Fair in the fall 1983, visitors from the USA, UK and Hong Kong ordered 107 microlight aircraft. In our country, people in agriculture, forestry, geology and sport showed their great interest in these aircraft. In addition some village organizations and even some individual farmers and herdsmen also showed their interests in constructing their own airstrips and buying their own airplanes. To meet the needs of national economy development and to further develop the microlight aircraft the MAI decided to bring the microlight aircraft development into line with the state plan, to strengthen the leadership and to increase the number of technical people. In addition, the Shijiazhuang Aircraft Factory and BIAA had been chosen to specilize in mass production of the existing microlight aircraft and in development of new ones.

2. The Hot—air Balloons

The hot—air balloon is a powerless and lighter—than—air aircraft and it consists of an envelope and a basket suspended underneath the envelope. Air is heated by a burner mounted on the basket and the heated lighter air fills the envelope and produces the float force so as to lift the balloon into the air.

The hot-air balloon is the earlist manned aircraft studied by mankind. It was with the hot-air balloon that the first human flight in the air was made by a French man in 1783. Hot-air balloons were no longer highly thought of after the appearances of hydrogen-filled and helium-filled balloons. More than one century had passed when it cameback in the late 1950s. The modern hot-balloon was developed by Americans, which was made of man-made fibres and used the propane as its fuel to heat the air. The hot-air balloon is so easy to operate that the flying technique can be mastered only after a short period of training. It is also safe and reliable in operation, convenient in maintenance, low cost in production and easy to handle. There are more than 30 countries in the world including U.S.A., Japan and France where the hot-air balloons are being used. The hot-air balloons are used not only for sports, but also aerial photography, sightseeing and advertising.

The development of the hot-air balloons in China began in the 1980s. Now two models, i.e. RQ7-1 and HGQ-1, have been certificated.

The RQ7-1 hot-air balloon was developed by the Hubei Parachute Factory. The envelope with volume of 2,160 cubic meters was made of 18 gores fabric and each gore with area of bigger than 20 square meters and each gore was made from 16 pieces fabric. This first Chinese manned hot-air balloon made its successful first tethered flight on January 30, 1985 in Beijing and flew across the Yangtze River in Wuhan on March 30 of the same year.

The HGQ-1 hot-air balloon was designed and produced by the Nanjing Parachute Factory. It had the basically same structure with the RQ7-1. It was 18 m in diameter, 20 m in height, 2,180 cubic meters in volume and 210 kg in weight. The lift of the balloon reached 790 kg and the payload was 580 kg. Its rate of climb was 5 m / sec. A total of six crew members could be carried. Its successful first flight took place in Nanjing in the spring of 1985. It made its free flight over the ancient Grand Canal in Yangzhou in April and the flight distance reached more than 10 km. In November of the same year it was used to measure the fog density at the altitude of 200 m and more over the Hefei airport to supply exact meteorological data to the airport. A manned flight demonstration was also made at the Fourth Asia and Pacific Area Trade Fair held in Beijing in the same month.

Although the development of the hot-air balloons in China was late but they began at a high technical level. During their development the international standards were referenced and a number of stringent tests were carried out. Among these tests were the normal tethered flight, free flight, horizontal cruise, climb as well as landing with maxium load in cold weather from high altitude.

3. Airship

Airship is a form of mechanically driven and lighter-than-air aircraft having a means of controlling the direction of its motion. It generally consists of a streamlined hull, a gondola, a tail unit and a power plant. So far the history of the airship has been more than 100 years since it appeared as the earlist manned and powered aircraft. It was used for military missions and commercial purposes in its early days but later its development was slowed down because of the appearance of airplanes. Since the 1970s the airship has comeback due to the progress in science and technology. A number of countries have begun to develop the modern airships on a new technical basis. Some of them will be used for offshore oil exploitation and the others will be used for ultra—heavy vertical lift applications.

The first Chinese airship was the Mifeng—6 designed and produced by BIAA. It was 30 m long and 17 m high. The envelope volume was 2,500 cubic meters. Its maximum flying speed was 20 km / h and flying altitude 3,000 m. There were 4 seats inside the gondala and its payload was 300 kg. The envelope was made of nylon, which could be folded and put into a big cloth bag after flight for easy transtortation by a truck.

The Mifeng—6 produced lift by heating the air inside the envelope and, hence, had VTOL capability. It was driven forward by engine thrust and its motion was controlled by control surfaces. It had the advantages of low cost, limited landing site and convenient operation but it was poor in withstanding storm. The hot—air airship could find its applications in aerial photography, aerial sightseeing, aerial remote sensing, air transportation in mountain area, vertically lifting in industry, aerial rescue and advertising. From July to August 1986 a Mifeng—6 airship was used to erect a 500,000 volt high voltage power transmission line which connected the Gezhouba power station and cities of Changde and Zhuzhou in Hunan province. Three sections of the power transmission line in the areas of numerous dangerously steep mountain peaks and valleys were successfully erected. Erecting power transmission line by the airship not only overcame the difficulty but also found a new way for power line erecting and made the first step towards the hot—air airship practical application.

The Chinese aviation industry has passed its 35th anniversary and its achievement in the aircraft development has been acknowledged worldwide. During the 35 years the rich experience in successes have been obtained as well as the lessons in failures. Because real knowledge comes from practice, these experience and lessons will certainly serve as valuable references to the further development of the Chinese aviation industry.

The scientific aircraft development procedure must be stringently followed. Based on experience accumulated in the past 30 years and more the Chinese aviation industry has sumed up a complete development procedure in the area of military aircraft. According to the procedure the development process of the military aircraft is divided into the following five phases: the study of operational requirement and feasibility in technology and cost; the conceptual definition study; the preliminary and detailed designs and mockup review; the prototype production and design certification; and the trial—operation and production certification. These five phases can also be used as a reference to the development of commercial airplanes. None of these five phases can be bypassed or surpassed because they are the integral parts of the development procedure. Special emphasis should be given to the first and second phases, i.e. the study of operational requirement and the feasibility in technology and cost and the conceptual definition study because they are the important prerequisite and the starting

Commercial Aircraft, Engines

65. Y7-100 passenger plane

66. Y7-100 taking off

67. Li Peng, Hu Qili and Yao Yilin visiting Chinese made aeroplanes.
    They took a ride aboard a Y7-100 at the end of their visit

68. Y7-100 passenger cabin

69. The Chinese made commercial aeroplanes exhibition

70. Y-8 medium transport aircraft

71. Y-8 night operation

72. A "Black Hawk" helicopter to be carried by a Y-8

73. A "Black Hawk" being pushed into a Y-8

74. A Y-8 at Lhasa

75. Y-8 cockpit

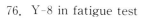

76. Y-8 in fatigue test

77. NC machining shop of an engine factory

78. A WJ6 engine being assembled

79. WS9 engine

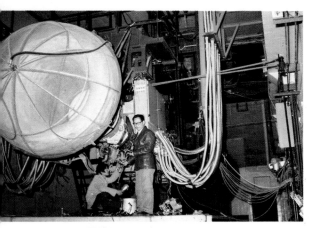

80. WS9 test rig

81. A WS9 engine in England for
altitude assessment running

You might as well count the number of times an aircraft takes off under Pratt power.

It happens almost every two seco[...]
Somewhere in the world another airc[...]
powers up with Pratt & Whitney engi[...]
Commercial airliners to military aircraf[...]
general aviation aircraft — even into sp[...]
We have the biggest engine fleet in [...]
skies.

Our achievements in China are equally impressive. We supply the power for air, and and sea. We sponsor technical exchanges, lectures and scholarships. China helps manufacture our parts. We are truly a partner in China's aviation development.

UNITED TECHNOLOGIES PRATT & WHITNEY

82. Y-10 big passenger plane

83. A maintenance hanger with a span of 72 meters

84. A Y-12 II passenger plane in flight

85. Y-12 II passenger plane

86. A Y-11 operating over the mountains

87. A Y-5 operating over a forest

88. A Mifeng 3 in flight

89. An old peasent aboard a
    Mifeng 2 microlight aircraft

90. Qingting 5 flying
    in formation

91. A canard in flight

92. A Qingting 6 in flight

93. A hot air balloon at Asia-Pacific
International Trade Fair

94. A Mifeng 6 airship erecting power transmission lines at
Gezhouba

95. Sports-3B parachute

96. Parachuting demonstration

97. A Chinese parachuting champion using a Chinese made parachute at the parachuting championship contest in France

point to the success of the later aircraft development. When an aircraft development programme is going to be launched a thorough study must first be made to its missions, potential opponents, operations, operational requirement as well as its alternative general configurations, engines and major airborne equipment. To make a technical decision, the tradeoffs between the requirement and the possibility, between the advanced technology and cost must be made. A thorough understanding of the present status and trend of the similar aircraft in the world and an investigation into the actual conditions in China are thus required. Based on the understanding and the investigation several different proposals should be made. After repeated comparisons and tradeoff studies a design concept of the new aircraft can be correctly defined.

Advanced R&D must be emphasized so that a proper technical base can be laid. Advanced R&D is the precursor and basis of the aircraft development. The development of new generation aircraft should not only inherit the proven technology but also incorporate some innovations. The innovations can be the breakthroughs and the applications of the achievement in basic research, or the ingenious combinations of the achievement in applied research, or the direct application of the advanced R&D achievement. In one word the innovations are related to advanced R&D in one way or another. If the advanced R&D has not been carried out the design activities can only be proceeded blindly and the development programme will fall into the following two cases: the aircraft developed will not incorporate any innovations and it will only mark time on a low technical level; or the technology used at the beginning of the design is not low but the development cycle will be prolonged, the development activities may be frequently interrupted by the unsolved key technical problems and sometimes the designers have to initiate their designs from the beginning. In the latter case the aircraft will be out-of-date when it is developed. In order to prevent the happening of the aforementioned cases advanced R&D must be strengthened. Subjects of the advanced R&D should be properly determined according to the world aircraft development trend, the Chinese strategy and policy, state of the art and financial resources so that the limited manpower and material resources can be spent at the most necessary and the most important places.

Scientific experiment must be fully conducted. The correctness of the aircraft design concept needs to be finally checked by the production and operation practices, but the design concept itself must be determined on the basis of a full range of tests to avoid any possible major deficiencies occured in the prototype production. During the prototype production another series of tests including the single equipment function test, individual system function test and the integrated function test have to be conducted. These tests should not only be fully carried out but also be conducted in simulated conditions which are as similar as the real conditions. To well carry out these tests the test methods and means must be gradually set up, improved and complemented so that they can meet the needs of the advanced aircraft development programmes.

The system engineering management must be put into practice. The aircraft development is a system engineering which embodies the achievements of modern science and technology and involves numerous disciplines and complicated technologies. The quality of development activities administration and the technical management directly affects the course of the aircraft development. The implementation of the system engineering management with the four aircraft development programmes, i.e. J−8Ⅱ, J−7Ⅲ, JJ−7 and Z−8, since the 1980s has showed that it enables the overall management, the centralized leadership, unified planning and coordination, the continuance in administration and management from design through tests, prototype production and flight test and, therefore, ensures the smooth progress of the aircraft development.

The Chinese aircraft industry, which is going to be mature, will use its historical experience accumulated in the past aircraft development programmes to catch up with the world advanced level and to achieve further and greater development.

PART THREE

Aircraft is the crystalization of modern science and technology. In addition to airframe, it consists of aeroengine, airborne equipment and weaponry. Since the founding of the aviation industry of China, relatively independent industrial departments of aircraft, aeroengine, airborne equipment and tactical missile were seperately established. They have their own respective R & D and production capabilities in considerable sizes and constitute the system of the Chinese aviation industry.

Over the past thirty and more years, the Chinese aeroengine, airborne equipment and tactical missile industries also evolved from repair to copy or licence production, product improvement and then development of new products on our own. To meet the needs of aircraft, a great variety of products with good performance were developed, produced in large quantity, delivered to the services of PLA and exported a certain amount. These specialized industrial departments gradually established a wide range of experiment and test facilities and other means and their research and design capabilities were increasingly enhanced.

Chapter VII   The Development of Aeroengines

Section 1   The "Heart" of the Aeroplane——Aeroengines

The function of an aeroengine is to provide necessary power to aircraft for flight. The flight history of mankind is closely related to the development of the flight power. And it was the birth of the internal combustion engine that made the powered, controllable, continuously flyable aircraft possible; the existence of the jet engine realized the supersonic flight; the tremendous thrust of the giant rocket engine brought man into space.

The "heart" of the aeroplane is of course the engine, and it plays the most important role. Its performance and structure has a direct influence on the tactical and technical performance, operational reliability and economy of an aeroplane. Normally, aircraft engines fall into categories of: piston engine, turbojet engine (turbojet), turbofan engine (turbofan), turbopropeller engine (turboprop) and turboshaft engine (turboshaft). As the aircraft engine has to operate for long hours repeatedly under high temperature, high pressure, high rotation speed and heavy load conditions, it must be of light weight, compactly structured, safe, reliable, and economical. Therefore the design must be carefully worked out, manufacturing must be precise and materials and vendor-furnished accessories must be of good quality, to make it a product of high technology and high additional value. Into its development are incorporated results of vast R&D in specialised technologies. Therefore the R&D of an aeroengine must be independent and in advance of that of the aircraft and under a stable development plan and a powerful leadership. Thus, nowadays in the world only a few industrially developed countries, such as the United States, the Soviet Union, the United Kingdom and France, are able to undertake the R &D for advanced aeroengines independently.

Its development has gone through three stages; initially, repair and overhaul, mastery of the production technology and research and development of new type aeroengines.

Starting with repair: In 1951, three aircraft engine repair factories were set up in Harbin, Shenyang and Zhuzhou. In the same year, they repaired and overhauled 337 engines of 4 types used on trainer, fighter and bomber aircraft. The establishment of these three factories laid a foundation for the development of China's aeroengine industry.

Mastery of the production technology: From the first half of 1952, through the manufacture of spare parts for repair and overhaul, these factories gradually increased their capability of production, which created the necessary conditions for the transition to manufacture of the complete engines. Starting from 1953, the two factories in Zhuzhou and Shenyang were expanded or newly established consecutively and the licence production of

M—11FR and WP5 aeroengines were successfully completed in 1954 and 1956 respectively. In 1957, the Harbin Engine Factory also succeeded in the licence production of Ash—21 engines. Production of these engines marked a significant phase in China's mastery of production technology for aeroengines.

R&D for new aeroengines: During the latter part of the First Five—year Plan, on the one hand the aeroengine industry had successfully established new factories in inland China, expanded production scales, undertaken the production of supersonic aircraft engines and high thrust aeroengines, and worked hard to improve its manufacturing technical levels. In the meantime, however, the first aeroengine design office (the predecessor of the Shenyang Aeroengine Research and Design Institute) was born in Shenyang. Other factories also began to establish their own product design offices. Beginning in the mid 1960s, some research and design institutes were successively established in Sichuan, Zhuzhou and Wuxi. Based on the mastering of production technology, through the ways of troubleshooting, life extension and modification programs for the existing engines and doing applied research, some engineering development programmes were launched and various types of engines successfully developed to power the trainer, fighter, attack aircraft, helicopter, transport and drone. With the accumulation in practical experiences, the expansion in test facilities and the progress in advanced R&D, the R&D capability of the Chinese aeroengine industry is continuously increasing.

It was during the development of the aircraft engine manufacture, that the primary foundation for the manufacturing technology of rocket engines became apparent. In the middle and later part of 1950s, one aircraft engine overhaul factory turned into a liquid propellant rocket engine manufacturer developing and producing large and medium liquid propellant rocket engines. In 1965, this factory and its tasks were assigned to the 7th Ministry of Machine Building. The development and production of the solid rocket engines for air—to—air missiles was undertaken by the Zhuzhou Aeroengine Factory (ZEF).

In the past thirty and more years, China's aeroengine industry has gained great achievements.

A number of factories and institutes have been established: 8 aeroengine manufacture bases, 4 research institutes and design institutes, and 5 factory—managed design institutes located all over the country. A strong and capable technical contingent has been formed including more than 10,000 engineers and technicians.

A total of about 27,000 engines in 30 types have been repaired or overhauled, among them more than 4,000 engines were overhauled during the Korean War. It provided the timely support for the operation and training of the Air Force.

Some 48,000 engines and a huge amount of spare parts in 25 types have been manufactured and delivered mainly for the Air Force and Navy, with 756 engines in 10 types for CAAC and some engines for foreign assistance and export.

Nine types of solid and liquid rocket engines for air—to—air, ground—to—air, ground—to—ground, and coast defence missiles have been manufactured.

About 40 improved versions and new types of engines have been developed and a substantial part of them put into series production for updating the equipments of the Services.

China's aeroengine industry has reached a stage where it has a good solid foundation. It's future plans are to learn from past experiences, adhere to the policy of "stand on our own feet", to strengthen international technology exchanges and improve the capabilities currently held in the research and design fields. The industry aspires to become, as quickly as possible, ranked among the world's leading and advanced aeroengine industries.

Section 2　Manufacture of the Piston Aeroengine

The piston engine is an internal combustion engine using gas to push the piston for the reciprocating movement and then through the linkage and crankshaft to turn it into the rotating movement of the shaft for driving the aircraft propeller or helicopter rotor. The piston engine was adopted for the aircraft industry at the beginning of the 20th century and went to its peak in the 1940s, with its power increasing from several dozens of kW to about 3,000 kW (4,000 hp). After World War II the piston engines were gradually substituted by gas turbine engines in military and large civil aeroplanes. The small piston engine, however, is more economical than the gas turbine engine, and therefore is still widely used in light and low speed transport aeroplanes, trainers, and, in particular, aircraft with specialized functions such as animal husbandry, agriculture, forestry, geographical survey, mapping and sports.

In the early 1950s, all of China's trainers, transports and bombers were powered by piston engines. Therefore, the production, modification and development of China's aeroengines started with the piston engines and in the 1960s a series of piston engines was formed.

1.　The Emerging of New China's First Aeroengine

On October 25, 1954, Chairman Mao Zedong of the Central People's Government issued a praise and encouragement letter to the Zhuzhou Aeroengine Factory to congratulate the successful licence production of new China's first batch of M−11FR aeroengines in that factory. It pointed out: "This is a good beginning for both the establishment of our country's aircraft industry and the strengthening of our national defence."

The M−11FR was produced according to technical documents provided by the Soviet Union. It was a 5 cylinder, radial, air−cooled piston engine with a take−off rating of 118 kW (160 hp) and a weight of 180 kg and fitted to the Yak−18 primary trainer. The M−11FR was the first aeroengine put into production by new China.

In Old China the industrial basis was particularly poor and it was under the guideline of "first overhaul and then manufacture" that the Zhuzhou Aeroengine Factory, which had previously been a shell manufacturer, actively set out to create the necessary conditions for manufacture of aeroengines.

When the factory was established in 1951, there were approximately 1,000 employees, none of whom had experience in the aeroengine industry. The factory had less than 100 sets of equipment, and those held were particularly old and of poor quality. The Government gave active support in manpower, materials and finance and the Soviet Union provided technical assistance. With a high conscientiousness of glory and duty for the construction of their Motherland's aircraft industry, the cadres, technicians and workers studied, overcame hardships and difficulties, and in that same year achieved the overhaul of 54 M—11FR engines. By the end of 1952 the factory had mastered the basic techniques of engine overhaul.

In order to solve the problems associated with the shortage of the imported spare parts necessary for overhaul, the factory started to make spare parts — both basic and complex — in 1952. In 1953, they produced piston rings, gear type oil pumps, casing rear covers and cylinders etc. This independent production of spare parts not only met the engine overhaul requirements of the factory, but also gave experience in manufacturing technologies. The production of cylinders with complex geometry and high quality requirements was a relatively all — round practice for the factory from the production preparation and blank casting, to the machining and assembly. The chlorinated refinement of the aluminium alloy and the casting of cylinder heads with cooling fins were the new manufacturing technologies at that time in China. The assembly of the cylinder head and barrel with interference fit, the boring of hyperbolas into

Fig.45　Wang Xiping at the Zhuzhou
Aeroengine Factory

the inner face of the cylinder barrel and the multicutter cutting of the cooling fins were all the technical challenges. Through the joint efforts of leaders, engineers and workers, these critical technical problems were solved one by one. Rong Ke, a casting expert, joined the team to tackle the key problem, and Zhou Yousheng, an engineer, played an important role.

To April 1954, the factory overhauled 575 M—11FR engines, and manufactured 322 kinds of parts and components, which accounted for 55% of the total parts and components of the engine. The employees were doubled and the metal cutting equipment and floor area increased by 3—5 times. Through the overhaul of the M—11FR engine and the manufacture of its spare parts the understanding to the structure and performance of the engine was deepened, the experiences in the parts and components manufacture and the engine assembly and test accumulated, and the production management improved. All these improvements laid down a good foundation for the licence production of complete engines.

In order to strengthen the leadership of the factory and speed up the licence production of the engine, Niu Yingguan, the Vice—Governor of Jiangxi Province, was assigned to be the director and Party secretary of the ZEF in January 1954.

In March, the Aviation Industry Bureau (AIB) issued a formal task for the trial production of M—11FR, and moved up the completed time from the National Day (October 1) 1955 to September 1954. Soon after, the Deputy Director of the AIB, You Jiang led a working team to the factory to provide assistance on the spot. To guarantee the licence production of the new engine on schedule, the factory took several measures: it formed a New Engine Licence Production Commanding System headed by chief engineer Yang Naichang; set up a production technical management responsibility system by the chief manufacturing process engineer, chief metallurgical engineer, chief production supporting engineer and chief production controller; strengthened the product quality inspection system; promoted and appointed engineering university graduates to be the heads of technical departments and some workshops; in the meantime, created a well—conceived plan for technical measures, in order for the whole factory to concentrate on the task, define the responsibility, coordinate the activities and achieve high efficiency and good quality. To deal with the problem associated with the need of a large amount of toolings for the production and the insufficient manufacturing capabilities, the factory set up a new tool room to increase the capability, and then appropriately reduced the number of toolings, and concentrated its efforts on the 1,320 most necessary toolings and equipments for the production. Thus in less than 3 months, all tasks were successfully finished. During this period, the parts production started while teams were organized to tackle the key technical problems. The first 3 M—11FR engines were finally assembled in July 1954 and the state acceptance tests were smoothly completed in August. On September 18 the Revolutionary Military Committee of the Central People's Government issued the approval to turn this engine into series production.

Thus, the aeroengine industry completed the transition from repair to manufacture in only 3 years after its start. That finished the long history of inability to make aeroengines in China.

2. HS5 Engine

In order to meet the requirement of the Y—5 multi—role aeroplane, ZEF started to produce HS5 engines in September 1956. These engines were manufactured after the Russian designated Ash—62IR with documents provided by the Soviet Union. It was a 9 cylinder, single row, radial, air—cooled piston engine with a single speed supercharger and a flat take off rating of 753 kW (1,000 hp) up to 1,500 m.

This engine was bigger than M—11FR, and also more complicated. The factory made full use of the production conditions for M—11FR engines and only added a few machine tools. According to the Russian technical documents, it was required to use large internal grinding machines and planetary gear thread milling machines for vital tasks such as the boring of the inner hole of the intermediate casing, the grinding of the hyperbola profile of the cylinder barrel's inner face and the milling of the sawtooth thread of the cylinder head. But the factory modified the conventional lathe and grinding machine to solve the problem.

The manufacture of the exhaust valve was a critical technology. The exhaust valve is hollow, filled with metal sodium of 40—60% of its volume and sealed. During the operation, the metal sodium vaporizes and sucks the heat, and then, through a guide sleeve, transfers it to the cylinder head. This reduces the temperature of the exhaust valve for extending its operational life. To make the exhaust valve, the following processes were needed: cutting of the hollow cavity, rolling of the rod, filling the sodium and sealing, chamfer of the mushroom head and coating of stellite alloy on the head of the value rod for wear—resistance corrosion—resistance. These processes were all highly difficult techniques and the filling of sodium and sealing was risky as explosion could occur. Jiang Xichung, the 8th grade skilled worker, and his colleagues actively studied and explored, and they worked together to solve the problems one by one. The exhaust valves made by this factory were not only used by HS5 engine but also satisfied the need for other types of engines.

Fig.46　New China's first aeroengine M—11FR

The production for HS5 engine was successfully completed in June 1958. In 1986, more than 2,600 engines were built, and out of them 402 were used for CAAC's Y—5 and Li—2 aeroplanes.

3.　HS6 Engine and Its Modifications

In 1957, China started to design its primary trainer, the CJ—6. Initially, it was decided to use Czechoslovakia's Doris—B piston engine as the powerplant. As the ordered engines could not be delivered in time, it was then decided to use our home—made M—11FR engine instead. As the two types of engines could not meet the need of the aeroplane, it was finally decided to adopt HS6 engines.

HS6 was a one row, radial, 9 cylinder, air cooled piston engine manufactured according to Russian AI—14R engine's documents. It was light weight with a good performance and its take off power was 191 kW (260 hp) which equalled 163% of the M—11FR's. ZEF commenced production in August 1960. Soon after the Soviet government ended the contract. All the staff members and workers of the factory relied on their own efforts and worked harder, and constantly improved their skills. With the efforts in one year and 9 months, they achieved the success of the licence production of HS6 engines in June 1962. They produced about 700 engines in total.

The performance of the CJ—6 using the HS6 engine was greater than that of the CJ—5. Users of the aircraft gave it high praise, but during flight above 2,000 m it lost much of its height, reflecting an insufficient thrust of the engine at high altitude.

In order to improve the aeroplane's performance and expand the operation range for training, at the beginning of 1963, the factory started to carry out modification designs on the HS6 engine to increase its rated power. The modifications mainly involved the redesigns of some 12 components including the cylinder, crankshaft, and supercharger, in order to increase the compression ratio in the cylinder, increase the r.p.m. of the crank at rated condition and increase the gear ratio of the supercharger. The rated power increased from 162 kW (220 hp) to 199 kW (270 hp) and the take off power from 191 kW (260 hp) to 210 kW (285 hp), gaining 23% and 10% respectively. The 600 hour bench test was carried out in October 1963 and the expected results reached. In 1964, a measure was undertaken by cutting the relief slot on the interface between the casing and the cylinder, that solved the major problem of the cracks on the intermediate casing. The substantial tests on the ground and in the air passed smoothly. In December 1965, it was approved for series production and designated as HS6A. The CJ—6 aeroplane with modified HS6A engine was much better: maximum level flight speed increased by 10 km, climb time reduced about 30%, service ceiling increased by more than 1,000 m and a substantial improvement in the height loss during vertical flight and aerobatics. HS6A engine won the first class award for the national industrial products in 1964. Until 1986, some 3,000 engines were built.

In 1975, in order to meet the requirement for Y—11 aeroplane the factory further modified the engine and renamed it the HS6D. By increasing the r.p.m., and strengthening the reduction gears, the engine's take off power increased to 220 kW (300 hp). In August 1980, the engine passed the ground test. It was a successful project.

The factory then further modified the engine as the HS6E. They modified or redesigned 36 parts such as the exhaust valve and reduction gears and further increased the compression ratio. The engine power was raised to 257 kW (350 hp) meaning it could now be installed on a new agriculture aeroplane.

Prior to that, the factory developed the HS6B engine in 1966 to improve the high altitude performance by adding a turbo—supercharger. From 1963 to 1970, the factory successfully modified and designed the HS6C for light helicopters. It was then used on China's "701" and "Yan'an Ⅱ" helicopters. The performance was good.

HS6 engine series are good quality, inexpensive, small piston engines modified by China. They have gained much praise for their applications to different aeroplanes.

4. HS7 Engine

The HS7 engine was made by Harbin Aeroengine Factory (HEF) using technical documents of Ash—82V engine provided by the Soviet Union. It was a large radial air—cooled piston engine with 14 cylinders in two rows and a two speed supercharger. Its take off power was 1,250 kW (1,700 hp) and its weight 1,070 kg. It was installed in the Z—5, the first helicopter made in China.

HEF was transformed from a weapon factory and in May 1951 also experienced a transition from overhaul to manufacture. Initially, a Russian field repair and maintenance train drove into the factory. The technical officers and soldiers did repair work and also trained the factory people in repair skills. Then the factory invited Soviet experts to help them speedily master the repair skills for Ash—21 and Ash—82FN engines. In five years, the factory totally repaired and overhauled more than 4,000 of the above—mentioned two engines and also made many spare parts to meet the overhaul requirements. Thus, conditions were created for the factory to turn wholly to manufacture. In 1957, the factory successfully made the trial production of Ash—21 engine. It was a single row, radial, 7 cylinders, air—cooled piston engine, with 515 kW (700 hp) take—off power and installed in the Russian Yak—11 medium trainer and UTB—2 bomber trainer. They produced and delivered 21 engines in that year. Then its production ceased as China did not make Yak—11 aeroplanes.

Trial production for the HS7 engine started in 1958 and its approval test finished in 1959. Due to the effect of the "big leap forward", there were quality problems. In 1961 a fresh try for the trial production was carried out and in September 1963, the engine got the approval with good quality. In 1966, design improvement measures were undertaken such as oil ejection lubrication in the main cylinder, to solve the scrapes on the cylinder and the flake off of the crank counter—weight sleeve that occurred during operation. That made the engine work more stable and reliable. By the end of its production in 1980, more than 1,500 engines had been produced. Some 200 engines were also exported to 8 countries.

5. HS8 Engine

HS8 was the first aeroengine successfully modified and developed in new China. It was used on 4 types of aeroplanes.

In the 1950s, there were a great number of Russian Tu—2s, Il—14s, Il—12s and American C—46s used as bombers and transport aeroplanes in China. They used the Russian Ash—82FN,

Ash—82T and American R—2800 piston engines respectively. These engines were in the same power class, but of different types and not interchangeable. In the long service of these aeroplanes, the engines needed several overhauls or replacement. There was demand in large numbers. In 1959, the operators requested improvements in the high altitude performance of the Ash—82T engine in order to enable Il—14 transport to fly into Tibet. In the early 1960s, due to the need of preparing for war, the Air Force increased their need for the above engines. But the imported supplies for these engines were completely cut off thus causing the grounding of a large number of aeroplanes. It was a very urgent and pressing task to supply the engines for these aeroplanes.

Wang Zuhu and his colleagues of the Engine Production & Technology Department of the AIB held many repeated studies and analyses on the proposal of producing R—2800 engine spares and manufacturing both Ash—82FN and Ash—82T engines. They felt these were not feasible from both the technical and economical point of view. Therefore, they refuted the idea of tackling all problems individually and proposed a modification and design programme which would use one engine for all applications. The people in HEF concurred, and in 1961 the actual programme gradually came out, i.e. integrating HS7 engine main body and its supercharger with Ash—82T engine's reduction gears. As a result a reliable new engine with a good altitude performance came out which could be used for the above—mentioned four aeroplanes, thus "killing four birds with one stone". This program gained the support from the leaders of the Ministry of Defence Industry (MDI) and the Air Force. The decision was made immediately by the leading organization that HEF would be responsible for this task. In September 1961, a leading team was formed by HEF, Harbin Aircraft Factory (HAF) and people from the Air Force Flight School. The chief engineer of HEF, Ou Deshi was appointed the team leader, and the work started immediately.

The design work was carried out by Wang Xiurui, Xue Weihua, Wang Zengyan and others. After test, they increased the power of the HS7 from 1,250 kW (1,700 hp) to 1,360 kW (1,850 hp) by raising the inlet air pressure, which satisfied the requirements of the Tu—2 and other aeroplanes. For the engine, 94.3% of the parts were adopted from HS7 and the new ones amounted to only 5.7%. After production, assembly and test, it reached the design target and was designated the HS8.

Towards the end of the development, a test flight team was formed by the Air Force, CAAC and AIB with Jin Sheng, Deputy Director of AIB, as its head. The engine was installed on the aeroplane for test in August 1962. The results proved that the new engine satisfied the flight training programs of Tu—2 bomber, slightly improved the flight performance of C—46, increased the empty load ceiling of Il—14 from 6,500 m to 9,060 m and greatly improved the reliability of Il—12.

After the endurance approval test, the HS8 engine was approved by the Certification Commission of Aero Products for series production in October 1963.

Up to 1980 when its production was stopped, there were about 1,300 units produced and out of them 195 provided for CAAC.

The success of the development of the HS8 engine enabled a large number of aircraft to fly again — particularly the Il−14 which could now fly into Tibet. The development period had been shortened, and at a relatively low cost − a considerable achievement for China for overcoming her temporary national economic difficulties. Furthermore, the development had earned China valuable experience whilst at the same time gaining support from end−users, producing a practical technical programme and enabling solid production.

Fig.47　HS8 engine used for 4 aeroplanes

At the end of 1963, Cao Lihuai, the Vice Commander−in−Chief of the PLA Air Force and Liu Ding, Vice Minister of MAI, attended a celebration meeting for HS8 engine. They all pointed out: "The modification and design of HS8 engine meets the principle of 'Seeking truth from facts', 'Advancing by regular steps'".Its success marked that China's aeroengine had marched one step—from copying to designing. Vice Premier He Long during his inspection trip to HEF also highly appraised it and said: "The modification and design as such is along the right track."

Section 3　A Breakthrough in the Manufacturing Technology of Turbojet Engines

The development from piston engines to the jet engines was a revolution in aeroengine history.

Due to its light weight, compactness, smooth running, high power and good altitude characteristics, the turbojet engine is much more superior over the piston engine at high speed and high altitude, particularly at the flight speed approaching the sound speed, when there is a tremendous shock wave drag called the "Sonic Barrier". Due to the power limit and dramatic reduction in propeller efficiency at high speed, the propeller aircraft powered by the piston engine could not overcome this barrier. The jet engine, however, can smoothly pass it because of the advantages mentioned above. Thus, the jet engines gradually replaced the piston engines for application in military and large civil aeroplanes.

The turbojet engine is formed by use of the core engine and a pipe. The core engine consists of the compressor, combustor and gas turbine. The high velocity gas from the core engine rushes out through the jet pipe creating the reaction force and pushes the aeroplane forward. The installation of the afterburner in the jet pipe forms the afterburning jet engine which can produce additional thrust for short periods. This type of engine is suitable for high speed aircraft. From the mid 1950s, China's aircraft industry started the trial production of turbojet engines. Firstly it completed the transition from the piston engines to the jet engines and then, in the configuration of the turbojet engine, completed the transition from the centrifugal flow compressor to the axial one and from one shaft to two shafts. It also successfully made large turbojet engines.

1. WP5——China's First Turbojet Engine

The WP5 engine was produced according to Russian technical documents of the VK−1F. It was a single−shaft engine with a centrifugal compressor and afterburner. The maximum dry thrust was about 26 kN (2,650 kgf) and wet thrust 37 kN (3,800 kgf). The engine net weight was of 989 kg and was installed in the J−5 aircraft. According to the First Five−year Plan, the Shenyang Aeroengine Factory (SEF) (hereinafter called the New Factory) was set up on the basis of the Shenyang Aeroengine Overhaul Factory (SEOF) (hereinafter called the Old Factory) from the first half of 1954 to the end of 1957 under the guidance of the principle "Carrying out the construction while starting the trial production." It was also required that the trial production of WP5 engine should be successfully completed before the National Day of 1957, at which time series production could begin in the New Factory.

Many high strength materials and high temperature alloys are used in the manufacture of the gas turbine engine which are difficult for machining. This difficulty is compounded by the high precision of nozzles, the complexity of blade profiles, and many thin wall welding parts in the combustion afterburner systems. Therefore, apart from precision machining and advanced heat and surface treatment technologies, they are also needed to set up precision casting and precision forging production lines which can make parts with little or no machining allowances, as well as various welding production lines such as seam welding, butter welding, DC electrode welding, hydrogen atom welding, high frequency brazing, manual and automatic argon arc welding, etc. Many of them at that time were of advanced technology and very difficult.

In order to fulfil the tasks of the construction of the New Factory and the trial production of the new engine at the same time, according to the principle of "The Old Factory is responsible for the construction of the New Factory" and "One director for two factories", Mo Wenxiang, Director of the Old Factory, Xu Xizan, the Chief Engineer, and the heads of each functional section and office and workshop, were given responsibility for the activities of both factories. Thus, it was possible to make full use of the conditions of the Old Factory for the construction of the New Factory and trial production. They made it possible for the factory to pick up equipment from reserved warehouses, and timely assigned nearly 9,000 staff members and workers to the New Factory. All these moves enabled the large construction project to be complete for trial and series production ahead of time.

In the meantime, preparation for the trial production of the WP5 engine was under way in the Old Factory which, with the assistance of the Soviet experts, trained a strong team in all necessary specialities through the overhaul, assembly and test of more than 3,000 jet engines in 4 different aircraft types as well as the production of nearly 3,000 part and component items in 2 years. They had a good handling of the manufacturing technology. The complete manufacturing documents of WP5 engines started to be translated and copied in April 1954 at the Old Factory. Through the joint efforts of both the New and Old Factories, about 12,000 toolings and equipments necessary for the trial production were produced in March 1956 and the trial production of parts also proceeded quickly.

Fig.48　Mao Zedong listening to the presentation of WP5 engine

　　To guarantee product quality in the trial production, the factory undertook a series of technical management measures including: organizing leading cadres, engineers and technicians concerned to attend the technical seminars; using cheaper dummy blanks for practice in the trial production instead of materials difficult for machining, expensive and used for long lead time parts. These were called the "Pilot Batch". Groups of parts were tested successively in order to expose and solve the problems at an earlier stage; In March 1956, after all parts and components were made, the full life ground test was carried out to expose and solve problems once again. These measurements were very helpful and effective to the success of the trial production of the new engine.

The first batch of trial produced WP5 engines passed the approval test and turned into series production in June 1956, one year and four months ahead of schedule. 40 engines were produced in the same year. At the end of September that year, the construction of the New Factory also passed the State's acceptance approval, eighteen months in advance of the original plan and the quality was regarded as "Superb". This showed that SEF had achieved two goals of factory construction and new engine trial production with good quality and at high speed. On the 10th September 1956, the Central Committee of the Chinese Communist Party and the State Council sent a congratulatory message to all the staff and workers of the SEF. In February 1958, Chairman Mao Zedong paid an inspection tour to the factory and viewed the jet engine produced by China.

The success of the WP5 trial production was a milestone, which marked that China's aircraft industry had stepped from the production of the piston engine to the jet engine and now it entered the era of jet. China became one of the very few countries in the world at that time who were able to produce jet engines in batches.

On the basis of the WP5 engine, SEF successfully produced the VK−1A engine (68% parts and components were the same as WP5 engine) in 1957, which was designated the WP5A and used for the Russian−made Il−28 light bomber of our Air Force. In 1958, the factory produced the RD−45 engine for MiG−15 fighters and made 30 units that year.

In 1963, China started to produce H−5 light bomber, and there was an increased demand for WP5A engines. It was decided that WP5A and WP5 engines would be transferred to Xi'an Aeroengine Factory (XEF) for continued production.

The construction of XEF started in August 1958, which was originally designed to produce high thrust WP8 engines for H−6 medium bombers. In the latter half of 1961, the factory carried out the mission of providing some spare parts of WP5 engines which were urgently needed by the Air Force. Then the State decided that this Factory would produce both WP8 and WP5 engines, and start immediately for the trial production of WP5A engines transferred from SEF. The factory took the organizational and technical measurements, strengthened the trial production teams and started the technical practices on the critical parts for the production, assembly and test of the "Pilot batch". Through the efforts of all the employees in the factory, the first batch of WP5A engines passed the acceptance tests in June 1965 six months ahead of schedule. In August, the Certification Committee of Aero Products proved the engine for series production. WP5A engine were used on both HJ−5 bomber−trainer and HZ−5 bomber−reconnaissance aircraft.

To work together with Chengdu Aircraft Factory (CAF) for the development of JJ−5 trainer, XEF modified and developed WP5D engine in 1965. In 1966, it successfully developed WP5B engines for the application to the Russian−made MiG−15bis fighter. In 1976, it completed the development of WP5C engines to be installed in the Russian−made all−weather fighter MiG−17. These engines were all turned into series production.

2. WP6——China's First Engine for Supersonic Fighters

WP6 engine was produced according to RD−9B engine's technical documentation supplied by the Soviet Union, and was for the application to J−6 fighter. Compared with WP5, the performance of the engine developed from subsonic to supersonic and the compressor from centrifugal flow to axial flow. Its maximum dry thrust is 25.5 kN (2,600 kgf) and the thrust with reheat is 31.9 kN (3,250 kgf), which are the same level as WP5. But the engine weight and maximum diameter were 30% and 48% less than those of the WP5. Thus the engine front area was great reduced, making the engine suitable for supersonic flight.

The trial production and the follow−on mass production were carried out by SEF. The Soviet documents arrived in the Factory consecutively in the first half of 1958. The factory selected the experienced technicians and workers for the trial production. The engine had 2,521 parts and components, which was 46% more than WP5 engine. Especially, the axial engine had more blades, pipes and the original WP5 production line could not meet the requirement. Thus a necessary technical reformation and expansion were undertaken and the production capability of blade forging and machining, pipe producing, magnesium parts machining and precision casting were strengthened. The technical lay−out of manufacture and assembly of parts was rearranged.

In the Summer and Autumn of 1958, under the influence of the "big leap forward" in the entire country, the policy was to "Speed up trial production" which caused great problems, namely poor translation of technical documents, copying was incomplete through lack of thorough study, vast cuts in tooling and equipment, poor quality of toolings and equipment and cancellation of technical management systems, particularly in control and inspection. Thus, when the first engine was tested at the end of 1958, the main performance goals were not reached. Then with new parts and components made in a hurry, the engine failed the second test again. In 1959, the engine passed the acceptance test after continuously troubleshooting. By the end of that year, the first batch of 60 engines had been built. Due to the poor quality, up to the end of 1960, the factory could not deliver a single qualified engine.

From November 1960, the factory rectified the quality, and started again on the trial production of the WP6 engine. The directors of the factory, Yu Xiaping and Li Mingshi led the cadres, from the top management down to carry out a deep education on "Quality First". They reorganized the technical management, strengthened the chief engineer system, restored the original rules and regulations, formulated product quality standards, and mobilized the enthusiasm of the massive staff members and workers. The trial production was sped up on the basis of ensured quality. In October 1961, the newly−made engine smoothly passed the endurance test and the quality was high. The State reorganized the appraisal and acceptance, and approval was granted for series production. That year 72 were delivered. In September 1963, the WP6 engine was installed into the quality approved J−6 aircraft and passed the flight test. The Military Commission of CCCPC issued a letter of congratulation to SEF and SAF. The engine was awarded the national first−class prize for new industrial products in May 1964.

The tortuosity and reversal of the WP6 trial production was a deep lesson on quality and scientific management to the employees in the aeroengine industry. It had also been good practice for solving key technical problems in design and testing. We accumulated experiences which were very useful for the promoting of engine development and production.

The WP6 engine was the powerplant of both the J−6 and Q−5 aircraft, and therefore there was a great demand for the engine. Later it was concurrently manufactured in SEF and the Chengdu Aeroengine Factory (CEF).

Fig.49   Deng Xiaoping, Li Fuchun, Bo Yibo visiting
WP6 engine in the factory

The construction of CEF began in October 1958, which was completely put in charge of SEOF. 60% of the manpower and other resources of SEOF were transferred to Chengdu with Yang Cheng and Cui Guangwei as the heads. Thus the production capabilities were soon formed in CEF. In the first half of 1959, trial production of the RD−500K engine for a coast defense missiles started. In July the following year the engine passed the acceptance test. The trial production of the WP6 engine began in the Spring of 1962. Great attention was paid to the training of new workers. By way of "Sending students out and inviting teachers in" CEF learned a lot from SEF. During the trial production more than 100 key manufacturing technologies were learned and mastered, such as abrasive belt dressing of blades, adjustment of complicated tracers, broaching of turbine disc firtree grooves, machining of precise holes in engine casings, refining of high temperature alloys, casting of magnesium casings and spraying of heat resistance ceramics. The engine passed the endurance test on September 15, 1964 and it was put into series production on October 11 after the State's appraisal.

SEF and CEF produced a large number of WP6 engines, which satisfied the requirement for J—6 and Q—5 aircraft. Some of them were also for foreign aid and export.

In the process of mass production of WP6 engines, the life extension programme and modifications were also carried out.

The overhaul life of the aeroengine means the operational hours between the delivery and the first overhaul or between two overhauls. The first overhaul life of WP6 was very short, only 100 hours, causing concern to both the manufacturer and the operator. At the beginning of 1965, the life extension programme was executed. After repeated tests and studies, 41 technical improvements were. adopted. When the modified engine passed the acceptance test, the first overhaul life of 200 hours was approved at the end of 1965. As there was no thorough understanding of the original design's weak points, by the end of 1969, the engine's turbine discs and combustion liners had major failures in operation and the overhaul life was reduced to 100 hours again.

In 1970, SEF reorganized the life extension work with emphasis on turbine discs and combustion liners. This took the fine adjustment of pitch and 3 other measurements, and the cracks on the firtree groove were cleared. They also made reference to the modified combustion liners of CEF, completely gave up the original design, used all air—film cooled combustion liners and solved the cracking problem on the liners. In addition, floating heat shield and other 20 technical improvements were adopted. In 1973, all these improvements were incorporated into the mass production engines and, as a result, the technical achievement of doubling the life (200 hours) of WP6 engine in 1965 was actually re—aligned.

CEF started to solve the problem of cracks and flakes of the combustion liners in 1968. They designed a complete new structure with all air—film cooling. After more than 300 single flame tube tests and nearly 100 engine bench tests and through more than 500 hours endurance test and 5 major flight tests under various operating conditions such as high speed at low altitude, high altitude with reheat—on and medium altitude acrobatic it was approved for series production in 1971 and designated as 4—71 type all air filmed combustion liner. That played an important role in the life extension of the WP6 engines.

Afterward, it was found that 4—71 type liners were difficult to start in very cold area. It was the disturbance period of the "great cultural revolution" and the factory stopped the production activities. But Qin Xueqi and other engineers, technicians and old workers were worried about what the operators were worried about and formed a special team covering all specialities. They adhered to carrying out further tests and, finally in October 1976, developed a new 4—76 type all air filmed liner. They then modified the manufacturing processes. In 1978, they produced a vastly improved 4—78 type all air filmed liner. Compared with the original liner, the new one had stable combustion under all flight conditions and good starting characteristics both on the ground and in the air. The engine thrust was increased and s.f.c. reduced. This liner won the national silver medal in 1982.

Their achievements in combustion liners also gained them a good reputation among the related manufacturers in the World. In 1983, they signed a contract with American Pratt Whitney company for making combustion liners for JT−8D series engines. The first two types of liners were produced by the end of 1984. After inspection by the American side, it was agreed to commence formal production in 1985.

When the life extension programme of the WP6 engines was being undertaken, the work to increase the strength of the turbine shaft was carried out. In the early 1970s, fractures of turbine shafts during operation occurred on the WP6 engines made by both CEF and SEF. In 1977, the MAI held a special meeting to analyse the failure. It appeared that the main reason for the failure was insufficient residual strength in the original design, particularly during spin. During the meeting, it was decided that CEF would be given responsibility to develop a new turbine shaft in order to meet the requirement of spin flight training. In 1978, MAI assigned to the factory the mission of "Study on the Structure Integrity Technology of the Aeroengine Shafts." This programme was headed by Gao Lianshen, Liu Dunhui, and Wang Changyuan. They carried out three major cycles of shaft modification design, test−piece production and fatigue tests; substantial progress was made in each cycle. The tests achieved satisfactory results by the end of 1979. The strength of the new shaft was greatly increased. It was reliable for long time operation under the spinning load for training purposes and able to sustain certain amounts of spin during normal flight operations. In 1981, the new shaft passed the flight test. In 1982, it was jointly reviewed by MAI and the Engineering Department of the Air Force and pronounced "suitable for practical operations." They also advised "it provides precious experiences for future design, test and study of other types of turbine shafts." It was approved for series production immediately.

Many modifications on the WP6 engine made its quality improved and life extended and the engine gained high appraisal from both domestic and foreign end users.

3.　WP7−−the Mach 2 Fighter Engine

The WP7 was made according to the Soviet R11−F−300 engine technical documents, and installed in the J−7 fighter. Its maximum dry thrust was 38 kN (3,900 kgf) and the thrust with reheat was 56 kN (5,750 kgf), which were 50% and 77% respectively more than those of the WP6. This axial flow, two shaft turbojet engine had 6 stages of compressor and 2 stages of turbine, which formed high pressure (HP) rotor and low pressure (LP) rotor. The LP rotor shaft went through the inner bore of the HP rotor shaft. The combustion liners were air filmed and inner and outside walls were coated with heat resistant ceramics. The improvement in the afterburner solved the problem of unstable reheat ignition of the WP6 engine at high altitude. The exhaust nozzle was variable and automatically controlled. This engine incorporated many new materials such as stainless steel and high temperature alloy on the compressor and turbine blades. The WP7 engine was more advanced than the WP6 engine both in performance and in structure, and the manufacturing processes were more complicated.

The preparation for trial production was formally started in 1963 in SEF. Having learned the lessons from the WP6 engine trial production, the leading organization placed high stress on having a thorough understanding of the technology before starting to cut the metal. Therefore, SEF organized 1 / 3 of its design and production engineers to form a team dedicated to the trial production of the WP7 engine. Shenyang Aeroengine Research Institute (SARI) and other science and research organizations also took the thorough—studying of the engine's techniques as its main task. They made analysis, calculations and rig tests and wrote technical reports.

According to the investigation, they corrected and supplemented 1,097 original documents which had errors or ommissions. Before the 3rd quarter of 1965, aeronautical factories and research institutes, as well as related organizations of the Chinese Academy of Sciences (CAS) and the industries of metallurgy, machinery, and chemistry had finished " tackling the key technical problems" included 26 new materials, 10 aero bearings, 46 new technologies and new production processes. For instance, the properties of the two kinds of high temperature alloy were even better than the Russian specifications. Through several years' hard work, the GH46 HT alloy was successfully produced by the joint efforts of the Ministry of Metallurgical Industry (MMI), CAS, the related factories, research institutes, colleges and universities of MAI. By using this alloy, only a small number of the turbine blades were rejected. For the imported blanks, due to hair cracks and the large forging grain size of the raw material, the rejected rate was over 50%. The deep hole machining of the turbine shaft was a critical process. The "three—in—one combining team" (consisting of workers, engineers and cadres) in the factory studied the machining experiences of the gun factory and Beijing Aeronautical Manufacturing Technology Research Institute (BAMTRI), and modified a machine tool which adopted the new technology of deep hole boring instead of the deep hole grinding specified in the original documents. That guaranteed the quality and improved the productivity. For turbine blades, they used new process of electrolysis to replace the original cutting. The Soviet Union did not provide the technical documents for the sea level ground test cell with heated inlet air. The factory solved this problem together with design and research institutes. The test cell of the WP7 engine was a complicated non—standard equipment. Normally, it would need 20 months to build. After thoughtful arrangement and continuous hard work, it was completed within only 7 months.

The all—round trial production started at the beginning of 1965. In October the same year, the final assembly of the first WP7 engine was finished. After three endurance tests which lasted more than one year, it was certified by the State and released for series production in December 1966.

The WP7 engine was made of indigenous materials, and the Soviet Union did not supply some of the key documents, thus showing that China's manufacturing technology of jet engines and the raw materials of the basic industries had come to a new and higher level.

According to the arrangement of the 3rd line (inland area) construction and as the production and development work in SEF was too heavy, in 1970, WP7 engines were transferred to·the Guizhou Aeroengine Factory (GEF) for production.

The set up of GEF started at the beginning of 1965. The SEF was responsible for the construction. In 1968, some parts of GEF started trial production and others were still under construction. At the end of 1969, the engine was trial tested in the ground test cell. As the factory was located in the Yun Gui plateau, the ambient atmospheric conditions changed greatly, which brought difficulties to the trial test. The engineers, technicians and workers made analyses and tests repeatedly and finally found a solution. In August 1970, the WP7 engine successfully passed the life test, marking the success of the transfer of production. Since that time, jet engines roar frequently among the previously—poor Miao Ling Mountains. Another great achievement in China's industry moving to the inland remote areas.

There were many shortcomings in the original design. During the operation, there were eight major failures including fracture of the first stage compressor blades due to flutter, which threatened flight safety. The manufacturers resolved to initiate the study and improvement. The designer, Cai Yunjin, and his colleagues of SEF designed the new reinforced first stage compressor blades and reduced the number of blades from 31 to 24. After laboratory, ground and flight tests under various conditions, the property of the new blades proved excellent, the structure reliable and the surge margin was enlarged. That effectively eliminated the stall flutter and cracking failure and greatly improved the engine reliability. Designer Jiang Hefu and his colleagues of GEF successfully incorporated the blade mistuning technology in assembly and treated the blades with shot peening. That further improved the new blades. Additionally, by enlarging the oil nozzle diameter for bearings GEF solved the engine shut—down problem caused by the over—heated intermediate bearing; the factory worked together with the Qiqihar Steel Plant to develop GH 33A heat resistance alloy with micro—elements instead of the original GH33 alloy. That solved the problems associated with the over—expansion of the first stage turbine disc; designer Wen Junfeng modified the structure design of the flaps of the afterburner nozzle, thus clearing the major nozzle failure of being unable to open or close. In 1979, GEF adopted 25 modifications and solved all the 8 major failures. That obviously improved the quality of WP7 engines. The above modifications were also incorporated in new versions of the WP7 family. The production of the original WP7 stopped in 1980 and the production of the WP7B engine began.

4. WP8——Turbojet Engine with High Thrust

The WP8, which was used for the H—6 medium bomber, was made according to the Soviet RD—3M engine technical documents. This engine was a relatively advanced high thrust turbojet engine at the end of the 1950s. Its maximum thrust is 93 kN (9,500 kgf), which is two times more than that of WP5 and WP6 engines. The weight was 3,100 kg and the maximum diameter was 1.4 m. The series production of such a large engine needed several hundreds of precision, special and large equipment and special test facilities. The production of each engine would consume 15 tons of high temperature alloy and 9.5 tons of non—ferrous metal. The blank of the turbine disc had to be forged by a 10,000 ton class hydraulic press. The manufacture of the high thrust engines reflected the economical strength and industrial level of the country. At that time only very few countries in the world could produce such engines of this size.

In 1958, in order to meet the requirements of the trial production for the H—6, it was decided that trial production of the WP8 engine would be jointly undertaken by HEF, SEF and XEF. In 1961, the aviation industry cut short its front line and trial production was temporarily halted. In 1963, it was decided that XEF would carry out the task alone.

The trial production in Xi'an was led by chief engineer Jiang Zutong and was carried out in planned phases. At the beginning of 1962, the factory sent out 132 staff members

Fig.50   Final inspection for WP8 engine final assembly

and workers to HEF and SEF to study and exchange experiences for the trial production and to accept the documents and materials concerned. From 1963 to 1964, some detailed parts started to be trial produced. In the latter half of 1965, the trial production began in an all—round way. In order to form the team quickly, the factory assigned some new workers to the WP5A production line and took out the experienced workers to the WP8's. They opened technical training classes for the production technology of the critical parts, and signed the teaching and learning contracts between the masters and apprentices using dummy blanks for training. That enabled the operators to grasp techniques quickly. Then, organized by Ma Shiying, the vice chief engineer, the trial production for 197 critical parts and components and tackling the key technical problems started. The Soviet Union did not provide the composition and work processes for the first stage nozzle guide vanes (NGV) casting alloy and they developed it successfully with the joint effort with the Beijing Aeronautical Materials Institute (BAMI) and Shanghai Jiaotung University. They also took many measures during the trial production to strengthen the quality control. Thanks to the joint efforts of the people from the top to the bottom and from the inside to the outside of the factory, the WP8 engine passed the State appraisal test in January 1967 and it was put into series production.

Since that time, China has had its home—made high thrust engines and its own factory for making such engines. Its medium bombers had reliable powerplants. This was major progress in China's aviation industry.

1,193 items of raw material, forging and casting blanks and finished parts and accessories were needed for WP8 engines. In 1960, about half of them could not be domestically produced. That became a major problem for the series production. The State relied on and developed indigenous materials. In 1967, the majority of problems were solved.

At this stage of WP8 trial production, the first time between overhaul (TBO) was 300 hours. XEF continued to undertake life extension work and gained great achievements. In 1974, the life was approved to be 500 hours, in 1979 extended to 600 hours and in 1983, further—extended to 800 hours.

Section 4   Development of New Turbojet Engines

1.   Attempt at Designing New Engines

a. PF—1A Engine

Soon after China successfully made its first jet engine, design and development of a new engine started. In August 1956, Shenyang Aeroengine Design Office (SADO) of SEF was formed. Wu Daguan was appointed its director and Yu Guangyu as chief designer. This office later became the Shenyang Aeroengine Research Institute (SARI).

The first design task given to SADO was to develop an engine with WP5 engine as reference, which had the thrust of 15.7 kN (1,600 kgf). The engine was named PF—1A and was going to be installed on the Chinese designed trainer JJ—1. The AIB pointed out: the task was not only to have the thing designed, but also " to train the engineers, accumulate data and to form the design team".

The preparation for the development started from the end of 1956 and the design and the preparation of trail production were completed in 1957. The fact that the engine was to be designed purely by China, gave fresh initiative to the workers. All the detail parts were finished within 100 days and the first prototype was assembled half a year later. After 20 hours' ground test, the engine

Fig.51   The first jet engine PF—1A designed by China

made its maiden flight on JJ—1 in July 1958. It proved the first step to the engine design was basically successful. Under the circumstances of lacking design experiences and basic test facilities, this design was practical. It met the principle of "do the things with one's ability and advance by regular steps." Later because the end user changed their training system, the development programmes for PF—1A engine and JJ—1 trainer were stopped.

b. "Hong Qi" (Red Flag) 2 Engine

The second task for SADO was to design an engine with 49 kN (5,000 kgf) reheat thrust based on the WP6 engine (the thrust was 50% more than that of WP6). The engine was designated as "Hong Qi" 2 and planned to be used on China's own designed high altitude supersonic fighter "Dong Feng" (East Wind) 107. The design was frozen by the end of 1958, and in the beginning of 1959 production started. As most of the materials and toolings needed were the same as those used on the WP6 engine, the work proceeded quickly. In September 1959, the first test engine was put to test cell. On the eve of National Day, the first ignition was successful. Then three phases of ground tests were carried out smoothly. When it was going to the normal test running, the higher level organization decided to design another "814" engine for "Dong Feng" 113 and stop the development of "Hong Qi" 2. However, as the target for "814" engine was set too high and the technology base was poor, it was also stopped in 1960.

2. WP6A Engine

The WP6A engine was modified and developed from the WP6 engine and used for Q—5I attack aircraft.

The mission profile of attack aircraft generally consists of penetration and ground attack at low altitudes and breakaway from the target area and return home at medium and high altitudes. It carries a heavy load of weapons and bombs, thus requiring the engine to have a high thrust, good acceleration rate at take—off and climbing, and minimum stable thrust when attacking the target. Therefore, the original WP6 for Q—5 aircraft needed to be modified.

SEF started the program of increasing the thrust of the WP6 by the end of 1964. The major requirements were to increase the turbine entry temperature (TET) and redesign the first stage compressor blades. The new engine was named WP6A. In 1966, it passed the endurance and flight tests. The thrust with reheat increased by 4.9 kN (500 kgf) and there was an obvious improvement in climbing characteristics. However, when the bleed valve was operated (in order to prevent engine surge, the bleed valve had to be opened to release some air at certain r.p.m.), there was a sudden change of thrust; and the r.p.m. of the upper surge limit moved up, which made the bleed valve open earlier. This phenomenon greatly reduced the engine's stable operation range and severely affected the aircraft performance. CEF and SEF seperately studied the variable geometry compressor vane to solve this problem. They gained good results. Yan Chengxiang and Shen Zhongming of SEF added a zero stage variable vane before the first stage compressor blade, which, together with the bleed valve, formed a "zero stage adjustable surge—preventing system". After tests, it effectively increased the engine stable working range, and could obtain the minimum stable thrust required by the attack aircraft. That was beneficial for the flight performance during fleet formation, penetrating clouds, aiming and shooting. In October 1979, it was formally decided that the WP6A engine would be the power—plant for Q—5I aircraft. After the appraisal by the State, the engine was certified in August 1983 and released for production and delivery.

At the end of 1984, Zhao Guangwu, Zhu Yuanhu, Zhou Zhiying and their colleagues at

Shenyang Aeroengine Company (SAC) (merged from SEF and SARI in 1979) supported by the company's leader Cheng Huaming worked together with Gao Ge a post—graduate of BIAA. They successfully applied the "stability theory on barchan dune" invented by Gao Ge to the flame holder of WP6A afterburner. They achieved reliable engagement of reheat and stable flaming both at poor and rich fuel conditions and cleared the problem of oscillatory burning which was most damaging to the flight. It also increased the engine thrust by 1.5% — 2%, and reduced the specific fuel consumption by 1 — 1.5%. The test acceptance rate was improved at the same time.

CEF made two improvements to the WP6 engine. One was the WP6A engine developed in 1969 for the application in Q—5 torpedo type and its thrust was 5.9 kN (600 kgf) more than that of WP6. The other one was the WP6B developed in 1970 for the J—12 fighter and its thrust was 7.8 kN (800 kgf) more than that of WP6. The two versions were all flight tested. As the developments of the aircraft were given up, the engine programmes were also cancelled.

3. WP7A Engine

The WP7A engine is the powerplant of the Chinese—designed high altitude high speed fighter J—8. It was developed from the WP7 engine by using some advanced achievements and a successful engine version.

In May 1964, the Chinese Aeronautical Establishment (CAE) held the first evaluation meeting on the design concept feasibility of the new fighter. In order to meet the aircraft's requirements of good performance at high altitude and high speed, good climb rate and long range, high thrust and low s.f.c. were required for the engine. There were two options: one was to adopt a single newly designed 12 ton (120 kN) thrust class big engine, another was to use two modified WP7 engines. On the second evaluation meeting held in October the same year, selection would be made between the two alternatives. As the lead time for a brand new designed large engine was too long, the single engine design could not meet the schedule requirement. The twice—modified WP7 (i.e.the WP7A) design with the increased thrust had difficulties in increasing TET by 100 ℃. The increase of TET could raise the useful energy of the gas, which in turn increased the thrust. However, the increase of the gas temperature would require new high temperature alloys, structure design and machining processes for the turbine blades; it gave the meeting a difficult decision to make. Rong Ke, deputy director of BAMI and a casting expert made a proposition. He proposed to modify the solid turbine blade to a hollow one, and induce cooling air to cool the blade. He advised that he had great confidence in developing the hollow blades with the materials and work processes already available. Despite the fact that this was still a relatively unadvanced technique, little—used abroad, and a major task to undertake, Rong Ke decisively expressed a wish to accept a "life or death order" to develop the hollow blades in approximately twelve months. Based on his many years of study in high temperature and work processes, the factory shared his confidence. Thus, his strong confidence at this critical moment made the twin—engined J—8 aircraft.

In May 1965, the leading organization formally approved the design targets of the J—8 aircraft and the development programme for the WP7A. It decided that the engine design and prototype manufacture would be carried out by SARI and SEF respectively, and that the hollow turbine blades would be jointly developed by SEF, SARI, the Shenyang Metal Research Institute (SMRI) of CAS, BAMI, BAMTRI, and the Steel Research Establishment (SRE) of the Ministry of Metallurgical Industry (MMI).

SARI specially set up a WP7A design office and deputy chief engineer Chen Jiheng was appointed programme manager and director of the design office. Zhang Hong, Chen Dafa, and Fang Wenfu were assigned to be responsible for this programme. Some 20 people of the design office, closely supported by other departments of SARI, worked hard on solid ground, and explored carefully. They carried out design and calculation work, issued drawings when urgently required and timely solved the problems occurred in the development.

The technical problem associated with hollow blades was the critical point for the success of WP7A. It was arranged that the casting and forging hollow blades were simultaneously developed.

On the casting blade side, SMRI had already developed a high property nickle—based casting high temperature alloy — the M17 — and the precision casting technology in SEF had also reached a certain level; thus the conditions were capable of fulfiling the task. However, to combine new materials and new work processes into an advanced component of the engine was still a task requiring advanced R&D and a prolonged period of time. The time limit was only one year, and the risks were great. With the full support from Director Li Xun of SMRI and Chief Engineer Chen Huaming of SEF, plus the involvement and guidance of Rong Ke, all worked hard to solve the problem. SARI was given responsibility to design the blade, SMRI endeavoured to make the 9 holed—hollow blade in the laboratory, and SEF made the industrial trial production. SMRI solved many technical problems such as the selection of core material, broken cores, core drawings, casting porosity, and blade straightening at room temperature. Work proceeded gradually.

BAMTRI, XEF, SRE, Fushun Steel Plant (FSP) and BAMI worked together in great tension to develop the 3—holed air—cooled forged blades. At that time the high temperature forging alloy was not available, the special machine for machining the blade was only a demonstrator and the advanced R&D in the hole shape and passage was just started. It was extremely pressing and demanding work, and for this all departments concerned gave their best efforts and kept close links with each other. After repeated tests, they solved the difficulties which had arisen in the new forging alloys, deep hole electrical spark machines, profile hole electrodes, wall thickness measurement of the deep holes etc, one by one. After some seven months, in January 1966, they presented their first set of forged hollow blades. This happy news promoted the whole development work for the new engine. Two months later, SEF assembled the first WP7A engine with forged hollow turbine blades. The bench test was conducted on April 12th, and all present felt tension in the air in anticipation of success. Following the order for starting, a loud rumble came, and the starting proved successful. The complete test procedures went on smoothly, and the engine performance reached its design goals for the very first time. Compared with the original version, the WP7A gained an increase of 12.8% in maximum dry thrust and a reduction of 13% in specific fuel consumption.

In September of the same year, the casting hollow turbine blade was also developed in the laboratory. In November, SEF precision casting production line cast one set of blades, and in December, the engine with casting hollow turbine blades was on the ground test bed. The result was most successful.

As the cast 9 holes blades had better cooling efficiency, higher residual strength, more simple manufacturing requirements and a lower rejected rate than the 3 big holes forged blades, it was finally approved that the cast hollow turbine blades would be the type certification blades for the WP7A engine.

This achievement in hollow turbine blades brought the birth of theWP7A engine. This hollow air—cooled blade technique was later applied to several other engines.

In July 1969, the J—8 aircraft with the WP7A engine made its first flight and it was successful. In 1970, the design task was transferred from SARI to SEF. Because of the interference of the "great cultural revolution", the work was semi—stopped. In 1974, the original design team of SARI was assigned to SEF for continuous development. The test run up of the engine on the sea—level test bed, the tests in simulated altitude test facility and the all round flight tests for performance were carried out individually. In June 1982, the WP7A engine was certified.

The development of the WP7A engine covered the complete process of design, trial production, rig tests, engine ground test, engine simulated altitude test, flight test and design certification. It also promoted the construction of test facilities and provided training for personnel. The success of the air—cooled hollow turbine blading proved that the creation and break through of the critical technique on the existing basis was the correct technical path. It also proved that only with the availability of new high temperature alloy and new work processes (i.e.technical base) such as forged and cast hollow blades, a breakthrough could be made in a relatively short period. The WP7A was a profound achievement in the development. It received 6 awards for achievements in science and technology beyond the provincial level. In 1985, together with the J—8 aircraft, it was awarded a special class national prize for science and technology progress.

4. WP7B Engine Series

The Guizhou Aeroengine Design and Research Institute (GADRI) was set up at the same time as GEF. On the basis of successful work on the troubleshooting and life extension of WP7 engines, they continuously made improvements under the principle of "doing things according to one's ability, and continuously marching forward with small steps." After a few steps forward, they developed the WP7B engine series.

The WP7B was derived from the WP7A and their main difference was in the length and structure of the afterburner. Because of the cracks on the first stage turbine blades, high rejected rate of castings and the higher wall temperature of the afterburner which "burned" the rear fuselage, the engine could not be certified and released for operation. GEF under took 24 improvements in structure, manufacturing processes, material and accessories. In order to solve the first stage hollow turbine blade problem, director Wang Xinming went to the workshop to organize tackling the key problems. Shi Changxu, deputy director of SMRI of the CAS gave his direction on the spot. After hard work, the strength of blades and an acceptable rate of casting were increased. To solve the problems of the afterburner, engineer Jiang Zhizhong designed a three sectioned heat shield, which reduced the wall temperature by 100 ℃, and the problem of burning the rear fuselage was solved. In the meantime, the Guizhou "Hongshan" Bearing Factory, Chongqing "Yiping" Chemistry Factory, Guizhou Aero—Rubber Factory, BAMI, etc. successfully developed high temperature aero—bearings, and high temperature synthesized oil and fluoride rubber sealing rings and the problems were solved one by one. By the end of 1978, the WP7B engine smoothly passed the State type certification test, with an increase of 6.1% in wet thrust compared with the original WP7 engines.

According to the requirements of the Air Force and the export market, the factory made further modifications to extend the operation life, with particular emphasis on the combustion liners. They modified the structure of the body and cover, increased the ability to sustain the ingested exhaust gas, modified the flange design to solve crack problems, and changed the three—sectioned air film cooling to five—sectioned, thus doubling the operation life. With other improvements, they extended the engine life from 100 hours to 200 hours and designated the engine the WP7B.

The factory then changed the seperate gasoline starter into the kerosene starter which took the fuel directly from the main pump. This change reduced the weight, improved the air starting both in time and in reliability and made field maintenance easy. This modification succeeded in 1981. In 1982, it was put into series production and exported. It gained much praise from the end—users, and was named the WP7B(M batch) engine.

At the same time, another design modification was carried out to reduce the engine weight by 17 kg, which satisfied the requirement of the export version (J—7M aircraft) to add drop tanks. It was released for series production at the end of 1982 and was named as the WP7B(BM batch) engine.

5. WP11 Engine

The WP11 was a low thrust engine installed on the WZ—5 high altitude pilotless reconnaissance aircraft. It could also be used as a powerplant of drones and short range cruising missiles. The development was carried out by BIAA, and Chen Daguang was nominated as the chief of the design team; ZEF and other organizations offered support to the development. The design started at the beginning of 1965 and with tremendous efforts, major progresses were made. However, the development work was halted by the "great cultural revolution". In 1967, about 30 teachers and students voluntarily formed a "continuing development team", and they further modified the inlet casing, compressor rotor, radial diffuser, etc. to increase the engine thrust by more than 8.3 kN (850 kgf). In 1969, the manufacturing of parts and components began. The first WP11 engine started ground test in June 1971. During the trial production and test, technical problems came out one after another. First, the precision investment casting of the integral impeller was extremely difficult. After repeated tests, it was solved. Then the radial diffuser distorted and seized the rotor during the test, which damaged the impeller and other two major components, the reason was the improper material for the inlet cone of the flame tube. This problem was solved by using a GH18 high temperature alloy aged sheet, which was jointly developed by BAMI, the Shanghai Steel Research Institute (SSRI) and Shanghai No.3 Steel Works. Then with 6 prototypes, various tests were completed before the type certification test. After the assessment by the State, the engine was certified together with WZ−5 RPV in 1980. This filled a gap in low thrust turbojet engines in China. The production of the engine was then transferred to Hunan Province.

6. WP13 Engine

The WP13 was the powerplant of J−7III and J−8II fighters. It was a twin spool turbojet engine developed on the basis of many years achievements in modification of the WP7 engines. Compared with the WP7, it had a better structure integrity; there was a major improvement on the compressor, which doubled the surge margin; an intermediate bearing was added to LP rotor to reduce the vibration; and titanium alloy was used on the compressor disks and blades, which reduced the engine weight. A metal chip detector was added to the oil system for condition monitoring. An apparent improvement was made in the engine operation stability and reliability. The TBO increased and the maximum dry thrust and reheat thrust were 5.1% and 14.9% more than those of the original WP7 engine respectively.

At this time a major reform occurred in that GEF and CEF formed a joint organization to coordinate the design, production and development of WP13 engines. The leaders of the two factories, Wang Xinmin and Wang Yunhan, were assigned as the Director and Deputy Director, and also Chief and Vice−Chief Engineer respectively. Yao Kepei was appointed Chief Engineer, and Wen Junfeng and Qiu Zizhen were appointed Chief Engineer and Deputy Chief Designer respectively. GEF was given responsibility for compressor casing, combustion and afterburner, and CEF was given responsibility for compressors, turbine rotors and turbine casings. The work−split between the two factories was roughly 50−50, and they exchanged parts and components and carried out final assembly, test and delivery separately. Following this, Vice Minister of MAI, Jiang Xiesheng, pushed forward the joint organization idea. The practice proved that this mode of operating, with two factories sharing the work, promoted cooperation and shortened development lead time. This was the first successful attempt at new management in engine development.

The development of the WP13 started in 1978. By the end of 1980, the first 3 engines were assembled separately in Guizhou and Chengdu and tested, and by 1984, simulated reliability tests, simulated altitude tests, open test bed calibration tests and pre–certification endurance tests had been completed with 10 engine prototypes. During this period, a total of 16 part and component tests, including the HP and LP compressor performance rig tests, thermal–shock tests on turbine blades, and overspeed test for turbine disc were carried out successfully. In 1985, the engine passed the State ground appraisal test and it was turned into the State flight appraisal test.

Based on the successful development of the WP13 engine, GEF and CEF both made further improvements to the engine. The major modifications to the WP13AII were: changing the 2nd to 7th compressor steel cases to titanium casting cases to reduce the weight; using hollow air–cooled blades for the first stage turbine blade to increase the thrust; and certain modifications on combustor and afterburner. After various tests by GEF, the WP13AII proved to be a reliable engine with good compatibility, a high residual thrust margin and stable operation.

Using the castings and forgings of creep resistant titanium alloy for the compressor disc and casing was a main feature of the WP13 engine. At the beginning of 1980, Cao Chunxiao and Gu Mingxin of BAMI and the Guizhou Aero–Forging Factory in cooperation with persons from Shanghai No.5 Steel works and CEF, developed the TC11 creep resistant titanium alloy for the die–forged part of the WP13 compressor disc, which could work for a long time at 500 ℃. They succeeded in 1982, and created the precedent for aeroengines to adopt the titanium die forged part. It was

Fig.52　Casting titanium casing of WP13 engine

greatly beneficial—both in economy and in technique. In 1983, it won the first class award of MAI science and technical achievements. In the meantime, Zhang Tixin and his colleagues of BAMI, supported by GEF, worked for 4 years and successfully applied the ZT3 creep resistant casting titanium alloy containing rare earth metals to the 4th to 7th HP compressor casings of the WP13 engine, which was first invented by Zhou Yanbang of BAMI. This reduced the engine weight by 12.6 kg. Xue Zhiyang and others successfully applied the ZT4 casting titanium alloy to the 2nd and 3rd compressor casings, which reduced the engine weight by 6.9 kg. The twomodifications in turn reduced the weight of J–7Ⅲ and J–8Ⅱ. It was the first time casting titanium casing instead of casting steel casing had been used in China. A considerable breakthrough in design and manufacture. The ZT3 and ZT4 casting titanium alloy and its WP13 compressor casing gained the MAI first and 2nd award for science and technology achievements respectively in 1984.

Section 5   The Development and Import of Turbofan Engines

The turbofan engine is developed from the turbojet engine by adding a fan and a bypass duct. The fan is driven by the gas turbine thus creating the bypass flow. Both the bypass flow and the hot gas expelled from the core engine create reaction thrust. The turbofan engine can be also equipped with an afterburner. This type of engine has better propulsive efficiency, low s.f.c., low noise and low gas pollution. It is suitable for large passenger aeroplanes and can be also used for long distance supersonic fighters, bombers and attack aircraft with a wide range of speeds.

China's aviation industry started to develop turbofan engines in 1962. Over the past twenty years, it has developed the WS5, WS6, WS6A, No 4 lift—fan, WS8 and WS9 engines. Although many of them were halted midway due to task adjustment, many valuable experiences were gained.

1. WS5 Engine

By the end of 1962, the operator asked CAE to modify the WP6 engine into a turbofan engine (after—fan type). At that time the turbofan was one of the development targets in the world for aircraft powerplant. It was an active and thoughtful arrangement to use WP6 engine as the basis. SARI was assigned to undertake the task, which was headed by Yu Guangyu, Zhou Gao and Wang Guodong. The development proposal was presented in January 1963 and it was named the WS5 engine.

Compared with the WP6 engine, the WS5 featured a rear fan, no afterburner, variable inlet guide vanes and stator vanes of the 1st, 2nd and 3rd compressor stages instead of a bleed valve. There were also other related changes. The modified engine achieved a gain in performance. The take—off power reached 35 kN (3,600 kgf) with a 35% increase; and s.f.c. at take—off condition reduced by 30%. The aircraft range had a fairly big increase due to the improvement of the compressor efficiency and lower s.f.c.. It was anticipated that the range of the H—5 aircraft re—engined with WS5 engine was expected to increase by 30%. The engine operating envelope was extended and there were improvements in starting and acceleration characteristics.

After completion of the WS5 engine paper work, SARI invited 7 experts outside of CAE including Professor Wu Zhonghua of CAS to review it. President Tang Yanjie of CAE presided over the review. These experts gave positive opinions on the development of the turbofan engine and the definition of the important parameters of the WS5 engine.

The design, manufacture and testing of the rear fan caused great difficulties. Among them, the manufacture of the "combined turbine − fan bucket" was a critical technology. After solving the problem, the first engine was assembled at the beginning of 1965. During test, cracks were found at the root of the fan blade portion caused by stall flutter. This problem was solved. In 1966, the engine's maximum thrust and s.f.c. reached the design targets. Then 7 prototype engines in two batches were built and after test and modification, some other problems were solved. In 1970, the engine passed the endurance test. In 1971, the H−5 aircraft with the WS5 engine had several taxings and the engine worked smoothly. Later, the operator decided that they would not re−engine the H−5. The development of WS5 ceased in May 1973. It was a successful try for the development of the turbofan engine. Some techniques such as the design of the supersonic & transonic fan blade, compressor variable vanes and their regulator were applied to many other engines later on.

2. WS6 Engine

In 1964, in a CAE meeting on the assessment of the design proposal for a new fighter, the design of a complete new engine for its powerplant was proposed. SARI made a comparison of 3 types of engines (two spool turbojet, one spool turbojet and turbofan) and 22 design proposals. It was agreed that the turbofan was of a higher standard than the other two types and thus the WS6 was selected. It would be a high thrust, two spool, bypass turbofan with reheat − the design initiated by China. Its maximum dry thrust was 71 kN (7,270 kgf), the thrust with reheat was 122 kN (12,460 kgf), the thrust to weight ratio was 5.93. The design was led by Wu Daguan, Yuan Meifang and Li Zhiguang successively. The total developments were divided into 3 phases of the drawing design, production of a prototype and engine test.

From October 1964 to April 1966, the design drawings were finished. At the beginning of 1966, SEF started to produce the prototypes. Up to 1969, two prototype engines had been made. It was the time of the "great cultural revolution" and the places for making the engines were changed several times so the development work was seriously affected. No single engine was produced for nearly 10 years. After 1978, the development was sped up and Wu Xia and other leaders of SEF took effective actions and strengthened the management. They timely expelled obstacles in production and greatly improved the situation. By 1980, 7 prototype engines had been made progressively, thus speeding up the development of the WS6 engine.

The engine test started in 1968. It covered the 5 milestones of running test, performance adjustment, endurance test, simulated altitude test, flight test, and the State type certification test. The engineers and technicians of SARI, persistently and dauntlessly did repeated tests, amended the design, carried out around 30,000 hours component rig tests and more than 300 hours engine tests and overcame more than 100 key technical problems. Finally the performance of the engine met the design targets.

Through 5 years' effort since commencement of the running test, the problem of poor efficiency of the compressor parts and the small surge margin of the HP compressor were solved. In 1974 the engine speed reached 100% design speed and entered high speed running test. The three critical technical problems of the unallowable vibration of HP rotor, surge at high r.p.m. and higher TET came out successively. After analysis and test, measures were taken to take out the inner of the HP compressor stator and improve the turbine sealing. Then the improper matching of the flow field between the fan and HP compressor and the dismatching of the power between HP turbine and HP compressor were eliminated. Thus the 3 key technical problems were cleared one by one. By the end of 1979, the engine could run at high r.p.m steadily for a long time.

In 1980, during the performance test the measured thrust and s.f.c. reached and exceeded the design targets. In January 1981, engine tests with afterburner were carried out and the measured wet thrust was 122 kN (12,490 kgf), which reached the design performance.

Then came the endurance test. In July 1981, the prototype engine was run continuously for 12 hours for the first time. In October, the 24 hours exploratory long run test was accomplished and in October 1982, the engine formally passed the 24 hours' "Preliminary Flight Rating Test"..

In 1980, a modification programme was launched to increase the reheated thrust to 138 kN (14,100 kgf) and thrust—to—weight ratio to 7.0, with the external dimensions of the engine remaining unchanged. In February 1982, the modified prototype test was carried out and the measured full reheated thrust reached what was expected. It showed the modified WS6 engine could have a thrust—to—weight ratio of 7.0.

China made major progress in designing the 12 ton (120 kN) thrust class turbofan engine with reheat. The development work trained and practiced personnel, sped up the construction for the test facilities and promoted the application and development of new technology, new material, new production techniques and accessories. Because of the insufficient technology base, the development of such a high performance engine was very complicated and extremely difficult. In addition, the task changed several times and the place for trial production changed frequently. It took as long as 18 years, to make the engine reach its ground performance target. In the meantime, the aircraft for which the engine was designed was stopped and the engine had to be given up.

3. WS8 Engine

The WS8 was a front—fan, axial flow, two spool turbofan engine with a short bypass duct. The take—off thrust was 80 kN (8,165 kgf), and it was developed for the Y—10 passenger aeroplane.

This engine was first developed by CEF in 1970. In September 1973, the task was transferred to the Shanghai Aeroengine Factory (SAF), which was built in the early 1970s. The work proceeded quickly under the support and assistance from all departments concerned. In June 1975, the 1st engine was released for test. Up to 1982, there were 8 engines on test: one finished 1,000 hours' endurance test, one completed 150 hours' airworthiness certification test, one was installed on aircraft for 8 takeoffs and nearly 22 hours proof flight tests. The results proved that the engine worked steadily, its performance was good, and it met the design requirements. With the cooperation and support within and outside of MAI, several new materials were used, with the titanium alloy amounting to about 17% of the engine weight. Some new production techniques were successfully developed such as the profile machining of the deep hole of the long shaft and the welding of the complicated casing. Some new surface treatment techniques were also used, for instance: the Ni—Cd diffused coating against corrosion at moderate temperature, graphite varnish against the titanium alloy being stuck together, and aluminizing siliconizing of turbine blades against high temperature corrosion. The needed parts and accessories were all ready and small batch production could begin. The development of the WS8 engine was a major achievement. Later, as the Y—10 aeroplane would not go on and there were no other applications, the engine did not get the type certificate.

For the development of the aeroplane and engine, an open test bed for the engine reverser was set up in Shanghai in the late 1970s, and was later retrofitted to be a standard open test bed for thrust calibration of new engines.

4.   Import of Spey Engine Technology

In the mid 1970s, China purchased the manufacturing licence of theSpey MK202 turbofan engine from Rolls—Royce, England. This engine was developed from the commercial Spey MK511. At the beginning of the 1970s, England re—engined their F4 Phantom fighters purchased from the United States with Spey engines. The United States also imported the engine, and used it on A7 attack aircraft. The purchase of the Spey Engine technology was a major decision for China.

At the end of 1971, at a conference on aero—product quality, Premier Zhou Enlai, with regard to the problem of declining quality and poor performance of China—produced aero engines, pointed out that the engine is the "Heart", and asked "How can one fight with a poor Heart uncured"! Following the meeting, he asked MAI to improve the quality of the products, and also to study how best to introduce foreign technology into China. Ye Jianying, Vice Chairman of the Military Commission of CCCPC, and Li Xiannian, Vice Premier, led the study and evaluation and decided to import the military version of the Spey from England. In May 1972, contact with the UK commenced, and a technical survey team was sent to the UK. In August 1974, the negotiations reached a substantial stage, and the technical import contract was signed on December 13th, 1975.

The Spey MK202 had a high thrust augmentation ratio (i.e. the ratio between the thrust with reheat and the thrust without reheat) comparatively low s.f.c., longer operation life, big surge margin of the compressor, high efficiency of components at various conditions and stable and reliable running. It had an air bleed system for the flap BLC (boundary layer control) to improve the take—off and landing performance of the aeroplane. However, the engine structure was complicated, the thrust to weight ratio was relatively low, and the thrust was insufficient at high altitude. It was, however, a good engine for China to import at that time.

The engine was designated as the WS9 and produced by XEF, and the State paid close attention to the development. Vice Premier Wang Zhen inspected the factory three times, and the Vice Minister of MAI, Mo Wenxiang, was assigned by the MAI to lead a team in the factory. They worked with Shaanxi Province to organize the relative factories, institutes, colleges and universities to translate technical documents and to produce toolings. The State allocated a specific fund for the trial production and the factory's technical reformation. The supply of domestic raw materials was also arranged.

Fig.53 Wang Zhen viewing the WS9 engine

The trial production in XEF started in 1976. The massive staff members and workers contributed all their efforts and completed the translation and copying of 420,000 pages of documents and finished about 30,000 tooling design drawings and the manufacture of these toolings. During the tooling manufacturing stage, Li Guofu, Qu Guangxin, Ma Shiying and other technical leaders of the factory organized the work to tackle the key technical problems and detail parts trial production, solving 76 critical techniques. The titanium alloy thermal forming was a unique process jointly worked out with BAMTRI, superceding the process specified in the supplied technical documents.

Through more than 3 years' effort, in the latter part of 1979, 4 WS9 engines were assembled in two batches. In November the same year, the 150 hours endurance test was completed in China jointly conducted by the British and the Chinese. From February to May 1980, the engine test in the simulated altitude test facility including cold starting at −40 ℃ and fatigue cycling test for 5 major components were carried out in England. All the results met the technical requirements. Documents were signed between the representatives of the two sides for clearance of the qualification test of the China−made WS9 engine.

The successful production of the WS9 engine enabled China to have a moderate thrust reheat turbofan engine.

The manufacturing techniques in the Chinese engine industry were brought to a much higher level through the production of the WS9 engines. The engine had a complicated structure, with many blades, precision parts, thin wall fabrications and complicatedly shaped pipes. Some existing Chinese materials used, however, were of poor quality. In order to solve this problem, new work processes and new technologies were introduced including the electro-chemical machining, electron beam welding, laboratory control, inspection and measuring, precision casting and precision forging. The parts and the toolings manufactured were one grade higher in precision than those previously used in China. During the production of the WS9, the factory mastered 13 items of advanced world technology such as the metal spray, vacuum heat treatment, pipe butt welding, vacuum brazing, NC pipe bending and electro machining, and in addition mastered 46 advanced technologies in China including soft die forming and creep feed grinding. Through the development of the WS9 engine, the manufacturing techniques and technical levels of China's metallurgical, chemical and machinery industries were also improved. Therefore, the gap between China and advanced aeronautical countries in engine manufacturing technology was considerably narrowed.

The imported 137 copies of design and calculation reports and test reports, as well as the complicated manufacturing documents of the Spey engine, were used as reference guides for design and development of our engines, and the manufacture of other western advanced engines.

The import of the Spey promoted the technical reformation of the factory, which purchased some 700 advanced machine tools and facilities from abroad. In its numerical control (NC) machine workshop, there were 26 NC machines both made in China and from abroad, supported by the capabilities of programming, setting, machining and inspection. There were 23 sets of special equipment for producing WS9 parts, which were modified by the factory from their existing capabilities. For example, the machining of the contours of HP and LP compressor casings was done in England by a special copy milling machine, at a cost of 800,000 Pounds Sterling. Niu Chunpu and his colleagues modified a conventional vertical milling machine, which performed the task perfectly. The precision casting and precision forging production lines all had first class facilities and work processes. It produced very few allowance forging and casting blanks, which greatly saved precious alloys, equipments and manhours. It served not only for other aeroengine factories, but also other military and commercial enterprises. XEF became an aeroengine manufacturing base with the manufacturing technique world competitive in the 1970s.

The introduction of the Spey was the starting point for China's aviation industry to further develop extensive international technical cooperation.

The main problem of the import of Spey engine was that there was no proper applications for the engine, which affects the full use of the benefit both in technology and economy.

Section 6   The Development of Turboprop Engines

The turboprop engine is a type of aero gas turbine engine which uses the gas turbines to drive the propellers. The power consists of the pull force from the propeller and the thrust generated by the exhaust gas. Compared with the piston engines, it has higher power, a lighter weight and lower vibration. Compared with the turbojet engine, it has lower s.f.c. and higher take—off thrust. Due to the restriction of the propeller, the turboprop aeroplane normally can fly at 550 to 750 km / h.

In structure, the turboprop engine is the turbojet engine plus more stages of turbines, the reduction gear box and propeller. This type of engine is widely used in commuter aeroplanes, long range transport aeroplanes and multi—role aeroplanes.

China set up a turboprop engine design office in HEF in 1958 and the office then endeavoured to design a turboprop engine. As the need for piston engines decreased, HEF and ZEF, under the leadership of their Directors Tang Qinxun and Guo Gubang, actively turned to producing and developing gas turbine engines. In 1968, Zhuzhou Aeroengine Research Institute (ZARI) was established. In the past twenty or so years, China has developed and produced several kinds of turboprop engines for application on transport and water—based bombers.

1.   WJ5 Engine

MAI decided in September 1965 that ZEF would develop the WJ5 engines. Its take—off equivalent power was 1,874 kW (2,550 hp) and it would be used in Y—7 transport aeroplanes. This factory had a very good foundation in technology and management, and the staff members and workers had high initiatives. Therefore, they soon finished the detail drawings; completed the design and manufacture of several thousands of toolings and equipments; solved about 50 technical difficulties such as the broach of turbine disc grooves and the welding of the annular combustion chambers; and produced and assembled the complete engines. By the end of 1966, the WJ5 prototype engine went through the 100 hours test. In 1968, because of the shifting of tasks, the WJ5 engine was transferred to HEF for continuous development. HEF made 13 times endurance tests using 8 prototype engines from the latter part of 1968 to 1976. The accumulated test time was 5,678 hours. They also did flight tests and actual operation and solved various technical problems. The design was certified by the State in January 1977.

2.   WJ5A Enigne

In 1969, in order to raise the take—off power and satisfy the need of a water—based aircraft, the development of the WJ5A started. The main points for design modifications were: to increase the take—off equivalent power from 1,874 kW to 2,315 kW (3,150 hp); to raise the power—weight ratio from the original 4.25 to 5.25; to increase the ambient temperature limit for keeping the above—mentioned take—off power from 25℃ to 30℃ to improve the take—off performance in hot area. For this the engine needed further 147 kW (200 hp) reserved power. Thus, at 30℃ temperature, the modification design had to increase the equivalent power by 588 kW (800 hp).

Soon after the task was defined, HEF formed a modification design team, and gained support from SARI and Harbin Military Engineering Institute. Through the evaluation of the proposals, it was decided to use hollow air—cooled turbine blades, for it could increase TET by 150 ℃, and hence there was an increase of 441 kW (600 hp) in power. When the aircraft took—off at high ambient temperature conditions, by increasing 500 r.p.m. of the engine for a short while, another 147 kW could be gained to meet the requirement.

During the modification design, attention was paid to the combination of inheritance and creation, they bravely adopted new techniques, new processes and new materials to make the critical parts related to the performance increase. For instance, in newly designed turbine parts, the blades and vanes were high temperature alloy castings which had good plastic property; the turbine casing had integral stainless steel double layer construction and the NGV was in segments as opposed to a welded single layer construction which could not sustain the high temperature. The turbine blade was designed short in airfoil, with 7 straight cooling holes, shrouds, deep root, less separations, and narrow chord, and was assembled in pairs. The adoption of the advanced technology ensured the improvement of the turbine efficiency, reduced the size, improved the heat resistance and stress conditions, maintained the long life structure and reduced the total weight by 14 kg. There were also some other technical improvements, but original parts were used to their maximum extent. Therefore, there were only 126 newly designed parts and components, which was 8% of the total number of the engine parts. The modification design of the WJ5A was to the full extent a combination of practicality, inheritance and advancement.

In April 1970, all modification design drawings were released and the first prototype was made in less than half a year and followed by the ground test. There were then difficulties in running tests and also a lot of troubleshootings. By the end of 1970, when the engine ran to 28 hours, an incident occurred in which the turbine blades were broken to pieces and the engine was on fire, Sha Lingpu, Director of HEF's Design Institute, and other engineers carried out in—depth investigations, inspected hundreds of flakes, analysed the trace of the trouble, and

Fig.54　WJ5A engine for water based bomber

found that the failure was caused by improper thermal centralization of the LP turbine outer shroud. During the operation the shroud shrank in bore diameter and hit the highly rotated turbine blades. They sought advice from domestic and foreign sources and used thermal centralization of free expansion of each stage's outer shroud, thus solving the problem. They finally completed the modification design, and in January 1980, the WJ5A engine was certified and released for small batch production.

The successful development of the WJ5A engine was a contribution to the SH−5 water bomber which would serve China's Navy air force. It also pushed forward the R& D of turboprop engines. In the meantime, it created conditions for the Y−7 aeroplane to serve the airline.

3. WJ5A Ⅰ Engine

The Y−7 aeroplane with the original WJ5 engines could not take−off with full load in the hot season and on plateau, due to insufficient power, thus greatly limiting the use of the aeroplane. In 1979, MAI decided that HEF would try to modify the WJ5A and to install it in the Y−7 aeroplane. During the re−engine process, a readjustment of the power distribution proportion between the turbine stages of the WJ5A engine was carried out to limit the take−off equivalent power to 2,132 kW (2,900 hp), and the ambient temperature limit was re−set to 38 ℃. This modified version was designated as the WJ5A Ⅰ engine.

The first batch of the modified engines passed the endurance test and then the performance matching flight test was completed. The result showed: the engine had high take−off power and good temperature characteristics and hence the aircraft had a greater climb rate and a faster cruise speed. The second batch of modified engines were stressed on the improving of the structure and the material, aiming at extending the engine operation life. The Y−7 aeroplane with WJ5A Ⅰ engines experienced flight tests in the hot season and on plateau. It took−off with full load of 21 tons smoothly from Wuhan airport when it was 38.5 ℃, and from Zhongchuan airport where it was 1,948 m above sea level and Keermu airport where it was 2,840 m above sea level. The modification of the WJ5A Ⅰ engine took 3 years. The engine was certified for series production in 1982.

4. WJ6 Engine and Its Modifications

In 1969, ZEF was tasked to develop the WJ6 engine — the powerplant for the Y−8 aeroplane which could also be used in the Soviet−made Il−18 passenger aeroplane. The take−off equivalent power was 3,124 kW (4,250 hp), and it weighed 1,200 kg. The transition from piston engine to turbine engine excited the staff and workers of the factory. With the cooperation of XEF, the design was completed by the end of 1969. In the meantime, the factory carried out technical reforms. During the construction of the WJ6 engine test cell, several thousands of the employees assisted and the work was finished 45 days ahead of schedule. In the trial production of the new engine, the technical people, workers and cardres were combined as one, and they solved 163 critical technical problems. In September 1970, the first engine prototype was built and the running test was started. By 1973, three endurance tests were undertaken smoothly. However, the accident of the oil pipe breaking at combustion chamber casing occurred twice in the 500 hours State appraisal tests in 1973 and 1975, and caused the failure of the test. The vice chief engineer Fei Binfang and WJ6 chief designer Cai Wangshui organized an investigation and repeated tests. They found that the two causes of the oil pipe breaking were not from the engine itself. One was the reverse flow in the test cell, which caused the engine vibration and another was the improper bleeding. They took measures to correct the insufficiency of the test cell and changed the way of bleeding. The problems were cleared. The third appraisal test was carried out in 1976, and passed smoothly. Following that was the 5 months acceptance flight test. The Y−8, which was being tested flew over 15 provinces and cities in China and covered a range of 60,000 km. They went to Hainan Island down in the South, and Hailaer up in the North. It successfully accomplished flight programs in very cold (−23.4 ℃), very hot (+38.1 ℃), and plateau (3,540 m above sea level) areas. The WJ6 engine was proved to be reliable in operation and its performance met the technical specification. In January 1977, the State issued the design certificate and it was put into small−batch production. After extensive tests and studies on its components and the complete engine, measures for improvement were taken, such as: the proper adjustment of the compressor vane installation angle, the adjustment of the clearances between the individual parts of the oil system and oil pressure, and modification of the combustor ignitor, etc.. The 4 remaining problems of insufficient power, high oil consumption, high exhaust gas temperature and short TBO were solved one by one. They soon increased the first TBO from 300 hours to 1,000 hours. In 1986 it was further extended to 2,000 hours. The in−factory tests of technical improvements for life extension to 3,000 hours was also accomplished. In 1984, the engine successfully passed the flight test to Tibet. In 1980, the engine was awarded the second class prize of the National Science and Technology Achievements.

After the WJ6 engine was released for production, the aircraft factory proposed to modify the Y−8 with a pressurized cabin and to increase its pay load capacity. They requested permission to increase the engine power. To this end, ZEF started the modification of the engine in 1977. They decided to use air−cooled turbine blades to increase TET and the r.p.m. The engine power was raised by 221 kW (300 hp) and it was named the WJ6A engine. The first prototype was built in early 1983, and after running tests, its performance reached the design value. In June the same year, the 150 hours reliability test was passed and it proved that the modification design was successful.

5. WJ9 Engine

The WJ9 engine was developed on the basis of WZ8 engine core, i.e. the turbo−shaft engine was turned into turboprop engine. Zhuzhou Aeroengine Company (ZAC), which was formed by merging ZEF and ZARI in 1983, was responsible for the development. Its take−off power was 500 kW (680 hp). The immediate application was for Y−12 aeroplane, and in the future it might be used on agricultural aircraft and other special purpose aircraft.

The work started in 1983. The axial flow compressor, gas generator and power turbine were the same as that on the WZ8. The jet pipe, reduction gears, accessory drive, oil and fuel system were all newly designed. The drawings were basically finished in 1984. The first two prototypes were built in 1985. In 1986 the component rig test and the complete engine test were conducted and, by the end of that year, the main engine and power turbine all reached 100% of the design speed. Engine performance parameters also met the design specifications, thus showing that the structure of the modification design was feasible. The development is still under way.

The WJ9 engine development was a good exercise for the technical team. The derivation of various types of engines from a common engine core is a trend in aeroengine technology development throughout the world. The development of WJ9 engine will promote the programme of using the WZ8 engine as the basis and turning it into various turboprop and turbo—shaft engines.

Section 7　The Development of Turboshaft Engines

The turboshaft engine is derived from the turboprop engine and used as the powerplant for helicopters. Its work concept and structure are basically the same as that of the turboprop engine. The power turbine drives the helicopter's main rotor and tail rotor through the transmission systems. As the speeds of the main and tail rotors should not be too high, it is necessary to have several reduction gears between them and the engine main shaft.

The turboshaft engine has higher power to weight ratio and longer life, and its s.f.c. is equivalent to that of superior piston engines. It can use the cheaper kerosene rather than gasoline. Therefore, from the 1950s, it has gradually replaced piston engines on helicopters. The use of turboshaft engines makes the design and manufacture of large helicopters become feasible.

China's aviation industry started to develop turboshaft engines from the mid 1960s. It has developed and produced WZ5, WZ6 and WZ8 engines.

1. WZ5 and WZ5A Engine

a. WZ5 Engine

In 1966, MAI assigned to HEF the task of modifying the WJ5 engine into the WZ5 engine. The designed shaft power was 1,618 kW (2,200 hp), with a weight of 700 kg and it would be used on the Z—6 helicopter. On this basis, the performance can be further increased and it can be used as a twin—packaged powerplant to provide more power for new helicopters.

The design concept was: to keep the flow path of the WJ5 engine unchanged, and to modify the mechanical transmission and free turbine governor. After intensive hard working, the first prototype engine was put to the running test. In 1968, the Zhuzhou Aeroengine Research

Institute (ZARI) was set up. The development of the WZ5 engine was transferred to ZARI. The manufacture of the prototype was still carried out by HEF. HEF and ZARI jointly formed a development team for the follow-up test and design amendments. The 400 hours endurance test was passed at the beginning of December 1969. On December 15, in the cold winds of Northern China, people were crowded along the two sides of the airfield at HAF. They excitedly witnessed the test flight of the first Chinese-designed helicopter to use the turboshaft engine.

After solving the problem of the loss of height during hovering in the flight test, the Z-6 helicopter was flight tested from a high airport for the first time in 1970, with excellent results.

In April 1973, the WZ5 engine was transferred to Jiangsu Province for continuous production. The engine passed the State ground test and flight test appraisal in October 1976. The result showed that the WZ5 engine had good performance at high ambient temperatures and on plateau. At Nanjing airport when the temperature was 38 ℃, it could take-off vertically with 1.2 tons maximum payload; at Gonghe airport in Northwest China, 3,170 m above sea level, it could take-off vertically and hover with maximum payload. Later, the Aero-Product Certification Commission formally certified the WZ5 engine.

b. WZ5A Engine

Due to the low pay-load and low level of safety with single engine operation of the Z-5 and Z-6 helicopters, the development of a new helicopter, Z-7, started in 1970. The design of the powerplant was carried out by ZARI. It was decided to use the twin-packaged WZ5A engines, the modified version of WZ5. The take-off shaft power of a single engine was 1,714 kW (2,330 shp). The modification design was finished in the first half of 1971, followed by the component rig tests such as the static stress and rigid tests for the load-bearing case of the free turbine and the zero load running of the elastic coupling, etc.. Because of the disturbance of the "great cultural revolution", the development work was adversely affected. The 50 hours endurance test was started as late as July 1978, and the performance reached the design target. Later as the development of the Z-7 was cancelled, the further development of WZ5A was also given up.

2. WZ6 Engine

In 1975, Jiangxi Helicopter Factory (JHF) started to develop the Z-8 large land and water based helicopter. The powerplant was WZ6 engine (each helicopter equipped with 3 engines). The engine would be developed by Jiangxi Helicopter Engine Factory (JHEF).

The WZ6 was a free turbine turbo-shaft with a rear output shaft engine. The take-off shaft power was 1,130 kW (1,536 shp) and the weight was 300 kg. The engine features were high speed, small size, precision detail parts, and many integral machined parts, precision casting parts, welded parts, balanced parts and curvic couplings, which were difficult in the cold and heat workings, the assembly and test.

JHEF was set up by HEF in 1969, with 1 / 3 of the personnel and equipment transfered from HEF. Therefore it had a fairly strong technical team. The WZ6 engine development started at the beginning of 1975. It was led by chief engineer Du Jingqing. Yang Ronghua and Chen Shiying were responsible for design. The design drawings were finished in 1976. In 1980 the first batch of engines were put for running on the test bed. The 500 hours endurance test was passed in 1982. The 2nd batch of engines after a series of appraisal tests in 1986, were then installed on the Z−8 helicopter for adaptability flight. The Z−8 flew for 46 hours. After the drawings and technical conditions for the pre−production batches were perfected, the third batch of the engines were produced.

3. WZ8 Engine

The WZ8 engine was made under the licence of the Arriel−1c turboshaft engine from Turbomeca, France. It was installed on the Z−9 helicopter (twin engines). The engine was developed by France in the early 1970s, and delivered for operation in 1978. It was installed in French Ecureuil (single engine) and Dauphin (twin engines) helicopters. The engine had simple structure, big design margin and good reliability. This engine used the modular design, with small size and light weight (118 kg), high power (515 kW, 700 shp), high speed (gas generator rotor at 51,800 r.p.m.). In the design new technologies were adopted such as supersonic compressor, curvic coupling, directionally−solidified superalloy blades, integral structure, thin wall structure and anti−salt corrosion. There are about 50% of the parts made of high temperature alloy and stainless steel. The design and manufacturing techniques are both advanced.

ZEF started to produce WZ8 engine in 1980. The work proceeded in 4 phases: first by using the complete kits from France to do the assembly and test; second by using the French raw material and blanks to produce some modules and together with other modules supplied by France to do the final assembly and test; third by using French raw materials and blanks to produce all 5 modules and then to complete the final assembly and test; fourth all raw materials, blanks, finished parts and accessories would be Chinese. In 1985, an all Chinese made WZ8 engine

Fig.55　The factory people are discussing problems in front of the WZ8 engine

passed the running tests conducted by the French and the Chinese and then it passed the assessment of various special processes. In June 1987, the French side issued the certification for the manufacturing under licence and also highly praised the quality of the product. Up to 1986,

35 engines were built and delivered to users for operation. According to the offset contract, 40 accessory gear boxes were delivered to France, which were well received. The development of indigenous materials and blanks were also carried out in parallel.

The WZ8 could also be used on armed helicopters. With modification, it could be converted to a turboprop engine for use on commuter airliners and agriculture aeroplanes.

In order to produce the WZ8 engine, ZEF took 12 items for technical reform, such as heat and surface treatment, physical and chemical metrology, non−destructive testing (NDT), N.C. machining, precision electric spark machining, electronic beam drilling, welding and plasma spraying. They funded the project with loans from the government and money raised by themselves. The Director of the factory, Wu Shenduo, insisted on handling the matter realistically and with careful calculation and strict budgeting. Those they could make themselves and could get domestically would not be purchased from abroad. For instance, the press forming equipment for the jet pipe was originally planned to be imported from abroad, and as it was too expensive, the workers and technicians pooled their wisdom and strength to produce it themselves. They succeeded. For the electron beam welding (EBW) machine, they worked together with BAMTRI, designed and manufactured it themselves, with only a few parts such as the high voltage power supply unit which they purchased from abroad. The performance met the international standards, and thus they saved more than 300,000 US Dollars. For the total technical reform of the factory, only 64 advanced equipments were imported and 35 million Yuan RMB spent, which met the targets.

The accuracy of the finished WZ8 engine was one grade higher than the factory's other products, and the requirement on the integrity of the heat and surface treatment was very strict. Taking the shot peening process as an example, the requirement on the equipment, measuring tools, coverage, strength and finish of the shot peening were very different from the previous processes. Facing the complicated manufacturing techniques, the chief engineer of the factory, Wang Jingtang, and the vice chief engineer Luo Guangyuan led the engineers and technicians to study in depth, testing repeatedly, and solving many technical difficulties such as the machining of the deformable thin wall rings, rolling of high hardness thread, and electric spark forming of deep blind holes. They became familiar with new manufacturing specifications such as the allowance system and finish standards, and quality control system. The factory made an obvious improvement in technology and management and achieved the capability of producing modern advanced small aeroengines.

4. Power Transmission System of Helicopters

The helicopter power transmission system is a gear train transmission unit which reduces the speed of the output shaft of the turboshaft engine or piston engine to the speeds required by the main rotor and the tail rotor. The system consists of the main reduction gear box, the intermediate reduction gear box, the tail reduction gear box and driving shafts. The main reduction gear reduces the speed of the engine output shaft from several tens of thousands r.p.m. to a few hundred r.p.m. through multi—reduction. Therefore, it requires compact structured, light weight reduction gears, which can reliably operate for long periods of time at high speed and high load conditions. Also they need to be smooth working, with low noise and even engagement and good matching. Therefore, the design and manufacture of the power transmission system is also an important subject in the aeroengine field.

China's aviation industry set up the production of the power transmission system for piston engine helicopters in HEF at the end of the 1950s. They produced the P—5 reduction gear box for the Z—5 helicopter in batches. Later they designed and developed the reduction gear box for the Z—6. Towards the beginning of the 1980s, the development and manufacture capabilities of the helicopter power transmission system were set up in South China, which included ZEF, ZARI and the Hunan Aero—Gear Factory. They developed the power transmission system for the Z—7 helicopter and carried out the development and production of the power transmission system for the Z—8 helicopter. The Z—9 helicopter's power transmission system was developed and produced by HEF and the Hunan Aero—Gear Factory.

Section 8　Industrial and Marine Gas Turbine Engines Derived from Aeroengines

The conversion of aeroengines into the industrial and marine gas turbine engines is an important business with a bright future.

The turbomachine which turns the energy of high temperature and high pressure gas flow into mechanical energy is generally called a gas turbine engine. Apart from its use as an aircraft power plant, the gas turbine engine is also widely used in industry and ships. Compared with conventional internal combustion engines and steam engines, the gas turbine has a much higher operating temperature. In its industrial application, the high temperature and high pressure gas expands and produces useful work through the turbine, which in turn drives the generator. The exhaust gas is still about 500 degrees C and it could go to the residual heat boiler, which in turn produces high pressure steam. The steam drives the steam turbine for electricity generation for the second time (the steam and the hot water can also be used directly). The waste gas from the boiler can be absorbed by the heat exchanger for the industry and daily uses. The heat energy of the fuel can be exploited in steps and the combined heat utilization rate will reach more than 80%. The gas turbine has the following advantages: light weight, small size, quick start, high reliability, no need for cooling water and adaptable to various fuels such as diesel, heavy oil, petroleum, natural gas, tail gas, low heat value gas, etc. It is easy to install or dismount, with a small amount of construction work, and can be remotely auto—controlled. Therefore, the gas turbine engine is a more adaptable, advanced, energy saving power plant. The industrial countries in the world all develop it with great efforts. Thus it plays an important role in the field of power and transportation.

The industrial gas turbine has developed in two directions: one is specially designed and developed for industrial use mainly heavy—duty; another is the design on the basis of aero—technology or to convert the aeroengines; they are normally lighter in structure, and called light—duty gas turbine (LDGT). After the 1960s, the aero gas turbine engines have made rapid progress, and the related technology has reached a mature stage. The reliability and economy are greatly improved, the compressure ratio is about 25, and TET reaches 1,400℃ .That is one generation ahead of the ground heavy—duty gas turbines. Therefore, most of the industrial and marine light—duty gas turbines are modified and developed from aeroengines. In this way, it can take the advantage of the advanced technology achieved by the aviation industry with a lot of manpower, material, money and time. In the industrial countries, all successful aeroengines have their industrial and marine versions.

In the 1960s China started to modify her aeroengines into industrial gas turbine engines. Starting from the 1970s, the gas turbine units derived from WZ5, WJ5 and WJ6 were used in oil fields for trial successfully. In 1981, under the leadership of the Machinery Commission, a gas turbine applied research team was formed, who carried out investigations, presented proposals and forcefully pushed forward the development. Since then a new era of the LDGT extensive development has begun. In September 1985, the LDGT Development Centre was set up in MAI, which conducted the management of the LDGT development. They gave priority to energy development and conservation, and transportation. Up to the end of 1986, they had delivered 51 sets (83 units) of industrial gas turbines, which were installed in oil fields all over the country, including Tibet.

1. The Use of LDGT in Energy Development

In energy development, especially in the petroleum industry, LDGT can be widely used.

a. Power Stations

An oil field needs to set up its own power supply as its main supply, or the peak time or emergency supply. If a new oil field is not connected to the normal power supply, an oil field power station is essential. The LDGT power generator group is movable and thus most suitable for the needs of the oil field where fuel supply is convenient. ZEF worked with the Beijing Heavy Electric Motor Factory and produced the YD—2000 container type movable

Fig.56　The gas turbine generator converted from WJ6 engine

power station, converted from the WJ6 engine. It could be quickly installed and moved, and its power rating was 1,800 to 2,000 kW. It could use light diesel, natural gas and the oil field gas.

—233—

Up to 1979, they had produced 17 sets, which were used in every big oil field. Single sets had already accumulated more than 10,000 running hours. The YD−1250 movable power station converted from the WJ5 engine by HEF was also in operation in Xinjiang and Daqing oil fields.

There are a lot of natural gas, oil field gas and oil refinery gas not fully utilized. The heat and electricity generator group converted from WP6 engine by SEF using natural gas. It first produced power and then provided steam through the residual heat boiler. The combined heat utilization rate reached 62%. In October 1984, it formally operated at Daqing oil field. To the end of 1986, it had accumulated 15,000 running hours with an average annual running time of more than 7,500 hours, and generated 62 million kWh and provided 176,000 tons of steam. As LDGT provided sufficient steam, and its temperature and pressure were stable, the recovery of the hydrocarbon gas was greatly improved and the daily output was doubled. The investment for the generator was fully recovered in less than one year. The operation and maintenance of the power station were managed by SEF, who bought the natural gas from the oil field and sold the electricity back to the oil field. This business was most welcome by the users. In 1986, SEF signed contracts with Daqing oil field and Zhongyuan oil field for the supply of 3 heat and electricity generator groups, 2 of which had already been put into operation successfully.

Fig.57   Gas turbine heat and electricity power
station in Daqing oil field

The Zhonghua Gas Turbine Company, jointly run by the Engineering Thermal physics Research Institute of CAS and XEF, worked with Beijing "Dong Fang Hong" (The East is Red) Oil Refinery Complex to implement an energy saving programme on gas−steam combined cycle. They converted the WS9 into a heat and electricity generator, which burned the residual gas from the refinery and generated electricity (4,500 kW), and then used a residual heat boiler instead of the original oil boiler to produce moderate pressure steam for the work process of the Refinery Complex. Thus saving on energy. The Wuxi Aeroengine Research Institute (WARI) also took part in the programme. This programme had entered the installation and commissioning stage by the end of 1986.

b. Water Filling Pump Power Station

Water filling is an important measure to guarantee the stable and high output of the oil field. It consumes about more than 40% of the total electricity of the oil field. The modified gas turbine can directly drive the water pump and make further use of the surplus heat. WARI converted 10 WZ5 engines in to water filling pump units, which were delivered for operation in Xinjiang oil field successfully from 1978. Up to 1985, the accumulated running hours were about 50,000, with the longest more than 13,410 hours for a single set. The water filling pump units converted from the WZ6 engine by JHEF were released for operation in Zhongyuan oil field in April 1985. To the beginning of 1987 it had run 5,000 hours in total and filled more than 410,000 cubic meters of water. The combined cycle unit converted from two WP6 engines by SEF was also installed in Daqing oil field for water filling and heat supply. The use of LDGT changed the energy utilization structure for water filling and saved energy.

c. Natural Gas Compressor Powerplant

The LDGT as a natural gas compressor powerplant can extensively be used for the compressing and feeding of natural gas, and in the hydrocarbon gas recovery unit. The hydrocarbon gas is the easiest part of the natural gas to be liquified. The natural gas is compressed by the compressor driven by LDGT and it is then cooled in the turbine expander, which in turn cools and liquifies the hydrocarbon gas for recovery. The remaining gas can still be used as chemical material or fuel. ZARI modified and developed the WZ5 engine as a turbocompressor unit; it was connected with the cooling turbine developed by the Hubei Aero—Accessory Research Institute (HAARI) and formed a hydrocarbon gas recovery unit. Four units were installed in Zhongyuan oil field; two of them had run 6,127 hours, compressed 62 million cubic meters of natural gas and recovered 5,800 tons of hydrocarbon by the end of 1986. It was estimated that after normal operation, the investment for the total installations could be recovered in two years.

d. Powerplant On Off—Shore Platform

LDGT is small, light weight, needs no water and can burn the nearby natural gas, oil field gas and petroleum and is easily switched over. It is the best powerplant on the off—shore platform. It is reported that some foreign deep sea platforms had 98% of their needed power supplied by LDGT. China has also started to work in this field.

e. Development for Further Energy Saving

The work involved in energy saving and making full use of LDGT to enable the LDGT to burn poor quality and low heat value fuel and form heat and electricity combined generator group of gas—steam cycle is of high priority. The aviation industry is currently cooperating with the chemical industry in testing and exploring this technique for small chemical fertilizer plants.

One of the note—worthy new energy saving subjects is the direct use of coal (after being gasified, slurried or powdered) as fuel for LDGT. Many countries in the world are studying this subject and China is also active in this field.

2. LDGT for Transportation

LDGT is also a suitable powerplant for trucks and ships. Some countries have already used it on ships, high speed locomotives and heavy trucks.

China still operates steam locomotives. They burn good quality coal with a thermal efficiency of only about 7—8% and their towing force and speed are low. The diesel motor has a higher thermal efficiency, but consumes much diesel oil, and is limited in power and weight; the towing force is also insufficient. The electrical locomotive is more advanced, but the construction expenses are very high. Therefore, their applications are all restricted. The adoption of LDGT as the power plant for locomotives, using heavy oil

Fig.58   The gas turbine for locomotive motor burning heavy oil

or coal as fuel has a bright future in China, soon to be realised. With the support from, and in cooperation with, the railway research departments ZEF has modified and developed the WJ6 engine as a locomotive motor. Its power is 2,574 kW (3,500 hp). The first modified prototype burning diesel was installed in a locomotive and tested at the end of 1985 running without load for 234 km and under heavy load for 53 km. The noise was low; starting acceleration good; starting success rate 100%; towing force climbing the slope was big; and there was no need for cooling water; necessary starting power was small, without diesel starter etc. The second step was the development of the gas turbine to burn heavy oil. By the beginning of 1987, the single tube and double tube combustion tests with heavy oil had been accomplished, the manufacture and assembly of the engine had been finished and the engine was ready for testing.

3. LDGT as the Powerplant for Ships and Tanks

In the past ships were powered by steam or diesel engines. As the gas turbine has higher power, lighter weight, smaller size, and good starting capability, fewer accessories, high reliability and low noise, its application was rapidly extended from aircraft to marine ships. It is reported, that there are more than 40 countries using gas turbines as the powerplant for their

Navy ships. There are several combinations of the ship powerplant, such as the gas—diesel combination (i.e. using gas turbine for high speed and diesel for low speed and cruising); gas turbine combination, (i.e. all power provided by the gas turbine). From the mid 1970s, in more than 1,300 frigates above 1,000 ton class newly built or to be build by various countries, about 88% are using the above—mentioned powerplant combinations. Operation has proved that tactical and technical performances of the ships are greatly improved by using gas turbines. For newly designed and built ships such as frigates, destroyers etc., the adoption of gas turbines as their powerplant is an important mark of powerplant modernization.

In the industrial countries, the powerplant for main battle tanks has been changed from high speed diesel engines to gas turbine engines.

China commenced study and development of modifying the aeroengine into marine powerplant from the beginning of the 1970s. ZEF worked in conjunction with the Harbin Marine Boiler and Turbine Engine Research Institute to develop the powerplant for hovercraft by modifying the WJ6 engine. It has passed the ground test and has come to the stage of being tested on hovercraft. XEF is also converting the WS9 engine into a 11,000 kW (15,000 hp) marine powerplant.

The use of LDGT for tanks has also entered into the exploration stage.

4. Other Applications of LDGT

LDGT can be used as fire fighting equipment in mines.

ZARI, working together with the Fushun Research Institute of the Coal Scientific Research Establishment, developed the DQ—1000 inert gas extinguishing device. It was one of the State level key technical programmes during the Sixth Five—year Plan and was certified by the State at the end of 1985. This device consisted of the gas generator of the WZ5 engine as its main motor (power section), the inlet anti—dust filter, plenum chamber, water cooling section and smoke channel, etc. During operation, the gas from the main motor was mixed with ejected fuel and burned for the second time in the plenum chamber, which reduced the oxygen content in the original gas from 17% to less than 3%. It was then cooled in the smoke channel by water ejection. It continuously produced the foggy inert gas mixed with rich steam which can extinguish fire or prevent blasting. When the mixed gas was ejected to the fire area, it rapidly deactivated the flammable gas and then extinguished the fire thus suppressing gas explosion. In December 1985, it was tested in a simulation of putting off a fire in a well of Pingxiang coal mine in Jiangxi Province. It showed that the performance was stable and it was a new type of device for putting off fire and preventing explosion in large mine wells. By the end of 1986, one DQ—1000 was delivered to Datong coal mine.

The development of industrial and marine engines derived from aeroengines has entered a new phase. The aviation industry has established cooperations with departments concerned in China. There are talks with related foreign companies on technology cooperation and trade combined, joint design and development, co—production and joint marketing. International cooperation will be widely carried out. The industry is working hard to rapidly form a series of LDGT from 440, 735, 1,470, 2,200, 2,940, 4,400, 9,550, 11,000 to 22,000 kW (i.e. from 600, 1,000, 2,000, 3,000, 4,000, 6,000, 13,000, 15,000 to 30,000 hp). It will continuously develop advanced engines, and contribute more to the "Four Modernizations", especially in the development of energy and transportation.

In August 1986, China National Aero-Technology Import & Export Corporation signed the FT8 gas turbine engine agreement with Pratt & Whitney in the United States for joint development, co-production and joint selling of gas turbine on the world market. The FT8 gas turbine is developed from the JT8D-219 aeroengine, which powered the large passenger aeroplanes of Boeing 727, Boeing 737 and MD 82 of the United States. The power rating is 24,000 kW (33,000 hp) and the thermal efficiency is 38.7%. It is an advanced gas turbine by present day standards and can be extensively used in industry and marine ships. The joint development of the FT8 gas turbine will promote the development of China's LDGT.

Over more than thirty years, China's aeroengine industry has achieved great success: it has established a large number of test facilities and considerable production capabilities; it has trial produced, modified, and developed many types of engines, which basically satisfied the need of the aircraft; it has trained and tempered a powerful technical team and gained precious practical experiences. All these have laid down a foundation for the development of new type aeroengines, and provided better services for the development of the advanced aeroplanes and other flight vehicles.

Due to insufficient experiences, China's aeroengine industry has gone through some detours in its development. The common problem had been the lack of a stable and long term plan. There had been too many changes to initial plans, and some developments were stopped half way; there was no effective accumulation of technical experiences; the performance of the products could not be improved step by step; the progress of constructions of research and test facilities was slow; there was no appropriate arrangement for the development and production teams; there were insufficient funds for the research and development; etc. All these have affected the progress of developing new engines. The special problem was that there was no thorough understanding of the features of the aeroengine development. This was mainly reflected in two aspects: one is that there was no sufficient understanding of the aeroengine industry as a relatively independent business. Very often the R&D of the engine followed the changes of the aircraft projects, i.e. when the aircraft project went, the engine project went; when the aircraft project was cancelled, the engine project was also cancelled accordingly, all of which was harmful to the development of the aeroengine technology. In fact, an advanced aeroengine can be developed into many versions for applications on different aeroplanes, and converted for industrial and marine powerplant. Therefore, the R&D of a new engine must be carried out in advance of, and independently of, the aircraft. In this way, the needs of the aircraft can be better satisfied. In the past, insufficient attention was paid to advanced R&D. Occasionally, a decision of launching a high performance engine programme was made when there was no sufficient technical base; when the core engine and component technology had not been solved, the development of the complete engine started. The result was "things went contrarily to wishes" and "more haste, less speed". Practice proved that the correct approach was to pay attention to applied research and prepare a solid technical base. On the one hand one should continuously use available technology and research results, and carry out improvements and modifications continuously on the existing engines; on the other hand, one should also actively develop advanced components and core engines.

Chapter VIII The Development of Airborne Equipment

Section 1 General Description

1. The Position and Role of Airborne Equipment in Aircraft

The airborne equipment is a general term referring to various equipments to ensure flying safety and to fulfil varieties of tasks of aircraft.

Aircraft are able to fly freely in the sky, over the ocean and perform varieties of tasks. Apart from aerodynamic characteristics and power produced by aeroengine, it also relies on functions of airborne equipment.

Usually, the performance and flying qualities of aircraft are described in terms of three aspects — airframe, aeroengine and airborne equipment. In the early days, airborne equipments were acting only as auxiliary devices. With the development of science and technology, the new achievements of various disciplines of science and technology have been applied to aircraft. The structure and systems of airframe and engine are getting more complicated, their performance being increasing rapidly. New requirements have been raised for airborne equipments, which greatly promoted the development of airborne equipment. The development tendency since World War Two shows that the position and role of airborne equipment in aircraft have been changing dramatically. The airborne equipment has become an important factor to improve the tactical and technical performance of aircraft, to increase its function, reliability, safety, comfort and economy. For some specific performance, the airborne equipment even plays the decisive role. The level of airborne equipment has already become one of the main criteria to judge the state of the art of aircraft.

Airborne equipment involves a broad spectrum of technology. Apart from traditional techniques, it uses newly—emerging techniques in modern technology such as infrared, ultrasonic, laser, electronics and computer. Especially, due to the application of electronics and computer technology in aviation, there has been formed a new subject of science — avionics, which improves the ability of communication, navigation, flight control, target acquisition, fire control and all weather flying etc.. The implementation of fly—by—wire technique and active control technique has greatly increased the manoeuvrability, adaptability and survivability, which has caused very profound change in aircraft design. Airborne equipment is very quick in the operational development and its types are getting more and more. The level of technical complexity is also getting higher and higher and the percentage cost of airborne equipment to total cost of aircraft has been increasing with time. Take Chinese—made fighter for example, this percentage occupies about 50%, and the tendency is going upwards constantly. The aircraft types and number of items of airborne equipment in main types of aircraft made in China are shown in Table 1.

Table 1   List of aircraft types and number of items of airborne
equipment in main types of aircraft made in China

fighter		transport		bomber	
type of aircraft	number of items	type of aircraft	number of items	type of aircraft	number of items
J—5	228	Y—5	140	H—5	342
J—6	301	Y—7	457	H—6	458
J—7	368	Y—8	677		
J—8	419				
J—7Ⅲ	434				
J—8Ⅱ	488				

Because the functions and roles of airborne equipment in aircraft have been constantly increasing, those countries developed in aviation field have put enormous amount of manpower, material and financial resources into research and development of advanced airborne equipment. To a great extent, the technical level of airborne equipment and the ability of integration in aircraft reflect the level of aeronautical technology and electronics industry of a country. China has become one of those countries in the world which are relatively highly self—sufficient in airborne equipment.

2.   The Development Process of the Airborne Equipment Manufacturing Industry in China

The scale of manufacturing of airborne equipment in old China was very small. Since the founding of new China, there has gradually been set up the airborne equipment industry which is relatively complete in types and combines production with scientific research. The development process can broadly be divided into following four stages:

a. The Setting—up Stage

In the early period of the founding of new China, the Korean War broke out. To be accommodated to the heavy tasks of aircraft repairing, the newly—set up aviation industry established repair shops of airborne equipment in three aircraft manufacture factories. It took over the Air Force's 21st factory which was quite strong in repairing airborne equipment (now is the Nanjing Aeronautical Accessories Factory) and the Tianjing Electrical Apparatus Factory (WEST) (now is the Tianjing Aeronautical Electrical Apparatus Factory) and the Pingyuan Machinery Factory in Xinxiang city from civil industries, and also established the Nanjing Parachute Factory. These factories were involved in repairing aircraft instruments, electrical apparatus, accessories, radio and armament equipment, and also trial—produced parachutes.

The production conditions then were very poor, the production shops were small and machinery old. The test and measurement instrumentation was simple and skilled technical people were not enough. But the staff was in high spirit, and they actively took up repairing task in such a difficult condition. This was the very beginning.

Since 1952, the aviation industry gradually widened the scope of repairing of airborne equipment from medium—scale repairing to overhaul and also increased the production of spare parts for maintenance. The repairing technique was completely mastered and the technical personnel were trained through practical work, making preparation for turning to production. Not long afterwards, reorganization and reform were carried out in each repair factory and shop, and major manpower was gradually shifted to production. In the process of turning from repairing to production, old factories played an active role. The Taiyuan Aeronautical Instruments Factory which was built on an old military camp, making use of the available conditions, reconstructed its old horse sheds into temporary production shops. Under the leadership of the director Yu Hui, technicians and workers were accomplishing repairing task on one hand, and on the other hand started trial production of new products. After only more than half a year, in 1954, the first batch of aeronautical instruments — pitot tube and magnetic compass were successfully copy produced. Zhu De, the Chairman of the Standing Committee of NPC twice visited the factory and praised it by using an old Chinese saying "Golden phoenix flies out of horse shed." He also warmly praised the hard spade working spirit of the staff. At the same time, the preparation to build a new factory was also under way. This was the setting up stage of the airborne equipment industry in China.

Fig.59　Zhu De visiting the Taiyuan Aeronautical
Instruments Factory

Fig.60   Chen Yi   visiting the Taiyuan Aeronautical Instruments Factory

Because the ability of repairing, manufacturing and integrating airborne equipment and associated spare parts in aircraft increased year by year, less and less were ordered from foreign countries. Compared with the year of 1953, the foreign orders reduced by 38% in 1955. The shortage of Chinese made airborne equipment in relation to airframes and engines began to be softened.

b. The Licence Production Stage

Roughly speaking, this stage was from the mid 1950s to the mid 1960s. Under the unified planning of the government, during the First Five—year Plan, five factories such as the Taiyuan Aeronautical Instruments Factory, the Tianjin Aeronautical Electrical Apparatus Factory, the Nanjing Parachute Factory, the Nanjing Aeronautical Accessories Factory and the Xinxiang Aircraft Accessories Factory were reconstructed or expanded. In Shaanxi province were newly constructed five airborne equipment factories which were among the 156 important construction projects of the government at that time. These five factories were engaged in production of aeronautical instruments, aeronautical electrical apparatus, accessories of wheel brake, aircraft accessories and engine accessories. These large and medium—scale factories were constructed within one year and a half to two years with fine quality and started production afterwards. They laid a good material and technique foundation for development of airborne equipment.

After trial production of primary trainer CJ—5 and J—5 aircraft was successfully completed one after another, the Bureau of Aviation Industry made the "Decision on strengthening the work on instruments, electrical apparatus and accessories" in Nov. 1956. To be accommodated to the needs of airborne equipment in home-made aircraft, the airborne equipment manufacturing industry, while making repairing and being constructed concurrently, put its main manpower and other resources to launch licence production of products in large scale. The first batch of products included gyro, magnetic compass, horizon, voltage regulator, DC generator, steering column, hydraulic pump, parachute and fuel accessories of jet engine etc., basically meeting the needs of these two types of aircraft. This was a mark that the airborne equipment manufacturing industry realized a historical turn from repairing to manufacturing. By the end of the First Five-year Plan, 275 items of airborne equipment needed by three home-made aircraft CJ-5, J-5 and Y-5 (not including repetitive items) were mostly provided by domestic manufacturers.

During the Second Five-year Plan period, according to the policy of "setting up new factories to make up with what was short, and turn the airborne equipment industry into a complete system" made by the Bureau of Aviation Industry, to further meet the needs of trial production of bombers, helicopters and new fighters, the second batch of mainstay airborne equipment enterprises were set up, including the Beijing Aeronautical Instruments Factory, the Lanzhou Aeronautical Instruments Factory, the Beijing Aeronautical Electric Motor Factory, the Lanzhou Aeronautical Electro-operated Mechanism Factory, the Xinxiang High-altitude Equipment Factory and the Baoding Propeller Factory etc.. Being followed with interest by Chairman Mao Zedong, the Baoding Propeller Factory was built very quickly, which made the production of propellers for primary trainers be based on the country itself. While new factories were being set up, some civil factories were being transferred and reconstructed, and some aviation schools were also reconstructed into airborne equipment factories, including the Suzhou Aeronautical Instruments Factory, the Wuhan Aeronautical Instruments Factory, the Chengdu Aeronautical Instruments Factory, the Hefei Oxygen Instruments Factory and the Hubei Personal Protection Equipment Factory etc.. Due to successive completion of construction of these enterprises and putting into production, the airborne equipment manufacturing industry was taking shape with relative completeness of various specialities.

During the Second Five-year Plan period, a large number of products were produced under licence, basically meeting the needs of airborne equipment for J-5, J-6, Y-5, and Z-5 aircraft etc.. Some relatively high-technology products such as autopilot, DC electric power system, fuel pump, fuel regulator and environmental control system of aircraft cabin etc. were put into batch production. Through licence production, the production skill of airborne equipment was mastered, which created conditions for further improvement and modification and independent design.

During the process of licence production, airborne equipment enterprises summarized their experiences and strengthened the management of production and technology. In August 1956, a chief engineer meeting of instruments, electric apparatus and accessories factories was held and presided over by Chen Shaozhong, the vice director of the Bureau of Aviation Industry. At that meeting, four production and technology management documents were made on design, manufacturing technology, inspection and regulation for licence production of new products, which laid a foundation for further improvement in systematic and scientific management of production and technology of the airborne equipment.

c. The Improvement and Modification and Independent Design Stage

Generally, airborne equipment factories were constructed after the pattern of copy manufacture factory. Through copy production of airborne equipment for several types of aircraft, research and design teams were gradually formed. From the mid 1960s to the mid 1970s, the main work in scientific research and design of the airborne equipment was improvement and modification of products. To be exact, the main contents were as follows: to partly improve products, to widen application scope, to reduce number of types and to make the range of products a complete series; to utilize new material, new elements and parts, to elongate life cycle and to improve performance of products; to improve structure of products, to improve manufacturing technology, to raise production efficiency and to reduce cost. During this period, in the so-called third line aera (inland) such as Guizhou and Shaanxi provinces were constructed a batch of airborne equipment factories and the scale of production was expanded. In many factories, research and design departments were set up one after the other, which started products design with reference to sample machines and some printed materials in order to meet the needs of J—7, Q—5, H—6 and Y—7 aircraft made in China.

The first airborne equipment research and design organization — the Aeronautical Instruments Design Department was established in 1957, which was later developed into the Aeronautical Automatic Control Research Institute. Zan Ling, an expert in the aeronautical equipment, was responsible for setting up the institute. In the early 1960s, he also presided over the design work of the first set of autopilot used in bomber, the performance of which was better than that of autopilot of the same type then copy produced.

Since then, rocket ejection seat for fighter, heading gyroscope, fluid—floated rate gyro assembly, 12 KVA variable frequency AC electric power system, 30 KVA constant frequency electric power system, miniature quick plug and socket and many types of parachutes etc. designed on our own, were successfully designed and formed in series in research institutes and factories, meeting the needs of home—made aircraft.

d. Commencing All—round Independent Design and Advanced Research Stage

Starting from the early 1970s, with the beginning of new aircraft design work, on the basis of design and research departments set up in factories, research and design work was further strengthened, research teams expanded and research and testing facilities added in various airborne equipment enterprises.

During this period, six specialized research institutes such as the Aeronautical Automatic Control Research Institute, the Avionics Research Institute, the Rescue Equipment Research Institute, the Aeronautical Fire Control Research Institute, the Airborne Radar Research Institute and the Aeronautical Accessories Research Institute were set up and strengthened. A number of large—scale laboratories were also established. A preliminary research and design system of airborne equipment was formed. By the end of the 1970s, research institutes and research departments in factories respectively became more specialized in their own work. To meet the needs of airborne equipment for new home—made aircraft, those research and design organizations vigorously developed new products by means of advanced tools such as electronic computers and various simulation facilities. A large number of new products and new parts such as flight control system, heading and attitude reference system, air data system, optical gunsight, Doppler navigation system, fire control radar, rocket launcher and electro—hydraulic servo valves designed on our own were successfully developed and put into production one after the other, meeting the needs of airborne equipment for Y—7, Y—8, J—7 and J—8 aircraft.

After the Third Plenary Session of the 11th Congress of the Central Committee of the Communist Party of China, the policy of putting scientific research in advance was seriously carried out by the airborne equipment industry. The work of "producing a generation, developing a generation, exploring a generation" started. At the same time, technical exchange and cooperation with foreign countries was actively under way. All these raised the level of design and manufacturing. Advanced research in many new fields of airborne equipment was started to match the development of a new generation of aircraft.

New achievements were made in R&D of the inertial navigation system, oil—spraying cooling AC electric power system, fire control system, avionics integrated system, fly—by—wire system and active control technique etc., which provided technical base for development of new products. New products such as AC electric power system with electro—magnetic constant speed driving unit, digital air data computer, flight control system for fighter and head—up display etc. were installed into new aircraft or were flight tested.

Since the 1980s, the airborne equipment industry in China has made an enormous progress in the application of electronics technology and computer science. For example, flight control system has been transferred from production of traditional autopilot and development of stability augmentation system to advanced development of digital redundant fly—by—wire FCS; navigation system has been transferred from production of traditional navigation system to development of inertial navigation system and integrated navigation system; fire control system has been transferred from production of optical gunsight and radar rangefinder to development of integrated fire control system combining head—up display, computer and radar, etc. During this period, the level of the airborne equipment has been increased remarkably. The airborne equipment industry is marching towards the aim of research and development of new technology and advanced products.

3. The Main Achievements of the Development of Airborne Equipment

a. After more than thirty years of construction, there formed a sound material and technical foundation in the airborne equipment industry. A relatively large—scale production ability and rather strong scientific research teams were established. Teams with good technical quality and fine political quality were trained in research and production practice. Facilities needed for development of new products have gradually been set up, including high altitude environmental simulation Lab, inertial navigation system Lab, dynamic emulation Lab for fire control system, dynamic emulation Lab for flight control system, electric power system Lab, wheel brake inertial test rig and avionics dynamic integrated emulation Lab etc. In these Labs, necessary precision facilities were equipped for scientific measurement and testing, which created conditions for tests needed for development of new products. Basically, the airborne equipment industry with complete categories and compatible specialities has been formed.

b. The airborne equipment products have met the needs of aircraft, aeroengine and some tactical missiles, and made contributions to the construction of the national economy. In more than 30 years, the Ministry of Aviation Industry, the Ministry of Electronics Industry and the Ministry of Armament Industry have developed and produced more than 3,000 kinds of airborne equipment products, which were used for more than 10,000 aircraft, more than 40,000 aeroengines and more than 10,000 tactical missiles made in China. The statistics for used products under batch production are as follows:

YEAR	1954	1957	1962	1965	1970	1975	1980	1985
Number of kinds	19	203	525	776	1558	1378	1486	2431

Besides, the airborne equipment factories and research institutes of MAI have also developed and produced technical facilities and products for other military departments and civil organizations and enterprises. Export products and civil products are also constantly increasing.

c. Scientific organization and management have been carried out, rules and regulations set up and made complete, which allows research and production running orderly.

During copy production period, management systems for trial production of new products, production preparation, job planning, production scheduling, design process and quality assurance etc. were set up. In the early 1960s, combined with the experience in checking quality of products, management system of trial production of new products was improved. It was made clear that there should be four stages for design process, which were preliminary design, trial production design, certification design and batch production design. A complete set of technical management regulations covering from trial production of new products to batch production was formed, which played a positive role.

Entering into the stage of improvement and modification and independent design, the regulation for development of new products was modified and refurbished. It was emphasized that the improvement and modification and the development of new products must go through five stages — conceptional study of design, preliminary design and trial production, demonstrator design and trial production, design certification and batch production, which ensured the quality of design and development work and increased the efficiency and economic benefits of new products development.

With the development of technology, the airborne equipment has gradually been evolving from single product to several systems which in turn are developing towards integrated systems. It is an irrevocable tendency to exercise system engineering management from advanced development to engineering development and from the whole aircraft to various systems. This requires making integrated study of relationship between systems and subsystems, parts and assemblies, systems and the external environment, and also organizing works such as system design, system development, system testing and system certification. That means taking various types of new aircraft as " lines", and taking various systems of airborne equipments as "columns" to form a matrix management network of system engineering. While exercising system management, the director designers of airborne equipment system of new aircraft and project designers for parts and components will be appointed; the three aspects —technology, cost and schedule — will be combined together for study and review of the development of new products; organizing, coordinating and managing will be carried out from four aspects — design, cost, quality and administration — to realize optimum design, control and management, achieving fine results.

After more than 30 years development, airborne equipments in China have been developed into 19 systems (refer to Table 2) and 16 categories of parts and assemblies (refer to Table 3). The development and production of these products are mainly based on the Ministry of Aviation Industry, and are also cooperated with the Ministry of Electronics Industry, the Ministry of Armament Industry and the Ministry of Machine Building Industry etc.. Some systems are cross—responsible by different Ministries and departments. In this chapter, except those systems specially noted, the rest of systems are all under the responsibility of MAI.

Table 2   Categorized General Table of Airborne
Equipments & Weapon Systems

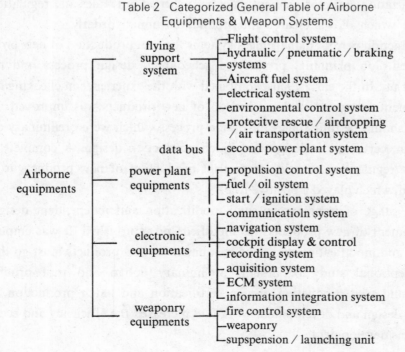

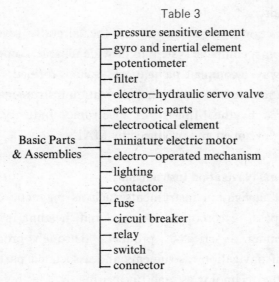

Table 3

Basic Parts & Assemblies
- pressure sensitive element
- gyro and inertial element
- potentiometer
- filter
- electro−hydraulic servo valve
- electronic parts
- electrootical element
- miniature electric motor
- electro−operated mechanism
- lighting
- contactor
- fuse
- circuit breaker
- relay
- switch
- connector

Section 2   Navigation System

Compass, as one of the four great inventions in ancient China, was the earliest direction finding instrument. It is also the plumule of modern navigation. The maritime compass appeared in the Middle Ages and the modern air magnetic compass were evolved and developed from the compass. However, it is far from sufficient for modern aircraft to rely only on the air magnetic compass, because during flight, all the time pilots have to know accurately and quickly that the aircraft is "where", "flying to where", "how fast flying?". To answer these questions, advanced navigation systems have to be used.

The functions of air navigation systems are to determine current heading, status and position of aircraft, and to guide the aircraft to fly according to predetermined flight route. In military aircraft, navigation systems have to perform concurrently the tasks of weapon delivery, reconnaissance, patrol, anti−submarine and rescure etc..

According to development stages, navigational systems can be divided into two large categories: one category is traditional navigation instruments and radio navigation equipments, and another category is navigation positioning equipments.

The traditional navigation instruments and radio navigation equipments mainly are: compass for indicating the heading of aircraft (including magnetic compass, gyro magnetic compass, radio compass, astronautical compass etc.); radio beacon receivers for indicating the direction of airport runway and identifying distance from and within airport.

For flying safety, these equipments and instruments are usually installed more than one set to make redundancy in order to prevent loss of information in case of failure of one or the other equipment.

Navigation positioning equipments refer to those navigation equipments which can determine the position of flying aircraft.

According to specific functional requirements of the aircraft, several navigational equipments can be selected to form a complete system to provide reliable, complete and accurate navigation information. By this way, a complete navigation system is formed.

Radio compass and beacon receivers of traditional navigation instruments and equipments etc. are developed and produced by the Ministry of Electronics Industry, and the rest of instruments and equipments are developed and produced by MAI.

1. The Development of Traditional Navigation Instruments

Since 1954, many types of navigation instruments such as magnetic compass, heading gyroscope, gyromagnetic compass, gyroscopic compass and heading system have been developed and produced, forming a series of products. Through production of these instruments, design technique of navigation instruments and associated parts and assemblies, various precision manufacturing technologies and measuring & testing techniques were mastered. Based on this, heading and attitude reference system and air data computer system were developed with emphasis.

a. Heading and Attitude Reference System

Gyroscopic magnetic compass and horizon indicating heading and attitude of the aircraft are important reference means for a pilot to steer aircraft. Their displays are located in the middle of cockpit central instrument panel. These instruments are based on gyroes as sensitive elements, which are composed of several miniature servo mechanisms. Compared with other instruments, they are more difficult to manufacture.

With constantly increasing of aircraft manoeuvrability, the aircraft attitude, especially aircraft banking, influences the heading displaying more and more, which results in great error. Hence, it is necessary to feed attitude information of the aircraft into gyroscopic magnetic compass to compensate. Thus, apart from two gimbals already existing in gyroscopic magnetic compass, it is needed to add one or two servo gimbals to receive attitude compensation signal, forming a three—gimballed or four—gimballed system. The structure of gyroscopic magnetic compass became more complexed and the number of servo mechanisms also increased.

So, in the early 1970s, the Baoji Aeronautical Instruments Factory launched development of two new products. One was suitable for use in small aircraft. Its function was relatively simple. It was a three—gimballed system and was still called gyroscopic magnetic compass. The other was suitable for use in large aircraft. Its function was more complexed with more output signals. It was a four—gimballed system and was integrated with horizon forming a complete system. It was called HZX Heading and Attitude Reference System. Wu Jinyu was responsible for the system design. Once the design scheme was fixed, the whole factory was mobilized to perform this task. Soonafter, the new demonstrator was developed and produced. In 1976, the design scheme of the Heading and Attitude Reference System was certified, and soon this type of equipment was used in new aircraft, forming a new generation of Chinese—made Heading and

98. Wumei colour parachute

99. Touwu-11 parachute

100. Life saving parachuts

Airborne Equipment

101. HZX heading and attitude system

102. KJ-11 flight control system components

103. JL7 firing
     radar in test

104. Generator driver

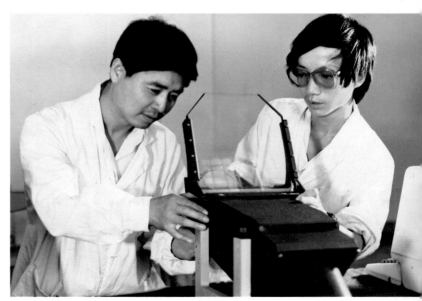

105. Adiusting a head up
     display

106. WP8 engine fuel control system

107. WS9 afterburner fuel system

108. Refrigeration component of a high pressure de-water environment control system

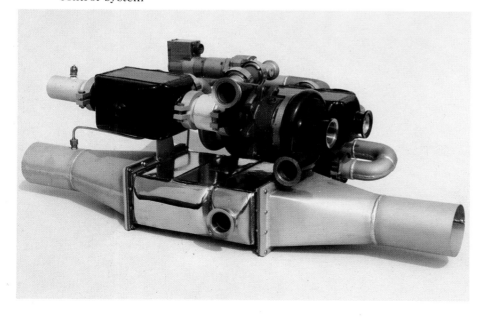

109. Environment control system test facility

110. 111. Turbine expander——the core component of an oil field gas recovery installation

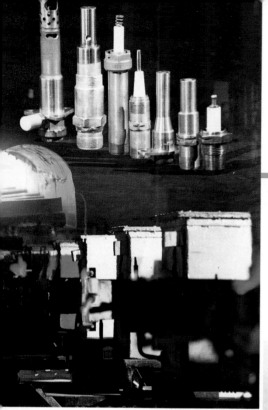

112. Aeronautical spark plug series

113. A State citation awarded
     for twin-engine starting box

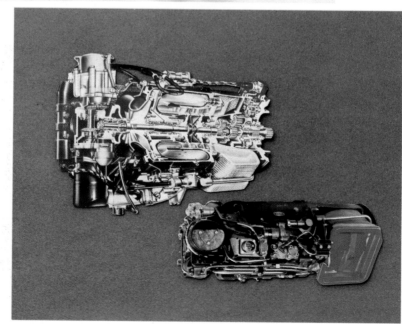

114. Gas turbine starter

115. Electronic anti-skid brake system

116. YM-9 hydraulic motor disassembled

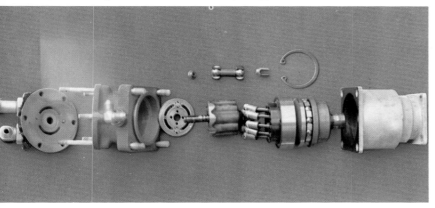

117. YZB-20 hydraulic pump disassembled

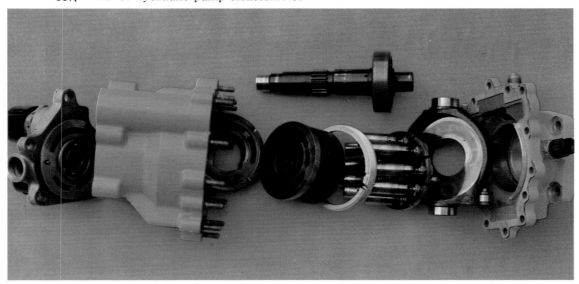

Working

Premier Li Peng establishes the potential for long-term cooperation with Mr. Brian Rowe, Senior Vice President of GE Aircraft Engines.

As the techno[...] of aircraft engin[...] progresses, so to[...] must the technol[...] base of the com[...] nies that manufa[...] them. Each day[...] industry become[...] more of a global[...] community, wit[...] each member na[...] contributing ski[...] resources and m[...] kets. It was wit[...] these facts in m[...] that GE Aircraft Engines made an agreeme[...] the early 1980s with the Shenyang Aeroeng[...] Factory of China.

Shenyang began subcontract manufactur[...] parts for GE's production of CF6 and CFM[...] commercial turbofan engines; and for CT6[...] turboprop and CJ610 turbojet engines. To [...] GE technical specifications and delivery sc[...] ules, Shenyang put in place manufacturing [...] technology and quality assurance programs [...] would satisfy the needs of the U.S. airwort[...] authorities.

GE wanted to expand this program to in[...] other Chinese aircraft engine factories. The[...] step was an order to the Xi'an Engine Comp[...] to manufacture turbine discs for the LM250[...] engine, GE's engine for ship propulsion and[...] industrial applications.

This was quickly followed by an import[...] step in technical cooperation - improveme[...] the performance and reliability of the Chine[...]

together

Dong Ruijun, Engineer from Harbin Engine
[Man]ufacturing Company, works on a design layout at GE
[Airc]raft Engines in the U.S.A.

A design review at GE Aircraft Engines includes (left to right) Audie Y. Mak, Project Program Manager GE; Zhang Ehne, Vice Director Shenyang Aeroengine Research Institute; Zou Zhong Yuan, Program Manager CATIC; Martin C. Hemsworth, Chief Engineer GE; Donald A. Brozenske, Engineering Program Manager GE; Feng Yong Chang, Vice Chief Engineer Harbin Engine Manufacturing Company; Jiang Yanying, Engineer Harbin Engine Manufacturing Company; and Stephen J. Chamberlin, Engineering General Manager GE.

[...]5A1 turboprop engine. Premier Li Peng and [GE]'s Senior Vice President, Brian Rowe agreed [that] engineers from both countries would work [tog]ether to further develop this Chinese design. [E]ngineers from the Harbin Engine Manufac-[turi]ng Company and from the Shenyang Aero-[eng]ine Research Institute would work with [eng]ineers from GE's engine factory in Lynn, [Ma]ssachusetts in the U.S.A. to redesign the [...]5A1 turbine section to improve fuel con-[sum]ption and to increase the service life of the [eng]ine.

[...] The first major phase of this program has [bee]n concluded successfully by the joint working [tea]m. The GE Aircraft Engine engineers were [ver]y impressed by the capability, professional-[ism] and enthusiasm of their Chinese partners; [as], indeed, of all of the Chinese engine industry [peo]ple with whom GE has worked. GE looks [for]ward to a long future of working together with [Chi]na on programs for the trunkliner engine and [eng]ines for commuter airliners.

GE Aircraft Engines

118. Transonic and supersonic wind tunnel (1.2m×1.2m)

119. Air tanks for FL-1 wind tunnel

120. An aircraft model in the test section of a wind tunnel

121. Keeping the wind tunnel in good condition

122. View of the engine altitude test facility

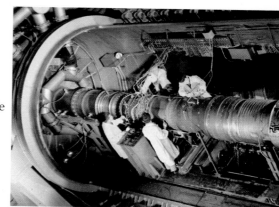

123. Engine altitude
test chamber

124. Control room for altitude testing

125. Calibrating an engine on an open door test rig

126. Engine rotor cyclic tester

127. Engine accessories casing test

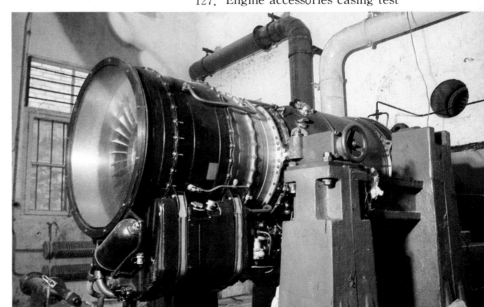

128. Doppler navigation system
dynamic simulation laboratory

129. Digital fly-by-wire system
ground simulation test

130. Clean room

131. Wheel brake inertia simulator

132. Aircraft fuel system test

133. Yang Shangkun, Wang Zhen and Yu Qiuli visiting landscape model for flight simulator

134. J-6 flight simulator

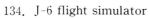

135. Flight control system simulation laboratory

Attitude instruments series. Because of its complete functions, it replaced original gyroscopic magnetic compass and horizon. It had many kinds of output signals with high accuracy. The display content was also expanded. It became a multifunctional flight compass and director horizon suitable for use in many types of aircraft and was welcomed by users. Since its coming out, 16 optional different assemblies have been developed to form 15 versions to meet different needs for fighters, bombers and transports etc..They have been used in 12 types of aircraft such as J−7Ⅲ, J−8, J−8Ⅱ, Y−8, Y−10, H−6, SH−5 and Z−8 etc..The successful development of this instrument was an important achievement in navigation instruments. It won the prize of the National Science Convention in 1978.

b. Air Data Computer System

The air parameters such as the height and speed of aircraft are important information. The pilot needs to know this information, and many systems in aircraft such as fire control system, flight control system and navigation positioning system, also need this information. In old aircraft, apart from air parameter displaying instruments such as altimeter and air speed meter, various air parameter signallers and transducers were also needed for different systems. But, among different air datum, existed requirement of mutual compensation and resolution to improve signal accuracy, which was impossible in original diaphragm−mechanical configuration. Air data system had to develop towards electrification and integration.

In the late 1960s, the Aeronautical Automatic Control Research Institute started to develop electro−mechanical analogous air data system. For the first time it successfully solved this problem. The system was based on one altitude transducer and one airspeed transducer. Through resolving by miniature power servo mechanism, the system could supply many air data signals such as altitude, altitude difference, air speed, Mach number, climb and dive speed etc. Later, this product was transferred to the Chengdu Aeronautical Instruments Factory to be further improved and produced. This system has been used in J−8 fighter.

With the development of electronics technique, the electro−mechanical analogous air data system became inferior by comparison. Since the mid 1970s, relevant aeronautical instruments factories and research institutes and institutions of higher learning started development of digital air data system and various new pressure transducers. They have achieved some progress in silicon−membrane resistor transducer and vibrating cylinder pressure transducer etc. and associated air data system.

Silicon−membrane resistor transducers with·0.1% accuracy are not only used in the aeronautical instruments, but also used in different sectors of the national economy. The vibrating cylinder pressure transducers with 0.01% accuracy have been used in the airborne equipment as core elements of digital air data system with microprocessor.

Having imported relevant technique from abroad, the Chengdu Aeronautical Instruments Factory established a high level production line of vibrating cylinder digital air data system. The Taiyuan Aeronautical Instruments Factory has also developed vibrating cylinder and air data system.

2. Navigation Positioning Equipment

Navigation positioning equipments are those equipments used to determine position of the aircraft during flight (position is represented by longitude and latitude or distance and bearing relative to a known position).

Many navigation positioning equipments determine the distance and bearing of the aircraft relative to the ground navigation stations by means of radio wave. They have to rely on the ground stations, so are called nonautonomous navigation positioning equipments. Astronomical navigation relying on stars and satellite navigation relying on man—made satellites also belong to this category.

Another category is self—contained navigation, which does not need to rely on external information, but completely rely on measurement and computation made by airborne equipment to get longitude and latitude of the aircraft or the distance (coordinates) from departing airport. Most common self—contained navigation systems are air data navigator, Doppler navigation system, inertial navigation system and their integrated systems.

a. Air Data Navigator

Based on airspeed measured by air data instrument, and according to heading and wind speed and wind direction reported by ground weather station, the air data navigator makes integrated resolution to determine aircraft ground speed. Then this ground speed is multiplied with flying time (integration), giving coordinates of flown distance. In this way, positioning is performed.

In the mid 1960s, the Taiyuan Aeronautical Instrument Factory copy produced HL—1 air data navigator. In this navigator, there was a miniature DC integrating motor, the rotor of which was made of single—layer drawing paper. It could be imagined how difficult it was to wire coils on thin paper shell and the performance was unstable. Later, Jin Huigen was responsible for designing a new HL—3 navigator. This navigator used miniature AC speed—voltage generator to form integration loop and its rotor was made of ferrite, which magnificiently increased performance stability, accuracy and production efficiency. More important, its system function was expanded to allow to be interfaced with newly—developed Doppler navigation system. So it no longer relied on inaccurate wind data reports from ground station and system accuracy increased a great deal. HL—3 navigator had replaced HL—1 navigator and was used in H—5, H—6, Y—8 and Y—10 aircraft etc., thus realizing the replacement of the old generation of air data system.

b. Doppler Navigation System and VOR / ILS Receiver

Doppler navigation system is such a navigation equipment which uses the principle of Doppler effect to measure aircraft ground speed. Since the late 1970s, the Aeronautical Electronics Research Institute started development of Doppler navigation system including Doppler Radar, digital computer and control display etc.. Key parts and assemblies such as magnetron, ferrite, high—voltage silicon pile etc. used in the system are all domestic—made. This system can be interfaced with heading and attitude reference system, air data navigator and autopilot etc. to realize automatic navigation. This system was certified for use in H−6 and Y−10 aircraft etc.. The institute has also developed another version of Doppler radar with higher technical requirement for attacker. Hu Mincai, the director of design department, made major improvement to the design of HF assembly.

Although Doppler radar is an effective means to directly measure ground speed of the aircraft, the measurement accuracy is often influenced by ground conditions (for example, desert etc.) and aircraft attitude. It is often used together with other navigation positioning means. Most often it is combined with the air data navigator. They can compensate each other to form a combined Doppler − air data navigator with high accuracy and low cost. In H−6 bomber, the Doppler radar was integrated with HL−3 navigator as a combined navigation system.

The Aeronautical Electronics Research Institute has also developed a VOR / ILS receiver for Y−10 transport. This is a nonautonomous radio navigation equipment. It can receive signals from ground navigation stations to provide short range navigation (direction finding and distance measuring) or approach and landing guidance. The performance of this receiver set conforms to technical requirement of ICAO and has been certified.

c. Inertial Navigation System

Inertial navigation system is an accurate and completely self−contained navigation system. It relies on its own accelerometer to sense and measure the motion of aircraft to resolve speed of the aircraft and flown distance. But, this kind of accelerometer must be accurate to within 1 / 10,000 of earth gravity acceleration or even within 1 / 100,000. Besides, in order to stabilize the accelerometer in a particular direction in space, it is necessary to use precision inertial−grade gyro. The drift rate of traditional gyro typically is 4 ° per hour. For more accurate gyro, this figure is 1 ° per hour, but it should be below 0.01 ° per hour for inertial−grade gyro. This kind of gyro and accelerometer use the latest technology, which has been mastered only by a few countries in the world. Inertial technique has become one of marks to judge the technical level of a country's aviation industry. The relevant organizations in China did not just wait and did nothing. Since the mid 1960s, research of inertial technique began. Technically guided and organized by Zhang Shouheng and Feng Peide, the Aeronautical Automatic Control Research Institute first started the development of inertial navigation system.

Inertial−grade gyro and accelerometer have many technical schemes: fluid−floated, air−suspension, electrostatic, flexural joint etc., and the common target is to reduce the friction force of gyro suspension. This institute and other relevant organizations in the aviation industry had tried every technical scheme, and at last they concentrated on two schemes—fluid−floated and flexural joint. Then, the development of the operational version of aeronautical inertial navigation system began.

In the development process of gyro, accelerometer and their platform, it was necessary to solve a series of difficult technical problems such as high roundness, manufacturing of high polish floating sphere, bonding and supporting structure, flutter, magnetic leakage interference, static balance of gyro and its floater assembly, dynamic balance, fluid filling, air filling and its sealing checking for leakage, manufacturing of constant elasticity flexural joint with thickness being only a few 1 / 10 mm, manufacturing of large frame with high concentricity and polishing problem of miniature bearing etc. With the assistance from material, parts and equipment departments, relevant factories, institutes and institutions of higher learning overcame these difficulties through constant efforts. They separately developed demonstrators for inertial—grade gyro, accelerometer, platform and the whole system.

In 1977, the first generation of fluid—floated inertial navigation system developed by the Aeronautical Automatic Control Research Institute as principle demonstrator was successfully flight tested. However, there still existed some faults caused by poor reliability of electronic parts. After electronic parts being replaced, in 1978, the system was flight tested again showing much improved reliability.

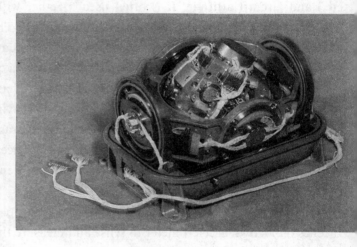

Fig.61　Type 563 INS platform

The second generation of INS was type 563 flexural inertial navigation system. The platform size was reduced remarkably and microprocessor was used, allowing the weight of the whole system reduced enormously. In early 1986, this system was tested in various flying conditions, which proved that the main performance characteristics reached the international level of the 1970s.

After more than ten years of construction, with the assistance of relevant organizations, now the Aeronautical Automatic Control Research Institute is equipped with a complete set of facilities used for development of IN technique, forming a scientific R& D base of the aeronautical intertial navigation systems.

Section 3　Flight Control System

Aircraft is operated through control surfaces such as elevator, rudder, aileron and flap. In the early days, pilots operated control column or control wheel and pedal to control various control surfaces through cables and link rods. Thus, aircraft attitude was controlled. Later, to reduce pilots workload during long flying, autopilot was invented and installed in aircraft.

Autopilot of early stages effected three axis stabilization through attitude gyroscope and heading gyroscope. When pitching, banking and heading conditions of the aircraft were slightly changed, gyroscope provided correction signal to operate associated control surfaces to make aircraft return to its original attitude and heading in order to maintain level straight flying.

With the development of flight control technique, there appeared damper or stability augmentation system used to improve flying dynamic process of aircraft. This system was mainly used for small aircraft such as fighter. Its main purpose was not to alleviate pilot's fatigue and to maintain level straight flying, but to improve flying quality of the aircraft.

Autopilot and stability augmentation system (SAS) operate control surfaces through a set of electro-mechanical devices, effecting stability and control of attitude and altitude.

Modern flight control system not only integrates functions of autopilot and SAS together, but also provides other important functions such as automatic navigation, automatic landing, low altitude anti-collision and hovering of helicopter etc.. To overcome shortcomings of nonlinear and elastic deformation of mechanical transmission system, the fly-by-wire system was developed which combines computer with redundancy technique. Now it is further developing into more advanced active control system.

1. KJ-3 Autopilot

In the mid 1960s, the Lanzhou Aeronautical Instruments Factory successfully copy produced the Soviet AP-5 autopilot. The "coordinatively balanced table" planning working method put forward by Shen Yuanfan played a positive role in copy production process. The level of this autopilot equaled to that of the autopilot used in the American B-17 and B-29 bombers during World War Two. But it became out-of-date in the 1960s. The AP-5 autopilot was used in H-5 and H-6 bombers. Its correction to aircraft attitude and heading was not sensitive and accurate, and its reliability was low with more faults, which made it not suitable for low altitude use. Facing this situation, the Aeronautical Automatic Control Research Institute decided to upgrade the type 601 autopilot originally designed for the "East Wind 107" aircraft, to take the place of AP-5 autopilot. The type 601 autopilot was proposed by Zhan Ling, the chief designer of the Aeronautical Instruments Design Department in 1958, and its design was organized by Cai Kefei, the director of the department.

The design of autopilot is not only designing electro-mechanical system, but also involves a series of theories and techniques in aerodynamic field. At that time, aerodynamic parameters of aircraft were not fully mastered, and designers had no experiences in autopilot design at all. The autopilot is directly related with flying safety with high requirement and heavy responsibility. In this case, the design work was even more difficult.

To overcome shortcomings of AP-5 autopilot (being unsensitive, unaccurate and unreliable), it was decided to change its control law from position-feedback propotional to rate-feedback integrating; accordingly, servoes were also changed from DC motor driving and cork clutch control to direct control by hysteresis AC motor, eliminating cork clutch. The volume, weight and power consumption were reduced dramatically. Because the accuracy of attitude gyroscope originally used in AP-5 system was low and its production was difficult, this gyroscope was redesigned. Besides, in order to make fixed altitude flying, a flying altitude holding mechanism was added. Later, this new autopilot was named KJ−3.

Developing autopilot needed ground simulation testing, so it was necessary to develop a three−axis servo turntable, which increased work amount of the development. Cooperating with Qing Hua University, the institute developed three−dimentional flight simulation turntable and unfolded emulation test work of flight control system.

In 1963, the first autopilot demonstrator, after being tested on ground simulation rig, was installed in H−5 aircraft to be flight tested. The squadron responsible for the flight test gave warm support to this flight test task. Based on very good preparation, the flight test was successfully completed. However, there still existed some problems, mainly: poor altitude hold capability; dynamic characteristics being not ideal; banking too large while aircraft making turns which even made bombing gunsight lose target. This was a new situation not predicted before.

Although the first flight test proved that the new control law was feasible, the problem of interfacing with gunsight and other shortcomings still needed to be solved. At the end of 1964, under the presidency of the chief designer, Zhan Lin, and the vice chief designer, Han Kuanqing, the second round of design started with participation of Yue Baokong and others. After investigation on bombing sighting pattern, the control law was modified and altitude hold mechanism redesigned. A miniature vertical gyroscope was developed. The vacuum tube amplifier was replaced by transistor amplifier. Besides, through flight testing, they further understood the urgent wishes of the Air Force and the Navy to fly at low altitude and decided to add low altitude safety measures into KJ−3 autopilot. Based on improved reliability of parts and assemblies, two acceleration limiters and two altitude drop limiting mechanisms were added, which allowed safe flight height of the autopilot to be reduced from originally 1,500 m to 300 m. This was one major improvement of KJ−3 autopilot. In October 1966, the second set of KJ−3 demonstrator was successfully flight tested. In Spring 1967, the final design was certified and the Lanzhou Aeronautical Instruments Factory started to produce this autopilot. The original version and its series products included 26 parts and assemblies, which were supplied by 16 factories in MAI. The Lanzhou Aeronautical Instruments Factory and relevant factories made lots of improvements and standardizations on the original design. During the "cultural revolution" disorder period, they overcame huge amount of difficulties and created conditions for batch production. In 1975, the technical coordination and final production certification of the whole system were completed. The system then steadily entered into batch production stage. A large number of systems were equipped in H−5 and H−6 aircraft. KJ−3 autopilot won the prize of the National Science Convention in 1978.

The successful development of KJ−3 autopilot offered valuable experiences for independent development of airborne equipment. These experiences were:

Firstly, it broke out the mysterious sensation of developing flight control system, which was an important breakthrough in the airborne equipment field. FCS is related with flying safety and its design is closely related with aircraft characteristics. The successful development of KJ−3 autopilot facilitated the emancipation of the people's mind and the development of FCS and other large airborne equipments.

Secondly, this development project was carried out in close combination with user's needs to solve practical problems both in production and in service. Its design targets were clear and it received strong support from the end—users.

Thirdly, many new techniques were boldly adopted in development process, which made the KJ—3 autopilot relatively advanced at that time, for example, the utilization of rate integration control law, altitude hold mechanism and acceleration limiting mechanism; the first use of hysterisis motor in servoes etc.. Especially, the application of transistor amplifier to the autopilot system was disputable at that time because of safety reasons. But later the

Fig.62   KJ—3 Autopilot

fact proved that the electronics technology progressed so rapidly that the technical policy of adopting transistor earlier was correct.

Lastly, it also told us that a large product turning to production in factory was an arduous process, and any neglegence was not allowed. Successful flight testing of the demonstrator was only the first step towards success. There was still a long way to go to run steady batch production. Design hastly being certified, hidden problems not being fully exposed and solved, problems of manufacturing in design and standardization not being solved, conditions for batch production being incompatible and on—site training and service work being not timely provided etc.,all these could bring about great difficulty for turning into production in factory and in practical use. So, it was necessary to strictly control the certification of the design, to strengthen the close cooperation between the development organization and the production enterprise.

2. Vigorously Unfolding the Development Work of FCS

With the development of control technique, the application of FCS is becoming more popular. It not merely is a special equipment for large transport and bomber aircraft. Fighter and attack aircraft also rely on FCS to improve flying quality and to raise manoeuvrability. Helicopters rely on FCS to solve its problems of hovering and reducing pilot's workload. Almost all modern aircraft need to install FCS with different requirements. Under the inspiration of the successful development of KJ—3 autopilot, relevant factories, institutes, universities and colleges in aviation industry have developed up to 20 types of FCS according to utilization needs of each type of new aircraft.

a. Further Development of Autopilot

In 1966, the development work on Y−7 transport began. In early 1970, Zhang Dingyuan, Chen Zhixiang and others of the Lanzhou Aeronautical Instruments Factory started developing KJ−6 autopilot for the Y−7 aircraft. The factory applied new research achievement — magnetic powder clutch and developed new electro−operated servoes. They also made minor modifications to several types of gyroscopes already under steady production to be used as signal sources to the autopilot. All this greatly reduced the work amount of the development and shortened development period magnificently. All development work including design, technical coordination, trial production, simulation testing and flight testing were completed within only 10 months. This system could be interfaced with heading and attitude reference system, air data navigator and Doppler radar to perform automatic navigation.

Apart from being used in Y−7 transport, KJ−6 autopilot was also used in Y−8 transport after being modified. As operating power needed by control surfaces in Y−8 transport was quite large, the electro−operated servoes were replaced by the hydraulic servo actuators. The modified version was put into batch production.

Since 1972, the Lanzhou Aeronautical Instruments Factory also developed the KJ−10 FCS for Y−10 transport. Its complexity and external interfaces much exceeded that of previous autopilot. Through these few times of practice, the factory has grown up as a fresh reinforcement in the development and production of FCS.

Since 1969, the Aeronautical Automatic Control Research Institute developed another type of autopilot for SH−5 bomber. This was a system with partially dual redundancy, limited authority, control wheel steering type model feedback. It used operational amplifiers. The system could be interfaced with navigation system and fire control system to perform functions such as automatic navigation, automatic target tracking, low altitude anti−collision and automatic pullup etc..It was a rather advanced system.

In the early 1970s, the Baoji Aeronautical Instruments Factory developed flight director system. This system could direct pilots how to correctly steer aircraft. It belonged to the FCS scope.

b. FCS for Pilotless Aircraft and Missile

Pilotless aircraft must rely on FCS and remote control system or programmed control mechanism for its operation. The development and production of FCS for pilotless aircraft in China began quite early.

In 1958, the Beijing Aeronautical Institute installed modified AP−5 autopilot in an Y−5 transport, and in it also installed independently−developed remote control and measuring system, radio altimeter, automatic landing system and engine control system etc. to perform automatic takeoff, automatic landing, air trajectory control and engine throttle operating. In February 1959, pilotless aircraft was flight tested successfully, which was praised by various circles. The aircraft was named "Beijing−5". This was a successful test.

In the early 1960s, the Aeronautical Automatic Control Research Institute and the

Lanzhou Aeronautical Instruments Factory developed in cooperation an autopilot for B—5 pilotless drone. It was a derivative of AP—5 autopilot, which could steer aircraft to perform automatic takeoff, cruise and automatic landing according to preset program. After the design being certified, this version was put into production together with AP—5 autopilot and was provided to the services. Later, it was modified again for installation in B—5A pilotless drone.

In the late 1960s, the Beijing Aeronautical Institute and the Nanjing Aeronautical Institute separately started development of high altitude pilotless reconnaissance aircraft WZ—5 and "sky—1" drone. They also developed associated autopilots. The autopilot of "sky—1" was developed on the basis of KJ—3 autopilot with some major changes. The control law was redesigned. The system performance was satisfactory. It met the requirement of highly manoeuvrable flying and autolanding. It was put into small—scale batch production.

The North—west Polytechnic University also developed a small remote control drone and simple but practical navigation system and FCS system. The drone was used for sighting and firing training of antiaircraft gun. The drone was small and cheap, and welcomed by the services.

Missile control system is used to guide the missile to fly towards the target. It is similar to FCS of pilotless aircraft in many ways. At the end of the 1950s, the Baoji Aeronautical Instruments Factory trial produced autopilots for ground—to—ground missiles and air—to—air missiles with the help of Soviet experts. The systems were put into small—scale batch production. Later, the autopilot for the ground—to—ground missile was transferred to the Ministry of Space Industry for carrying on production. In the mid 1960s, under the leadership of the director, Chen Daming, the Beijing Aeronautical Instruments Factory succeeded in the trial production of the autopilot for "SY—1" ship—to—ship missile. This system was turned to batch production and was used in missiles in large quantity and with good quality. In the 1970s, they again developed autopilots for "SY—1A", "SY—2" missiles, and made contributions in improving low altitude penetration capability.

c. Fighter FCS

The development of FCS for fighters started with developing flying damper. The J—7 fighter was trial installed with damper and the result was positive. When the development of J—8 fighter started, there was a proposal of trial installation of damper in the J—8. Because of the disorder of the "cultural revolution" and the fine flying quality of the J—8 fighter, longitudinal and lateral dampers developed by relevant factories and institutes could not be installed for flight testing and used in the aircraft, which affected the progress of FC technique for the Chinese—made fighter.

Since 1977, the development of J—7Ⅲ and J—8Ⅱ fighters began one after another. Both aircraft required installation of autopilots which were to be produced by the Beijing Aeronautical Instruments Factory. These two systems were respectively named KJ—11 and KJ—12 autopilots. Li Yunbao, the chief designer, was appointed to be responsible for these two development tasks. Both systems had such functions as stability augmentation, automatic triming, automatic level—out, altitude hold and limited authority steering. KJ—12 system had also function to automatically pullup from hazardous low altitude. Although the factory had some experiences in producing autopilots of coast defence missiles and upgrading design, the original technical and material conditions seemed not to be sufficient to deal with the new problem of fighter autopilot. But the technical personnel in the factory, on one hand, were developing FCS, on the other hand, were designing dynamic simulation lab and facilities for the system. After only half a year, the lab was constructed, and steering system simulator, simulation turntable and acceleration simulation rig were also successfully developed. The computer and other equipments were installed and tested. All these works matched the schedule of testing. Due to strict quality control, responsibilities of different ranks of designers being made clear according to system engineering method and technical coordination being properly settled, the development and simulation test process was quite smooth. In 1984 and 1985, these two systems were separately flight tested. The test results of KJ−11 was good, but there appeared oscillation phenomenon of pitching instability in the flight test of the KJ−12 autopilot. This involved matching problem between the autopilot and the air data system. Through a large amount of tests and analyses, both systems were modified. The problem was smoothly settled and certification design stage began.

d. Helicopter FCS

The way of working for helicopter FCS is quite different from that of fixed wing aircraft, but helicopter FCS also has channels of heading, pitch, banking and altitude hold.

Since the late 1960s, the Aeronautical Automatic Control Research Institute started developing autopilot for the Z−6 helicopter. At that time there was no experience in using autopilot in helicopter, and the aerodynamic characteristics of helicopter were not complete. The FCS designers were not familiar with features of helicopter, so the design work of FCS started with difficulties. The young designers of the institute, on one hand were learning, on the other hand, were making derivation of motion equations on their own. After more than one year of hard working, the control law of helicopter was finally determined.

According to the original design scheme, the system was a traditional autopilot with three channels. In 1973, the principle demonstrator with three channels was flight tested. Then it was decided to advance in large steps technically, i.e. to develop an automatic FCS with control column steering and air speed hold capability, to add rod displacement transducer and command model, and to redesign a better electro−hydraulic servo actuator.

After the development of Z−6 helicopter was interrupted, this system was turned to be installed in Z−5 helicopter and was expanded into a complete four−channel system. In the Autumn of 1977, a performance flight test was conducted, and proved that its characteristics reached design requirements: pilot could directly steer the aircraft in each condition without system shutoff and the stability quality of helicopter was remarkably improved. In 1980, the system passed design certification flight test.

In the late 1970s, the Dong Fang Aeronautical Instruments Factory in Shaanxi province started developing KJ−8 autopilot for Z−8 helicopter. In 1985, the flight test showed that its design principle and basic functions worked.

In the early 1980s, the Lanzhou Aeronautical Instruments Factory imported foreign technique and started developing FCS for Z–9 helicopter.

3. The Development of New FCS

a. Type 622 Control Augmentation System

In FCS, control and augmentation are a pair of contradictions: control requires sensitivity, but augmentation requires stability. Control augmentation system is a kind of FCS to solve this pair of contradictions. In control augmentation system, the amount of steering or steering force of control column is transformed into electrical signal through rod displacement transducer or rod force transducer, which is fed into FCS loop and is combined with stability signal from gyroscope. After resolving, the unity of control and augmentation is realized.

Type 622 FCS developed by the Aeronautical Automatic Control Research Institute for new aircraft was a digital–analogous hybrid system, with high authority control augmentation and built in test (BIT) capability. It was a triple redundant system with redundancy management and monitoring. For this purpose, electro–hydraulic redundant servo actuators applying BIT technique and hydraulic logic switching technique, and triple redundant control stick force transducer were developed by the institute. In 1985, the whole system finished physical simulation test, proving that yaw channel reached "fail–safe", and pitch and roll channels reached "fail–operational" redundancy level. This system could ensure flying safety at high speed and low altitude and has now entered into the system integration testing stage.

b. Variable Stability Aircraft FCS

Variable stability aircraft is a research experimental aircraft which utilizes installed FCS, through adjusting system parameters, to change operational and aerodynamic characteristics of the aircraft. An aircraft like this can simulate and replace many types of aircraft. So it is very valuable for flying quality research of aircraft, study of new steering system and pilot training of new aircraft. It can be called a multifunctional flying lab. The key of variable stability aircraft is its FCS. Since 1977, the Aeronautical Automatic Control Research Institute started developing this system. It was divided into two subsystems — aerodynamic characteristics variable stability and artificial feeling simulation, and this system was a dual redundant, digital–analogous hybrid fly–by–wire steering system with full authority. In 1986, ground simulation testing of the whole system was completed and the system was ready to be flight tested.

c. Terrain Following FCS

To avoid the search of hostile radar and raise attack accuracy on ground targets, fighter aircraft is required to reduce its flight height and follow terrain. In this case, hills and tall buildings on the ground become fatal obstacles. During high speed flying, pilots have no time to avoid these obstacles. They have to rely on FCS with terrain following function. This system needs a terrain acquisition radar to early detect obstacles, and also needs a flight control computer to automatically resolve the optimum climb trajectory. The Aeronautical Automatic

Control Research Institute and the Nanjing Aeronautical Institute are studying this system according to different anti—collision laws.

4. The Development of Main Parts and Assemblies of FCS

The main parts and assemblies of FCS are servoes and electronic assemblies etc. The R&D of these parts and assemblies is the basis for the advancement of FC technique.

As for servoes, at the early stage, the executing mechanism of FCS mostly was electro—operated servo. Later, because of its insufficient power, hydraulic servo actuator started to be used in most cases. Hydraulic servo actuator has features such as large power, soft action and quick response etc. and is composed of electro—hydraulic servo valves and hydraulic actuators. When larger output power is required, one more hydraulic booster can be added to form combined hydraulic servo actuators. In the late 1970s, FCS was developed into redundant system, also called " multiple FCS" , which was a highly reliable system using two or more subsystems to perform the same control function. It also required its executing mechanism to apply redundancy and BIT technique. Hence, the Aeronautical Accessories Research Institute developed quadruple redundant force summing hydraulic servo actuator. The four servo actuators formed a loop using position feedback, resulting in double " fail—operational" capability. The Aeronautical Automatic Control Research Institute also developed triple redundant force summing hydraulic servo actuators with software monitoring, resulting in double "fail—operational" capability. The failure detection rate reached over 98%.

Besides, the Aeronautical Accessories Factories also developed and produced varieties of servo valves and hydraulic servo actuators for use in various types of autopilots, making contributions to the progress of FC technique. The Xi'an Aircraft Accessories Factory also developed a complicated transmission mechanism for maneuvering flaps.

Electronic parts and assemblies form the nerve centre of the system. They have undergone the development processes of electronic tube amplifier and magnetic amplifier, transistor amplifier, small scale integrated circuit operational amplifier, medium scale and large scale integrated circuit and microprocessor. In the mid 1970s, operational amplifiers started to be used in the control system of "SY" 1A coast defence missile and in type 651 FCS. The triple redundant analogous computer in inner loop of type 622 FCS used a few hundred operational amplifiers, analogous switches and a large number of digital logic circuits, having quite sophisticated computation and logic control capability.

Since the mid 1970s, numeric control technique has been developing very quickly. The Aeronautical Automatic Control Research Institute started developing digital computer for FCS and soon entered into the microprocessor application stage. After the demonstrator was flight tested in open—loop manner, which proved the principle was feasible, microprocessors were incorporated in digital computer dealing with aerodynamic stability variation of type 671 system and in digital computer in outer loop of type 622 system. The performance of microprocessor met the requirements of both systems.

Section 4   Aircraft Electrical Power System

With the continuous increase in the number of airborne equipments, especially electronic equipments, electrical power consumption in aircraft is getting higher and higher. Aircraft electrical power system (also called aircraft power generating system) of a modern large aircraft has installed capacity as high as more than 1,000 KVA, which equals to the electrical power consumption of a small town. Aircraft requires that the electrical power system should not only have sufficient capacity, but also meet stipulated standards for power supplying qualities such as voltage accuracy, frequency accuracy, voltage transient and voltage shape etc..

Aircraft electrical power system typically includes main electrical power, emergency electrical power and secondary electrical power systems.Both main electrical power system and emergency electrical power system belong to primary electrical power systems. The main electrical power system consists of generators driven by engines and associated regulators and control protection devices; the emergency electrical power system generally refers to accumulator or other independent electrical power system not relying on the aircraft engine; the secondary electrical power system refers to those units which transform part of the primary electrical power into another form of electrical energy.

The evolution and development of the electrical power system in Chinese—made aircraft has undergone several stages of production and development, which are: low voltage DC, variable frequency AC, constant speed constant frequency AC, variable speed constant frequency AC and high voltage DC electrical power systems. The capacity of a single system increased from a few hundred watt (DC) to dozens of KVA (AC).

1. Low Voltage DC Electrical Power System

Most of the old types of aircraft made in China used 28.5 V low voltage DC electrical power system.

The first set of low voltage electrical power system (350 W output power) in China was copy produced by the Tianjing Aeronautical Electrical Apparatus Factory in 1957. In the same year, the construction of the Xingping Aeronautical Electrical Apparatus Factory was completed ahead of schedule and production began. The factory soon became the mainstay in manufacturing aeronautical electrical power system in China. From the mid 1950s to the mid 1960s, these two factories copy produced and developed DC generators with seven different power ratings ranging from 350 W to 18 kW, DC starter generators with power rating from 6 kW to 18 kW and control protection units associated with above—mentioned generators. In 1969, the Xingping Aeronautical Electrical Apparatus Factory again successfully developed DC starter generator with power rating 24 kW. By that time, a complete series of low voltage DC electrical power systems for aeronautical use in China was formed. In the development process of these products, the Xingping Electrical Apparatus and the Beijing Electrical Motor Factories solved problems such as electrical motor overheat, large commutation spark, "brush lightning" and low isolation resistance etc., and thus achieved successful development and fine quality of products.

With the improvement and perfection of DC generator series, control units such as voltage regulator of generator etc. also advanced accordingly. A series of carbon slice voltage regulators were basically formed. The rapid progress of electronic technique provided possibility for DC control unit to advance towards wide application of electronics technology, miniaturization and integration. In the 1970s, the Aeronautical Accessories

Fig.63   QF-18 DC power system and starter box

Research Institute developed small and light transistor DC voltage regulator, which was used in fighter. In 1981, according to the modification requirement of Q-5 aircraft, Guo Yonghou and other engineers in the Xingping Aeronautical Electrical Apparatus Factory, succeeded in developing combined transistor voltage regulator, which had multiple functions of voltage regulation and protection etc. and got high sensitivity, light weight and small volume, and could be used in various DC electrical power systems with power rating below 9 kW. Wang Xien and others in the Hubei Aeronautical Electrical Motor Factory, also developed DC combined control unit for use in J-8 II aircraft. The successful development of the combined control unit indicated that the aeronautical DC electrical power control unit in China has progressed from the single function separate type to the multifunction combined type, and reached a new level.

2.   Variable Frequency AC Electrical Power System

Although low voltage DC electrical power system has advantages of simple structure, easy supply of power in parallel and being used as starter at the same time, but also has problems such as heavy weight, difficult heat dissipation and low reliability in high altitude and high speed working condition. In solving these problems, AC electrical power system gradually developed.

Variable frequency AC electrical power system is composed of variable frequency (VF) AC generators driven by aeroengines and voltage regulation and protection units. It has advantages of simplicity and high reliability, light weight and low cost. Since the early 1970s, China started to develop VFAC electrical power system with power rating 12 KVA for Y-8 transport, which later was modified again for J-7 III aircraft. This kind of AC generators had brushes and were air-cooled. It had sliding electric connectors such as brushes and slip rings, so its high altitude performance was not satisfactory and it was not convenient for maintenance. To overcome these shortcomings, the development of brushless AC generator was accelerated.

In the early 1960s, advanced research in brushless AC generator started. The excitation of the generator was provided by coaxial exiter and rotary rectifiers. The key parts were high temperature—resistant, high strength rotary rectifying diodes. Since its founding, the airborne equipment manufacturing industry has always attached great attention to the development of parts and assemblies, and later, to the guiding principle of paying equal attention to system and to parts. From the mid 1960s to the mid 1970s, the Xingping Aeronautical Electrical Apparatus Factory, cooperating with the Xi'an Rectifier Research Institute, succeeded in developing rotary rectifying diode with 40 A current rating. It could withstand centrifugal acceleration 5,000 g and the reverse voltage was 200 V. The junction temperature was 190 ℃. The Xingping factory especially established a research section of rotary rectifiers. This section altogether developed 5 types of rotary rectifiers for AC electrical power systems in Y−7, Y−10 and SH−5 aircraft. The highest junction temperature reached 230 ℃ and centrifugal acceleration was 8,000 g. The success of developing rotary rectifiers created conditions for the development of brushless AC generator. In the early 1970s, based on this condition, under the direction of Liu Chen, the Xingping factory was successful in developing 30 KVA brushless AC generator. During development process, difficult technical problems such as fatigue fracture of soft axis etc. were solved, and sufficient tests were made using high altitude large test facility set up by the factory. Later, the product was modified and upgraded, and installed in Y−7 and SH−5 aircraft.

3. Constant Speed Constant Frequency AC Electrical Power System

To overcome the shortcomings of the variable frequency power system, e.g. wide range of frequency variation and being unable to parallelly supply power, the constant speed constant frequency (CSCF) power system was developed. In this system, the variable speed of aeroengine is transformed into constant speed through constant speed driving unit (CSDU), then this speed is applied to the shaft of the generator, which maintains the frequency to be stabilized on the same value (400 Hz). The structure of this kind of power system is more complex, but it has large capacity and good performance. So this system was widely used in aircraft requiring large power consumption and high performance.

From the mid 1960s to the mid 1980s, four mechano−hydraulic and three electromagnetic CSCF electrical power systems were developed.

The mechano−hydraulic CSDU was a power transmission unit commonly performed by mechanics and pressurized oil. Its efficiency was as high as above 85%, and was light−weight. This kind of unit was suitable for large power AC generator. This kind of electrical power system was the key to develop the aeronautical electrical power system in China. In the mid 1960s, the development of 20 KVA mechano−hydraulic CSCF AC power system started. The CSDU was developed by the Aeronautical Accessories Research Institute and the generator was developed by the Xingping Aeronautical Electrical Apparatus Factory. In the generator, cyclic oil cooling heat sink and brush structure were applied, and for magnetic excitation and voltage regulation, phase compensated compound excitation technique was used. The ground integration test of this power system was completed, and it was used as a ground secondary power system. Since the early 1970s, 30 KVA CSCF AC power system was developed for Y−10 large transport. Four systems could be working in parallel. Its CSDU was developed by the Nanjing Aeronautical Accessories Factory. It was a hydraulic CSDU using axial differential gears. The electrical section of the system was developed by the Xingping Aeronautical Electrical Apparatus Factory. The generator was an air−cooling brushless architecture. The voltage regulator and control protector used transistor circuits, performing eleven functions including voltage regulation, active and reactive equalization and protection etc.. In 1979, the whole system passed ground integration test. The test showed that the performance was stable and reached the original technical specification. This was a rather complicated power system with relatively complete functions developed in China. In 1977, the Aeronautical Accessories Research Institute also developed a 30 KVA cyclic oil cooling brushless AC power system.

Oil spraying cooling generator was a kind of generator emerged in the 1960s. Its cooling method is to directly spray fogged oil onto heat parts such as windings of generator and rectifying diodes. Oil fogger has two types —— nozzle and dam. Nozzle type unit uses tiny holes to spray the oil to make it fogged; dam type unit forces the oil to be overflown to make it fogged. Because cooling liquid directly contacts heat parts, the cooling area is large and its heat dissipation capability is strong, which further reduces the weight of generator. In the mid 1970s, China started to develop this generator. The dam type oil fogger was a key difficulty. Li Zongfu and other technical personnel in the Xingping Aeronautical Electrical Apparatus Factory, cooperating with workers, developed 40 KVA dam type oil spraying brushless generator after numerous tests and research work. The generator used highly−magnetized iron−cobalt−vanadium alloy steel sheet, high strength insulating wires and high temperature−resistant insulating material, decreasing weight−power ratio of the generator to 0.46 kg / KVA, which was about half of that of air−cooling generator with the same capacity. During development process, new manufacturing techniques were applied, including magnesia−insulated coating, vacuum electronic beam welding and dip impregnating varnish etc. to improve product quality. This product laid a sound foundation for developing combined driving power generating system. At the same time, the Aeronautical Accessories Research Institute also developed a 40 KVA nozzle type oil spraying cooling generator, the weight−power ratio of which was about 0.45 kg / KVA.

Electromagnetic combined driving power generating system was so configured that electromagnetic constant speed driving unit and generator were coaxially installed in a common shell. Electromagnetic CSDU used electromagnetic action to transfer mechanical power and to maintain output rotational speed constant. Compared with mechano−hydraulic type, it was simpler in structure, but was lower in efficiency. It was suitable only for low power AC power system. In the early 1980s, Jiang Zonghai and others in the Hubei Aeronautical Electrical Motor

Factory succeeded in developing a 6 KVA electromagnetic combined power generating system. This system was used in J−8Ⅱ aircraft. During development process, some important and difficult problems were solved. According to the original design, phase compensated compound excitation would be used in the motor. But tests showed that the output power in high temperature was not enough and the quality of supplied power was poor. In the situation that new aircraft urgently needed this system, the factory utilized the results of advanced research — using rare−earth material to make the magneto — and resolutely made use of the permanent magnetizer to replace the phase compensated compound exciter. After the change, above problems were easily solved. In flight test, power cutoff in the air repeatedly occurred. Investigation showed that the reason was that there appeared voltage transients (i.e. voltage peak and surge), causing transistors broken through and hence power cutoff. After measures to restrain voltage transients were taken and protection time was properly elongated, this fault of power cutoff in the air was removed. The successful development of this power system symbolized that China has mastered the design and manufacturing technique of constant frequency AC power system with low power electromagnetic CSDU.

4. Variable Speed Constant Frequency AC Power System and High Voltage DC Power System

Since the 1970s, the development of LSI circuits, large power electronic parts and rare−earth permanent magnet high energy magnetic steel, has created conditions for developing new types of electrical power systems. Variable speed constant frequency (VSCF) AC power system supplies constant frequency AC electrical power through electronic frequency converter, eliminating CSDU which is complex in structure, expensive, vulnerable to faults and difficult to maintain. High voltage DC power system utilizes new techniques such as solid state electronic parts and brushless DC motors, and has advantages of both low voltage DC and AC power systems. The common advantages of these two systems are high efficiency, high reliability and simple maintenance etc.. These systems are very promising. To match the development of new aircraft, China has made advanced research in this field. In the late 1970s, the Aeronautical Accessories Research Institute developed an AC−DC−AC type 10 KVA frequency converter, laid a technical foundation for the development of VSCF AC power system. In the early 1980s, the Nanjing Aeronautical Institute, cooperating with the Xingping Aeronautical Electrical Apparatus Factory, began to develop a 30 KVA AC−AC type VSCF power system. The system had two functions — starting and power generating. The system used new techniques such as samarium cobalt magnetic steel and microprocessor control. They made some progress with it.

5. Emergency Power System and Secondary Power System

While the main power system was being developed, emergency power system and secondary power system were also developing accordingly. They were supplementing each other to meet the needs of various types of Chinese−made aircraft. On the basis of the requirements by the Chinese−made aircraft, the Hubei Aeronautical Electrical Motor Factory successively developed

3 KVA AC emergency power system and cyclic oil cooling generator with AC / DC double outputs (20 KVA / 4 kW).

A whole series of aeronautical secondary power systems were also developed including DC step−up transformer, inverter, transformer, transformer rectifier and static inverter. DC step−up transformer ranged from 11−300 W. Single−phase and three−phase inverter ranged from 40−4,500 VA. The capacity of transformers and power of transformer rectifiers respectively reached several KVA or kW. These products not only met the utilization needs of various Chinese−made aircraft, but also were used in some missiles and tanks.

Static inverter using power semiconductor parts and transforming DC power into AC power belongs to the secondary power system. Because static inverter has no moving parts, no noise, high efficiency, light weight and is simple to use and maintain, it is gradually replacing inverter. Since the late 1960s, the Guizhou Aeronautical Electrical Motor Factory and the Nanjing Aeronautical Institute have successively developed single−phase and three−phase static inverters with power rating being 17−750 VA. These products have basically formed a series and been used in Chinese−made fighters and helicopters.

Section 5   Environmental Control System and Protective Rescue System

Modern aircraft is a complete "man—machine" system engineering. In this system, man plays the leading role.

When aircraft carries man to the sky, its altitude, speed and attitude are changing all the time, which greatly influences man's physiological functions and working conditions. Thus, a series of protective and rescue units are needed to assure flying crew's and passengers' safety and to provide them with proper living and working conditions. These units respectively belong to the environmental control system and the protective rescue system. The protective rescue system includes three subsystems: ejection escape, personal protection and parachute.

1. Environmental Control System

The function of ECS is to provide crew and passengers in cabin and airborne equipment with necessary environmental condition for normal working, i.e., to maintain proper pressure, temperature and humidity. Because the power of electronic equipments in modern aircraft has increased by large magnitude and as air transportation quickly advances, the passengers' requirement for comfort is constantly increasing, thus more stringent requirements for ECS were voiced.

ECS includes subsystems of cabin pressurization, cabin air supplying distribution, pressure control, cooling and temperature control and humidity control. Among them, cooling unit is a technically difficult equipment.

In more than thirty years, China has produced more than 80,000 sets of ECS for ten and more types of aircraft, among which cooling turbine unit is a typical product. As its air flow paths are extremely narrow, it is necessary to increase the rotational speed of the turbine to maintain a proper efficiency. Typically, the rotational speed is between 40,000 RPM and 100,000 RPM. In the late 1950s, copy produced cooling turbine unit for fighter had low efficiency and short life cycle for improper selection of bearing type and backward design of lubricating and cooling structure. It was a key technical problem for a time. After bearing and lubricating structure were modified, the design was certified for production. Afterwards, the first generation of new cooling turbine unit was developed, in which air flow paths were redesigned and improved, and closed wheel brazed with aluminium was adopted, increasing efficiency from 50% to 75%.

Then, the Aeronautical Accessories Research Institute developed the first set of long blade cooling turbine unit of reverse force type allowing refrigerating efficiency exceeding 80%. These products have been used in SH—5 and Y—10 aircraft.

To further raise refrigerating efficiency, under the leadership of Yang Yansheng, an air static—pressurized bearing research team was formed. This kind of bearing used air as lubricating medium, separating bearing spinning at high speed from bearing sleeve, which decreased friction and increased working life. Because there was no need for oil, it eliminated pollution, improved maintenance condition and reduced the number of parts by 2 / 3. This type of cooling turbine unit was successfully flight tested in Y—7 transport in 1975, and won the prize of the National Science Convention in 1978.

Considering that the "sky lights" lit day and night in petroleum industry and wasted large amount of oil field gas, in 1979, the research team modified the aeronautical cooling turbine unit which was succeeded in cooling oil field gas and in liquifying mixed light hydrocarbons and recovering it. The recovered light hydrocarbons amounted to one hundred million Yuan (RMB) every year. This achievement was praised by premier Zhao Ziyang and awarded the prize for technical development by the State Economic Commission. In the mid 1980s, the team even reached a higher level through international cooperation.

Fig.64　Air static pressurized bearing

In the early 1980s, to reduce bleed gas from engine to decrease power loss of engine, to solve problems of high temperature of cooling medium, large temperature variation and high humidity of cooling air, to improve reliability of electronic equipment and to provide pilots of military aircraft and electronic equipment with proper environment, R&D of high pressure water separation — boosting air cycle cooling system and application study of electronic technique in the environmental control system were carried out.

2. Aircraft Ejection Escape System

The function of aircraft ejection escape system is to allow pilot to escape from aircraft quickly in emergency, and to safely return to ground with the help of parachute. When aircraft's indicated airspeed (IAS) exceeds 400 km / hr, it is impossible for pilot to escape from aircraft relying on his own physical strength. It is only feasible to eject pilot within one second together with seat to a safe height by means of an ejection escape system, then to open parachute for landing.

The R&D of ejection escape system in China has been carrying on in such a way that specialized research institutes play main role and research, production and utilization departments are closely cooperating each other. Thus, technical manpower from various fields has been mobilized to jointly solve difficult technical problems. In a short time, four rocket ejection seats suitable for physiological features of Chinese pilots were successfully developed.

At the end of 1960s, because the performance of ejection escape system of J−6 aircraft was backward, emergent escape below 300 m could not work properly to save pilot's life. The Air Force and MAI decided to jointly establish a team to improve ejection escape system of J−6 aircraft. The primary target was to ensure pilot escaping from aircraft and save his life at zero altitude and at level indicated airspeed of 250−850 km / hr. Major improvement was made to original structure of ejection seat, i.e., to add rocket pack, seat / man separation unit, drogue and drogue launching unit etc. The improved seat was named type I rocket ejection seat.

During the development process, a key problem was to run rocket sled test on the ground to simulate the flight test. In comparison with flight test, this kind of test can accurately and repeatedly simulate preset velocity and acceleration and is easy to observe the test and collect measured data. Parts and assemblies also can be recovered. The whole facility for rocket sled test consists of three parts: track, rocket sled and testing and measuring equipments. The technical requirements of these facilities are very high and only a few countries in the world have these facilities. The construction work of rocket sled test range in China began rather late. However, the ejection escape test was related with pilot's life and was followed with interest by many people, no delay was allowed. The Flight Test Research Institute taking responsibility of making test the earliest, decided to start test with simple facilities. In May 1970, on a feeder line of railway in Shaanxi province, the institute tested self−made first rocket sled. Although initial starting weight was light (350 kg) and skiing distance was short (170 m) with slow sled speed, this was a good beginning anyway. Based on this, the sled design was improved using two rocket engines of larger thrust, which resulted in 630 km / hr sled speed and 1,270 m skiing distance.

By October of that year, 31 tests of rocket sled were carried out altogether, and animals such as dogs and monkeys were used in tests. When these animals landed safely after the ejection, their physiological reaction was normal, proving that the design was feasible.

Due to the limited length of the straight line segment of this feeder line, the sled speed could not be further increased. In November 1970, the special railway line of the Capital Airport was used as test range. The rocket sled was improved to install the cabin section of J−6 aircraft and type I seat on sled, and rocket engine of larger thrust was employed. After 45 tests of rocket sled (among them, three times were done at high speed, the maximum sled speed was 850 km / hr), the first ejection test in aircraft with real pilot in China was conducted, with a risk of the pilot's life from the Air Force. In 1973, type I ejection seat design was certified and then put into use in J−6, Q−5 and JJ−6 aircraft, improved reliability of ejection escape and safe escape range.

The original version of the ejection seat in J−7 II aircraft was made in such a way that the seat and canopy were automatically engaged each other, and would automatically be disengaged after leaving aircraft. This method often led to failure of escaping. The Chengdu Aircraft Factory considered the urgent needs of the Air Force and developed type II ejection seat with reference to the results of type I ejection seat. The tests of type II ejection seat were carried out in sled range in Henan province, meeting the safe rescue specification of zero altitude and within 250—850 km / hr IAS. In 1979, the design of type Ⅱ seat was certified and then used in the services with good results.

In 1973, the Rescue Equipment Research Institute started to develop type Ⅲ rocket ejection seat for J—8 aircraft. The main technical specifications were as follows: safe ejection escape speed in level flight was 130—850 km / hr and safe ejection altitude in level flight was from zero to aircraft ceiling. Under the leadership of Shen Erkong, the chief engineer, the forced drogue opening technique was employed, i.e., to use drogue gun to fire out drogue and life—saving parachute to shorten the parachute opening time and to improve low altitude rescue performance of the system, and to use more automatic ejection operating and separation programmed system. In five years of development, 38 sets of seat test

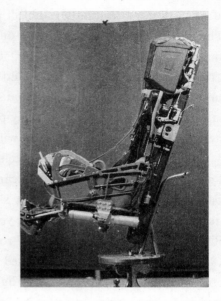

Fig.65　Type Ⅲ rocket ejection seat

samples were produced, and 67 ejection tests of ground "zero altitude — zero speed" were conducted. Also carried out were 61 high and low speed ground tests and 15 air ejection tests. The maximum speed of the sled reached 926 km / hr. A large number of tests showed that this ejection escape system had excellent performance and was equivalent to foreign products of the same type. The design of this system was certified in 1977. In 1983, a J—8 aircraft of the Air Force had an accident during flight training, entering a dive of nearly 90 ° with left rolling. In this extremely adverse attitude, the pilot used the ejection seat successfully, without any injury. The practice proved that the performance of type Ⅲ rocket ejection seat is reliable and safe.

In 1980, the Rescue Equipment Research Institute began developing type Ⅳ rocket ejection seat for J—7Ⅲ aircraft. Based on type Ⅲ but modified, the type Ⅳ used rocket pack of small impulse and changed drogue, life—saving parachute and parachute opener. The height of seat increased to be better accommodated to the figure of Chinese pilots, which further improved the performance of seat and operational safety. In 1984, the design of type Ⅳ ejection seat was certified.

After more than ten years of hard working, China has developed 4 types of rocket ejection seats, meeting the needs of fighter, attacker and fighter trainer. Ejection seats of fine quality have been supplied to the services and success rate of ejection rescue has been raised, which was praised by the Air Force and the Navy. In recent years started research work on ejection escape system which will work while aircraft is in an adversly complicated attitude with speed being

0—1,100 km／hr.

3. Personal Protective System

Military aircraft crew have to be prepared for abnormal environment and conditions such as high altitude (low pressure), acceleration, collision, high speed air flow, dropping into water, low temperature and high temperature. Therefore, personal protective systems are required, including oxygen supply system, pressurized helmet, high altitude compensating suit, pressure vest, anti—G system (anti—G regulator valve and anti—G trousures), protective helmet, immersion suit, rescue vest, armpit life—saving unit, ventilated suit and water—cooled suit

Fig.66　Duan Zijun visiting the Aeronautical
Rescue Equipment Research Institute

etc. Their functions are to ensure normal working efficiency of flight crew during flight, also to provide protective rescue in emergent case, on the sea or in desert etc..

In more than 30 years, China has developed four new types of oxygen supply systems and 35 kinds of new products, meeting needs of various types of aircraft. In 1978, the oxygen supply system for large passenger airliner was successfully developed. Because the old oxygen supply system in Y—8 transport could not contain the required oxygen volume for all parachuters onboard for four hours, the Hefei Oxygen Equipment Factory started to do the research on the principle of airborne "closed circuit oxygen supply". This new principle can increase utilization efficiency of oxygen in aircraft by five times. In 1977, the feasibility study of new principle was completed. This achievement won the prize of the National Science Convention. Afterwards, the engineering development of a chemical regeneration oxygen supply unit for Y—8 transport was carried out. Technical personnel overcame the difficulty of reaction capability decrease of the drug after long time storage in low temperature. After physiological tests and flight tests being made, the system design was certified in 1983.

In 1980, R&D of molecular sieve oxygen generation in aircraft began. In 1984, the key material "351" molecular sieve for generating oxygen was basically developed and ground oxygen generation process test was completed, making a big step forward.

When flying altitude of fighter exceeds 12,000 m, it is necessary to use personal protective apparatus——high altitude pressurized helmet and high altitude compensation suit. Once aircraft cabin losses air tightness, this kind of protective apparatus can maintain the pilot's survivability for five minutes to allow him to reduce the aircraft altitude. The compensation suit and open pressurized helmet developed by China use new structure and advanced technique. It passed wind tunnel test, water tank test, rocket sled test and flight test. In 1986, the design was certified. In the development process of the pressurized helmet, computer-aided design was first used, which improved design quality, shortened development period and accelerated development schedule. Besides, anti-nuclear flash helmet was also developed for pilot's use in nuclear test situation. In the past several nuclear tests, it worked properly.

Immersion suit is such a protective suit which, once aircrew drop into water and is immersed in cold water, can keep the body temperature to maintain physiological functions for some time. In 1977, the Hubei Personal Protective Apparatus Factory started developing immersion suit. Cooperating with the Shanghai Textile Institute and the Chongqing Textile Industry Research Institute, the factory developed air-ventilated but water-proof textile and made a series of tests of immersion suit in the sixth Research Institute of the Navy, including live low temperature physiological test and live tests on the sea in winter etc.. In 1986, an armpit life-saving unit was developed which, after being immersed into water, could automatically be charged with air.

4. Parachute

The function of parachute is to increase motion drag of airdropping human body and object, to reduce the speed, to stabilize the motion attitude and perform safe landing. At the beginning of the 20th century, parachute already started to be used for rescue. During the Second World War, parachute was widely used for airdropping armament, mines, torpedoes and for air rescue. In 1974, drag parachute started to be used for fighter to shorten rolling distance of aircraft landing on ground and landing on deck. At present, parachute is widely used in paratroopers dropping, air rescue, airborne drop, air vehicle speed decreasing, recovery and parachuting sport etc..

The design, development and production of parachute are very specialized and the technical requirements of strength, parachute opening procedure and safety device are very strict. Especially for man-carrying parachute, it is related with man's life, and a slightest negligence would lead to disastrous result. Apart from that the design and manufacturing process needs strict quality control, many kinds of tests are required including wind tunnel test, tow test, powered launching test, static test, impulse test, ejection test and airdropping test. The airdropping test is the most popular test item. For life-saving parachute, paratroop parachute, sport parachute, reserve parachute and cargo parachute etc. usually dummy, balancing weight and real objects are used in transport to make airdropping test or live parachuting test. Each improvement of paratroop parachute and sport parachute generally has to undergo a few hundred or thousand live parachuting tests. The birth of each new product involves the hard working and the spirit of brave devotion of parachuters.

Parachute was the airborne equipment the design and research of which started earliest in the aeronautical industry. Since the 1950s, with the purpose to meet the military and civil requirements, the policy of combination of factories and institutes, of research, manufacturing and utilization, and self—reliance has been adhered to. All materials, designs, manufacturing and testing were based on domestic resource, and products were constantly upgraded. In more than thirty years of development, 11 series of more than 260 types of man—carrying parachutes and cargo parachutes were produced, which met the requirements of national defence, research tests and sports. Part of products have been exported. So far, the following parachutes have been designed and produced: life—saving parachute and stabilization—brake parachute for zero altitude—low speed ejection escape system; various types of life—saving parachutes with instant opening speed being 400—600 km / hr and minimum safe opening altitude 100—60 m; paratroop parachute and reserve parachute with escaping speed being 180—400 km / hr and minimum safe altitude 300 m; cargo parachute with airdropping weight being from 6 kg to 4.5 tons; parawing sport parachute with lift drag ratio being 2.6—3 and the maximum horizontal speed 12 m / sec; various types of drag parachutes with aircraft landing weight being 6—48 tons and landing speed 200—320 km / hr; various aerial bomb parachutes with aircraft speed being 900 km / hr and aerial dropping altitude 50—10,000 m; various types of flare parachutes being able to open in supersonic speed condition; nuclear test parachute; and specialized parachutes for ECM, laying cable at the bottom of sea, rocket blast, rocket mining, drone aircraft, air—sounding instrumentation recovery and air—refueling etc.. During the development process of new products, many types of new materials were timely developed by the textile industry of China, including synthetic fibre textile of high strength and mini—ventilation, which played an important role for the birth of new types of parachutes.

a. Man—Carrying Parachute

Man—carrying parachutes include life—saving parachute, paratroop parachute and sport parachute etc..

Life—saving parachute is a kind of life—saving apparatus used for pilot to escape from aircraft in emergent case. It can be used independently or together with ejection seat.

In 1959, Guo Ruiquan, a designer and others overcame high mountain reaction and adverse weather condition and made investigation in Qingzang plateau crossing a long distance. At last, they developed the life—saving parachute suitable for use in plateau areas, making contributions to the national defence.

In 1973, after more than 3000 tests and more than 160 ground and air integrated tests, the life—saving parachute and seat stabilization parachute used for type I rocket ejection seat were developed. The function of stabilization parachute was to steadily decrease the speed of seat to ensure life—saving parachute to open safely and to ensure the seat maintaining a proper attitude before separation of man and seat, which facilitated the separation of man and seat and opening the main parachute.

In 1976, the Hubei Parachute Factory developed type 10 life—saving parachute. The parachute could instantly open at maximum horizontal speed 550 km / hr at altitude 60—12,000

m. The parachute could carry oxygen rescue boat and various rescue objects. Its landing speed was not larger than 6 m / sec, satisfactorily solving low altitude safe ejection escape problem for J−6 and J−7 aircraft. It won the prize of the National Science Convention in 1978. In 1979 and 1985, the factory again developed seat stabilization drag parachute and life−saving parachute ejected by drogue gun, meeting the needs of J−7, J−7Ⅲ and J−8Ⅱ aircraft and solving low altitude and high speed rescue problem. It won the first class prize of major science achievement of the industries of national defence.

Paratroop parachute is an equipment used for paratroop operation and for parachuting training. From 1952 to 1984, 10 types were developed, technical performance of which reached the level of the same kind of foreign products.

The type 4 paratroop parachute developed in 1970, all used polyamide fibre material. It had light weight and low volume, and could be used for armed parachuting for Y−5, Y−8 and other aircraft. This parachute had been used by Chinese paratroops. The accumulated number of parachuting came nearly one million. This parachute caused positive response both from home and abroad.

The type 6 paratroop parachute developed in 1976, used new structure of variable area stabilization parachute. It had both functions of stabilization parachute and pilot parachute, and solved the parachuting problem of two queue dense escaping in the Y−8 transport aircraft. The escape speed was 180−400 km / hr, increased by 80 km / hr compared with the original maximum utilization speed. It could use delayed opening. The minimum safe altitude is 300 m. It improved the fighting ability of the services. It won the prize of the National Science Convention in 1978.

Sport parachute is a sportsman−used chute for games, training and demonstration. The sport parachute made in China had quite large horizontal speed and excellent operational performance, and received praise from sportsmen of various countries. Since 1958, there were developed altogether 35 kinds. Using this parachute, Chinese parachuting sportsmen achieved good scores in international games many times, winning honour for motherland. In May 1960, Chinese National Parachuting Team firstly broke world record using Chinese−made parachutes in the international parachuting game in the Soviet Union. The team won three champions and four runner−ups among eight game items.

In 1978, Wu Ruzhang, Sun Jiaqi and others in the Nanjing Parachute Factory developed the first generation of type 6 parawing sport parachute in China. This parachute used the principle of wing lift. When the parachute is gliding down, a lift will be generated. The lift drag ratio reached 2.6−3, which allowed pilot gliding down at a horizontal speed greater than descending speed by 2−3 times (9−12 m / sec). Also its steering was flexible and the performance of landing deceleration was good. There could be seen some technical innovation. The successful development of parawing sport parachute increased parachuting score. Chinese sportsmen used this parachute and updated all national parachuting records and achieved excellent results in international games. In August 1980, using home−made parachute, the Chinese team got the second place in women collective fixed point parachuting, and the fourth place in women's team event in the fifteenth international parachuting championships in Bulgaria.

In 1980, the second generation of type 8 sport parachute started to be developed. It used high strength polyamide fibre. Its weight was lighter than that of the type 6 sport parachute by 24% and horizontal speed reached 10—20 m / sec. Its apperance was nice and stability was good. It was easy to control. It reached the international level of the same kind of products. The design was certified in 1983. In September 1984, in the 17th World's figure and fixed point parachuting game, Chinese woman parachuters achieved the championship of woman's personal fixed point parachuting and the second place of collective fixed point parachuting. In 1984, parachuting formation sport parachute was developed. It was comfortable to wear and the opening procedure was simple. "Sparrow landing" with it was easy. In 1985, after the type 6 sport parachute was modified, it could be used for treading parachuting performance. The Chinese sportsmen have successfully twice won the world championship of quadruplet treading parachuting. China also developed more than 20 types of demonstration parachutes. They have got varieties of colours and patterns, and also used in celebrating holidays.

b. Cargo—Carrying Parachute

Cargo—carrying parachutes developed in China include cargo parachute, aerial bomb parachute and nuclear test parachute etc.

The function of cargo parachute is airdropping various armaments, vehicles and materials. The Parachute Factory developed many types of cargo parachutes to meet the needs of the national defence construction. For example, in 1982, a cargo parachute was developed, the total airdropping weight was 2.5 tons. It could be used in Y—8 transport to airdrop lightweight field vehicles or 150 W radio station vehicle. In the same year, also was developed a cargo parachute with an airdropping total weight of 4.5 tons, it could airdrop field vehicle or 85 mm cannon. The rocket blast parachute played its role in mine sweeping in the defensive fighting against aggression.

Aerial bomb parachutes refer to those parachutes used to airdrop bomb, mine, torpedo and flare bomb. By the year of 1984, there were altogether developed 24 types of various aerial bomb parachutes. In 1958, after repeated testing, technical personnel developed mine parachute with 2 stages opening structure for H—5 aircraft to airdrop 500 kg mine, which allowed mine dropping speed of aircraft to be increased from 360 km / hr to 700 km / hr. In 1967, a mine parachute to airdrop 1 ton mine was developed and the performance was better than that of the same kind of foreign products.

The function of nuclear test parachute is to ensure safe descending of nuclear bomb, and to ensure explosion, measurement, effect and safety, and to ensure nuclear bomb reaching preset space position in preset time. All these need accurate and reliable opening procedure, accurate trajectory and enough strength. So it was very difficult to develop. The nuclear test parachute developed by China was first used together with successful aerial nuclear explosion in June of 1967 and later was successfully worked together with aerial nuclear tests, which received praise by the State Council and the Military Commission of CCCPC. Among them, the new nuclear test parachute of wave ring structure has even more accurate and strict opening procedure, which raised trajectory accuracy and assured test quality. This nuclear test parachute won the National Gold Medal in 1979.

Section 6   Fire Control System and Suspension and Launching Unit

1. Fire Control System (FCS)

When fighting, in order to accurately attack the target, military aircraft must acquire, track and identify target, and it is also necessary to guide the aircraft along a favourable trajectory to approach the target, and to control the launching of its rocket, missile and gun, and the delivery of bombs. The system responsible for these tasks onboard is called fire control system. It consists of various equipments controlling the direction, density, proper time and time duration of aircraft weapon firing. The performance of FCS directly influences the hit rate of weaponry. Hence, aircraft performance, FCS and pilot's operating skill are typically called three important elements of an aircraft's fighting capability.

Aviation—developed countries in the world have always attached great importance to the development of FCS. During the Second World War, only single optical sight was used in military aircraft. In the mid 1940s, with the development of electronic technology, radar rangefinder was combined with optical electro—mechanical sight, forming the early stage FCS. It was also called radar sight. Radar ranging replaced optical ranging, and increased the range of target measurement and measuring accuracy, and the automation of range measuring was realized. In the 1950s, the multifunctional firing radar able to measure range and direction was developed. Combined with an optical sight it formed a new generation of FCS, making the daylight fighter an all weather fighter. In the 1960s, due to the emerging of the electronic display technique, appeared the electronic sight——head—up display. It combined digital fire control computer, firing radar and air data computer to form an integrated fire control system, which greatly improved system function and sighting accuracy and pushed FCS to a new development stage. Since the 1970s, new achievements in various scientific fields began to be applied to FCS. The constituent parts of FCS have been constantly updated and system performance increased. For example, the application of infrared and Laser acquisition units increased the attack capability at night and in complicated weather conditions; the application of pulse Doppler radar provided aircraft with look—down and shoot—down capability, and the attack on low altitude targets became possible etc..

The development stages of FCS in China are similar to those abroad. In the late 1950s, the Ministry of Armament Industry copy produced optical gunsight for J—5 aircraft. In the early 1960s, optical gunsight was copy produced for J—6 aircraft. The Ministry of Electronics Industry also copy produced radar rangefinder and firing radar for J−6 aircraft. In the mid 1960s, the Ministry of Armament Industry and the Ministry of Electronics Industry separately copy produced several types of optical bombsights and bombing radar for H−5 and H−6 aircraft. In 1970, the MAI established the Aeronautical Fire Control Research Institute and the Airborne Radar Research Institute responsible for the development of various types of fire control equipments and systems. The advanced three−dimentional dynamic emulation lab for FCS and the system test lab for airborne radar have been constructed and test facilities improved to ensure quality of research results. Since the 1970s, enterprises have developed FCS equipments and systems such as many types of optical gunsights, advanced head−up displays, various firing and bombing radars, infra−red direction finders and Laser rangefinders etc.. Compared with FCS equipment copy produced before, the working range was increased and sighting accuracy and system functions improved. Thus, the fight capability of Chinese−made aircraft strengthened.

a. Aeronautical Optical Gunsight

Type SM−8 aeronautical optical gunsight was a FCS equipment developed for use in J−8 aircraft. It consisted of optical display, semi−floated computing gyroscope, analogous electronic computer and control box. In 1975, the prototype was trial produced and installed in J−6A aircraft to make simulated attack test and air drone live firing test. It showed following advantages: short ring stabilization time, bright ring, good anti−vibration performance of gyroscope and quick reaction. In 1976, the design was certified.

In early 1979, it was upgraded as type SM−8A. The main features of the modified version were: standardized semi−floated rate gyroscope replaced specialized semi−floated computing gyroscope to measure aircraft angular velocity; it was more reliable, had longer working life and higher system accuracy; the light ring consisted of light points of diamond shape, the range display being added and the brightness of the light ring being increased; a high accurate and stable integrating circuitry was developed solving the system damping problem; it had multiple working modes suitable for air−to−air and air−to−ground sighting and attack with various types of weapons. In May 1979, the flight test of the principle demonstrator showed that live firing accuracy was high, meeting the requirement of the improved design. This was the first time to successfully use rate gyroscope as measuring unit of a fighter sight to form a sighting system in China. In November 1980, it was put into operational test after technical appraisal. Later, the chief engineer Jiang Chengying, vice chief engineer Wu Xiuren of the Aeronautical Fire Contorl Research Institute organized technical personnel to solve technical problems such as ring fluttering, serious spurious colours of display and not being able to normally work in strong interference etc.. The design and technical problems were solved. The design was certified in November 1982, and the system started to be used in J−8 daylight version and all−weather version. Then, based on type SM−8A and with partial modification, many versions of type SM−8 series were developed and installed in various types of fighters, trainers and bombers.

b. Head−up Display

When pilot is fighting, if he uses traditional optical sight to aim, sometime he has to raise his head up looking outside to search target, and other time he has to lower his head down to look at instruments, which distributes his attention. Especially for high speed aircraft, it would influence the aiming and even affect the fighting. Hence the head—up display appeared. The head—up display is installed above the instrument panel, in front of pilot's eyes. Through semi—transparent and semi—reflective display screen, pilot can see the front and outside scenery, and also can watch the aiming picture and instruments—generated information superimposed on outside scenery, thus improving aiming accuracy.

In early 1979, the Aeronautical Fire Control Research Institute began developing head—up display, using cathode ray tube and high speed large capacity digital computer. In December of the same year, the first principle demonstrator was produced. In February 1980, it was tested interfacing with digital electronic computer, and five dynamic pictures were successfully displayed. In 1982, it was installed in J—6A aircraft for flight test. The demonstrator had many working modes and dynamic pictures such as

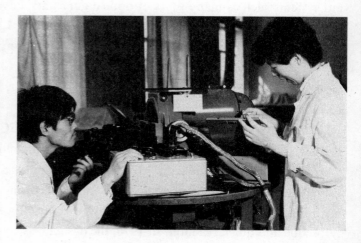

Fig.67   Technical personnel adjusting and testing optical gunsight

lead tracking, tracer—line snapshot, missile attack and navigation. The results of various tests and flight test showed: the design principle of the demonstrator was correct; the scheme was feasible; the whole system worked coordinately; pictures were bright and clear; tracer—line tracking was changing smoothly; response was quick; the impact point of firing to air drone was basically coincident with the tracer—line.

The development of the head—up display was a spade work in China. It was very difficult. Some key technical problems should be solved such as computer interface and software design for generating dynamic pictures. Xi Liyun, an engineer, was responsible for the development of HUD computer. After a cancer operation, he was still working on computer adjusting and testing. He actually solved the problem of computer interface and improved the reliability of the product. Engineer Ye Xiaofeng was responsible for the system software. He finished the design of the symbol generator after hard studying. Due to the joint effort of the scientific researchers and technicians, they developed a HUD principle demonstrator of fine quality at last. In November 1982. the MAI organized technical appraisal of the demonstrator. Based on the principle demonstrator, in 1984, the prototype of HUD used for J—8 II aircraft was developed and interfaced with a digital air data computer developed by the Taiyuan Aeronautical

Instruments Factory. In May 1985, it was installed in J-7 II aircraft and successfully flight tested. The new head-up display had complete functions. Its technique was advanced and it was convenient to use. Its reliability was high and all interfaces worked properly. All pictures were stable and lines smooth. Symbols were clear and easy to be identified. Under strong light pictures were clear. Its anti-G capability was better than that of optical gunsight. This successful development has filled in the gap in this field in China, which symbolized that the aeronautical FCS in China entered into a new stage. This provided technical basis for upgrading FCS in Chinese-made fighter, attacker and bomber.

Besides, in August 1985, the HUD developed for a new bomber was retrofitted and installed in Q-5 aircraft for R&D flight test, and bomb dropping test was made with good results.

One of the important reasons why HUD could be developed in such a short time was that the advanced research was given enough attention. It prepared a good technical storage for the HUD development. For example, the tracer-line snapshot principle was the theoretical basis for the general scheme of HUD. In 1972, the Aeronautical Fire Control Research Institute began the basic theory study. In 1975, the principle demonstrator of snapshot sight was flight tested. Symbol generator was another technical hardnut. Through advanced research, its key techniques were mastered. These advanced research items laid down technical basis for the engineering development and shortened the gap with foreign advanced level.

c. Airborne Firing Radar

Firing radar is a fire control equipment for fighter to perform all-weather tasks in complicated weather conditions. It is interfaced with optical sight to search, acquire and track targets. It provides FCS with target information. China has developed many types of firing radar. Type SR-4 was the first airborne fire control radar independently designed by China. The design scheme review was mainly carried out by the South-west Electronics Research Institute of the Chinese Academy of Sciences and the development task was given by the Ministry of Electronics Industry to the South-west Electronics Research Institute of the Ministry. The task of developing 142 items of parts and raw materials were clearly defined and carried out, including large power magnetron, isolator, thyratron, double gun storage display tube etc..The first set of the principle demonstrator of the radar passed through stages of design, trial manufacturing and the system integration testing. In 1971, it was installed in aircraft and flight tested. The results showed that the design scheme was successful, and design performance of acquisition, interception, tracking and anti-interference met desired requirements. But there still existed some problems such as long search period, easy breakthrough of microwave parts in high power condition and mechanical resonance of antenna system.

In early 1971, the development task and personnel of this radar were transferred to the Airborne Radar Research Institute newly formed by the Chinese Aeronautical Establishment. After being modified in design, trial produced and flight tested, five prototypes were produced by the Sichuan Airborne Radar Factory, and more than ten large-scale ground tests were conducted. In 1981, the radar was installed in J-8 aircraft for R&D flight test. Its tactical and technical performance basically met the design requirements. In 1982, the design certification flight test and ground to air tests of the radar were performed. The chief engineer Zhu Kexin of the Airborne Radar Research Institute and his technical team worked very hard at flight test range all the year to solve difficult technical problems. They solved various technical problems caused by installation of radar in aircraft, including false target interference of aircraft inlet, corona of antenna feed source case in high altitude environment, and fluctuation phenomenon of hydraulic system of installed radar etc. paving the way for the certification of the radar. In 1984, the radar design was certified and installed in J−8 aircraft, turning the daylight version into an all−weather version.

At the early stage of type SR−4 radar development, due to the system that the chief designer had the technical responsibility and the responsibilities of technical personnel at each rank were clearly defined, the first set of principle demonstrator was produced within one year. However, because of the disorder of the "cultural revolution", regulations were loosened and management was changed. As a result, the development organizations were changed four times and test facilities were in shortage, which resulted in such a fact that after eight years of coming out of prototype, the R&D flight test then began, elongating development period.

The type 317 radar, developed at the same time with type SR−4 radar, was a multifunctional fire control radar, and had following functions such as air−to−air and air−to−ground acquisition, terrain mapping, terrain avoidance and ground ranging etc.. Based on type 317 radar, type 317A multifunctional monopulse radar was developed. Compared with type 317 radar, it reduced volume, weight and power consumption, expanded waveband and added anti−interference measures. Flight test proved its excellent performance and it was certified in 1981. Its technical results were applied to new generation of firing radar type JL−7.

Type JL−7 was an airborne fire control radar with air−to−air functions being main tasks, and air−to−ground functions being secondary ones. Compared with other fire control radar, it had advantages such as small volume, light weight, low power consumption and high anti−interference capability, and it was suitable for fighter use. In 1980, the Airborne Radar Research Institute undertook this development task, and Li Hongfan was appointed chief designer. To expand radar operating range, attention was given to solve key techniques such as the increase of repetition frequency, the increase of video accumulation and reducing of noise figure etc..In 1982, a radar demonstrator for ground testing was produced. In 1983, environment tests such as high temperature, low temperature, low atmospheric pressure, vibration, impulse and high altitude thermal simulation were completed. Ground integrated testing of FCS showed that interfaces were correct, and static accuracy met the requirements of FCS. Type JL−7 radar was also installed in fighter for inlet interference test, and the interference of false target echo was removed. The radar worked properly. In 1984, three sets of radar were trial produced and R&D flight test was finished. In 1986, the design certification flight test was carried out.

Besides, China has also developed and produced other fire control equipments, such as missile allowable launch distance computer, aeronautical infra−red observing unit and airborne

Laser rangefinder etc. and has launched advanced research on diffraction optical head—up display, airborne side—looking radar, airborne phased—array radar, terrain—following radar, pulse Doppler fire control radar and avionics integrated system.

2. Suspension and Launching Units

The armament of military aircraft, including bomb, nuclear bomb, rocket and missile etc. are suspended or installed in aircraft by some kinds of units. While in fighting, they are delivered or launched through electro—mechanical control units. Generally, these units are called suspension and launching units.

a. Suspension Unit

Suspension unit refers to electro—mechanical control unit in aircraft to suspend and delivery weapons, including various bomb racks. Since 1960, the Henan Aeronautical Accessories Factory has developed more than 20 various suspension units for many types of aircraft, including special bomb carrier and bomb shackle and missile carrier etc., which satisfied the needs of traditional bomb and nuclear bomb.

In 1966, the Government decided to develop a special carrier to suspend atom bomb for H—6 aircraft. The Henan Aeronautical Accessories Factory finished this task only within four months, ensuring successful test of the first Chinese atom bomb. This unit was certified for production.

Traditional shackle makes delivery by gravity, i.e., shackle opening is controlled by electro—magnetic force, then the store will be separated from carrier aircraft under the action of its own gravity. The speed of this separation is slow, only suitable for low speed aircraft. If used for high speed aircraft, there possibly would happen problems such as "adherence" and collision with carrier aircraft. To avoid occurence of these phenomena, in 1972, a bomb shackle of jettison force delivery was designed, i.e., the high pressure gas generated by ignition of initiator pushed a piston to open the schackle, at the same time also pushed jettison rod, instantly applied huge thrust onto the store to make it rapidly separate from the carrier aircraft.

In 1983, an ejection bomb schackle was developed for J—8 II and J—7 III aircraft. This unit had some innovations in ejector reset, controllable attitude delivery etc.. By controlling the powder composition of the initiator, the jettison speed was increased. The structure of combustion chamber and initiator was also improved and the reliability of induction ignition increased, which made suspension unit turning from single point jettison to double point jettison, from attitudeless control to attitude control. The process towards standardization, seriation and generalization then began.

The missile carrier developed for H—6D bomber could carry air—to—ship missile. Its main feature was using integrated configuration to combine release mechanism with carrier structure. In November 1985, the carrier design was certified and put into batch production, thus forming a new series of air—to—ship missile suspension and launching units combining shackle with carrier together in China.

b. Missile Launching Unit and Turret

Missile launching unit is an electro—mechanical control unit to suspend and launch missiles. It is divided into rail type and jettison type.

Since 1964, the Air—to—Air Missile Research Institute and the Henan Aeronautical Accessories Factory have developed more than ten air—to—air missile launching units for J—7 and J—8 Ⅱ aircraft.

Rocket launching unit is used for suspending and launching rocket. Since 1958, more than ten rocket launchers have been developed for use in more than ten types of aircraft, meeting the needs of the services.

To meet the needs of bomber and military transport, since the 1960s, the Xi'an Aircraft Accessories Factory has produced many types of turrets. Turret is a remote—operated follow—up system. Its structure is complex and the manufacturing work amount is large. One turret has to use nearly 10 thousand parts, assemblies and standardized parts, a few hundred boughtout items, more than ten thousand specialized manufacturing equipments and more than 100 items of test equipments. After being produced, the turret has to undergo firing test, so it is very difficult to produce. The factory not only has developed a series of products, but also produced in batch a few hundred sets of turrets, which have been provided to the services.

Section 7　Hydraulic, Aircraft Fuel, Engine Control and Starter Systems

To ensure flying and to control flying power, aircraft and aeroengine also should be equipped with numerous systems with different functions. These systems mainly are: hydraulic, pneumatic and wheel brake system used to operate aircraft; aircraft fuel system to feed fuel; engine control system to control flying power; starter—ignition system to start engine and other specialized units and devices of various types. During the development process of airborne equipment in China, the above—mentioned parts, assemblies and equipments were generally called aeronautical accessories. With the advance of science and technology, these systems are getting improved.

The basic feature of these systems is that the mechanical structure is the main body, with some electrical apparatus in certain cases. Starting from the 1960s, electronic technique began to be applied. Then, a series of electro—mechanical products were developed which were progressing towards digitization and integration in terms of automatic control functions. Because these systems need to be working reliably in complicated environmental conditions, they are quite different from ground mechanical products. Their functional features are high automation, quickly working, mutiple configuration, small volume, light weight and being accurate and reliable.

The structure of these systems mostly are quite complicated and need precision processing.

For example, fuel regulator and gas turbine starter both have more than one thousand parts and assemblies. The production of some complicated parts and assemblies often need dozens of manufacturing technologies and associated equipments, need to use several hundred of specialized toolings and pass through several hundred processes. Even though technical tooling is quite modernized today, manufacturing of some parts and modules and assembly of some products still require skill of experienced workers. Assemblied products have to pass through various tests, such as static, dynamic, environmental, working life and simulation tests etc..Also, various special testing facilities are required, including high altitude lab and inertial test rig etc.

1. Hydraulic, Pneumatic and Wheel Brake Systems

Hydraulic, pneumatic and wheel brake systems are mainly used to retract and extend landing gears, to steer control surfaces, to open and close cabin doors, to charge gun, to operate wheel brake and for emergent operating etc..The main accessories of these systems are hydraulic pumps, hydraulic motors, pneumatic motors, brake discs, and valves, filters, boosters, actuators, servoes of various types. Their features are: a. to realize remote steering; b. to achieve boosting effect, for example, some control surfaces need a few tons of steering force; c. quick response.

In the 1950s, to meet the needs of Chinese—made CJ—5, J—5 and Y—5 aircraft, associated hydraulic, pneumatic and wheel brake systems were copy produced, basically matching the development of aircraft.

In the 1960s, the trial production of hydraulic system (the system for J—7 aircraft was a representative) was put on the agenda. The J—7 aircraft had good manoeuvrability and dogfight capability, good takeoff and landing capability and operating performance. Aerodynamic heating at high speed made the environmental temperature of the hydraulic system go up to 110 ℃. The force required to operate control surface at high speed in large manoeuvrability flight reached 56.9 kN (5.8 tons), and working pressure of hydraulic system increased to 2,059.5 × 10^4Bar (210 kg / cm^2). The improved performance increased the accuracy of precision parts of the hydraulic system by an order of magnitude. Also, a number of new materials were used, including fluorinated plastics, silicone rubber, heat—resistant high strength stainless steel and graphite inpregnated with resin etc..To check the reliability of the hydraulic system, some more strict tests such as six degree—of—freedom loading, heat impulse, dynamic oscilloscope recording were added. Under the leadership of Zhang Ning, the director of the Nanjing Aeronautical Accessories Factory, the hydraulic system for J—7 aircraft was successfully trial produced and put into batch production, symbolizing that the manufacturing technology of the hydraulic system and the ability of meeting domestic requirements were raised to a new level.

In the 1970s, the stage of independent development of hydraulic system began. New hydraulic systems were successively developed for Q—5, J—8 and Y—10 aircraft.

In the 1980s, a batch of new products were developed for J—7Ⅲ, J—8Ⅱ, Y—7, Y—8, H—6 and Z—8 aircraft, including hydraulic pump, hydraulic motor, high precision filter, various switches, servo valves, boosters and servoes etc..Compared with the hydraulic pump copy produced in the 1960s, the new hydraulic pump increased rotational speed from 2,000 RPM to 4,000 RPM, flow capacity from 36 litre / min to 80 litre / min. The power—weight ratio increased by four times. The pressure regulating quality from zero flow capacity to full flow capacity was improved from about 14% to about 3.5%. In the late 1970s, to meet the needs of new aircraft, the production technology of variable delivery hydraulic pump was imported. But apart from product drawings and basic process information, the technical information of key processes and the third party's license were not available. These numerous manufacturing technology difficulties and key raw material problems were solved by related domestic factories. The Nanjing Aeronautical Accessories Factory and the Guizhou Hydraulic Accessories Factory, through thorough study, developed manufacturing technique of hydraulic pump, independently designed and produced integrated test equipment using microprocessor control and test equipment for friction couple parts of fuel pump, and raised the level of test technique. In 1984, this hydraulic pump was successfully trial produced, and passed performance qualification test.

Before the 1970s, the domestic wheel brake system had mainly been inertial antiskid automatic braking. Since the 1980s, due to combined application of mechanic, hydraulic and electronic techniques, electronic antiskid brake system was developed. Stopping efficiency increased from 60% to above 90%. It has been used in Y—10 aircraft.

The performance of brake, to a great extent, depends on friction coefficient and high temperature—resistant performance of the friction material of brake block. In the 1950s, the brake block copy produced by the Xinping Aircraft Wheel Brake Accessories Factory, used asbestos—rubber friction material and the wheel brake torque could not reach technical specification. Since the 1960s, many types of friction materials such as phenol—asbestos base, plastics—iron, cupper base powder alloy, iron base powder alloy, bimetallic friction couple were successively developed. They increased friction performance. In the 1980s, the development of friction couple using carbon—carbon composite material started and has made some progress.

In more than 30 years, China has established a complete network of research and production bases and test centers of wheel brake system. The test equipment can make inertia test from medium and small wheel brake of 10 tons and 15 tons to large wheel brake of 46 tons. The large inertial test rig can test tyre of maximum diameter 1.8 m. Its radial load reached 46 tons. The peak power of electric motor is 9500 kW. It employs digital display, and uses electronic computer to perform automatic monitoring and test appraisal.

2. Aircraft Fuel System

Aircraft fuel system is a complete system used to store fuel and to ensure continuous and reliable feeding of fuel to engines in specified flying condition and according to desired pressure and flow rate. Aircraft fuel system in copy produced aircraft before the 1960s, used manual gravity refueling when being refueled on the ground. Its pressure and flow rate were low. It required quite long time for refueling, which was not suitable for preparing fight. Besides, there still existed some disadvantages such as control of flow rate being not accurate, sealing being not tight and that it needed a large amount of work for the ground personnel. Later, the Aeronautical Accessories Research Institute developed a closed automatic pressure refueling system, and also successively developed hydraulic centrifugal pump, AC electric pump, ejector pump, electric double-faced pump with inverted flight capability, and mechanical multiredundant flow proportioner and numerically-controlled flow proportioner which could automatically adjust the flow rate to each tank and maintain the balance of CG of the aircraft. While the development was going on, large simulation test facilities were set up. Among them, the two-dimentional integrated simulation test rig for aircraft fuel system, which can simulate working status in air, won the prize of the National Science Convention in 1978.

3. Engine Control System

Engine control system (propulsion control system) is used to control the working status of engine to meet the requirements of different flight conditions of the aircraft. It can be divided into two large categories — mechanical, hydraulic, pneumatic control and analogous / digital control.

The development and production of engine control system in China has undergone a process from simple to complex and from copy production to independent development. In the 1950s, the Xi'an Accessories Factory and the Nanjing Accessories Factory copy produced many types of control systems for piston engine and jet engine. From the end of the 1950s to the mid 1960s, under the leadership of Li Shifa, the chief engineer, the Xi'an Engine Accessories Factory successively developed engine control systems for WP6, WP7 and WP8. In the late 1960s, two control systems for turboprop engine were developed, and also control systems for turboshaft engine and turbofan engine. These products had complex structure and high precision. For example, the geometric tolerence of precision couple is 1 μm, so the workers had to be careful to select them and match them while being assembled. Poor storage also could lead to deformation of some parts. For some parts, while being measured, the temperature of hand also could influence its dimension, making measurement inaccurate. In the manufacturing process of accessories, one key technique not been solved for a long time was the influence of polluters on working reliability of precision assemblies. The cleaning work on "three evils" (metallic powder, grinding paste and foreign objects) in multiple crossed, thin and long fuel feed pipes in regulator case had been carried out for many years. In some cases, there were 88 crossed fuel feed pipes with tiny holes of 3—5 mm diameter, among which there were 27 blind holes and more than 140 crossings. In these places, it was quite natural to have deposition such as metalic powder and grinding paste, but it was a relatively steady area of fluid flow. It was impossible to clean it with traditional method. But it was this case in which were installed more than 10 precision valve couples, the matching gap being 5—8 μm. If being stuck, there possibly would be unsmooth motion, even seized, heavily influencing performance. Even worse, it could possibly lead to a shutdown of the engine and catastrophic result of the aircraft. At the end of the 1970s, the Guizhou Engine Accessories Factory, led by the chief engineer Tan Su, organized technical personnel to solve this problem of "three evils". After three years of hard work, they summarized a complete set of technological processes to get rid of "three evils", achieving good results.

In the late 1970s, engine control systems for WS9 and WZ8 engines were imported, also associated precision cold and hot manufacturing equipments and test equipments for product performance and environmental testing. A batch of new products were trial produced. Taking engine fuel accessories for example, compared with old versions of products, new products were improved from single parameter closed regulation to combined parameters integrated regulation and the number of regulated parameters increased from a few to more than ten. Through trial production of these products, technical processing level was remarkably heightened and super-precision processing, NC processing and many kinds of heat treatment and welding technologies were mastered, making processing accuracy increased by one order of magnitude.

Fig.68   Chen Shaozhong visiting the Xi'an Aeronautical Engine Accessories Factory

Modern aircraft faces complicated combat and flying environment, which requires that engine control system be developing towards multiple functions, multiple parameters, integration and high reliability. So, with the development of electronic technique, there have successively been appeared analogous and digital electronic control system.

To master this advanced technique, the Xi'an Engine Accessories Factory started this research with electronic regulating system of ground turbine engine. In 1982, the analogous electronic control system of WJ6 engine ground power generation was successfully tested. In 1985, the dual-redundant digital electronic control system (for use on ground) of WJ6 engine was successfully trial run. In 1984, the digital electronic control system of WZ6 engine was developed, and has been used in power machinery set of pumping station in oil exploitation. This symbolized that some fine results have been achieved in transferring application of engine control system to civilian use. Based on this, at present, the development work is concentrated on full functional, digital aeroengine control system.

4. Starter and Ignition System

Starter and ignition system is a complete set of units used to drive engine, to make it gradually accelerate from static status, to ignite gas, and to have engine entering into steady working status. Starting engine needs large torque. It should be easy to operate — "one push starts it immediatly". For Chinese—made engines, there are many types of starts such as electrical start, high pressure air start and gas turbine start etc..Electrical starter is widely used in various types of fighters. Gas turbine starter has the feature of independence from ground equipment, and can be used as auxiliary power unit (APU) of the aircraft.

In 1957, the Xingping Aeronautical Electrical Apparatus Factory copy produced electrical starter. At the end of the 1950s, the Nanjing Aeronautical Accessories Factory developed powder turbine starter. To suit multiple working conditions, dual energy supply starter was developed which could also be driven by high pressure air. Since the 1960s, many types of air turbine starters and gas turbine starters were developed. For example, the air turbine starter used in Y—10 transport could start engine within 30 seconds. The key part of this starter was power turbine, which was made of titanium alloy of high strength and toughness. The profile of blade was complicated and the blade was of integrated structure. It was difficult to manufacture by means of traditional mechanical processing. Through large number of technological tests, at last the electro—chemical machining was employed successfully.

To speed up the progress of starters, the Nanjing Aeronautical Accessories Factory imported production technology of gas turbine starter from abroad. During trial production process, many sets of precision test equipments such as starter inertia test rig were independently designed and produced. More than 9000 items of toolings were made by the factory. The factory also solved the processing technique of key precision parts. In the early 1980s, the design was certified for trial production and it was named type DQ—23. Afterwards, new versions began to be developed to match the progress of R&D of new aircraft.

The ignition of Chinese—made engine mainly uses electrical ignition system, the key part of which is spark plug.

The manufacturing difficulty of aeronautical spark plug lies in ceramic parts. The raw material used was completely different from raw material used for high voltage ceramic parts of other electrical apparatus. If its production was arranged together with other products on the same production line, it would mutually affect the quality of products. So, some factories did not want to develop high temperature—resistant ceramics. In the mid 1950s, the production of spark plug was "in shortage". In 1958, when the minister of the second Ministry of Machine Building Zhao Erlu was visiting the Xingping Aeronautical Electrical Apparatus Factory, he encouraged the factory to have spirit and not to be afraid of the small spark plug. He also decided to set up a spark plug shop in the factory. The director Li Zhongyuan, acting chief engineer Wang Tianming organized the trial production of spark plug. The carpenters' shop was reconstructed into a suitable shop. They also set up a tunnel kiln by themselves. In the case of no proper ceramic material, they made comparision tests on porcelain clay from different places. After more than one year, they found proper material and trial produced many types of spark plugs. They put its production and supply on a domestic basis.

In the early 1960s, Zhang Linyu of the factory and Ge Houshen, the military representative from the services, together developed high voltage ceramic spark plug to replace mica spark plug relying on imported golden mica.

In the mid 1960s, Zhan Xinxiang and others launched the research of semiconductor material used for spark plug. After many years of hard work, they found out proper composition and processing parameters, which provided the necessary condition for the development of semiconductor spark plug. In the mid 1970s, the factory developed titanium oxide semiconductor spark plug which made Chinese—made engine to use semiconductor igniter system of low voltage and high energy for the first time with success. At the same time, the factory also developed catalyst ignitor used for WS9 engine.

During more than thirty years of development of airborne equipment, great achievements have been gained, but also learned some lessons and experiences. The following are main ones:

a. Airborne equipment, while ensuring general requirement of aircraft, must be actively developed. Airborne equipment is serving the needs of aircraft and engine, and is an important constituting part of the whole aeronautical industry. It is directly related with the performance, flying quality and fighting capability of the aircraft. Under the general arrangement of MAI, it has to obey and match the general technical and schedule requirement. At the same time, advanced technical equipment for aircraft should also be actively developed according to the features and laws of the progress of airborne equipment itself. One of the important features for modern airborne equipment is to constantly absorb the latest results of scientific research, especially in electronics, automatic control and computer techniques, and to develop completely new products in order to greatly increase the performance of aircraft and engine. Its development does not simply depend on aircraft, but to a certain extent, plays a pushing role of increasing the performance of aircraft and engine. So airborne equipment must actively develop. It is necessary to predict the development tendency of modern science and technology and aircraft, and based on requirement and possibility to timely make plan for development of airborne equipment, to arrange advanced research subjects and to carry on R& D of new principles, new techniques and new principle demonstrators in order to prepare sufficient technical storage as options for aircraft and engine and be prepared to turn to the development of new types of equipment or operational improvement. The development of airborne equipment should start before the aircraft and engine design are certified. Only in this way, when development of aircraft and engine is launched, there could exist off—the—shelf advanced airborne equipment to meet the needs of the aircraft and engine, enabling a great increase in aircraft performance.

b. The coordinated development of airborne equipment requires centralized system engineering management. Because there are many systems of airborne equipments and varieties of types, their technical relationships with aircraft and engine are complex, with many subcontractors and numerous related factories. And it was quite often in the past that the technical requirement was released rather late, but work schedule was tight. Hence, it needs centralized system engineering management.

Experience shows that to execute management in this field needs to properly settle three relations: (1) relation among aircraft, engine and airborne equipment. Airborne equipment should obey and serve the general requirements of aircraft and engine. It is a subsystem of the primary system. In the meantime, it also should play an active role to develop advanced products making contributions to the primary system. (2) relation between the internal and external cooperation. In more than 30 years, the MAI has established quite complete R&D and production organizations and enterprises of airborne equipment. The most R&D and production work were led and organized by MAI, which is necessary and correct. This is an important condition for development of the aeronautical industry. But the internal cooperation within the aeronautical industry could not include everything, and the wide cooperation with industries of electronics, armament and machinery is needed. To combine the centralized leadership of MAI and cooperation with other related industries then is a complete and all—round work relationship. (3) relation between self—reliance and technical importation. With the implementation of the open policy, it is necessary to import technology and to buy some products from foreign countries. The purpose of importing technology is to better execute the policy of self—reliance. The imported products will gradually be manufactured by domestic enterprises. Through this way, the technical level of airborne equipment and the capability to meet the needs of aircraft and engine will be constantly increased.

c. Scientific research must be combined with production. The way of development of airborne equipment in China was having the production ability first and having the research and design ability second. Many research and design organizations grew up out of manufacture factories.

The scientific research work on airborne equipment has been always "walking with two legs", i.e., to have independent specialized research and design institutes and also to have some research and design units in factories. Thus, the research and design network of airborne equipment was formed.

Scientific research is always advancing ahead of production, and the production is a continuation and an outcome of the scientific research. Only the combination of these two will produce good results and effects. But scientific research also has its own law of development. Research institutes are responsible for system development. Because they do more advanced research, and they have a wide scope of work, it is better to set them up independently. For those research and design institutes belonging to factories, it is proper to execute dual leadership both of the Ministry and the factory, with leadership of the factory being primary one.

Historical experience shows that the main tasks of research institutes are to develop new technology and new products. It is essential to equip them with necessary research manpower and test facilities and to have small batch production ability in order to make preparation for the transfer of a project from research to production. Independent research and design institutes should create a condition for its connection with relevant production factories for the benefits of development of research and production.

d. Insisting on system first and parts second. With the wide application of electronic computer and rapid progress of automatic control theory and technique, the composition and functions of airborne equipment are experiencing important changes. Individual equipments have given way to more combined and integrated system, thus forming a multifunctional system.

The advanced level of system technology of airborne equipment is directly related with the performance and flying quality of aircraft, but the advanced level of parts in turn affects the advanced level of the system. The parts should serve the technical requirements of the system and also provide new technical basis for the system development. Hence, it is necessary to pay attention to the technical development of both system and parts. These two sides should progress coordinatively and promote each other. Otherwise, the technical development of system would be like "water without a source".

Between parts and system, not only exists a relationship of locality and entirety, but also some parts often are key elements of the system, which play decisive role in technical performance of the system. Once an element employing new theory and new technique is successfully produced, it often symbolizes a breakthrough in a system. So, for the development of parts and assemblies, one should be far—sighted, start work early and be not afraid of running risk. It is necessary to make full use of advantages of each enterprise within and beyond the profession, and to have cooperations in a wide scope. Experience shows that except that common parts and assemblies have to be supplied by relevant industries, a large number of specialized parts and assemblies must be developed by the aeronautical industry on its own initiative, and they should be given equal attention as to airborne systems.

Chapter Ⅸ The Development of Tactical Missile

Section 1 General Introduction

Missile is a weapon which started to emerge in the 1940s of this century. Missile is a pilotless vehicle which has guidance system either onboard or outboard. It can automatically control its flying trajectory according to the information transmitted from the ground or the carrier (aircraft or warship), missile body itself and from target, in order to deliver the warhead and to destroy predetermined target. Except that a few missiles use turbojet engine and ramjet engine as power units, the majority of missiles utilize liquid or solid propellant rocket engines. So, missile is also generally called controllable rocket.

According to their usages, missiles can be divided into two large categories — strategic missile and tactical missile. The strategic missiles are those missiles which are used to destroy hostile important strategic targets and to defend strategic points of one's own side. Those missiles include long range ballistic missile, long range cruise missile, submarine-to-ground missile and anti-ballistic missile etc..The tactical missiles are those missiles which are used to destroy hostile targets in battle or in tactical depth or those various missiles which are used to directly support fighting actions of the services. The tactical missiles include ground, airborne and shipborne missiles, such as antitank missile, short range ground-to-ground missile, ground-to-air missile, air-to-air missile, air-to-ground missile, tactical cruise missile, air-to-ship missile, ship-to-ship missile, ship-to-air missile and coast-to-ship missile etc..

Missile is a new stage of the weapon development. In the later part of the Second World War, Germany first used V-1 and V-2 missiles. The V-1 was an air-supported ground-to-ground missile and V-2 was a ballistic ground-to-ground missile. After the War, some industrially developed countries further developed techniques used in these two missiles. According to different requirements, they constantly applied the latest achievements in science and technology, and developed a variety of missiles having different functions for various warfares.

In more than 40 years after the War, the accumulated number of varieties of tactical missiles has amounted to more than 300. In local wars happened in the world since the 1960s, the role and position of the tactical missiles have become more important. It caused the change of penetration tactics in modern war, making the pattern and way of war to be changed. At present, to a certain extent, the types, number and level of missiles in a country often determine whether the country could gain the initiative control in the war, thus becoming one of the important marks for the modernization of the national defence and an important means for judging the strength of the military power of a country.

The development of tactical missile in China began since the mid 1950s. According to the requirement to strengthen the construction of the national defence and catching up with the world's advanced level, the Central Committee of CPC and the State Council decided to establish the missile industry. In April 1956, the Government set up the Aeronautical Industry Commission, Nie Rongzhen was appointed the director, and Huang Kecheng, Zhao Erlu deputy directors. The commission was responsible for leading the development and production of aircraft, rocket and missile. In May of the same year, the Bureau of Aviation Industry was cooperating with the Chinese Akademy of Sciences, the Air Force, the Beijing Aeronautical Institute, the Harbin Military Engineering Institute to start research in jet and rocket technology and responsibilities for research in 40 subjects such as aerodynamics and combustion process etc. were defined for each agency. In October of the same year, the 5th Establishment of the Ministry of National Defence (MND) was formally established, specialized in missile R&D. In October 1957, the Chinese and the Soviet Governments signed an agreement on new technology. It was stipulated in the agreement that the Soviet Union would supply several tactical missile samples and technical information, and send experts to China to help with licence production. Since then, the trial production of tactical missile formally began in China.

Generally, the development of Chinese tactical missile could be divided into two periods:

1. The Starting Period of the Tactical Missile Industry (1958—1965)

To start work on tactical missile industry, the Government made an important decision that the 5th Establishment of the MND take the overall technical responsibility and the aviation industry be responsible for licence production of the first generation of missiles.

The reasons why the Government decided to use the manufacturing technology of the aeronautical industry to trial produce missile were as follows: firstly, missile and aircraft have many similarities and commonalities in structure, appearance and manufacturing technology; secondly, after large—scale construction and progress during the First Fine—year Plan, the aviation industry already had a certain scale and technical base, so it had the condition and ability to do the trial production; thirdly, because of the limited condition at that time, the Government could not set up independent missile industry, but the construction of the national defence urgently required missiles. The practice proved that this decision was completely correct and played a very important role in quickly setting up and developing the missile industry.

The way adopted by the aeronautical industry to trial produce tactical missile was, according to category of products, to select factories specialized in products similar to missiles as main manufacture factories responsible for trial production, final assembly and delivery of main parts (body and engine), and to distribute tasks for the rest systems of the missile, equipments, new devices and new material to various cooperating factories. The cooperating factories not only included many factories in the aeronautical industry, but also enterprises in other industries such as armament, electronics, shipbuilding, metallurgy, machinery, chemical industry, light industry, construction material and petroleum etc.. Basically, no new factories were built for missile production. Factories in the aeronautical industry were technically reformed for missile production with available technical and production conditions. On original trial propuction lines were set up some production lines which sometimes were combined with aircraft production but in other times separated. Modular assembly and general assembly shops and labs were separately set up. Production preparation and cold and hot processing facilities were shared with aircraft production wherever possible. This method on one hand made full use of existing technical and production conditions, on the other hand ensured the relative independent position of missile production. At that time, it was called "one house with two courtyards, combined and separated alternatively".

The trial production of tactical missile during this period was based on the technical information and samples supplied by the Soviet Union and four categories of tactical missiles were produced under licence including ground—to—ground, ground—to—air, air—to—air and coast defence missiles. The 5th Establishment of the MND sent technical personnel to factories of various industries. These persons, on one hand, participated in trial production and assisted factories to solve technical problems, on the other hand, digested and thoroughly studied technical information to raise R&D level.

a. Short Range Ground—to—Ground Missile

The first short range ground—to—ground missile produced by China was P—2 ballistic short range ground—to—ground missile produced under licence on the basis of technical information supplied by the Soviet Union. Under the unified planning of the Government, in April 1958, one factory in the aeronautical industry was transferred to the 5th Establishment of the MND and that factory undertook the responsibility for licence production, final assembly and delivery of the body of the P—2 missile. As for rocket engine, the Shenyang Aeroengine Factory in the aeronautical industry undertook the responsibility for manufacturing the majority of parts and the Rocket Engine Factory was responsible for manufacturing some parts, general assembly and testing. The 10 factories such as the Baoji Aeronautical Instruments Factory were responsible for manufacturing 33 items of accessories.

The largest difference between the rocket engine of missile and the turbojet engine of aircraft lies in that the rocket engine carries comburant and oxidizer by itself, and it need not absorb oxygen from the air for combustion. The liquid propellant rocket engine used in missile has high technical requirement and is rather complicated. For parts and assemblies of the engine, some of them have to withstand high temperature and high pressure (3,000 degrees C and 20—30 atomospheric pressure), and others have to withstand low temperature and high pressure (—183 degrees C and 200 atomospheric pressure). This raises crucial requirement to structural strength, tightness of the engine and the reliability of various systems. Thus, trial production of rocket engine was a difficult task.

From July to November 1958, the technical information for rocket engine continually reached the factory. In October 1959, the factory started trial production. The trial production was organized by Qi Kefei, the vice chief engineer of the engine factory. In September 1960, the first batch of rocket engine were assembled and passed 90 sec. typical test. The performance data totally met specification. On the 5th of November, 1960, the Chinese made P−2 missile installed with rocket engine successfully passed firing test. Since then, China has owned domestic−made short range ground−to−ground missile and large rocket engine. In the mid 1960s, the large rocket engine used for ground−to−ground missile independently developed by China was also put into production.

b. Ground−to−Air Missile

Ground−to−air missile was produced under licence on the basis of technical information and samples supplied by the Soviet Union. The domestic designation was HQ−1. This missile consisted of two stages of rockets. The first stage was solid propellant booster, on which four stabilizing tails were installed. The second stage was liquid propellant main engine and the autopilot, radio control unit, radio fuze and warhead were installed within the missile body.

The body of the HQ−1 missile was trial produced by the aircraft factory and the rocket engine was trial produced by the rocket engine factory. There were also more than 20 main factories supplying finished parts. To meet the needs of trial production of ground−to−air missile, in the aircraft factory was set up missile design section and newly established modular and final assembly shops for missile. Also was reconstructed magnesium alloy processing shop and set up high pressure air supply station.

In March 1959, the Soviet technical information arrived at the factory. In August 1960, the factory began to prepare trial production. In March 1961, parts manufacturing started. By 1963, six batches of rocket engines were produced altogether. The general assembly of simulated missile of the missile was completed. In July of the same year, the first flight firing test was conducted and the trajectory was normal. In August, the general assembly of one dummy missile was finished for ground test and practicing. By the end of 1963, the operational missiles were produced. From May to October of 1964, altogether three firing tests were completed with good results. In the firing test of drone, one missile hit the target. In December of the same year, the HQ−1 ground−to−air missile was certified for batch production.

Since 1964, the missile design section of the aircraft factory modified and upgraded the HQ−1 missile. The modified version was designated HQ−2 missile and it successfully passed firing test in June 1965. Compared with HQ−1, it raised the height of killing area and maximum range.

c. Air−to−Air Missile

Air−to−air missile was produced under licence on the basis of two types of air−to−air missiles supplied by the Soviet Union. Their Chinese designations were respectively PL−1 and PL−2. The PL−1 is a radar beam guided missile, and the PL−2 is a passive infrared homing missile.

Since the second half of 1958, the Zhuzhou Aeroengine Factory started to create testing and production conditions for the air−to−air missile, then began to trial produce PL−1 missile, which was certified for production in 1964.

Fig.69   Marshal Peng Dehuai inspecting the AA missile factory

Since 1964, the factory started to establish a production line for PL−2 missile. To match the trial production of two versions of missiles, the AA missile design institute and the missile subsidiary factory were constructed in the factory, which became the first specialized factory capable of AA missile trial production, modification and batch production in China.

In Autumn of 1961, to strengthen design and research teams of AA missile, the Aeronautical Armament Design and Research Institute was set up in the Chinese Aeronautical Establishment. This institute was responsible for design and research of AA missile, airborne radar, sight and armament.

Fig.70   Wang Zhen inspecting the coast defence missile
shop of the Nanchang Aircraft Factory

d. Coast Defence Missile

In 1959, the Nanchang Aircraft Factory started to copy produce SY-1 ship-to-ship missile under licence on the basis of technical information supplied by the Soviet Union. The engine used for the missile was copy produced under licence by the rocket engine factory. This air-supported missile had many similarities with aircraft in structure and manufacturing process. In March 1960, the Nanchang Aircraft Factory set up integrated trial production department — "40 office" combining design, initial assembly, general assembly, testing, processing and metallurgy. He Wenzhi was appointed the director of the department. In 1964 and 1965, the ground firing tests and shipborne firing tests were separately made with success.

During 1958-1965, China developed the ground-to-ground, ground-to-air, air-to-air missiles and put them into small batch production, and ship-to-ship missile firing test also started. By then, the production and technical conditions for the tactical missile industry were basically set up, and the tactical missile industry began to advance from licence production to operational improvement and independent design.

2. The New System for Missile Development (Since 1966)

Before 1966, the 5th Establishment of MND and MAI (Bureau), which belonged to two different systems — the Defence Science and Technology Commission and the Defence Industry Commission — were respectively responsible for the research & design and trial production of missiles. It was difficult to highly unify and coordinate the leadership, planning, work distribution and cooperation. This situation was not helpful for the missile industry to transfer from licence production to independent development. In November 1964, the Government decided to readjust R&D and trial production / production system, to combine the relevant units and to execute unified leadership and to set up the Seventh Ministry of Machine Building (later called the Ministry of Space Industry), which was responsible for the R&D of the strategic and large missiles and the development of space activities. After some preparation, starting from January 1966, the leadership of the rocket engine factory, the ground-to-air missile production shops in the aircraft factory and one aeronautical instruments factory in MAI were transferred to the Seventh Ministry of Machine Building. In terms of work division, the MAI was responsible for the design and production of AA missile and part of coast defence missile, the ground-to-ground missile and ground-to-air missile were under the responsibility of the Seventh Ministry of Machine Building. In 1970, the research and production of ground-to-air missile were transferred back under the leadership of MAI. This situation lasted until the setting up of the Eighth General Bureau of Machine Building.

After the new system was set up, the aeronautical industry concentrated on the development of AA missile and coast defence missile and further strengthened the research and production capability in this area. Since the mid 1960s, the Air-to-Air Missile Research Institute was formed on the original basis of the Aeronautical Armament Research Institute. Two specialized missile factories and design institutes in these factories were successively set up in the inland area for producing AA Missile. One missile test equipment factory was reconstructed for producing ground measuring / test and maintenance station for AA missile and ground measuring / test equipment for coast defence missile. The Pilotless Aircraft Research Institutes in the Nanjing Aeronautical Institute and in the North—west Polytechnic University were set up for research and production of drones used for appraisal of missile testing. In 1984, to meet the needs of developing new AA missile, the AA Missile Research Institute was expanded into the AA Missile Research and Development Center. In research and production of coast defence missile, a research and production system was formed in which the Nanchang Aircraft Factory was the main manufacture factory (the System Design and Research Institute of Coast defence missile in the factory was responsible for overall technology) and more than 40 main factories in the country were acting as cooperating enterprises. A technical manpower source consisting of about 1000 specialized technical personnel and 10000 technical workers was formed. Generally speaking, a quite complete and relatively independent research and production system of AA missile and coast defence missile was formed in the Chinese aeronautical industry and the system had the capability to develop new missiles.

In more than 20 years, a number of AA missiles and coast defence missiles have been developed in MAI, ten of which have been certified, put into production, and used by the Chinese Air Fore and the Navy.

Section 2   The Development of AA Missile

AA missile is a kind of missile launched from aircraft to destroy air target. Generally, it consists of body, power unit, guidance unit, warhead and fuse system. AA missile, combined together with fire control system and launching unit of the aircraft and ground measuring / test and maintenance equipment, forms a weapon system of AA missile. In China, AA missiles are carried in various types of fighters. Its main targets are hostile fighters, fighter bomber and bomber.

1. Copy Production of the First Generation of AA Missile
   a. PL−1 AA Missile
   This was a radar beam guided missile. It consisted of radio fuze and warhead (first section), the steering part of autopilot (second section), rocket engine and batteries (third section), the stabilizing part of autopilot and pneumatic system (fourth section) and radio control part (fifth section).
   After being launched, the missile was guided by radar beam of aircraft guidance radar, and the equipment onboard the missile controls the missile to fly along the centerline of the beam until it hit the target. It could be used in all weather conditions, and multiple missiles could be launched using the same beam.

In 1958, the trial production of PL—1 missile began. The Zhuzhou Aeroengine Factory was responsible for manufacturing missile body and rocket engine, general assembly, adjusting and testing and delivery. Zhu Zhuanqian was the chief designer. The factory set up a missile shop and test labs for missile's general configuration, weather, dynamic environment and static strength, ground ignition test rig for solid rocket engine and radio and autopilot labs. Also established the cooperation relationship with factories of the Ministry of Armament Industry in warhead and grain of solid rocket engine, lead and initiator. The factory also established cooperation relationship with factories of the electronic industry in radio control unit and radio fuze.

In March 1960, the factory trial produced the first AA missile. In July of the same year, the first batch of missiles passed ground test. However, the first firing test experienced setback: all four live firings missed drone. In 1961, the quality consolidation was carried out. The reason found out was that the aircraft guidance radar had not been calibrated before the missile being launched. In 1962, the trial production resumed and 27 missiles were produced in October. After regular tests, in March 1963, air component tests for major parts were conducted, and the results were satisfactory. During this period, Marshal Ye Jianying inspected the missile subsidiary factory of the factory and inscribed "You have a bright future, you can fly over ten thousand km, and climb to the summit of technology, you are advancing everyday."

In November of the same year, missiles were sent to test base for the second firing test. After the airborne radar was accurately calibrated, 20 missiles were launched for various conditions. Two of them were launched against drone and both hit targets, which showed that the performance met the technical specification.

In April 1964, the Special Weapon Certification Commission of the State Council approved the PL—1 AA missile for formal production. In May, the missile won the State's first class prize for industrial new products. The PL—1 missile has been put into service with the Chinese Air Force.

b. PL—2 AA Missile

In 1962, China imported the Soviet MIG—21F fighter and its AA missile. Then, the licence production of this missile began and the domestic designation was PL—2. This missile was a passive infrared homing missile. The whole missile consisted of five sections — automatic heat—homing head, servo section, nonimpact fuze, warhead, solid rocket engine and tails. It used canard aerodynamic configuration.

Fig.71 PL—1 AA missile

While in use, after aiming onto the target and having launched the missile, the carrier aircraft could fly away and forget it. Afterwards, the

Afterwards, the homing head of the missile entered into automatic tracking working mode. It received the infrared ray radiated from target. This information, after being optically modulated and processed, gave position parameters of the target. These parameters were used by the control units of the missile to control missile's flying and made the missile automatically acquire the target.

In 1963, the PL−2 missile was produced under licence mainly in a factory of the Ministry of Armament Industry, with relevant factories and research institutes cooperating. In July 1966, the first batch of missiles were assembled and tested. In November 1967, the design was certified for production.

In October 1964, the MAI began to trial produce PL−2 missile. The Zhuzhou Aeronautical Engine Factory which was responsible for general manufacturing task, set up a production shop and test facilities required by infrared optical technique on the basis of trial production of the PL−1 missile. At the same time, technical personnel were sent to relevant departments of the Ministry of Armament Industry to study optical technique. In October 1965, parts manufacturing began. In April 1966, the high altitude simulation test, the aerodynamic heating simulation test and the flexible ignition test were successfully conducted. At the end of the year, 18 missiles were trial produced for certification batch firing test. From May to July 1967, the integrated certification tests including air firing were completed smoothly. Because of the influence from system reorganization during the "cultural revolution", the certification of the missile was not timely organized. It was not until August 1970 that the Aviation Industry Leading Group certified the design for production.

Since the 1970s, two factories in the inland area also started to trial produce PL−2 missile. The number of produced missiles of this type occupied the first position among all tactical missiles.

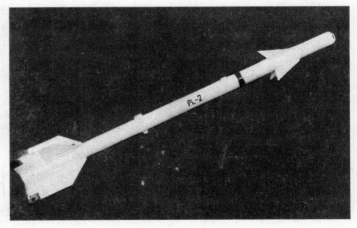

Fig.72   PL−2 AA missile

2. The Operational Improvement and Derivation

To meet the Air Force's need to improve its operational capability, the MAI decided to make better derivatives out of the original version of the missile in order to solve existing problems of the PL−2 missile such as poor anti−interference capability of the guidance system and early burst of the infrared fuze. The derivation was undertook by an AA missile specialized manufacture factory in the inland area. The derivative was designated PL−2B.

The main improvements of PL−2B missile were: higher sensitivity of the sensor, greater detecting range of the homing head, better anti—interference capability against the sun and the sky background, reduction of the possibility of early burst of the fuze, higher average velocity of the missile and longer firing distance at low altitude. The number of changed parts caused by the above modification occupied about 40% of the total of the missile.

In 1978, the modification work and trial production were launched in the factory. Zhang Hesheng and Yuan Jihong, the two leading designers, organized all designers to work very hard. With reference to foreign technique and combining technical reserve of the factory, they carefully and accurately finished all drawings for the modification. The first stage of the trial production was to tackle key technical problems. More than 10 key technical problems were solved one after the other. By the end of 1979, three principle demonstrators of homing head were produced. After testing, its characteristics such as anti—sun interference and detection range were remarkably improved.

The second stage was making trial production of the firing batch of missiles for the whole missile flying test. At that time, there was no strontium titanate — the material used to manufacture immersion lens of sensor. Through scientific analysis, engineers found out a proper replacing material and also removed the flutter faults of control surface at control section. In March 1980, the factory produced 20 PL—2B missiles. In firing test at the base, the problem of high early burst rate was noticed and solved. Then another 10 fuzes were trial produced and test results were all normal.

The third stage was making trial production of the design certification batch of missiles. In January 1981, 23 missiles were produced which passed all checks stipulated in the design certification test program from April to June of the same year. In December, the Aero Products Certification Commission formally certified the design of PL—2B missile.

The PL—2B missile was the first AA missile modified and produced by the Chinese tactical missile industry independently and successfully. The main improvements were: big increase of anti—sun interference, some improvement of trajectory stability of infrared fuze and remarkable decrease of early burst rate, some increase of detection range and tracking angular velocity. It was put into batch production and delivered to the services.

3. The Independent Design of AA Missile

Since the mid 1960s, China has independently designed and produced PL—3 and PL—5B AA missiles.

a. PL—3 AA Missile

The PL—3 was developed on the basis of PL—2. The control surfaces were enlarged to improve high altitude manoeuvrability. New immersion sensors were added to increase target acquisition range and attack range. Fuse delay automatic control system was also added to improve the matching ability of the initiation system. New warhead was designed to increase the lethality of the missile. The structure of rolleron was modified to improve the control performance in roll, pitch and yaw channels for the purpose of hitting the target at longer distance, more accurately and more heavily. The apperance and aerodynamic configuration of PL−3 was generally similar to that of PL−2, but the geometric dimension and weight slightly increased.

The development task of PL−3 missile was undertook by the AA Missile Research Institute and the Zhuzhou Aeroengine Factory. The research institute was responsible for drawing design, general technical management, system adjustment and component test, and Liu Yongheng was appointed the chief designer. The factory was responsible for manufacturing parts and assemblies such as engine, control surfaces, servoes, general assembly and testing.

In 1965, the design drawings of principle demonstrator was completed. In 1966, the first batch of principle demonstrators were trial produced. The main parameters met design specification. In 1968, the second batch of demonstrators were trial produced. The ground firing test proved the correctness of the design. In 1969, the third batch of missiles (certification batch products) were trial produced. During testing at a base, there occurred a few early burst phenomena. During the process of solving the early burst problem, the researchers of the AA Missile Research Institute boldly innovated and designed an automatic speed measuring and computing unit. The fuze circuitry was improved, and the manual adjustment of infrared fuze onboard aircraft and the automatic adjustment of delay time onboard missile were realized. The early burst and late burst problems of the fuze were also well solved. In 1972, the ground−to−air moving drone firing tests were conducted and the fuze was working properly. In November 1974, the firing tests were conducted again. The J−7 aircraft was used to launch PL−3 missile and hit target by one shot. In April 1980, the Military Products Certification Commission certified the design of PL−3 missile.

b. PL−5B AA Missile

The PL−5B belonged to the second generation of missile. Its appearance was similar to that of PL−2. The aerodynamic configura− tion also was canard, and the head section of the body was of small obtuse egg shape. The areas of the control surfaces and wings were quite large. The guidance was infrared homing.

The working principle of the missile was similar to that of PL−2, but performance increased notably.

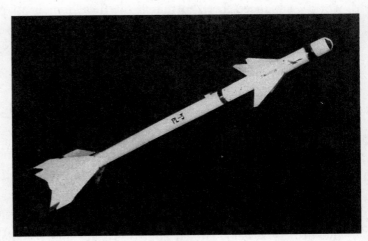

Fig.73 PL−3 AA Missile

It could effectively track targets with large manoeuvrability, increase acquisition sensitivity and enlarge angular range of acquiring targets. The manoeuvreing acceleration almost doubled. The infrared fuze worked reliably and firing range increased.

For the PL—5B missile, the Huang Bin and Hu Rongchao of the AA Missile Research Institute were chief designers for the engineering development one after another. In 1966, when the development work started, it advanced quite quickly. After only half a year, two ground principle demonstrators were built, and field component tests on components such as rocket engine, radio fuze and safety and arming device were carried out. But later the schedule of trial production was slowed down and had many zigzags. From 1967 to 1979, altogether five batches of products were trial produced. Ground firing and flight firing were made. Later, the testing stopped because of high early burst rate of radio fuze. After two years of hard working, the "infrared integrated circuit fuze" with strong anti—interference capability was developed and it worked well. In 1984, the sixth batch of products were produced. In 1985, the design certification drone firing tests of the PL—5B missile equipped with the infrared integrated circuit fuze were completed. In September 1986, the State Council and the Conventional Military Products Certification Commission of the Military Commission of CCCPC endorsed the design certification of this missile.

In the 1980s, China again developed PL—7 infrared dogfight AA missile. This missile used infrared guidance, had dogfight capability and could automatically search, acquire and track target. The PL—7 missile was independently developed by the Zhuzhou Aeroengine Company. Wu Shenduo, the manager of the company, was also the chief designer. In 1985, 20 PL—7 missiles were trial produced. At the end of 1986, drone firing test was successfully carried out only by once. In April of 1987, it passed technical certification.

The achievement of AA missile in China is remarkable, but there is still some gap between the Chinese development level and the world's advanced level. The new target is to aim at the world's advanced level, to match the development of new advanced fighter, and to progress towards the missile with all altitude, all direction and all— weather performance in order to supply more accurate and fine weapons for the modernization of the national defence.

Section 3   The Development of Coast Defence Missile

The coast defence missile is a general term for missiles launched from coast or ship to destroy ships on surface. It includes coast—to—ship missile and ship—to—ship missile. It generally consists of the body, power unit, automatic control system, automatic guidance system, warhead and initiation system. The coast—to—ship missile, together with the target acquisition and display system, launch control system and technical support equipment on the ground, forms the coast—to—ship missile weapon system. The ship—to—ship missile, together with the target acquisition and display system, horizontal stabilization unit, launch control system and technical support equipment etc. on the ship, forms the ship—to—ship missile weapon system.

The coast defence missile production in China began at the end of the 1950s. The first generation of missiles were introduced from the Soviet Union and produced under licence. The

Nanchang Aircraft Factory set up a missile design department and a special production line for the coast defence missile. In more than 20 years, through several development stages such as licence production, operational improvement and independent design, altogether 5 types were formally produced. These missiles equipped destroyers, escort vessels, missile fast patrol boats and bases.

The coast defence missiles produced by the aeronautical industry mainly are SY and HY two large series.

1. SY Series Coast Defence Missile

a. The First Generation of Ship—to—Ship Missile —— SY—1

In 1959, China introduced air—supported ship—to—ship missile and its manufacturing technology from the Soviet Union and the licence production was undertook by the Nanchang Aircraft Factory. The terminal guidance radar, autopilot, fuze, warhead, solid rocket booster, liquid rocket engine of the missile were produced under licence by other factories. Its domestic designation was SY—1.

The missile had normal aerodynamic configuration and the head section of the missile was of obtuse egg shape. The middle section was cylindrical, and the tail section was a shrinking part of round shape. The wings were trapezoidal wings of small aspect ratio. The horizontal tails had two trailing edge elevator surfaces. The parallel solid boosters were in rear lower part of the missile and automatically separated from the body after finishing working. The control mode was self—contained plus automatic guidance. The missile could be used to equip various light weight missile fast patrol boats, middle class escort vessels and large fighting destroyers, and was an important anti—ship weapon for patrol and attack on the sea.

In March 1960, the preparation work of the licence production of SY—1 missile began and the certification test was completed in November 1966. The whole process took seven years. During this period, the designers in the Nanchang Aircraft Factory, on one hand, made a series of reverse design to get themselves familiarized with the work and to digest design information in the original language, and finally they understood the reasons for selecting these design parameters for SY—1 missile system and problems in aerodynamic configuration and strength computation. On the other hand, they tackled key techniques of manufacturing process in trial production of the missile through hard work and gained excellent achievement.

To tackle key techniques in trial production of the missile, Su Min, the chief engineer, organized several key task teams consisting of technologists, designers and workers. The key task team of fiberglass reinforced foam plastics radome started work with the purpose of finding out the material composition and the technical specification, and developed shaping process of the radome after more than 300 tests. In 1963 the qualified products were produced. Later, in 1966, according to the experience in aircraft honeycomb nose radome, missile radome of fiberglass reinforced plastics honeycomb sandwich structure was produced which was simpler in processing, and lower in cost than that of foam plastics but met the same requirement.

To solve the key technical problem in aluminium alloy extrusion casting of wing panel, the factory concentrated experts in machine tool design, electrical design and casting process, and sent them to the Shanghai Casting and Machine Research Institute to study. After repeated review and tests, in 1965, the large extrusion casting machine was produced. This solved problems such as panel shaping, dimension, weight, mechanical performance and shape correction of heat treatment, which filled a gap in this technical field in China.

Fig.74   The general assembly shop of the coast defence
missile of the Nanchang Aircraft Factory

The solving of key techniques removed obstacles on the road to trial produce the missile. The total trial production process was divided into three steps: (1) the ground simulation missile, (2) sea simulation missile of a mixed type and telemetry missile, and (3) certification missile with all parts made in China. In October 1963, parts manufacturing began. In August 1964, the missile smoothly passed the static test. In November and December, the first batch of three ground simulation missiles were successfully firing tested. From August to November 1965, six shipborne simulation missiles were successfully firing tested. During this period, the engine and autopilot of the missile were separately trial produced by the Rocket Engine Factory and the Beijing Aeronautical Instruments Factory. From April to July 1966, the telemetry missile flight tests of SY−1 ground−to−sea and ship−to−ship versions were conducted and fine results were achieved. In November, the missile certification test was smoothly passed with a score of 8 hittings among 9 firings and completely met the requirement of the test program — 6 hittings among 9 firings. In December of the year, SY−1 missile design was formally certified.

In early 1966, the Chairman of the Standing Committee of the CNPC Zhu De (aged 80) inspected the Nanchang Factory. He touched the SY−1 missile, repeatedly praising "well done!"

SY−1 missile has enjoyed good reputation both at home and abroad for its good quality. From July to August 1982, flight test of the SY−1 missiles, which had exceeded its service life and were treated by life−extending measures, also showed excellent results with 8 hitting among 9 firings.

Through practical work in licence production, reverse design and production, a technical contingent engaging in R&D of the coast defence missile rapidly grew up.

b. Modified Version of SY−1 Missile —— SY−1A

The SY−1 missile had high hit rate and stable quality, but there also existed some drawbacks:

− It used aneroid altimeter and the altitude control error was big. The missile always lost height during flight.

− It used conic scan radar and its counter ECM capability and anti− sea clutter performance were poor.

To solve these two problems, the Nanchang Factory made some preliminary modification tests, which controlled the missile to climb normally and then turn to level flight and maintain flying at a preset height until hitting target. The good results were gained with 3 hitting in 3 firings.

In July 1974, the Defense Industry Office of the State Council formally issued the modification task. The main contents were two items: to install cm waveband monopulse transistorized miniature radar to replace the old one and to replace the original old altimeter and vertical speed sensor with radio altimeter. The modification development started. Under the leadership of Jiang Longtan, the Beijing Aeronautical Instruments Factory developed radar altimeter to replace air pressure aneroid altitude hold mechanism, applied integrated circuit operational amplifier, designed analogous computer for control. All these resulted in remarkably decrease of missile's flying altitude and raised the low altitude penetration capability. In 1975, the low altitude test was done with results of three hitting in five firings. It indicated that at altitude close to the sea, the missile could track and acquire target properly.

From 1977 till 1980, the SY−1A missile successively made three design certification tests, but they were all failed. In February 1981, He Wenzhi, the vice minister of MAI, presided over a product fault analysis and coordination meeting and decided to take technical measures to make integrated management and strict control of the quality of the finished parts. In the fourth quarter of 1982, the fourth design certification test was completed in success. In December 1983, the design certification of SY−1A missile was approved. This successful development was one step forward towards raising missile flying performance at very low altitude and anti−interference capability.

At the same time, the factory also carried out improvement study of second lowering height of SY−1A missile. The so−called " second lowering height" means that during the process to fly to target, the missile will descend from level flight height to the lower flight height and after the radar acquire target, descend to altitude close to the sea and continue flying. When close to target, the missile then directly attacks target, thus realizing very low altitude sea−skimming flight. In 1980, this test succeeded, which prepared a technical base for developing new products.

c. Independent Development of SY−2 Ship−to−Ship Missile

SY−2 was a miniature supersonic ship−to−ship missile independently developed by China. It was light, but could fly at high speed, and had strong anti−interference capability.

In 1970, the development of SY-2 (liquid) using liquid rocket engine began. Peng Lisheng was appointed director designer. Because production order was disabled during the "cultural revolution", the development schedule was impeded again and again. It was not until 1975 that the firing test of the ground simulation missile succeeded. In 1980, the firing test of ground telemetry missile was completed. By this time, the development of SY-2 (liquid) was temporarily terminated. Through this research, deep understanding was gained of the flying characteristics and quality of miniature low altitude supersonic missile both in theory and in practice. In 1976, according to new equipment requirement put forward by the Navy, the development of SY-2 (solid) missile using solid rocket engine was put on the agenda. By 1986, results were gained from scientific research in this respect.

2. HY Series Coast Defence Missile

During the process of developing coast defence missile, there was ship-to-ship missile first, and coast-to-ship missile second. The HY series missile was derivative of the SY missile. It was moved from "shipborne" to "ground", then again developed into a common missile both for coast and ground.

Fig.75　The missile destroyer making live firing
test of HY-1 missile

a. HY-1 Coast-to-Ship Missile

In order to meet the services' need for a coast-to-ship missile, Chairman Liu Shaoqi instructed to develop the HY-1 missile.

In December 1964, the Nanchang Aircraft Factory made a report on the development scheme of HY-1 missile. In April 1965, Zhao Erlu and Qian Xuesen presided over a design scheme review meeting of HY-1 missile in Beijing. The design scheme, reported by the head of missile design section He Wenzhi, was selected by the Government. The main research site was the Nanchang Aircraft Factory. The terminal radar, autopilot, solid rocket booster and liquid rocket engine used in the missile were modified and developed by relevant factories. After development work started, Sun Zhiyuan and Liu Ding listened to reports made by on-site technical staff many times and helped them to solve problems. Liu Ding wrote to the Aeronautical Automatic Control Research Institute asking them to arrange the simulation test of the autopilot, which speeded up the development process. In 1966, this missile was put into small batch production. But in the same year and the year next, three firing tests were failed because of self-guidance radar faults occurred at the instant while the booster was ignited.

In trouble analysis, the third Establishment of the Seventh Ministry of Machine Building, responsible for designing missile launcher and ground command system, suggested to shorten the launcher guide rail to reduce the shock and vibration interference source of the booster plume. This suggestion was accepted. Later, other technical measures such as increasing rigidity of the body and expanding the self-guidance distance of the terminal radar were taken, and after many tests the problems were solved. In May 1972, acceptance flight tests were made using three HY-1 missiles, all hitting targets. In 1974, the design and production certification of HY-1 coast-to-ship missile and its engine were formally granted.

b. HY-1 Shipborne Missile

In 1967, the MAI ordered to modify SY-1 into shipborne missile to equip the missile destroyer independently developed by China. The technical scheme of modification was defined and it was decided to transversely launch the missile.

The main difference of the two types of HY missiles were: the environmental condition for shipborne version was more adverse and the temperature and humidity were more severe. Thus some units of the radar need modification and a follow-up system needs to be added in the autopilot. Also, electrical circuitry had to be changed accordingly.

The Nanchang Aircraft Factory undertook this development work and made rapid progress. At the end of 1968, two simulation missiles were launched from ship, which proved the feasibility of transverse launching from ship. In September 1971, two simulation missiles were successfully launched from the missile destroyer independently developed by China. In September 1973, again on the same ship, the live firing tests were conducted. Two single launches for fixed target and moving target were separately carried out and also two salvo launches. The result was excellent — 4 hittings in 4 firings. The Vice Chairman of the Central Committee of CPC, Ye Jianying and Li Desheng were present on the test range and watched firing tests.

From 1968 to 1975, there were 5 firing tests of HY-1 shipborne missile and 13 missiles were launched, achieving expected result. In January 1976, the State Council and the Military Commission of CCCPC certified the design of HY-1 shipborne missile.

To reduce the number of types and to facilitate the use and maintenance for the services, it was suggested to make a common version of HY-1 coast-to-ship missile and HY-1 shipborne missile for both usages. The main modification and coordination tasks were the radar, autopilot, electrical parts and slide block of the body etc..Since 1978, through technical modification by the Nanchang Aircraft Factory, the HY−1 missiles produced by the factory could be used both for the coast and ship.

The batch production of the HY−1 missile (including both coast−to−ship and shipborne versions) began in 1975. This missile has equipped the Chinese Navy and provides a new weapon for the construction of the national defence.

c. HY−1A Shipborne Missile

In 1983, to raise the tactical and technical characteristics of HY−1 shipborne missile and to meet the needs of sea fighting in new conditions, the Nanchang Aircraft Factory began to develop HY−1A shipborne missile. The main improvements were: to raise the counter−ECM and anti−sea clutter interference capability, to lower the level flight height and to expand the range of the missile. From July to September 1985, the first flight test of the HY−1A missile was conducted on firing range with a good score of 4 hitting in 4 firings. In October 1986, after technical certification, it was put into production and delivered to the services for use in 1987.

In the aeronautical industry, a development road of coast defence missile has been paved, which is self−reliance, in cooperation with other industrial departments, to make full use of each one's advantages and with less investment and high efficiency. From now on, under the guidance of the open policy, taking self−reliance as main body, with reference to foreign advanced technology and to unfold international cooperation, China will advance towards developing coast defence missile of higher performance.

PART FOUR

Advances in aeronautical science and technology have a decisive impact on the development of aviation industry. The products of aviation industry — aircraft, aeroengines, airborne equipment and weapon systems — are the crystalization of modern science and technology. The development of aeronautical science and technology is closely related to the growth of national economy and defence. Its achievement is one of the important marks signifying the levels of science and technology and industry of a nation. The rapid development and international commercial competition of the aero products are, in the final analysis, the results of the competition in aeronautical science and technology. In order to gain technological superiority and economic payoffs, major industrial countries in the world put vast investments in the aeronautical research and development (R&D) — one of the high technology fields.

Since the mid 1950s China has made great progress in aeronautical R&D and now in the 1980s it is marching forward to a more ambitious goal.

Chapter X Aeronautical Research and
Development in New China

Section 1   General Description

Following the licence production of the Soviet aircraft, aeronautical R&D in new China began to exist and evolved. At the beginning R&D efforts were concentrated on materials, manufacturing technology and flight test to meet the needs of licence production; then transfer - red to operational development and engineering development of aircraft, aeroengines, airborne equipment and weapon systems; and then extended to advanced R&D of new concepts, technologies, materials and manufacturing technologies according to short term and long term plans for new products development. In contrast with developed countries the aviation industry in China is characterized by such a reverse process of R&D and production, that is the production came in first, product development second and advanced R&D last. The history of aeronautical R&D in new China can be divided into following three phases.

1.   Transition from Repair to Licence Production and Mastery of Manufacturing Technologies

The aviation industry in new China began with the aircraft repair. According to the guiding principle of "manufacturing spare parts for aircraft repair, giving consideration to technology development and actively trying to produce new aircraft", the variety of manufactured parts was rapidly increased and the factories were technically updated and expanded, laying a basis for new aircraft production. In the period of the First Five – year Plan, China bought the licences of Yak–18, MiG–17 and An–2 aircraft and their engines and airborne equipment. Technical documents in large quantities were translated into Chinese and thoroughly studied and products manufactured under instructions of Soviet experts. Through the licence production the Chinese learned manufacturing, inspection and metrological technologies. Some Chinese material specifications were established and, in compliance with these specifications, materials were developed and evaluated. As a result the proportion of Chinese materials used in aircraft was progressively increased. Physical and chemical laboratories, static test laboratories, engine test stands and other test facilities were constructed for product performance checkout. In the meantime the factory managers learned how to organize a modern production. During this period the Aeronautical Materials Research Institute, the Aeronautical Science and Technology Information Institute, the Aeronautical Manufacturing Technology Research Institute, the Flight Test Research Institute and the Aircraft Instrument Department were established under Bureau of Aviation Industry and aircraft, aeroengine and aircraft accessory design departments were also established in related factories to suit the needs of aircraft production.

2. Transition from Licence Production to Product Design and Start of Aeronautical R&D

In 1956 the Science and Technology Planning Commission of the State Council decided to develop jet propulsion technology as one of the five measures to catch up with the advanced science and technology level of the world. The decision greatly inspired the scientific and technical workers. Starting in the second half of 1956 the Bureau of Aviation Industry assigned some factories to design three types of aircraft: a jet fighter–trainer (JJ–1), a primary trainer (CJ–6) and an attack aircraft (Q–5). The development of these aircraft were based on the experiences gained in the licence production. Technical equipment owned by factories and universities and calculation facilities in certain organizations were used. Through the design and manufacture of these aircraft a team of young aeronautical engineers and scientists became tempered. They met with many technical problems in subsonic aerodynamic configuration, structure strength, flutter and hydraulic, fuel and control systems as well as equipment installations, and solved them all with simple means and limited resources. They mastered some basic technologies in aircraft design and manufacture, and got familiarized with the aircraft development process and associated problems. As a result, their abilities were enhanced and a good foundation was laid for further aircraft development.

During the period of the "big leap forward", aircraft were nationwide designed and manufactured. But some of them only flew into the air to report a success and then no more, because the designs were not carefully studied and therefore they had no value of application; others came to a premature end because of the unrealistic design goals. Lessons were learned from both the positive and negative sides.

In the late 1950s China began to develop a supersonic fighter but had difficulties in technical base and test facilities, and besides, the Soviet Union had broken off contracts and withdrawn its experts from China. These led to the necessity of speeding up aeronautical R&D. In 1961 the Military Commission of CCCPC decided to establish Chinese Aeronautical Establishment (CAE) and individual research institutes under it. At that time the tasks were to thoroughly study the design philosophy and key technologies of MiG–21 aircraft and its R–11F300 engine, K–13 air–to–air missile and other airborne equipment and develop necessary manufacturing technologies and materials. From the end of 1961 all the drawings and technical documents given by the Soviet Union under the procurement contracts were translated into Chinese, copied and checked by related research institutes in cooperation with factories. Then the identified key technical problems were tackled with theoretical calculations and tests. Through "thoroughly studying" Chinese designers learned the design methods of supersonic aircraft and accumulated a certain amount of experiences, with which they began to develop a high altitude and high speed fighter — J–8. Through the successful development of J–8 Chinese designers mastered the basic techniques of aircraft design and learned some management skills in aircraft development. In the meantime, the importance of technical base and advanced R&D

was further recognized.

The "great cultural revolution" seriously sabotaged the aeronautical R&D. Effective work procedures, rules and regulations were abandoned; aircraft development programmes were hastily launched; aircraft could not be qualified or certified long after its first flight; constructions of test bases and equipment were interrupted from time to time, bringing about adverse effects on aeronautical R&D.

3. Unified Planning for a New Developmental Period

The National Science Convention held in March 1978 provided guidelines and impetus to aeronautical R&D. A comprehensive survey on aeronautical R&D was carried out by experts at the request of MAI. After careful preparation a meeting on aeronautical R&D was held in July 1978. The meeting emphasized the unique importance of aeronautical R&D in the development of aviation industry and pointed out that aeronautical R&D should be given the highest priority in the industry. Historical experiences in aeronautical R&D were summed up and a new plan for aeronautical R&D was formulated with emphasis on the construction of test equipment and facilities.

This plan had set up goals that should be achieved in major fields of aeronautical science and technology. Particularly it emphasized the important role of advanced R&D in the developments of aero products. Eight key items — high performance propulsion, active control, CAD / CAM, advanced fire control, fatigue and fracture control, electronic and digital techniques of aircraft systems, applications of titanium alloys and composite materials and advanced hot forming technology — were highlighted in the plan. And nine other items were also been emphasized. Since then aeronautical R&D began to go ahead with well−defined goals, carefully set plans and effective measures. In order to ensure quick achievements in R&D, MAI gave priority to the constructions of research and test bases. With limited funds the bases for flight test, structure strength, propulsion, and life escape system as well as institutes for flight control, fire control, computational technology and science and technology information were constructed or expanded. In addition, a certain amount of advanced test equipment were imported. By 1986, flight data real−time processing system, 100 point computer−based loading system, engine component test and control processing system and wheel brake inertia test equipment had been constructed, an avionics test aircraft procured and automatic data acquisition and processing realized.

During this period, computers were widely used in conceptual definition, design, manufacturing, test data acquisition and processing, flight simulation, process control and management. Several single−computer networks were set up and a multi−computer network was linked and put into use in Xi'an. Combined with data base technology the computer network realized information sharing and improved efficiency and economic payoff. Development of the multi−function computer aided design, manufacturing and management (CAD / CAMM) system marked a new level of computer application in aviation industry and,

136. Aircraft electrical network test

137. Engineers and test pilots
     discussing flight programme

138. The Flight Research Institute at night

140. Real time flight data processing system, flight monitoring room

139. Real time flight data processing system, working room

141. A corner of real time flight data processing system working room

142. Airborne test bed for engines

143. Real time flight data processing system, computer room

144. Vertical launcher

145. A pilot in simulator

146. Rocket sled test

147. Missile fuze test area

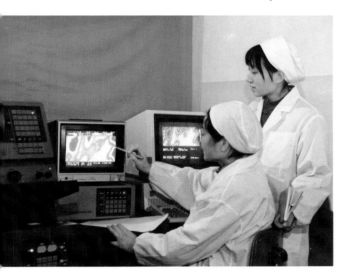

148. Infrared background
radiation tester

149. Optical machining shop

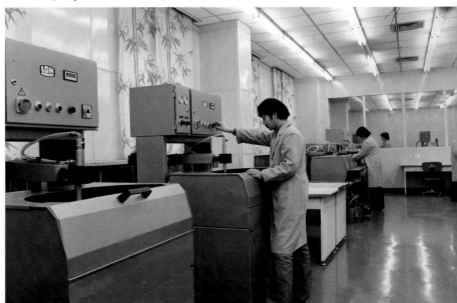

150. Atmosphere environment exposure test area

151. Siemens 7760 computer room, exterior

152. Paint specimen being
tested in atmosphere
environment

153. Engineers working in
microwave anechoic
chamber

ANCES IN TECHNOLOGY THAT CHANGE THE FUTURE OF FLIGHT.

In 1935 the DC-3 became the first airplane in which technology was integrated with commercial practicality. At McDonnell Douglas we continue to look at every new technological development that might improve performance and bottom line. Everything from aluminum lithium matrix composites to ultra high bypass engines. Flying by wire to flying by light. Soon, a whole new breed of aircraft will fly better and more economically. Because that's what the airline industry needs, that's what we're working on—right now.

WE WERE THE FIRST. AND WE ARE THE FUTURE.

MCDONNELL DOUGLAS

154. 50 ton hot press

155. Directional precision cast
hollow turbine blades

156. Three coordinates
measuring device

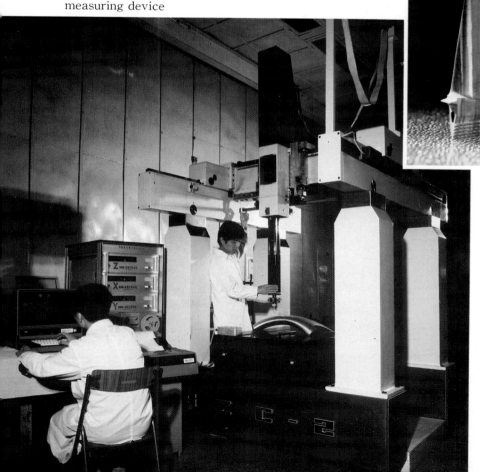

Economical and Technical Cooperations with Foreign Countries

157. Deng Xiaoping visiting CATIC's Shenzhen Industry and Trade Centre

158. Zhao Ziyang visiting Shanghai Aircraft Factory

159. The Soviet first vice minister Arkhipov visiting
Shenzhen Industry and Trade Centre

160. CATIC quartz watch production line at Shenzhen Industry and Trade Centre

161. British Foreign Minister Geoffrey Howe visiting Chinese aviation industry stand at Farnborough Air Show

162. Zhang Jinfu visiting Chinese stand at Hannover International Trade Fair

163. Receiving visitors at Chinese stand

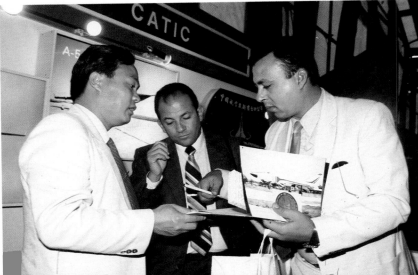

164. Y-7 aircraft model at exhibition
in Singapore

165. Other exhibits at Singapore
exhibition

166. Discussing trade problems
     with foreigners

167. Introducing Chinese aero
     products to foreigners

168. A Chinese made precision
     machine tool

169. King Hussain of Jordan posing with Chinese engineers after his visit to houses built under contract by Chinese engineers and workers

170. Houses built by Chinese engineers and workers

171. Training foreign users in China

as a result, programming automation and software engineering and standardization would be progressively realized.

Much attention was paid to the application and popularization of new technologies in the aviation industry. A research institute specialized in this area was established together with some technology exchange and popularization stations, forming a network for technology popularization. From 1970 to 1986, more than 500 items of advanced manufacturing techniques and technologies were developed and popularized and significant technical and economical payoffs gained. Since 1983, the commercial technology market was opened, which paved a new way for applying defence technologies to commercial products.

Since China carried out the open policy, CAE began to have extensive technical cooperation and exchange with its counterparts of foreign countries in line with the agreements on science and technology cooperation between the Chinese and foreign governments. Visits were exchanged and cooperation agreements on science and technology signed between CAE and DFVLR, FFA, NASA and ONERA. The establishment also got in contact with the scientific and technological circles in Italy, Romania, Belgium, etc. Through these activities, Chinese experts exchanged their experiences and knowledges with their partners.

Since 1978 more rapid progress was made in aeronautical R&D due to the correctness of guideline, implement of intellectual policies and adjustment of tasks (cancellation of unnecessary development pro—grammes). By 1986, 35 independent research institutes and product design institutes in total had been established, some fundamental test facilities completed, and several regulations for scientific achievement management formulated; as a result, aeronautical R&D had been promoted and a lot of achievements gained. Among these achievements

Fig.76   A technical cooperation agreement being
signed by representatives of CAE and DFVLR

287 items were awarded the National Science Convention prizes, 152 items the prizes for major scientific and technological breakthrough in defence industry and 53 items the national prize for scientific and technological progress. Among these prizes were 68 national prizes for science invention. Some achievements reached or nearly reached the advanced world level. These achievements strongly supported the developments of new products and pushed the aviation industry of China to a new height.

Section 2 Following the Law of Development of Science and Intensifying Advanced R&D

Experiences obtained from the research and development of aeronautical science and technology for more than thirty years have shown that aeronautical R&D has its own law, which must be followed if we want to avoid detours.

1. Paying Great Attention to Advanced R&D and Establishing Technical Base

Aeronautical research and development (abbreviated as aeronautical R&D) includes all the activities in research and development of aeronautical science and technology.

Aeronautical R&D in China is divided into five phases: basic research, applied research, advanced development, engineering development and operational development. Basic research includes all activities in exploring fundamental natural phenomena related to aeronautics, extracting new ideas and expanding and enriching knowledges in aeronautical science and technology, aiming at progress in knowledge instead of direct payoff. Applied research is to explore the possibilities of applying existing theories and results from basic research to the development of aeronautical technologies and create new design concepts and methods, new technologies, manufacturing technologies and materials. Advanced development is to verify or demonstrate the feasibilities of applying the results from applied research or new technologies, materials, products, manufacturing technologies and methods published at home or abroad to aeronautical engineering. Technical demonstrators and engineering demonstrators can be manufactured in this phase. The technical demonstrator is to demonstrate the feasibility of new technologies in an aeronautical system. Engineering demonstrator is the first embodiment of type specification of an aeronautical system. The above-mentioned three phases can also be called "advanced research and development (abbreviated as advanced R&D)". Its task is to establish technical base for development of new products and application of new technologies. Research institutes under MAI are mainly engaged in applied research and advanced development. Engineering development is to develop specific products, i.e. to design and manufacture new aero products. This is the main task of design institutes and factories under MAI. Engineering development is characterized by its vast investment, long cycle and high risk. Engineering development programme of a specific product can be launched only when a thorough definition has been carried out. Operational development includes all efforts to enhance the performance and find new applications of a certified product.

All the five phases of aeronautical R&D are closely related and interacted. Basic research and applied research are the base for advanced development. Engineering development would be a mirage without a sound technical base laid by advanced development. New requirements on engineering development, in turn, promotes advanced development. These five phases of aeronautical R&D constitutes a complete and integrated process of the development of aero products. The product engineering development can be misled or result in prolonged cycle or reduced performance or premature end, causing heavy losses in time and money if the law of development of science is not followed and advanced R&D ignored. It does not mean that all the aero products must be developed from the basic research of one's own. Achievements by other people at home and abroad can be, of course, utilized. So, most scientific and technical efforts of aviation industry in China should be put into applied research, advanced development, engineering development and operational development.

2.   Speeding up the Construction of Test Equipment and Facilities

Test equipment and facilities are the important basis of aeronautical R&D and one of the symbols of the modernization of aeronautical science and technology. Test equipment and test technology are decisive, to a certain degree, in determining the future of aeronautical technologies, aero products and even aviation industry.

Various test technologies and equipments are needed for scientific experiments during all the phases of aeronautical R&D. In research and design, new theories, new technologies and the feasibility of design concepts have to be verified or demonstrated by tests. In product development and manufacturing, products have to be checked for their manufacturing quality and evaluated for their performance. In operation, necessary tests have to be conducted on the products to obtain operational information feedback for product improvement. The backwardness of aeronautical R&D in China is, to a great extent, in test equipment and facilities.

Since 1978 priority was given to and more funds were invested into the construction of test equipment and facilities, and the poor situation of test equipment and technology in product development was improved. More attention has still to be paid to the development of test equipment and technology so far as the construction of a modern aviation industry is concerned.

3.   Formulating a Development Plan for a Longer Term

A development plan of aeronautical R&D for a longer term must be formulated and implemented if we want to achieve tangible results from it and keep it growing steadily.

Based on predictions of development trends in aeronautical R&D, the plan should clearly define the goals in the main fields of aeronautical science and technology and enhance the technical base of key technologies according to the philosophy of "producing a generation (of aeronautical system), developing a generation and exploring a generation". The plan should iteratively be adjusted in accordance with the progress of individual R&D projects. In the light of the long term goals and technical base a relatively short term plan should be also formulated for the engineering development programmes. In the formulation of the plan decision—making procedure must strictly be followed to avoid the error that was once made, of "launching a programme today and cancelling it tomorrow". In the early 1980s an analysis was made of the funds invested in engineering development programmes. It showed that about 40% of the total funds was spent in the programmes which resulted in certified products, or were still under way or with promising future; another 40% in the programmes which were postponed or cancelled; and the remainder in the programmes which had few production orders or little economic payoff. That was the consequences of the hasty decision making and lack of careful conceptual definition. Therefore a scientific and democratic decision making system should be established for the major development programmes. Technical and economic definition must seriously be carried out by leaders and experts in accordance with a scientific decision making procedure. Alternatives should be compared and then the best chosen. A major development programme needs a lot of funds and other resources and lasts for a long time, so it should be prudently studied before the launch. In the conceptual definition the advanced technical goals should be well balanced against realistic feasibilities. The targets should timely be frozen and the programme kept stable when it is approved. Then the loss caused by incorrect decision making can be minimized.

Chapter XI Research in Aerodynamics and
Structural Strength

Aerodynamics is a science which studies the movement of air and other gases and the interactions between air or other gases and solid bodies moving therein, with emphasis on the flight theory of vehicles flying in the atmosphere. In flight the aircraft is supported by a lift created on it when the coming airflow moves through the aircraft. In the meantime a drag against the aircraft movement and a resultant force are generated, which affects the aircraft balance. Aerodynamics provides a theoretical base for the development of effective combat aircraft and efficient commercial aircraft.

The aims of the research activities in aerodynamics in aviation field are, through wind tunnel tests, numerical calculations and flight tests, to seek the optimal aircraft aerodynamic configuration and determine the forces and moments acting on aircraft over the flight envelope to meet the requirements on performance, controllability and stability.

The task of the research activities in structural strength is to ensure the safety and reliability of the aircraft structure during flight and ground movement. Critical flutter, divergence and control reversal may occur under high dynamic pressure due to the interaction between structural elastic, inertial and aerodynamic forces. A borderline science to deal with these critical problems is aeroelastics. As the automatic control technology is widely incorporated on aircraft, the complexity of the aeroelastic problem is increased, resulting in a new science — servo aeroelastics. All these new sciences support the development of new aircraft.

Section 1 Research in Aerodynamics

The research in aerodynamics is an important part of aeronautical R&D and a "pioneer" of the aircraft development. Wind tunnel test, computer calculation and simulation, and flight test are the three basic tools for the research in aerodynamics.

By the mid 1980s, China had owned a group of wind tunnels with various test sections and speed capabilities, providing means for conventional tests in aircraft development. The development of the computational aerodynamics provided means for determination of the aerodynamic characteristics of aircraft. On these bases studies on advanced aerodynamic configuration were carried out for development of new aircraft. In addition, new progresses had been made in studies of aeroelastics.

1. Studies on Airfoil Profiles and Aerodynamic Configurations

While aircraft designs increasingly evolve, studies on advanced airfoil profiles and aerodynamic configurations for future aircraft are also under way.

In the early 1970s an airfoil profile with augmented load at trailing edge for high subsonic transport was studied and verified by wind tunnel tests in NPU. NPU2 and NPU3 supercritical airfoil profiles were thereafter studied for transport aircraft design.

Starting in the late 1950s studies on straight wing and its airfoil profile arrangement suitable for subsonic aircraft were conducted. They were put into application to trainer and transport designs under the guidance of Professor Zhang Guilian, an aeronautical educationist and aerodynamicist of China. In the early 1960s studies on sweptback wing configuration were carried out and the problems in the design of transonic attack aircraft solved. In the study on the delta wing configuration a great deal of tests and analyses were done particularly in the conical twist of the delta wing. The results obtained from these studies were successfully used in the design of J-8 fighter. After the 1970s a large amount of calculations, tests and analyses were carried out on various configurations of advanced fighters, such as strake wing, variable sweptback wing, canard configuration and conventional configuration with foreplane. Winglets were studied and successfully used on Y-7-100 commuter.

Single slot flap, double slot flap and blown flap were studied for lift augmentation. In improving the leading edge design, studies on leading edge flaps and slotted flaps of the wing with high sweptback angle were conducted besides the twist of leading edge. And now a study on spanwise blown leading edge is under way.

In inlet system, configurations of two side inlets for subsonic aircraft, normal shock inlet for transonic aircraft, and axisymmetric inlet with variable conical spike and two dimensional ramp inlets on both sides of, or beneath fuselage for supersonic aircraft, as well as isentropic and axisymmetric inlet for Mach 3 were studied in China.

2. Wind Tunnel Test Technology

The purpose of the wind tunnel test is to determine, by similarity criteria, aerodynamic forces and moments acting on an aircraft in flight with the data measured on static subscale models in airflow generated in wind tunnel. The airflow field in a wind tunnel can not fully represent the actual airflow field in flight because of the limits imposed by its walls. In addition, the subscale model can not simulate all details of the aircraft and viscosity of air has different effects on subscale models and aircraft, i.e. different Reynolds numbers. All these factors make the aerodynamic data measured in wind tunnel differ from that in flight. In order to obtain reliable aerodynamic data, large cross-section of the test section or high total pressure in the wind tunnel must be provided. This, in turn, needs a large power capacity of wind tunnel and much funds for its construction. After the founding of new China, several relatively large wind tunnels for teaching and studying purpose were built in some aeronautical universities and colleges such as the low speed wind tunnels with test sections of 1.5 m diameter in the Harbin Military Engineering Institute and BIAA under the guidance of Professor Ma Mingde. It provided useful data for trainer aircraft design. In the early 1960s an intermittent subsonic, transonic and supersonic wind tunnel with a test section area of 0.6m x 0.6m was put into operation in the Shenyang Aerodynamic Research Institute, followed by a low speed wind tunnel with maximum airflow velocity of 90 m / s and a test section area of 4m x 3m in the Chinese Aerodynamic R& D Center. This wind tunnel played an important role in aircraft design. After the 1970s a transonic wind tunnel with a test section area of 1.2m x 1.2m and several low speed wind tunnels with various cross section areas of the test sections were constructed and they provided a technical base for several aircraft development programmes.

In developing the instrumentation and control equipment for wind tunnels, a data logger was first developed with the advances in electronic measurement technology. In 1974 a "708" system was successfully developed for FL–1 wind tunnel. The system could transfer outputs of linear or angular displacement into electric signals and check them, and then output the digital results. In 1979 the programme control of variable angle of attack at constant Mach number was realized in the FL–1 wind tunnel, which was awarded the scientific and technological achievement prizes of the Defence Industry Office of the State Council and MAI. Automation of the test procedure control and data acquisition and processing system was achieved for other major wind tunnels of China, which significantly increased the stability, reliability, flexibility, productivity and quality of wind tunnel tests.

Fig.77   Test at high angle of attack in a
3.5m x 2.5m low speed wind tunnel

Wind tunnel balance is a principal tool for measuring aerodynamic forces and moments on models and it must be highly sensitive and accurate and not easily to be influenced by ambient conditions such as stings and temperatures. Since the 1970s the mechanical balance once used for low speed wind tunnel tests was gradually replaced by strain gauge balance and the wind tunnel measurement developed from single balance to multi–balance combination, the maximum combination consisting of 7 balances and 32 output channels. Now the development of the strain gauge balance used for high speed wind tunnel test is tending towards standardization and seriation. The six–component internal balances of 2.4 mm and 3 mm diameters can be now developed in China, with an accuracy of 0.5%. Large balances with a maximum measurement range of 31.3 kN have been installed in some low speed and large size wind tunnels. For pressure measurement, a transducer system with a scale range of 0.03—6 bar and an accuracy of 0.5% was built, which can simultaneously measure the pressures at 200 points. The measurement of pulsation pressure with a frequency band of up to 20 kHz was realized and successfully used in inlet transient distortion and aircraft buffet tests. In low speed wind tunnels the fluorescent tuft technology was used for flow observation besides the traditional smoke flow, hot wire and oil flow methods and it was awarded the national prize for science invention. The colour flow image photos with 7 colours and 15 zones were obtained by colour image display technology developed by the Harbin Aerodynamic Research Institute. In high speed wind tunnels, the flow observation and photographic technologies such as laser colour schlieren, fluorescent oil flow method, water spray method and laser holography were used besides the traditional shadow and schlieren methods.

In the 1970s China owned 25 wind tunnels for aeronautical R&D including 12 low speed and 13 trans−supersonic ones, by which following tests and measurements could be conducted: forces and pressures on aircraft models; inlet distortion and performance characteristics; velocities and directions of airflow; pulsation and buffet pressures, and unsteady pressure distribution on airfoil profiles; delivery trajectories of various dynamically similar models; flutter and elastic characteristics of structurally similar models; jet simulation; and various blown and boundary layer controls.

In order to apply the results of wind tunnel tests to aircraft design, correlative studies between the wind tunnel and flight tests were carried out. At first the results of the wind tunnel test were calibrated with a calibration model and then the calibrated results compared with the results of flight test to obtain the correction methods. The test data obtained from 0.6m x 0.6m and 1.2m x 1.2m subsonic, transonic and supersonic wind tunnels can be used for design of high speed fighter and data from 3.5m x 2.5m, 4m x 3m and 8m x 6m low speed wind tunnels for design of subsonic airliner in China.

3. Research in Computational Aerodynamics

Computational aerodynamics consists of theoretical aerodynamics, numerical mathematics and computer technology. The rapid advances in numerical mathematics and computer technology opened a new way to shorten aircraft development cycle, reduce development cost and achieve better design.

In aerodynamic design of modern aircraft, preliminary screening of design concepts is first conducted by computer in accordance with the operational specification and then tests on the selected design concepts in wind tunnel and further screening are carried out, to determine the preliminary aerodynamic configuration. Thanks to the computerized preliminary screening of aerodynamic configuration concepts, much time of wind tunnel test was saved and both the computational aerodynamics and wind tunnel test became necessary for design concept screening.

Research in aerodynamic calculation of airfoil profile is a fundamental advanced R&D activity. By the early 1980s advanced calculation methods such as Theodorsen's, source and sink, and panel methods had been introduced in China for development of subsonic, transonic and supersonic airfoil profile series. Wind tunnel tests proved that the performances of a subsonic airfoil profile and two transonic supercritical airfoil profiles developed by China were good.

In the 1970s research in aerodynamic calculation of the wings was conducted. Based on the linear potential flow theory, the method of singularities for subsonic and supersonic thin and thick wings was successfully used. Attention was given both in China and abroad to the calculation of aerodynamic characteristics of transonic wing because modern high speed aircraft fly mostly in the transonic regime. A calculation method of transonic small disturbance was at first developed for the wing and then an accurate velocity–potential equation was applied to leading edge of the wing to improve the small disturbance method. Studies on the viscosity and strong shock wave interference on the transonic wing were also conducted to provide methods of viscous correction for inviscous calculation or inviscous–viscous coupling iterative calculation in the range of low angles of attack. Preliminary computer codes were also developed for calculation of slender wing, considering seperated vortex from leading and side edges at high angles of attack.

In aerodynamic calculations of wing–fuselage combination and aircraft, computer programmes of the method of singularities for aircraft pressure distribution calculation at subsonic and supersonic speeds and of finite difference for aircraft pressure distribution calculation with small disturbance at transonic speed were developed and calculation for preliminary concept screening could be accomplished according to the operational requirements. In the 1970s Professor Luo Shijun, an aeronautical educationist and aerodynamicist of China, sponsored and completed the studies on aerodynamic calculation of transonic aircraft and its application and published more than 20 papers and books such as "Theory of Slender Body and its Applications", "Theory of Conical Flow and its Applications", "Mixed Difference Method of Transonic Steady Potential Flow" and "Longitudinal Aerodynamic Difference Calculation of Combined Body at Transonic Speed". Studies on the aerodynamic calculations of aircraft with external stores and of subsonic aircraft in lateral direction were also carried out.

In respect of inlet flow, principal research work was on two dimensional subsonic diffusors with attached and seperated boundary layers and UIM (unitized integration method) method was developed by combining theoretical calculation with test. In order to take account of the compressibility of airflow the UIM method did not consider, an integration calculating method that combined UIM with BOWER method was developed. This combined method can be used for calculation and definition of two dimensional or asymmetrical subsonic diffusor with optimal performance.

4. Publication of the Aerodynamic Handbook

In order to provide aircraft designers with aerodynamic data for aircraft design the compilation of the Aerodynamic Handbook was completed in October 1983 by nearly 30 experts from 11 organizations of CAE, in which calculation methods and scientific achievements available in China and valuable calculation methods from other aerodynamic handbooks and new scientific achievements made in the 1970s in other countries were also included.

The Aerodynamic Handbook is a comprehensive reference book with relatively high technical level and practicality. It unified aerodynamic nomenclatures and collected the advanced aerodynamic calculation methods. Its publication improved the chaotic situation caused by referring to handbooks from several foreign countries and laid a sound foundation for a Chinese aerodynamics system.

Section 2   Research in Structural Strength

The research in aircraft structural strength is to study the aircraft's capabilities of load—bearing and environment—resisting. It is a major means by which the aircraft aerodynamic configuration and design can be realized and a prerequisite for the safety and reliability of the aircraft structure.

Research activities have been extensively carried out in the following areas: static and dynamic strength, vibration, fatigue strength and thermal strength. Relatively complete test equipment have been constructed, software development considerably advanced and a number of high—level scientific achievements gained in China.

1.   Research in Fatigue, Fracture and Structural Stability

In 1953 and 1954 the "Comet" airliner of the United Kingdom had several flight accidents due to explosions of the pressurized cabin. In 1969, a F—111 fighter crashed because of shedding of the wing. Great attention was attracted by these accidents in aeronautical field and research activities in fatigue and fracture were stimulated.

Advances in fatigue fracture research broke the design philosophy in accordance with which any crack was not allowed and crack initiation should be postponed as long as possible in aircraft structure. That led to the assumption that unexpected initial damages or defects could not be avoided. Thus the aircraft damage tolerance philosophy based on the fracture mechanics was established. In the mid 1970s studies on the fracture mechanics began in China and by the mid 1980s the research activities in linear elastic fracture mechanics had entered practical phase. Through the tests and studies on fracture control of the wing—frame of H—6 bomber the operational life and fail—safe strength were given for the wing—frame with overtoleranced oxidated film. And fracture control methods and improving measures were also proposed for the defects caused in manufacture processing and the design of structure details. The major problem in the production of H—6 bomber was then solved, gaining a very high economic payoff.

The development of a new high speed fighter led to the need of calculation of structure stability. In the early 1970s studies on calculation methods and tests of the net—type integral stiffener curve panel were conducted and an "effective width method" was developed for the development of the fighter, in which the effect of local instability on total instability was considered. Much work was also done on developing analytic methods, analyzing and calculating typical structures, considering the effect of boundary conditions and finding the analytic solution for stiffener panel. Studies on non—destructive test technique for related plate—shell under lateral pressure were carried out and such tests were done. The successful study of aeronautical structure analysis system provided a calculation method for stability of large complex structure and effectively solved some engineering problems.

Aerodynamic heating caused by friction between the air and the skin of high speed vehicle raises the skin temperature to a range of 200—800 ℃, reduces the structure stiffness and strength, produces thermal stress and strain, and even causes the catastrophic flutter. In the meantime it also raises the environment temperature in cockpit and makes oil and fuel become volatile and diluted. Research in thermal strength is to determine the load—bearing and environment—resisting capabilities of aircraft structure under these high temperature environments. In the mid 1970s research activities in thermal strength test and analysis started in China and completed projects included nonlinear analysis, thermal stability and ground simulated thermal flutter test and calculations of creep and fatigue at high temperature and large strain at moderate temperature.

In strength research, measurements of the following parameters must be made: strain fields in complex structure area, notches and crack tips, contours in tests on axial—compressed shear stability and W—directional displacements. Therefore studies on stress analysis were carried out. Completed research projects included stress analysis of photoelastic model test, applications of microgrid fringe method and image fringe method, and stress analysis of strain—gauged photoelastic test. A certain amount of achievements were made and put into use.

2. Study on Engineering Numerical Calculation Methods and Development of Applicable Softwares

The study of engineering numerical calculation methods is an important field of the research in structural strength. The methods under study included finite element method and aeronautical structure analysis system.

Based on the variational principle a zone with definite solution can be divided into nets, points, and line, surface or body elements in any forms according to the finite element method. And on the basis of the division, the stripped low power interpolation function can be established. Therefore the quantitative analysis and calculation can be performed for actual engineering structures and boundary conditions with an accuracy higher than that from classical structure mechanics. With the computer this method can be used not only in large scale analysis on a whole aircraft structure, but also detail analysis on a complex structure. Now it has become a conventional method for aircraft structural analysis. In the early 1970s studies on the application of this method began in China and many achievements were made particularly in the systematization and theorization of the mixed—stiffness finite element method. " First Class Hybrid Finite Element Analysis" and "Finite Element Method for Mixed—stiffness Curved Hexahedron" developed by Zhou Tianxiao, an expert of the finite element method from the Aeronautical Computation Technology Institute were respectively awarded the prize from the

State Science and Technology Commission and the national prize for science and technology progress for their ingenuity and practicality.

The study on aeronautical structure analysis system (abbreviated as HAJIF) is fruitful. Aviation industry is one of the first departments where electronic computers are used for structure analysis. At the early stage the computer programmes were developed for individual structure analyses and had no commonality. As early as 1958 Feng Zhongyue, a late structural expert, made a study on the matrix displacement method and used it to develop a wing stress analysis programme on a first generation computer. His work took the lead in China at that time. In thoroughly studying the MiG—21, a certification computer programme was developed by using substructure analysis technology and direct stiffness method and it was used for analysing the stress and deformation of the wings of J—8 fighter. With the rapid progress in finite element method and computer technology a HAJIF project team was formally established and development activities in this large analysis system were carried out in full swing under the leadership of Feng Zhongyue.

In November 1979, the Aeronautical Structure Static Analysis System (HAJIF—I) successfully passed evaluation. This system had good commonality, high efficiency and excellent reliability. It provided a new analytical tool for analyzing and calculating the large complex structure in aircraft development.

The Aeronautical Structure Dynamic Analysis System (HAJIF—II) was completed in 1981. It incorporated new technologies developed in China and abroad in the mid or late 1970s. This system had functions for calculating natural vibration characteristics, flutter characteristics (taking account of active control system) and partial gust response of structures. HAJIF—II proved to be reliable through demonstrations of calculating 57 examples such as SH—5 aircraft structure, J—8 aircraft and wing structures (with or without missiles) and wing structure model of a new fighter. This system was characterized by the improved simultaneous iteration method, improved hypermatrix technique and dynamic integration technology of multilevel substructures. The dynamic integration technology provided a new analytical method for dynamic characteristics calculation of the structures with various external stores. Thus some difficult problems were solved.

The Aeronautical Structure Nonlinear Analysis System (HAJIF—III) successfully passed evaluation in 1985. This system could be used in analyses of static linear, thermal stress, elastic—plastic, stability and large displacement or deformation of aeronautical engineering structures. It can also be used in research projects such as new solution of nonlinear equations, new element and new material model. Verified by seven nonlinear calculation examples on such as J—7 fighter, the system proved its reliability and solved some urgent problems in aircraft development and engineering application. HAJIF I, II and III are also applicable to structure analyses in space industry, shipbuilding, chemical machinery, dams, tunnels and other civil engineering projects.

The Multiconstraint Optimization Design System of Aircraft Structure (YIDOYU—I) successfully passed evaluation in November 1982. This was a computer aided design software system used in conceptual definition and preliminary design of wing surface of new aircraft. It provided the aircraft designers with a design method, with which, according to the defined operational requirements and selected structure configuration, the weight of the wing surface can be minimized within the design constraints in material strength, stability of the structure element, maximum displacement and natural vibration frequency of the structure, static reversal speed of the wing surface, efficiency of the control surface and flutter speed of the wing, i.e. an optimal solution could be automatically gained by computer. This was a great progress in technical level and design productivity compared with the past method, with which a smaller weight solution was chosen by the designers, according their experiences, from limited alternatives. It played an important role in improving design quality, shortening development cycle, raising work efficiency and reducing cost, as well as in facilitating the modernization of aircraft structure design method. This achievement was awarded the second — class national prize for science and technology progress. The work on "a Series of 4 and more than 4 Nodes Wrapped Quadrilateral Shear Plate Elements" done by Liu Xiashi, a finite element expert of China, developed methods for the static and dynamic analyses on large structures and optimization design of multiconstraint structures.

3. A Moderate Size of Test Equipment and Facilities

During the development process from design to flight test and certification, tests on aircraft structures and elements to be studied or demonstrated must be conducted to determine their behaviors and resistant capabilities under loading and certain environmental conditions and verify their strength calculations. The structure tests include static, dynamic, fatigue and thermal strength tests. The test facilities are large in size, variant in type and complex in technology.

a. Static Test

The strength, stiffness and deformation distributions on aircraft structures and elements should be verified on the ground by applying static loads on them to simulate the loads which may be encountered in various flight conditions. Then destruction tests should be carried out under the ultimate load conditions (the ultimate load condition varies with the type and application of the aircraft) to see if the strength is enough and the safety and reliability of the aircraft is ensured.

In the 1950s, small scale test facilities were constructed in some aircraft factories to meet the requirements of copy production. At the end of 1966, a static test facility of the Aircraft Structure Strength Research Institute was completed, where full—scale airframe static tests of large aircraft can be conducted. In 1978 the static test of Y—10, a China—designed and manufactured airliner with 150 seats, took place under 163 load cases in 42 test items. Take the full—scale airframe suspended destruction test for example, 3,064 up—load points and 3,435 down—load points were applied on the airframe, with the total up—load and down—load of 307 t each and a maximum load of 3.3 t. The loads were increased incrementally and coordinately from zero. Few countries in the world can built the large static test facilities like this and do appropriate tests.

Fig.78   Full—scale airframe static test of Y—10 airliner

In combination with a computer—controlled automatic system, a computer—based proportional loading system and servo control hydraulic loading system developed by China were used for the loading in static tests. The automation of loading and data measuring and processing was realized in the test procedure, with a data sampling speed of 3,000 times per second and a system accuracy of ± 3%.

In the 1980s the full—scale airframe static test of the aircraft in 120 t class could be carried out in Chinese static test facilities. A structure static test system for transport, bomber, fighter, attack aircraft and helicopter was formed with the Aircraft Structure Strength Research Institute as the backbone supported by structure strength test organizations in related factories, research institutes, universities and colleges in aviation industry. Full—scale airframe static tests for 25 aircraft types have been completed, offering scientific findings for flight test, certification and production of new aircraft.

b. Structure Dynamic Test

Aircraft is subject to the thrust variation of its engine(s) and unsteady airflow in flight, the impact at landing and the bump during taxiing on ground. All these may cause aircraft vibration and the vibration, in turn, may cause destruction of the structure elements and malfunction of its instruments or control systems within the structure, even resulting in faults or accidents. Vibration and associated noise have adverse effects on human body's physiology, psychology and behavior, thus reducing the function of central cranial nerve, diverging one's attention and making one tired. Structure dynamic test is an important means to demonstrate the dynamic characteristics of the aircraft structure and evaluate the dynamic analyses made on the structure. It includes the full—scale airframe ground resonance test (i.e. dynamic characteristics), environmental vibration test, nose landing gear hunt, landing gear drop and impact tests and so on.

The aim of full—scale airframe ground resonance test is to measure the vibration parameters such as natural frequency, natural vibration mode and damping on aircraft structure in order to provide test data for flutter, strength and life analyses and flight tests and ensure that no flutter, divergence and other aeroelastic unstable phenomena will occur on the aircraft in development. In the 1960s studies on this field began in China. In the early 1980s, thanks to the fruitful cooperation between CAE and DFVLR, a full—scale airframe resonance test system was developed by using new technologies such as indicator function method and graphic display control force. The measurement system had a capacity of 250 channels and a data acquisition speed of 10 samples per second and was equipped with 150 channel vibration transducers and amplifiers. The automation of exciting vibration, measuring and data acquisition and processing was realized. Satisfactory results of full—scale airframe resonance tests were obtained with the system.

Fig.79　Full—scale airframe ground resonance test of H—6 bomber

The task of environmental vibration test is to demonstrate the vibration—resistant strength and anti—vibration stability of aircraft components or accessories under the specified vibration or impact environments. The technical level of vibration test of the 1970s in China equaled only that of the 1950s in advanced countries. In the 1960s and 1970s, drop test facilities for landing gear and hunt test facilities for nose landing gear were constructed. In the late 1970s, research activities in the measurement and analysis of vibration environmental data, data processing and induction method, vibration destruction theory and test standard formulation were carried out. In the early 1980s, a 15 t hydraulic vibration machine and SKD—1 random vibration control system were developed. This system had relatively sophisticated analysis and control software with a higher frequency resolution and analytical function. In the meantime, a DVC—50 random vibration machine and related measuring, recording and analysing equipments were installed. In 1983, the aircraft vibration standard and related instructive documents were prepared and studies on combined environmental vibration test technology were also carried out. By the mid 1980s the combined environmental vibration tests at high and low temperatures had been conducted, studies and analyses on impact, cannon shake, bird impact, constant acceleration and shake tests were carried out and a certain amount of associated test equipments installed, most of them being put into practical use. The technical level of China in aircraft environmental vibration test was significantly raised.

c. Structure Fatigue and Fracture Tests

In view of the fact that most of the catastrophic flight accidents were caused by fatigue damages and fractures of aircraft structures, studies and tests on aircraft structure fatigue and fracture were of great significance. The fatigue fracture tests of small parts and elements were carried out on universal fatigue test machine and crack detection equipment. The fatigue tests of large full—scale components and airframes were technically more complex and need a computer—based multi—point loading rig. At first, the loading test of pressurized fuselage was carried out in a large water tank and then in a test hall with an air supply to pressurize the fuselage. The test procedure consisted of endurance test and damage tolerance test. Its task was to determine the safe operation life and inspection interval and identify the weak points of the structure, thus providing test data for improving aircraft design and manufacturing technology and for the preparation of operation and maintenance manuals.

Before the 1960s real structure full—scale airframe fatigue test could be done only on a few loading points and in one or two load cases in China. In the mid 1970s, variable loading was realized by using a computer—controlled loading system with 40—50 loading channels and cases, with an accuracy of 1—2%. In 1983, a 622—type computer—based multi—channel loading system was developed, which could be used for the fatigue tests on aircraft elements and landing gears. It had some ad-

Fig.80　Computer—based 100 channel loading system

vantages such as high accuracy, good reliability, flexible and convenient generation of load spectrum, safe operation and provisions for the quick increase of the control channels. In the meantime, a computer—based 100 channel loading system was imported, which could automatically control the test procedure. Data automatic acquisition and high speed real—time processing on the parameters such as strain, deflection and crack propagation could be realized with an accuracy of 1% of the actuator's full scale—range. This system could be used for not only the fatigue and damage tolerance tests but also the full—scale airframe static test.

Fatigue fracture failures were often caused by the propagation of cracks initiated due to undetected defects or damages, so, the key point of structure fatigue and damage tolerance characteristics tests is the crack detection and failure monitoring based on the criteria of crack propagation rate. After fatigue fracture failure, the aircraft structure must be disassembled and checked and fracture surface analysis conducted. Then the safe life and inspection interval can be given for the aircraft to prevent the unexpected failure. In China, there have been several pieces of equipment for crack detection and fracture analysis, including the 1032D acoustic source orientation system with 32 channels.

d. Structure Thermal Strength Test

When flight speed exceeds Mach 2.4 the aircraft structure is subjected to high temperature caused by aerodynamic and friction heating, i.e. the so—called "heat barrier". It has some adverse effects on the structure strength: first, the basic properties of materials will change at high temperature; second, thermal stress will occur due to the temperature gradient in the structure. Therefore the structure thermal strength test is essential to the development of high speed aircraft and missiles. In this field, there are various tests for transient thermal stress, structure thermal stability, high temperature creep, high temperature vibration, thermal aeroelasticity, thermal fatigue, thermal fracture and so on.

In the late 1950s small scale thermal strength test facilities were established in China. In the early 1970s a transient thermal stress test hall and a thermal stress laboratory were set up in the Aircraft Structure Strength Research Institute. In the mid 1970s the analogue computer and data logger were developed in China. In 1981, a HIDIC—80E digital controller system was imported. With 110 control channels, it had a system error of less than 3%, 2,100 data channels and a sampling speed of 5,000 samples per second as well as the functions such as automatic control of heating and loading, automatic data acquisition and high speed real—time processing and failure monitoring. It could be used not only for thermal strength test, but also for thermal fatigue test. In China, a creep test oven with an internal volume of 1,600mm x 1,500mm x 1,500mm was built, equipped with a computer—controlled forced convection thermal strength test system for high temperature creep, vibration and fatigue tests.

Chapter XII   Research in Aeroengine Technology

The tactical and technical performances and cost effectiveness of aircraft depend on, to a considerable degree, the advances in aeroengine technology. Capabilities such as sustained supersonic cruise, short takeoff and landing, stealth, non—conventional maneuver, high survivability and low life cycle cost of aircraft are closely related to the aeroengine technology. The research and development activities in aeroengine are characterized by sophisticated technology, long cycle and high cost and risk because the engine operates under the conditions of high temperature, pressure and speed and heavy load, and its aerodynamic, thermodynamic and structural conditions are more complex and crucial than those of airframe.

The Chinese aeroengine industry evolved progressively from copy production to operational development of existing engines and then to engineering development of new engines. In the mid 1960s, the design work on a large augmented turbofan engine began. In the late 1970s an advanced R&D programme of high performance propulsion system started. Now the aeroengine industry has possessed some specialized research and design institutes, various test equipment and facilities for R&D and production, a scientific and technical contingent with considerable academic level and, as a result, the capabilities for developing aeroengines.

Section 1   Research in High Performance Propulsion System

In the late 1970s, the aforementioned advanced R&D programme of high performance propulsion system was listed in the aeronautical technology plan as a key item in order to establish a technical base for developing new aeroengines in China. Headed by Yuan Meifang, a senior engineer of the Gas Turbine Research Institute, the programme was carried out with system engineering method. It involved more than 600 scientific and technical staff from 24 factories, institutes and universities in a nationwide transindustry cooperation. The key points were three core components: high pressure compressor, short annular combustor and heavy load, high temperature transonic turbine. By 1986, 1,217 technical papers and 218 computer codes had been completed; 446 theses presented on seminars and journals at home and 114 theses on international seminars and journals; and over 50 scientific and technological achievement prizes of MAI were awarded for the results obtained from the programme. This was the first large scale transdepartment and transdiscipline aeroengine advanced R&D programme in the aeronautical R&D history of China.

In compressor, studies on the design and calculation methods for high performance compressor were carried out on the basis of the three dimensional flow theory developed by

Professor Wu Zhonghua. A compressor design system under inviscid flow condition was developed and studies on three dimensional flow calculation method taking account of flow viscosity are under way. A selective range of main parameters for tandem—airfoiled cascade was obtained from the study on circulation calculation of two dimensional cascade.

For raising the stable operation margin of compressor, the variable stator was investigated leading to increases of 30% and 10% in the surge margin and efficiency of compressor respectively and a more accurate method of predicting the surge limit developed. Significant progress was made in single stage transonic compressor designed on the basis of three dimensional flow theory and S_2 flow surface aerodynamic calculation, as well as in the development of trans—supersonic

Fig.81　Compressor test rig

compressor and multistage high pressure compressor. In the flutter aerodynamic study on turbomachinery, Professor Zhou Sheng of BIAA made predictions on the subsonic chocked flutter and sub—transonic stall flutter limits for the first time in the world by using numerical analysis instead of experimental method or coefficient and studies on the mechanism of flutter initiation and method of flutter prevention.

For the main combustor, research activities were concentrated on the short annular combustor. Studies on the damp diffuser and suction diffuser were accomplished, obtaining a lot of data on the optimal divergent angle and drag coefficient. The flow coefficients for holes in various forms were measured and computer codes for calculating one dimensional and three dimensional flow distributions developed. In the fuel injection and combustion research, airblast nozzle and vapourizing nozzle were investigated and their operating characteristics obtained. Segment tests of the short annular combustor under medium and high pressure were finished and combustion process and temperature distribution were good.

In the heavy load and high temperature transonic turbine, some calculation methods and corresponding computer codes of aerodynamic design, shaping and cascade circulation were developed, a set of more accurate calculation methods for aircooled high temperature blades provided and temperature reduction capabilities of the ceramic coatings preliminarily investi-gated. Now the heavy load transonic turbine operating at 1,600 K can be developed in China, which has a stage expansion ratio of 3.71, an efficiency of 0.88 and an enthalpy drop of 418.6 kJ / kg (100 kcal / kg). In two dimensional cascade of the transonic turbine, good results were achieved in the loss coefficient and performance under variable operating conditions.

In engine cycle parameter optimization and propulsion system integration, the analyses on engine steady and transient performance characteristics and the selection procedures of optimal engine cycle parameters, airframe—engine performance integration and propulsion integration were completed and the flow distortion simulation techniques for inlet—engine compatibility study preliminarily developed. With regard to the engine structure analysis, research activities were centered on the strain fatigue theory and technologies of mode analysis and time—space analysis. The powerplant mathematic modelling technology and emulation test method were developed for digital electronic engine control system.

All these achievements obtained from the high performance propulsion system programme laid a technical base for the development of new engines, the operational development, troubleshooting and life extension of the engines in service and the thorough study of imported products and technologies and found their applications in the design, production and operation of aeroengines and the economic construction of the nation. Some of them were the first achievements of their kinds in China.

Section 2   A Major Breakthrough in Flameholder Design Theory

A design criterion which was followed in design of the flameholder of the aircraft turbojet engine for a long period was: "higher the drag, more stable the flame". In order to solve the problems associated with the unstable flame in the afterburner of a jet engine, a vast amount of studies were carried out by many countries but, in principle, concentrated on the V — gutters. The phenomenon of "snow drift" was investigated in the United States with the emphasis on the three dimensional profile curve of snow drift. Under the guidance of Professor Ning Huang, a famous expert in the combustion theory of aeroengine, Gao Ge, a Ph.D. student of BIAA, developed a new criterion for flame stability and improved the existing flame stability theory while he was devoting himself to the studying on stable vortex associated with the combustion aero—thermodynamics. The Ph. D. student issued a paper "Local Stability Theory on the Vortex" and developed a rapid solution method of the three dimensional Navier—Stocks equation for calculation of the stagnation vortex flow field behind the dune. With the help of Chao Minghua, a lecturer of BIAA, Gao Ge designed the "barchan dune flameholder" on the basis of flame stabilization mechanism behind the dune. Compared with the V—gutter flameholder which had been used for 40 years, its drag was reduced 4 times and stable operation margin increased more than 7 times. Ground and flight tests of the WP6A turbojet engine with the barchan dune flameholder demonstrated that not only the critical oscillating combustion could be easily eliminated but also the augmented thrust of the engine was increased by 2%, specific fuel consumption reduced by 1—1.5% and the successful rate of the acceptance tests of production engines raised from 30% to nearly 100%. This achievement brought China to the leading position in this field. Its originality and practicality were fully affirmed by authoritative experts. Gao Ge was awarded the first—class national prize for science invention for his achievement.

Professor Wang Jiahua and Professor Zhang Xunan of NAI also made some important achievements in the unconventional flameholder. Under contracts from the office of the high performance propulsion system programme, they systematically investigated the mechanism of V—gutter pilot flameholder and obtained its design criteria and method. Ground and flight tests of the WP6 turbojet engine with this new flameholder proved that significant improvements had been made in the augmented specific fuel consumption, probability of successfully lighting the afterburner at high altitude and operation stability of the afterburner during acrobatic flights. This flameholder was simple in structure and it found wide applications in aeroengines.

Section 3　Research Activities for Operational Development of Aeroengines

In addition to the founding of technical base, research activities in the aeroengine technology were carried out also for improving the performance of operational engines.

1.　Parameter Measurement and Investigation through the Engine Flow Path

In order to obtain main cycle parameters and component parameters of the WP6 engine, more than 200 measurements were conducted on 649 measuring points and, as a result, 110,000 data recorded. On the basis of these data, the aerodynamic parameters at all flow stations, main cycle parameters, component loss coefficients, flow distributions and curves were determined for WP6 under the normal, maximum and augmented conditions and a great deal of reliable information was provided for derivative design and flight characteristics calculation of the engine.

2.　Research Activities for Engine Performance Improvement

At first, the first stage of the WP6 compressor was redesigned and turbine inlet temperature raised by 50 ℃ so that the thrust of the engine was increased by 15.4%. Then a new annular combustor was developed for the engine, resulting in a further thrust increase of 2%, a specific fuel consumption decrease of 1.5%, an improvement of 6% in combustor exit temperature factor and a fall of 60 ℃ in temperature at the hot spot. An 11% increase in thrust and 14% decrease in specific fuel consumption for WP7 engine were realized by incorporating the aircooled and shrouded turbine blade, raising the turbine inlet temperature by 100 ℃ and improving the afterburner fuel system and manifold.

3.　Research Activities for Enhancement of the Stable Operation Limits

The surge margin and stable operation limits of the WP6A engine were enhanced by adding a variable " 0 " stage stator after the problems associated with the stator's shaping, cascade performance, configuration, strength and deicing had been investigated and solved. In order to avoid engine shutdown of the J—8 fighter in flight, tests of stability limits, distortion tolerant capability, inlet exit flow field and compressor efficiency were done for WP7A engine and, as a result, the operating stability of the engine was improved by a method of case treatment called "spoiler in small stagnation cell". In addition, the high frequency oscillation in the afterburner of WP7A engine was successfully eliminated by readjusting the fuel concentration distribution and designing a antioscillation screen with large diameter holes. By the way, the design, calculation and test methods and procedures of antioscillation screen were developed for the afterburner with small augmentation ratio and small diameter.

4. Research Activities in Stall Flutter of the Compressor Blade

Through tests and analyses, the cause of the compressor blade failures of WP7A engine in flight was found to be the poor aeroelastic —vibration characteristics of the blades, which had a wider operating range of stall flutter. It was found through comparison tests of different blade frequency differences that the flutter characteristics of the blades on any engine could be improved by installing the blades with large frequency difference between them. Safe and reliable operation of the engine of the J—8 fighter was ensured over the flight envelope. This was the first time in China to investigate the effect of blade mistuning on the stall flutter and to use the blade mistuning technology.

The publication of the "Aeroengine Strength Design Handbook" provided a practical reference book for aeroengine strength design. It included the experiences obtained from the aeroengine strength design and test in China and the useful information extracted from related books and papers in foreign countries.

Section 4   A Moderate Set of Test Facilities

In the mid 1960s, the Shenyang Aeroengine Test Station was established. It accommodated more than 10 engine types one after another for various kinds of testing and offered a large amount of data for production and scientific research in the Chinese aviation industry. In the meantime the station also provided test and equipment design data and reference documents for nearly 100 organizations in 22 provinces and municipalities as well as the ministries of railways, water conservancy and power and metallurgical industry and the Navy of PLA. In the 1970s, more than 60 engine component test rigs and facilities were constructed in Hunan and inland China. Over the past thirty and more years, nearly 300 test rigs and facilities have been built for large, medium and small engines in several factories and design and research institutes and the first construction phase of the simulated altitude test facility has been completed.

The Gas Turbine Research Institute is a test and research center of aeroengine and its task is to provide the technical base for other aeroengine design and research organizations and users. Beginning in 1965, a complete set of test rigs and facilities was built up, consisting of one simulated altitude test facility, one ground test stand and more than 40 engine component and system test rigs and facilities. Some of them were relatively advanced, such as the supersonic inlet wind tunnel, trans–supersonic two dimensional cascade wind tunnel, single stage and multi–stage axial compressor test rig, high pressure main combustor and annular combustor test rig, integrated turbine test rig, turbine disk overspeed test rig, physical simulation unit for main fuel governing system and inlet flow distortion generator. Imported automatic data acquisition and real time processing systems were used for these test rigs and the test capacities greatly increased.

Among these test facilities, the engine simulated altitude test facility is the largest and most complicated in technology. The actual flight conditions (temperature, pressure and flow rate) at engine inlet can be simulated in this ground facility. The engine to be tested is installed in the test chamber with controllable inlet air conditions and ambient pressure and temperature. The steady and transient performance characteristics can be measured over the flight envelope with a maximum Mach number of 2.5 and a maximum altitude of 25 km.

This simulated altitude test facility is a direct–connected one with a continuous air supply in moderate size. It comprises air supply, air treatment unit, refrigeration turbine, heating system, test chamber and exhaust cooling system. The temperature of the air flow ducting to the engine inlet can be reduced from 40 ℃ to −65 ℃ by the cooling turbine system or raised from 150 ℃ to 500 ℃ by the heating system. The temperature of the hot exhaust gas from the engine can be reduced from a maximum of 1,800 ℃ to less than 50 ℃. Larger engines can be tested in the test chamber.

Great progress was also made in the construction of engine strength test equipment. In the 1980s, 4 sets of strength test equipment were imported for the licence production of Spey turbofan engine, which enhanced the strength test capabilities of aeroengine industry of China.

Instrumentation technology and equipment play an important role in the aeroengine test and research. Research activities were carried out in test and instrumentation tech - nologies for the high performance propulsion system. Important achie -

Fig.82　The air supply station of the simulated altitude test facility

vements obtained in this field are as follows. In the compressor operation stability, a new approach for predicting the rotation stall and surge was found through measuring and analyzing the wake of the compressor rotor and its variation. In the simulation technology of engine inlet flow distortion, a wake mathematic model for single simulated plate was developed by combining the two dimensional wake theory with experimental method and a further mathematic model for multiple simulated plates also developed for calculating the complex simulated flow field. These models were used in the inlet flow distortion tests of the engine for J−8 II fighter. In the flow distribution measurement for small holes on the combustor wall a test method called "one−side accumulated hole−blockage method" was developed to determine the flow distribution from the small holes. A non−contact displacement and vibration measurement unit was developed, which could be used to measure the radial and axial displacements and moving trajectory of turbine, compressor and fan shafts. In the engine structure tests the problems associated with the computer−based multipoint coordinate loading and the imposing of vibration torque and cyclic compression load on the main torque were solved, thus improving test accuracy and productivity. A microprobe and automatic traversing mechanism were also developed, which made it possible to measure the thickness of boundary layer at any position on a wall. Advances in the laser technology greatly facilitated the aeroengine test and instrumentation technologies of China. Laser holography, laser fuel particle sizer, laser fuel vapourization analysis unit and double focus laser anemometer were successfully used in engine tests. Electronic computer found its wide application in engine and component tests and gave a new drive to the development of aeroengine test technology.

Chapter XIII   Research in Avionics Technology

Generally speaking, the avionics technology includes communication technology, navigation, radar and identification technology, electronic countermeasure technology, automatic flight control and aircraft instrument system, electric system, fire control technology, flight data recording and training simulation technology and system as well as air traffic control technology and system. With the rapid development of microelectronic and computer technologies great changes took place in the airborne equipment, i.e. the traditional classic control theory gave way to the modern control theory, the electronic equipment replaced most of the mechanical and electrical equipments, the software development dominated over the hardware development, the optics and electronics separation turned to the optics and electronics combination and the discrete equipments evolved into integrated one. As a result a new discipline of avionics emerged. Before the 1950s the electron tubes were dominantly used in the communication, navigation and radar ranging equipments installed on the aircraft. After the 1960s new equipments which featured transistor and integrated circuit gradually substituted for many airborne mechanical and electric equipments. Since the 1970s, due to the wide application of the large scale integrated circuit and very large scale integrated circuit, the development of airborne equipment was directed toward compactness, all electronic, integration and digitalization. This made it possible to develop high manoeuvrability and low altitude penetration technologies and provide snap-shot, look-down and shoot-down, panoramic display, active control and self-adaptive electronic countermeasure capabilities for the military aircraft and to improve the safety, economy and comfort for the civil aircraft. The technological level of avionics has become an important factor in judging the performance of a modern aircraft.

Since the late 1970s the advanced R&D activities in the integration and digitalization of avionics and in the key technologies of advanced weapon system for dogfighting and interception attack began in China and exciting results have been achieved in a short time.

Section 1   Active Control Technology

A revolution is taking place in the aircraft control system. With the traditional design philosophy, designers at first select the reasonable aerodynamic configuration, structure and powerplant and then arrange the flight control system. With the development of modern control theory, microelectronic technology and computer, it is possible in the initial design phase that the functions of flight control system can be considered in combination with the selection of optimal aerodynamic configuration and structure. This is the so—called active control technology. It can significantly enhance the capabilities of manoeuvring, tree—top and allweather flights and improve the flying quality. For the military aircraft, active control technology can effectively raise the combat effectiveness and survivability, and for the civil aircraft, the safety, economy and comfort.

In 1958 the Chinese aviation industry began to develop aircraft autopilot. In 1965 the design, loop analysis and simulation test of the autopilot of a coast defence missile started. In 1967 the research activities in aircraft autopilot and control augmentation system were carried out, various electrohydraulic servo—actuators developed with the simple redundance technology and applied research activities in the analog hardware redundance technology conducted. A technological breakthrough was made in the parametric self—adaptive adjustment over a wide range of flight conditions for the energy—balanced self—adaptive flight control system and the partial active control technology was explored for the gust alleviation system.

After 1978 the active control technology was listed as a key subject in the aeronautical R&D plan. The Aircraft Accessory Research Institute and the Aircraft Automatic Control Research Institute made considerable progresses in the fly—by—wire and redundance technologies. Under the guidance of senior engineer Li Mingquan the airborne quadruple redundance fault—tolerant computer developed by the Aeronautical Computation Technology Institute was successfully flight tested.

In the meantime the applied research activities in the maneuver load control, direct force control and active flutter suppression were accomplished. They laid a foundation for the further development of active control technology and the research of the fire / flight and propulsion / flight integration controls.

Section 2　Avionics Integration Technology

The avionics developed from discrete to integrated, from analog to digital and from using individual computers to a central computer and then to a hierarchical and distributed network of electronic system. Before the late 1950s the avionic units were individually developed according to the aircraft operational specification and the related technical base at that time. Each unit had its own function as well as its own antenna, receiver and transmitter, cable, controller and display, which resulted in a low equipment utilization and a heavy system weight. By the late 1960s the digital technology was incorporated in partial system and partial function integration was realized with a central computer. But the volume, weight and power of the aircraft electronic system continued to grow due to the seperate functions of each transducers and the seperate developments of each subsystems. In the 1970s the system integration technology brought out a digital and integrated aircraft electronic system, which could combine the functions such as communication, navigation, identification and anti—collision into a multifunctional and multifrequency system, transfer various information such as voice, picture and data, execute synthesized computation and real–time control and realize redundance and source sharing. As a result the weight, volume and cost of the total system were reduced and its reliability, maintainability and anti–jamming capability doubled.

In the late 1970s priority was given to the avionics integration technology in aeronautical R& D in China. As the first step the Avionics Research Institute developed an integrated subsystem of communication, navigation and identification. This multifunctional integrated system could not only reduce the system volume and weight, but also make a reasonable use of radio frequency band and signal and, in turn, it could reduce internal interference and satisfy electromagnetic compatibility requirement. It could be also used for the classified and anti–jamming data transfer, digital communication and voice communication. Considerable progress was made in this field.

In the meantime the research activities were carried out in the avionic digital integration system, which could integrate the functions of information acquisition, transfer, processing and display on board so that the subsystems could share the common source to get more benefits and higher performance. The system developed in China incorporated the hierarchical distributed computer network structure consisting of four core components: i.e. digital multiprocessor, dual–redundant multichannel data bus, integrated control and display unit and mission software. Subsystems of the airborne electronic equipment were linked to the bus via terminals constituting a complete integrated information system. The mission processing computer used in the system was a second class airborne computer and belonged to the medium level computer of the airborne computer series developed in China, which was suitable for the real time control and data processing. It passed technical evaluation and its good performance was proved. The data exchange speed and distance of the data bus were 1,000,000 bits per second and 100 m respectively. The integrated control and display unit was developed by a related organization and it included the head up display and head down display. The head–up display developed by the Aircraft Fire Control Research Institute could display eight clear, bright and stable pictures related with fire control, navigation, etc. The head–down display developed by the Suzhou Aircraft Instrument Factory proved to be almost comparable with foreign product of its kind in the picture number and character clarity. The mission software consisted of main executive software and partial executive software so that the system could perform its functions for a variety of flight missions.

Section 3 Aircraft Fire Control Technology

The combat effectiveness of a modern fighter depends on, to a great extent, its fire control system. Advances in the fire control technology provide the modern aircraft with an increasing combat capability. So the airborne fire control system has become an essential part of modern combat aircraft. The development of aircraft and its weaponry and changes in the air fight tactics have a direct influence on the development of the fire control system. Modern airborne fire control system has evolved into a navigation and attack system which operates with the pulse Doppler radar as main detector, the head—up display as display terminal, the distributed computer network (in which radar, inertial navigation system, air data computer and other related equipments are linked by a data bus) as the analysis and calculation device and combat flight procedure software as the management system, so that the multifunction, multiweapon, multitarget treatment and multitransducer requirements on modern aircraft can be realized and the weapon attack accuracy and aircraft combat effectiveness raised.

On the basis of the first generation monopulse multifunctional airborne radar for fire control and bombing and the head up display, the advanced R&D activities began in the mid 1970s in the airborne radar of coherent pulse Doppler system and phased array system, diffraction optics head—up display, strapdown inertial navigation technology, laser ranging—finder and associated softwares and since then considerable progress were made.

The first all—coherent pulse Doppler radar demonstrator developed by the Airborne Radar Research Institute proved, through tests, to be able to detect and track the flying target in clutter environment.

The instantaneous field of view of head—up display is one of the important performance goals of airborne fire control system. The desirable field of view is 60 ° in azimuth and 35 ° in pitch, but the field of view of existing refraction optics head—up display is only 17 ° and 11 ° respectively. Since the diffraction optics head—up display can provide a larger field of view and higher brightness of picture, the Aircraft Fire Control Research Institute launched an advanced R&D programme in this technology in the 1970s and satisfactory results were achieved.

The strapdown technology is one of the focal points in the development of inertial navigation system. While in the conventional inertial navigation system gimbals of its stable platform simulate the inertial coordinate system and local coordinate system respectively, in the strapdown inertial navigation system with its transducer directly installed on the airframe the computer and corresponding software perform the functions of the stable platform. The strapdown inertial navigation system has some advantages such as small volume, light weight, low cost, multiredundance and high reliability. On the basis of successful development of the platform inertial navigation system the Aircraft Automatic Control Research Institute conducted the research activities in the strapdown inertial navigation technology and good results were gained.

Section 4　Precision Guidance Technology for Advanced Weaponry

In modern war the air combat is still an effective means for gaining air superiority. The fast changing and fierce air combat imposes increasingly requirements on the main air combat weapon — air—to—air missile, e.g. the all—altitude, all—direction and all—weather attack, target acquisition and weapon launch at large off—boresight angles and self—contained target acquisition after launch. Therefore many countries are devoting their major efforts to developing new theories and technologies for more advanced air—to—air missile, including the optimal guidance law and correctional proportional guidance law, banked turning control, thrust vector control, active radar guidance system, millimeter wave active radar guidance, etc. As a result great improvements have been made in range, accuracy and lethality of the tactical missile.

Satisfactory progresses have been made in research and development of the advanced air—to—air and coast defence missiles. The Air—to—air Missile Research Institute has made substantial progresses in the application of modern control theory to choosing the control law of air—to—air missile, nonlinear control and filtering, compact combined guidance system, active radar guidance and self—adaptive digital autopilot. Big progress has been also made in the digital information processing and control, system emulation, infrared and radar background radiation, target characteristics and anti—jamming. The research activities in the technologies of television guidance, stare focal—plane array multielement imaging and anti—radiation and laser guidance are smoothly under way.

Banked turning control of air—to—air missile is an advanced technology, which can significantly improve the maximum g, maneuvering capability and guidance accuracy of a missile by positioning the missile at the optimal banking angle and constantly guiding it to the maneuvering plane of the target with a certain degree of accuracy. The research goal has been basically met through the static characteristics measurement in control chamber and physical simulation test on the banking system.

Off—boresight aiming is one of the important research subjects in the fire control technology of air—to—air missile. Analysis and test proved that the off—boresight aiming can improve the target acquisition probability and night acquisition capability of missile and guide several missiles to their targets respectively. This is of great significance in enhancing the combat capability of the air force. The Air—to—air Missile Research Institute won the science and technology achievement prize from MAI for its research activities in this field.

Another new technology developed in the 1970s for the coast defence missile was the "on—the—deck" flight, which could improve its penetration capability. Beginning in the mid 1970s the Coast Defence Missile Design Institute conducted the "on—the—deck" flight test of coast defence missile with two successful flights at reduced altitudes and two hits.

Chapter XIV Research in Aeronautical Materials and Manufacturing Technology

Advanced aircraft and engine designs can be realized only when the required aeronautical materials and sophisticated manufacturing technology are available. Modern aircraft demand that the aeronautical materials must have high strength and stiffness, low weight (i.e. high specific strength and stiffness), excellent corrosion resistance, high reliability, good workability and so on. Various materials and manufacturing technologies are required for different aircraft parts and components and furthermore special equipment and manufacturing method are needed for many structure elements and materials. These requirements are promoting the development in aeronautical materials and manufacturing technology and, in turn, the achievements in these fields are helping enhance the aircraft performance. In the 1950s the Aeronautical Materials Research Institute and the Aeronautical Manufacturing Technology Research Institute and again in the early 1960s the Precision Machinery Research Institute were established in China.

At the very beginning of the aviation industry of new China, a guideline for the development of aeronautical materials was laid down, i.e. the aeronautical materials should be domestically made and new materials developed on the basis of new material technologies and achievements from foreign countries and full utilization of domestic resources. New achievements in this area were frequently made in cooperation with the ministries of metallurgical industry, petroleum and chemical industry, building material industry, light industry and textile industry, related research institutes of the Chinese Academy of Sciences and universities and colleges.

In 1963 an aeronautical material team was formed under the sponsorship of the Defence Science and Technology Commission and CAE. The team consisted of many famous experts in metallurgy, chemical engineering and material science from its 190 member organizations. Under the guidance of the team leader Li Xun, the development direction of aeronautical material science in China was discussed and determined and the "Development Plan of Aeronautical Materials 1963—1972" formulated. This transdepartment team made an important contribution to the development of aeronautical materials in China with the support of related ministries and commissions under the State Council and the Chinese Academy of Sciences according to the unified plan.

In the meantime the manufacturing technologies were mastered by the factories in aviation industry through repair and licence production. In the development of new aircraft, engines, instruments, electric equipment and accessories, the Aeronautical Manufacturing Technology Research Institute and the Precision Machinery Research Institute as well as the factories in aviation industry carried out extensive research activities in manufacturing technologies, offered a great deal of achievements and made their contributions to the mastery and popularization of advanced manufacturing technologies.

Section 1   Aircraft Materials and Manufacturing Technology

1. Aircraft Materials

Aircraft materials consist of metallic materials and nonmetallic materials. The former mainly includes aluminium alloys, structure steels and titanium alloys, and the latter transparent materials, resin matrix composites, adhesives, rubbers, sealants, paints and coatings, engineering plastics and textile materials.

a. Aircraft Metallic Materials

Aluminium alloy found a wide application in aircraft structure due to its high specific strength and stiffness, good chemical stability and excellent workability. For a modern aircraft about 50——80% of the structure weight are of aluminium alloy. Since the 1970s aluminium alloy has been further widenning its application in aircraft structure because of new breakthroughs in the stress corrosion resistance, fracture toughness and fatigue resistance of aluminium alloy and developments in the aluminium—lithium alloy and rapid solidification powder aluminium alloy.

In 1956 the Northeast Light Alloy Plant was set up in China and it produced various wrought aluminium alloys of Soviet specifications. The development of new aluminium alloys began in 1958. Now both the wrought and casting aluminium alloys of Chinese specifications can be produced in series.

In the high strength wrought aluminium alloy, LC4 (i.e. the Soviet specification B95) could not be widely used because of its high sensitivity to the stress corrosion and notch and low fatigue strength. To seek a better aluminium alloy, a research team was formed and, after analyzing the development trend of aluminium alloys and considering the domestic resources, it successfully developed in 1965 the LC9 high strength aluminium alloy under the guidance of Liu Duopu, a light alloy expert, and in cooperation with the Northeast Light Alloy Plant. Compared with LC4, LC9 was

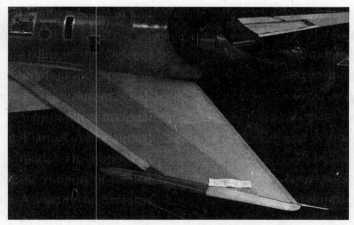

Fig.83   The horizontal tail panel made of high strength aluminium alloy

better in stress corrosion and crack propagation resistance, machining deformation and form correction and could be used for the load—bearing elements of aircraft, such as longerons, stringes, frames, skins, panels, wing ribs, attachments, landing gears and actuators. The horizontal tail panels and other 26 forgings of J—8 fighter were made of LC9. The nose landing gear of J—12 fighter made of this alloy proved to be good in performance by flight test.

In the casting aluminium alloy series, HZL205 was developed by Liu Bocao and other engineers, which had higher tensile strength and good plasticity and toughness. The weights of J—7 and J—8 fighters were reduced due to the application of this alloy to them. The middle pulley of a five—pully block used for erecting ultra—high voltage transmission lines was once made of HZL205 casting aluminium alloy and its weight reduced and the erecting work facilitated.

Starting in 1958 Su Caiye and other engineers began to develop the high strength structural steels. For saving nickel they explored the Cr—Mn—Si—Mo—V(Ti) steel series and finally developed a superior ultra—high strength steel, GC—4. Proved in the operational tests of J—6 and Q—5 aircraft the landing gears made of GC—4 were lighter than those made of the 30 Cr—Mn—Si—Ni steel copied according to the Soviet specification. Then the GC—4 steel was formally used for the nose landing gear, main landing gear and spar of the horizontal tail of J—8 fighter and, as a result, the aircraft structure weight also reduced. This achievement was award - ed the third—class national prize for science invention.

Another breakthrough in the high strength steel in China was the successful development of a low—alloy high strength baintic shaped steel, GC—11. Its inventors were Wu Shize, a structural steel expert, and others and they were awarded the second—class national prize for science invention for their achievement. This steel has excellent formability and weldability and its heat treatment processing is simple. After being austenitized and then air cooled the GC—11 steel has a strength equal to that of the 30 Cr—Mn—Si steel after being oil quenched and tempered and even better hardenability, moderate—temperature property and endurance strength. It has a general property equal to that of the steels of its kind in foreign countries and filled up the nation's blank in this steel category. GC—11 has been widely used in eight types of aircraft with good results in ensuring the product quality, raising the productivity and reducing the intensity of work.

Compared with other structural materials the newly—developed titanium alloy has a higher specific strength and better corrosion resistance. TC1 and TC4 are the main titanium alloys used in Chinese—made aircraft. TC1 sheets in 800 mm wide and 3,000 mm long were produced in the Sujiatun Non—ferrous Metals Plant and the Fushun Steel Plant and pressed into J—7 fighter's parts such as the fore section of tail fairing, horizontal tail and fairing skin. This titanium alloy was also used for J—8, Y—7, Y—8 and Q—5. In order to reduce the structural weight and improve the tactical and technical performance of the J—8 II fighter, it was decided to extensively use the TC4 titanium alloy for fabricating the load—bearing elements of the aircraft. Through more than three years' hard working on key problems, 5 large close—die forgings and 20 open—die forgings were made resulting in a lighter structural weight.

Brake materials are the key to the effectiveness of wheel brakes and wheel brake disks are the critical parts for safe landing. Before the 1960s the wheel brake disks of domestic aircraft were made of asbestos—rubber brake material. In 1962 the Soviet MK—11 iron—base brake material was copy—produced in China. Then several sintered powder metallurgy brake materials were developed on our own. Before the 1970s all the brake materials for commercial aircraft were imported. Later on it was difficult to order the brake materials from abroad and some aircraft were faced with a difficult situation of being grounded. Therefore the State Planning Commission assigned a task to develop brake materials for commercial aircraft on our own and in a cooperative manner and ensure the scheduled flights. After receiving the task Li Dongsheng and other engineers successfully developed a single—metal brake pair made of a new sintered iron—base brake material F245. The brake pair could be still used after 2,000 takeoffs and landings accumulated on the An—24 commuter aircraft and, for comparison, the actual operation life of the former brake pair was 400—600 takeoffs and landings. Thereafter it was used on other commercial aircraft and exported. This scientific achievement was awarded the third—class national prize for science invention. The performance of the Chinese—made steel brake disks on the Trident airliner also reached that of foreign brake disks. As a result all the brake materials could be made in China and a lot of foreign currency was saved for the nation. In 1976 research activities in carbon—carbon composite brake disk began.

b. Aircraft Non—metal Materials and Their Moulding Techniques

Both in variety and weight the proportion of non—metal materials in aircraft structure is continuously increasing. Composite materials play an important role in reducing the aircraft structural weight and improving the aircraft performance. Transparent materials and their moulding techniques make it possible to configure a new canopy structure with arc windscreen. New adhesives and adhesive—bonding techniques as well as new sealants and their proces-sing techniques, all contribute to the aircraft performance in their own ways. Most of the aircraft non—metal materials are high molecular materials or their products. High static strength and fatigue strength as well as good aging—resistant and weather—resistant properties are the main requirements on the structural elements made of non—metal materials.

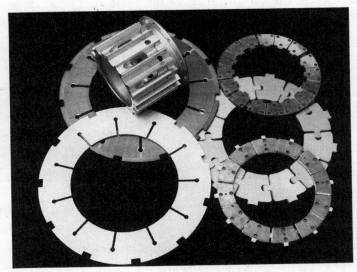

Fig.84　The brake disk made in China

Research activities in aircraft non—metal materials in China began with the copy production of the Soviet materials. Starting in 1958 the research activities in new non—metal materials and their moulding techniques were carried out under the guidance of Fan Tang, an aircraft non—metal material expert. The seriation of the Chinese made non—metal aircraft materials was realized, step by step, through the efforts of MAI in cooperation with the related research institutes and factories of the ministries of petroleum and chemical industry, light industry, textile industry and building materials industry as well as the Chinese Academy of Sciences.

Non—directional acrylic plastics was once used as the canopy material but it tends to craze, crack and damage. In order to obtain higher impact toughness and craze resistance of the material, development activities in the directionally stretched acrylic plastics began in the 1960s. The moulding technique is rather difficult because the acrylic plastics must be hot—moulded under the tensile stress and within a strict dimension tolerance. In the 1970s a hard and fixed canopy made of directionally stretched acrylic plastics was fabricated for the J—8 all—weather fighter on the basis of the previously developed new materials, equipments and moulding techniques and its static test, ground static and dynamic jettsioning tests of canopy, temperature and pressure simulated test and flight test proved its material properties and fabrication techniques.

Fig.85　The composite material panel of vertical tail

The sealed cockpit and metal integral fuel tank are the prerequisites for supersonic flight. The requirements on the sealing materials vary with seal processings and while a seal processing is being developed, a seal material suitable for the processing needs to be developed. In order to meet the requirements of new aircraft development Hu Shaozhi and other engineers developed room temperature—vulcanized sealants of polysulfide rubber and silicone rubber matrices and ever—wet putty based on cis—butadiene rubber, arylonitrile—silicone rubber and phenylene—silicone rubber matrices. The former are suitable for the faying surface sealing and fillet sealing and the latter for filled sealing and channel sealing. In addition a liquid seal shim was developed for sealing the engine joint face and a sealant series for different surrounding mediums and temperatures was formed.

Compared with steel, aluminium and titanium the advanced composite materials have a much higher specific strength, specific modules and fatigue strength and are in a highlighted position in the aircraft structural materials. The development of resin matrix composite material reinforced with carbon fiber began in the early 1970s and continued in the 1980s. Significant progresses were made in raw material, fabrication processing and product quality control. On the basis of the achievements in the lay—up design and strength calculation and the results from the high temperature stiffness test, fatigue test and lightning test on various typical structural elements, the carbon fiber composite panel of vertical tail of the J—8 aircraft and all composite vertical tail of the Q—5 aircraft were successfully made and their static tests, fatigue tests and flight tests passed. This indicated that China had entered a new phase in the fabrication and processing of the composite material structure and the application of composite materials to the aircraft structure.

2. Aircraft Manufacturing Technology

The aircraft manufacturing technology in China evolved when the aircraft industry developed from copy or licence production to development of new aircraft on our own. The research activities carried out by aircraft factories in this field are for the aircraft production, existing technology's improvement and factory's facelifting while the Aeronautical Manufacturing Technology Research Institute, the Precision Machinery Research Institute and aeronautical universities and colleges explore new manufacturing processes and technologies. Factories, research institutes and universities and colleges often do the research work in a cooperative way.

The aircraft manufacturing technology includes the integral panel manufacturing, aluminium honeycomb structure bonding, sheet forming, titanium sheet hot forming, shear spinning, NC machining, CAM, composite material fabricating and so on. The research activities in these fields were carried out one after another and achievements gained.

Integral panel is the main load—bearing structural element of aircraft. Its manufacturing technology was a key problem associated with the J—7 aircraft production. The Aeronautical Manufacturing Technology Research Institute developed chemical milling and tracing milling methods. A chemical milling section was set up in a aircraft factory, in which qualified integral panels of the fuel tank of the J—7 aircraft were manufactured. The integral panels of the J—8 aircraft and large panels of SH—5 aircraft were successfully produced with the tracing miller designed on our own and awarded the national prizes for new industrial products. The corresponding peen forming technique improved the product quality and raised the productivity by 5—6 times.

Adhesive bonding technique is one of the three main joint techniques in the contemporary world. The aluminium honeycomb sandwich is a lightweight structure and it is fabricated with the adhesive bonding technique. In the early 1960s the adhesive bonded metal rotor blade of the

Z—5 helicopter was developed by Hu Jianguo and other engineers and put into production. In the late 1960s the movable rudder and elevator made of high temperature adhesive bonded honeycomb was successfully developed and produced for the J—8 fighter. In the development also emerged such problems as unstable product quality, structure leakage and separation of the skin from the core due to adhesion failure. To solve these problems, a quality control procedure in the adhesive bonding process was formulated, phosphyric anodizing technology of adherend surface of aluminium alloy and durable aluminium alloy honeycomb core were developed and honeycomb without holes was incorporated instead of the honeycomb with holes. Therefore the operation life of adherend structure under high humidity and temperature conditions was increased. In the meantime the adhesives for the honeycomb without holes, which could be cured at different temperatures, was developed and a series of adhesives for metal structure formed.

In the 1970s the fabrication technology for all—adherend structure of metal sheet—sheet was studied and the all—adherend vertical tail panel of J—8 fighter and then the all—adherend fuselage panel of SH—5 bomber were developed, laying a foundation for the application of all—adherend structure to aircraft. After 1980 the fabrication technology of the honeycomb made of Kevler paper was mastered so that this new technology was available for J—8 and J—7Ⅲ production and China's adhesive bonding technology reached a new height.

The old sheet forming technology used for aircraft production in the 1950s remained in use for a long time and, as a result, the mechanization level and product quality were low. The rubber hydraulic press, which were used in the early period had some disadvantages, i.e. a low pressure (only 19.6—24.5 MPa in actual operation) and serious leakage in the hydraulic system. A research team headed by Professor Chang Rongfu of BIAA made a thorough investigation into the high pressure cylinder winded by steel wire, and successfully developed a technology demonstrator of the rubber hydraulic press with a pressure of 58.8 MPa and in the late 1970s two cylinder—type rubber hydraulic presses in cooperation with the Shanxi Special Equipment Factory and the Taiyuan Heavy Machinery Factory respectively. The Xi'an Aircraft Company also manufactured a press with the tube—type tyre made of polyurethane rubber. A foundation of sheet forming mechanization was then laid. The Harbin Aircraft Factory incorporated such a new manufacture processing that the forming and correcting of aluminium alloy parts were performed during their aging time after quenching since the aluminium alloy sheet had good plasticity at that time. Correspondingly, the multi—roll correcting machine, gearless shrinking machine and corner—dressing machine were designed and together with the refrigerator and cylinder type rubber hydraulic press, a new production line was set up. Hence China's backward situation in sheet forming was changed.

The hot forming technology of titanium alloy sheet was a research project in the 1960s and one of the technical keys in J—7 aircraft production. The Shenyang Aircraft Company conducted the research activities in this field and made a success. In order to cope with the increasing need of titanium alloy sheet parts on J—7Ⅲ, J—8, Q—5, Y—7 and Z—8 aircraft and their engines, the first generation hot forming press (RX−1) was successfully designed, the deformation mechanism of titanium sheet studied and new lubricating protective material developed. As a result, nearly ten thousands of titanium sheet parts in several hundreds of varieties were manufactured with good quality. Soon the second generation hot forming press (RX−2) came out in succession.

The shear spinning technology is a manufacturing method for thin wall spinning parts of aircraft and engines. Various parts such as the bodies and tungsten nozzles of missiles and rockets, nose domes of aircraft, and inlet cone, front case, combustor case and tail cone of engines were manufactured with the SY shear spinning machines designed by the Aeronautical Manufacturing Technology Research Institute.

Fig.86　The three axis NC plane milling machine

NC machining and CAM is the only way to realize automatic production and suitable for the complex and precise parts of aero products in large variety and small batch. As early as the late 1950s the development of NC technology hardware and software began. Deng Hongchou and other engineers took up these research activities. In 1968 the first extrapolation NC milling machine came into use in the aircraft production, and then the NC drafting machine and three axis and four axis NC plane milling machines were put into production. A large mul-

Fig.87　The four axis NC plane milling machine

tiaxis NC plane milling machine was also developed in cooperation with France, laying a foundation for designing the NC machines on our own.

The advanced R&D on CAD / CAM began in the mid 1960s. At first some engineering softwares were developed on the domestic computers. In the late 1970s several universities and colleges and factories developed applicable mathematic models for analysis and calculation and engineering softwares and software packages for drafting and machining and with interactive functions. In 1983 a research team led by engineer Li Shengyuan completed CAM251 CAM integration system, which synthesized the functions of mathematic modelling of aircraft configuration, NC drafting and NC machining. This system was used for the production of 19 aircraft types with good technical and economic payoffs. According to an incomplete statistics, the production cycles of some prototypes were shortened 1.5 times, the standard toolings for some types of aircraft reduced 2 times, the large production toolings for other types of aircraft reduced nearly 1.5 times, the machining productivity of the complex toolings and large parts raised by 3——5 times and the machining and assembling accuracy of some parts improved by an order of magnitude. In the 1980s the Shenyang Aircraft Design and Research Institute and the Aeronautical Manufacturing Technology Research Institute began to develop the CADEMAS software system in cooperation with MBB of the Federal Republic of Germany, and two NC programming softwares were completed. In the meantime the graphic input and output system, automatic programming system of interactive NC and interactive three dimensional geometry configuration system were imported, which pushed the CAM technology of China to a new height. Some softwares developed within MAI were popularized and applied in more than 30 departments outside the ministry and even abroad.

Section 2　Engine Materials and Manufacturing Technology

1.　Engine Materials

Engine materials mainly include high temperature alloys, steels and titanium alloys as well as some aluminium—magnesium alloys.

In the metallurgy history of old China there were no high temperature alloys. After the founding of aviation industry of new China the Government gave priority to the development of high temperature alloys and the Ministry of Metallurgical Industry put a great deal of manpower and other resources on it. In 1956 the first high temperature alloy of China was developed due to the joint effort of the metallurgical industry and aviation industry organized by the Government. Then the metallurgical industry successfully developed several high temperature alloys for the aviation industry. It was only from then on that China had its own high temperature alloys.

Starting in the late 1950s China developed the high temperature alloy series adaptable to domestic resources. Senior engineer Huang Fuxiang and others did a lot in this field. The iron—nickel base high temperature alloy GH140 developed with their participation was used to make the combustor and afterburner parts and components of aircraft and industrial gas turbine engines operating at 850 ℃ and its nickel content was only two thirds of that of the similar nickel base alloy. GH140, of which over 50 part items of 12 engine types were made, had the highest production output among the high temperature alloys in China. It yielded considerable economic payoffs and saved a large amount of the strategic material — nickel. Other iron—nickel high temperature alloys such as GH15 and GH16 developed by Huang Fuxiang and the others were also used in engine production. These scientific achievements were awarded the second—class national prize for science and technology progress. Huang Fuxiang was titled the "outstanding expert" of MAI.

In the 1970s the GH128 high temperature sheet was developed under the leadership of engineer Fu Hongzhen of the Iron and Steel Research Establishment of the Ministry of Metallurgical Industry and with the participation of the Fushun Steel Plant and others. Combustor made of this material could operate with a temperature range of 900—950 ℃. Fan Juchen of the Qiqihaer Steel Plant and Wuxi of the Guizhou Aeroengine Company developed GH33A alloy with high yield point. It was widely used to make turbine disks for several engine types and awarded the second—class national prize for science invention. The GH132 high temperature alloy was successfully developed due to the joint effort of the Daye Steel Plant and the Chengdu Aeroengine Factory. It substituted for GH36 in the turbine disk of WP6 engine, solving the corrosion problem associated with the original alloy and in turn extending the operating life of the disk. For the development of new engines the Fushun Steel Plant, the Iron and Steel Establishment, the Chengdu Aeroengine Factory, the Aeronautical Materials Research Institute and the Great Wall Steel Plant jointly developed the GH698 and GH220 alloys for turbine disk and blade, which had a superb high temperature property and general property.

The casting high temperature alloy was usually used to make turbine blades and vanes. With the improvement of engine performance the turbine inlet temperature increased to about 1,400 ℃. In combination with sophisticated blade cooling scheme and configuration, the casting high temperature alloy with better high temperature property than that of the wrought alloy progressively took a dominant position in the blade materials of the high performance jet - engine.

Under the guidance of Rong Ke, a casting expert of China, a nickel base or iron—nickel base casting alloy series was developed including K1, K3, K5, K6, K12, K14, K17 and K19. Of them the K14 iron—nickel base alloy was an desirable material for turbine vanes due to its simple composition and exclusion of rare and noble elements, which suited China's resources situation. Compared with nickel base alloys K1 and K12, its nickel and chromium contents were respectively reduced by 30—40% and 20—30% and its strength and allowable operating temperature exceeded those of K12 by 49 MPa and 50 ℃ respectively.

In 1968 the vaccum melting equipment for the directional solidification alloy was built and a directional solidification and single crystal alloy series such as DZ3, DZ4, DZ22, DZ17G, DZ38G and DD3 were developed. In 1986 the first stage net shape casting hollow turbine blade made of directional solidification alloy was successfully manufactured for a new engine. It was a breakthrough in the blade manufacturing technology in China. In comparison with the conventional casting blade this blade had an increase of 50 ℃ in the allowable metal temperature. Compounded with a reduction 300 ℃ in the blade surface temperature it reached the advanced technological level of the 1980s in the world.

In order to meet the requirements of high thrust—weight ratio engines the development activities in more advanced directional solidification, single crystal and powder metallurgy superalloys and mechanical alloying superalloys are under way and preliminary achievements have been gained.

Titanium alloy is widely used in the aeroengines. As early as 1956 the Titanium Alloy Laboratory, with Professor Yan Minggao—— an expert in metal physics as its director, was established in the Aeronautical Materials Research Institute. Now it can not only develop both the wrought titanium alloy and casting titanium alloy, but also produce the precise castings of titanium alloy in compliance with the international aerospace standard, and has made a great deal of achievements over the past thirty and more years.

In the development of a new engine started in 1978, the development of TC11 titanium superalloy became a major challenge, which made up 13% of the structure weight of the engine. Research institutes, metallurgical plants, aeroengine factories and related universities and colleges were organized to tackle this key problem. Through a three years' joint effort, problems associated with the metal melting, forming and die forging of the compressor disk as well as the metallographic structure and property were solved. Compressor disks made of this alloy were successfully manufactured on high velocity hammer forging machine and explosive die forging machine. In the meantime the Fushun Steel Plant and the Baoji Non—ferrous Material Fabrication Factory manufactured the TC11 titanium discuses and the Southwest Aluminium Fabrication Factory the TC11 titanium compressor disks. This breakthrough in the materials not only reduced the import of materials and in turn saved the foreign currency, but also promoted the material technology and the export of titanium forgings to foreign countries including the United States.

Through the fabrication of titanium compressor disks and blades and their operational tests on several engine the die forging technology for titanium disks and the die forging and high speed extrusion technologies for blades were mastered. In addition the sub—β forging technology was developed for the titanium alloy, with which the titanium forgings of basket—type structure could be made. This structure raised the hot strength and fracture resistance of the forgings under high temperature and heavy load conditions. The sub—β forging technology marked a new height in titanium forging technology in China.

In the casting titanium, ZT3 and ZT4 were developed and used to make the compressor casing of a new engine. As a result the engine weight was reduced by 19.5 kg, the material utilization rate raised from 7% to 30% and the corresponding amount of machining decreased nearly 1.5 times, in turn gaining payoffs both in the engine performance and economy.

2. Engine Manufacturing Technology

New structures and materials must be incorporated in modern aeroengines if higher thrust, lower weight and longer life are required. This in turn needs new manufacturing technologies for air cooled structure, titanium alloy structure, special welding, special manufacturing, special coating and so on.

The air cooled structures are incorporated on the highest temperature parts and components of the aeroengines such as combustors and turbine blades and thousands of small holes or hollow passages must be made on these superalloy structural parts. Hence the manufacturing technology is a key element in the engine production. In the late 1960s a comparative study on the electrochemical machining, electric spark machining and laser processing as the alternatives for small hole manufacturing was carried out. First an electric pulse machine and its brush—type electrode was developed. With this machine 2,105 small holes of 0.5 mm diameter were made on the flame tube of the WP7A engine and an air cooling film was formed over its inner side, thus doubling the operating life of the flame tube. Later a laser processing research team developed a special equipment and made small diameter holes into the turbine blades of WS6 turbofan engine. The mean metal temperature of the blade was reduced by 300—330 ℃. Two prizes of the National Science Convention were awarded to the above—mentioned achievements. In 1985 the film cooling holes of small diameter and high precision were made into the first stage turbine blades with good quality and no reject.

For machining the blade dovetail, the Aeronautical Precision Machinery Research Institute and engine factories developed an emery wheel and diamond wheel used for the creep feed grinder and completed the processing parameter test. The creep feed grinder was designed on our own in 1980 and then improved for several times. Now a series of creep feed grinders are available for machining the blade dovetails of various engines.

The electric chemical machining (ECM) for titanium alloy is a key point of the research activities in the manufacturing technology. The major progresses in this area were as follows: the blade of WP6 engine were successfully machined by ECM; the manufacturing process from die forging of the blank to direct polishing by ECM was realized for the titanium blade; and the titanium integral disk of WS9 engine and the convection cooling passage in the turbine blade of WP7 engine were

Fig.88　The superplastic formed titanium sample parts

made by ECM. In addition the combined superplasticity forming—diffusion bonding technology of the titanium alloy was developed, which extended the application of this alloy.

In the engine the thin wall structure is mainly applied to the compressor disk. The twin face hydraulic tracing lathe and corresponding processing technique can be used for machining the compressor disk with a wall thickness of 0.17 mm. The compressor disk of the Spey turbofan engine manufactured with the imported twin face tracing lathe could not meet the accuracy requirements but the disk manufactured with the Chinese-designed machine could. Now the latter machines are widely used by the engine factories of China.

Welding is playing an important role in the aircraft and engine production and has become a special welding technology. Its research scope includes the weld properties of metal materials, the welding process and equipment for structure parts, the test method for weld property and so on. Successes were made in the longitudinal seam welding for the engine cylindric parts, the automatic argon arc welding for the flanges of engine cylindric parts and suspended welding for thin cylindric parts. On the basis of these achievements and the mechanisms of welding stress and deformation developed by Guan Qiao, a welding expert, the welding deformation on the thin cylindric parts of aircraft and engines were successfully controlled. Important progress was also made in the high temperature brazing. In development of a new engine it was required to braze a porous seal of powder metallurgical material on the turbine blade shroud. The melted brazing filler metal could penetrate into the seal and then the sealing would be affected if the conventional brazing was used. A unique foretreatment processing was developed, which could prevent the liquid brazing filler metal from being sucked into the seal. Thus a key problem associated with the engine development was solved. Thanks to the high temperature brazing filler metal and the new constant-temperature diffusion treatment technique, the remelting temperature of the welding seam was raised, which facilitated the manufacture of the directional solidification hollow casting blade. In addition the electron beam welding was studied and high voltage electron beam welding machine built. A micro beam plasma welding process was developed by a research team led by engineer Ding Peifan, with which the 0.1 mm thick parts could be welded.

Main functions of the special coatings on the engine parts are to enhance the thermal stability, corrosion resistance, abrasive resistance and sealing effectiveness and, in turn elongate their operating lives and improve the engine performance. In 1956 the research activities in the high temperature enamel coating began. After 1961 the W-2, V-1000 and EV-300 coatings were developed in succession. Of them the W-2 high temperature enamel coating was the first protective coating developed and produced in China. It had excellent antioxygenic and corrosion-resistant capabilities and were used for making the combustor, ignitor, afterburner flameholder and variable flap of the nozzle of several engine types. In the late 1970s and the early 1980s the detonation spraying and associated equipment were developed, with which the high temperature and room temperature abrasive-resistant coatings as well as abrasive-resistant seal and thermal coatings could be made. The lives of such coated parts could be raised by several times to several dozens of times. In the meantime the plasma sprayed coatings such as the cobalt-tungsten, nickel-chromium-boron-silicon plus titanium carbide and tungsten-cobalt carbide coatings were applied to the turbine and fan blades of aeroengines with good results. Several coatings were further developed for the seals of the compressor and turbine casings and as a result the turbine exhaust temperature was reduced by 13—14 ℃, thrust increased and specific fuel consumption lowered by 0.8—1.0%. A thermal coating with nickel—aluminium as primer and aluminium trioxide as upper layer raised the life of the combustor burner of an engine by more than 100%. The GP—80 high energy plasma spraying equipment developed in the late 1970s was awarded the national golden dragon prize. The plasma spraying developed within MAI was popularized to other economy fields in 28 provinces and municipalities.

Section 3   Precision Alloy and Precision Machining Technology

1. Precision Alloy

The precision alloy, i.e. the functional metal material, is a metal or alloy with special physical properties. It can transform the values in optics, acoustics, magnetics and thermodynamics as well as pressure, displacement, angle, weight, speed and acceleration into electric signals, or transform the value of one physical property into that of another, hence performing the functions of the energy and signal sensing, transformation and transmission. The precision alloy includes magnetic alloy, elastic alloy, expansion alloy, thermal bimetal, resistance alloy, electric contact material, measurement alloy and so on. They are used for making aircraft instruments, electric and microelectronic equipments and automatic control equipments and are indispensable for the compact, integrated and digital automatic control system and electronic equipment of the aircraft.

The research activities in the precision alloy began in 1958 when the first instrument alloy research section was established in the Aeronautical Materials Research Institute. It developed the wires, belts and tubes from 11 noble metals such as platinium—iridium and palladium—iridium. The Kunming Noble Metal Research Institute undertook to produce the noble metals for the aviation industry and became the first research and production base for the noble metals.

According to its natural resources China developed the gold base alloy to gradually replace the platinium—iridium and palladium—silver alloys. In April 1966 the fine wires, bars and thin sheets of gold base alloy were successfully substituted for those of platinium base and palladium base alloys in 31 components of 17 products manufactured by six factories.

The purified smelt—casting technology for platinium—iridium alloy was developed to eliminate its metallurgical defects such as bubbles, lamination and inclusion. With the advantages such as good stability and repeatability this advanced technology was widely used in the noble metal production, resulting in the improved material quality, product reliability and material utilization.

Through nearly thirty years' effort a complete series of precision alloys were developed and produced in China and the aviation industry's need for this metal was met.

2. Precision Machining Technology

The precision manufacturing technology has a very important position in the production of aircraft instrument, accessory, electric equipment and control equipment. Some products and parts have special manufacturing specifications, e.g. a concentricity allowance of 0.5 μm for the thin wall floating cylinder and vibration cylinder of several dozens of micrometers thickness and a micro—unevenness allowance of 0.05 μm for the spherical dynamic pressure support made of pure beryllium and sprayed with antiabrasive material. The machining accuracy is not only required in the dimension, but also in the form and position, which are more difficult to control. Special equipments and toolings were developed for machining such parts with unique specifications. Relatively advanced special equipments developed in the 1950s and the early 1960s were: 62—type universal profile grinder, precision double—face lathe, two-axis and four—axis precision com-

Fig.89 The four—axis precision combined borer

Fig.90 The four—station combined machine

bined borers, six—station multi—function combined machine, 12—station precision combined automatic machining line, four—station combined machine, extraprecision machine for the floating ball manufacturing, precision gyro dynamic balancing machine, dynamic balancing machine for the rotor of micromotor, laser automatic balancing machine and so on. In addition some precision toolings were also made such as tooling microscope, 1″ goniometer, interferometer, precision goniometer, optical index head, "0" grade worm wheel and "0" grade leading screw. For machining the precision capsule components, a bench—type low—voltage electric beam welding machine was made and it became the first electric beam welding machine exported from China.

Achievements were also made in the optical technology and related equipment. In the early 1960s the 10" optical index head developed by the Precision Machinery Research Institute was exported and later came out a series of instruments and equipments such as optical filing machine and two—coordinate non—circular gear inspection instrument.

A very high accuracy can be achieved of the assembly, installation and measurement of aircraft, missile and large equipment if the optical instruments such as the alignment projector, plumbing mirror and transit square are used for establishing a reference line or point. The laser alignment projector was developed in the early 1970s and used for the installation of aircraft assembly jig in 1975. The optical tooling rule developed in 1982 was used for the installation and adjustment of large facilities in the space and nuclear industries with good results. These two achievements were awarded the National Science Convention prize and the national prize for science invention respectively.

Section 4 Aeronautical Materials Test and Inspection Technologies

The damage tolerance design criteria began to be gradually implemented in designing metal material parts and components to prevent catastrophic failure and ensure flight safety. Therefore it is required that besides the material data of physical property, chemical property, mechanical property and corrosion—resistant property, other material data should be provided, particularly the data of fracture toughness, initial crack and crack propagation rate under the simulated operation condition. In order to obtain and provide all these data, various tests must be conducted on the aeronautical materials, test techniques to simulate the operation conditions developed and various material property handbooks and standards prepared. Professor Yan Minggao began to study the mechanism of the strengthening of superalloy and the fatigue fracture of metal and made important achievements in the application of the aeronautical materials and the troubleshooting and life extension of the aero products. Under his guidance and based on tests as well as experiences from foreign countries, the "Test Methods for the Fatigue Crack Propagation Rates of Metal Materials" and the "Fatigue Crack Propagation Rate Handbook for the Aeronautical Metal Materials" were prepared. These documents provided the aircraft design, production and operation departments with the basic data for the damage tolerance design and fatigue crack propagation rate measurement. Professor Yan Minggao was elected the chairman of the council of the Fifth International Material Mechanical Behavior Conference.

The Aeronautical Materials Research Institute studied and worked out the "Test Methods of Plane Strain Fracture Toughness of Metal Materials" for promoting the damage tolerance design and new material application and on the basis of the accumulated data prepared the

"Aeronautical Metal Materials Fracture Toughness Handbook and Data Collection". Through fatigue tests this institute also prepared the "Aeronautical Metal Materials Fatigue Property Handbook", which filled the gaps in this field in China. In order to get reliable data, test pieces were made in same shape and same way, the dynamic loads of the material testing machines were strictly corrected and test methods and data processing were unified according to the concrete conditions of China. The mid−value life of the intermediate life range with a 95% confidence was measured with the group−test method and the fatigue life of the long life range measured with the raising and falling method. So the fatigue property curves obtained were reliable and they were put into use. These curves played an important role in facilitating the fatigue test and research, and were very valuable to the aircraft design, life determination and life extension as well as the material research.

The research activities in the interaction between metal creep and fatigue and the high temperature fracture were carried out for the material selection and life prediction in the aeroengine design and development. These activities included the creep fatigue tests of nine commonly−used materials for different duration, analyses on the mixed mode damage and cycle intensifying mechanisms, design of the creep / fatigue mixed mode testing machine and the test and research on the creep crack propagation for five superalloys.

The tests on the corrosion resistance to atmospheric environment and aging resistance of metal and non−metallic materials were conducted to evaluate the general property of the materials and verify the results and methods of the accelerated test. From 1957 several atmospheric environment test stations were established in Hainan, Nanchang, Beijing, Shenyang and Qinghai and tests on the environmental adaptability of materials were carried out. The Bei − jing Atmospheric Environment Test Station developed three test methods including the continuous sampling method for measuring the hydrogen nitride, sulfur dioxide and salt particle contents in the atmosphere. In 1983 this station was designated as the national class atmospheric environment test station.

Correct determination of the aging resistance of rubber is a prerequisite for predicting the operation life of a rubber product. The more than ten years' atmospheric environment aging test on more than 10 rubber materials and rubber products were simultaneously conducted in Hainan, Nanchang, Beijing, Shenyang and Chengdu and accelerated aging tests were correspondingly carried out. Based on the test results, storage life and operation life were determined for various rubber products. The storage life of domestic rubber products determined through tests was elongated by 2−−3 years in comparison to that in the original specification and the output of rubber products of a factory has increased by 1.5−−4.0 times.

In order to ensure the material and product quality a great amount of research activities were carried out in the nondestructive inspection. Some advanced inspection techniques and methods were learned and used, such as the eddy current inspection, penetrative inspection, radiographic inspection, ultrasonic inspection, acoustic emission inspection, infrared inspection, liquid crystal inspection, laser holography and ultrasonic holography.

Chapter XV　Research in Flight Test Technology

Flight tests of the aircraft, powerplant and airborne equipment are conducted under the real flight conditions. Only through the flight test can be finally verified the new concepts and technologies and the results of the ground simulated tests, can be checked and fulfilled the operational specification and airworthiness requirements of an aviation product and can be provided the operating envelope for safe and reliable operation. The flight test includes research flight test and evaluation flight test. It is an essential phase for certification of new aircraft and other aero products, an important foundation for development of aeronautical technologies, and also one of the three principal means for aerodynamics research.

Fig.91　Li Xiannian visiting the Flight Test Research Institute

Superior flight test pilots are needed for flight test because of its airborne nature. The flight test pilot is required to have more aeronautical knowledge than other pilots. He must be highly skilled, indomitable and devoted himself to the aviation cause. Through the past thirty years' flight test practices a good number of heroic flight test pilots were trained and tempered. In new aircraft flight tests Lu Mingdong was brave in doing highly difficult maneuvers and exploring the boundary of flight envelope. He has made great contributions and won many prizes. Wang Ang and Hua Jun were awarded the title of "Scientific Flight Test Hero" and the first—class hero medal of the People's Liberation Army for their outstanding achievements in flight test.

They assiduously studied aeronautical theories and hardly practised flying skills and so could keep calm and take resolute actions when serious failures occurred to save the aircraft and thereafter provide the clues of the failure to aircraft designers and related research staff.

Various measurement means are also needed for flight test and real—time monitoring and data acquisition should be made during the test. Through the more than thirty years' construction the Flight Test Research Institute and flight test stations in factories have come into a moderate size. The institute now has owned more than 50 flight—beds, necessary ground equipment and relatively advanced airborne measurement and ground processing system as well as a comparatively complete flight support system and control system. Since its founding the institute has accomplished evaluation flight tests and scientific flight tests of nearly 30 aircraft, more than 20 engines and a lot of electronic, fire control and life escape products for the State. They developed a set of flight test methods and had the capability of conducting the relatively difficult and dangerous flight tests.

The flight test can be generally categorized into the test for specific research subject and the test for flight test method.

Section 1   Flight Test for Specific Research Subject

Flight test for specific research subject is conducted on a test object according to its specified technical requirements. The Flight Test Research Institute has accomplished extensive flight tests on various subjects posed in aircraft development, production and operation and a great deal of achievements has been achieved.

1.   Model Free—flight

Model free—flight is a complement to the wind tunnel test and flight test and it has become an important means of aerodynamic experimental research. During the tests, aircraft (or other vehicle) models will be intentionally delivered into the air. It features low cost, less time and low risk, and particularly suits some dangerous tests such as stall, spinning, flutter, highly maneuver and envelope boundary flight, and it is often used for the tests, the conditions of which are difficult to be simulated in the wind tunnel. Under the guidance of senior engineer Ge Ping more than 40 research subjects of model free—flight were completed for more than 10 aircraft types and versions. In technology the qualitative measurement of parameter gave way to the quantitative of some parameters and then to the quantitative of all parameters; in test method the remote controlled airborne recording was changed into the remote control and telemetry; in remote control method the manipulation was turned into the proportional control; and in complexity the test subject was developed from the simple spinning to the stall characteristics and then to the stall / spinning characteristics, thus reaching a higher technological level. In addition the model free—flight test for low speed dynamic derivatives was successfully carried out and the rocket—boosted model free—flight test was started. More than 20 research subjects were conducted on a modified carrier of the free—flight model, including the delivery test of external wing tank and external fuselage tank from the carried J—7 model, the delivery test of the A—bomb model and the carried intercontinental ballistic missile model, and satisfactory results were obtained for all the tests.

2. Spin Flight Test

The forces acting on an aircraft are balanced when it is in steady flight. The aircraft will lose the balance due to lift decrease, drag increase and pressure redistribution when its angle of attack exceeds the critical value. As a result, vibrations on the airframe, rudder and tail and then stall occur, leading to the autorotating and rapid descending of the aircraft. During a relatively long period in the aviation history many pilots got killed from sudden spin and its difficult recovery. To verify an aircraft's spin recovery capability one must intentionally force the aircraft into a spin and test it under various spin conditions. This is a very dangerous test. After the 1970s the research activities in the spin theory and its prediction method were carried out in China and technical papers such as the "Investigation into the Aircraft Stall and Spin Theories and their Prediction Methods" and the "Stall and Spin Movement Prediction of the Large Aircraft" were completed. A set of spin recovery methods were developed through a great number of spin tests on JJ—5 and JJ—6 aircraft, with a total of 3,782 spin—enterings and recoverings in 512 flight sorties.

3. Engine Flight Test

The task of engine flight test is to measure the engine thrust and specific fuel consumption and check its stable operation margin and air start capability. The engine flight test and the ground simulated altitude test are complements to each other. Under the guidance of senior engineer Shan Fengtong a Soviet Tu—16 bomber was modified into a flying test bed and 13 engine types and versions were tested on it.

4. Research in the Influence of Weapon Launch on Engine Performance

The engine shutdown may be caused by launching airborne weapons including cannon, rocket and air to air missile and it would not only bungle the chance of winning a battle, but also endanger the flight safety. In the mid 1960s the Flight Test Research Institute began the works on this subject. On four aircraft types, five engine types were tested with various weapons being launched, their influences on engine operation and the cause of the engine shutdown studied and a great amount of data measured, providing a scientific basis for preventing the engine from surge and shutdown during the launching of weapons. Research work was also done for the preventative measures of engine shutdown during the derated throttle operation, emergency starting and encountered starting. This research institute used a flying test bed with a missile simulator to create the engine intake temperature distortion so that the engine could be forced into surge and shutdown and the operating procedures of the shutdown—preventing unit and its reliability be checked. The surge—inducing method and dynamic measurement system were developed and a breakthrough in the accurate control of the surge—entering time was made, laying a basis for the further research in engine operation stability.

5. Weightlessness Test

The weightlessness tests are needed for the development, production and operation of aerospace products. In order to create a weightless environment the load factor of a test aircraft must not exceed $\pm$ 0.2 g and 5—6 parabolic flight segments must be flown in a flight sortie with a minimum weightless time of 30 seconds each. For an unmodified aircraft the parabolic flight segment and "weightless pagoda" can create a very short duration of weightlessness and the above—mentioned requirement can not be met. The Flight Test Research Institute modified an aircraft for weightless test with emphasis on the fuel and lubrication systems so that the modified aircraft could reliably operate under the weightless condition for a long period. To keep the weightlessness for a long period, the pilot has to control the aircraft in an abnormal way when the aircraft is in the parabolic flight segment, and the pilot must not make any erroneous control otherwise a catastrophe will come. The Chinese test pilots splendidly fulfilled these tasks with 5—6 weightlessness parabolic flight segments per flight sortie, three load factors within $\pm$ 0.2 g and a maximum weightlessness duration of 49.5 seconds. These achievements not only made contribution for the space flight but also laid a foundation for the low load factor test, flowing characteristics test and low load factor shake—damping test of the liquid propellant system.

6. Air Ejection Test

After the ground ejection test and rocket sled ejection test the air ejection test should be done for the aircraft ejection escape system. The first special ejection—test aircraft was a modified Soviet Il—28 light bomber and then a high speed ejection—test aircraft was built. It could undertake the air ejection test for developing the rocket ejection technology.

7. Flight Test of Avionics and Fire Control System

In the avionics the emphasis of research activities was put on the signal characteristics of target. In the early 1970s the measurement of the radar cross—section area of target in "S" frequency band was conducted on the J—5 and J—6 aircraft and then the transient measurement of the vertically polarized radar cross—section area of target in "X" frequency band was done for the J—6, H—6 and J—7 aircraft. Through measurements the radar cross—section areas of several aircraft in the same frequency band were obtained, providing the data for radar design, target identification and evaluation flight test. In the meantime a set of flight test methods were also developed. In addition the research activities for specific subjects were carried out such as the current measurement of static discharge, multifunction antenna, flight test of the range and angle finding accuracy in "ground to air" simulation experiment and flight test method of the radar tracking accuracy of the fighter as well as special tests on the fire control system required by the Government. The Flight Test Research Institute owned three avionics test aircraft, which could be used for the flight test of airborne equipments such as communication and navigation equipment, radar and flight instrument.

As the research activities in flight test developed, the flight measurement technology was significantly improved. The computerized real—time processing of the flight test data and the ground data acquisition and processing were realized so that the test and measurement capabilities were greatly increased in the number of measured parameters, frequency band, measurement accuracy and data processing speed. This made it possible to record 500 pulse—code modulation (PCM) parameters and 144 high frequency signals such as vibration simultaneously on an aircraft and to real—timely monitor about 150 parameters from the ground equipment.

To facilitate the flight test technology the "Flight Test Handbook" was compiled. It was a Chinese flight test directory and played a positive role in the research activities.

Section 2   Research in Flight Test Method

In China the research activities in the flight test method began with learning and mastering the foreign test technologies and theories and then embarked on the independent development of the flight test method on the basis of the accumulated experiences in flight tests.

In the 1960s the flight speed and climbing performance of the CJ—6 aircraft were determined with the differential—correction method. Then the J—5 aircraft was tested to explore new flight test methods. Through a lot of flight tests, the conventional flight test method for single research subject was thoroughly mastered and, thanks to the studies on the relatively advanced dynamic flight test technology, the synthesized characteristics—curve method for determining the synthesized aircraft performance was also in hand.

Controllability and stability are main aspects of the aircraft flight performance and they should be quantitatively evaluated through the flight test. In the early 1960s, for solving the problems associated with the directional stability of the J—8 aircraft, the J—7 aircraft was tested to determine its directional stability derivative and aileron efficiency and then its control derivative was derived with the frequency response method. In 1973 the Newton—Raphson method commonly used in the world was studied and used to gain the dynamic derivative which could not be obtained from the wind tunnel test. It was a new digital method to derive the aerodynamic derivatives through the computer matching of aircraft transient response. After the initial values and weights had been determined, this method was successfully applied to the flight test for determining aerodynamic derivatives on the J—6 flight simulator. Through the tests the static and dynamic derivatives and control derivative were obtained and progress in the flight test for determining the aerodynamic derivatives was made.

The task of flight flutter test is the prerequisite to verify the flight envelope at low altitudes. Flutter is a dangerous vibration mode and the aircraft will breakdown in a few seconds if flutter occurs. The critical speed for flutter has to be determined through flight test since the flutter prediction can not be accurately made with existing analytical and computational means. In 1963 the development of vibration—exciting equipment began under the leadership of senior engineer Zhang Kerong and in 1971 the first flutter test was made on the J—8 aircraft equipped with a small rocket for vibration—exciting. The aircraft was intentionally vibrated, its dynamic characteristics was measured and analyzed and the damping characteristic curves for some important structures were plotted. Then the critical flutter speed was extrapolated out of these curves and reliable data gained. Later this vibration—exciting equipment was successfully used in the flutter flight test of the J—6 aircraft. Thus a new method for flutter analysis was developed.

Strength and load measurements in flight are needed for the certification flight test of a new aircraft. An airborne camera was used to measure the curves of wing elastic deformation, the wing maneuvering loads and the application point of their resultant loads in flight were measured with the ground—loaded strain gauge method, landing gear load and load spectrum of various aircraft were measured with the stain gauge method and gravity center overload method, and aircraft's loads and moments under various load conditions were measured with the strain load—measuring method.

In the flight test research of the helicopter, successes were made in determining the polar curve of rotor blade, multivariant regressive analysis technology of the test data, determination of the helicopter aerodynamic derivatives with the Kalman filtering technique and so on.

In the flight test method and measurement technology for engine flight characteristics the engine thrust in flight was measured with the "internal measuring method" and then the swinging rake probe. In the early 1970s the in—flight negative thrust measurement technology was studied and success was made in measuring the positive and negative thrusts of the engine in flight. In addition the performance conversion method was explored on several typical engines and feasible performance conversion method was obtained. The problems associated with the evaluation flight test for the flight performance characteristics of various aeroengines were then solved.

The research activities in the environment—airworthiness, environmental test method for the engine, flight test method for the life escape equipment and ground and flight simulation test technologies were carried out with positive results.

Chapter XVI   Research in Aeronautical Fundamental Technologies

Aeronautical science and technology information, measurement, metrology and inspection and standardization are the important fundamental technologies and an integral part of the aeronautical R&D.

Section 1   Science and Technology Information

Aviation industry is one of the industrial departments which established their special science and technology information organizations in the earliest time. In 1956 the Aeronautical Science and Technology Information Institute was established on the basis of the Document Translation and Edition Section of the Bureau of Aviation Industry. The science and technology information sections were also erected in factories, research institutes and universities and colleges. Over the past thirty and more years a great deal of valuable information were provided for the formulation of long–term development plan, decision–making, production, R& D, technical import and foreign trade in different development phases of the aviation industry. The aeronautical science and technology information system played its consultative and advisory role indeed.

1. Evolution of Aeronautical Science and Technology Information System

In the aviation industry seven technical information networks were organized for different specialities, i.e. aircraft, engine, instrument, electric equipment, accessory, life escape system and test equipment and measurement. The information institute and information sections constituted a complete aeronautical science and technology information system with multichannel, multilevel and multifunction. It owned several thousands of professional information staff. About 4.5 million pieces of technical documentation were collected through various channels such as procurement, exchange, request, entrusted collection, exhibition, technical seminar, international academic symposium, international cooperation and technical achievement evaluation. Among them were 0.67 million pieces in the Aeronautical Science and Technology Information Institute covering technical books, document retrieval books, papers, audio and video materials and 2,416 magazines from China and abroad. Some modern equipments such as computers, duplicators, microfilm readers, audio and video equipment and printing machines were available for information research and service.

The document retrieval is the most important means to acquire the technical information.

In order to find out the needed document from the rapidly increasing storage of technical documents and books and utilize the information resources for technological progress and product renewal, a scientific document retrieval method, a computerized document retrieval system and a modern information transfer network are needed.

Over 140 document retrieval books are available in the documentation department of the Aeronautical Science and Technology Information Institute. The institute established two document retrieval systems: the card system and journal system, in which the title names of all the documents collected and stored by the institute and the abstracts of part of these documents were included. The annual amount of indexing was 17,000 titles. Beginning from 1971 a monthly retrieval journal "Indexes of Foreign Aeronautical Science and Technology Documentation" was published with about 1,200 index items each. In 1985 the "Abstracts of Aeronautical Science and Technology Documentation" was added to the retrieval journal series. In addition, this institute published the "Title List of Foreign Technical Documentation (Aeronautics and Astronautics)" as well as the title list, bulletin and specific subject index of the Chinese technical documentation non-periodically. The former was included in the national technical information journal series. Then a complete multichannel retrieval system was formed.

The document retrieval method used in the aeronautical science and technology information system was the thesaurus method, which was proposed and propagated by Yang Jinfu an aero information expert, who had foreseen the development trend of document retrieval methods and compared the merits and demerits among various retrieval methods. Under his leadership the preparation of the "Subject Headings of Aeronautical Science and Technology Documentation" lasted 14 years (1963—1977). It comprised more than 10,000 subject terms, totalling over 4 million Chinese characters. The normalized terms (i.e. subject terms) worthy of retrieval were listed according to their Chinese phonetic alphabetic order. Besides the advantages such as direct perception, good specificity and easy to learn, this book is convenient for input and output on the computer and can be used as a basis of the software system for the computerized retrieval. It blazed new trails in the document retrieval theory and architecture. The "Subject Headings of Aeronautical Science and Technology Documentation" was popularized in the aviation industry and included in the national thesaurus system in 1974. It was awarded the National Science Convention prize in 1978.

The electronic computer found its application in the document retrieval and good results were obtained in the computerized document retrieval for specific research subjects. On the Z-80 microprocessor a checking-for-duplication programme was developed, a documentation database established and an "English-Chinese and Chinese-English Subject Heading" prepared.

2. Aeronautical Publications

The aeronautical publications are an important medium for information transfer. Through adjustment, development and enhancement a complete aeronautical publication series was formed in different publishing cycles and for different readers. Some of the publications won the readers' praises for their comprehensive, correct and timely information.

A total number of 127 publications including 87 periodicals were edited and published by organizations in the aviation industry with an increasing circulation. The International Aviation (China) was issued to 10 countries and two regions. Its editorial department established exchange relations with editorial departments in Japan, the United Kingdom, Belgium, Switzerland, France and the United States as well as Hong Kong.

3. Aeronautical Information Research and Service

The task of the aeronautical information research is to provide users with valuable information. The aeronautical information research evolved through the following three phases:

a. Translating, editing and reporting of the technical documents, books and information;

b. Preliminary information research for specific subjects, which could only provide the valuable information obtained from foreign countries;

c. More advanced information research, which, through analysis and comparison, resulted in an information paper with valuable materials, findings and suggestions.

The information research staff paid attention to the three combinations in their work, i.e. combinations of the information analysis with the domestic needs, of the technical and economical analysis with the military strategic and tactic analysis, and of the qualitative analysis with the quantitative analysis. With the experiences accumulated they made significant progress in their synthetic analysis capability.

Over the past thirty and more years the Aeronautical Science and Technology Information Institute provided nearly 100 fundamental information documents such as yearbooks, handbooks, essentials and dictionaries and several thousands of the information papers on various subjects. From 1978 to 1983 it gained 35 information achievement prizes, among them were five prizes from the National Science Convention or the Defence Industry Office. In 1982, 53 information achievement prizes of MAI were awarded to the information sections of factories and research institutes

The aeronautical information research provides services in the following fields:

a. Formulation of development strategy, plan and programme;

b. Key technical problems emerged from the aeronautical R&D and production;

c. Technology import;

d. Improvement of enterprise management;

e. Factory's technical transform and technical innovation;

f. Non-aero production and application of the military technology to the civil production;

g. Fundamental reference books.

Main publications included more than 20 fundamental materials such as the "Reference Materials on the Development of Aeronautical Science and Technology" and the "Statistic Data Collection of Foreign Aviation Industries"; more than 50 handbooks such as the "Foreign

Aircraft Handbook" and the "Aeronautical Materials Handbook"; more than 10 directories such as the "Aircraft Designer's Directory" and the "Aircraft Strength Design Directory"; and 17 dictionaries such as the "Russian—Chinese Aeronautical Engineering Dictionary" and the "Science and Technology Dictionary of the Aviation Industry". These publications played an important role in the decision—making, aeronautical R&D and production.

To accommodate itself to the development of aviation industry, the aeronautical science and technology information community is striving for its equipment modernization, high efficiency management, high density storage, rapid transfer and high quality service, as well as its leading position in the science and technology information community of the country.

Section 2   Measurement Technology

With the development of modern electronic technology, fundamental changes have taken place in the measurement equipment and instrument itself. For example parts and elements are becoming modulars and monolithics, the measurement equipment and instrument are being given artificial intelligence and interfaces are being standardized. The measurement function also developed from the single channel and discrete measurement toward the full automatic measurement and control and the system emulation, i.e. the computer—based full automatic control and handling would be realized for the measurement and control equipment (e.g. transducer, data acquisition, processing and control, output peripheral equipment and terminal) as well as the environmental emulation and real—time control of the test equipment and test objects. This is of great significance for the aeronautical R&D and aviation industry as a whole.

During the copy or licence production period, most of the performance measurement technologies and equipment were imported and their capacities were limited and working conditions poor. Most of the nonelectric parameters were measured with the old mechanical measuring equipment except that the electric parameters were measured with the universal electric meter in a single—channel and discrete way. In the mid and later parts of the 1950s the resistance stress gauge and static and dynamic strain gauges developed by BIAA greatly promoted the material and structural strength test and research of the country. After the founding of the Flight Test Research Institute the measurement equipment was improved and the professional measurement staff reinforced. A number of transducers and equipments were copy produced and then improved. The development of the simulation and emulation technologies and associated equipment were also started. As a result China's first generation simulation turning table was produced and the second generation was in development. The development of FM tape recording system and airborne digital tape recording system used for flight test began in the mid and later parts of the 1960s. In 1967 a temperature data logger (200 channels and 400 samples per second) for the thermal strength test of aircraft and its components was successfully developed, paving a way to the measurement automatization in the aviation industry of China.

—370—

By the mid 1970s there had been four research institutes (the Precision Machinery Research Institute, the Metrology and Inspection Research Institute, the Aeronautical Manufacturing Technology Research Institute and the Flight Test Research Institute), two measurement equipment manufacture factories and 14 related organizations involved in the research, development and production of measurement technology or equipment, with about 4,000 professionals. A good amount of measurement equipment and instruments were successfully developed to meet the needs of the aeronautical R&D and the production. Some of them were rather advanced. For example two FM tape recording systems of quick—varying parameters and three PCM tape recording systems for slow—varying parameters were used in the flight tests of the Z—6 and Z—8 helicopters and the J—7 and J—8 fighters with good results. In addition the following equipment were also developed: the 10—point computer—based loading system for full—scale airframe fatigue test, low sampling speed and high accuracy multipurpose data logger (100 channels and 100 samples per second), rate turning table for precise gyro test, polar axis table and servo turning table, frequency response test rig, precise double—axis optical turning table, three—coordinate measurement machine, three—axis simulation turning table, universal high power electro—hydraulic vibration rig and mercury—free pressure gauge as well as a variety of transducers (including the wire strain gauge type, piezo—resistance type, null pressure—differential angle of attack type and small inertia atmospheric temperature type).

After entering the 1980s significant progresses were made in the application of small— and micro—computers and the integration of measurement and control in the aeronautical measurement and test. The SRC—2G high speed data acquisition system (12,000 samples per second), HSC—1000 data acquisition and control system (20,000 samples per second) and HSC—186 high speed data acquisition and control system (50,000 samples per second) were developed in succession. In the simulation and emulation system there were single—axis and three—axis hydraulic and electric turning tables in a series. The static and dynamic pressure simulators and negative load simulator played an active role in the performance test and measurement of the aircraft automatic control systems and accessories. In 1983 the first Chinese computer—controlled J—6 panoramic flight simulator was successfully evaluated and accepted and through its development many important achievements were made in the computerized control technology, software technology, six degrees of freedom hydraulic simulation system and optoelectronic vision simulation system. The emulation technologies of the aircraft systems also advanced with great strides and several system emulation facilities were built which were more realistic, accurate and close to real—time operation, such as for the flight control system emulation, dynamic emulation of the fire control system and three dimensional mixed real—time emulation of the infrared control system of the air—to—air missile. The wide application of emulation technology in the aeronautical R&D made it possible to reduce R&D cost, shorten R&D cycle and get more high level achievements. Significant progresses were also made in the measurement technologies for special test such as the microwave anechoic chamber test, electromagnetic compatibility test and anti—microvibration test.

Section 3   Metrology and Inspection Technology

The metrology and inspection technology is to deal with problems associated with the metrological value transfer, inspection and supervision and management and features its accuracy, uniformity and legality. Throughout the research, development and production it provides accurate and reliable data for verifying the basic theories and rationality and exactness of design method and ensures the quality and technical performance of products, components and parts. This technology makes the individual subsystems and different phases of an aeronautical system operate accurately, organically and coordinately in accordance with the expectant quantitative relation. So it is an important technical means for ensuring the overall quality control and obtaining the maximum economical payoffs.

1.   Establishment of Metrological System

In the early years of new China the metrological activities were gradually carried out to meet the requirements of the production development but suffered from lack of necessary technical management and regular transfer means of the metrological value. From 1953 rapid progress began to be made in the metrological activities within the defence industry. By 1955 a moderate scale metrological system had been established, which could transfer the metrological value step by step.

In 1961 the Metrology and Inspection Research Institute was formally founded. By 1962, through adjustment and reinforcement, a relatively complete metrological system had been formed including the length, temperature and mechanics metrologies. Then the electricity metrology was added to the system and the construction of the regional metrological stations over the country reinforced. The basic tasks of the Metrology and Inspection Research Institute are as follows:

a. Establish the metrological standards and transfer the metrological values (metrological center — 60 regional metrological stations — more than 100 metrological sections in the grassroots organizations of the aviation industry and other defence industries);

b. Evaluate measuring instruments;

c. Carry out the arbitral measurement.

2.   Role and Achievements of the Metrological Technology in the Aviation Industry

The metrological technology plays an important role in the aeronautical R&D and the production of aero products.

In aeronautical R&D, accurately calibrated measurement equipments are needed to obtain accurate and reliable data. The metrological values in common use are in force, pressure, vibration, temperature, length, flow rate, time, frequency, etc.

In material research activities such as composition, analysis and property test, the directly related metrological values are in force, pressure, temperature, mass, etc.

In production the metrological values associated with the machining precision and quality inspection include surface roughness, hardness, angle, flow rate, electrical parameters, etc.

The success probability of flight test mainly depends on the accuracy of the data measured on the ground, which in turn depends on the advance in the measurement and metrological technologies.

The development of the aeronautical measurement technology gave a great impetus to the metrological technology. The corresponding metrological standards should be established for new measurement techniques such as laser, microprocessor, holography and acoustic emission.

Over the past thirty and more years commonly—used 18 metrological standards (totalling 74 practical standards) in four categories (i.e. length, temperature, mechanics and electricity) and their

Fig.92 The rated shock wave tube dynamic pressure calibration device with a diameter of 100 mm

Fig.93 100 t standard material dynamometer

transfer system have been established and a certain amount of precise measurement equipment developed, such as the g—meter for ejection escape system, impact g—meter for missile, trajectory measuring equipment for helicopter rotor blade and digital diaphragm capsule displacement meter.

Section 4　Standardization

With the development of aviation industry a moderate scale standardization system was gradually established. The development of the standardization system also went through the transition from learning and importing the foreign standardizations to formulation of the Chinese ones. This system played an active role in shortening the product development cycle, ensuring the product quality, enhancing the economical payoff and finally promoting the development of aviation industry.

1.　Development of the Standardization of Aviation Industry

The development of the aviation industry's standardization went through following four phases.

a. Introduction of Soviet Standards

In 1953 the standardization activities, at first in the toolings, began on the basis of the imported Soviet standards. By 1957 altogether 809 standards on the cutting toolings and measuring instruments and 1,036 standards on the parts and assemblies of the toolings had been issued.

b. Formulation of Chinese Standards

In 1965 MAI began to formulate the basic standards and part and component standards. In 1968, the Government required that the Chinese standards should be formulated and implemented. Through several years' effort the standards issued by MAI were applied to the technical document for foreign assistance and Chinese technical documents were prepared for new aircraft development and production.

c. Restoring and Rectifying Old Standards and Formulating New Ones in an All-round Way

During the "great cultural revolution" the product quality was deteriorated due to the abolishment of rules and regulations. In 1972, according to the arrangement for raising the product quality set by the State Council, the necessary rules and regulations were restored or newly established and the aviation standardization work also began to restore and develop. In the same year an aviation standardization working conference was held, the corresponding regulation and plan were formulated, the "Aviation Standardization" magazine was initiated and the formulation of new standards was started. In order to meet the requirement of raising the quality of aero products, an all-round rectification and revision were conducted to more than 2,000 existing standards. Another aviation standardization working conference held in 1976 called for formulating a certain amount of standards to lay a foundation for establishing a complete and advanced standard system and realizing the product quality standardization, product seriation and part and component commonality. After the conference some organizations were assigned as the specialized agencies in charge of the standardization and related test respectively. They were furnished with test equipments, extensive research and test activities carried out and various standards formulated. Performance and quality standard developed from that of individual products to the performance standard and specification of aeronautical systems such as aircraft, engines and missiles, to provide the specifications for the tests of new aeronautical systems. The formulation of Chinese system specification marked a new development phase of the standardization in the country.

· d. Establishing the Aviation Standard System

The aviation standardization working conference held in 1981 decided to steadily establish the Chinese aviation standard system to meet the requirements of the development and production of new aircraft. Therefore various standards were formulated in an all-round way and the "Technical Standard System of the Aviation Industry" was prepared. On the basis of the product standard, the standards of aircraft system and its subsystem such as the structure were formulated. Through the analyses on related foreign military specifications the formulation of product specifications was set up and in addition the preliminary environment standard and specification were worked out. To meet the need of the transition from military production to civil production, the civil aircraft airworthiness regulations and standards as well as the standards of other non-aero products were laid down.

2. Role and Achievements of the Aviation Standardization

a. A standardization contingent was trained and brought up. Over the past twenty years the standardization sections have been established in most of the factories and research institutes under MAI, including five specialized agencies and 13 test stations and totalling more than 700 professionals. This professional contingent was trained through the formulation of new standards. For example over 300 technical staff members were organized to formulate three standards on aircraft electric motor and electric equipment and a great deal of test activities carried out. The ambient temperature measurements were conducted at various typical places throughout the country, e.g. Hailaer in the Northeast, Shanshan in the Northwest and Hainan in the South. As a result a large amount of data were obtained and the situation of applying mechanically foreign standards changed. Our capability of formulating standards was gradually raised through formulation of the toolings standards at first and then the basic standards, product standards and system specifications.

b. Nearly 140,000 standard documents were accumulated, laying a foundation for establishing a complete and advanced aviation standard system. Of the nearly 2,000 standards formulated on our own 30% reached the technical level of the world in the 1970s. A total of 126 achievement prizes were awarded, among them were 19 national prizes.

c. By 1986 more than 4,000 technical standards were available in MAI. In order to have a rational structure of the aviation technical standards and conduct the standardization activities orderly, the "Technical Standard System of the Aviation Industry" was prepared. It clearly defined the interrelationship between the structure and the system of the aviation technical standards, identified the gap between the Chinese standards and foreign advanced standards and indicated the direction for formulating standards in the future.

d. Good results were obtained from application of new standards to the development and production of new aircraft and other products. The "Aircraft Cockpit Red Light Illumination" standard substituted for the fluorescent illumination system in the Y-7, J-7III and J-8II aircraft. The "Water-vapourproof Barrier with Desiccant for Aircraft Auxiliary and Accessory Products" ministerial-level standard formulated on the basis of extensive test elongated the preservation period of the aircraft auxiliary and accessory products by 5—10 years. The aluminium alloy castings and magnesium alloy castings must be inspected for pinholes and microporosity respectively to ensure their quality. Through extensive test and production verification a classified standard for the pinhole and microporosity in the castings was formulated and it was listed in the aviation industry standards. With this standard the classification of a casting could be done without destroying the casting. It filled a blank in the inspection standards of the Chinese machine building industry. In the production tooling for "zero batch" of the J-7 aircraft three million pieces of standard parts were used and the manufacture cycle was shortened by six and half months.

e. Various specifications for the aeronautical science and technology were formulated. In 1972, based on the investigation into domestic and foreign technical documents and the statistics of examples, the "Strength Specification of Normal Land-based and Water-based Aircraft" was prepared and published and the situation of following foreign specifications in this field was changed. In the mid 1970s China's first "Flying Quality Specification" was compiled through five years' effort of pilots and flight dynamics research personnel under the guidance of Professor Zhang Guilian of BIAA. It provided a guide for studying the aircraft control safety. In 1984 the "Military Aircraft Strength Specification" was also compiled. Based primarily on the life cycle design and secondly on the damage tolerance design, it stipulates that the damage tolerance design and ground airframe strength test should be carried out for the main structures which are very critical to the aircraft integrity and crew safety. This specification could be used not only as a guide to aircraft engineering development but also as a basis for the analysis and test on fatigue and damage tolerance characteristics. In addition a great deal of research activities in the test methods for measuring the basic properties of related materials were carried out and corresponding standard test methods were developed and issued as the state standards or ministerial-level standards.

In 1980 the formulation of the "Aircraft Engine General Specifications" began, including the "Aircraft Turbojet and Turbofan Engine General Specification", the "Aircraft Turboshaft and Turboprop Engine General Specification" and the "Aircraft Gas Turbine Powerplant Flight Test Specification". These specifications were formulated with reference to the related foreign specifications and the experiences obtained from the development, flight test, production and operation of turbojet, turboprop and turboshaft engines in China. The "Aircraft Engine

General Specifications" is an important basis for the engineering development, operational development and quality control of the turbojet, turboprop and turboshaft engines.

More specifications for the aircraft engines were also formulated such as the "Correction Specification of the Effect of Atmospheric Humidity on the Engine Performance Measured in Ground Test", the "Correction Specification of the Effect of Atmospheric Temperature on the Engine Performance Measured in Ground Test" and the "Correction Specification of the Engine Performance Measured in Simulated Altitude Test". These specifications played a positive role in promoting the development of aircraft engines of China.

f. International exchange activities were carried out. After China had joined the International Standardization Organization (ISO) in 1978, foreign experts were invited to give lectures, and foreign standards were introduced in this country, such as the U.S. military standards and specifications, the U.S. SAE space standard, the European civil aviation electronics organization standard and the space standard of the Federal Republic of Germany. Through analysing the foreign standards the "Aviation Industry Technical Standard System" was improved and some major technical problems were solved. Since 1981 MAI sponsored the 10th Technical Conference of Hydraulic System and Assembly Subcommittee and the 7th International Conference of Aeronautical Materials and Manufacturing Technology Subcommittee of Aerospace Technology Committee of ISO in Beijing and organized six technical seminars on the standardization topics such as aircraft hydraulic system, high temperature flame—resistant hydraulic oil and aircraft engine.

172. Beijing Institute of Aeronautics and Astronautics

173. Aircraft on show at the Chinese Aviation Museum

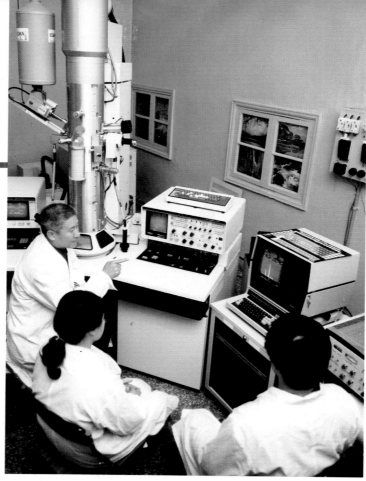

174. Analysing a metal material with an eletron microscope
which can amplify 800,000 times

175. A laboratory of the aircraft department of BIAA

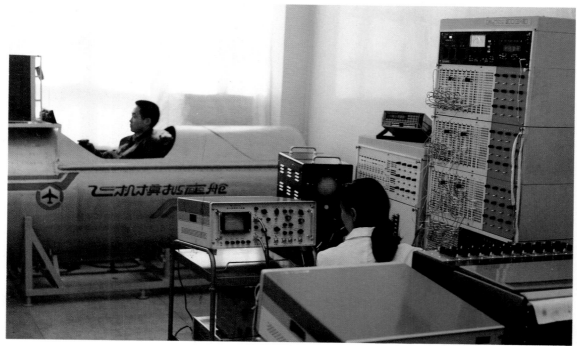

176. A bird's eye view of the North-West
Polytechnic University

177. A linguistic laboratory of NPU

CATIC
GEC *Avionics* Projects Ltd
co-operation

F-7m

GEC-Marconi

SEEING

...IS BELIEVING

178. A NPU student with a parachute glider made by themselves

179. A nationwide youngster's summer camp at Yan'an sponsored by NPU

180. The Library of the Nanjing Aeronautical Institute

181. A wind tunnel with two
test sections at NAI

182. High altitude environment test

183. Summer Campers
visiting aircraft

184. Awards to winners in a national youth
contest on aviation knowledge

185. A diploma of honour
for the magazine
Aerospace Knowledge

PART FIVE

Educational undertaking, capital construction, management system, quality control, ideology and style construction of staff and workers and international trade and academic exchange, all have two sides: spiritual and material. They are the important parts of aviation industry. They played an important role in the 35 years' development of aviation industry. So, it's quite necessary for us to present their histories and achievements, and summarize and analyze their features and main experiences.

Chinese Society of Aeronautics is a transdepartment academic society under the leadership of Chinese Association for Science and Technology. It is affiliated to the Ministry of Aviation Industry. Its activities will also be reported in this part.

Chapter XVII   Educational Undertaking of Aeronautics

Section 1   General Description

After liberation, the aviation industry of China had an eager demand for qualified scientists, technicians and managers and skilled workers. But there were only a few qualified persons from the old China remained. So it was a pressing task to initiate the aeronautical education and educate personnel with great effort. A guide principle was set up at the initiation of the aviation industry of new China, that was, to build up factories as well as colleges and pay attention to production as well as education of personnel.

Aeronautical universities and colleges were built up on the basis of adjusting former aeronautical colleges and faculties of several universities. The first step of adjustment to the former aeronautical faculties was taken in 1951. The aeronautical faculties of Qinghua University, Beiyang (North Sea of China) University, Northwest Institute of Technology and Xiamen University were merged into the Aeronautical College of Qinghua University; The Yunnan University's aeronautical faculty was combined with the Sichuan University's; and the aeronautical faculties of the Central Polytechnic Training School and North China University were merged into the Aeronautical Faculty of the Beijing Institute of Technology. In December this year, Premier Zhou Enlai instructed that all factories should run training classes to train urgently needed professional personnel wherever conditions exist. And aeronautical universities and colleges should also be initiated. In May 1952 the "Resolution on the Construction of Aviation Industry" was passed by the Military Commission of CCCPC, which decided to make preparations for setting up aeronautical institutes based on all former aeronautical faculties. Before long, a further adjustment of the aeronautical faculties was made. In 1952, the Aeronautical College of Qinghua University, the Aeronautical Faculties of Sichuan University and Beijing Institute of Technology were merged into the Beijing Institute of Aeronautics and Astronautics (BIAA). Also in this year, the aeronautical faculties of former Central University, Jiaotong University and Zhejiang University were merged into the East China Aeronautical Institute, which was moved to Xi'an in 1956 and renamed as the Xi'an Aeronautical Institute. In 1957, the Northwest Institute of Technology was merged into the Xi'an Aeronautical Institute with a new name of the Northwest Polytechnic University (NPU). In the early 1970s, the Air Engineering Faculty of Harbin Military Engineering Institute was also merged into NPU. In 1952, the Nanjing Aviation Industry School was founded, which was upgraded to the Nanjing Aeronautical Institute (NAI) in 1956, and in the same year, NAI merged the Suzhou Aviation Industry School. By then our aviation industry owned three aeronautical institutes (for their evolutions, see tables 5, 6 and 7). During this period, a training school of Russian language was taken over from CAAC.

Table 5   The Evolution of BIAA

(The figures in brackets are the calendar years when the institutes and faculties were founded, as appropriate)

Aeronautical Engineering Faculty of
Qinghua University (1934)

Aeronautical Engineering Faculty of   Aeronautical
Beiyang (North Sea of China) University (1935)   College of
                                                                       Qinghua
Aeronautical Engineering Faculty of   University
Northwest Institute of Technology (1938)   (1951)

Aeronautical Engineering Faculty of
Xiamen University (1944)   BIAA
                                                                                               (1952)
Aeronautical Engineering Faculty of   Aeronautical
Yunnan University (1944)   Faculty of
                                                                       Sichuan
Aeronautical Engineering Faculty of   University
Sichuan University (1945)   (1951)

Aeronautical Engineering Faculty of   Aeronautical
Central Polytechnic Training School (1949)   Faculty of
                                                                       Beijing
                                                                       Institutee of
Aeronautical Engineering Faculty of   Technology
North China University (1950)   (1951)

Table 6 The Evolution of NPU

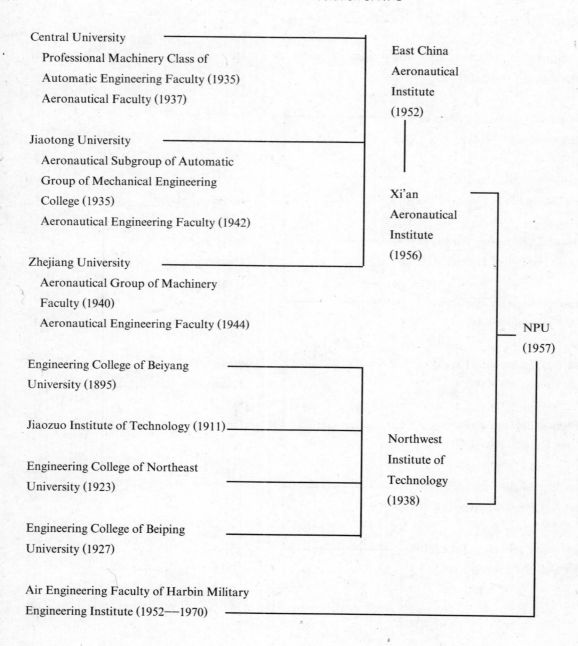

Central University
   Professional Machinery Class of
   Automatic Engineering Faculty (1935)
   Aeronautical Faculty (1937)

Jiaotong University
   Aeronautical Subgroup of Automatic
   Group of Mechanical Engineering
   College (1935)
   Aeronautical Engineering Faculty (1942)

Zhejiang University
   Aeronautical Group of Machinery
   Faculty (1940)
   Aeronautical Engineering Faculty (1944)

Engineering College of Beiyang
University (1895)

Jiaozuo Institute of Technology (1911)

Engineering College of Northeast
University (1923)

Engineering College of Beiping
University (1927)

Air Engineering Faculty of Harbin Military
Engineering Institute (1952—1970)

East China Aeronautical Institute (1952)

Xi'an Aeronautical Institute (1956)

Northwest Institute of Technology (1938)

NPU (1957)

Table 7 The Evolution of NAI

Nanjing Aviation Industry School (1952)	NAI
Suzhou Aviation Industry School (1956)	(1956)

While aeronautical universities and colleges were set up, aeronautical secondary schools and skilled—workers' training schools were also initiated. The first four aeronautical secondary schools were located in Beijing, Harbin, Nanchang and Shenyang. By the end of the First Five—year Plan, 8 technical secondary schools and 11 skilled—workers' training schools had been set up in the northeast, north, centralsouth, southwest, northwest and east of China.

At the early time of each institute or school, everything was waiting to be initiated. The starting was difficult. Capable cadres were transferred from army and local government departments to the leadership of institutes and schools by the State, such as Wu Guang, Zhao Pinsan, Liu Haibin, Shou Songtao, Deng Yongqing, Wu Jizhou, Wang Dachang, Chen Guyin, Zhang Shichao and others. They led teachers, administrative staff and workers to work arduously and made contributions to laying the foundation of aeronautical education.

According to the " Instruction on Developing Spare—time Education for Staff and Workers" issued by the Government Administration Council in 1950, various kinds of in—service education were initiated in the early stage of aviation industry, including on—the—spot trainings. Teaching and learning contracts were signed between masters and apprentices. Schools for eliminating illiteracy, primary schools, junior and senior middle schools, technical secondary schools and spare—time engineering college for the staff and workers were set up. By 1956, all factories had established educational management organizations and various rules and regulations. A relatively complete education system for the staff and workers was preliminarily formed. During this period, the educational undertaking of aeronautics grew healthily.

After the beginning of the Second Five—year Plan, there was a further development in the aeronautical education. During the period of 1958—1960, a lot of new schools were established, quite many old schools were upgraded and a mass movement of "a factory a school, educational revolution and work—study programme" was set off. In order to meet the needs of aeronautical R&D and production, the aeronautical universities and colleges added some new specialities, established some research departments and carried out research activities in aerodynamics, aeroengine, structural strength, instrument and automatic control, manufacturing technology, etc. Every institute and school made great efforts in running factories and produced electromechanical products to equip itself and support local construction. It was a matter of profound significance for aeronautical universities and colleges to start to combine education with scientific research and production. However, under the erroneous influence of the "left" which neglected objective laws and basic conditions and was overanxious for quick results, there were not a few faults in the work during this period. First, the number of aeronautical institutes and schools was sharply increased from 23 (1957) to 55 and it was an overrapid development. A number of technical secondary schools and skilled—workers' training schools were upgraded to higher technical schools and technical secondary schools respectively. Because of the shortage of teachers and teaching equipments and facilities, the quality of education could not be ensured. Most of the new schools had to close down one after another. There was a great up and down. Second, the regular pattern of education was neglected. Political activities, productive labour and scientific research projects occupied too much time of the teachers and students and broke the regular teaching order. Finally, the enthusiasm of the teachers was deeply damped because of the denying of the role of intellectuals and the leading role of teachers in teaching. These faults caused an obvious falling of quality of aeronautical education at that time.

In 1961, the number of aeronautical institutes and schools were adjusted and reduced according to the eight — character (Chinese) —policy of " Readjustment, Solidification, Substantiation and Improvement". Next, CCCPC issued the "Provisional Regulation (draft) on Educational Work in Universities and Colleges under the Ministry of Education" (the Sixty—Point Decision on Higher Education). The National Defence Science and Technology Commission made an adjustment on the tasks, development orientation, specialities and the subordinate relationship of universities and colleges of national defence; correspondingly, the Defence Industry Commission and Ministry of Defence Industry made a provisional decision (draft) on the teaching work of technical secondary schools and skilled—workers' training schools. Accordingly the work on "Four Fixations" was carried out in every school, i.e. fixing tasks, sizes, specialities and staff. The guiding principle of "Teaching and Learning First" was implemented in every school. Teaching, scientific research and production were arranged as a whole, rules and regulations were observed and so the order of teaching was established. At the same time, the Party's policy towards intellectuals was implemented. More attention was paid to further training of teachers, so the teaching and learning activities in institutes and schools returned to normal. By the end of the adjustment in 1962, 38 institutes and schools were cut down or merged, 3 universities and colleges, 8 technical secondary schools and 6 skilled—workers' training schools remained. Later, 4 institutes and schools were set up in concert with the inland construction.

In 1964, an important instruction on two kinds of education and labour systems were issued by CCCPC. It said that the work (farmwork)—study programme should be considered as regular education and labour system. The programme was tried out in aeronautical secondary schools in Zhuzhou and Shanghai and skilled—workers' training schools in Xinxiang. Altogether 42 part—work and part—study technical schools were set up by factories. By 1965, the work—study programme was brought to all technical secondary schools and training schools. It was a necessary probing. But the method of "cut at one blow" caused a declining of teaching level and quality in some schools which had good teaching quality before.

In 1966, at the beginning of "great cultural revolution", education had to bear the brunt, classes were suspended and "revolution" was made in schools, so that the aeronautical education was seriously destroyed. In 1969, technical secondary schools and skilled—workers' training schools were all cut down or transformed into factories. The aeronautical education which had been created for more than ten years faced disintegration. Though worker—peasant—soldier students were enrolled in universities and colleges from 1970 and a few technical secondary schools turned to train skilled—workers in 1972, the enrollment of students in universities and colleges or technical secondary schools and skilled—workers' training schools had been suspended for ten or seven years respectively. The catastrophe caused dozens of thousands of youths to miss their chance to be trained as scientific and technical staff or skilled—workers, resulting in a shortage of various kinds of staff in aviation industry. It was a great loss for the nation.

Fig. 94   The teaching building of the Zhengzhou Management
Institute of Aeronautical Engineering

After the downfall of the "Gang of Four" in 1976, the aeronautical education entered into a new historical period of development. After the Third Plenary Session of the Eleventh CCCPC, through bringing order out of chaos, redressing the injustice, false and wrong cases and implementing the policy towards intellectuals and cadres, vast numbers of teachers and cadres worked more diligently with ease of mind. Based on this, every school carried out conscientiously the policy of "Readjustment, Reform, Consolidation and Improvement" and the reissued "Regulation on the Work of National Key Institutes of Higher Education" by the Ministry of Education. Teachers were awarded professional titles as appropriate to their qualities, the management and construction of schools strengthened, and the teaching staff replenished. Normal order came back again to teaching and learning. During this period, the aeronautical secondary schools both in Shenyang and Nanchang were upgraded to the Shenyang Aeronautical Engineering Institute and the Nanchang Aeronautical Engineering Institute respectively. The Zhengzhou Aeronautical Secondary School was also upgraded to a management technical school, later to the Zhengzhou Management Institute of Aeronautical Engineering. Thus, there were altogether 6 aeronautical universities and colleges, among which BIAA, NPU and NAI were three national key institutes of higher education. These key institutes set up their graduate systems and enrolled graduate students for Master's or Doctoral degree. BIAA and NPU even established graduate schools. The professional education in factories was greatly improved. Teaching quality of each school was obviously raised, new achievements were frequently gained in scientific research, interschool cooperations with foreign universities and international academic exchanges were progressively developed. A picture of prosperity appeared before the educational undertaking of aeronautics.

For more than thirty years, the aeronautical education passed through a tortuous path, yet the achievements gained were enormous. Owing to upholding the principles of education for socialist construction, combination of theory with practice, integration of teaching, scientific research and production, and implementation of running school industriously and thriftily, now the aeronautical education has grown into a considerable scale and formed a system with multidiscipline multilevel, multinorm and multiform. It is supplemented by in-service education. By 1986, there had been 6 universities and colleges, 3 technical secondary schools and 2 skilled-workers'training schools directly under MAI; and 26 professional engineering colleges and 32 technical secondary schools for staff and workers run by enterprises and institutions and 46 skilled-workers' training schools run by factories. Besides, there had been 6 night schools, 6 correspondence schools and 183 classes of TV institutes and technical secondary schools run by enterprises and institutions. Within MAI, 500 postgraduates and 4,000 graduates can be annually sent to the nation from aeronautical institutes and schools, 700 graduates from technical secondary schools and 5,000 graduates from various kinds of skilled-workers' training schools. Over the past thirty five years, 120,000 senior and middle-rank technical and managerial personnel and 100,000 skilled-workers were trained in total. This not only satisfied the personnel needs of the initiation and development of aviation industry, but also provided technical personnel for the Air Force of PLA, the Ministry of Space Industry and the Ministry of Nuclear Industry.

For aeronautical education, a solid foundation has been laid. By the end of 1986, 11 institutes and schools under MAI had owned 19,210 teachers, staff and workers, 6,000 of them were teachers and 1,265 of them with titles of professor, associate professor or senior engineer. The total area of school buildings was 1.4 million square meters. There were 60,000 sets of test equipment for teaching. The number of teachers, staff and workers of the schools run by enterprises and institutions was increased to 9,836, 3,349 of them were full-time teachers, supported by 8,257 sets of teaching test equipment. In all aeronautical universities and colleges, scientific research activities were actively carried out while teaching task was completed, and there were altogether 7 research institutes or centers, 32 research departments and 3 computer centers, which could annually undertake several hundreds of research projects. They became an important force in aeronautical R&D. During the new period of development, the aeronautical education is being geared to the needs of the modernization, the world and the future. It is marching towards a new goal.

Section 2   Higher Education of Aeronautics

1.   Size, Specialities and Curricula, Educational Structure and Teaching Plan

In 1952, BIAA, the East China Aeronautical Institute and the Nanjing Aviation Industry School had 10,760 students in total. After the adjustment, the number of students of BIAA, NAI and NPU increased to 14,760. After setting up three aeronautical institutes in Nanchang, Shenyang and Zhengzhou in 1978, the number of students reached 18,000, an increase of 67% compared with that in 1952.

The number of the specialities offered in aeronautical universities and colleges also gradually increased. In the early 1950s, in order to meet the need of aviation industry's transition from repair to manufacture and then design, eleven specialities, such as aircraft design and manufacturing technology, aeroengine design and manufacturing technology, aircraft instrument, aircraft electric equipment and machining, were set up, based on the experiences from the Soviet Union. Later, more specialities were added, such as computer, radio communication, radar, automatic control, rocket, missile, metal material and enterprise management. In 1961, the number of specialities reached 76. After 1978, according to the principle of strengthening basic theories, widening the range of specialities and renewing course contents, to give students more adaptability to their future work and to better meet the requirement of civil production, specialities were adjusted and reformed. First, the specialities on defence products were reduced and the specialities for general purposes were added. For instance, some engineering specialities on material science, computer engineering, industrial management, industrial foreign trade, industrial and civil architecture, heat energy engineering, environmental protection and nondestructive testing, liberal art specialities on technical foreign languages, archives and political ideological education, and science specialities on applied mathematics and physics were added. Second, the range of specialities were widened and some product—oriented specialities were changed into technology—oriented type to train versatile scientists and technicians. For instance, the former specialty of aeronautical electric machine and equipment was changed to electric technique and the specialty of aircraft altitude equipment to vehicle environmental control and life—saving. After the adjustment, there were altogether 57 specialities in 8 categories offered by 6 aeronautical universities and colleges : vehicle design, aircraft powerplant engineering, aircraft instruments and control, aircraft electronic and electric equipment, aircraft machining and hot working, underwater weaponry, applied science and technology, management engineering and others.

　Undergraduates as well as postgraduates are educated through aeronautical higher education system. The system of educating postgraduates was set up as early as the 1950s, suspended during the "great cultural revolution" and resumed in 1978. Postgraduates began to be enrolled for Doctoral degree in 1981. BIAA and NPU established graduate schools successively in 1985 and 1986. During the years from 1981 to 1986, postgraduate education in aviation industry developed rapidly. During this period 1,935 students got Master's degree, which was 83 percent of 2,319 postgraduates trained in more than thirty years. 24 students got Doctoral degree. Approved by the State Council, the Doctoral degree could be awarded for 39 specialities in aviation industry, among them were seventeen in BIAA, fourteen in NPU, seven in NAI and one in the Aeronautical Materials Research Institute with 82 instructors in total assigned. The Master's degree could be awarded for 119 specialities, among them were forty in BIAA, thirty six in NPU, nineteen in NAI and twenty four in research institutes and there were almost 1,000 instructors.

The following is the list of the specialities and instructors for awarding Doctor's degree in aeronautical universities and colleges:

Solid mechanics: Wang Junkui, Wang Derong, Gao Zhentong, Zhu Dechao, Huang Yushan, Yang Nansheng, Chen Baiping, Zhang Azhou, Zhu Demao; Aerodynamics: Chuang Fenggan, Lu Shijia, Wu Liyi, Li Chunxuan, Wu Jianming, Wang Peisheng, Luo Shijun, Lin Chaoqiang, Yang Zuosheng, Dai Changhui, Huang Mingke; General mechanics: Huang Kelei, Ji Wenmei; Mechanology: Zhang Qixian, Zhang Xisheng, Chen Yansheng; Aircraft design: He Qingzhi, Xia Renwei, Yang Qingxiong, Zhao Lingcheng, Wang Shicun, Qiao Xin, Fan Xuji; Aeroengine: Yan Litang, Cui Jiya, Ning Huang, Chen Maozhang, Zhou Sheng, Nei Jingxu, Wang Hongji, Zhou Xinhai, Chen Fuqun, Zhang Shiying, Peng Chengyi, Wu Guozhao; Navigation and control system: Wen Chuanyuan, Wang Xingren, Chen Xinhai, Guo Suofeng; Aircraft production engineering: Tang Rongxi, Hu Shiguang, Zhu Xinxiong, Yang Pengji, Peng Yanwu, Chen Shuxun; Aircraft gyro and inertial navigation: Lin Shie, Zhang Hongyue; Flight mechanics: Zhang Guilian, Chen Shilu, Liu Qiangang; Casting: Zhou Raohe, Fu Hengzhi; Machinery engineering: Chen Dingchang, Yu Chengye, Zhang Youzhen; Metal material and heat treatment: Chen Changqi, Yan Minggao, Kang Mokuang, Zhen Xiulin; Computer application: Kang Jichang; Experimental mechanics: Zhuang Fenggan, Lian Qixiang; Aircraft instrument and measurement engineering: Tao Baoqi; Communication and electronic system: Zhang Qishan; Computer software: Li Wei; Hydraulic control system: Wang Zhanlin; Aerospace system and management engineering: Feng Yuncheng; Aircraft electric engineering: Yan Yangguang; Automatic control theory and its application: Gao Weibing, Dai Guanzhong; Torpedo design: Ma Yuanliang; Solid rocket and propellant: Wu Xinping; Numerical mathematics: Zhou Tianxiao.

About the length of schooling and teaching plan. The lengths of schooling at the early stage were five years for regular college course and two and half years for special college course.

At that time, attention was paid to both the education of political ideology and the teaching of basic courses, basic specialized courses and specialized courses; furthermore emphasis was put on the combination of theory with practice as well as education with productive labour; importance was attached to the practical teachings such as experiments, practice and course design and graduation design; and besides, a certain period of time per year for physical labour was arranged. All these yielded good results. Yet, there were some problems, e.g. rigid teaching plans and neglect of domestic conditions, and experiences obtained both at home and abroad were over-looked. These dampened and confined the enthusiasm and creativeness both of teachers and students. During the "great cultural revolution", worker–peasant–soldier students were enrolled, the length of schooling was shortened to 3 years, no strict cultural examination was taken before students' entrance, and physical labour and production was overemphasized in teaching plan. These weakened the teaching of basic knowledge and theory and caused a serious falling of teaching quality.

Fig. 95   A corner of the campus of the Shenyang Aeronautical Engineering Institute

After the resuming of national unified examination system in 1977, the length of schooling of regular college course became four years. Thanks to the open policy, universities and colleges started learning experiences in aeronautical education from foreign countries. On the basis of more than thirty years' practices of running schools a set of teaching plans for aeronautical higher education has been progressively worked out. That is: thoroughly carrying out the educational policy laid down by the State; correctly handling the relations between politics and vocational work, theory and practice, teaching and scientific research, basis and specialized courses, and required and optional courses; with emphasis on teaching basic knowledge, basic theory and skill, ameliorating the intelligence structure of students and cultivating the students' ability to analyze and solve concrete problems and work independently.

The concrete steps are as follows. The first is to strengthen the teaching of basic theory courses by renewing or setting up new basic and specialized basic courses such as engineering mathematics, automatic control theory and computer theory while reduce required courses and add optional courses in order to widen students' knowledge. The proportions of class hours are: general and basic courses make up about 80% of the total class hours, specialized courses 15% and optional courses 5%. The second is to cultivate vigorously the abilities of mastering foreign languages, doing calculations and making experiments. The third is to reduce simple demonstration experiments, add comprehensive and design-oriented experiments, and even open computer course in an all-round way and use computers for design-oriented calculation and experimental research. In the four years in school, students' computer-time should be no less than 100 class hours and experimental teaching time no less than one-eighth of the total class hours. Also the students should do teaching and productive practices and make course designs and graduation designs to train their ability for scientific research. The fourth is to pay attention to the education of Maxism-Leninism theory, raise students' socialist consciousness and cultivate their communist moral character and the spirit of serving the modern socialist construction. All institutes and schools have set up the credit system, and some of them have even tried a sifting system for their students. As a result, the students' initiative and creativeness in learning have been mobilized.

2. Textbook, Teaching Experiment and Productive Practice Facility and Library

Textbook is a principal part of the school infrastructure. In the early days of the higher education of China the Soviet textbooks were introduced for most of the courses. The contents and structures of these textbooks were more theoretical and systematical. Textbooks for courses of manufacturing technology formed a relatively complete system. Combined with the productive practice and course design the textbooks played an important role in training the students' abilities to work independently. Some textbooks in relatively new disciplines were good for teachers in raising their specialized knowledge level. During the period from 1958 to 1960 a great quantity of textbooks were prepared by various schools, but most of their stresses were laid on practices at the expense of theoretical contents and systematical structures. After the implementation of the "Sixty-Point Decision on Higher Education" in 1961 attention was paid to cancelling the old contents from the textbooks and introducing new ones into them. By 1966 BIAA, NPU and NAI had prepared and published 159 textbooks and then the teaching quality was ensured. Since the end of the "great cultural revolution" the preparation of textbooks was further strengthened and a textbook edition organization set up in MAI. During the period from 1977 to 1983 BIAA, NPU and NAI prepared 2,390 textbooks and teaching materials in total, 153 of which were selected as the national unified textbooks. The "Automatic Control

Theory" and the "Transducer Theory" prepared by NAI were chosen by some national key institutes as their textbooks. The "Machine Design" prepared by NPU was printed in more than 460,000 copies and the "Mechanics of Materials" compiled by BIAA was well received by its readers.

For strengthening the teaching and scientific research great attention was paid to the construction of laboratories for not only the basic courses such as physics, chemistry, mechanics of materials and electrotechnics but also the specialized basic courses and specialized courses. By 1956 BIAA, NPU and NAI had constructed low speed wind tunnels and intermittent wind tunnels of 1.5 m, 1.0 m and 0.75 m diameters. By 1966 these three schools had owned 54, 65, and 32 laboratories respectively. As regards the large experimental facilities BIAA owned the supersonic wind tunnel, ramjet and liquid rocket engine test stands, simulated altitude test facility, etc.; NPU the wind tunnel, engine test stand, swinging test rig, helicopter rotor test stand, etc.; and NAI the transonic—supersonic wind tunnel, hydraulic three degree of freedom flight simulation table, large low pressure turbine air supply, etc. After 1978, these laboratories were restored, rectified, expanded and renewed. First, some advanced experimental instruments and equipments were imported, e.g. the scanning electron microscope, X ray diffractometer, multi—point vibration—exciting measurement device, hot—wire anemometer, computer—controlled universal material test machine, high speed camera, transmission electron microscope and electron probe. Second, advanced measurement instrument and data acquisition system were incorporated, e.g. the computer—based steady data acquisition system for the jet engine test stand and laser anemometer for the engine fuel system laboratory. Third, several important test facilities were constructed, e.g. the single and twin—stage compressor test rig, water test tank, acoustic water tank and high speed water tunnel, variable—Mach number supersonic intake wind tunnel, rotor fatigue system and automatic control emulation equipment. Forth, computation centers and measurement centers were set up in BIAA, NPU and NAI. Fifth, modern teaching equipments such as the color video system were imported and audio—video teaching centers and producing centers and linguistic laboratories were established, from which teaching films, video tapes and slides could be produced. All these played an important role in strengthening the teaching and scientific research capabilities.

Subsidiary factories were also set up to provide the students with the sites for productive practice, manufacture the test pieces for scientific research activities, conduct the intermediate test and produce and repair the equipment. The factories subsidiary to the six aeronautical universities and colleges had 2,600 workers and staff, a shop area of 100,000 square meters and more than 1,300 machines in total. Through the productive labour the students improved their productive skills. Thanks to the combination of teaching with scientific research and production, military and commercial products were developed and produced such as the pilotless aircraft, ultra—light aircraft, instruments and motorcycles.

Library is an essential facility for the universities and colleges. In the 1980s the existing libraries were expanded and new ones built in the six aeronautical universities and colleges with a total floor area of more than 40,000 square meters and 3 millions of books. NPU is the biggest collector with 1.09 millions of books.

3. Teaching Staff

The teaching staff of the aeronautical universities and colleges comprises two kinds of personnel. The first is the professors and technical experts in aeronautical engineering or other technological fields from old China, such as Shen Yuan, Wang Derong, Lu Shijia, Wang Junkui, Ning Huang, Lin Shie, Zhang Guilian, Ji Wenmei, Jiang Changying, Wang Hongji, Wang Peisheng, Huang Yushan, Chen Shiping, Luo Shijun, Xie Angu, Xu Xianong, Fan Xuji, Zhang Azhou, Zhang Shiying, Zheng Yannie, Yu Chengye and Cheng Baoqu, and the second is the graduates, Masters and Doctors trained since the founding of new China. In 1952 three aeronautical universities and colleges had 238 teachers, among them were 61 professors and associate professors and 23 lecturers. Thanks to the concern of the Government, with the help of the Soviet experts and through hard working, they raised their ideological and teaching level rapidly and became the first teaching staff in the aeronautical education of new China. Many of them became the leading scientists and instructors who can award the Doctoral degree. Due to the rapid expansion of higher aeronautical education it was an urgent task at that time to strengthen and train the teaching staff. The corresponding measures were: to assign new graduates as teachers, to train the postgraduates to be teachers by the professors with high academic level, and organize the teachers to learn from the Soviet experts. Altogether 66 Soviet experts were invited to China to give lectures and a certain number of excellent young teachers and students were sent to the Soviet Union and the eastern European countries to study or engage in advanced studies. By 1965 the aeronautical universities and colleges had owned a contingent of approximately 3,000 teachers with relatively high academic level.

After 1978 the following measures were taken to raise the teachers' professional level. First, various classes for advanced studies in new theories and technologies were all provided. Second, the young teachers were encouraged to study for the Master's or Doctor's degree or take the postgraduate courses and examinations and experienced teachers assigned as their instructors. Third, domestic and international academic exchanges were extensively carried out and famous foreign experts and professors invited to give lectures in China totalling to several hundred persons by 1986. In addition some Chinese experts were invited as part-time professors, such as Wu Zhonghua, director of the Engineering Thermophysics Institute of the Chinese Academy of Sciences, Yang Nansheng, vice president of the Fourth Research Establishment of the Ministry of Space Industry and Yan Minggao, Gu Songfen and Zhang Yanzhong, experts of MAI. Fourth the middle-aged and young teachers were sent abroad for advanced studies, or as visiting scholars or to study for the Master's or Doctoral degrees totalling to more than 300 persons, and some of them were qualified, after returning home, to be the instructors who can award the Doctoral degree. Fifth, some teachers were sent for advanced studies on their specialities in other domestic universities and colleges. These measures had positive results in enhancing the professional level of the teachers and strengthening the teaching staff.

By the end of 1986 the six aeronautical universities and colleges had owned 5,279 teachers' in various specialities, among them were 238 professors, 975 associate professors, 2,148 lecturers, 1,344 assistant and 574 other teachers. Through diligent work this teaching staff loyal to the aeronautical education cause made a great contribution to the training of the aeronautical scientific and technical staff and the modernization construction of the nation. Many teachers were cited by the Government for their remarkable achievements in the teaching and scientific research, e.g. Professor Zhou Yaohe and Professor Zhang Litong (female) were respectively awarded the titles of the national model worker and the national "March 8" (the International Working Women's Day) red—banner pacesetter.

A great number of teachers did well in the campaign of "training the students to be the socialist minded and professional experts". In 1982 Professor Zhao Lingcheng of NPU was praised by MAI for his meritorious deeds in the campaign and awarded the title of the ministerial model worker. Professor Li Xincan was awarded the honourable title of the national excellent teaching worker for his remarkable achievements in the campaign and the "May 1" (the International Labour Day) medal. Most of the teachers paid attention to the ideological education and gained positive results.

4. Scientific Research Activities

Aeronautical universities and colleges are an important force in the aeronautical R&D. They are actively engaged in basic research and in the meantime put their main resources into applied research and development to meet the requirements of the aviation industry and other economic departments. In accordance with the trends in science and technology the universities and colleges also explore the boundary and new disciplines.

In the mid 1950s BIAA, NPU and NAI began to carry out the scientific research activities and hold academic seminars at regular intervals. During the period from 1958 to 1960, according to the aeronautical science and technology plan and the decision of "Establishing Several Research Points at Several Universities and Colleges of the Ministry of Higher Education", these three aeronautical universities and colleges established a number of research departments for aerodynamics, aircraft structural mechanics, jet engine theory, aircraft manufacturing technology, instrument and automat, gyro, computational technology, control system, rocket engine, etc. In the meantime, for implementing the educational policies of the combination of education with scientific research and production and part—work and part—study, the senior students were required to do the "real things" in graduate design and so involved in the design and development of some new flight vehicles, such as: light passenger aircraft, high altitude meteorological rocket, high altitude and high speed drone and pilotless aircraft in BIAA; light helicopter, two—seat air cushioncraft and high altitude atmosphere rocket in NPU; and target drone in NAI. The developments of these flight vehicles were ambitious attempts made by vast numbers of the teachers, students, staff and workers. Through the whole development process of design, manufacture and flight test many teachers were tempered both in ideology and professional ability and senior students trained in basic professional skills. But the teaching was affected since too many scientific research and development projects were arranged in a relatively short period and too much time of the teachers and students spent in these projects.

In 1961 the scientific research and development activities in the aeronautical universities and colleges were adjusted with emphasis on basic and applied research and application of the scientific research achievements to the teaching and economic construction. Thanks to the adjustment more achievements were made. In 1965 twenty two research projects accomplished by BIAA were assessed and among them the gyro dynamic balance machine with an accuracy of 0.02 μm, high temperature and high strength aluminium alloy, high temperature (400 ℃) strain gauge and 28 channel telemetric equipment were the first ones of their kinds. The NPU—I type target drone was certified, mass—produced and exported.

Fig. 96   The contact welding laboratory of the Nanchang
Aeronautical Engineering Institute

During the period from 1966 to 1976 many achievements were also made in spite of the chaos of the " great cultural revolution" . In November 1972 the high altitude pilotless reconnaissance aircraft developed by BIAA made its maiden flight. In 1975 this institute sent 150 teachers and other technical staff from 11 disciplines to take part in the preliminary design of the J—6 aircraft simulator. In the country it was leading in some applied theories such as the theoretical research and computation of transonic compressor and fracture mechanics and in some technologies such as the magnetic powder clutch, 6,000—ton and 1,500—ton cylindric rubber oil presses, cyanogenless plating and cadmium—titanium alloy processing. In 1970 NPU successfully developed the NPU—II type target drone, which was put into batch production and service. From 1971 to 1975 this university carried out a great deal of research and development activities in 337 applied theories, new technologies and products including the transonic aerodynamic calculation, airfoil profile theory and design and numerical calculation on the internal and external flow fields of the static exhaust system of the engine. The pilotless drone research department of NAI was awarded the title of the national advanced collective in science and technology for successful developments of its high altitude target drone and sampling aircraft for nuclear test. Of the 58 achievements which gained the National Science Convention prizes were 26 items from BIAA, 21 items from NPU and 11 items from NAI.

After 1979 a flourishing new period began for the scientific research in the aeronautical universities and colleges. Due to the implement of the policy that the economic construction should be put on the foundation of the development of science and technology and the development of science and technology oriented to the economic construction, these three national key universities and colleges highlighted the applied research, reinforced the basic research and gave consideration to the product development. By the end of 1984 all the three universities and colleges set up academic committees at both the university or college level and faculty level, restored or established seven research institutes or research centers, expanded 36 research departments and stations. In the meantime a new system combining teaching, scientific research and production was established. It brought the scientific research in line with the teaching and gave the senior students an opportunity to join the research activities. Therefore positive results were gained both in bringing about the scientific achievement and training the student for self studying and working abilities. From 1978 to 1984 BIAA, NPU and NAI won 459 prizes at the state level or ministerial, provincial or municipal level. Only in 1984 were seven national prizes for science invention awarded to the three universities and colleges.

During this period the scientific research activities in the aeronautical universities and colleges had the following features.

First, major achievements were made in basic research, applied research and development and quickly transformed into the productive forces. Under the guidance of Professor Nin Huang, Gao Ge, Ph. Doctor student of BIAA won the first class national prize for science invention for his theoretical research and application achievements in his barcharn dune flame holder. Achievement made in the finite element theory research activities under the leadership of Professor Wang Derong were successfully used in the engine troubleshooting for flight accidents associated with failures of turbine shaft. It was awarded the National Science Convention prize. The research activities for reinforcing the main spar of the J—5 aircraft wing conducted by NPU shortened the inspection interval by 50% and in turn extended the aircraft life by 3—5 years for a fleet of nearly 1,000 aircraft. NAI successfully utilized the results of the ground resonance research activities to the helicopter ground resonance test and analysis.

Second, with the multidisciplinary resources that the aeronautical universities and colleges owned, some flight vehicles were developed, which filled the blanks in the inventory of the Chinese Air Force. Developed by BIAA, the WZ—5 high altitude pilotless reconnaissance aircraft was certified by the State in February 1980 and then was put into production and delivered for service. The J—6 flight simulator was jointly developed by BIAA, the Aeronautical Precision Machinery Research Institute and the Beijing Aircraft Electric Motor Factory, with BIAA in charge of the overall design. It passed the state evaluation in 1983 and was delivered for service. This achievement was awarded the first class national prize for science and technology progress. The performance of the Changkong 1 low altitude, high manoeuvable target drone developed by NAI reached the world's advanced level of its kind.

Third, research activities in the rising and boundary disciplines and the interdisciplinary and high technology fields grew rapidly, such as computer software, noncrystalline physics (optical information storage), fiberoptical communication, robot, composite materials, flexible manufacturing system, computer simulation and emulation, reliability engineering and CAD / CAM.

Fourth, with aviation industry as the main user, the scientific research activities were oriented to other economic fields in multiform and through multichannel. Besides the research projects from MAI the aeronautical universities and colleges also undertook research projects from other economic departments and science research foundations and engaged in the product developments in cooperation with some local research institutes or departments. BIAA developed the "Bee" ultra—light aircraft series, which could be used for various purposes. Its quadruple tension control system with magnetic powder clutch was used in the colour offset press and hence the domestic offset press was improved and exported. Then the system was incorporated by more than 100 factories in ship—building, automobile and clock—making industries. This institute also developed a computerized system for character and word frequency statistics and made a contribution to the reform of the writing system. The multipurpose pilotless reconnaissance aircraft developed by NPU found its wide application in the topographic survey and geophysical exploring. This university also developed a gas—launched dry—chemical fire extinguisher and a new magnesium—casting nontonic foundry sand. The former got a patent; and the latter could be substituted for the tonic foundry sand, thus improving the working conditions and reducing the cost. NAI engaged in the application of microprocessor with good results. A microprocessor—controlled lathe produced by the institute won an order at the largest amount on a national new technology and product exhibition of the machine—building industry. The Nanchang Aeronautical Engineering Institute developed a new conventional anodizing process for aluminium alloy, which omitted the refrigeratory equipment and reduced the power demand. The Shenyang Aeronautical Engineering Institute won the national prize for science invention for its hydraulic piston pump used in petroleum extraction.

Fifth, rapid progress was made in the international academic exchange and cooperative development. After 1978 the aeronautical universities and colleges sent teachers and other technical staff abroad to investigate, give lectures and engage in advanced studies as well as to take part in the international academic activities. BIAA staff members had joined more than 10 international cooperative research projects in fluid mechanics, composite materials, brazing technology, etc. In 1985 the adjustable gear box designed by Associate Professor Chen Shixian won a gold medal on the 13th World New Invention Exhibition held in Geneva. The micropressure—type transducer invented by Professor Tao Baoqi of NAI won a gold—plated prize on the 14th World New Invention Exhibition held in Geneva. Several hundreds of academic papers were published or presented on some famous foreign academic journals or international academic conferences. Professors and experts from 21 countries and regions were invited to give lectures, visit and install equipment, totalling over 1,100 person—times by 1986. BIAA, NPU and NAI also established the inter—university cooperative relationships with some famous universities in foreign countries.

5. Training of Qualified Scientists and Technicians

The aeronautical universities and colleges always take it as their main goal to train the senior technical and managerial experts with socialist consciousness. Over the past thirty and more years more than 70,000 students graduated. Most of them had good political quality and sound scientific knowledge. They are doing a good job at their posts. Just like "young bird sings better than the old", the old generation of scientists and educationists trained a young generation which even surpass them. Out of the young generation, some took the leading posts in the government at various levels, as well as in the enterprises and research institutions of MAI, some took charge of important development projects in high technology fields, such as long range missiles, satellites and aircraft, some became professors and experts enjoying good prestige both at home and abroad, some won the honourable titles such as the scientific flight test heros, top—class model workers or advanced workers and some won the national prizes for science invention. Most members in the leadership and technical backbone of every organization under MAI graduated from the aeronautical universities and colleges of new China.

To send students and teachers to study and engage in advanced studies in foreign countries is another way to train the senior scientists and experts. Of the students and teachers sent to the Soviet Union and the east European countries to study 207 remained to work in MAI. They became the leading members in charge of technical affairs and made their contributions to the modernization of the aviation industry. Those who worked in universities and colleges started new specialities or became the leading scientists in their own disciplines and the instructors of the graduate students for the Doctoral or Master's degree. For example Professor Cao Chuanjun president of BIAA took part in the preparation of the rocket engine speciality of this institute and was the chief designer of the first Chinese atmosphere rocket engine; Professor Chen Shilu of NPU devoted himself to the flight dynamics and initiated the missile speciality of this university.

From 1978 to 1986 MAI sent approximately 1,000 people to foreign countries for advanced studies. They studied assiduously, made considerable progress in their studies and received good comments from the organizations where they studied and from their instructors. After returning home these people are playing active roles in various technological fields. Many of them became scholars of higher attainments and achieved greater success in the disciplines and specialities they were engaged in. For example, lecturer Huang Qingsen of BIAA, who studied in England, won three patents in the industrial robot and mechanical arm. The robot and mechanical arm designed by him were called the "Huang's machines". Teacher Xun Ji of BIAA took his degree of Ph. Doctor at the Stuttgart University in the Federal Republic of Germany. In this country he won a patent with the method presented in his doctoral dissertation. After returning home he developed a microprocessor—based numerical control system, with which old NC millers could be retrofitted into NC millers with new functions at a small expense and won the first—class prize of the national microprocessor application for this achievement. Zhang Lingmi of NAI made a breakthrough in his research activities in vibration when he worked in the Structural Dynamics Research Center of the Cincinnati University of the United States and was engaged as a research consultant. In the cooperative research with DFVLR of the Federal Republic of Germany Associate Professor Zhou Mingde of NAI made a great success in the transition technique and he was invited twice by the research establishment to give instructions to their research workers. Associate Professor Zhu Depei of NPU developed a new concept in plastic strain modes when he studied on the finite element theory of solid mechanics in the Federal Republic of Germany and he was awarded the Humboldt scholarship. Teacher Li Wei of BIAA took the degree of Ph. Doctor at the Edinburgh University of the United Kingdom. Having returned home he achieved outstanding success in CAD of the large scale integrated circuit and he was soon promoted to be a professor — the youngest professor in aeronautical universities and colleges who qualified to train research students for the Doctoral degree. In the new development period these scientists and experts returned from abroad achieved splendid results and became the nucleus of the scientific and technical contingent working in aeronautical education, R&D and production.

Section 3   Vocational Education of Aeronautics

Vocational education of aeronautics is an important part of the educational undertaking of aeronautics and its task is to cultivate middle—rank technical and managerial personnel. Generally, aeronautical secondary schools enroll junior middle school graduates and their schooling length is three or four years. In 1952 and 1953 aeronautical secondary schools were set up in Beijing, Harbin, Hankou (later moved to Nanchang) and Shenyang, from which the first students graduated. Though there were a few technical high schools in old China, but they had very little to hand down in aeronautical field. So, in the early 1950s people were quite short of experiences in how to run technical secondary schools well. With the help of Soviet specialists and the endeavour of all teachers, students, staff and workers of these four aeronautical secondary schools, the construction and teaching were soon led into the right path. Teaching quality was raised and experiences in running schools were progressively accumulated.

Through adjustment and development the number of aeronautical secondary schools was increased to 13 in 1965. During the "great cultural revolution" all technical secondary schools were closed and transformed into factories. In 1972 things began to resume and by the 1980s there had been altogether three aeronautical secondary schools in Xi'an, Chengdu and Dayong. In these schools the teaching and practice equipment and facilities were quite good and furthermore there was a contingent of teachers and cadres with abundant experiences in teaching and management as well as a whole set of teaching plans, programmes and textbooks. In 1980 both schools in Xi'an and Chengdu were qualified as the key technical secondary schools of the country.

Fig. 97   The front gate of the Xi'an Aeronautical Secondary School

Altogether 32 specialities in four categories were set up one after another in aeronautical secondary schools. The first category included 10 specialities of aviation products; the second, 18 of general purpose such as cold and hot working, chemical engineering, tooling manufacturing, power engineering and computer; the third, two of management; the fourth, two of architecture. After 1978, according to the principle of strengthening basic theories, widenning the range of specialities and giving students more adaptability to their future work, further adjustment to the specialities was made: new specialities were added, such as computer application and maintenance, electronic instrument and measurement technology, industrial electricity automation, heat energy engineering, heating and ventilation, industrial and civil architecture, and water supply and drainage, while a few specialities were merged or cancelled. After the adjustment there were altogether 12 specialities and 15 speciality stations in the three aeronautical secondary schools. These specialities were universal and hence they suited well the policy of producing both aero products and non—aero products in aviation industry.

Teaching plan of aeronautical secondary schools had the following features: general knowledge courses made up 40—50% of the total class hours, so as to ensure the students' cultural level comparable with that of the senior middle school graduates and enable the students not only to easily acquire basic technical and professional knowledge but also to lay a foundation for advanced studies; attention was paid to the training for basic knowledge and skill, with practice courses making up 20—30% of the total class hours and the students were required to master the skills on a certain level; attention was also paid to the combinations of theory with practice and teaching with productive labour; again attention was paid to political and ideological education, so as to enable students to develop morally, intellectually and physically. In 1979 MAI set up a typical teaching plan for four—year technical secondary schools on three specialities including aircraft part machining, industrial electricity automation and electronic instrument and measurement technology. Making reference to the typical teaching plan every school set up its own teaching plan on other specialities. The teaching plan defined that the theoretical courses (including general courses, basic technical courses and specialized courses) should cover 3,544 class hours in total; the ratio of the practice and productive labour time to the total class hours of the theoretical courses was 1 : 5.84.

Before the mid 1950s aeronautical secondary schools adopted the unified teaching programme on general courses and basic technical courses issued by the Ministry of Education. But the teaching programme on specialized courses was set up by Soviet specialists. Later the teaching programme on specialized courses was revised to accommodate itself to the development of the aeronautical R&D and production. By 1966, 58 textbooks as well as various tooling books, reference books and guide materials for teaching were compiled. After 1978 a whole set of textbooks were recompiled. These new textbooks not only met the requirements of the teaching programme, but also reflected new achievements in science and technology. They played a positive role in enhancing the teaching quality. Some of them were widely adopted by technical secondary schools all over the country.

To adhere to the principle of combining theory with practice and strengthening objective teaching, every aeronautical secondary school set up progressively research rooms, showrooms and laboratories equipped with aero products such as aircraft, aeroengines and airborne equipment, so that they could offer all experimental courses in accordance with the teaching programme. Electronic computers and audio—video teaching equipment were also installed. For training the students in basic productive skills, every school set up practice factories with considerable scale and the students could receive the training of the fitter and mechanic operation and the basic skills required for their own specialities. These practice factories also produced mechanical and electrical products when they were not occupied by the teaching practices.

Teachers of aeronautical secondary schools consisted of college graduates assigned by the State and the professors and associate professors transfered from universities and colleges and senior engineering personnel from industrial departments, such as Zhang Benlu, Tao Li, Jiang Baisheng, Wu Yucang, Fan Tongkang, etc. As for the young teachers' continued training, at the early stage, Soviet specialists were invited to give instructions and example lectures; and later, advanced studies were arranged for them. Through several adjustments and continuous training there were altogether 556 experienced teachers in the three schools, among them 168 teachers had titles of lecturer and above. Some teachers were invited to give lectures in foreign schools. In 1982 and 1984 lecturer Pei Jiadu and teacher Cao Wangji of the Xi'an Aeronautical Secondary School were invited by an American agricultural and engineering college to give lectures on electronic computer application, and theoretical mechanics and computer graphics respectively. Some had made excellent achievements in their research activities. Teacher Qu Mengyun of the Chengdu Aeronautical Secondary School presented a paper titled "Dyad Green's Function for Microstrip Antenna" on an annual meeting of IEEE held in 1984 in Boston. It was called as the "Third Theory of Microstrip Antenna".

Aeronautical secondary schools trained a large number of excellent technical and managerial personnel for aviation industry. By 1986 altogether 46,000 students graduated. These graduates could quickly become familiarized with the technical and managerial work as well as the practical operation on their posts since they were already well trained in political ideology, professional knowledge and practical skill. The first 1,418 graduates from the aeronautical secondary schools in 1955 were exceptionally welcome after they were assigned to factories, because they were all outstanding youths chosen from the military units and had the cultural level of graduates from junior middle schools. At that time all factories were generally short of middle-rank technical personnel, so their timely coming provided timely help for the factories which were in the transition from repairing to manufacturing. In the 1950s graduates from technical secondary schools made up 60—80% of technical and managerial personnel of each factory. Though this proportion dropped to about one-third in the early 1980s they still played an active role in production, scientific research and test, construction and management and made great contributions to the development of Chinese aviation industry.

Section 4   Skilled-workers' Education in Aviation Industry

Skilled-workers' education in aviation industry began in 1951. In 1953, 13 junior technical schools and skilled-workers' training classes run by factories were transformed into regular skilled-workers' training schools. These schools enrolled graduates from junior middle schools and trained them to be grade 3 or 4 skilled-workers. The schooling length was two or three years. Through more than 30 years' industrious effort in running schools the number of schools has increased to 47. They own a lot of teaching equipment and an experienced contingent of cadres and teachers and they have been continuously training skilled-workers in middle grades for aviation industry.

These skilled—workers' training schools offered courses for altogether 27 types of work in production, among them 17 were for general purpose, five for special purpose and five for others. They mainly included wooden mould, casting, forging, heat treatment, surface treatment, painting, turning, milling, grinding, planning, fitting, welding, sheet forming, riveting, stamping and pressing, aircraft and engine assembly, instrument, radio, electricity and parachute—making. In the 1960s the type of work for aircraft and engine assembly was cancelled while those for electric equipment assembly, electric equipment maintenance and instrumentation equipment maintenance were added. From the late 1970s 21 types of work were offered mainly for general purpose.

After 1979 a new schooling system was set up. Under this system a schooling length of two years with 3,180 class hours was for the students enrolled from senior middle school graduates and a schooling length of three years with 4,600 class hours for the students enrolled from junior middle school graduates. The ratio of the theory courses to the practice ones was approximately 1 : 1.4.

It is a main course of the skilled—workers' training school to train the students for the operating skills through productive practice. The education principle is "take the teaching as main task, carry out thoroughly the productive practice programme and make the production serve the teaching better". In the early 1950s the productive practice made students receive relatively good training in basic skills; however the practices were wasteful because of paying no attention to the utilization of the products made by students. In 1953 the Shanghai Aeronautical Skilled—workers' Training School found out a way of combining teaching practice with production. Several dozens of gear lathes and hydroelectric sawing machines made in teaching practices were utilizable. In 1955 the Ministry of Labour held a national meeting of the skilled—workers' training schools and formally set up a principle, i.e. the schools should take teaching practice as their main task and combine teaching practice with production. After the meeting all the aeronautical skilled—workers' training schools followed this principle and organized conscientiously productive practice. As a result the teaching quality was improved and material wealth created for the society. The products made in productive practices included lathes, millers, grinders, planers, stampers and drillers, from which the schools gained benefits.

Theoretical courses consisted of cultural knowledge, general technologies and specialized theories. Every school strengthened the teaching study, improved the teaching methods and set up laboratories of physics, chemistry, electrotechnics, metallography, material test, measurement, metal cutting, electrical engineering and electronics, showrooms for general knowledge of aeronautics and classrooms for specialized and practicing courses, to make students learn and master cultural and specialized knowledge more deeply and comprehensively.

Work—study system is a good tradition of the skilled—workers' education in aviation industry. At the early stage of new China all neglected tasks had to be undertaken. In order to race against time schools enrolled students while they were under construction. School buildings were either old shabby earthern houses or mat sheds and bamboo houses. In some cases the students even had classes in the open-air. Fearing nothing of hard conditions the teachers, students, staff and workers took part in the school construction enthusiastically and set to work for a better condition for running school and a good environment for teaching. The good work style of starting an undertaking through arduous effort was inherited and further developed in the teaching and productive practice. The Xi'an Aeronautical Skilled-workers' Training School was a model in carrying out the work-study programme. This school was rebuilt in 1953 on the basis of a training class run by a factory. There were only 90 sets of machine tools in the school, of which 60% were the belt driven lathes made in the 1920s and 1930s. Learning from the spirit of the Chinese People's Anti-Japanese Military and Political College all the teachers, students, staff and workers built school buildings and made machine tools on their own to improve the teaching conditions. Under the teachers' instruction the students made not only general lathes and electromechanical equipment but also a gyro-balancer with relatively high accuracy, which was exhibited at the Leipzig International Fair. During 1958—1960 this school gained an output value of 23.62 million yuans (RMB) and reached a status of self-sufficiency even with a surplus. It constructed teaching buildings at its own expense, bought more machines and equipment and took on everything for setting up another new school of its kind.

In January 1958, while making an exposition on the "Sixty-Point Decision on Method of Work" at a meeting held in Nanning, Chairman Mao Zedong praised the Xi'an Aeronautical Skilled-workers' Training School for its work-study programme and self-sufficiency. He pointed out, "all technical secondary schools and skilled-workers' training schools can set up their own factories or farms and accomplish self-sufficiency or half-self-sufficiency when the conditions exist ... ." On 22th, January of the same year the "People's Daily" published a news titled "Work-study Programme, Self-sufficiency", introducing the experience on work-study programme of the Xi'an Aeronautical Skilled-workers' Training School. In May the vice-president Jiao Qiming of this school attended the Second Conference of Eighth National Congress of CPC as a nonvoting and specially invited representative, and he delivered a written speech on the experience on work-study programme of his school. Also in this year an on-the-spot meeting was held at the school by the First Ministry of Machine Building, the Second Ministry of Machine Building and the Ministry of Labour, at which leading cadres from 17 cities and 73 technical secondary schools, skilled-workers' training schools and universities and colleges were present. The meeting called all schools to systematically learn from the experience of this school on work-study programme. In 1960 this school was elected a national advanced organization.

Promoted by this model, work-study programmes were widely carried out in aeronautical skilled-workers' training schools. From 1958 to 1961 production profits of schools in Harbin, Nanchang and Xi'an were increased and self-sufficiency in finance was realized. Using the funds raised by themselves, they built teaching buildings, enlarged practice factories and bought more teaching equipment. Things were greatly improved in the schools. It was proved that the work-study programme was a way of running skilled-workers' training schools with less investment and training more skilled—workers.

Over the past thirty and more years aeronautical skilled—workers' training schools trained more than 100,000 skilled—workers altogether. In the 1950s 345 excellent school graduates and skilled—workers were sent to the Soviet Union for study. After coming back they were assigned to the departments of aviation, electronics and shipbuilding industries. During the period of the First Five—year Plan a large amount of graduates from the skilled—workers' training schools were assigned to factories, strengthening the worker contingent and meeting the need of the development of aviation industry. They became the backbone in production and made contribution to prototype manufacturing and mass production of aircraft, engines and airborne equipment. The graduates were also an important worker source for many newly—built factories. Of the workers of new factories one—third were from old factories, one—third from the graduates of the skilled—workers' training schools and the rest from the apprentices. So new factories could began production as soon as their constructions were completed. By 1965 the graduates from skilled—workers' training schools made up 60% of the total number of workers in aviation industry, forming a reasonably—structured skilled—worker contingent.

The graduates from the training schools grew quickly to maturity because they had a certain level of special knowledge and manufacturing skill. Many of them made outstanding achievements in activities of production labour and technical innovation and hence they were either elected model or advanced workers or promoted to leading posts at different levels. According to a survey to the Zhuzhou Aeroengine Factory in 1959, the graduates from training schools made up 54% of the total number of the workers, 21% of the group leaders in workshops, 90% of the model or advanced workers and

Fig. 98   Students of a skilled—workers' training school working on engine assembly line

65% of initiators of major technical innovations. A statistics to 30 enterprises and institutions under MAI in 1983 showed that among the graduates from the training schools three people won titles of the national model workers, 18 were provincial or municipal model workers, six won the prizes of the National Science Convention or second—class prizes for science and technology achievement of MAI.

Section 5   Professional Education in Aviation Industry

In the past thirty and more years a guiding thought has been followed in the professional education in aviation industry that professional education should serve production, scientific research and economic benefits of the enterprises. Its purpose is to build up a staff contingent with modern scientific, technological and managerial knowledge and a skilled—worker contingent with middle grade workers as its main body. According to the principles of "serving production, arranging things coordinately, teaching students in accordance with their aptitudes and adopting flexible methods", various forms of professional education have been taken for staff and workers and their political, cultural and technical levels were raised.

There are three levels in the professional education hierarchy in aviation industry: higher professional education including professional colleges, radio and TV colleges, night colleges, correspondence colleges and various advanced training courses; secondary professional education including professional secondary school, radio and TV professional secondary school, training courses run by technical secondary schools, professional senior middle schools and various kinds of technical training courses in middle level; and primary professional education including various kinds of technical training courses in primary level for people before or after employment. Besides there are training courses for senior skilled—workers. The forms of professional education are flexible and varied. Most of the staff and workers are engaged in spare—time study or part—work and part—study, only a few are fully released from their regular work for study. The professional education consists of the systematical training with diploma and on—post training and other educational forms such as the complete course system and credit system have been also tried out.

At the early stage of aviation industry staff and workers of the factories came from all directions and most of them lacked production and management knowledge related to aviation industry. So, adhering to the principle of "grasping construction, production and education simultaneously" every factory organized on—post training for its staff and workers. Workers were organized to learn general knowledge, operation instructions of equipment, operation and service of machine tools, mechanical drafting, and theory, structure and manufacturing method of products, technical staff to learn Russian and manufacturing process as well as production techniques from Soviet experts, and managerial staff to learn management knowledge. At that time massive staff and workers in the industry set off an upsurge of learning with great enthusiasm. According to an imcomplete statistics there were 110,000 person—times involved in various courses of spare—time cultural, technical and professional knowledge in the first six large factories of aviation industry. After 1955 professional education stepped on the stage of regularization and systematization. Spare—time cultural schools, technical secondary schools and engineering colleges were set up one after another. By the end of 1956 the number of regular spare—time professional schools and colleges had been increased to 26, among them were seven spare—time professional engineering colleges being approved and registered by the Ministry of Education as the first batch of their kind. There were altogether 27,000 students in seven spare—time technical secondary schools, which made up more than 26% of the total number of staff and workers in aviation industry. Before 1966 spare—time professional education went on smoothly and a large number of staff and workers raised their cultural, technical and professional levels on their posts. After 1978 cadres at all levels paid attention to the intelligence development and took the development of professional education as a strategic task. Thus professional education resumed and developed very quickly. Besides various forms of on—post training, systematic training with diplomas at different levels were also developed. By 1986 the number of full—time professional schools and colleges had been increased to 14 with more than 14,000 students, among them were 10,000 students in engineering colleges and the rest in technical secondary schools.

Thanks to the continuous education and training the graduates from universities and colleges, technical secondary schools and skilled—workers' training schools had made up 60% of the total number of staff and workers in aviation industry by 1966. But the 150,000 young staff and workers who came into aviation industry during the "great cultural revolution" were not competent for their jobs because they had not received systematic cultural and technical training. After 1978 cultural and technical courses were offered for these people (called "making up two kinds of missed courses"), with more than 10,000 persons in junior middle school course and 90,000 persons in primary technical courses. By the end of 1984 the task of "making up two kinds of missed courses" was finished, one year ahead of schedule set by the Government.

Before 1966 the hierarchical grade structure of the workers in aviation industry was relatively reasonable, but it became unreasonable by the latter part of the 1970s with 48.04% (including 3.77% of apprentices) of the workers in grade 1—3, 48.9% in grade 4—6, and only 3.06% in grade 7—8. In order to improve the unreasonable hierarchical grade structure of the workers the training for middle—grade workers was carried out to make the workers on key posts or operating key equipment have the cultural level equivalent to that of the graduates from skilled—workers' training schools. Therefore 45 skilled—workers' training schools run by enterprises or institutions enrolled annually 6,000 students from in—service young workers for middle—grade training. Depending on the cultural and technical levels of the students schooling length was one or two years. After training and examination students would be given graduation certificate of the skilled—workers' training school. In order to raise the proportion of senior skilled—workers in the worker contingent six skilled—workers' training schools with good conditions made attempts to offer training courses for senior skilled—workers and enrolled the workers under 35 years old who had the cultural knowledge equivalent to or above that of the graduates from skilled—workers' training schools and the operating skill equivalent to or above that of the grade 4 workers. After two years' training the students should acquire the knowledge and skill equivalent to senior skilled—workers. The first 200 worker—students took the course in 1986.

Aviation industry is a newly–developed industry in new China. Training senior technical and managerial personnel from in–service staff and workers is an important way of improving their quality and meeting the need of development of aviation industry. In the early 1950s a special course for cadres was offered in BIAA and it enrolled leading cadres sent by factories. In the same decade 60 leading cadres from factories were sent to the Soviet Union for practice in its aeronautical factories. After 1956 spare–time engineering colleges and technical secondary schools were set up in some factories, which created a favourable condition for massive cadres and workers to study in a systematic way. In 1960 the first batch of 78 graduates from the spare–time engineering college of the Shenyang Aeroengine Factory returned to the production post and then became the backbone quickly with some being promoted to leading cadres of the factory. At that time the People's Daily, Guangming Daily, Wenhui Daily and other national newspapers reported their deeds and filmed news documentaries to introduce their practices. In 1961 and 1962 the spare–time engineering colleges of three aeronautical factories in Shenyang, Zhuzhou and Tianjin turn out 247 graduates again. According to an imcomplete stastistics the spare–time engineering college and technical secondary schools had turned out more than 2,300 and 1,000 graduates respectively by 1966. From 1980 to 1986 altogether 4,555 students graduated from the spare–time engineering colleges. Many of them achieved great successes on their posts. After graduating from the spare–time engineering college, Liu Hongchang,a tool worker in grade 8 of the Shenyang Aeroengine Company,improved the materials of broaches and hence the Chinese broaches surpassed imported ones in quality. Liu was honoured as the "Broach King" and became the chief engineer of the tool factory of the company. After his graduation Chen Zude,a worker of the Nanjing Parachute Factory,developed a special equipment and new manufacturing process, resulting in an increase of productivity by more than ten times.

Since 1978 several other approaches for training staff and workers were also taken besides spare–time engineering colleges and technical secondary schools. Aero - nautical universities and colleges held 16 terms of training course to train the managers, directors, party secretaries, chief economists and chief accountants for the national unified examination and 1,073 people completed their course. To the staff who were engaged in planning, production management, statistics, quota management, finance, distribution of materials, marketing

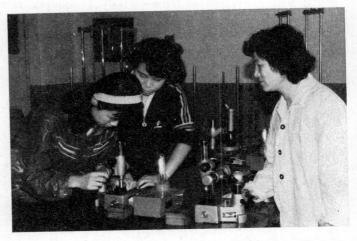

Fig. 99 Students of a spare–time engineering college are doing physical experiment

and other special managerial works, training courses on managerial knowledge were offered in bureaus and factories under MAI. By 1986 more than 80,000 person—times had been trained. For the scientific and technical personnel, programmes of continued engineering education were launched. Under these programmes the scientific and technical personnel were organized to learn foreign languages, electronic computer, new manufacturing technologies, value engineering, system engineering and information retrieval and processing in the light of their works. Thus they replenished and renewed their knowledge. By 1986, 150,000 person—times training had been accumulated.

After 1978 the teaching staff of professional education began to grow up and expand. By the end of 1984 the total number of teachers, staff and workers had amounted to 9,836. They worked diligently and perseveringly, devoted themselves to professional education and made great achievements. Willingly bearing the burden of office for decades on end, Zhao Changyou, vice—chief engineer in charge of training of the Shenyang Aeroengine Company, made an important contribution to professional education. Entrusted by UNESCO, he went to Japan in 1984 to investigate Japanese adult education. Zhao Zhong from the professional engineering college of the Shenyang Aircraft Company, Jiang Mingyang from the professional secondary school of the Shenyang Aeroengine Company, Gong Yinben from the professional engineering college of the Harbin Aircraft Factory, He Lijun (female) from the professional engineering college of the Harbin Aeroengine Factory, Ji Tingkun (female) from the professional engineering college of the Xi'an Aeroengine Accessory Factory, Chen Jianjun from the education office of the Xinxiang Aircraft Accessory Factory and others were entitled the national excellent teachers of professional education. Many professional colleges, schools and departments were entitled the provincial or municipal advanced organizations of professional education. The wealth of experiences accumulated in the professional education in aviation industry not only contributed a lot to the development of aeronautical education, but also had a bright page in the adult education history of new China.

Chapter XVIII   The Capital Construction of the Aviation Industry

In more than 30 years, the capital construction of the aviation industry has generally gone through three stages. The period from 1951 (setting up) to 1965 was the foundation—laying stage. The period after 1965 was the inland construction stage and the period since 1979 was the new stage of technical transformation in which under the guidance of the reform, open policy and vitalizing the economy, the capital construction of the industry is gradually advancing towards the self—dependence development.

Section 1   Building up the Material Base of the Aviation Industry

In fifteen years from 1951 when the first batch of Soviet experts came to China to help with designing the aeronautical factories until 1965 when the inland construction began, the sound material foundation was laid down through consistant and large—scale construction. This 15 years period again could be divided into the first half (first 7 years) and the second half (latter 8 years). The first seven years included the economy recovery period and the First Five—year Plan and was the period in which the capital construction of the aviation industry was going on most smoothly and most efficiently. The later eight years included the Second Five—year Plan period and three years of readjustment. During this period, although there was the setback caused by the "big leap forward", the capital construction of the aviation industry still made new progress in filling up shortages and adjusting enterprise distribution through its readjustment and consolidation.

The economy recovery period was the intense stage of the Korean War. The most urgent task faced by the newly built aviation industry was to repair by all means aircraft damaged in the war. At that time, on one hand, the industry had to repair aircraft and engine sent by the Air Force, making full use of the Soviet repairing trains and those simple repairing factories transferred from the Air Force, on the other hand, actively built up relatively sophisticated repairing factories to undertake heavy repairing task.

In June 1951, the first batch of 20 Soviet experts arrived at Beijing to assist in construction of the aeronautical factories in China. They came from the Aviation Industry Design Establishment of the Soviet Union and covered specialities such as technological process, construction, electrical apparatus, power and piping etc. They brought complete sets of design standards, specifications and related design information and helped Chinese technicians to design the aeronautical factories. At the same time, the Government tried its best to mobilize technical personnel and with priority distributed dozens of polytechnic university graduates who were in great shortage then, to the capital constructions departments of the aviation industry.

Besides, under the support of Premier Zhou Enlai, a batch of Russian translators who used to study technology in universities, were allocated to the aviation industry from the Air Force. At the very beginning, from the second half of 1951, this technical team of less than 100 persons, started their work on reconstructing and expanding six large repairing factories under the direction of the Soviet experts, thus lifting the curtain on the capital construction of the aviation industry in China.

The six large repairing factories then were the Harbin Aircraft Repairing Factory, the Harbin Engine Repairing Factory, the Shenyang Aircraft Repairing Factory, the Shenyang Engine Repairing Factory, the Nanchang Aircraft Repairing Factory and the Zhuzhou Engine Repairing Factory. To make these factories form their repairing capability at highest speed, the design departments of the capital construction spent much painstaking efforts. According to the practical experience of the Soviet experts

Fig. 100   Designers working

working in China, taking reference to the experience that the Soviet Union quickly moved their factories in the western part of the country to the eastern part during the War, they resolutely adopted simplified method of design procedure after being approved by their higher authorities. That was to simplify the traditional design procedure of three stages (preliminary design, technical design and construction drawing design) to directly making construction drawing design on the basis of the preliminary design. By this way, the design of six large repairing factories was completed in less than one year. These factories also adopted measures for three aspects of design, construction and production to go on in parallel, which led to rapid formation of the repairing capability of these six large factories.

The policy of turning from repair to production not only directed the development of the aeronautical production and technology, but also directed the road for the capital construction to advance. While these repairing factories were designed, consideration also was given to the prospect of transforming them into manufacturing factories in future. But manufacturing factories and repairing factories belonged to two different categories and their technological process, shop composition, equipment selection and factory scale were quite different. For example, aircraft repairing factory required disassembly and check shop, but manufacturing factory did not have this process at all. The manufacturing factory required lofting and fixture shops, but repairing factories did not need them. Especially for heat treatment, surface treatment and power departments, if a factory was designed as a manufacturing factory, it would need more capital and also could not meet the then urgent needs to rapidly form the aircraft repairing capability. If a factory was designed as a repairing factory, it would happen that when it develops into manufacturing factory, some part of the factory would have to be dismounted and rebuilt. To solve these contradictions, the design departments of the capital construction again successfully applied the principle of combining far future with near future, i.e., in terms of general layout and general plan view of factories, to insist on long term requirement and reasonable arrangement with long term requirement being taken as primary. For the design of costly and time—consuming heat treatment, surface treatment facilities and power station etc., meeting the requirement of repairing would come first. For some part which would possibly be dismantled in future, temporary measures were taken for the time being. Some heat treatment shops were located temporarily in wooden structured houses. In the meantime, the parts manufacturing and production preparation capability of repairing factories were also intentionally expanded, which prepared in advance favorable conditions for smooth transfer to manufacturing. The facts proved that this way of simplified design procedure and the principle combining far future with near future suited the then historical condition.

During the economy recovery period, following the policy of reconstruction and expanding of old factories, thirteen reparing factories (six aircraft and engine repairing factories, seven airborne equipment repairing factories) and seven secondary technical schools were set up. The 2,020 sets of metal cutting equipments were installed and factory construction area reached 162 thousand square meters. All these basically met the aircraft repairing requirement of the Korean War and created a good beginning for the future development of the aviation industry.

In 1953, China and the Soviet Union signed an agreement on assisting China with construction of 141 projects (later increased to 156 projects), among which 13 were aeronautical projects. Since then, the capital construction of the aviation industry was turning from reconstructing and expanding repairing factories to a new stage of setting up manufacturing factories in large scale. Although these projects were all key engineering projects of the First Five—year Plan, they were not advancing in parallel and in an all—round way. But rather they were constructed in batches, in the order of the schedule requirement of the development and production of new aircraft, and also in consideration of the growing up process of technical staff. At the very beginning, the emphasis of construction was put on two main factories ("main" here refers to airframe and engine) — the Nanchang factory and the Zhuzhou factory to ensure the trial production of the Yak—18 aircraft and the M—11 piston engine in 1954, and their timely turning into batch production. In 1955, when the largest amount of construction work of the above two factories were just over, the emphasis of construction work was moved to two main factories in Shenyang to ensure trial producing the MiG—17F aircraft and the Bk—1F jet engine in 1956. Since 1956 when the pair of main factories in Shenyang were basically set up, the emphasis of construction work was swiftly moved to setting up five new airborne equipment factories in the North—west and reconstruction of several airborne equipment factories in

Tianjin, Shanghai, Shenyang, Xinxiang, and Taiyuan. While the construction work of factories speeded up, the Beijing Aeronautical Institute, the Nanjing Aeronautical secondary technical school (it was promoted to an aeronautical institute in 1956), the Eastern China Aeronautical Institute (it was combined with the North-west Polytechnic Institute in 1957 forming the North-west Polytechnic University) and eight secondary technical schools located in Harbin, Shenyang, Beijing, Nanchang, Zhuzhou, Xi'an, Chengdu and Shanghai and also 11 technical workers schools were successively built up during the First Five-year Plan. During this period, the number of projects formally given by the Government to the aviation industry was 15, but in fact, 19 factories were newly built up or expanded and 4 warehouses and 19 schools were constructed (the aeronautical institutes and universities of higher learning were not included). The constructed area was 2,999 thousand square meters, of which 1,049 thousand square meters was factory construction area. The number of metal cutting equipments amounted to 11,160 sets, increased by 5 times in comparison with the year of 1952. These equipments included large specialized equipments for aircraft manufacturing such as the skin stretch machine and profile bending roll machine and precision machine tools for manufacturing aeroengine such as high precision grinder, borer and broaching machine. These equipments belonged to rather advanced equipments in the world then and they formed a material prerequisite for the aviation industry to be transferred from the original backwardness to manufacturing jet aircraft using modern technological process.

During the economy recovery period and the First Five-year Plan period, the capital construction of the aviation industry was quite smooth. Not only the construction speed was quite high, but also the quality of all projects was good, most of which belonged to excellent categories. The investment benefit was also good. At the end of 1957, the newly added fixed capital used for putting into production occupied 82.7% of the total investment during the First Five-year Plan period. Just because the construction plan originally stipulated for the First Five-year Plan was overfulfilled ahead of schedule, in early 1956, the aviation industry was advancing after gaining success and actively started to construct the second batch of projects.

The primary reason why the capital construction of the aviation industry gained great achievement during the First Five-year Plan period was that the Government established correct guiding principle for development and active but stable technical policy and made full use of the industrial base and technical manpower in the coastal area. From the Central Government to local governments, leaders of various ranks all gave great concern and support to the aviation industry. As early as in April 1951, the Party's Central Committee issued a notice to every central bureau and subsidiary bureau of the Party, regional military command and local financial committee, pointing out: "the construction of the aviation industry is a new work, which has high technical and political characters", "to successfully finish this difficult task, all organizations of the Party, government, the services and industrial departments should try hard to assist in the work". So, at that time, all projects in the aviation industry were treated as prominent tasks, and were asked to finish in time with all available manpower and resources.

Take the Nanchang Aircraft Factory for example, with the support of the Party's provincial committee and the provincial government, a feeder railway line of 3.3 km long was completed only in 9 days. When the factory was short of refrigerating equipment, the provincial government then decided to allocate refrigerators of the Nanchang Ice Manufacturing Factory to be used by the aviation industry, which decreased the freezing and ice manufacturing capability in the city of Nanchang. Apart from these correct guiding principles and policy, the following points were also worthy of being mentioned:

1. A stable and practical long term plan was an important guarantee for smoothly going-on of various works. The plan of the aviation industry during the economy recovery period, which was called "three to five years development plan" then, was defined under the guidance of Premier Chou Enlai and approved by Chairman Mao Zedong and Commander-in-Chief Zhu De. The First Five-year Plan of the aviation industry made on the basis of the above plan, was reported to higher authorities by the Bureau of Aviation Industry in September 1953. In December of the same year, this plan was formally approved by the State Planning Commission and became the legal construction program for the aviation industry during the First Five-year Plan. These plans were stable and practical, and all departments strictly executed them. They set the target clearly before the people for them to strive for. Capital and resources were concentrated on these construction projects.

2. The coming of Soviet experts who were complete in specialities to China to participate in design work played an important role in improving construction quality and quickening the construction speed. Because of adopting this decision, the design documents and drawings could be dispatched in batches and the design and construction could be conducted crisscrossingly, which provided favorable condition for preparing materials in advance, performing organization and design of construction and purchasing equipments etc. resulting in greatly shortening the construction period. To compare the Baoji Aeronautical Instruments Factory designed in the Soviet Union with other 10 factories designed with participation of the Soviet experts in China, the schedule of the former's construction was delayed for one year, which was a clear contrast. Also, because the Soviet experts worked in China, they understood the on-site situation clearly, made design more compatible with practice and could timely solve problems encountered in design and construction.

3. Sufficient preparation before the construction of the factory provided reliable basis for smoothly carrying on the capital construction. For the capital construction during the First Five-year Plan period, a series of works including the definition of projects, writing task documents, selecting factories, measurement, drilling and surveying, writing design documents, organizing construction teams, preparing construction base, ordering materials and equipments, arranging general schedule of construction, making preliminary financial plan for construction, carrying on preparation for production technology, training qualified technical workers and management personnel etc. were going on in a coordinate and orderly way. On the basis of almost completion of these advanced preparation works, the construction, installation and

adjustment / testing were launched. And also according to the order of the production process, sufficient manpower and resources were concentrated to solve key problems. As soon as one shop was completed it was put into production immediately. When all shops were completed, the whole factory was delivered for production. The reason why projects during the First Five—year Plan period were going on smoothly was the result of respecting objective laws and insisting on handling affairs according to the procedure of the capital construction.

4. The setting—up and strengthening of the management organization of the capital construction and strictly executing various management systems played an important role in ensuring the quality of projects and accelerating the construction speed. There were set up the management and design sections of the capital construction in leading organizations of the aviation industry. Also, in each construction units, relatively perfect functional organizations were established, and leading cardres, technical personnel and technical workers were allocated to form a complete set. They were representing the construction units during the whole process starting from the advanced preparation before the factory was set up until the final completion of construction and acceptance, and delivery for use. And they were completely responsible to the Government. With the purpose of smoothly carrying on the construction of projects and gaining support and cooperation from relevant departments, the factory construction committees were set up for the construction projects during the First Five—year Plan period participated by the heads of the relevant provincial and municipal governments as leaders and also the relevant departments and constructing units were invited to participate. The cooperative work organizations were set up on—site, which played an active role in coordinating various relations, unifying working schedule and ensuring quality. With the large scale unfolding of the capital construction, under the organization and leadership of Fan Ming, the deputy head of the bureau, who was responsible for the capital construction in the Bureau of Aviation Industry and with the assistance of the Soviet experts, necessary systems were set up including the planned task documents and the writing and approval procedure for the preliminary design, project management, quality checking, construction completion acceptance, planning, finance, statistics, material and management of equipment etc., which made the capital construction have laws and rules to follow and all works run orderly. This helped to shorten construction period, ensure the quality of projects and early put into production. During the First Five—year Plan period, after each project was completed, usually the account was cleared up with the construction finished. The excess material was immediately moved to new construction site, and the construction personnel also quickly went to new construction site, which was due to the sound system and the strict management.

Because of the interference from the "left" error, these successful experiences in the First Five—year Plan period were not well applied to the Second Five—year Plan. Sometimes things were going on just to the contrary of the above experiences and caused great loss. In early 1958, during the Second Five—year Plan period, the investment for aviation industry was 127% of that of the First Five—year Plan and was practical. But later, with the start of the "big leap forward", a large plan was blindly put forward "to finish the Five—year Plan in three years", " the investment of the Second Five—year Plan increaing by three times compared with that of the First Five—year Plan and the number of staff increasing to 300 thousand." In 1959, after Lin Biao was put in charge of the work of the Central Military Commission, he made a big plan to double the number of the military factories in three years, which made the capital construction scale of the aviation industry expand larger and larger. In 1960, more than 20 factories started to be built at the same time, which greatly exceeded the practical possibility then. Under the governance of the high target quota, blind command and boasting and exaggeration, a slogan of "to build two factories with the investment of one and with half the time" was raised out without any grounds. The objective laws were disobeyed and the procedure of the capital construction was not followed. The advanced preparation work was neglected. The design standard was arbitrarily decreased. For example, the safety factor of the main structure of shops was lowered from above 2.0 to 1.4—1.6. The standard for living area structure was also forced to be lowered. In some places, so called "quick constructing" was practiced paying no attention to the quality. In most construction sites management was in disorder. All these were resulted in popular low quality of the construction. Later, after check up, it was found out that 1,020 thousand square meters construction area had to be repaired and strengthened. At the same time, because of too large scale, diverse investment and material shortage, construction work for many projects had to stop and resume from time to time. The construction period was lengthened and production capability could not be formed for a long time. The 51 projects start-ed successively from 1958 to 1960, but no one of them was put into production during the Second Five—year Plan period and 20 newly started of them were forced to stop, which led to loss of investment worthy of more than 100 millions RMB. If repairing and strengthening cost was added, the 20% of investment during the Second Five—year Plan period was vainly wasted. The lesson was very profound. It was not until August 1961 after the national defence industry meeting held in Beidaihe resolutely carried out the eight charaters (Chinese) policy of "readjustment, consolidation, substantiation, improvement", that the passive situation of too large sclae capital construction, serious quality problem and disorderly management in the aviation industry started to turn to a favorable direction. It goes without saying that the loss caused by the "big leap forward" to the capital construction of the aviation industry was serious. This was because of the "left" erroneous influence, being anxious to success, shortage of experience in the economic construction, and also caused by arrogance and self—satisfaction appeared after smoothly finishing the First Five—year Plan. But, the people had the strong desire to change the economic and cultural backward status of our country. Through carrying out the eight characters policy and three years readjustment during 1963—1965, the massive workers and staff in the aviation industry corrected the deviation in the "big leap forward" and many methods not conforming to science. Many effective measures of the First Five—year Plan period were restored and the policy of "projects lasting for generations call for good quality above anything else" was again carried out. Management was strengthened. Also, attention was paid to making full use of the investment and to checking the execution of the construction plan. Great achievement was made in making up what was short of and setting up factories that were necessary to form a complete system. So, for the Second Five—year Plan and later, the three years readjustment, although setback caused by the "big leap forward" was experienced, the capital construction during this period still had important meaning for the development of the aviation industry.

a. A batch of backbone enterprises were built up in the inland area. In the First Five—year Plan period, to quickly form the production capability, most enterprises were established on the basis of old enterprises in the coastal area. Since the starting of the Second Five—year Plan, according to the general strategic arrangement of the country, new large aircraft and engine factories and important aeronautical instruments and electrical apparatus factories were arranged to be situated in Sichuan, Shaanxi and Gansu provinces, which made the distribution of the aviation industry start to be improved. Among these constructed factories, there were two sets of aircraft and engine factories and nine airborne equipment factories. Some of them had new requirement in techniques. Taking the Xi'an Aircraft Factory for example, its floor area was 400 thousand square meters. The design and construction of its reinforced concrete roof truss of the paint—sparying shops, which had 60 meters span with hanging cranes, was the first try of this kind of technology in the country. Special equipment used in this factory increased by an order of magnitude compared with same category of factories during the First Five—year Plan, which indicated that the development of the aviation industry entered a new stage.

b. The missile production capability was basically created. Because there were many similarities between aircraft and missile in manufacturing process, the general assembly task of air—to—air, ground—to—air and coast defence missiles started in 1958 and ground—to—ground missile engine and some finished parts manufacturing were undertaken by the aeronautical factories. To save time, the policy of utilizing existing equipments to make trial production on one hand and creating relevant cooperating conditions on the other hand was followed. By 1959, the missile production bases in some aeronautical factories which occupied dozens of thousand square meters and were of subsidiary character were set up in the North—east, North—west and the South areas. Among them, the highly clean shops needed by the assembly of missile instruments were associated with many new technical areas and very high technical standards in such fields as purifying filtering, sealing isolation, constant temperature and constant humidity, ventilation, testing and measurement technique, decorating material and high brightness lighting. The design departments whole—heartedly did their design and construction units strictly did their construction. The strict responsibility system was established for key work. For key locations of parts and items, the templets were made first and then the construction quality of large area was checked against the templets, thus ensuring the delivery with fine quality. From 1964 to 1966, the aviation industry successively developed and batch produced the air—to—air, ground—to—air and coast defence missiles. This was a big achievement by the aviation industry utilizing its existing conditions.

c. The construction of the research organizations and test facilities was strengthened. During the First Five—year Plan period, the aviation industry owned only a few test facilities primarily used for licence production. The material and technological process research institutes just began to be built then and the aircraft, engine and instrument design sections also were short of necessary testing facilities, so scientific research and independent design was greatly limited. In 1958, the first transonic—supersonic wind tunnel in China began to be built in Shenyang. This was the first large testing facility for the aeronautical research. Due to strong cooperation from various departments especially from relevant departments in Shenyang and Shanghai, the construction was going on smoothly. In February 1960, it was completed and put into use, which provided an important testing means for the independent design of supersonic aircraft and other flight vehicles in China. In 1961, after the Chinese Aeronautical Establishment was formally set up, in addition to the several research organizations set up during the First Five—year Plan period which were continuously being constructed, the AA Missile Research Institute and some aeronautical accessories research institutes including aircraft accessories and electrical apparatus also began their preparation work for construction in the South— central area. The Aeronautical Automatic Control Research Institute was moved to a new place resuming construction and the Flight Research Institute was also expanded on the original basis.

d. A batch of complementary airborne equipment factories were added. At the end of 1958, to match the engine production in the North— east area, the Aeroengine Accessories Factory was set up in Jilin province. In 1959, after the ten great buildings including the Great Hall of the People were completed, the Beijing municipal government welcomed another batch of construction projects to be built. In this background, the Aeronautical Electrical Motor Factory and the Aeronautical Instruments Factory were constructed since they belonged to precision machinery projects with less industrial pollution. In the early 1960s, when the capital construction scale was compressed in large scope and a large number of construction projects were stopped or terminated one after another, to fill the blank in the aeronautical products, it was approved after strict inspection that in the aviation industry, the Aeronautical Miniature Electrical Motor Factory, the Gyroscope Instruments Factory and the Hydraulic Accessories Factory went on construction and the Aeronautical Propeller Factory, the High Altitude Cabin Factory, the Oxygen Instruments Factory and the Magneto Factory were newly built up. Among them, the propeller factory was constructed at a high speed and its engineering quality was also of high grade.

In short, in the First and Second Five—year Plan and readjustment periods, the capital construction of the aviation industry in China made great progress. Although there were setbacks sometimes, but valuable lessons were learned. The practice indicated that the contingent of the capital construction of the aviation industry was a strong power working all the year round on the construction sites. Just due to their hard effort in more than ten years, the solid basis was laid down for constructing an aeronautical industrial system.

Section 2   Large Scale Inland Construction

In 1964, from the working meeting of the Party's Central Committee in May to the Secretariat's meeting of the Party's Central Committee in August, Chairman Mao Zedong raised the problem of the inland construction many times. In October of the same year, the "Work Plan of the National Defence Industry in 1965" approved by the Central Committee, asked various departments of the national defence industry to resolutely adjust the coastal area and be concentrated on the inland area construction. According to these requirements, in early 1965, the MAI made a decision to resolutely stop or terminate projects under construction in the coastal area and the middle area, to move the enterprises in the coastal and middle areas to the inland area and to move six airborne equipment factories in Shanghai, Tianjin and Nanjing to the inland area, thus lifting the curtain of the inland area construction.

The all-round unfolding of the inland area construction happened in the "cultural revolution" period. The disaster lasted for ten years long and caused serious damages to the inland construction of the aviation industry. However, due to hard struggle of the broad mass and the government's large amount of investment, under the guidance of the policy of getting prepared for war, a batch of construction projects were completed by the aviation industry during this ten years.

During this period, two sets of quite large scale aircraft production bases were established in Guizhou and Shaanxi provinces. A set of helicopter factories were established in Jiangxi province and a water-based aircraft factory was established in Hubei province. In two above-metioned production bases and in the western part of Sichuan province, the western part of Hunan province, the western part of Hubei province, a batch of airborne equipment factories and other complementary factories were set up. At the same time, more than ten factories in Shanghai were reconstructed and expanded for developing and producing large airliner.

During this period, the construction of research organizations also progressed prominently. The Aerodynamic Research Institute and the Aircraft Structure Strength Research Institute were basically constructed. The various ground test beds for the whole engine and components were built up in the Aeroengine Research Institute and another batch of research institutes were also taking shape.

Because most of the inland construction projects were in the mountains and valleies, the traffic was difficult and the local economy was backward. The work amount of making road clear, setting up electricity supply, water supply and leveling up the construction sites were very large. When the aeroengine factory in the Guizhou base was constructed, there were no high-tension wires. The construction workers and staff of the construction preparation departments of the factory and their relatives set up these wires by themselves. They stood in cold water to erect up posts and drank a mouthful of corn wine when feeling too cold.

The construction contingent of the aviation industry in the inland area was basically belonging to the Ministry of Construction Engineering. In early 1969 when the construction task was in intense stage, Chairman Mao Zedong also personally issued an order to transfer the construction engineering troop to strengthen the construction contingent in Guizhou area. Besides, a large number of local peasants were mobilized to take part in the construction work. Take the construction sites of the water-based aircraft factory and the research institute for example, there were more than 13,000 peasant workers. There were even more peasant workers on work sites in two bases — Guizhou and Shaanxi. There were many people on work sites with songs and flags everywhere. The work of traffic, electricity and water supply and site-leveling was basically finished by the local peasant workers with simple tools.

Although roads used for construction were paved, it was still very difficult to transport some large equipments into valleies. Many equipments were transported to the construction sites by manual pulling with steel tubes underneath the machine bottom as rollers. The shimmy test bed in the Structure and Strength Research Institute had a large flywheel 5 m in diameter, wheighing 67.3 tons which exceeded the loading capability of a bridge which the transportation had to pass through, causing great difficulty. The director of the institute, Chen Baozhen, organized the modification of the transportation means through use of actuator to start lifting. The bridge was also strengthened and reinforced and the driver steered the vehicle calmly and bravely to make constant speed advance. At last, the transportation problem was solved.

In the ten years from 1966 to 1976, through very hard effort, more than 40 projects were set up in the aviation industry. They played an active role in forming a complete system of the aviation industry, changing its geographical layout and promoting the economic development of the inland area where most of the minority nationalities lived.

But because of the serious "left" mistakes during the "cultural revolution", the lessons of the "big leap forward" were not drawn earnestly in the inland construction. The construction scale was made too large. At the time when the inland construction plan was made, the aviation industry was basically "scattered in general and concentrated in particular", i.e., to deviate from big cities, large industrial areas and important transportation junctions, to build medium and small scale factory group in a concentrated way and to make planning and design on this basis. However, all these reasonable working principles were totally neglected and the war preparation requirement was overemphasised. The policy of "along mountains, scattered and hidden" and "entering into cave" was followed, resulting in every factory and shop being spread over a large area. The Aircraft Component Assembly Factory in the Guizhou base was spread over an area of nine square kilometers and there were more than ten boiler houses. A landing gear factory was built with too many parts unnecessarily hidden under the ground, which not only wasted large amount of investment, but also made production organization difficult. Living conditions were also too simple, and houses were build with clay bricks and of low standard, which also caused many difficulties for workers and staff. The serious results brought about by these "left" working methods were exposed in the late 1960s. The broad cadres, masses, especially some cadres who had been engaging in the capital construction for long time, were feeling that it needed to be rectified. Hence, in 1970, when the so called "entering into mountains" and "build clay houses" were unfolded again for the capital construction, workers and staff in the Guizhou and Shaanxi bases and some other construction units refused to execute them, thus reduced some losses.

In addition, the locations of the factories were selected very hastily without detailed reviewing and surveying, the results were very serious. Take the Shaanxi Transport Component Assembly Factory for example, the location of the factory was selected in a hurry without knowing the geographical condition. In 1974, a large scale landslide happened and buildings of more than 50 thousand square meters were influenced. Some pillars of the shops were broken and walls slipped. The situation was very dangerous. Later, huge anti—slide pillars were driven deeply into the ground with investment of more than ten million RMB, then the landslip was tending to be stabilized. The Large Aircraft Design Institute was built for seven years, but it had neither airport nor railway in the mountains. Information was blocked and the life was inconvenient. At last, this institute was moved back to a city to be rebuilt with economic loss of 20 million RMB. Because the construction period of new factories in the inland area was long and the investment was quite large, resulting in high cost, the products were short of competitive capability. Some projects belonged to repetitively—building projects and the production ability was expanded blindly, which made the production tasks insufficient and new factories and old factories were competing for "food". The after—effect of the inland construction brought about very hard adjustment and reform task later. Since the latter part of the 1970s, after many years' continuous adjustment and rectification, the situation was getting better.

Section 3   Reconstruction, Innovation, and Self—dependence Development

In late 1978, the historically significant Third Plenary Session of the 11th Central Committee of CPC corrected the "left" error and afterwards defined the policy of "Readjustment, reformation, rectification and improvement" for the national economy. Based on this, the principle "to shorten battle line, to stress on major projects, to do what is in accordance with one's ability strength, to do well and get achievements" was defined for the capital construction of the aviation industry, and the construction of a batch of projects which were quite beyond its reach and more difficult were stopped or terminated, thus readjusting the capital construction to a reasonable scale. After that, the stress was shifted from building new factories and expanding old factories to technical transformation.

The aviation industry, a newly—emerging industrial sector, had to build up a batch of factories and research institutes at the initial stage. But after a certain base was established, frequent technical transformation should be carried out to maintain its vigour. In the mid 1960s, some efforts were made in this area. For example, in the new factory construction and old factory reconstruction, new technological processes and new techniques such as electrolytic processing, bonding point welding, chemical milling, precision casting and precision forging, non-metallic structure, shot peening and aluminium impregnation were applied. In aircraft factories, new equipments such as NC machine started to be used to promote the development of technology and to improve the capability of enterprises. In the mid 1970s, to develop two new aircraft — J-8 and Y-7, the technical transformation was separately carried out and the production lines were set up in the Shenyang Aircraft Factory and the Xi'an Aircraft Factory. The investment was only equal to that used to set up a factory to produce Y-5 small transport in Hebei province. The practice proved that this kind of transformation raised the technical level of old factories, and the investment effect was also good.

However, because there was a period isolated from the outside world, this made the application and development of new technological processes and new techniques more difficult. Also because in the ten years of the "cultural revolution", most investment for the capital construction was all used in the inland construction and the depreciation funds of enterprises were totally turned over to the higher authorities, the capital which could be used for the technical transformation of old factories was very limited. All these led to the ageing of enterprises. Thus, after entering into new period of the historical development, it became very urgent for the development of the aviation industry to take the road of self-dependence, i.e., through technical transformation to raise the technical level of old institutes and factories. The technical transformations in this period were mainly as follows:

1. Carrying out the technical transformation in connection with important technical import projects. In the late 1970s, through unified arrangement of the Government, centered on trial production of "Spey" engine, technical transformation, reconstruction and expanding at different levels were carried out in the Xi'an Aeroengine Factory and five relevant airborne equipment factories. A large batch of modernized production and testing equipments were imported, some of which were of the advanced world level at that time. This made those factories set up in the 1950s and early 1960s advance a large step forward in machine tooling and in the level of process technology. In the 1980s, centered on trial production of the "Dauphin" helicopter, technical transformation was carried out in the Harbin Aircraft Factory, the Zhuzhou Engine Factory, the Harbin Engine Factory and three airborne equipment factories (including propeller factory). Some production and testing conditions of high technical requirements were added in areas of composite material, heat processing etc., thus providing these factories with the capability of producing advanced helicopter, engine, main gearbox and tail gearbox etc..

2. Carrying out technical transformation in order to receive orders for aircraft parts and components from foreign countries. The Xi'an Aircraft Factory and others are manufacturing aircraft parts and assemblies for foreign aircraft companies of the United States, Canada and so on, and are learning the foreign advanced process technology. They also reconstructed some technically weak points in heat process technology etc..This method needed less investment and

its goal was clearly defined. Its transformation period was short and it was helpful for technical progress.

3. Importing measuring and testing equipments from abroad to improve research and testing conditions. During this period, some important and large testing facilities were imported such as the real time data acquisition and processing system for flight test, the coordinative loading and detection system with 100 points for the whole aircraft fatigue testing, the large electronic computer, the inertial test rig for wheel brake. Most construction of these imported projects occupied only a few percentage of the total investment, at most more than ten per cent, representing the principle of self-dependence. To install the real time data acquisition and processing system for flight test in air-conditioned shop of large area, to build the "Spey" engine test bed and to build the base of and to install the engine strength testing equipment etc. were quite complicated. To match the contract schedule signed with foreign contractors, the capital construction departments worked very hard and met the various requirements in a relatively short time.

4. Carrying out self-transformation with fund collected by enterprises and organizations. Since the 1980s, the reform of economic system widened the self-managing rights of enterprises, increased the depreciation reserve of fixed assets, thus mobilizing enterprises' initiative. The capital construction and the technical transformation also more and more relied on enterprises' own power. During the Sixth Five-year Plan period, the construction fund accumulated by the enterprises and organizations of MAI and MAI itself was 50% more than the investment of the State's budget in the same period. Most of this fund was used for the technical transformation of enterprises and organizations and its target was clear. It penetrated into various links and was more active than large scale construction and reconstruction projects. In the meantime, these small reconstruction projects were accumulated together and also promoted the technical progress of the whole trade connecting one another and advancing steadily.

5. Concentrating the State's capital on reconstructing key enterprises and organizations, to strengthen the weak links and to compensate for the "debt of construction" in the past. Because enterprises and organizations had raised their own capital, the capital construction investment of the budget which was allocated by the State to MAI for its direct control could be more used for the research and education cause. Although the aircraft design and research institutes in Shenyang and Chengdu had been set up for many years, but their research conditions and testing facilities were still weak. It was not until this period that they were strengthened and constructed with emphasis. This created necessary condition for the development of two new intercepter aircraft. In order to recover and develop the education cause, from 1979 to 1985, intensive support was given to six universities and institutions. The investment of the capital construction in seven years was equal to the total of previous 28 years and 385 thousand square meters of houses and buildings were newly built, which preliminarily improved the teaching environment and the living conditions of teachers and students. Besides, initiatives from various aspects were mobilized to construct houses for staff and workers in the whole profession, thus

alleviating the intensive housing situation accumulated for long time.

Section 4   Progress of the Design and Technology in the Capital Construction

The design and technology of the capital construction in the aviation industry were constantly improving and blazing new trails with the progress of the construction work and the accumulation of the practical experience.

1. Roof Truss of Large Span and Shop

Because the dimension of aircraft continuously increased, the span of shops for aircraft assembly, paint—sparying and maintenance hangar also was getting larger and larger. For the intercepter factory built up during the First Five—year Plan period, the shop with 36 m span was sufficient. In 1958, the maintenance hangar in the Capital Airport and the paint—spraying shop of the Xi'an Aircraft Factory required 60 m span, which greatly exceeded that of the ordinary shops. To save steel material, Lan Tian, an engineer of the Fourth Design Establishment (later was called the Fourth Planning and Design Establishment of MAI, abbreviated as the Fourth Establishment in the following text) and his colleagues designed prestressed steel—reinforced concrete roof truss which was assembled by 19 prebuilt triangular structures and upper chord bar of double slope trough type. Because the weight of the roof truss was as heavy as 67 tons and the span was large, the hoisting was a difficult problem. The Fourth Establishment, the factory and the construction organization together devised a scheme to put two roof trusses on the ground to make a large roofing panel, forming a roofing unit of 60m x 6m. Its weight was 200 tons. Then the pillar jacks were used on both ends to jack steel band to raise the roofing unit and gradually raised to the top of pillars.

Among the industrial shops in our country, this steel—reinforced concrete roofing system had the largest span. Its design and construction methods were suitable for the situation of our country. The steel was saved and cost reduced. The jack with large lifting weight was avoided. The construction work was simple, safe and stable. It had many advantages. The complete set of drawings were sent to the International Fair in Poland for show and won the prize of the National Science Convention in 1978.

For the general assembly shop in the Shaanxi Aircraft Factory built in the 1970s, its span increased to 72 m, and a crane of 15 tons would be hung up. Engineers Gu Guizhang and Zhao Yuming and others from the Fourth Establishment, applied heavy trapezoid steel roof truss in the design of structure. Its upper and lower chords were of welded manganese steel H shape section. The rigidity of the roofing was increased by 9 m large pillar spacing and 9 m prestressed large layered panel. Thus the number of supporting structures was decreased. The construction hoisting also used the method of lifting the whole roofing unit with steel bands.

Then, the maintenance hangar in the Capital Airport designed by engineer Liu Shutun and others also used steel roof truss with 72 m span. But because the construction work with riveting was inconvenient and it was difficult to ensure the quality of large number of rivets. So the roof truss bars were connected by means of high—strength bolts. However, the abrupt rupture of the high—strength bolts in use was a problem not solved yet in foreign countries. The Fourth Establishment made a large number of tests in the selection, design, manufacturing and construction of the bolts and summarized a set of solutions, which were used in that hangar. The hangar has been used for more than five years and there has been no one rupture among more than 50 thousand sets of bolts. This achievement was praised at the Bridge and Structure Engineering Workshop participated by more than ten countries including China, the United Kindom, the United States and Japan etc. in 1982 and won the second class prize for major science and technology achievement of MAI in 1984.

Fig. 101   The aircraft general assembly shop with 72 m span

In the 1970s, the design of large span shops was developing towards space network structure. The space network structure had advantages such as good integrity, good anti—vibration performance and was easy to hang cranes etc.. This structure was applied in the hangar and led to decreasing the number of pillars and the door could be opened laterally, which allowed aircraft going through conveniently and increased the flexibility of changing the variety of aircraft, thus raising the integrated production capability by about 25%. In 1975, when the Fourth Establishment designed a hangar for the Air Force, the bolt ball knot network structure was used, the pillar network being 40 x 36 m². Engineer Ding Yunsun and others changed the round ball shape knot commonly used in foreign countries into mine shape knot, which decreased the weight of knot from 40 kg to 19 kg. It not only saved material, but also could be carried by one man, thus greatly facilitating installation work. The method of high altitude separate installation using moving platform was applied on construction sites, which saved large tooling and rigs, reduced the cost and accelerated the schedule. This design won the National Gold Medal of Fine Design in 1984 and received praise internationally.

In 1984, when the maintenance hangar with 80 m span was designed at the Baiyun Airport in Guangzhou, the advantages of the same category of hangars in Japan and the United Kindom were applied and modified. To suit the features of high tail wing and low fuzelage of the Boeing 747 airliner, the whole roof truss was designed in a structure of fold line type space network, the height of the low chord of the high span being 26 m and that of the low span being 17.5 m. At the interfacing location of the

Fig. 102   The mine shape bolt ball knot network

high and low spans, space combined truss was used to solve the problem of stress concentration. In order to save door hangar and make the structure look beautiful, the space truss at the front gate was designed as hanging type. This was the hangar with the largest span in our country.

2. Clean Shop

The highly clean shop designed for assembling the air-floated gyroscope in 1961 was the earliest of this category in our country. For this category of shops, the dust partical in workers' breathing had to be considered. Engineer Liu Xingjie and others actively collected various reference information and finished the design scheme through summarizing the experience and theoretical computation in previous ventilation design work. A special room was established in the Air Conditioning Research Institute of the Architecture Science Establishment of the Ministry of Construction Engineering. In this room, the 1:1 full scale simulation test of the air flow organization was performed. The test result completely met the desired requirement. After the construction work was meticulously carried out, the clean shop was handed over as a complete project of fine quality. Although the performance of the air filter then was poor, it still met the utilization requirement. Because this was the first large clean shop in China, within more than one year after completion of the shop, more than 100 technical visits were received. Some guiding ideas related with meeting purification requirement and principles worthy of being considered were included into the national standard. The structure drawing of dense layout of the wind opening disperser had fine effects. It has been used for more than 20 years and has been the national standard drawing.

In 1970, with reference to foreign information, the Forth Establishment and relevant organizations jointly designed and trial produced the clean shop of assembly type of 1,000 grade with 300 square meters clean area and complete set of equipments. The number of dust particles of 0.3 – 1 micro m diameter per cubic foot was less than 1,000 (i.e., the number of dust particles per litre of air was less than 35), and was the first set of assembly type shop of this category in our country. The Aeronautical Gyroscope Instruments Factory tested it and put into practical use, and the various specifications reached the design requirements.

In the 1980s, China already could produce highly efficient air filter and the design and construction technology of the clean shop were getting mature. In 1984, the Fourth Establishment designed a clean shop of large area, in which 25 square meters belonged to 100 grade and the diameter of dust particle was limited to less than 0.5 micro m. This is the highest grade included in the international specifications today.

3. The Design of the Internal Environment and Large Special Equipment of the Memorial Hall of Chairman Mao Zedong

The construction of the Memorial Hall of Chairman Mao Zedong was a special task at the end of 1976. Because the Fourth Establishment had abundant experience and fine record of practical work in the design of constant temperature, cleaning and equipment, the Government quickly decided that the Fourth Establishment undertake the design task of the indoor environment and large special equipment to preserve the remains. Engineers Qu Yansong, Chen Shenyu and others immediately started work. This project was unprecedented and had no reference material. The time was urgent and it should be absolutely safe. So it really was a very arduous task.

It was mandatory to keep relatively constant low temperature and rather high humidity within the crystal coffin, and while the remains being looked up with reverence, this condition should be kept without being influenced by the indoor temperature and crowd. After repeated study, computation and comparison, at last they devised a scheme to use low temperature air film to isolate and cool the crystal coffin. But there should not form dew in the coffin because of the low temperature air and no sound to be heard or sensed by the crowd. For the sake of caution, a number of tests on 1:2 model were carried out and proper parameters were found at last.

In order to meet the requirement of keeping constant temperature and high cleanness in the small chamber where the coffin was kept, the highly efficient filter and other measures were adopted. The practice proved that the work effect was good. To lift up and down the crystal coffin between the storage area and the looking up table, the Fourth Establishment designed a scissor type lifting mechanism, of which the hydraulic tank was provided by the Xi'an Aircraft Factory. The Shenyang Aircraft Factory manufactured the tank. This lifting mechanism met the requirement of making the crystal coffin quickly and steadily lift up and down.

In August 1977, the whole system was successfully tested just for once in the Memorial Hall of Chairman Mao and won the prize of the National Science Convention. After many years' use, it is still working well.

4. Minivibration—Isolating Shop

The testing of the inertial navigation system and its gyroscope and accelerometer in the Aeronautical Automatic Control Research Institute required very high precision and the influence of the outside vibration had to be reduced to the minimum. The minivibration—isolating shop designed by the North—west Industrial Construction Establishment, which had already been put into use, used air bag on its deep foundation to support the testing area. The air—conditioning machine room, which worked for this shop and also produced mechanical vibration, was located 70 m apart. This ensured that the outside vibration influence on testing was less than 10^{-5}g, and less than 10^{-6}g at the best time. That had the highest technical specification for shops of this category in our country.

5. Engine Test Bed

The engine test bed is a necessary facility for production, modification and development of the aeroengine. In the 1950s, it was designed basically under the guidance of the Soviet experts. In the early 1960s, the Fourth Establishment began independent design of the test bed. The first design task was the No.9 test bed in the Shenyang Aeroengine Factory. This test bed was required to simulate the status of the temperature increase of the inlet air in high speed and low altitude flight, which had not been required for all previous test beds. The design team of the engine test bed of the Fourth Establishment headed by Zhong Siguang suggested to put an engine in the front of the engine inlet and to utilize its exhaust to heat the inlet air of the test bed. Tests showed that this scheme worked properly. Since then, in construction of test beds of the Flight Research Institute, the Chengdu Aeroengine Factory and the Shanghai Aeronautical Industry Company etc., the design work at various links was improved and much experience was accumulated.

In the mid 1970s when the British "Spey" engine was imported for the licence production, if its test bed and measuring and testing equipments had also been imported from abroad, the cost would have been much higher. After the analysis made by the Fourth Establishment, it was found out that although the measuring / testing accuracy defined for the test bed was higher than that of those available test beds in China in many respects, China still could design them on the basis of many years' experience and the Xi'an Aeroengine Factory was also in a position to produce it. Only the measuring / testing system had to be imported for the research purpose.

After more than two years, through the common effort of the technical personnel of the Fourth Establishment and the Xi'an Aeroengine Factory, the test bed for the "Spey" engine was independently designed and manufactured, and its installation and testing was also completed. In July 1979, the measurement and test were carried out again according to the British aeroengine test program with all British measuring and testing instrumentation. It was appraised by the Chinese and British parties that this test bed was of the highest level. It had advantages such as compact structure, high measurement accuracy, open field of view and being easy to operate. The horizontally movable noisekilling section was adopted. Its design concept was clear and innovative, and it could improve the inlet flow field. A British engineer said: "in some respects, this test bed is better than the existing test beds of the same category at R.R. company in U.K.".

The total cost for developing and constructing this test bed was only equal to several tenth of the quotation of the foreign manufacturers. This project won the First Class Prize for the Science and Technology Achievement from MAI.

China independently designed and manufactured this test bed, which not only saved large amount of capital and foreign currency, but also trained staff, raised technical level and strengthened confidence. In February 1980, in the report made by MAI on this test bed, the State Council viewed and pointed out: "we should believe ourselves, and not underestimate our own capability. If only the initiative of the broad masses is mobilized and the material foundation laid down during more than 30 years is fully utilized, we could perform many things."

The technically more difficult test bed was the high altitude simulation test bed of the Aeroengine Research Institute. Its design scheme was explored and studied for many years. At the end of the 1970s, the Fourth Establishment and the Aeroengine Research Institute completed the design through foreign consultation and surveying of the test bed of the same category. Most of the main equipments of the high altitude test bed such as high altitude test cabin, exhaust coller, diffuser, mixer, large refrigerator, large air compressor, large motor and large valve were the largest in our country or firstly–developed non–standard equipments or large installations, which had high technical requirement and were difficult to manufacture. The State Economic Commission and the State Construction Commission called many meetings and a batch of factories were selected nationwide to undertake the manufacturing task of these key equipments. This project is one of the State's main projects. The first stage engineering has been finished and the follow–on engineering is under intensive construction.

6. The Wind Tunnel Construction

In 1958, the first intermittent transonic–supersonic wind tunnel for industrial use was constructed by the aviation industry in Shenyang. With reference to the technical information of the Soviet AT–1 wind tunnel, the Fourth Establishment supplied the complete set of design drawings, including flow field calibrating / measuring instrumentation and all drawings of the electrical system. The First Ministry of Machine Building and the Liaoning province organized broad cooperation for the supply of equipments, instrumentation and material, and for the construction and the installation. This key task was fulfilled smoothly and with good quality.

In early 1960s, the Fourth Establishment and the relevant research institutes of the Ministry of Aerospace Industry cooperated and designed a complete set of new wind tunnels, including hypersonic wind tunnel, high—vacuum wind tunnel simulating stratosphere status and plasma zone wind tunnel simulating the status for space vehicles to reenter atmosphere etc. and all these tunnels worked successfully.

In the mid 1960s, the construction of large scale subsonic wind tunnel and the largest low speed wind tunnel in Asia began. To construct this category of wind tunnels, the First Ministry of Machine Building specially manufactured 3 sets of extra large fans with 2,600 kW power. In order to stabilize air flow field of the large working section, the technical personnel of the Fourth Establishment and the South—west Aerodynamics Research and Test Base, against the interference of the "cultural revolution" and using the facilities of the North—west Polytechnic University, carried out varieties of model tests. At last they found out the way to use metallic louver and metallic net to get rid of the influence of outside gust and rain on test section and solved this difficulty.

In the early 1970s, an all open—section wind tunnel of 2.5 m diameter was constructed for testing parachute with 90 m / s wind speed. During the construction, a problem of the building resonance occurred. Later, spoilers were added at the air feeding nozzle and compression relief openings on the cylinder wall at the air suction section, thus properly solving this problem. This wind tunnel incorporated a XYZ three component force scales to measure the drag of the parachute. In 1972, it performed trial running and totally reached the utilization requirement.

This batch of wind tunnels of different sizes, different wind speeds and structures developed by Chinese engineers made an active contribution to the development of the aeronautical and astronautical cause in China.

7. The High Altitude Simulation Test Lab of the Aeronautical Electrical Power System

The high altitude simulation test lab of the aeronautical electrical power system is a key facility used to simulate the heating status in high altitude environment, high and low temperature environment and at high speed, and the air feeding parameters in various flying conditions etc.. In the 1950s, there was no such facility in China, so the aeronautical electrical power system had to be sent to Moscow for checking and testing in high altitude conditions. In the early 1960s, the Soviet Union stopped performing this kind of tests for China, and it became a key technical problem then.

In 1964, the Fourth Establishment collected a group of senior technical personnel to tackle this problem and they solved problems such as forward and reverse rotation, large acceleration, large load, large noise, short operating life and the sealing of high speed rotating elements. Those testing conditions were reached to generate intake temperature and flow rate simulating the flying altitude and the environmental temperature, pressure, climb rate from the ground to high altitude and rolling speed etc. at associated height. The stable accuracy was 0.5% and the flying Mach number approached 2.5. This set of equipments has been stably working for more than ten years, playing a positive role in the production, research and development of the aircraft electrical power system.

Apart from the above—metioned achievements, there were also some other achievements worthy of mentioning. For example, the 603 slice type waterproof material solved the problem of roof rain leakage and underground infiltration. The H80 epoxy coat had strong anti—acid and anti—alkali performance and was in wide use. Also, there were negative pressure reverse flow regenerated Natrium for softening water for boiler use, hydrogen ion exchanger, dust—cleaning apparatus to solve powder dust damage, sodium hypochlorite generation unit for small scale water processing, electrolytic air—floated method for processing polluted water from plating, self preheating nozzle of energy—saving industrial boiler, the cyclic use of the processed fluorecent wasted liquid, microcomputer—controlled telemetry, remote communication and remote control units used for factory power plant system and various automatic production lines and minivibration—isolating research on multi—storied shops etc.. All achieved good results.

Section 5   Growing—up of the Capital Construction Contingent in Practice

After 35 years practical work, the capital construction contingent of the aviation industry accumulated strong manpower in surveying, design, installation, engineering management and responsibility system etc.. The Fourth Establishment of MAI was gradually developed from the design section of the Bureau of Aviation Industry set up in 1951. This design section was one of the design units which were set up the earliest in Chinese industries. At the beginning, there were only 97 persons and specialities were not complete. At that time, the construction task of the aviation industry was very heavy and urgent, and the engineering design was the highest priority task to be solved. With the Government's support, the Bureau of Aviation Industry invited a number of Soviet design experts in complete specialities to come to China for on—site design. At the peak time, there were 49 persons. According to the agreement between the Soviet Union and China, the Soviet side was responsible for design and the Chinese for cooperation. The Fourth Establishment arranged newly—graduated students to work together with the Soviet experts and to learn from them. These students got good quality and had received systematic and sound professional education. They were vigorous and able to absorb new technique and new knowledge. Soon, they took up the tasks for the Chinese side and got the practical training of how to use the advanced technique and to build modern industry.

In February 1955, the design section of the Bureau of Aviation Industry was changed into the Second Establishment. In 1956, it was changed into the Fourth Establishment and Li Zhaoxiang was appointed the director of the Establishment, Liu Zhenghui, Tang Lizhi and Xu Xizhen chief designers. There were altogether 1,560 persons then. The technical personnel in the engineering design grew up quickly through the practice of the First Five—year Plan period. In 1958, the responsibility system of the Soviet experts was changed into the consultation system. In 1960, when the Soviet Union withdrew all experts, the Fourth Establishment began to take the responsibility of the design task of the aviation industry construction. Since then, it has been the main force of the engineering design in the aviation industry. This Establishment not only had all the specialities such as the technology, construction and power plant for the industry and civil construction design, but also set up a powerful equipment design contingent at the end of the 1950s, which designed some complexed equipments such as aeroengine test bed, wind tunnel, various test apparatus and industrial furnace. Besides designing projects in factories, institutes, establishments and universities under MAI, this Establishment also designed some projects for the Air Force, the Navy and the Civil Airline. These projects mainly were aircraft and engine repairing factories etc.. Since the early 1960s, they also undertook design tasks for foreign countries such as Albania, Vietnam, Tanzania, Korea, Pakistan, Romania, Egypt and Jodan.

In 1979, after this Establishment was approved to be one of the first batch of surveying and design units making experiments of acting as an enterprise, the technical and economic responsibility systems were carried out in the Establishment. The Establishment also tried hard to serve the whole society and to open up new service area. The work amount finished in 1985 was four times more than that in 1978, of which more than one third belonged to jobs of other professions. For example, engineer Tu Chuanxiao and others designed a 43 storied aeronautical building in Shenzhen, and helped in the design of the technical transformation in the Tianjin Bicycle Factory to raise the annual production of the "Flying Pigeon" bicycle from 2,000 thousand to 3,500 thousand. For the production line for deeply processing soybean of the soybean integrated processing factory of the San Jiang foodstuff Company in Heilongjiang province, its equipments and technology design were imported as a package from abroad, and its general configuration design, construction and power system were designed by the Fourth Establishment. This production line can process 100 thousand tons of soybean per year. The technology design of the "August the First" Textile Factory in the Xinjiang province was performed by the Design Establishment of the Ministry of Textile and its general configuration, construction and power system design were also performed by the Fourth Establishment. The Establishment also set up a consultation and development department to carry out feasibility study and consultation service, and also opened up channels to jointly make design with foreign countries.

The Changsha third Design Establishment of MAI was set up at the end of the 1970s with 300 staff members. It was a complementary power in factory design of MAI.

The Integrated Surveying Establishment of MAI was developed on the basis of the surveying section of the Second Ministry of Machine Building set up in 1952. In 1986, there were more than 600 staff. It had manpower in hydrographical geology, engineering geology, measurement, physical surveying and engineering piling and has been undertaking all surveying tasks in the construction of the aviation industry. They have been to most part of China to search water source in dry areas such as loess plateau and karst topography and areas of complicated hydrographical geological conditions, and also dealt with various complicated engineering geological problems such as wettable macropore soil, swelling soil, landslip, collapse, fault and spongy foundation. They performed tasks such as large area, high precision and large scale measurement for rocket sled test range and accumulated abundant experience. In the early 1960s, an engineer Zhou Jiaqi and others used slurry drilling to replace sleeve drilling, breaking up the Soviet specifications then. This not only saved a large amount of seamless steel tubes and reduced the drilling cost, but also was highly efficient and of good quality. They also used directional exploder to avoid some popular accidents such as oblique lower part of portal, drilling stick and drilling burrying and the results were good. The DJ—1 type on—site large straight scissors instrument and light—weight induration instrument were successfully developed to deal with landslip, which played a great role in the construction of the mountainous area where landslip frequently occurred. These products won the major research achievement prize of the National Science Convention in 1978.

Since the 1980s, on the premise of fulfilling surveying tasks of the aviation industry, the Establishment actively entered into contracts for other work. On the basis of the original specialities, they widened business scope and undertook works such as engineering construction of the base piling, physic—chemical washing of the water well, dynamic and static load measurement and test, and protection and monitoring of the envinonment. This Establishment is gradually developing towards a department with integrated surveying capability.

The North—west Installation Company of MAI has more than 1,000 persons and it has undertaken many installation works of heavy and large equipments for the capital construction of the aviation industry. It has a lot of experienced and skilled workers and now is actively opening up new business fields.

Besides, in every enterprise and organization under MAI, there are a batch of leading cadres and management cadres engaging in the capital construction, who are working on the construction sites, for example, Liu Yaxin, Yuan Yangfeng and others, who have organized construction work of several large factories and production bases. They have made a lot of hard but meticulous management work from the factory selection preparation, committed design, acquisition, material storage and organization of construction contingent to the project acceptance and delivery to production departments. They have made their contribution to the development of the aviation industry.

In the 1980s, one important reform in the capital construction system is setting up engineering contracting company, which helps overcoming disadvantages of "being reimbursed for what one spends" and "big rice bowl" in the capital construction and can bring the ability of the specialized cadres in the capital construction into full play. There have been set up four engineering contracting companies. The China Aeronautical Engineering and Development Company in Beijing is based on the Fourth Establishment. Its business covers the feasibility study of construction projects, serveying design, enquiry and selection / purchasing of equipment, material ordering, engineering construction and construction completion and delivery. It can sign contracts seperately and also contract the whole process, i.e., contracting "turn—key" projects. This company is also actively engaged in inter—profession cooperation and developing and spreading new architectural material.

Generally speaking, the contingent of the capital construction is a contingent of good political and technical quality. It is highly experienced and innovative and hard working. They will make new contribution for the further development of the aviation industry and for the four modernizations of our country.

Chapter XIX The Management System of the Aviation Industry

In the 1950s when the Soviet technology was imported to China, the Chinese aviation industry learned the management idea from the Soviet Union and gradually established the enterprise management system of modern large industry. At the same time, the Government executed centralized management system of enterprises. Afterwards, although there were a few times of changes, and zigzag and consolidation were experienced, the basic mode of the management system had no essential changes. Since the third Plenary Session of the 11th Central Committee of CPC, the reform of the economic system was launched nationwide. To meet the requirement of developing the socialist commodity economy, centered on tasks to adjust the product structure, to strengthen research, to speed up updating aircraft, and to raise economic benefits, aiming at the drawbacks of the original management system, the exploration of the management system reform was carried out in the aviation industry. They mainly were: setting up the military–civil combination system, vitalizing enterprises of the aviation industry, carrying out the reform of the foreign trade system, advancing the reform of the scientific and technical system and executing system engineering management of the development of new aircraft. These explorations of reforms achieved some progress. But it was only a beginning. The reform of the whole management system is gradually deepening.

Section 1 Establishment of the Management System of the Aviation Industry

1. The Establishment of the Enterprise Management of the Modern Large Industry

At the early stage of the aviation industry, factories mainly consisted of repair factories transferred from the Air Force and also some factories transferred from the armament departments. The task undertook by these factories was to repair aircraft with the Soviet–made components. In the enterprise management, basically the system and method of the ordnance factories at the revolutionary bases during the war period was used. After 1951, with the help of the Soviet experts and according to the requirement of repairing tasks, the production management system began to be built; the technological specifications for repairing started to be carried out; and the quality checking work was strengthened. But, the management work then got a feature of repair and was short of the strict scientific planning management, technical management and economic accounting required by the large–scale production.

After 1953, with the carrying out of the First Five–year Plan, the large–scale capital construction began and large enterprises were set up one after another. Especially, the enterprises' task was changed from repair to manufacture, so the original management was no more applicable. At that time, the number of components needed to make an airframe was dozens of thousand kinds made of several thousand kinds of materials. Only in aircraft manufacture factory, dozens of shops and sections and departments were involved in design, technology, production preparation, components manufacturing, assembly, testing, flight test and delivery. There also were some other factories to cooperate with. The technical coordination in aircraft manufacturing process was even more complicated. Unified technical standards and technical specifications had to be followed and strict quality check had to be carried out etc..If any link in these chains was not properly planned or some cooperation failed, the production would not go on normally and the aircraft would not be rolled out. At that time, all people in the aviation industry from leaders to ordinary workers were short of experience to organize such complicated large—scale production. Hence, setting up the management system to match modern large—scale production became an urgent problem for the aviation industry. During the First Five—year Plan period when the Soviet technology was imported, the enterprise management was also systematically imported and the management organizations, rules and regulations required by enterprises of the modern aviation industry were also set up and gradually improved.

In 1954, according to the instruction from the Ministry of Defence Industry, to fully carry out the "one man leadership system" in enterprises was a central task for the whole year. According to this system, the director of the factory executed unified direction on the production, technology, economy and so on, and he was totally responsible to the Government. Under the leadership of the director, the chief engineer (first deputy director) and other deputy directors respectively responsible for the production, finance, material supply, capital construction, personnel matters and welfare, formed the factory's administration which was the core of the decision—making and control in the enterprise. Generally, the management structure was divided into six sub—systems — the production plan management, technology management, quality control, business management, personnel matters and education, administration and welfare. Some large enterprises also had the capital construction system. The responsibility system of the main administrative heads was set up at different levels of the factory: the factory top, workshops and sections headed by the factory's director. Each business functional system again set up functional responsibility system and post responsibility system for workers. Through the combination of these responsibility systems, every job was being attended to; every person was being allocated his responsibility; and the phenomena of imcomplete organizations, vague responsibilities, acting according to one's own will and nobody being responsible occurred during the stage of transition from repair to manufacture in enterprises was effectively overcome.

The enterprise responsibility system was centered around the development of new aircraft and production task. To ensure the orderly running of trial production and production, the management of production plan was strengthened and the execution of production plan was treated as the central work in enterprises. At that time, it was emphasized that the production plan was the law and the programme of action for enterprises. The plan was made according to three requirements: (1) to ensure the fulfilling or overfulfilling of the plan in terms of kinds and quantity of products; (2) to organize balanced production; (3) to shorten the production period to the minimum. Not only the monthly job plan was made, but weekly or calendar day job plans were also made. The plan making also promoted various quota management. To organize and monitor the execution of the job plan, a powerful dispatching and directing network was set up from the factory's administration to shops in enterprises. Production organization and management in aircraft and engine factories were very complicated. Combining with their own situation, these factories learned from the Soviet experience and gained good effects. For example, in aircraft factories, the parts of an aircraft were divided into several sets according to the technological processes and their processing period, so that the sets of parts could be delivered before their time. The grouped parts were supplied at different assembly process steps by a specially set up centralized store according to set delivery cards, thus ensuring the production running orderly. Because the management of the production plan was strengthened, by the end of the First—Five—year Plan period, the normal production order was set up in most of aeronautical enterprises and in some factories balanced production was realized.

At that time, the technology of licence production of new aircraft was complicated, so the technical management was widely strengthened in enterprises. The ways were following: under the chief engineer, a production chief responsible for organizing production was appointed and a chief technologist responsible for technology, a chief metallurgist responsible for metallurgy, a chief designer (early called the head of design section) responsible for design and a chief mechanic—power supply head responsible for equipment maintenance and power supply system running were also appointed simultaneously. The responsibility system of the production technology at different levels was established and headed by the chief engineer. The technical management was all—roundly strengthened. The management systems for design, technology and metallurgy, the equipment utilization and maintenance system, the technical safety responsibility system, and systems for material, tooling, technological equipments and power supply etc. were set up. Then, the Bureau of Aviation Industry clearly stipulated that the technological specifications were the laws in production and production was not permitted without technological specifications. On production sites, "white paper specification" (i.e. the temporary specification without being blueprinted) and "black specification" (the specification without formal approval) were not allowed. The technological specifications were also treated as one of the main marks of the trial production certification of new aircraft. New aircraft were not permitted to put into production without technological specifications being reviewed and approved. The technological disciplines were strictly executed and the responsibility should be investigated if quality accident occurred due to disobeying the technological disciplines. These ways of strengthening technical management played an important role in overcoming "the repair style" of manufacturing not strictly according to the technological specifications, in raising the workers' technical skill and in making the production quality conforming to specifications.

For the aviation industry, the quality of products was a management problem of life—or—death. So, the quality control was under direct leadership of the director. The quality monitoring system consisting of the technical check section, department and station was established under the direct leadership of the directors in all enterprises, and a complete set of quality check system was set up starting from material arriving at factory, through manufacturing, assembly, testing (flight test and ground test) and ending at the product delivery. Also, the field service system after delivering products was established. The Air Force and the Navy of PLA set up the product acceptance representatives stationed in all factories and the system of military representative stationed in the factory. Because these quality control and monitoring measures were adopted, the quality of the aeronautical products steadily improved and the reject rate gradually decreased in the First Five—year Plan period. There was no fatal accident due to quality problem. Thus remarkable achievement was gained in ensuring operational safety.

To set up and improve economic management and execute economic accounting were also an important aspect of strengthening enterprise management. In enterprises, organizations of economic planning, finance accounting, labour wage and material supply were set up and management systems in finance, labour, quota, cost and material etc. were established. The economic accounting was strengthened, and activities of economic analysis and the assignment of economic targets to each shop were carried out. In income distribution, graded wage system was adopted for technical personnel and management personnel, and eight grade wage system and time—based bonus system were executed for technical workers. For some part of workers, piece rate wage system was implemented. The socialist labour competition was widely unfolded.

During the First Five—year Plan period, formal cadre on—position study and worker training systems were popularly established. Schools of technology were set up in most enterprises and also staff part—time technical colleges were set up in some enterprises. Short period study courses and training courses were very popular. Leading cadres, technical cadres and workers all participated in culture, technology and business study. Special persons were assigned to learn from the Soviet experts. A technical worker was allowed to take the post only after his training being appraised and be allowed to raise their grade only after testing. Every year, a large number of graduates from universities, secondary technical schools and schools of technology were also allocated to take part in the technical and management work at grassroots and to be workers at the production lines. The quality of staff in the aviation industry increased year by year, and this was an important guarantee for various technical and management measures to be correctly carried out.

In the First Five—year Plan period, the aviation industry learned the enterprise management established by the Soviet Union which underwent some zigzags in later development, and some adjustment and changes were also made. For example, in order to solve the problems of neglecting democratic management and weakening ideological and political work, the "one man leadership system" was changed into the director responsibility system and the staff representative congress system under the leadership of the party committee. Workers participated in daily management of production team and cadres participated in production labour with "three—in—one combination" consisting of cadres, technicians and workers. It was emphasized to combine the fine traditions formed during the long—term revolutionary struggle with modern large production and to combine the political and ideological education with material encouragement. Also were strengthened three basic works — the grassroots work of enterprises, the management work and the basic skill training of staff. Many new regulations were formulated to strengthen the scientific management of the research and development of new aircraft. Some of the above measures were modifications and improvements to the enterprise management system, but the base was still the management system established during the First Five—year Plan period.

2. The Zigzag History and Experiences and Lessons of the Enterprise Management

From the late 1950s to the end of the 1970s, two big relapses were experienced in the enterprise management of the aviation industry.

During the three years "big leap forward" period, because of the influence of "left" errors, it was onesidedly emphasized to vigorously unfold mass movement leading to unproperly dismissing organizations and management personnel, and weakening and disturbing the unified control system of production and administration. It was especially serious that the " four director engineers and one chief" system was cancelled and a complete set of technical and quality control systems of product design, technological specifications, equipment maintenance, tooling manufacturing and quality check etc. were abandoned and seriously changed, which damaged the strict responsibility system and the fundamental work of production and technology. In the work of developing new aircraft, so called "quick trial production" was conducted, and the technological specifications were arbitrarily simplified. The necessary technological tooling was reduced. The scientific working procedure was violated and products were put into production without being design—certified. This caused confusion in the production order, loosed technical management, relaxed quality check and led to falling down of the industrial production and product quality. All these resulted in a serious setback in the development of the aviation industry.

In 1959, the rectification of product quality began in the aviation industry. In the early 1960s, according to the eight characters policy of the Party's Central Committee of "adjustment, consolidation, solidification and improvement", " Regulations of the state—owned industrial enterprises (draft)" (i.e. "70 points for the industry") issued by the Party's Central Committee, was all—roundly carried out. The production and administration control system of enterprises headed by director was restored, and the production technology responsibility system headed by the chief engineer was set up and improved. In all enterprises, raising product quality was taken as central work and carrying out technological process as key points; the sound consolidation of the design management, technology management, technical monitoring and check system etc.,in the whole production process was carried out. The economic accounting system was improved and planning management was strengthened. The finance responsibility system headed by the chief accountant (or the deputy director responsible for finance) was established. At the same time, the post responsibility system in various fields was strengthened. Through such consolidation process, by the year of 1963, the products in the aviation industry passed tests with good quality. In 1965, various management systems were all-roundly restored.

When the management of the aviation industry was going towards normalization and the production of enterprises went up day by day, the serious damage was caused by the "great cultural revolution". All practical management experiences and methods accumulated in long time were treated as revisionist and were neglected, thus causing great disorder and large setback in the enterprise management work. The situation of production without planning, operating without specifications, quality without check and labour without quota occurred once in some enterprises. The anarchism was widely spread over and the quality of products decreased seriously. From the late 1960s to the mid 1970s, Premier Zhou Enlai, and Ye Jianying and Deng Xiaoping who presided over the daily work of the Military Commission of CCCPC, grasped the quality problem and enterprise consolidation work in the aviation industry. But because the "Gang of four" played the bully then, the situation could not be dramatically changed. It was not until the crash of the "Gang of four", especially after the third plennary session of the 11th Central Committee of CPC and a few years of recovery and consolidation, that the enterprise management in the aviation industry gradually came back to normal status.

Although the two zigzags in the enterprise management of the aviation industry caused damage at different degrees(the latter one was more wide-spread and serious than the former one), their common features were: bringing about serious quality problems of the aeronautical products and great setback in the development of the aviation industry. The experience of these two setbacks told us that for the aviation industry being a knowledge-intensified and technology-intensified profession, its development relied not only on the continuous progress of technology, but also on setting up and improving the strict scientific management. The quality of the aeronautical products often reflected the working status of various aspects of the enterprises, and especially was a sensitive indicator of reflecting the technique and management status of the enterprises. When the quality problem occurred, the leaders of the enterprises had to acutely be vigilant, and seriously check the correctness of works in various aspects (ideology, technique, management and work style of the enterprises), especially the management situation of the enterprises, to timely solve existing problems.

The scientific management of the enterprises is the basis to ensure the quality of products and normal running of various works of enterprises. Generally speaking, the enterprise management of the aviation industry has two functions — to reasonably organize productive forces and to adjust relations of production. In the enterprise management, those features representing the production technology in the aviation industry, and the systems and methods to ensure the quality of products and normal running of the production reflected the objective laws of the production technology, which should be strictly obeyed and should not arbitrarily discarded. Otherwise, punishment would come. In the two above-mentioned zigzags, because the systems and methods such as technique management, production management, quality control, the strict responsibility system and staff training system which reflected the objective laws of the production technology were violated, the management base ensuring the quality of products and normal production was damaged, which led to serious results.

However, the enterprise management is not always unchangeable. With the development of science, technology and production, the changes of social production relationship, superstructure and objective conditions, those management systems and methods not suitable to new situation also need to be changed. But, speaking of reform, the principle of insisting on everything being proved through test should be followed. Especially, for those parts reflecting the features and laws of the production technology of the aviation industry and related with ensuring the quality of products and reasonably organizing production, it is necessary to follow the scientific procedure and to pass sufficient tests and strict approval. The change could only be made after the new method is proved to be accurate, reliable and practical. In the two zigzags, many so called reforms had not passed any test and were performed arbitrarily, so it was inevitable to cause serious disorder. This lesson is very deepgoing.

To pay attention to the scientific nature of the enterprise management, to strictly execute the systems and methods conforming to the features and laws of the production and technique of the aviation industry, and to insist on the principle of every new method passing tests for the management reform etc., in final analysis, are to persist in the ideological line of that the practice is the only criterion to check the truth. This is an important historical experience for enterprise management of the aviation industry. Sticking to this point is essential for the future reform of management and the realization of management modernization.

3. Centralized Management of Enterprises by the State

The enterprises of the aviation industry, which were successively set up since the 1950s, were enterprises of the ownership by the whole people and related with the nation's lifeline. Through the Ministry of Defence Industry and the Bureau of Aviation Industry (the Ministry of Aviation Industry since 1963), the State executed the centralized leadership and management over these enterprises. The development direction, production scale, number of staff and total wage amount of these enterprises were determined by the State, and the capital construction and technical reform were invested by the State. The scientific research and production plans were assigned by the State and the products were distributed by the State. The profit and depreciation fund were handed over to the State and the fund was allocated by the State. The organization of departments and units and the number of staff of the enterprise was approved by the leading authorities and its main cadres were appointed and removed by the leading authorities. The material was allocated and transferred by the unified material supply system of the leading authorities. The technical and management staff were allocated by the State from the graduates of universities and secondary technical schools. The main targets such as gross output value, yield of main products, trial–production of new products, important technical and economic quotas, cost reduction rate, total number of staff, total wage amount, labour productivity and profit etc. were all assigned by the State in order to check the enterprise. In this centralized administrative management system, the personnel, finance, material, supply, production and sale were all decided by leading authorities and the basic task of enterprises was to totally fulfill the instructive plans assigned by the State.

The Bureau of Aviation Industry not only executed centralized management of the plans, labour and material etc. of enterprises, but also executed centralized production scheduling and strict quality monitoring. This was one important feature of the management system of the aviation industry. Since the 1950s, the Bureau of Aviation Industry set up complete production scheduling system. In the 1960s, after MAI was established, it was emphasized to strengthen the mainstay line of the production and technology. In the offices of MAI, not only bureaus responsible for production and technology (e.g. the Aircraft Bureau, Engine Bureau, Airborne Equipment Bureau and Bureau responsible for missile) were set up, but also the Production Scheduling Bureau was established. These departments executed daily organization, scheduling of the production of the aeronautical products, solved various problems encountered in the production, especially the cooperation problems among factories. They also monitored the fulfillment situation of the national plans. The production scheduling unit timely understood the dynamic situation of the whole profession every month and every ten days. The leading authorities and grassroots of enterprises communicated each other and coordinated their working pacing. In the responsible bureaus of the Ministry, director engineers responsible for every factory were also appointed to timely understand and help factories with the key problems in production and technology. Sometimes, the important problems of coordination in production and technique were also discussed and solved at the production scheduling meetings presided over by the vice ministers responsible for the production. There also set up the Quality Bureau in MAI and a powerful quality monitoring system was established from the leading departments to the grassroots in order to strictly ensure the quality of products to meet required standards.

This centralized system played an active role in the history of the aviation industry, which could be summarized as follows:

a. Many factories in the aviation industry were set up with the purpose of the national defence. Their construction investment was big and the recovery period was long which made the profit of products quite low. Just because of the State's investment and the centralized management, these factories could be quickly set up and put into use.

b. The technical coordination in aircraft manufacture was very complicated. Aeronautical factories were scattered all over the country. The relations among enterprises were weak. In this situation, a unified production plan, unified technical standards, unified scheduling and powerful administrative management effectively solved complicated coordination problems and ensured normal running of trial production of new products and batch production.

c. Because aircraft flies with man onboard and military aircraft has to fight in air with man onboard, its quality requirements are different from ordinary civil products and also different from products of other defence industries. The aviation industry had to have very strict quality control and production order. The centralized management system contributed to the realization of such a quality control and production order without interference to ensure the quality of products.

However, some problems of the centralized management system were also exposed. They were as follows. The leading authorities overcontrolled enterprises and made enterprises becoming the attachments of the government's departments. They lacked self—managing rights. The management way of unified income and unified expending made the producers not to be concerned with business running, which caused the production, research and business running separated from one another, the responsibility, rights and profit separated from one another and also deprived enterprises of invigoration. Purely instructive plans, single structure of military products, and closed production system made the progress of technology short of stimulus and power, and also made cooperation difficult to further expand. The coordination of production mainly relied on administrative means. The government was busy with daily production affairs, but was unable to pay enough attention to the macroscopic management from long—term point of view.

To solve the overcentralized problem of the management system, in the late 1950s, the State tried the double leadership (central and local departments) system with the central as primary. In the mid 1970s, another double leadership system with the local being primary was tried. But because these reforms only touched subordination relationship, the basic mode of the centralized management did not change substantially and its drawbacks still existed.

Section 2 Exploration of Reform of the Management System of the Aviation Industry

In 1978, the third Plenary Session of the 11th Central Committee of CPC raised the task of reforming economic management system and the eight characters policy of " readjustment, reformation, rectification, improvement". In 1984, the third Plenary Session of the 12th Central Committee of CPC made "The decision on the reform of the economic system". In 1986, the Party's Central Committee, the State Council and the Military Commission of CCCPC made a decision on changing the system of military industry, which put MAI under the direct leadership of the State Council. These important decisions showed clearly the correct direction for the reform of the management system of the aviation industry.

Since 1978, with the unfolding of the reform of the economic system in our country and the development of the aviation industry, more and more urgent requirements were raised for the reform of the management system of the aviation industry. Firstly, with the change of the international situation, the required quantity of the military products by the State decreased by a large magnitude. The industrial structure of the aviation industry should be turned from the production of purly military products into the combined production of military and civil products. This required that the management system be turned from the single system of the military industry primarily serving the construction of the national defence in the past, into the military—civil combination system serving the four modernizations. Secondly, with the development of the socialist commodity economy and the transform of the aviation industry from the industrial economy to the planned commodity economy, enterprises had to develop new products, to engage in sale business, to make full play of their potential power and to actively vitalize economy. This required to reform the past management way of unified income and unified expending, to eliminate drawbacks of enterprises' being short of vigour and to give self—managing rights to enterprises. Thirdly, with the execution of the open policy, China was entering the international market step by step, and importing technique and expanding export had become an important strategic problem of whether the aviation industry could speed up its development, which required to change the past closed status of the management system, to create open system, to reform the foreign trade management and to mobilize the initiatives of enterprises to expand their export. Fourthly, because of the damage caused by the "cultural revolution", the gap in the aeronautical technique between China and the world's advanced level became even wider. This situation could not meet the requirement of the modernization construction and required that the aviation industry resolutely carry out the strategic guiding principle that the economic construction must rely on science and technology, and the science and technology must face the economic construction. To strengthen research and to accelerate aircraft renewal became the first priority item on the agenda. The management system of the aeronautical research had to be reformed. All above—metioned measures aimed at promoting close combination of research with production and speeding up the application of scientific achievement and their transformation to commodity. Fifthly, with the turning of the aviation industry from licence production to independent design and development, the technical coordination and management in the development of new aircraft were getting more and more complexed and the original management way was no longer suitable. The old management system had to be reformed according to the principle of system engineering, and to be combined with the reform of the contract system and the responsibility system, and to create the system engineering management for the development of new aircraft. All these indicated that the reform of the management system of the aviation industry was an inevitable trend.

1. Setting Up the Military—civil Production Combination System

In peace time, the aviation industry originally should be the military—civil production combination system, and produce both military aircraft and civil aircraft. Also its residual production ability can be used for producing civil products to serve the national economy. However, after the Korean War was over, the aviation industry in China was often in a pre—war preparedness status. Also, in the early 1960s, improper criticism on the development of civil products by the departments of military industries was made, so the civil aircraft and civil products in the aviation industry were not suitably developed. That led to the long time existance of the single structure of military products and its associated system.

Since 1979, the State emphasized that the military industries should carry out the military–civil combination policy. Deng Xiaoping suggested many times that the system of military industries should be properly solved to end the isolated situation of the military industries. In 1983, the State Planning Commission, the State Economic Commission and the Scientific and Industrial Commission of the National Defence jointly convened a meeting to further promote the military–civil combination and to develop civil products in the departments of military industries. During this period, Premier Zhao Ziyang clearly suggested that "the enterprises of military industries should be a military–civil production combination system". In the early 1986, when Premier Zhao Ziyang met 20 experts of the Ministry of Aviation Industry and the Ministry of Armament Industry, he further explained the problem of setting up military–civil production combination enterprises. He pointed out that the concept of the so-called military–civil combination was completely different from the concept that enterprises of military industries produced civil products. It should produce both military and civil products. This was related with the enterprises' development strategy, long term planning, technical transformation, leading method and business management etc.. In July of the same year, the Party's Central Committee, the State Council and the Military Commission of CCCPC decided to put the Ministry of Nuclear Industry, the Ministry of Aviation Industry, the Ministry of Armament Industry and the Ministry of Space Industry under the direct leadership of the State Council. This further created conditions for these departments to go beyond the "small arena" of military production and to participate in the construction of the four modernizations.

According to the policy of military–civil production combination stipulated by the State and the spirit of the State leader's speech, a military–civil production combination system was gradually set up in the aviation industry while the structure of products was readjusted in successively few years, starting forming a model. Its main representations were as follows:

Military–civil production combination, civil production being primary, aeronautical production being basic and diversified economy were defined as the guiding principle for the development strategy and the reform of management system of the aviation industry, and has gained remarkable progress in practical work. Through a few years continuous readjustment, the service direction of the aviation industry has turned from primarily serving the construction of the national defence into military products taking priority, overall arrangement, serving both the construction of the national defence and the development of the civil aviation, serving the technical transformation of various professions of the national economy, serving the market of the light industry and serving the export of foreign trade. According to the requirements of the aeronautical production being basic and diversified economy, while the development of military aircraft goes on, the civil aircraft is also being developed with stress and full use has been made of the aeronautical technique and its residual capability to produce non-aeronautical products. Because the structure of products was readjusted, there emerged a trend for civil aircraft to be developed quicker. During the Sixth Five-year Plan period, the production lines of large, medium and small airliners and the production lines contracting many kinds of the aeronautical parts and assemblies of foreign countries were set up one after the other. The small civil aircraft such as Y-5, Y-11, Y-12I and Y-12II and Z-9 helicopter were put into short route air transportation and the general aviation use in agriculture and forestry, surveying and oil industry. The Y-7, Y-7-100 feeder airliners and Y-8 medium cargo transport have been put into regular passenger and cargo flight. The first MD-82 large airliner assembled in China has also been delivered to CAAC and is in scheduled flights now. More than 50 sets of the aeroengines have been retrofitted into industrial gas turbines which are used in various oilfields in our country. The civil products serving the economic construction also developed quickly. The percentage of the output value of the civil products of the whole profession in the total industrial output value was 6.4% in 1978 and rose to 61.2% in 1986.

The military-civil combination structure is taking form now. There are a batch of civil aircraft manufacture factories, such as aircraft manufacturing companies and factories in Shanghai, Harbin and Shijiazhuang. Civil aircraft production lines have been set up in some military aircraft factories such as the Xi'an Aircraft Company. Other aircraft factories have undertaken or are preparing to undertake the manufacturing task of civil aircraft, assemblies and aeronautical parts and assemblies of foreign countries. In the meantime, the production lines, shops and subsidiary factories producing non-aeronautical products are emerging continuously in the aeronautical enterprises. During the Sixth Five-year Plan period, 60 important production lines of civil products were established. There are appearing three categories of enterprises: military-civil combination enterprises with the aeronautical products being primary, military-civil combination enterprises with non-aeronautical products being primary and enterprises totally engaging in non-aeronautical products.

The distribution of the main production elements such as capital, manpower and equipments was changing towards the direction of military-civil combination. While the State ensured the capital for developing military aircraft, since 1985, the capital for developing civil aircraft has been included in the State plan. Some part of the capital owned by the enterprise was also transferred to the production of civil products. This capital plus the bank loan, the State's subsidies and the subsidies of the relevant professions became the capital source for developing civil aircraft and civil products and for making technical transformation to undertake the production of the aeronautical parts and assemblies for foreign companies. At the same time, a quite large portion of the leading cadres, technical personnel and workers were moving towards the production of civil products. While a small number but highly trained manpower of enterprises was used for developing military aircraft, the design organizations, business and sales organizations and production lines for civil aircraft and civil products have been substantiated and strengthened.

The business practice was also changing according to the military–civil combination requirements. In conformity with the features that the production and sale of the civil aircraft were adjusted by both planning and market, the sale and service practice of the civil aircraft were also diversified. Apart from that the civil aircraft were produced and supplied to the Civil Airline through the channel of the State's instructive plans, the cross–professional cooperation with local departments also started to be established. For example, in the aviation industry, cooperating with the Navy and departments in the oil industry, the Chinese Off–shore Helicopter Service Co. was set up. Cooperating with departments in the geology and minerals field, the special aircraft for mine–surveying were produced and supplied. Assisting the Xinjiang Production and Construction Corp., the Agriculture Air–service Squadron was set up and the Aircraft Service Squadron was formed by relevant factories and so on. The international trade cooperation of the aeronautical products also began. The cooperation relationships with companies of Federal Germany, United States, United Kindom, Canada, France and Italy have been set up successively on various programs.

The aviation industry's turning from single military industry system to military–civil combination system was an important reform task, and also an arduous readjustment task. It already made a good beginning. It is also necessary to go on exploration in this field according to the government's policy to solve this problem step by step.

2. Vitalizing Enterprises

In more than 30 years, the aviation industry has grown up into a fairly large–scale industry. In addition to fulfilling the military and civil research and production tasks, there remains relatively large potential. However, in the highly centralized management system, the responsibilities, rights and profits were separated from one another and the enterprise lacked initiatives to use their remaining potential to open up new production areas and to raise economic benefits. Since 1978, in point of this situation, on the ground of the government requirements on reform, opening to the world and vitalizing economy, a reform of the management system was carried out in the aviation industry. The core was to change the situation of the leading body's overcontrolling of enterprises, to give enterprises self–managing rights, to vitalize enterprises, to make enterprises really become relatively independent economic entities, become manufacturers and managing organizations of the socialist commodity with autonomous management and assuming sole responsibility for their profits and losses, and to have the capability of developing products, opening up market, self–reforming and self–developing.

Hence, MAI adopted a series of reform measures. Since 1980, according to the government's policy of fixed amount of profits to be handed to higher authorities and the extra part being remained with and controlled by enterprises which would be unchanged for six years for MAI, MAI conducted the responsibility management system the center of which was the profit contracting responsibility for enterprises. In 1984 and 1985, MAI issued " Temporary regulations to further expand self—managing rights of the aeronautical enterprises" and "The complementary regulations to further expand enterprises' self—managing rights to advance the reform". In 1987, MAI again issued "Temporary regulations to further expand enterprises' self—managing rights to strengthen enterprises' vitality". Reform also promoted the change of MAI functions. In summary, there are four focal points of the reform. They are as follows:

a. Reforming the Planning System and Expanding the Management and Decision—making Rights

According to the principle of "concentration of the aeronautical products and diversification of civil products", MAI gradually reduced the scope of instructive plans and expanded the scope of guiding plans and the market adjustment.

For aeronautical military products such as aircraft, engine, missile and airborne equipment, the instructive plans are carried out, at the same time, conditions should be actively created to change the instructive plan to contract system. That is to say, the buyers directly sign contracts with the main supplier (companies) and the main factories (companies) again sign contracts with the cooperating factories (companies). The relationship between various fields are connected through contracts. For task assignment in new aircraft development, the policy of combining planned assignment with bidding to choose the best manufacturer is carried out. The MAI gradually reduces its direct instruction and is mainly responsible for monitoring, coordination and service work during the execution of contracts.

For civil aircraft, different management methods are used for various types of airliners. For civil transport and general aviation aircraft, the method of combining the instructive plan with opening up market is adopted. For microlight aircraft, then the manufacturers have total control rights.

The industrial gas turbine is a major product transferred from the aeronautical technique to the non—aeronautical application. This product and other civil products organized by MAI for export are primarily controlled by instructive plans. As for all other civil products, guiding plans and the market adjustment are executed. For some important backbone products, enterprises need assistance during their development stage. Then these projects will be taken into the State's plan of technical transformation. But in operation, manufacturers are still provided with their self—managing rights.

Through this reform, enterprises have relatively large decision—making rights in business. They can independently adjust the structure of their products in a large scope and continuously develop and produce more products needed by the State and the market. Thus, since last several years of reform, the output value and varieties of civil products in the aviation industry have grown up quickly. From 1978 to 1986, the yearly growth rate of the output value of civil products in the whole profession was 37.4% on average and the assortment of goods of the civil products increased from more than 200 to more than 3,000. Apart from aircraft and various civil electro—mechanic products, more than 400 specialized equipments, instruments, instrumentation and production lines were also provided for the technical transformation of 28 trades such as the energy, transportation, textile, light industry, foodstuff, construction material, medicine and environmental protection. More than 3,000 components and spare parts replacing imported ones were provided for imported large oil, chemical—industry, chemical fibre and metallurgical equipments. This indicated that the reform measures vitalizing enterprises played a positive and promotive role in raising economic benefits.

b. Executing Responsibility Contracting System (with Profit Contracting as the Main Content) to Give Enterprises the Pressure and Impetus to Run their Business

The practical methods were as follows: For profitable enterprises, MAI executed a policy "to contract a basic profit to be handed over to the above, and to divide the surplus profit according to a preset percentage" or " to divide the whole profit according to a preset percentage". For minor profitable enterprises, a policy of "a fixed part of profit totally handed over, all the extra remained with the enterprise" was applied. For planned lossing enterprises, then the policy of "verifying a limit, fixing a date to change the lossing status, dividing the part of revenue less the limit, getting no compensation for extra lossing and, all profit will be the enterprise's" was carried out. The enterprise's depreciation fund was gradually changed from partly being handed over to the above to being totally remained with the enterprise, which was mainly used for the technical transformation and equipment upgrading. The economic contracting system was also conducted for the enterprise's research projects and the saved research expense could be used by the enterprise according to relevant regulations. The enterprise has rights to utilize its own capital to develop transprofessional cooperation and make investment to other enterprises according to the principle of mutual benefits. Enterprises also could combine research fund, production development fund, depreciation fund and overhaul fund together for reasonable use.

After the profit contracting system went into effect, enterprises felt pressed in business and tried every means to develop products and open up market, improve management, increase income and save expense, which pushed enterprises to change itself from a purely production organ to a production, business running and developing organ. At the same time, after making profit and having same amount of profit remained, enterprises strengthened their economic power. According to statistics, during the Sixth Five—year Plan period when profit contracting system was executed, the total profit amount of the whole trade increased three times compared with that of the Fifth Five—year Plan period. About 40% of the enterprises' remaining profit was used for expanding production capacity. This capital plus the depreciation remaining fund and overhaul fund, became an important capital resource for the enterprise's technical transformation and products development. Enterprises also made use of the remaining profit and self—collected capital to solve some welfare problems for their staff. In the Sixth Five—year Plan period, the area of staff's housing increased 33.2% per year on average in comparison with the Fifth Five—year Plan period.

c. Reforming Labour and Personnel System and the Management of Wage and Bonus Distribution to Mobilize Staff's Initiatives

The main contents of the reform were: executing contract system with new staff, executing a rotating system for heavy physical labour and those kinds of work detrimental to health, entrusting enterprises with some recruitment rights, an enterprise's total standard wage and bonus amount being linked to its profit, extra bonus to encourage the production of civil products and for the development of new aircraft etc.. At the same time, MAI also trial executed the overall amount of wage contracting method, adding more persons without increasing the total amount of wage, reducing the number of staff without decreasing the total amount of wage, wage saved from the reduced number of staff being controlled by the enterprise. These reform measures reflected the spirit of selecting better staff, reasonable distribution of manpower, rewarding better workers and punishing worse ones, which promoted the full play of staff's initiatives, strengthened the staff's disciplines, increased income and labour productivity. In 1986, the total labour productivity in the aviation industry was increased by 28.4% in comparison with the year of 1978.

d. Conducting the Internal Reform within Enterprises to Vitalize Enterprises

The delegating of rights by the leading bodies created conditions to vitalize enterprises, but to really vitalize enterprises required the internal integrated reform. Following measures were taken: to reform the internal leadership system within enterprises and to change the director responsibility system under the collective leadership of the Party's Committee into the director (manager) responsibility system, to connect the director's term target responsibility system with the enterprise's economic contracting responsibility system, to execute economic responsibility system with responsibility being subcontracted at different levels within enterprises, to give rights to subsidiary factories etc.. At the same time, transprofessional, transregional economic combinations were developed in many ways. These reform measures reflected the spirit of proper separation of the enterprise's ownership and management rights and the combination of responsibility, rights and

Fig. 103 The civil product of the Shenyang Aeroengine Company — glass curtain wall

profit and created conditions for enterprises to unfold democratic management and to mobilize staff's initiatives, thus advancing enterprises' production, development and management. During reform process, in the Shenyang Aeroengine Company, the development, production and business of the main product (aeroengine) were under the company's direct leadership.

Meanwhile, six subsidiary factories were set up in the company. Among the six were factories of the industrial gas turbine, aluminium profile and gas meter etc..They also established economic relations with more than 60 enterprises, research institutes and village—run enterprises. The production of civil products in enterprises grew quickly and business was vitalized. According to statistics of the whole profession in 1986, enterprises in the aviation industry established 273 combined enterprises with 698 organizations and agencies of 23 provinces and cities, most of which gained good economic benefits.

3. Reform of the Foreign Trade System

To reform the foreign trade system, to mobilize the enterprise's initiatives and to expand export were important measures for the aviation industry to carry out the open policy and to speed up self—development. Since the CATIC was set up in 1979, the reform work on the foreign trade system in the aviation industry has been constantly carried out.

The export of aeronautical products was the mainstay of the export for the aviation industry. To promote the export of the aeronautical products and to make the export work proceed orderly, different ways were adopted for different kinds of products.

Because of the special features of military aircraft, its export was managed solely by CATIC and participated by relevant enterprises. After contracts with foreign countries were signed, these contracts were included into the national unified plans and the economic contracts were signed between CATIC and enterprises. Enterprises could retain a percentage of foreign currency for the export, and get bonus, and the bonus was connected with three targets: received foreign currency, profit and performance rate of the contracts.

The export of civil aircraft and the aeronautical parts and assemblies was also controlled and managed by CATIC, and a policy of foreign currency retention for enterprises was carried out.

The export of civil electro—mechanical products was up to enterprises to make business. Enterprises could independently select export channel. The CATIC is now both doing business for some enterprises and representing the others in regard to the export of civil products. It will gradually become a representative for civil product export. The percentage of foreign currency retention for export of civil products was higher than that of the aeronautical products, so as to encourage enterprises to actively open up their international market and develop civil products for export.

Those enterprises which had backbone products for export and high foreign currency income, could be approved to be the foreign trade bases or enterprises with expanded rights in foreign trade. These enterprises could have favorable conditions to run foreign trade. By the year of 1986, there were six foreign trade bases and 15 enterprises with expanded rights in foreign trade.

These measures mobilized enterprises' initiatives to expand export. Before 1982, the Chengdu Aeroengine Factory had had no export of the aeronautical products at all. But by

1986, through 5 years hard work, this factory had produced 66 kinds and more than 40 thousand parts and assemblies of aeroengine. These items were exported to the United States and won U.S. Pratt Witney's confidence for their good quality and timely delivery. Thus, both sides established long–term cooperation and trade relationship. In 1986, both sides further signed a contract to jointly develop and produce FT8 industrial and shipborne gas turbine. In the meantime, this factory also signed 26 export contracts with 15 companies of the United States, Canada, the United Kindom and the Federal Republic of Germany. In 1985 and 1986, this factory was approved to be the enterprise with expanded rights in foreign trade and foreign trade base respectively by the State Council and the Sichuan province. In the whole aviation industry, there are 49 enterprises supplying export products, such as aircraft, aeroengine, aeronautical parts and assemblies, industrial gas turbine, parachute and many kinds of electro–mechanical products. With the unfolding of the reform of the foreign trade system, the export and foreign trade in the aviation industry in China is steadily advancing.

4. Reform of the Science and Technology System

After the National Science Convention, the reform of the science and technology system in the aviation industry gradually started. After the Party's Central Committee made the "Decision on the Reform of Science and Technology" in 1985, under the guidance of the strategic principles that the economic construction must rely on science and technology, and the science and technology must be oriented to the economic construction, the reform was further pushed forward.

The focal point of the reform of the science and technology system in the aviation industry was to promote the combination of the product design units with the production units to speed up replacement of old generation of the aeronautical products. According to different situations of product design units, different forms of combination were adopted.

To set up the product design institutes in factories was a form of close combination. In the late 1950s, this kind of design institutes already emerged and were set up since then one after the other. Since the 1970s, this kind of design institutes developed more vigorously. For example, the aircraft design and research institute, the missile design institute in the Nanchang Aircraft Factory and a number of airborne equipment design institutes belonged to this category. Practice proved that this kind of combining research and production could speed up the development process of new products, shorten development period and make products quickly to be put into production and delivered for use. Support and assistance should continuously be given to this kind of combination.

That the independent product design and research institutes join enterprises was another form. In 1979, the Shenyang Aircraft Design and Research Institute joined the Shenyang Aircraft Factory and the Shenyang Aeroengine Design and Research Institute joined the Shenyang Aeroengine Factory, forming the Shenyang Aircraft Company and the Shenyang Aeroengine Company. In 1985, the Zhuzhou Aeroengine Design and Research Institute and the

Zhuzhou Aeroengine Factory were merged forming the Zhuzhou Aeroengine Company. That the aircraft research institutes and the engine research institutes were respectively merged with relevant factories in the inland area also belonged to this category. The main feature of this combination was that the design and research institutes were still relatively independent entities, but acted as main development departments of companies and undertook the development task of the aeronautical products. These institutes closely combined the design, trial production and production together under the companies' guidance. After the new products designed by the design institutes were put into production, some organizations also executed the policy of connecting the institute's income with the product sale, making design institutes gain practical interests from the commercialization of their research achievements. This kind of combination fostered a relationship of relying on each other, helping each other and promoting each other between powerful research organizations and production units, thus accelerating the development speed of new aircraft. After the research institutes and factories were combined, the Shenyang Aircraft Company performed the design certification of J—8 and J—8I aircraft at high speed and conducted the maiden flight of the independently developed J—8II aircraft ahead of schedule. The Zhuzhou Aeroengine Company performed the combination of the factory and the institute and speeded up the development of the WJ9 engine.

Fig. 104   The building of the design and research institute of the Nanchang Aircraft Factory

The independent design and research institutes were combined with relevant factories, forming product development centers with research taking the lead. This was a combination emerged in the 1980s. The AA Missile Research Development Center was an example of this category.

Another form was a combination between the factories and the institutes to fulfill particular tasks, for example, the combination between the factories and institutes to develop J-7Ⅲ aircraft and WP13 engine, and the combination formed around the system development task between the research institute and relevant factories with the research institute taking the leading task of system development of airborne equipments etc..

In the early 1987, the State Council issued " Some Regulations for Pushing Further Forward the Reform of the Science and Technology System" and "the Regulations to Push Research and Design Units Entering the Large and Medium-Scale Enterprises". Under the guidance of these two documents, the work of combining research with production in the aviation industry is advancing even further.

During this period, the MAI also made reform to strengthen advanced research, to change research fund allocation system and to promote the commercialization of research achievements.

Since 1979, advanced research has been put on a prominent position, and an all-round systematic plan was made. Key projects and important research subjects were made prominent. There was no fund for advanced research in the past. Research programme can only be funded when the programme is linked to a product project, but this was changed. It has been decided that 30% of the State research fund will specially be used as the advanced research fund. This reform provided an important guarantee for the steady development of the advanced research.

Since 1984, according to different categories of the research organizations, reform on the appropriation system for research organization has been carried out. For those design and research institutes whose main tasks were product design or research and development, the operational fund would be gradually reduced and the contract system would be used for undertaking design and research tasks. For those research institutes, whose main tasks were applied research or experimental research, then the operational fund would be

Fig. 105 The production line of the viscose rayon long fibre compression washing machine developed by the Shenyang Aeroengine Design and Research Institute

partially reduced and the technical and economic responsibility system would be used for undertaking research tasks. For those research institutes whose main tasks were to provide integrated services, the operational fund would be allocated by the State and the fund responsibility system would be used. Meanwhile, the bidding system was trial-used for advanced research subjects and new product development in a limited scope. The purpose of these reforms was to stimulate research units to do a better work, to speed up the commercialization of research achievements and to make the research work better serve the development of the aviation industry and the economic construction. This reform already got some good effects. The utilization efficiency of the research fund increased and the operational expense reduced. After performing reform, the Shenyang Aeroengine Design and Research Institute not only cooperated with relevant factories and institutes and made great progress in the development of new aeroengine, but also made full use of its potential and advantageous points and fulfilled more than 300 items of technical services, technical transformation and difficult technical problems for the Civil Aviation, petroleum, chemical industry, metallurgy, coal and textile industries. Good social benefits were gained and the economic income of the research institute also increased.

5. System Engineering Management for the Development of New Aircraft

Since the transition from licence production to independent design and development stage, the development of new aircraft raised higher requirements for the management.

Modern aircraft includes a few large categories — airframe, engine and airborne equipments and each category consists of various equipments and systems and subsystems. There exist complex interconnection and numerous interfaces within each system and among systems. During the whole aircraft development process from the general configuration review, test, design, trial production to batch production, participants include many industrial departments in the central government and several hundred factories, research institutes, universities and institutions of higher learning and operational departments all over the country. Its planning, technology, production and management are very complicated and the cost is high. Also, the development of new aircraft involves very strong timeliness and large risk.

During a long period in the past, when a decision was made to start or to terminate the development of a new type of aircraft, there was often existed a phenomenon of one–sidedliness in considering some major factors — technical performance, schedule and cost. It was quite common that the administrative leading bodies such as MAI had to directly deal with the technical coordination problems, schedule coordination problems and detailed cost allocation problems of the whole system. The offices in the ministry were too busy to deal with so many problems coming from various fields and it was difficult to properly settle these problems.

Since 1980, the MAI summarized the historical experiences in aircraft development in the past, learned the scientific methods in system engineering management from the space industry and drew lessons from foreign system engineering theory and practical experiences, and the system engineering management started to be used in the development of new aircraft, which made the scientific management of new aircraft entering a new stage.

a.   Making a Scientific General Scheme for the Development of New Aircraft

The first important thing in the system engineering management of developing new aircraft was to define a general scheme for development of new aircraft. The practical procedures were as follows. After the development project of new aircraft was approved by the State, according to the performance requirements raised by the operational departments, the MAI organized aircraft, engine and airborne equipment factories and design / research institutes and various experts to make multiple technical schemes, carrying out a "three—dimensional" integrated review of the technical specification, cost and schedule. These schemes then were compared, studied and reviewed from various points of view to optimize the general scheme for the development of new aircraft.

Then, the system engineering technique was used to make system analysis of the general scheme of the development of new aircraft. The Military Aircraft Bureau or Civil Aircraft Bureau responsible for practicing system engineering in the Ministry of Aviation Industry made use of operations research, information theory and cybernetics, as well as experimental data accumulated in many years with the aid of electronic computers to make schedule distribution of the general development period, and found out critical stages, critical links and critical lines for developing new aircraft, so as to optimize the coordination of the development schedule of each system (such as engine, flight control system, communication system and navigation system) and then to put the development plan of new aircraft in a zero level network diagram. The zero level network diagram was the main content of the general development scheme of new aircraft. After being approved by the State, it became an instruction from the State which every development department including those both within and outside the Ministry should obey strictly. This was the main basis to control the whole process of new aircraft development.

b. Setting up the Designer System

Since 1980, when the system engineering management for the development of new aircraft was carried out in the aviation industry, the designer system was set up for the development of new aircraft such as J—8 II and J—7 III. This system was called designer's responsibility system. It was the center of the technical management for developing new aircraft. The Defense Science and Technology Industry Commission respectively appointed Gu Songfen the chief designer of J—8 II fighter and Song Wencong the chief designer of J—7 III fighter.

The designer's responsibility was clearly defined in the "Working Regulations for Weaponry Development Designer System and Administrative Control System" issued by the State Council and the Military Commission of CCCPC as follows: "the designer system of the weaponry development is a cross—departmental technical management system consisting of designers at different levels, and is responsible for the design work in the weaponry development". The chief designer was the head of the designer system.

Designers at different levels were heads responsible for their own technical systems, responsible for the design work in their special fields and they followed the technical leadership of designers of higher ranks. There were four levels in the designer system, which were the chief designer, system chief designer, director designer of equipment and subsystem, and designer in charge of products. Take the designer system of J—8 II fighter for example, there was one chief designer, five deputy chief designers and three assistants to the chief designer totally responsible for the management of the design work. Below these persons, five system chief designers and seven deputy system chief designers responsible for important systems (engine system, fire control system etc.) were appointed (or held concurrently by deputy chief designers). Below them, 25 director designers and deputy director designers of equipments and subsystems were appointed. Below the director designers, 35 designers in charge of products were appointed. The designer system of J–8 II fighter involved three Ministries of Industry and 47 factories and design research institutes.

The setting up of the designer system for developing new aircraft broke up the limits among departments, changed the traditional management patten of purely relying on the administrative means and the vertical leadership, brought the technical coordinative function of designers at different levels into full play. This was a kind of matrix management. It strengthened the technical responsibility system of designers at different levels and established a complete set of management systems and work regulations of the technical documents of the designer system.

After the designer system of J–8II fighter was set up, through three technical coordination meetings, the chief designer of the fire control system properly solved some important technical problems such as the system accuracy allocation, missile launching procedure and the interfaces among radar, sight and missile control, which were related with many factories and institutes of three Ministries of Industry.

The development of a new aircraft has a strong exploration character. Through technical information feedback of the designer system, designers at all levels could timely find out problems and make decision to ensure the technical coordination in developing the new aircraft. When the preliminary design of J–8 II aircraft was finished, it was noticed that the electrical subsystem of the aircraft A.C. electrical power system exceeded the preset weight. The chief designer informed the director designer of the electrical power factory of this situation. The

Fig. 106   Technical documents about the maiden flight of J–7 III   aircraft

director designer considered the overall requirement, adopted some measures and modified the design of generators, thus reducing the weight.

The whole process of technical management of system engineering for developing new aircraft was divided into stages, and was called management of "milestone" check points.

Generally, the whole development process of new aircraft in the aviation industry was divided into six stages: a) tactical / technical and technical / economic feasibility study; b) general configuration review; c) technical design and mock—up approval; d) detailed design and test / trial production; e) flight test and design certification; f) trial operation and production certification. The review meetings were participated by various experts from operational and industrial departments to review every stage. Every subject on agenda was analysed one after another with all opinions on table. Also the consultation groups of the engineering design were set up in MAI, which provided technical consultation and technical assistance at each stage in developing the new aircraft.

c. Executing Powerful Administrative Control

As developing new aircraft needed strict schedule coordination, the MAI set up a powerful administrative control system for every project of new aircraft. For the development of some important projects such as J—8 II and J—7 III aircraft, vice ministers of MAI hold the posts of general managers of the projects and on—site working offices of every important project were set up in main aircraft factories. Cadres with rich experiences were appointed on—site general officers, acting on behalf of the Ministry. They executed on—site coordination and control, and together with chief designers directly tackled and solved various problems among the main factories and institutes, main factories / institutes and auxiliary factories / institutes during the development of new aircraft. Meanwhile, the Military Aircraft Bureau and Civil Aircraft Bureau were set up in MAI to practice the system engineering management. Thus, a system engineering matrix management with both vertical and horizontal controls was formed.

A basic content of the system engineering management was to carry out schedule coordination strictly according to the network diagram. In developing new aircraft, the on—site working offices of J—8 II and J—7 III aircraft earnestly and carefully carried out the network diagram, actively performed the quality control and cooperation work and together with the technical system set up on—site service groups for the aircraft development, ensuring a smooth schedule coordination of development for these two aircraft. The on—site working office set up at the main manufacturer of J—8 II aircraft —— the Shenyang Aircraft Company, according to the requirements of the zero level network diagram, shortened the time period from the trial production preparation to the maiden flight to only 18 months. They took the schedule as major control target, precalculated the time parameters of each item of the critical path and reasonably allocated this 18 months period. They analysed the trial production period using statistics calculation method and made four—level network plan. The parallel and cross working procedure was carried out in large scale. The actual result was one month ahead of preset development schedule.

The focal point of schedule coordination in developing new aircraft was to strengthen the administrative leadership and schedule control over key stages, key links and key paths. The administrative control system in the development of J—8 II aircraft found out through analysing schedule and tracking and surveying, that the key of the whole aircraft system was the flight control system and the key of that system to be solved was a kind of potentiometer. The deputy minister in charge of J—8II aircraft made a detailed survey in the potentiometer factory and the flight control system was successfully solved.

The flight test stage was an all—round check stage for new aircraft performance and was critical to the success of aircraft development. In 1985, the flight test working office was set up by MAI and a deputy minister in charge of the flight test held the post of general manager, who coordinated the design certification and flight test of a few new aircraft and made a detailed flight test network diagram. The flight test working office executed unified control at the Flight Test Research Center (the Flight Research Institute) and solved some important problems under the support of the Air Force.

d. Practicing the Scientific Control over the Development Funds of New Aircraft

For a long time, the development funds of new aircraft in the aviation industry was allocated by the government to the relevant administrative organizations and the government would reimburse for what was spent, which made the development organizations short of cost—effective consciousness. This often led to the expenditure of the development funds out of control. To solve this problem, since 1981, the MAI trial executed the technical and economic responsibility system of the development funds for J—7M and Q—5Ⅲ aircraft and later organized responsibility systems for 19 aircraft (such as J—8Ⅱ and J—7Ⅲ), 9 engines and more than 1,100 airborne equipments projects. The chief accountant system for each project was set up and the chief accountant of each project was appointed. The position and role of accountants at all levels in the engineering development of new aircraft were established. The systematic budget management method of the research and trial production cost was gradually formed.

In general scheme, the budget responsibility and staged bonus method were defined and the MAI organized main factories and institutes to sign the technical and economic contracts with cooperating factories and institutes in terms of aircraft, engine and missile projects. The responsibility, rights and liability of each party was made clear, and the bonus and punishment conditions were also stipulated.

During the development funds contracting process, every target of contract had to be reviewed and approved to make the scheme optimum. The economic review not only promoted the optimization of the technical scheme, but also saved money. The zero altitude ejection rescue system test of J—7M aircraft, after jointly studied and reviewed by the Chengdu Aircraft Factory and the Flight Test Research Center, was conducted using H—5 aircraft to roll and eject on runway. The test was succeeded at the first time. That saved a few months time than if the test was to be carried out at rocket rail range, and saved a lot of money.

As an important link of the system engineering management, the development funds responsibility of new aircraft basically solved the problem of separation of technology, schedule and cost, primarily broke up the "big rice bowl" of the development funds and mobilized the initiatives of development organizations, thus promoted the development of new aircraft and improved the utilization benefits of the funds. Due to this system, the Shenyang Aircraft

Company saved 6% of the money in developing J−8II aircraft.

The system engineering management of new aircraft was generally organized according to the aircraft project. Because the technology of the aeroengine was complex and its development period was long, it is necessary to be independently developed in advance. Hence, the system engineering management was also used for the engineering development of new engine. And also, this management method was used for airborne equipment systems and weapon systems such as missiles which need to be developed independently and in advance.

Because the system engineering management of new aircraft development was carried out in the aviation industry, it facilitated the development of new aircraft. A batch of newly developed aircraft such as J−8 II, J−7 III, JJ−7 and Z−8 made their maiden flight timely or ahead of schedule. Their flight test and design certification also proceeded smoothly. The utilization of the development funds for new aircraft became more reasonable and effective. This is a good beginning for Chinese aviation industry.

Chapter X   Quality Control of Aviation Industry

Strict quality standard and scientific quality control are objective requirements for research, development and production of aviation industry.

Airplane is a kind of product which will be used repeatedly for manned flight over a long period of time, so it must have high safety, reliability and economy. Poor quality of aero product is liable to cause a catastrophic crash. If used as a weapon, it will lead to lose a battle in wartime, even jeopardize national security. As compared with common mechanical product, airplane works in much more harsh conditions. It has to adapt itself to various adverse circumstances, such as high altitude, high speed and extreme temperatures, and bears all sorts of complicated loads. Among thousands and thousands of airplane parts and components a single small part which sometimes loses effectiveness or has been carelessly omitted in manufacturing will incur a disastrous accident and great economic losses. Therefore quality of aero product has particular importance and strict quality standard has to be adhered to.

As a big system airplane consists of many subsystems of airframe, aeroengine and all kinds of aircraft equipment as well as armament etc.. In view of the process of research, development, production and marketing it also includes phases of advanced research and development, design, trial production, production and product support etc.. In order to ensure that tens of thousands of airplane parts and components will achieve the required reliability and life target after final assembly, so that the complete airplane meets its quality standard, it is necessary to carry out quality control by means of systematic scientific method in every respect of the whole system and in every phase of the whole process.

The policy of quality first for aero product was put forward even at the initial stage of the construction of China's aviation industry. In 1954, when the first airplane was made in new China, Chairman Mao Zedong stressed in his letter to the workers and staff of aircraft and aeroengine factories, in praise of their work saying: "It is necessary to further master technology and improve quality of product." For the last thirty years and more the organizations of aviation industry have been continuously going against neglecting product quality and making every effort to improve quality of product.

Section 1   Development of Quality Control

The development of quality control of new China's aviation industry can be roughly divided into three stages:

1. Stage of Fundamental Construction of Quality Control

In 1951, the Military Commission of CCCPC and the Government Administration Council pointed out in "Decision on Building Aviation Industry" that in order to raise the quality of production to meet the specifications required for operating and training, the Bureau of Aviation Industry must set up an inspection organization, and the Air Force Command an acceptance unit. From then on all sorts of aircraft parts and components made, repaired and renewed by aviation factories had to be inspected and passed as qualified by inspection and acceptance organizations, then handing over procedure would be gone through. At the initial stage of the building of the aviation industry various problems of product quality arose because of weak foundation, backward technology, poor management of production and lower technical level of the personnel. In view of this situation the Bureau of Aviation Industry put forward in early 1952 the policy of quality first for aero product, and demanded to pay more attention to technological management centering on quality. With the beginning of the First Five—year Plan, aviation industry stepped into a stage of large—scale construction, turning gradually from repair into manufacture. Quality problem was put on the important agenda. In 1954 the Bureau of Aviation Industry pointed out in its instructions given to the factories that while the focal point of the work in aviation industry gradually turned from repair to manufacture, how to ensure quality of trial production and keep the quality stable in the following mass production became a very important question in quality control. At the same time the Bureau set a demand that starting with quality education and stressing on carrying out technological process the Soviet quality control method be studied and introduced in combination with the specific conditions of China, so as to carry out the fundamental construction better. From then on regular quality control was set up step by step.

First, carrying out the education of quality first repeatedly, mobilizing the workers and staff to make joint efforts to ensure the quality of product. At that time custom and work style of the cadres and workers did not change from that of the stage of repair, and were no good for ensuring quality of product. In machining workshop spread a saying: "If a shaft is larger, lathe it smaller; If a hole is bigger, inlay a sleeve to it; If a crack exists, weld it again; Beat it to place in assembling and make do with defects with repairs and patches." This was the reflection of that kind of work style. For example, more than 2,700 parachutes had to be scrapped in the early 1950s because of neglecting technological rules, and changing technical standard at will in production and letting the products leave the factory perfunctorily. This is impermissible in production of high precision aero product.

In order to solve the problem of underestimating product quality, education on quality in many forms was conducted every year over the period of transition from repair to manufacture, and general checking out on product quality was regularly carried out to discover the hidden peril to quality. Measures for improvement were also taken. The workers and staff, and enterprises had all to be tested with regard to quality targets, the superior ones got rewards and the inferior ones punishment, thus enhanced their quality consciousness.

Second, carrying through the technological rule and rigorously enforcing technological disciplines. At that time 2/3 to 4/5 of quality problems resulted from going against technological disciplines and not observing technological rules. In order to change this situation, the Bureau of Aviation Industry issued an order " Work must be done according to technological rules" which emphasized that technological rules are laws for production. During the stage of licence production the process of manufacturing was also the process of ensuring product quality. Technological management was enhanced and technological rules were strictly followed. They played a decisive role in stablizing product quality, and also pushed forward the workers and staff to master production technology and foster rigorous and careful work style.

Third, learning the method of quality control of the Soviet aeronautical factories and introducing the complete set of rules and regulations on quality inspection from the Soviet Union. In 1954, the Bureau of Aviation Industry issued " Twelve—article Technological Regulation of Quality Inspection" with reference to the relevant regulations of the Soviet aeronautical factories, including inspection procedures of manufacturing process, such as control of unqualified products, handing over of technological equipment for examination, appraisal of instruments, identification marking of parts and selection of standard parts etc.. Through using the complete set of this working methods and combining it with the experience gained in practice, the aviation industry made great improvements in quality control in a short period of two to three years.

In this period the quality inspection work was gradually strengthened. A system of chief inspector was established in every enterprise. Veteran workers with good political consciousness and high level of techniques were appointed inspectors. The proportion between inspectors and workers was about 1:10. The characteristics of quality inspection work then were as follows: 1) Keeping control of the whole process of production. Supervision of quality was conducted from feeding in the material to processing, assembling and delivery. 2) Paying attention to taking precautions. It was stipulated that raw materials and semi—finished product had to be strictly examined (re—examined) before being put into production, technological equipment and instrumentations used in process of production had to be appraised regularly, and that the inspection units had the right to supervise and examine product production and production preparations so as to avoid waste product. 3) Setting up strict system of responsibility for quality. The main working procedures and main parts in process of production had quality record. Unqualified products were carefully classified and counted, and stored in isolation, then the responsibility was defined. Through all these, the aviation industry in the later part of the First Five—year Plan formed a relatively integrated system of quality inspection ensuring the first domestic propeller—driven and jet airplanes to fly successfully in 1954 and 1956, and turning into mass production smoothly. Meanwhile rich experience was gained. This was the stage when the foundation of quality control of aviation industry was laid. In addition, from the beginning of 1952 a system of resident military representatives in factories was put into effect. The military representative was responsible for supervision and acceptance of aero product and played an active part in helping the factory to improve and increase their product quality.

2. Stage of Rectifying and Advancing Through Interferences and Setbacks

In 1958, owing to the influences of the erroneous Left ideology of the "big leap forward" on aviation industry, working in accordance with scientific laws was considered as taboos and commandments. In trial production of J−6 fighter and Z−5 helicopter due to lopsidely seeking high speed in production without studying thoroughly the technical documents, technological rules were simplified, technological equipment reduced and quality control weakened so that the qualities of the new airplanes were not good and a great deal of products returned to factories for repair thus causing a great downturn of the aero product quality. This was a penalty of acting contrary to scientific management. In the 1960s, Eight−character (Chinese) Policy "Readjustment, Consolidation, Substantiation and Improvement" was carried out. For the first time the aviation industry underwent quality rectification and strictly conducted "70−article Regulation on Development of Industry."

The State Council and the Military Commission of CCCPC reiterated once more the policy "In all national defence production 'quality first' must be definitely put forward, and quantity must be increased on the basis of ensuring quality." It resolutely combated erroneous views of concentrating on quantity and output value without regard to quality. Through three year's arduous working, all products of aviation industry became excellent by the end of 1963, quality control restored and developed. These can be summed up as follows:

Centered on ensuring product quality, an all− round and realistic rectification was conducted in every respect of design management, technological management and technical inspection of the whole production process in order to make all products excellent. Rectification was done on the basis of three different cases: One case was that if there were problems in all the drawings, specifications, inspection standards and finished products, it was necessary to do it all over again; Another case was that if there was no problem in drawing and technological rules, but quality of product was not good, then it was necessary to trial−produce new products again according to technological requirements and quality standards; Still another case was that after reexamination design, technology and inspection were all up to quality requirements, then series production continued while quality was even more stressed.

The system of productive and technical responsibility with chief engineer as the head was reactivated. On the basis of ensuring product quality, the chief engineer of the factory was fully responsible for the productive and technical work of the enterprise. In so doing, design, technology and technical and professional work were organized integrally and the phenomena that no body was responsible for technical quality and the disorder that existed in the "big leap forward" were completely changed, so that ensuring product quality became the main point of system of productive and technical responsibility.

Meanwhile, the inspection manpower was readjusted and reinforced and inspection system was perfected. The mass participation in quality control was further developed so as to further perfect the activities of quality analysis at the team or group level.

After rectification, quality of aero product took on a new aspect, large numbers of high-quality airplanes such as J-6 fighter, Z-5 helicopter etc. were manufactured in succession. Quality of such new airplanes as J-5A fighter, J-7 fighter, H-5 bomber and H-6 bomber etc. and their aeroengines were ensured in process of trial production, thus speeding up greatly the progress of trial production. The "cultural revolution" which took place from 1966 to 1976 was the decade during which quality control was seriously sabotaged. All the quality control organizations, systems, regulations and methods set up in last rectification of aviation industry were destroyed. Quality of product dropped down terribly, so that a large number of airplanes could not be delivered. In 1969, Premier Zhou Enlai timely criticized this mistake. At the end of 1971, he entrusted Ye Jianying, Vice-chairman of the Military Commission of CCCPC to hold a forum on quality of aero product and put forward a policy "three graspingnesses and three promotings." That is grasping foreign aid and promoting quality; grasping J-6 fighter and promoting other planes; grasping aviation industry and promoting national defence and nonaero industries. Beginning from 1972, the second rectification of aviation industry was carried out, which lasted till the late 1970s.

Through these two setbacks and rectifications in about twenty years the masses of cadres and workers of aviation industry from both positive and negative experiences realized that "Quality of product is a comprehensive reflection of the overall work of an enterprise," "To solve quality problem, we have to be on the offensive side and combat the key technical problems," "We have to combine prevention with inspection, and put prevention first." They also realized that "If there is no quality in aviation industry, there will be no quantity either. If serious problem of quality takes place, the overall situation will fall into a passive position. Only quality—the foundation becomes consolidated, can aeronautical research, development and production as well as the other work be successfully developed." Although the new realizations were established, the basic reason causing quality problems still had not been really found out. Therefore an important break-through in quality control was impossible and after twice rectifications quality control work still basicly remained at the level of examination after the event.

3. Stage of Carrying Out Total Quality Control

After smashing the "Gang of Four" and on the basis of setting things to right, enterprise consolidation with stress on general inspection of quality was unfolded and quality control enhanced in all round way. After entering the 1980s, aviation industry shifted its particular emphasis from production to scientific research and development and the development of new aircraft, from production of only aero products to combination of aero products with nonaero products, from pure production to the combination of production with trade, from mere domestic market to both domestic and international markets. The new situation of research, development and production and economic reform posed new requirements to quality control, thus ushering in a new period of development for quality control of aviation industry. A series of important improvements and enhancement in scope and method of control took place in this period.

a. Quality control was extended from production process to design, trial production, production and product support, that was the quality control over the whole process. In order to improve an enterprise's quality control capability from the beginning of aircraft design, classification of the functional characteristics and reliability assessment were made. Quality review and evaluation in design stage, reexaming before the first flight were carried out. In production process not only the main procedures of processing, heat treatment, assembling and testing were controlled, but also a complete set of controlling method was put forward on critical parts. Field service turned trouble—shooting only into product support. System of technical service and system of quality information feedback were established both at home and abroad.

b. Supervision over quality control was enhanced. Quality control work changed from inspection after the event into stressing on precautions and inspections, thus forming an integrated quality control system including quality legislation, quality inspection, quality supervision, and combination of field service with quality information feedback.

c. Strengthening quality legislation and carrying through quality standards. In the 1980s, documents and standards like "Quality Control Regulation of Aviation Industry," "Quality Inspection System of Enterprise of Aviation Industry," "Classification of Aero Product Elements and Principle of Quality Control" were worked out in succession. Quality control regulations, "Quality Control Handbook" and "Quality Assurance Programme" were compiled for different types of aircraft, aeroengines and aircraft equipments. The requirements for quality assurance were stated in the form of directive documents and were as authoritative as design and manufacturing technological documents.

d. Using successful experiences of other countries to carry out overall quality control. Cadres and workers were organized step by step as planned to learn total quality control and then use the knowledge they learned in production. Meanwhile foreign experiences were applied to the actual situation in China, a quality control method more suitable to the aviation industry was sought.

For example, inter—factory quality assurance system for joint programmes of aircraft and its matched equipment was set up by using system engineering method, so as to improve product quality together, and remarkable success was achieved.

Through more than 30 year's efforts, although difficulties and setbacks were experienced in this period, great success of quality control in China's aviation industry was achieved. Quality assurance system applicable to the situation in China and the characteristics of aviation industry and a set of scientific quality control method were established. By the end of 1986, 12 enterprises, such as Suzhou Aero—instrumentation Factory, Shenyang Aircraft Company, Chengdu Aircraft Company, Xi'an Aircraft Company, Nanchang Aircraft Company, Zhuzhou

Aeroengine Company, Chengdu Aeroengine Company, Chengdu Aero-instrumentation Factory, Guizhou Engine Accessories Factory, Guizhou Aeronautical Electrical Apparatus Factory, Baoji Aero-instrumentation Factory and Shaanxi Hydraulic Accessories Factory etc. all won prizes for quality control from the Ministry of Aviation Industry, among which Suzhou Aero-instrumentation Factory won national prize for quality control. 19 groups were elected national excellent quality control groups, 180 groups were elected excellent groups of the Ministry of Aviation Industry and 159 groups were elected advanced quality control groups. Because improvement of quality control level promoted higher quality of product, the records of safe flight made by the Air Force and Navy armed with domestic aircraft and aeroengines were much better. Since the practice of awarding prizes for excellent quality products was started in China, the Ministry of Aviation Industry won 10 national gold medals including 8 for aero products and 2 for nonaero products, and 45 silver medals including 27 for aero products and 18 for nonaero product. The national gold medals were, among others, for the CJ-6 basic trainer in 1979, the ejection seat of J-7 fighter and a table-tennis ball projector in 1985, and a model airplane engine in 1986. In addition, 374 products were named ministry level excellent products by the Ministry of Aviation Industry.

Section 2   Quality Control in the Process of Production

The process of manufacturing is the key link of quality control of aero product. The objective of quality control in the process of production is to ensure that the quality of products is in conformity with the quality standards.

1.   Carrying Out Technological Rules and Strictly Enforcing Technological Disciplines

Technological rules are the basis for manufacturing. Only the technological documents are well-compiled and products made strictly according to the papers, can the quality of production process be ensured. If the technological requirements are changed improperly and technological discipline is not strictly observed or any careless omission in manufacturing and assembling occurs, quality accident will often arise. Due to smaller fillet both on the bottom diameter of threat neck of a helicopter rotor hub and the neck of turbine shaft of a jetengine and roughly manufacturing, break-downs of the shafts occurred. Even more critical was that in production of WP6 aeroengine, the technical personnel changed the small galvanized spring tongues in the compressor disk into cadmium-plated ones without proof and "cadmium embrittlement" took place in operation, so that compressor disks were broken down three times in succession within half a year, thus causing replacement of parts and components for thousands of aeroengines with heavy losses. In order to ensure conducting technological rules, every enterprise set up its strict technological disciplines. All the technological papers had to be strictly examined and approved, otherwise they were not allowed to be used in production. The approved technological rules became law of production process, which was not allowed to go against.

While the technological disciplines were strictly enforced, the tendency for opposing trial production and production procedure, and lowering quality standards were checked. In the history of aviation industry, the progress was once pursuited lopsidedly and all the necessary procedures were cancelled and "high—speed trial production" was carried out. As a result more haste, less speed, the quality was difficult to ensure and the product had to be made all over again. There was another situation that a new product was put into production before evaluation and approval of prototype, or modified version of some old products was rashly put into production without being fully tested, thus causing endless troubles for the future. After summing up these lessons, the development procedure of new aircraft, management method of design variation and that of operational development were worked out again, so as to ensure that research, development and production were conducted in accord with scientific procedures.

2. Carrying Out Working Procedure Quality Control

In the late 1970s, according to their functions in aircraft the parts of main types of aircraft were classified as critical parts, important parts and common parts. Quality control of key working procedure was conducted on critical parts and important parts. On the basis of strict technological rules the work directory and control chart of critical parts, important parts and key working procedure were compiled to keep production in a standard control, thus ensuring stable working procedure quality. Take J—7 II fighter as an example, after implementation of the working procedure quality control, the critical and important parts which were 14.4% of the whole parts met the standard of excellent product, making the aircraft excellent. In 1982, on the basis of this typical case the main points of the working procedure quality control were highlighted:

a. A clear objective; Written directory for key work procedure; Work by special persons and inspection strictly according to the work directory, so as to keep a regular control.

b. To solve difficult problems on the basis of all—round control. To grasp the key link influencing the quality, and the technological engineer, inspector and operator (three—in—one combination) recorded the problems and took measures to improve the quality.

c. To pay more attention to the weak link, especially to key positions like engine compartment, cockpit, hydraulic control system and power supply system etc. The rule of " Every procedure must be passed successfully" was strictly followed, thus ensuring no unnecessary thing and no more trouble. After conducting the quality control for key procedure, the creation of excellent aircraft was effectively ensured. 435 steps in gyro motor production procedure at Baoji Aero—instrumentation Factory were 100% under control, with an effective rate of 88.6%. In order to ensure the quality of assembling and testing, Suzhou Aero—instrumentation Factory established inspecting and awarding methods for the key procedure control. Its rate of qualified products reached 100% for 43 months in succession, all passed the checks by military representatives.

3. Quality Control of Special Technology

The quality of heat treatment and surface treatment of materials, and manufacturing technology, such as welding, forging, rolling, electrolysis and chemical milling is very important to aero product. Any problem occurs in quality often leads to catastrophic accident. The Ministry of Aviation Industry decided that the control method and inspection items in this respect be determined by the quality control departments. Regular examinations would be done on operators and inspectors. All the technological rules, equipment and instruments had to be examined and evaluated by the quality control departments. Inplementation of these stipulations was not purely to inspect but mainly to control and supervise the product quality. After the 1970s, all the aviation factories paid even more attention to work in this respect and were equipped with special instrumentations, in particular made technical reformation on heat treatment and surface treatment technologies. They posed a set of scientific inspection methods and complete instrumentations. The heat treatment and surface treatment of the aircraft components made by Xi'an Aircraft Company for Boeing Aerospace Company (U.S.A.) and Canadair Limited (Canada) came up to the international standard of the same profession.

4. Arranging Production in an Orderly Way, Strictly Enforcing Batch Control

It is impossible to make the product of high quality in a dirty and disordered environment because aero product poses very strict demand on production environment. The aviation industry requires high level of clean production environment. Effective use of parts, tools, materials and equipment is all strictly examined as a technological discipline. " Uncivilized work" and putting parts in disorder are forbidden. No scratch bruise marks and unnecessaries are allowed to exist on the products. In rectification of enterprise in the early 1950s and the mid 1960s, the advanced experience in this respect was spread. The typical experience of the afterburner assembling group of Shenyang Aeroengine Factory and Xingping Wheel Brake Accessories Factory was introduced, so as to promote strict control of production site and keep the production environment clean and in good order.

It is extremely important to carry out batch product management, because there are tens of thousand kinds of parts and assemblies in each airplane and each aeroengine among which some parts and assemblies are processed in succession by dozens of equipment undergoing hundreds of procedures in process of production, as well as many batches of the same part and assembly are stored in the same place of storehouse. Beginning from the licence production, all factories made their products according to the type and batch of variety of production. Every part had its original record of quality written in accord with the working procedure and circulated along the technological process. Quality file of each aircraft, aeroengine and finished part had to be carefully recorded and kept in the archives, thus ensuring traceability. Nanjing Aero Accessories Factory was one of the factories which had done well in batch product control. This factory had great variety of products and large quantity of batches. In the past, because of poor management and incomplete original quality record, it was difficult to define the scope covering the problem even if a minor problem occurred, batches of products made many years ago could not but be checked and repaired. This not only wasted time, but also incurred avoidable economic losses. In rectification of quality in 1960, they carried out batch product management. They had not only complete quality record of production process, but also quality achieves in which you could check up on each batch of product. In January 1980, hydraulic pump pressure in two airplanes of the Air Force was dropped down in flight. After disassembling the malfunctioning part it was found that there was a crack on swashplate resulted from the defects of forging. Nanjing Aero Accessory Factory looked up all the original records within only four hours and found out the batch number of the product and went to 15 units in time to get rid of hidden perils from 557 hydraulic pumps.

5. Enhancing Metrological Management and Improving Detection Techniques

Metrology and detection are basic and important technical medium in quality control. In 1956, the aviation industry established professional metrological organization and developed supervison and management of metrological instrument. After that, metrological stations were set up widely in enterprises, and metrological centers were set up in major enterprises, specialities and regions. The metrological centers were provided with good detection equipment and more competent inspectors to do key detection, standard calibration, supervision and inspection, so as to ensure accurate and reliable transfer of the measured data in production and management. Metrological verification rules were compiled in different professions, and regular mandatory verification was made strictly according to the procedure on all the metrological instruments and instrumentations. The verified metrological instruments and instrumentations were marked "Qualified" or "Using is forbidden", so as to avoid causing quality problem in workshops of a factory or inter-factories (institutes), because of inaccurate measurements. The detected environmental conditions, such as temperature, humidity, vibration and cleanliness etc. were also controlled.

In order to raise the technical level of quality inspection, departments of the aviation industry continuously renewed the means of metrology and detection according to production characteristics. In respect of detecting geometric value, they mainly checked on high precision, multi-size and complicated shape. The geometric detection technique which mainly consists of optical projection and digital display was widely used. Multi-coordinates measurer and profile projector were used in manufacturing aeroengines to check out porous case housing of complicated shapes and in production of bend pipe with different space angles. Multi-point electro-metering technique, such as image pointer and graphical analyzer were used in process of production of blade and high precision parts. In physical and chemical detection, non-destructive detection, such as ultrasonic detection, electro probe, eddy flow detection, scanning electro-microscope, infrared beamsplitter and laser holographic techniques were used not only in quality evaluation of parts and components, raw material and work blank, but also in analysis of quality defects. The above mentioned detection techniques basically came up to the international standard of the same profession in cooperative production with foreign countries.

In the process of carrying out quality control in an all—round way, all the enterprises of aviation industry paid special attention to detection technique reform and training detection persons. Zhuzhou Aeroengine Company set up a detection technique research laboratory, which designed and manufactured blade chord width detector of engine and profile checkout device, greatly improved detection accuracy and efficiency. The aviation industry already owns three state— approved detection centres and three detection units for examining and issuing

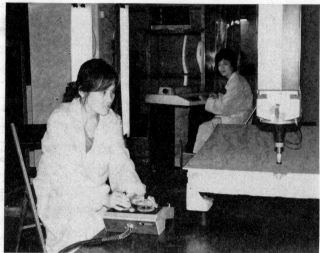

Fig.107   20 m diameter antenna reflector being measured by the technical personnel

production licence. They undertake the detecting task for the State and defence industry.

6.   Seeking and Summing—up Management Methods with Chinese Characteristics

At the beginning of its development the aviation industry brought the fine tradition of the Communist Party of China and the People's Libration Army of China into aero production management and in learning and using the Soviet experience the tradition was also carried forward in combination with the specific condition. In quality control work special attention was paid to relying on the masses and summing up the good and practical experience from the masses, which was spread and used in time. This method of work became a system. At the later stage of the First Five—year Plan period, in quality control system of aviation industry were introduced many quality control methods which had been created by the masses and were in conformity with scientific management principle, such as "Three fixings", "Three inspectings" systems, "Three no letting—offs" principle, and the three—in—one combination of specialists with masses, quality analysis meeting, system of customer visiting and key problem tackling in a coordinated process etc.

"Three fixings" means fixing working procedure of products, fixing operators and fixing machine tools in production process. "Three inspectings" means that when the first part of each batch is finished by each shift, it will be put into mass—production only after self—inspected by the worker, re—inspected by the team or group leader, then inspected and considered qualified by the special inspector. " Three no letting—offs" is that in quality inspection, not let any problem off when it is discovered but the reason for that has not been found out yet. Not let it go, if the responsibility for the problem is not clear, and not let it go, if not taking measure to improve. In so doing the product quality was ensured, waste of batches of products were averted, technical level of the workers was pushed higher, making the inspection no more a mere supervision after event.

The purpose of three—in—one combination of specialists with masses is to mobilize the masses and rely on the workers to take part in quality control. In solving important quality problem the special inspector, technician and worker work together to analyse the reasons, to take measures for troubleshooting. On the basis of this, worker quality controllers were organized in the production team or group and quality analysis meeting of three—in—one combination held regularly to collect good ideas and mobilize everyone to control the quality, thus achieving good results.

System of customer visiting is to inquire about product quality timely in the process of operation. Through customer visiting the target for improving the product quality was defined, so as to increase the performance and reliability of products.

Tackling key problem in a coordinated process is to solve the key quality problem in a coordinated process. Every step and every workshop in a procedure are coordinated to solve key weak points in production. This is a good method developed from creating excellent quality in the 1960s and proved highly effective. In order to solve the crux of the variation of engine turbine blade grain, a team of tackling key problems in a coordinated process of forging, heat treatment and processing was formed in Shenyang Aeroengine Factory to solve key technical problems.

These experiences were systematized and brought into the whole quality control, thus making the quality control a typical Chinese one.

Section 3   Quality Assurance of Air Materials

Air materials consist of raw materials and vendor—furnished parts and components. The quality of these materials is the basis of the quality of the complete aircraft. The most important task for air materials supply is to ensure the quality of air materials to meet the quality standard of aero products.

At the initial stage of the development of aviation industry, selection of materials strictly according to the standards was taken as an important integrated part of the quality control. After that, with the establishment of production bases of air materials in China, and in order to effectively control the quality of bought materials, the aviation factories worked together with the material manufacture factories to increase the quality control of materials, making the quality control of the coordinating factories an extension of quality control of aero products. Effective control methods were established for that purpose.

1. The Formation of Air Material Standard

The technical standard of air material is the norm which must be observed both by the manufacturer of air material in their production and by aviation industry's factories in their acceptance test of the material. It serves as a basis of quality control for both sides. The process of the formation of the air material technical standard of China was as follows: At the beginning of the development of aviation industry, the Soviet air material technical standard was used as a temporary standard. During the First Five—year Plan period, the departments of metallurgy, chemistry, petroleum, machine—building, building materials, light industry and textile industries etc. accumulated a great deal of data in production and each formulated its own ministry—issued standard which combined its own specific conditions with foreign experience, and gradually replaced the temporary standard. However these commonly used standards could not completely cover the quality requirements of new aero products. In order to solve this problem, the Bureau of Aviation Industry and its subordinate Air—materials Research Institute organized technical personnel from both supplying and demanding sides to work out a Chinese air—materials technical standard on the basis of the Soviet air—materials standard and the Chinese commonly used standard. In the 1970s, the Air Standardization Research Institute was set up and the air materials standard of the Western countries was introduced, thus promoting the technical level of air raw materials production. Through rectifications and improvements, up to 1985, 4,572 air materials standards were worked out in China, which laid a reliable foundation for ensuring quality of air materials.

2. Quality Control of Air Material Production

In order to produce qualified air materials, the material producers took measures for strict quality control. Manufacturing process for each air material was laid down according to the technical standard and strictly carried out after being approved by the management of both sides. For example, Fushun Steel Works established a production system for high—quality steel named "A" steel, which was specially used for aero product. It was stipulated that this "A" steel must be produced strictly according to the approved manufacturing process from preparations of raw materials to delivery of the finished steel, so as to keep the quality stable. Some important air material producers set up closed production lines for military materials, under the management of a factory—level director. Capable technicians and skilled workers and the best equipments were provided. The inspection and test systems for the production lines were strictly followed. After being approved by the State Council the aviation industry from 1955 sent its resident representatives to major materials manufacture factories to provide the technical quality information to the factories and supervise the production and check the quality before delivering products. This not only ensured the quality of air materials, but also increased economic benefit for both sides. However, in the "cultural revolution", this system was allegedly a product of "not believing in the working class of the material industry and an unnecessary repetition of work" and was cancelled. As a result such materials with serious defects in quality as the delaminated sheets, cracked bars and forged pieces with slag etc., flew into the aviation factories, thus causing great losses. In the rectification of quality this mistake was corrected, and the rational system restored.

Systems of exchanging visits, data information and personnel etc. were established between the Ministry of Aviation Industry and other departments of raw materials industries and between aviation factories and material manufacture factories, so that they could promote each other. In 1956, when the static test of the whole plane for the licence produced MiG—17 fighter was conducted, the Bureau of Aviation Industry specially invited the leaders of related departments of material industries and directors of factories to view the tests on—the—spot, so that they got a deeper understanding of the importance of air materials' quality to aircraft performance and reliability. After 1979, both sides carried out total quality control. The quality control became even more scientific and systematic, and the relations between supplying and demanding sides even more closed. After 1983, more than 100 air materials manufacture factories jointly set up an inter—factories quality assurance system for jointly producing excellent products. The system further ensured and improved the quality of air materials, thus making great contributions to creating aero product of high quality.

3. Quality Control in the Storage and Turnover of Materials

The departments of aviation industry have been carrying out a dual check system. Besides strict check before the delivery by the manufacture factory, the materials have to be inspected before both getting in storage and putting into production in aviation factories so as to strictly prevent unqualified materials from mixing up in production line.

The material supplying departments of aviation industry placed orders for materials with certain factories strictly according to the air materials technical standard and the specifications approved by their higher authorities. The supplying departments had no right to revise the specifications and change the manufacture factories. Every aviation factory set up its own air materials inspection unit, and strictly observed the inspection system for acceptance of the air materials. In February 1953, the Bureau of Aviation Industry issued "The Inspection System for the Materials Bought at Home and Abroad before Being Put In Storage" which stipulated that the air materials accepted by the aviation factory had to have the quality certificate given by the manufacture factory, in which the test data had to be written completely. After entering the factory the materials had to be first put in receiving storeroom where the technical documents, quantities and packages of the materials were checked. If there was no problem, the materials would be sent to the "waiting—for—check storeroom" where samples of the materials would be re—checked. If the re—checked materials were qualified, then they were transfered to production storeroom. Each piece of the stored bars and sheets had to bear a mark number and a heat number to avoid being mixed up with other materials. Qualified materials and unqualified ones, un—checked materials and re—checked ones were also clearly identified.

The air materials in stock had to be taken care of strictly according to the requirements of the "Air Materials Storage Manual" and kept from rust and corrosion. As to non-metallic materials like rubber and paint etc. the storage life, pot life and the temperature, humidity of storehouse had to be strictly controlled. The factories and materials supplying stations also summed up a lot of experiences and methods in management of storehouse, so they made everything in good order. After 1979, some factories used classification management and computer aided management.

Before leaving the storehouse, the air materials had to be inspected as qualified by the inspector, and handed out only after going through releasing procedures. For the materials used by segments the mark number and heat number had to be retained. Before processing, the worker should check the mark and heat number again. In manufacturing processes, batch management method was used and the complete original record was made for long-time preservation. When any mistake and omission occurred, it was possible to find the cause in time. Therefore the stipulation that the unqualified materials were not permitted to be put in storage, taken out of the storehouse and put into production was completely and seriously carried out.

A national model worker of the material supply department, Chen Xiukang, the director engineer of Beijing Storehouse No.403 made an outstanding achievement in this respect. He checked the air materials before putting them in and getting them out of the storehouse and adhered to the standards. Quality of each piece of materials was re-checked and all the unqualified materials were sent back. He picked out the unqualified imported materials and made claims, thus reducing the economic losses of the country.

Section 4   Quality Control in the Process of Engineering Development of New Aircraft

The quality control in the process of engineering development of new aircraft is the basis of quality assurance of new aircraft. In view of the engineering development experience of the Chinese aero products, critical quality problems which occurred when some new types of aircraft came out mostly resulted from design and trial production phases of new aircraft development. Along with the progress of new product development, the quality control in the process of engineering development of new aircraft was paid more attention to day by day. This work was overall unfolded in the late 1970s, and perfected gradually till the first half of the 1980s through engineering development of J-8 II, J-7 III fighters.

1.   System of Chief Quality Engineer for Project

Development of aircraft is a large system engineering, coordination of various circles and at all levels is very complicated, so imperfection of responsibility system will lead to hidden quality peril. Therefore from the every beginning of the development, a strict technical quality responsibility system must be set up. That means the chief designer is responsible for the quality assurance of the whole aircraft. Under his leadership, the chief quality engineer for the project helps the chief designer ensure the quality of the project.

Aircraft design is a dynamic process. From conceptual design to design certification many corrections and reexaminations will be done. In order to use new material and technology to improve aircraft performance and operating life and to meet the requirements of the user, it is still neccessary to further revise the design, even after the design certification. To harmonize and match the aircraft with its systems, a quality assurance system was formed, under the leadership of the chief designer and the chief quality engineer, to ensure the quality of every component and every system. Intersections between components and professions and disputed problems of structure and strength, structure and material etc. were coordinated and solved all by the chief designer and chief quality engineer. In this process the chief quality engineer of the project is responsible for implementing quality responsibility, laying down quality legislation, controlling focal points and arranging design quality review and quality recheck in various phases etc..

2. Quality Control in Design Phase

Airplane design is divided into three phases i.e. conceptual study, technical design and detail design phases.

In order to control the quality of conceptual study, the Ministry of Aviation Industry has mapped out the general design specifications. After defining the operational requirements and specifications, in combination with the practical situations in China the correctness of the selection of specifications and their implementation are strictly examined, so as to ensure the rationality of the airplane configuration design.

With the beginning of the technical design the main task of quality control is to solve the problems of harmonization and matching between the components and systems, and to strictly control weight, according to the quality control documents of technical design, such as airplane harmonization rules, aircraft preliminary design regulations and aircraft weight limits etc..

In detail design phase on the basis of the "Classification of Parts and Elements of Aero Product and Quality Control Principles," the airplane parts and components are divided into three parts, critical part, important part and common part according to their functions and importance in regard to the safety of aircraft. On the basis of the classification, reliability design is carried out. In design, the operational reliability has to be taken into account and the failure regularity of each kind of parts has to be summed up and preventive measures against failures should be taken. This quality control method helps ensure product quality. It can also test the economy of the design concept.

After the technical design and detail design, and before the first flight of the aircraft, system evaluation review and quality re-check will be conducted. Only the quality target in evaluation review is considered qualified, can the work be continued into the next phase.

Verification of design work is mainly ground simulation test. All the structual design, system design and design of the important parts must pass through simulation test to ensure the correctness of the design principle, the load-carrying capability and the computation method.

The quality department must take part in the test work. According to the conclution of tests the chief designer and chief quality engineer for the project will approve the design office to send out drawings and begin trial production.

The chief quality engineer for the project organizes experts, designers and quality controllers from different fields to participate in system quality evaluation review, quality re-check and test verification of the design work. The fact has proved that it is possible in so doing to overcome the limitations of examination by the chief designer alone, and to do away with mistakes of design by all means in drawing design and ground test phases, not let design problems go into production, thus realized the saying: "Be serious and conscientious, thoughtful and careful, make everything safe and reliable and no chance for anything going wrong."

Fig.108   A check on the land view model of a flight simulator

3.   Quality Control in Trial Production

Trial production is also to verify the design. The "Quality Control Regulation for Aircraft Engineering Development" worked out by the Ministry of Aviation Industry stipulates that the design departments must cooperate closely with the trial production departments to jointly ensure the quality of trial production. The design personnel must go down to the trial production site and through trial production to find defects in design and further perfect the design. The trial production unit strictly enforces the quality control in the process of trial production to reduce tolerance and raise the quality of prototypes. By seriously unfolding design quality control, quality evaluation review in phases, quality control in trial production and quality re-check before first flight, the development work of new fighters, J-8 II and J-7 III was greatly facilitated. The manufacturing technique was good and harmonization and matching were quite good, and the aircraft successfully made its first flight.

Quality control of new aircraft engineering development not only ensured quality of new aircraft design and trial production, but also opened up a new prospect for quality control of new aircraft engineering development.

Section 5 Quality Control in the Process of Operation

Quality control in the process of operation (product support) is an important link of total quality control. Product support is mainly divided into two stages: Before 1980, the first stage was to do field troubleshooting of product for the user, but after 1980, it was an overall technical service stage.

After the first batch of Chinese—built airplane was put into service, the aviation industry established a field service setup. In the early 1960s, when the military services were equipped with a great deal of Chinese—built airplane, the people for field service numbered more than 300. Because the military services had considerable experience of maintenance and logistics for their aircraft produced under licence and modified, there was no need to have more technical service from the manufacturers. Therefore, for a long time the field service was mainly limited to troubleshooting and information feedback.

Round about 1980, the focal point of aviation industry shifted to engineering development, model certification and production of even newer type of airplane. While the new airplane was put into service, new changes began to take place in product support. In early 1980, the Chinese naval air force began flying modified J—7 fighter. Owing to short training time, pilots and ground crew were not familiar with the new airplane, two accidents took place in succession. Therefore the Ministry of Aviation Industry and aviation factories paid more attention to these and decided to dispatch service group of higher technical level to do service work in various forms on—the—spot, from thoroughly explaining technical problems to on—the—spot maintenance. The pilots and ground crew of this unit mastered the knowledge of operating and servicing this type of aircraft very soon, thus ensuring proper operation of the aircraft. In so doing the aviation industry preliminarily found and summed up the method of product support. In November 1981, a meeting on field service of aviation industry was held and definitely put forward that the focal point of field service was to shift from troubleshooting only after event into overall technical service.

Soon afterwards the enterprise of military industry underwent an important renovation: to shift from production to production and trading. A new generation of aircraft developed in aviation industry began to go into service, the production of civil airplane was increasing year by year. Aero product began to sell abroad. All of these urgently called for an extension of quality control from the process of production to that of operation, i.e. to unfold an overall technical service.

In the period of seven years from 1980 to 1986, product support was suited to the above mentioned shift and developed continuously. Apart from product support at home, 86 service groups including 664 people were dispatched abroad to more than ten foreign countries. The scope of service was extended as follows: training air and ground crew of the customers;

dispatching on–the–spot technical service personnel; periodic inspection and repair; providing much–needed spare parts and materials; supplying technical data and service bulletin and information feedback with regard to quality.

The field service is a kind of hard and complicated work. The person for this work not only has to know well the aircraft structure and production technique, but also can operate skillfully. The technical service people usually work in extreme weather conditions and face many difficult problems. Together with the operating personnel they have to try their best to ensure the operation and the maintenance of the airplanes. The field service group of J–8 fighter from Shenyang Aircraft Company set a good example. The group leader, Zhang Peiwu worked all the year round on the aircraft. He was praised by the Air Force as the best field service worker. His group was praised and cited by the Military Commission of CCCPC for their excellent field service in aerial view in the 35th Anniversary of National Day in October 1984.

Section 6 Producing Excellent Product

Although there was strict quality control in production process in the 1950s, knowledge and practice were very little as to the coordination and quality control of the work going on in different departments, organizations and industries. In the 1970s, because quality problems came out repeatedly in the process of design, trial production and certification of J–6III fighter, Q–5 attacker, J–8 fighter and their engines, airborne equipments, the aviation industry summed up experiences and lessons. Beginning from the 1980s, according to the principle and management method of the system engineering, the Ministry of Aviation Industry set up an inter–factory, inter–industry and inter–city quality control system for aircraft, aeroengine, missile and their accessary producers to work cooperatively, with the director or manager of the main factory as the leader, and the vice directors or chief engineers of the accessary producers as its members. " Provisional Regulations of Quality Control System" , " Quality Information Feed–back Method" were laid down and enforced.

Quality control system office was set up in the main factory, which directly exchanged with the liaison–man of the member factories information on the progress in tackling difficult problems. In addition, the office supervised and sped up the progress irregularly and held liaison–man meetings to sum up and exchange experiences. In order to commend the good quality of their products and their achievements in tackling difficult problems, the Ministry of Aviation Industry held a meeting every year to introduce their good deeds. By the end of 1986, quality control system was set up for three types of aircraft, three types of aeroengines and one type of missile, with participation of 171 enterprises, among which J–8 I , J–7II fighters, WP7B, WP7 II aeroengines and PL–2 II missile were up to excellent quality standard and named excellent quality products by the ministry. Of the accessories to these aircraft, aeroengines and missiles, 160 items were named excellent quality products by the ministry, in which one was awarded national gold medal, and ten were awarded national silver medal.

The fact shows that this form of quality control system suits to the Chinese conditions and the peculiarity of quality control of the aviation industry and is an effective way to ensure aircraft quality.

Setting up quality control system and working cooperatively to produce excellent quality products promoted direct negotiation between factories and raised working efficiency. For instance, mutual interference between various kinds of radio equipments of J-7 II fighter existed for a long time, hampering the operation of the equipments. This problem related to six factories in aviation and electronic industries. After setting up the system, a trans-department joint group for tackling key problems headed by aircraft factory was formed. After repeated tests, the source of the interference was found. Each factory took measures for antijamming through increase of shielding to reduce interference level from 20V to 0, so that the problem existed for many years was solved within only five months.

This system also sped up the process of tackling difficult problem in products. It promoted technical development and extended product life. High temperature seepage and poor tightness etc. problems once existed in aircraft flexible tank and sealing tape. After establishment of quality control system, the North-western Rubber Factory formed quality control groups and enforced quality control on 105 working procedures. They used new materials and new technique to solve the problem, so that anti-seepage capability of the flexible tank increased by 10-fold, rate of qualified sealing tube increased from 30% to more than 80% and operating life ten times as much as before. There was a critical problem of final power amplifier diode burn out in 50W single sideband radio. By their hard work the rate of qualified products increased from 60% to more than 90%. Failure rate of pipper up-drift of SM-7 I sight was as high as 70%, but after solving the key problems, its qualified rate amounted to 100%. Tianjin Aeronautical Electrical Apparatus Factory solved contact adhesion of aeroengine igniter and the life of the contact increased from 1,000 times to 2,000 times. Quality of products was higher and times for troubleshooting much less. Take J-7 II fighter flight test as an example, successful test items for the first time increased from 91% to 97%, aircraft controlling stability, acceleration and reliability were all up to or beyond the required standard and well received by the customers.

Section 7 Airworthiness Management of Civil Aircraft

Airworthiness research and management of civil aircraft is an important link in constructing a modern aviation industry and a guarantee of quality control in the whole process of development, production, operation and maintenance as well as import, export of civil aircraft and of international cooperation project. Before the civil aircraft airworthiness management organization was formally established by the State, in order to meet the requirements of the

—479—

development of civil aircraft the Ministry of Aviation Industry formed an airworthiness management laboratory in the Aeronautical Standardization Research Institute with the approval of the State Council on October 30, 1980. On the one hand it functioned as an acting airworthiness authority for the State and trained airworthiness management personnel, on the other hand, it was doing airworthiness research and management work of civil aircraft developed by the aviation industry. In 1985, the State established airworthiness management committee of civil aircraft, which was responsible for issuing type certificate, production certificate and airworthiness certificate. The airworthiness management laboratory of the Ministry of Aviation Industry was mainly responsible for airworthiness research and management of civil aircraft designed and produced by the enterprises of the aviation industry.

On the basis of a great many investigations the airworthiness management laboratory using American Federal Airworthiness Regulations (hereafter referred to as FAR) began to compile airworthiness regulations, procedures and certification program including quality control and test in the whole process of aircraft development, production, operation and maintenance, and control of airway, examination of air and ground crew and airfield and servicing station etc.. All these reflected the contents of various flying qualities of aircraft and made the qualities standardized and normalized, and ensured air safety of all the aircraft used in airline.

Compilation of airworthiness regulations began from 1981. Through systematic investigation and accumulation of data, airworthiness documents of light aircraft, transport, helicopter, propeller and super–light aircraft and agricultural aircraft, aeroengine and noise etc. were mapped out one after another, which played an active part in promoting normalization, standardization and routinization of quality control for civil aircraft.

Since 1981, the American FAR has been taken as a standard to enforce airworthiness examination, type certification and production certification of Y–11 and Y–12 transports made by Harbin Aircraft Company. By 1985 ten airworthiness examinations have been made on the above two aircraft, including a number of very difficult "marginal flight" which are confirmed to be up to the airworthiness requirements. In December 1985, CAAC, on behalf of national airworthiness authority issued the first type certificate to Y–12 transport. Meanwhile, according to the requirements of "Production Approval and Supervision Procedure" and "Certification Program" CAAC carried out three times evaluation and examination of Y–12 and an overall inspection of development and production process. The experience of examination of Y–12 transport was widely used for other types of aircraft, thus creating a good beginning for the Chinese civil aircraft to apply to international airworthiness requirement, and meet domestic and foreign needs.

Section 8 Quality Control Structure

With the development of scientific research and production, quality control structure in the aviation industry underwent a process of development and improvement.

In the early days of development, in order to successfully realize the transition from repair to manufacture and ensure product quality of mass—production, a forceful quality inspection system was set up in every enterprise in accord with strict quality inspection requirements and the Soviet control method. To ensure the quality inspection organization to carry out tasks without any disturbance, the Bureau of Aviation Industry decided that it would exercise its functions independently under the leadership of the director of the factory and was responsible for product quality of the whole factory. In August 1955, it was definitely decided at the conference of inspection work of aviation industry: " The inspection organization of an enterprise is an independent one led by the factory director under which there is a chief inspection engineer. In enterprise the inspectors are all under the leadership of the chief inspection engineer, and their main task is to accept or reject parts and components strictly according to the drawings and technological process. If there is any divergence, the inspection organization will directly report to the Bureau of Aviation Industry." The chief inspection engineer had a technical inspection office, below this office there were inspection sections in different work or production regions, and inspection labs in different workshops. Inspectors were provided according to different working procedures. In production it was strictly observed that no unqualified material was allowed to put into production, no unqualified parts and components were allowed to assemble and no unqualified product to leave the factory. This structure effectively ensured the delivered product to meet the quality standard, helped implement the policy of quality first and coordinate the quality standards. It promoted development of inspection personnel and raised inspection technical level. This was an important and successful basic construction of enterprise management of the aviation industry during the First Five—year Plan period.

This quality inspection structure of aero product managed in high degree of centralism was heavily pounded both in the "big leap forward", and the "cultural revolution". Then the quality inspection organization of the enterprise was weakened or even broken up leading to neglect of inspection and supervision and serious degradation of quality. Afterwards it could not but reactivate and amplify this effective structure through difficult rectification. The fact shows that it is absolutely necessary for the complicated system of aircraft which demands high quality and so many technical coordinations to enforce the highly centralized quality inspection structure to strictly control the quality, and that will not be changed arbitrarily.

Since the aviation industry developed to design stage, the quality problems resulted from variation of product design and insufficient tests were increasing day by day, and the quality problems of new products exposed and feeded back in the process of operation took place very often. Therefore it was obviously far from enough that the original task of quality inspection organ was only to control the quality in the process of production. It had to be extended with the development of situation. It was necessary to shift quality control mainly after event to quality control mainly in advance, to extend quality control mainly in the process of production

—481—

to the whole process from advanced development, design, trial production, production, test, inspection to product support after delivery, thus setting up quality control in the whole process. To conform to this situation in the late 1970s, the aviation industry unfold total quality control step by step with reference to foreign experience, and the system organization made new progress accordingly. In November 1983, National Defence Science, Technology and Industry Commission issued " Provisional Regulation Regarding the Quality Control of Military Products." According to the principle of this regulation the aviation industry laid down " Quality Control Regulation of Aviation Industry" and " Inspection System of Aviation Industry's Enterprise." The implementation of these documents made the construction of the quality control system of aviation industry enter into a new stage.

At the new stage quality control organization of the enterprise is divided into two parts: One functions in unified organization and coordination of quality assurance between different departments of the enterprise and promotion of quality control, another functions in quality supervision and inspection. The characteristics of the setup are that the quality control and quality inspection are clearly divided in functions and powers. Generally, in large factories, they have both quality control and quality inspection offices which take on these two functions separately. In small and middle factories the organizations can be merged into one, but must have both quality control and quality inspection functions. In order to help the inspection department concentrate their efforts to find quality problems and enhance preventive control, task for handling the unqualified products is assigned to quality control organization or unqualified product handling committee. The quality control department is responsible for plan, organization, direction and coordination of quality control and exercises effective supervision for quality responsibility system of every department. The two functioning organizations are under the leadership of the chief quality engineer of the factory, work in cooperation and jointly ensure product quality. They form an organic whole. The chief quality engineer is also responsible for organizing quality assurance system formed through combination of different departments within the enterprise.

The Ministry of Aviation Industry sets up Quality Bureau which directs vocationally quality control and quality inspection of the enterprises. Its main tasks are: all-round planning, working out general quality target of the whole profession; putting forward guiding principle, mapping up quality standard and quality control law and supervising and examining their implementation; organizing quality assurance system for creating excellent quality product of trans-department, trans-profession and trans-region projects, and arranging interfactory competition and exchange; handling serious quality problems. This structure forming a quality control system from the leading bodies to the grass roots enterprises may well exercise various quality control functions of offices and enterprises. It is helpful to set up closed-loop control of quality legislation, quality control and supervision, quality inspection and quality information feed back, shift quality control from " rule by man" to " rule by law," thus promoting total quality control in the aviation industry.

Reviewing the development process of the quality control of China's aviation industry, people are aware that: In order to ensure its own healthy development, to effectively serve the national defence and economic construction, the aviation industry must stick to the principle "quality first", take quality control as a main link to make products of good quality. In history, whenever it keeps to do so, enterprises will develop and industry flourish. Otherwise quality of products will drop down, the enterprises fall into difficult position and all the aviation industry meet with setbacks. Therefore in any time and under any conditions the aviation industry has to struggle against negligence of quality and quality control. When any contradiction exists between quality and quantity, quality should be put in the first place.

To conduct unremitting and effective supervision and examination on related quality laws, inspection system and technological discipline is an important and indispensable measure for ensuring product quality and an important task for quality control department. A large number of quality problems are usually caused not by lack of rule and standard, but by not seriously implementing them. Therefore it is necessary to bring the functions of quality control department into full play and to strictly enforce quality responsibility system.

In addition, raising the quality of aero products must rely on technological progress. Application of new technology, realization of design improvement and technical innovation as well as break through of key technical problems may often lead to greatly raising performance and quality of product. Therefore promoting technical progress is an offensive measure for bettering product quality and should be an important content of quality control program. But the promotion of technical progress often needs to be combined with necessary technical reformation, then can get double results with half the effort. The quality control department should push forward technical development to help improve product quality.

An important respect for increasing product quality is to enhance the quality of man. High sense of responsibility, adherence to the principle for ensuring quality a hundred percent, serious and careful, conscientious and meticulous style of work, consciousness for providing the first class products to the customer should become occupational ethics of the workers and staff in aviation industry. Every department of enterprise including quality control department should exert efforts to cultivate this occupational ethics and raise the technical level of the workers and staff. Routine quality education, system of quality analysis meeting, and adherence to education on prevention of defects in advance, as well as grasping "three basic constructions" (basic team, basic professional construction and basic training of workers) to enhance their technical level, and the rule that operator is not allowed to come to work without certificate etc. all should be persistent. It is even more important to do so at the new historical stage when the veteran workers are to be replaced by new ones.

The aviation industry is developing, so is the quality control. In the process of development, it is necessary both to accumulate its own experience, and to incorporate the advanced experience of foreign countries; both to persist in the traditional effective method of quality control, and to learn to use modernized control method; both to control quality by special persons and by the masses. It is the industrial workers who directly ensure product quality. Without the mass's control it is impossible to put so many factors incurring quality troubles under effective control.

Chapter XXI   Cultivation of Ideological Style
in Aviation Industry

A good ideological style is an invisible force. At the initial stage of its development, the aviation industry made efforts to strengthen the ideological style of the workers and staff, so as to ensure the improvement of quality of the ranks, and promote the production development. For more than thirty years, the ranks of the aviation industry have formed their own ideological style of work through continuous education and practice, which is mainly as follows: the revolutionary ideal of devotion to the aviation cause, the strong sense of duty to serve the people, the consciousness of "quality first," the strong will of working hard and building an enterprise through arduous effort. All these have been deeply rooted in the ranks.

Section   1   Fostering the Revolutionary Ideal of
Devotion to the Aviation Cause

China's aviation industry always considers it a fundamental task to build ideological style of ranks to carry forward the fine revolutionary tradition, to teach the workers and staff to set up the revolutionary ideal of dedication to aviation cause, and to initiate the revolutionary spirit to defy personal danger for the motherland and cause.

At the beginning of the construction of the aviation industry, the Korean War was going on. The workers and staff of the factories had to watch out for surprise attacks by hostile airplanes, when repairing airplanes from morning till night. The workshop was taken for battle—field, and the tool as a weapon. Many moving deeds and excellent persons were emerging when they fulfilled their tasks and solved difficult problems in repairing. Ma Deyou, a worker of Shenyang Aeroengine Factory, lived a hard life before liberation. After the founding of new China, being master of the country, he did not forget the hardship in the old days, he invented cylinder grinder, innovated washer and rebuilt engine test rig, thus rendered his outstanding service in rush—repairing the engines returned from the front line. Therefore, he was chosen as a national model worker.

At the initial stage of the aviation industry, widespread propagation of Ma Deyou's deeds played a good role in educating the vast mass of the workers and staff to love their motherland and the aviation cause and in fostering the ideology of contributing to the country. To build up the aviation industry became the strongest will of the whole workers and staff. Many skilled workers from the big cities in the South came to aviation factories in the North. They overcame the cold weather and unusual living conditions, and devoted themselves wholeheartedly to building new factories, repairing and manufacturing airplanes. Chen Ayu, a worker from Shanghai, offered all his abilities and unique skill in making standard samples and jigs, thus contributing greatly to trial production and production. He was chosen as a model worker of Liaoning Province.

In the 1950s, when the aviation industry began to turn from repair to manufacture, under the care of the Party Central Committee hundreds of leading cadres were transferred to the aviation industry from the civil service and the military service. As soon as these long-tested revolutionary cadres heard of that they would manufacture aircraft with their own hands, they got very much excited. From then on, they made up their minds to take the building of aviation industry as their life long cause, and devoted their lives to it. Although at that time many of them knew nothing of industry, not to mention making airplanes, they kept in minds Chairman Mao Zedong's words: "The serious task of economic development confronts us. What we are familiar with is going to be set aside in part, while we are compelled to do what we are not familiar with." "We must learn what we don't understand." A lot of people spared all their time available from rest and recreation on learning with great eagerness. Finally, a great deal of leading cadres changed from laymen into experts. Hu Xichuan from Shenyang Aircraft Factory was a typical example. Originally he worked in Shanghai, but he voluntarily applied for leaving Shanghai for the North-east to participate in building aircraft factory. Facing the new work and complicated technology, he studied very hard. In less than one year, he could take on the leading and organizing work of the design office under the guidance of Soviet experts. The Soviet experts suggested that the factory give him awards because of his hard study and work. Afterwards he was appointed chief engineer of Harbin Aircraft Factory, and participated in organizing and leading trial production and production of two types of aeroplanes. Called on by the Government and with the leading cadres taking the lead, a great upsurge of learning culture and technology, and marching towards science rose rapidly in the aviation industry. Leading cadres, technical and management personnel all joined in learning culture, technology, management and all kinds of production skills as well as the Soviet technology and experience. At that time, the people were busy at production by day and went to have class by night. It was the lofty ideal of devotion to the aviation industry that gave an impetus to rapid development of the aviation industry at its initial stage.

In the 1960s, when the national economy encountered temporary difficulties, the development of aviation industry suffered setbacks too. It was necessary to answer the question whether to blame Heaven and others, and keep waiting or to work hard to overcome difficulties. At that time, the Ministry of Defense Industry called on all the workers and staff to learn from oil workers the spirit of working hard to extract much oil for the motherland. In 1961, a team headed by Wu Rongfeng, vice director of political department of the Ministry of Defense Industry, went to Yumen Oil Field for learning, their learning finding report was noted by Sun Zhiyuan, Minister of Defence Industry and distributed throughout the Ministry. Then, the Ministry launched a series of activities of learning from the "Iron Man Spirit" of Daqing Oil Field, learning from P.L.A and Lei Feng.

At the same time, the aviation industry called on its people to learn from Ma Chuanwu and Gao Fangqi. Ma Chuanwu was a worker of Nanchang Aircraft Factory. When raging flames endangered the factory building, he ignored his own safety to remove the fire source bravely, and thought of state property even when he was severely burned. Gao Fangqi was a chief engineer of Shenyang Aircraft Factory. He had been the director of Shenyang No.53 Factory — the first model factory after the founding of new China. He was given the title of a model worker many times. After being transferred to Shenyang Aircraft Factory in 1953, he devoted himself to the aviation cause and succeeded in organizing trial production and production of the Chinese fighters like J—5, J—6 and J—7, thus making great contributions to the aviation industry. When his heart disease got very serious in 1965, he led in person a team to visit every air force base to solicit opinions. With his swollen legs, he made great efforts

Fig. 109   Gao Fangqi introducing J—5 fighter to Premier Zhou Enlai

to check airplanes on board or on the ground. He visited air force and navy bases in Qingdao, Hebei, Zhejiang, Jiangxi, Guangzhou etc. gathered hundreds pieces of opinions about the plane quality, which he managed to solve as soon as he returned to factory. After Vice Premier Chen Yi heard of his illness, he let him have a health check when he attended a meeting in Beijing, which deeply moved him. After returning to factory, he worked even more diligently regardless of his heart disease and till he collapsed suddenly and could not be rescued with many measures at the beginning of 1966, which fully showed the thoroughgoing revolutionary spirit of selflessness and fearlessness of a communist. These advanced deeds formed a strong force to encourage all the workers and staff to work hard and surmount various difficuties, and also promote more advanced workers to emerge. It was an important factor for the aviation industry to go through readjustment and rectification to prosperity in the earlier stage of the 1960s.

In the mid 1960s, inland construction of the aviation industry began. Large numbers of workers and staff had to leave the factories built by themselves and the working posts familiar to them, and the big cities where they lived with favourable conditions for remote, backward places to break new ground. All the organizations that would move to inland and undertook building of inland enterprises had been mobilized with political ideological work. Constancy of revolutionary ideal and sense of conscious discipline became fundamental guarantee to fulfil tasks. The broad masses of workers and staff actively applied for participating in inland construction. At that time, there were altogether 200,000 workers and staff in the aviation industry. 40,000 of them moved to outlying mountain areas within two to three years. Tianjin Aeronautical Electrical Apparatus Factory was divided into two parts. Each part was composed of a complete set of man force. They came from afar to inland and established a new aeronautical electrical apparatus factory in the mountain area. They spent less than one year in building the factory and soon started production. Within only a few years, modern aviation factories towered over the inland mountain areas one by one. These new factories were built by the workers from old factories and local people with selfless spirit.

After stepping into new stage of development, the focal point of work shifted to modern socialist construction. For one thing, in building modern socialist aviation industry, it was necessary for the whole workers and staff to participate wholeheartedly in the difficult work of adjustment, reform and development, so as to keep abreast of the times, for another, an erroneous tendency " doing every- thing purely for money" arose while carrying out the open policy and revitalizing the economy. In this case, building–up of the revolutionary ideal

Fig.110　Inland construction is in full swing through arduous effort

of dedication to aviation cause and style of work became even more urgent and important. Therefore, the Ministry of Aviation Industry unfolded education both in the Party's line and policy and in professional ethics with emphasis on "loving aviation and one's own job, devotion to one's duty and quality consciousness." In order to train the young workers politically in an all–round way, a course "To Be a Qualified Aviation Worker" was tought. These training and instruction resulted in good effect. The vast number of the workers and staff studied hard for "four modernizations" and determined to give their lives to aviation cause of the motherland. When they were invited to work with high salaries and live in favourable conditions, many of them gave no consideration and insisted on making contributions to the aviation cause in difficult circumstances. Feng Zhongyue, the director of Aircraft Structural Strength Research Institute, was suffering from an incurable disease, but he still persisted in scientific research till he stopped breathing. Wu Minxing, deputy chief engineer of Chengdu Aircraft Factory, went on directing airborne radar test until he completed the task although he knew well that his tumour had spread widely. Wang Songqing, a lecturer of Shenyang Aeronautical Institute held on giving lectures and was in charge of a class even he had suffered a serious heart disease and lung's lobe haemorrhage. Shen Zuxian, an expert of aircraft instrument returned from U.S. in his early years worked wholeheartedly dozens of years like one day to establish and develop new China's aircraft instrument, so he was respected by the people and elected a representative to the National People's Congress and a member of the National People's Political Consultative Conference, and awarded the title of model worker of the Ministry of Aviation Industry. Regardless of his heart disease, he thought of and worked for the cause, at last he stopped breathing at a symposium, so that he fulfilled his pledge "sacrifice myself to heed the call of the motherland." They were all great heroes of the aviation industry.

The spirit of selfless dedication is the glorious tradition of the revolutionary ranks under the leadership of the Chinese Communist Party. The veteran revolutionary leading cadres brought it to new China's aviation industry and carried it forward. There were many moving deeds in this respect. Liu Ding, once a vice minister and adviser of the Ministry of Aviation Industry, was typical of them. He was an old revolutionist, and a veteran expert who joined the Party in the 1920s, and took part in the revolutionary activities and learned military engineering in Germany and the Soviet Union. In the revolutionary war he experienced white terror and was behind the bars, and rendered outstanding service in Xi'an Incident and construction of military engineering in the base areas. After the founding of new China, he became an important leader of defence industry and aviation industry. In his long revolutionary career, no matter how hard he had suffered, he always took care of the revolutionary and construction cause, and paid no attention to personal safety and honour or disgrace. During the "cultural revolution", he was persecuted and put in prison, but he was still concerned about the aviation industry and wrote down a summary of technological work of 200,000 words in extremely difficult conditions. When he was released from the prison, the first words from him were about the aviation industry. He kept always in mind the aviation industry until his last days on deathbed. The dedication spirit embodied in a lot of excellent persons and rooted in the ranks of workers and staff step by step is the precious heritage of the aviation industry. It will be handed on from generation to generation and developed greatly.

Section 2　Carrying Forward the Strong Sense of Duty to Serve the People

Educating the workers and staff to serve the people heart and soul was carried through in the whole process of the aviation industry's construction with emphasis on different points at different stages.

As early as 1951, when preparations were made for the establishment of the Bureau of Aviation Industry, it was decided that active service for the Air Force was the main content of all trade style cultivation. The factory director meeting held in the same year called on the workers and staff to serve the Air Force and to serve war and asked them to act according to this principle. In the war—ridden years, there was a firm belief that the demand in the front line of the Korean War was an order. No matter what kind of hardship they would bear and how tired they would be, so long as the Air Force required, they would resolutely fulfil their tasks. At that time there was great needs of external tank in battlefield, Shenyang Aircraft Factory which was then under construction undertook this task. However, they had neither drawing of the external tank, nor aluminium sheet for manufacturing the external tank. The needs of war compelled them to think about and test. Patriotic feeling and sense of responsibility encouraged them to advance. After many failures, they successfully made the external tanks out of galvanized iron sheet instead of aluminium sheet and with reference to real tank, so as to satisfy the needs of war.

In the early 1960s, according to combat readiness requirement at that time, the aviation industry carried out deeply and painstakingly in the ranks of workers and staff the national defense education, war education and education on serving the construction of national defense and armed forces. Vice Premier He Long and Minister of Aviation Industry Sun Zhiyuan said many times: "The most important thing is to serve the national defense and the armed forces construction, that is to serve the people," and they emphasized repeatedly on serving the people well and making the people and the armed forces satisfied.

In 1961, the Air Force and Navy were forced to shorten the flight training time because of lack of components and spare parts, resulting in grounding of hundreds of aircraft. At that time, there was contradictions between the production of fragmentary components and spare parts and that of the complete aircraft, and there was great difficulty to organize production of the fragmentary components and spare parts for old types of aircraft, but the Ministry of Aviation Industry firmly carried out the policy, "To give first priority to production of components and spare parts, and accordingly give consideration to trial production of new aircraft," so as to meet the pressing needs of the armed forces. The aviation factories adjusted more than seventy production lines, the total production value of components and spare parts produced within three years was 2.1 times that of the past nine years. Once the Air Force urgently needed an aircraft force arm regulator, but unfortunately the aircraft factory had no such regulator in stock. The leader of the factory decided resolutely to take one off the aircraft which had been assembled in the assembly line, and send it to the air force unit. Some factories launched competition for winning the honour of "serving the armed forces".

With the gradually deepening reform, the open policy and revitalization of the economy at the new historical stage, the aviation industry enlarged its scope of service, not only continuing to serve the national defence construction, but also offering its service to economic development, market and export. In order to realize smoothly this major transition, the Ministry of Aviation Industry called on the workers and staff to leave the "small world" of the military industry production for the "big battlefield" of serving the "four modernizations" in the way of combination of military products with civil products. Every enterprise tried to bring the technological advantages of aviation industry into full play, and actively served every department of national economy. In order to ensure safe work at pit bottom and reduce the rate of accident to the minimum, the Ministry of Aviation Industry in cooperation with the Ministry of Coal Industry, successfully developed the KJ—4 safety monitor system for coal mine. It was up to the international standard in the 1980s and had Chinese characteristics. On the common base—flying in the sky or working underground — both involved human life, a number of research and test personnel of Beijing Instrumentation Technology Research Institute etc. with deep feeling for coal miners worked carefully and kept on doing experiments in severe underground conditions in the process of development. This system was tested operationally on a working surface of coal mine, where gas spilt over frequently. It gave alarm correctly 110 times within six months realizing successfully continuous monitoring. This success was a new achievement of technological development as well as a new progress of the service spirit.

The Ministry of Aviation Industry also asked the whole industry to observe the following principles: "The leading body serves the grassroots unit; The preceding working procedure serves the following procedure and the enterprise serves the customer." Suzhou Aircraft Instrument Factory not only developed an advanced wire cutting machine, but also provided high quality of technical service, so as to serve the customer even better. In 1985, they actively went to visit the customers for installing and debugging 859 sets / times of NC wire cutting machines and training more than 400 operation and maintenance personnel for 29 organizations. Owing to excellent quality of product and good service, the factory enjoyed widespread renown and its products were sold both at home and abroad.

"To serve four modernizations" has already been carried through in every field of the aviation industry and in the whole process of production, research, development and management. It has become step by step a conscientious act of the broad ranks of workers and staff.

Section 3   Cultivating the Consciousness of Quality First

The special use of aero product determines the special importance of product quality. Without the consciousness of "quality first," one can not be a qualified member of the workers and staff of the aviation industry. It is the concentrated expression of heart and soul service of the workers and staff of the aviation industry and an important task for ideological style cultivation of the workers and staff to cultivate the sense of responsibility a hundred percent for product quality and provide consciously the State, the people and the customer with first rate products.

In 1952, the Bureau of Aviation Industry put forward distinctively the policy "In aero product, quality first" and in particular, educated the workers and staff to attach importance to product quality and cultivate strict and careful style of work. Education on quality was listed as an obligatory course for a new member of the workers and staff entering the factory, and strict observation of technological discipline was brought into the factory regulations and laws of enterprise, so as to constantly strengthen quality consciousness of the workers and staff. Shenyang Aeroengine Factory once scrapped all the nozzles produced in four months, because workers did not follow the technological process. The Bureau of Aviation Industry circulated a notice of the event in the whole industry, and unfolded a mass movement on discussing about the nozzle event and carried out a general inspection of quality for a period of three months, thus giving a deep quality education to the masses of workers and staff.

Cultivation of quality consciousness of the workers and staff was conducted repeatedly through practice. Because of the influence of high targets and confused orders, putting undue emphasis on quantity and paying no attention to quality, sense of quality first was broken off, causing serious degradation of aero product quality in 1958. In the early 1960s, when the aviation industry rectified product quality on a large scale, it reiterated the policy of quality first and further called on the broad masses of the workers and staff to be conscientious and meticulous. The unqualified new aircraft should be scrapped and rebuilt, and trial production be carried out again. Shenyang Aircraft Factory and Shenyang Aeroengine Factory mobilized the workers and staff to learn a lesson from this bitter experience of neglecting quality. Beginning from inspection of the drawings of technological processes of J−6 fighter and its engine piece by piece, they made tooling and parts again, then assembled aircraft of excellent quality. The factory worked out standard of excellent quality for each link of trial production. It was not permitted to put into production, if any link was not up to the standard. Once in Shenyang Aircraft Factory one standard sample of main beam was overproof in processing. The shape of this sample was complicated and required high accuracy, the period of manufacturing was very long, but in order to foster serious and careful style of work and ensure product quality, Lu Gang, the director of the factory, decided to reject it and to have it remade. This overproof product was hung over the factory area as a negative example to teach the workers and staff a lesson of " quality first" . From then on, whenever rectification of product quality was conducted, it was emphasized that strict and careful, conscientious and meticulous style of work should be carried through, closely combining cultivation of style of work with rectification of product quality to form step by step a serious and careful mood, and a conscious practice.

Strengthening the sense of quality of the workers and staff and cultivating the conscientious and meticulous style of work were expressed first in strict requirements of the leading cadres at all levels for product quality. The Minister, Sun Zhiyuan emphasized time and again that: " Quality of aero product can not be overemphasized and there is no trifle as quality is concerned. Leaders at all levels must correctly handle the relations between quantity and quality." The Ministry of Aviation Industry made a rule for enterprises, i.e. "The first thing for a new director of a factory to do when he assumes office is to grasp product quality. To judge the contribution of a factory director is to see first of all whether he has done something to improve quality." Therefore, to set strict demands and ensure product quality became the first duty of a factory director. Immediately after he assumed office, Zhou Jiquan, director of Suzhou Aircraft Instrument Factory instituted working policy centralizing on assurance of product quality and issued strict management system. He also exercised veto power in distribution of bonus. Those who made unqualified products would be deprived of his bonus. Through three to four years' efforts the factory became one of the national advanced factories with products awarded every year. After Tang Qiansan, manager of Shenyang Aircraft Company assumed office, the first order he issued every year was a document dealing with assurance of product quality. He had the major quality accidents in the factory compiled and published in book form. It was used as a teaching material for new members of the workers and staff to study after entering the factory. The director wrote personally "Quality Regulations for the Workers and Staff," and stipulated three "hundred percent." Those who did not follow the regulations and discipline should be registered a hundred percent, reported to the leader a hundred percent and deprived of the current month bonus a hundred percent. Because of the strict demand and clear distinction between rewards and punishments, quality of product was improved continuously, so that the factory won prize of quality control from the Ministry of Aviation Industry. Xie Ming and Hou Jianwu, the former and the follow on directors of Chengdu Aircraft Company both regarded the hidden perils as an unerupted "volcano", and should be exposed and solved one by one without the slightest degree of carelessness. In order to put an end to unnecessaries inside aircraft, 105 check points were defined in procedure of assembling and checked one by one, then recorded for reference. Strict demand of the leaders was a decisive factor to cultivate a good sense of quality of the workers and staff.

Intensifying the sense of quality of the workers and staff was also embodied in adhering to the policy "three no letting—offs" in dealing with quality problems: i.e. no letting off when the reason for the problem is not clear, no letting off when the responsibility is not definite and no letting off when there are no measures for improvement. When Su Zhi, director of Shaanxi Aircraft Accessory Factory, once found a hair in a brake accessory, he organized successively workers to discuss the matter and then took measures to prevent similar event, thus putting an end to a bad style of neglecting quality. This was not only a painstaking management work, but also a work of tempering a conscientious and meticulous style.

For intensifying the sense of quality of the workers and staff a factory had to persist in educating the workers and staff with "quality first". This kind of education already became a common practice of each organization of the aviation industry, and they reminded themselves of this frequently, repeatedly and constantly. Many leading cadres, technical personnel and workers realized from experience: "For quality of aero product there is no minor problem," "Quality of product makes an impact on result of a war and safety of pilots and passengers," and "We would rather be troubled for hundreds and thousands times, but not let pilots run a bit risk." Through choosing quality pacesetter by public appraisal and spreading advanced experience, more and more workers recognized that as the workers of the aviation industry, they had to be responsible for product quality all his life. It's a glorious thing to make high quality product, but a shameful thing to produce rejected product. Product had to be of good quality, style of work be serious and careful, and skill be perfect. To ensure product quality, the workers generally attached importance to training their basic skill and raising technical level. Chen Xikun, a model worker of Zhuzhou Aeroengine Factory had not produced any waste product for seventeen years. His experience was   to be strict, careful and exquisite. i.e. strict thought in ensuring quality; careful operation in each step; exquisite technique in key working procedure. On the basis of raising consciousness, many enterprises unfolded in the ranks of workers delivery without fault for many years. Products made by Yi Zhixiang, a model worker of the Ministry of Aviation Industry were free of scrapping, free of fault and free of overproof, realizing delivery of high quality products every year. He deemed that a worker of the aviation industry should look up to product quality as important as his life. Wang Lanfen, inspector of Shaanxi Aircraft Landing Gear Factory tried every means to get to the bottom of the matter concerning product quality, even if there were only traces of fault. She often said: "I must be assured myself of the quality before I can assure the user of the same." Once in inspecting oil return valve, she found the difference of the bore diameter from the previous ones. Although the processing of this part was in conformity with the technological process, she was still in suspense. She found at last that the technician had written a wrong figure of size on the original drawing, so that an event of rejecting products in batches was avoided.

In the period of transition of the aviation industry to combination of military product with civil product, the Minister of Aviation Industry, Mo Wenxiang exhorted cadres at all levels and the whole staff that product quality was still a matter of life and death. In arranging production of military and civil products, many factories adhered to the principle of living on quality, developing on quality and benefiting on quality. Baoding Aircraft Aggregate Fixture Factory was aiming at building the first rate factory, manufacturing the first rate product and providing the first rate service. Starting from management, they intensified the sense of quality of the whole staff, used quality of work to ensure quality of product and did all they could to be a cut above others in quality. Because of the excellent quality and low price of its products, this factory won market in competition. In Machining Tools and Equipment Exhibition held in U.K. in 1986 this factory won optimum tooling prize for modern equipment.

The Consciousness of "quality first", the conscientious and meticulous style of work are becoming professional ethics and prevailing customs of the workers and staff in the aviation industry.

Section 4   Carrying Forward the Glorious Traditions of Building an Enterprise Through Arduous Effort and Self-reliance

The Government paid more attention to building of the aviation industry from its very beginning and invested in it as a focal point. But at that time the Korean War was still going on, the State had financial difficulty, and the industrial base was very weak, the aviation industry had to foster the Yanan Spirit to build an enterprise by thrift and diligence and hard struggle. In the past thirty years, China's aviation industry has been educating its workers and staff with this spirit, let them carry forward this spirit in building factories, institutes and schools. In every organization and every historical period were left the traces of the arduous efforts of the pioneers: At the initial stage of the construction of Taiyuan Aeronautical Instrument Factory, they produced the first China's aircraft instrument in the workshop which had been rebuilt from a horse shed; In Zhuzhou Aeroengine Factory the workers used the enamel ware for daily use to produce small copper-plated spare parts which were urgently needed; For the first rocket skid rail, a number of rocket slide tests were done on a special-purpose railway, etc.. These were not only victory of material progress but also songs of the spirit of arduous efforts and self-reliance. In memory of the great achievements in inland construction made by the workers and staff of the aviation industry, Guizhou Aeroengine Blade Factory engraved "Building an Enterprise Through Arduous Effort" on a cliff in Chinese. These words will last from generation to generation to encourage the people of today and tomorrow.

In the development process of the aviation industry, the spirit of building an enterprise through arduous efforts and self-reliance was closely combined with the ambition of scaling new heights. In 1951, when the construction just began, the acting Minister, He Changgong urged the leaders of factories, "To build up China's independent aviation industry as soon as possible, and to have aeroplane made by ourselves." On the eve of the success of the licence production of the first jet aircraft, director of the Bureau, Wang Xiping had convened a forum of experts to work out scientific research plan and began to organize the scientific research and design contingent. In the 1960s, the Soviet Union broke off his supports, the young China's aviation industry met with new difficulties. Vice Premier He Long pointed out promptly: "Self-reliance is the invariable principle of our Party. Under this circumstance, the aviation industry still must be prepared to undergo hardships and work with a will to make the country strong." The Minister, Sun Zhiyuan said: "Leaders at different levels must keep a close watch on overall situations, plan and prepare for the future and conduct scientific research through self-reliance, so as to attain and surpass advanced world levels." For more than three decades since the founding of Nanjing Parachute Factory, they have developed 170 types of 19 assortments of parachutes relying on the spirit of self-reliance. Nearly all the parachutes used in China were designed and manufactured by this factory, some of which have approached or attained advanced world levels in performance. Among these products type 4 paratroop parachute was developed successfully through 1116 sets / times various tests in order to meet the needs of improved aircraft speed. In the first nuclear bomb drop test, China also used nuclear test parachute designed by this factory at its primary stage. After watching the tests, Premier Zhou Enlai warmly commended the design institute of this factory for their achievements and talents. Nanchang Aircraft Factory was a primary trainer manufacture factory in its early days.

In order to change the backward situation that only piston—engined aircraft could be produced, with little investment from the Government, the workers and staff of the factory sticked to the principle of self—reliance and building an enterprise through thrift and hard working, built test facilities thriftily, carried out technical reformation, conducted trial production at the intervals of mass—productions, and at last designed and produced jet attacker Q—5 aircraft. The Ministry of Aviation Industry propagated widely these deeds of the two factories' workers and staff to carry forward the spirit of building an enterprise through arduous effort and designing aero products by themselves. Cultivated by this spirit, many advanced departments emerged in the aviation industry. The Unmanned Aircraft Research Institute of Nanjing Aeronautical Institute was one of them. They developed four types of unmanned aircraft in succession, of which the highly maneuvering drone was comparable to the same sort of planes of the world. It took only one year to develop this drone. In order to test the highly maneuvering drone, the fifty members of the test flight team of this institute strived arduously in cold weather in Gobi desert for more than one hundred days. Some of them worked in the field at −36 ℃, with their fingers injured by cold metals. This team was highly praised by higher authorities as a test flight team which could bear hardships, tackle key problems, and overcome difficulties.

With the spirit of building an enterprise through arduous effort, and the ambition of scaling new heights, a lot of difficult problems could be resolved. There was an important load—bearing member—radial flexible hub made of composite material in Z—9 helicopter. This hub had to be moulded by 50 tons special moulding press. At that time only a few countries had this special—purpose equipment. Foreign merchants contacted Chinese government many times to sell this kind of hot—press and claimed that if China did not buy this machine, it would make historical mistake. The technical personnel and workers of Beijing Aero Precision Machinery Research Institute overcame difficulties and tried to produce this equipment with indigenous methods. Instead of tall building of workshop, they built a big matshed in the open air which was used as workshop for assembling and debugging the main body of the equipment. Each time they hoisted a big component, they had to lift the roof of the matshed. For dustproof, a plastic curtain was made around the precision parts. In the height of summer, they debugged the machine inside the curtain, the working conditions were very hard. It was just by dint of high aims and lofty aspirations, and the spirit of hard working as well as scientific management and powerful research capabilities that the special 50 tons hot—press was successfully developed within only two and half years. Foreign experts could not help praising that it was " an outstanding achievement."

If the building of the aviation industry with military product as a main purpose in the past was called the first pioneering work, then in the new historical stage, to build the aviation industry into a military—civil type industry would be in fact the second pioneering work. Compared with the first, the second pioneering work was quite different from the first one in breadth and depth. It needed even more courage of building an enterprise through arduous effort and spirit of working with all one's might. Changzhou Aircraft Factory was a small factory which had been rebuilt from local factories. There were only a few workshops, inadequate funds and difficult conditions. For six years from 1979 to 1985, they adhered to self–reliance, did not wait for, did not rely on and did not ask for help from outside. They advanced along the road of building an enterprise through arduous effort, developing nonaero products and creating new level of quality. In three successive years from 1983 to 1985, this factory was elected national advanced organization. With funds raised on their own, factory buildings were enlarged from 1,000 square metres to 60,000 square metres, the number of equipment increased from 56 to 601. In 1986, they netted six million Chinese Yuan, and manufactured a small–sized unmanned plane. The factory began to take shape.

The experiences in cultivation of ideological style are as follows:

1. Pay attention to the cultivation of working style of the workers and staff, while carrying out economic development. To judge the capability of the workers and staff in scientific research, production and construction is to see not only their technical and professional quality, but also their political and ideological quality. It is an indispensable duty of the leading body of an industry to cultivate the ideology and style of its workers and staff through technical and professional work. On the basis of this, the aviation industry has been attaching importance to the ideological construction of the ranks. The Bureau of Aviation Industry made in 1951, a seven–point decision on the style cultivation of the ranks, which was approved at the first factory director meeting. From then on, at the annual meeting of the enterprise leading cadres every year, they put forward definite objectives and requirements for the construction of the ranks. After stepping into the new stage, according to the new situation of the open policy and revitalizing economy as well as the succession of the new to the old of the workers and staff, meetings of political work of the aviation industry was held two times first in 1981 then in 1984 to unify the understanding of the importance, principle and task of the ranks' ideology and style cultivation in new stage, to rectify the tendency of ignoring ideological and political work and put stress on educating the young workers so that the construction of the contingent could also enter a new stage.

2. The examples of leaders are silent commands. Good style of leaders plays a strong leading role. Just because there was a good leader—Tan Su who had held the posts of chief engineer, director and the Party secretary of an aero oil pump factory in an extremely cold and remote mountainous inland area, the factory could become a national excellent enterprise in ideological and political work. He not only enforced strict demand and strict management in production technology and product quality, but also attached great importance to ideology and style cultivation of the leading bodies at all levels and the ranks of worker and staff. He worked actively to criticize the evil trends and encourage healthy trends. He was strict with himself in working and living. Led by him, the workers and staff of the whole factory were in a calm, unruffled mood and production was becoming more and more flourishing. Therefore, it is necessary to grasp persistently the style cultivation of leading cadres in the style cultivation of the ranks of the workers and staff.

3. The more and deeper the workers and staff understand Marxism–Leninism, Mao Zedong Thought and task, principle and policy of the government at every stage, the stronger the sense of a master's responsibility will be and the better ideological basis the style cultivation will have. The aviation industry has consistently paid attention to conducting normal education of situation and task, education of principle and policy and education of ideology and politics. After the "cultural revolution," through setting things to right, and getting rid of the working methods of Left trend, the aviation industry upheld the practical and realistic ideology line based on that the social practice is the only criterion for judging truth, adhered to the four cardinal principles and policies of reform, opening and revitalization and carried out ideological and political education of the workers and staff.

4. Persist in unfolding activities of learning from and catching up with the advanced persons and organizations. The advanced ideology and fine style were most concretely and lively represented by the advanced persons. The Ministry of Aviation Industry kept on frequently choosing advanced workers and launching widespread socialist emulation campaign in every organization of the ministry. In the 1950s, the deeds of the national model worker Ma Deyou were widely propagated. In the 1960s, Ma Chuanwu and Gao Fangqi were set up as pacemakers of the whole industry. These activities were still going on even in the period of ten years of chaos—the "cultural revolution." At that time production of many organizations were at a standstill or at a half standstill. But Li Linzhuang, a worker of Zhuzhou Aeroengine Factory persisted in working hard, he operated two sets of machine tools himself. For many years he fulfilled several years' amount of work in one year. Regardless of some body's opposition the Ministry of Aviation Industry firmly set Li Linzhuang up as an example for the whole industry to learn from and conferred him the title of honour "The Man Advancing Ahead of Time". To cite Li Linzhuang timely was also to protect the productive initiative of the most of the workers and staff who stood fast at their posts then.

After the Third Plenary Session of the 11th Central Committee of the Party, to learn from and catch up with the advanced elements became even more invigorating. In 1979, Li Linzhuang, Yan Deyi, Li Xiangchen, Yu Long and Zhou Yaohe etc. were all awarded the title of "the National Model Worker." In 1984, the Ministry elected such seven people as Tan Su, Li Linzhuang, Shen Zuxian, Gu Songfen, Zhang Zixiang, Zhao Lingcheng and Yi Zhixiang etc. as "the Model Workers of the Ministry of Aviation Industry" making the activities of learning from and catching up with the advanced elements develop continuously in depth. Every organization kept on electing its own advanced elements and taking them as backbones to guide the workers and staff to emulate even high standard and constantly enlarged the contingent of the advanced workers thus forming a "chain of model workers" to push forward the cultivation of good style.

To foster good style of the ranks is an important component of the building of socialist culture and ethics. The Ministry of Aviation Industry summarized the following words as professional spirit: "vitalize the aviation industry, serve the four modernizations, reform and progress, quality first, hard struggle and unite and observe discipline." It is either a summary of building the contingent in the past years, or the objective of cultivation of ideological style in the new stage. All the workers and staff are asked to carry forward this professional spirit, act as a model worker to inherit traditions and as a vanguard to blaze new trails to the four modernizations.

Chapter XXII   Economic Relations, Trade and Scientific and Technological Exchange with Other Countries

Exchange of aeronautical scientific and technological results and experiences between countries and reciprocal international trade and technological cooperation are indispensable conditions for giving impetus to the development of the aviation industry. From the beginning, China's aviation industry attached importance to technological cooperation with foreign countries. After 1978, China started to carry out the open policy. It brought favourable conditions for the aviation industry to cooperate with other countries and develop foreign trade in a larger scope. In early 1979, the State Council approved the forming of China National Aero–Technology Import & Export Corporation (CATIC) by the Ministry of Aviation Industry to generally organized import and export trade of the aviation industry. Afterwards a good situation of rapid development emerged in foreign technological and economic cooperation and trade of China's aviation industry.

Section 1   Import of Technology

From its beginning, new China's aviation industry actively imported advanced technology from other countries. This was taken as a major measure and an important way to raise the level of aero–technology, enhance self–reliance capability and advance the aviation industry.

In the 1950s, Premier Zhou Enlai, vice premiers Chen Yun, Li Fuchun, Nie Rongzhen directly led and organized import of technology of the aviation industry. In 1951, a protocol for building China's aviation industry with the Soviet assistance was signed by the Chinese government and the Soviet government. In the agreement of 141 projects (increased to 156 projects in 1955) of Chinese economic development assisted by the Soviet Union, signed by the two governments of China and the Soviet Union in 1953, and in the Soviet assisted projects of the Chinese Second Five–year Plan negotiated in 1956, the construction projects of China's aviation industry were all arranged. In this period, manufacturing technology of seven types of aircraft, nine types of aeroengines, five types of tactical missiles and several hundreds of airborne equipments were imported in succession from the Soviet Union. During the First Five–year Plan period, the Soviet Union helped build thirteen key projects, and 847 Soviet consultants and experts were invited to work in 32 units of offices, factories, research institutes and colleges of China's aviation industry. In the meantime, China sent a total of 353 leading cadres, technical personnel and workers to the relevant Soviet factories for training. The total amount of the expense of technological import was about three hundred million new Roubles. This was the period in which China's aviation industry imported on large–scale foreign advanced technologies.

Beginning from the 1960s, the Soviet Union broke off the contracts signed with China. The Western countries like U.S.A. continued to enforce blockade and embargo on China, so technological import of the aviation industry was basically at a standstill.

In the 1970s, the conditions for China's aviation industry to conduct international associations were getting better. Under the direction of Ye Jianying, Vice Chairman of the Military Commission of CCCPC, Spey Aeroengine was imported from U.K. This was the beginning of import of advanced technologies from the Western countries.

After smashing the "Gang of Four", especially after the Third Plenary Session of the 11th Central Committee of the Party, the open policy became a long-term national policy of the country. The association of the aviation industry with other countries and import of technology were increasing day by day. From November to December 1978 for the first time the Delegation of China's Aviation Industry headed by Lu Dong, Minister of Aviation Industry paid a visit to F.R.G., France and U.K. In April and May 1985, Mo Wenxiang, Minister of Aviation Industry led Chinese Aviation Delegation to investigate and visit the aviation industries of U.S.A. and Canada for a period of one month. According to statistics from 1978 to 1986 delegations and groups sent abroad by the aviation industry travelled all over Asia, Europe, North America, Latin America, Africa and Oceania. Through these contacts, understanding of foreign aviation industries was increased, a lot of information of technological import and economic trade gained, thus created conditions for China's aviation industry to unfold trade and cooperation with other countries. From 1980 to 1985, the aviation industry successively imported from 10 countries dozens of items of aero and nonaero technologies and about one hundred items of important facilities for aeronautical scientific research and test.

At new stage import was conducted according to the following policy and principle: a. Stress on technology import, but not on purely purchasing of products with the aim to raise the starting point of the development of aeronautical science and technology. b. Import of complete set of equipment should be done carefully and by a small amount, but single item of technology should be imported selectively to strengthen the weak link of the aviation industry. c. Attach importance to importing advanced research and test equipments and instruments enabling the aviation industry to have modern scientific research facilities. d. Fully study the items to be imported, carefully make decisions and arrangements, so as to ensure a full utilization of the imported items. e. Import of foreign technology should be considered in conjunction with domestic scientific research. Only those items urgently needed and could not be obtained in time through domestic research and development were allowed to be imported. The imported items should be fully studied, transplanted and updated.

Thanks to the correct policy and principle, import of technology has played a remarkable role in promoting the development of the aviation industry.

1. The Process of Mastering Advanced Technology Has Been Accelerated in the Aviation Industry

New China founded its aviation industry on an extremely weak basis. Just because China had imported repairing technique and manufacturing technique of aircraft, aeroengine and airborne equipment etc. from the Soviet Union and with the support of the Soviet experts, it could manufacture trainers and fighters during the First Five—year Plan period and advanced from repair to mass production. Only ten years after the first practical jet fighter appeared in the world, China could master the manufacturing technique of the first—rate jet fighter at that time. In the late 1950s, the first generation of supersonic jet fighter was also made, which broke through "sonic barrier", and realized a leap of quality in manufacturing aircraft.

In the mid 1950s, speed of jet aircraft increased to Mach 2. After the Soviet Union successfully developed MiG—21 fighter with the speed of Mach 2 and a flight altitude of 19,000m in 1956, China imported this airplane in the early 1960s and succeeded in its licenced production in the mid 1960s. In addition, China also produced transport aircraft, helicopters and bombers under licence. Correct policy of technology import helped Chinese aero products leap into the advanced ranks of the world. In the meantime for manufacturing products, the Government set up many advanced aeronautical factories, research institutes, design establishments, universities and colleges, and secondary technical schools, thus laying a solid foundation for the future development of China's aviation industry.

2.　A Gap Has Been Filled Up and Technology Obtained

In 1975, production licence of Spey engine was introduced from the British Rolls—Royce Co.. Trial production of this engine came off all right in 1980, thus filling up a gap of turbofan in China's aeroengine and accordingly obtained engine manufacturing technique.

In 1980, CATIC and the French Aerospatiale and Turbomeca SA signed the contract on transfer of production technology of Dauphin helicopter and its Arriel engine and the contract of purchasing their parts of aircraft and engine, as well as raw materials respectively. After that, CATIC and other French companies signed contracts on the supply and technology transfer of autopilot, hydraulic booster and stagnation pressure pick—up etc. required by the helicopter. To start with, a batch of the complete machine was accepted. Then final assembly and test were done followed by parts and components production until all the parts and components became Chinese—made. By the end of 1986, thirty two helicopters have been produced, and already delivered to CAAC, Air Force, Navy and Chinese Marine Helicopter Co. Trial production and mass production of this kind of helicopter have met the needs of geological prospecting, marine investigation, contamination monitor, hoisting equipment, petroleum extraction, forest fire—fighting, agriculture and fishery work, mountain areas and ocean short—distance transport, rescue and salvage as well as public security and tourism etc.. Through technical reform manufacturing technology of domestic helicopter has been improved a great deal.

3.　Performance of Aircraft Has Been Improved and Use of Aircraft Enlarged

After opening to outside world on the basis of self—reliance, China's aviation industry waited for an opportunity to enforce flexible policy of using foreign advanced parts to match its own aircraft. Good results were achieved in introducing foreign technology to modify Chinese existing aircraft for the improvement of their performance and use.

In 1980, CATIC with two British electronic equipment companies, Marconi and Smiths Co. signed contracts for purchasing airborne radar and head-up display as well as part of these electronic equipment's manufacturing licence to modify Chinese-built J-7 fighter. Before long flight test and fire target practice were completed. It proved that the modification of J-7 fighter was successful, and this aircraft exported to foreign countries very soon.

In the early 1980s, CATIC imported electronic equipment from American Litton Industries Corp. and Collins Radio Co. to modify Y-8 transport. After modification, this aircraft could carry out self-contained navigation, fly 2,000 km away over the sea and became a good sea patrol aircraft.

4. Building of Modern Research and Test Facilities Has Been Strengthened

The international scientific research and test equipment and instrumentation developed with each passing day and already became an effective factor for promoting the progress of aero-technology. After the 1980s, research and test equipments imported into China's aviation industry equipped and reformed its scientific research and design organizations and enhanced its research and test capacity.

These test equipments include: Citation II aircraft with airborne datum test equipment, which was purchased from the American Cessna Aircraft Company and was used in many kinds of research and test of airborne equipments for newly developed aircraft. French DAMIEM III flight test data acquisition system can acquire various data of aircraft, aeroengine, radar test flights, and those measured from aircraft intake and flow field; French DAMIEM V flight test real-time data system can do real-time observation of main flight parameters and critical parameters on the ground; American MTS aircraft fatigue coordinated-loading system has a loading accuracy of 1% ; Accuracy of the instrumentation system of test rig of engine components is up to 0.5% ; A set of advanced large-sized computers and microcomputers can do computation work on design, research and test of aircraft, engine and airborne equipment, providing modern medium for enterprise and scientific research management.

5. Ways of Co-production of Aero Product with Other Countries Have Been Opened Up

In March 1985, Shanghai Aero Industry Co., China Aero Materials Co. signed an agreement of co-production of aircraft with American McDonnell Douglas Corp., which was approved by the Chinese Government and became effective on April 15th of the same year. The main contents of the agreement are as follows:

a. With the help of McDonnell Douglas Corp. Shanghai Aero Industry Co. uses parts and components, and assembling technique provided by McDonnell Douglas Corp. to produce twenty five MD-82 passenger aircraft before 1991 and sell to CAAC.

b. Aircraft quality must be in conformity with FAA standard. This will be accomplished by Shanghai Aero Industry Co. and McDonnell Douglas Corp.

c. McDonnell Douglas Corp. helps Shanghai Aero Industry Co. produce three big components of MD-82 and recruit CATIC for development of an aircraft project with newly-designed propfan engine.

d. 30% of the general contract value is for compensation trade. To execute this contract, Shanghai Aero Industry Co. will dispatch about 200 engineers and skilled workers to U.S.A. for training, while McDonnell Douglas Corp. will send about 70 experts to work in Shanghai Aero Industry Co. According to the plan, parts and blanks of the first aircraft were transported to Shanghai in January 1986, and through riveting, assembling and test flight, the first aircraft was already completed in July, 1987, and delivered to CAAC.

In 1986, China's aviation industry signed an agreement on co-development of FT8 gas turbine with the American Pratt Whitney Corp. and an agreement on feasibility study of the 75 seats propfan passenger aircraft with MBB of the Federal Republic of Germany.

6. Capability of Technical Reform of Aero Factory Has Been Increased

For use of advanced technology, through effectively reforming some backward technologies of aero factories, China's aviation industry introduced manufacturing techniques of NC machine. In 1980, Chinese Aeronautical Technology Research Institute signed contract on introduction of NC miller production licence with French FOREST-LINE. Maximum working surface of this machine amounts to 9m x 4m , total weight 160 tons, 5 coordinates, accuracy 0.06 mm. It can be used to make aircraft parts. The Chinese side bought from this company design drawings, technical documents, test standard and many kinds of manuals of this machine, and organized to produce it in China. The proportion of home-made parts and components was enlarged gradually, and already amounted to 60%.

Aircraft factories used this kind of machine to change traditional design and production flow. For example, airframe originally composed of various kinds of parts and components changed into an integrated body, so as to increase strength, save preparation manhours and processing manhours, reduce technological equipment and shorten assembly period. This kind of equipment was adopted by both aircraft factories, and departments of automobile and ship-building industries.

7. Production of Nonaero Products in Aero Enterprises Has Been Sped Up

In the 1980s, China's aviation industry turned considerable part of technical equipment, scientific and technological personnel and skilled workers to production of nonaero products. In order to push forward this transform, the Ministry of Aviation Industry selectively imported some technologies of nonaero products. By the end of 1986, the Ministry has achieved good results in introducing technology for making advanced tourers, micro-automobiles, refrigeration equipment and high pressure water cutting machines etc.. Take the advanced tourers as an example, it is a much— needed means of transportation for tourist trade and a suitable product for aircraft factories to produce. In the early 1980s, Shenyang Aircraft Company introduced RM80G advanced medium—sized tourers from Fuji Heavy Industries Ltd., Japan for manufacturing. Up to 1986, the proportion of Chinese—made parts amounted to 70%.

Section 2 International Exchange and Cooperation of Science and Technology

Beginning from 1979, China's aviation industry unfolded planned and organized exchange and cooperation of science and technology with other countries, including scientific and technological cooperations between governments, attending international academic conferences, going abroad for technological investigations, inviting foreign experts to give lectures in China and sending students to study abroad, dispatching engineers to work in foreign companies etc.. It expanded the Chinese association with aviation industries and academic circles of many other countries, promoted friendship between them and exchanged academic achievements.

1. Scientific and Technological Cooperation between Governments

According to agreements signed between the Chinese Government and other countries' governments on cooperation in science and technology, the aviation industry of China and aviation circles of other countries developed cooperations in science and technology. In March 1979, Professor H.L. Jordan, Chairman of the Executive Board of the German Aerospace Research Establishment (Deutsche Forschungs—und Versuchsanstalt fur luft—und Raumfahrt e.V. —— DFVLR) led a delegation to visit China. In September of the same year, Xu Changyu, Vice Minister of Aviation Industry and President of Chinese Aeronautical Establishment headed a delegation to visit F.R.G. In April 1980, both sides signed the special agreement between CAE and DFVLR on scientific—technological cooperation in civil aeronautical research. In October 1979, Mr. Sunden, Director General of the Aeronautical Research Institute of Sweden (Flygtekniska forsoksanstalten —— FFA) led a delegation to visit China. In October 1980, Vice President of CAE Xu Mingxiu headed a delegation to visit Sweden and both sides signed a protocol on scientific and technological cooperation. In June 1980, Dr. A.M. Lovelace, Deputy Administrator of National Aeronautics and Space Administration (NASA) led his delegation to visit China; In September of the same year, Xu Changyu headed CAE delegation to visit U.S.A. The two parties signed the protocol on cooperation in aeronautical science and technology in May 1983. In May 1984, Mr. A. Auriol, President of the National Institute for Aerospace Research and Studies (Office National Detudes ET De Recherches Aerospatiales —— ONERA) led a delegation to visit China; In January 1985, Vice Minister of Aviation Industry and President of CAE Gao Zhenning headed a delegation to visit France and both sides signed a protocol on cooperation in aeronautical science and technology.

Apart from the above four countries China carried out scientific and technological cooperation with some other countries, such as Italy, Romania and Belgium etc.. Forms of cooperation include joint research, holding academic conference, exchange of experts and information and documentations. Through these channels China's aviation industry sent in succession 140 men−times of engineering and technical personnel and experts to the above countries to visit and do cooperative research. In the meantime China's Aviation Industry also received 87 experts from these countries to conduct aeronautical scientific and technological activities in China.

Remarkable achievements were made in these exchanges and cooperations. Chinese and foreign experts jointly wrote dozens of valuable academic theses. Some of them were read at international symposia, some published in internal publications of both sides. Aeronautical research institutions of China and F.R.G. jointly compared German and Chinese low speed wind tunnel test results, studied measuring technique of turbulent flow boundary layer, structural stability analysis, calculation of 2−3 demensional boundary layers, experimental strap−down inertial navigation system, instrumentation technique of engine cascade, artificial boundary layer transition as a tool for subsonic wind tunnel testing, experimental investigation of micro−mechanism of aluminium alloy, analysis of buckling of composites structure and fatigue crack growth behaviour under spectrum loading etc.. Good results from the above research were achieved. Topic of artificial transition research was advanced in technical thinking, but very difficult to fulfil. It created a precedent of successful research of boundary layer artificial transition with thermo−pulse in wind tunnel. Six−component balance designed jointly by Chinese and German experts and made in China was a high quality balance.

Another example of successful cooperation between China and F.R.G. was the development of ground resonance vibration technique of aircraft as a whole. According to annual program of scientific and technological cooperation between CAE and DFVLR in 1980, the Chinese side dispatched two engineers to DFVLR to work for three months. They familiarized themselves with test facilities and methods of DFVLR, especially the advanced technique which uses exponential function and pictorial display to control adjustment force and developed a set of Chinese software system. In 1981, German experts came to China and together with Chinese experts did resonance vibration test on an aircraft with the above system. The test proved that performance of the software system was stable and came up to advanced world standards. After that the two parties carried out joint tests and also achieved good results. A summary of this was published in scientific and technological reports of DFVLR. The cooperative result of this research pushed forward the development of China's aircraft ground test technique.

In aeronautical science and technology cooperation between China and Sweden, experts of both sides jointly researched wind tunnel testing equipment and testing and calibrating techniques, Laser Doppler Velocimetry (LDV) techniques used in wind tunnel testing, boundary layer evaluation from flight test, aerodynamic calculation for configurations consisting of wing, body pylon and nacelle, theoretical research and numerical calculation of transonic slotted wind tunnel wall interference and fatigue crack propagation etc. The effects of all the above topics were satisfactory.

Through these cooperations of science and technology, Chinese experts tempered themselves and learned advanced technology from cooperators of other countries. They also provided their own experiences, therefore both sides were mutually benefited.

2. Attending International Academic Conference and Exchanging Science and Technology

From 1979 to 1986, China's aviation industry sent 545 men / times to attend 240 international academic conferences held the world over. At the same time five international conferences were held in China. Through these international conferences new achievements of academic and technical research were comp— rehensively exchanged between Chinese and foreign noted scholars, scientists and engineers. They gained benefits from each other's wisdom. For instance, at the 11th European Microwave Conference held in Holland

Fig. 111   Officials of F.R.G. visiting China's aeronautical industrial exhibition stand

technical ideas on antenna radiation pattern, antenna gain, antenna polarization and antenna impedance were exchanged, which played an active part in the development of microwave technology in China's aviation industry. Another example is that at AIAA 11th Aerodynamic Experimental Conference technical experiences of presentations of fluorescent tuft fluid state, coloured pictorial fluid, helium bubble fluid state and coloured optical—fiber flow field etc. were exchanged. This enlightened Chinese experts on their work and helped China's aviation industry raise the level of wind tunnel testing. Still another example was that attending international standardization conference to exchange experience provided good reference for China to institute its own standards.

At the international conferences, experts sent by China read many papers of high level, which won favourable comments from foreign counterparts. For example, at the 4th international experimental mechanics conference, Chinese expert, Professor Wu Zongdai read his report "Development of Self—compensating Resistance Strain Gauge under 700 ℃ High Temperature." This subject is being studied nowadays all over the world, and it aroused the attention of each related expert.

In September 1985, Gas Turbine Division of the American Institute of Mechanical Engineer (AIME), CATIC and CSAA co-sponsored Beijing International Gas Turbine Symposium and Exposition. During the symposium a total of 154 pieces of theses was read among which 75 pieces were read by the Chinese delegates. The contents of these theses included 35 topics of design and production, combustion and fuel, cascade flow of aeroengine and turbine etc.. During the symposium 35 foreign companies, such as American General Electric Company, Avco lycoming Div., British Rolls Royce Ltd. French Turbomeca SA etc. exhibited their products. CATIC also exhibited its own products. Through the symposium and exposition Chinese scholars and experts broadened their horizons, associated with many friends and learned some new knowledge. Scholars and experts from other countries got profound understanding of work and production in respect of gas turbine, which had been done in China. This kind of symposium laid a foundation for further development of academic exchange between Chinese scholars and international counterparts.

3. Inviting Foreign Experts to Give Lectures and Attend Technical Seminars

From 1979 to 1986, China's aviation industry invited 235 experts from twelve countries to come to China for giving lectures in a short period and attend technical seminars. Making use of these opportunities many professors, experts, engineers and technical personnel of aviation industry directly exchanged knowledge and experience with foreign experts. This was good for teaching, scientific research and production in China. In this respect BIAA, NPU and NAI did much more work. After inviting a professor from Aachen to China to give lectures, BIAA put the contents of lectures in their teaching materials for postgraduate and applied it to repairing engine parts e.g. repairing of a batch of engine guide vanes which would have been scrapped, by means of vacuum repairing welding, and they succeeded and these vanes passed through 400 hours long-term test run.

4. Detailing Students and Engineers to Study and Work Abroad

Since opening to outside world, apart from dispatching students to study abroad at the expense of the Ministry of Education, the Ministry of Aviation Industry specially allocated funds to additionally detail students to study abroad. The total number was 949. By the end of 1986, thirty one of the returned students received doctor's degree. In addition, the Ministry also sent 110 engineers to foreign companies to work. While working they learned technology and management from the foreign companies. They were dispatched to twelve countries such as: U.S.A., U.K., F.R.G., Japan, Canada, Switzerland and Sweden etc..

Most of the students studying abroad were diligent in their studies and specialized in a field of study. Many of them made inventions and some won patent rights abroad.

Section 3 Export Trading

1. Export Trade of Aero Products

From 1979 to 1985, China signed 141 contracts with more than ten countries and areas including Egypt and Pakistan etc. for sales of aero products. China already exported many types of aircraft and aeroengines, and repaired quantities of aircraft and aeroengines for friendly countries.

The reason why China could make notably achievements in export of Chinese aero products within such a short period lies in:

a. Chinese aero products were practical and cheap, and had a strong attraction in international market. J—6, J—7, Q—5 and Y—12 aircraft as well as various kinds of trainers exported in quantities from China all had good performance and were more useful aircraft. Because of their reasonable prices they were more competitive in international market, in particular, attractive to the developing countries.

b. To actively modify aircraft to satisfy the needs of customer countries. Aerodynamical configuration, structural strength, flight speed, altitude and manoeuvrability of Chinese aircraft were all good. Although avionics and engines of some types of aircraft were not good enough, in order to meet the requirements of customer countries for increasing aircraft performance, China's aviation industry managed to keep up the advantages and replace the unsuitable parts by means of importing equipment, modifying aircraft and raising performance etc. or modifying aircraft in cooperation with other countries. Q—5Ⅲ and J—7M aircraft were exported after being modified by this way.

c. To elaborate product—support. In export of aero products China did technical training for customers before delivery of goods and did product—support after delivery. In so doing the customers were able to correctly use these products with high proficiency and bring them into full play, and problem was solved in time when it occurred. In order to keep exported products always in good conditions in the customer countries, CATIC also helped the customer countries build ten repair lines and production lines of aircraft, aeroengine, mechanical instrument and gyro motor etc. as required by them.

With the growth of export quantity, amount of product—support work doubled and redoubled. After being approved by the State Council in October 1981, China Aero—Technology Service Company was set up under CATIC, which manages and coordinates completely product—support work for exported aero products. From 1980 to 1986, they trained for foreign customers more than 900 of various kinds of aircrew and ground crew, arranged about 1,200 hours flight training and more than 8,000 hours instructing on ground, trained a number of technical backbones for the customer countries.

In order to help the customers understand specifications of Chinese products, CATIC specially compiled and published about 7,000 sets of more than 400 kinds of different aircraft and engine technical documents (English version), and timely distributed Technical Bulletin and Aircraft and Aeroengine Life Extention Bulletin. More than 700 men-times of 86 technical expert groups were sent to the customer countries to help them install equipment and conduct test flight, and tackle about 500 important technical problems, answer 1,150 technical questions, so as to ensure the customers to operate and maintain the products normally. Meanwhile technical experts were dispatched with equipment and instrument to the customer countries to calibrate and repair their periodically inspected instrumentations. The customers were provided with 20,000 pieces of urgently needed components and spare parts of 2,400 items in 70 batches.

To accelerate the customer's solving technical problems in operation and maintenance, CATIC organized the customers to visit Chinese manufacture factories and operation bases, to study and exchange the operation and maintenance experiences of the same models of aircraft and aeroengines. Through these activities Chinese aero products won higher reputation, and the customer countries had much more faith in Chinese products.

2. Export of Aero Components and Spare Parts

To ensure exported products in good conditions for operation, CATIC arranged to produce and export components and spare parts on a large scale. These were supplied to 17 countries and areas satisfying the needs of maintenance of old aircraft and aeroengines exported twenty five years ago and that of the latest aircraft and aeroengines with a total of thirteen types of aircraft and a variety of 150,000 articles. CATIC provided components and spare parts not only for aircraft and aeroengines but also for ground equipment, measuring and testing instruments and machine tools of overhauling production lines, and also provided enroute repair kit and aero-materials etc.. One hundred and twenty factories in the whole country took on this task.

To organize production of components and spare parts was a complicated and tedious task. Because some kinds of components and spare parts were too old to be produced in the factories, and the quantity needed was very small, to produce them again was not worthwhile. However the customer countries needed them urgently, without them their aircraft could not fly. To serve the customers, China's aviation industry often spent a lot of money to organize production of these components and spare parts. Aero components and spare parts to be supplied were of many kinds and varieties, and in big quantities ordered by a lot of customers. To ensure supplies of components and spare parts of quite different specifications and numbers to the customers timely and correctly, CATIC used computer aided management and set up completed storage and transport system. In general, the components and spare parts were exported by sea, or by air if they were in urgent needs.

Production preparations and manufacturing period of aero components and spare parts generally took three to six months. To meet customers' crying need special measures of production and storage of components and spare parts were taken:

a. Set up storage of vulnerable components and spare parts. One could take out any kind of the stored parts at any time when needed.

b. CATIC and manufacture factories assigned special persons to be responsible for orders of urgently needed components and spare parts and arrange special vehicles to transport these components and spare parts.

c. CATIC representative offices in those countries where more Chinese aero products were ordered installed their own telex by which the information of urgent order was sent back to China immediately, and transmitted on the same day to relevant factories.

d. CAAC gave priority to transportation of urgently needed component and spare parts sending out these goods by the latest flight. Generally components and spare parts needed urgently could be delivered to customers thirty days after the order, of which 80% were delivered within only twenty days. Correct and high efficient supply of components and spare parts satisfied the needs of the customers, thus won their praise and trust.

3. Compensation Trade and Sub—contracting

Following international practice, when China buys goods of high value from a foreign company, the company should purchase from the Chinese side Chinese products as compensation which occupy a certain proportion (generally 30%) of the total price of the contract. This is internationally known as compensation trade. It is varied in forms one of which is to manufacture products according to supplied drawings, samples and materials by the seller to be resold to the seller. It is called sub—contracting production. This is a main form by which China's aviation industry exports its processed products.

By the end of 1986, China has gained nearly a hundred million U.S. dollars of compensation trade from ten aircraft manufacturing companies such as the American Boeing Company, McDonnell Douglas Corp., Sikorsky Aircraft Div., British Aerospace Co. Ltd., French Aerospatiale, etc. due to purchasing their aircraft. China has also gained tens of millions of U.S. dollars of orders from the following aeroengine companies: American Pratt Whitney, General Electric Corp., Allison Div., Avco Lycoming Div., British Rolls—Royce Ltd., French SNECMA and Turbomeca SA, Canadian Pratt—Whitney etc. due to purchasing their aeroengines.

Products which were processed according to contract for compensation trade for aircraft are: different kinds of doors, main gearboxes, centre wings and flaps, vertical tails, wing ribs, mechanical parts, titanium forgings and aggregate fixtures etc., for aeroengines are: turbine blades, guide vanes, compressors and turbine discs, combustion casings and flame tubes, stator rings, seals, stub shafts, accessory cases, all kinds of rings and gears etc.. Many factories made good achievements in compensation trade. For example, in early 1982, Xi'an Aircraft Company signed a contract with Boeing Company for manufacturing 70 pieces of Boeing 737 access door. Delivery started in January 1985. When Boeing Company received products, they did not find any problems through evaluation, and considered the quality reliable. When receiving the seventh product, they asked to reorder 100 sets more.

Compensation trade and sub–contracting production stimulated technical reformation and management improvement of the enterprises which took on the tasks. Most part of compensation trade products were used on aircraft and aeroengines of foreign airlines, so the requirements of product quality and the methods of quality control were extremely strict. The relevant foreign companies carried out surveys of production conditions in advance, and the production contract was signed officially only after the conditions had been confirmed to attain the standard. To undertake to produce aircraft components for Boeing Aircraft Company, Xi'an Aircraft Company has reformed more than 20 production lines and will continue to reform according to the tasks. After signature of production contract the Company carried out trial production, then the product was inspected and passed and licenced, if it was an important part and then put into production formally. Boeing company has already issued 12 technological production licences to Xi'an Aircraft Company. At the same time, according to international standards the company has instituted systems and methods of quality control and worker's skill assessment as well as management in the whole process from raw material purchase to product delivery, storage and transport, so as to raise management level and create favourable conditions for undertaking production of more parts and components for international market. This is an important approach for China's aviation industry to step into international market. Now there are six Chinese aviation factories undertaking sub–contracting production, and the number is increasing.

4. Export of Nonaero Products

Since the 1980s, export of nonaero products has been increasing too. They are mechanical products such as gages, cutting tools, aggregate jigs, forgings and castings, optical glass and granite platforms etc. The market is becoming bigger and bigger.

Most of the Chinese mechanical products on the international market are also required in quantities by the aviation industry itself. These products are of advanced technology, easy to produce for aviation industry, and proved sound in operation. Therefore when these products were put on international market, they were all welcomed. The "sea gull" stainless steel calliper made by Chinese aviation factory had an accuracy of 5 micron and sold well on international market. It was received very soon by the European and American markets.

To keep good quality and cheap price of goods is another important factor to win markets. Cutting tools exported in quantities by CATIC were made of special quick–cutting steel and processed with special heat–treatment technique, therefore not only the knife–edge was very sharp, but also the service life was several times longer than the commonly used ones. However the price was much cheaper than that of common cutting tools. It was favourably received on international market. The American "Industry Weekly", "American Mechanist", "Cutting Product", "Blue Book of Tools" etc. journals published reviews and comments of the users in praise of "Hang Jian" brand cutting tools that their performance was good and service life three times longer than the common ones, but the price was 15—20% less than the market price. The American Los Angeles Standard Tools Company said that efficiency of "Hang Jian" brand cutting tools doubled that of the other ones, so that the production efficiency increased by 40%. Users of this kind of cutting tools rapidly spread to American mechanical, aerospace and military industrial processing departments. American Hughes Helicopter Company made a conclusion on testing of Chinese milling cutter saying: "Efficiency of CATIC milling cutters doubles that of the American trump cobalt 42 high speed steel cutters. If the user processes one part, he has to use 10 American milling cutters and finishes it in 8 hours; Whereas he uses only two CATIC milling cutters and finishes the work in three hours; Furthermore it can be used to process titanium alloy." American Whitney Cutting Tools Company made comments that if CATIC milling cutter was used to process stainless steel, the cutting speed and feed could be increased by a factor of 4—5, service life 3—4 times that of cobalt high speed steel.

Sales of nonaero products underwent a process — from lack of experience to gradually gaining experience. For example, China has more than twenty year's experience of production and operation of aggregate jigs, the users spread about 100 factories of the whole aviation industry. However when they appeared on the British market for the first time in 1980, nobody cared about it because people didn't know how to use them. Later CATIC Representative Office in London changed their selling technique: In the forgings and castings exhibition held in 1981 in London a foreman of much experience from Harbin Aircraft Manufacturing Company gave a demonstration of the techniques of the aggregate jigs then and there. After that he went to British Aerospace Co. Ltd., Rolls—Royce Ltd. and Dowty company to demonstrate and help assemble. CATIC also entrusted an agent to sell them in Europe. Civil Aircraft Div. of British Aerospace Co. Ltd. bought and tried them out in production of aircraft, the effect was quite good. From then on the aggregate jigs were gradually sold to some other companies, and started to have a foothold on the Western European market. Finally they found a good sale on the world market.

Section 4   International Contracting Engineering

Through more than thirty years' construction, China's aviation industry has formed a contingent of about ten thousand capital construction people with rich experience in architectural design and construction management. When the Government began to carry out the open policy in 1979, CATIC immediately organized a contingent of project construction people, and with support of and in cooperation with Ministry of Metallurgical Industry and Ministry of Nuclear Industry advanced towards international market to unfold international contracting engineering. CATIC stuck to the following principles: less risks, minor profit, high quality, to put reputation first, act according to its own capability, advance steadily and honour its commitment to users. Contracted engineering projects are mainly in Jordan, Kuwait and the

United Arab Emirates (UAE).

In 1980, with the approval of the State Council CATIC set up a Design and Construction Engineering Company. In June of the same year, it was on recommendation of the Chinese Embassy in Jordan that the company signed contract with Jordan General Construction Ltd. on Jordan Swaqa Rehabilitation Center Project. In December 1980, the company was registered and officially formed in Jordan with the business licence issued by the Ministry of Industry and Commerce, Jordan. In the same year it won another contract on Abu Nuseir District housing project. From 1981 to 1983, the company signed a series of contracts, such as Maan Glass Factory construction project, A Hassan housing project, six schools projects in Abu Nuseir New Town, sewage treatment plant project, main transformer and two substation projects, and South Cement Factory housing project etc..

In contracting the above projects the guiding ideology of CATIC was not only to earn foreign exchange, but most important was to help the third world friendly countries in construction. CATIC used the best techniques and asked cheap price and exerted every effort to guarantee the quality and period of completion of construction projects. During three years, they kept up low price and high quality which won full confidence of the local government and the users. On August 16th, 1983, His Majesty King Hussein of Jordan, accompanied by Prime Minister, Commander of the Three Armed Services, Minister of Urban and Rural Affairs and Environment, Governor of Maan Province, General Manager of Housing Company inspected Maan housing construction site. He highly praised that CATIC abided by an agreement, quality of construction was good and progress could be ensured. He wrote a few words of appreciation as follows: " We highly praise the Chinese brothers who have made contributions whole—heartedly to the most important project of Jordan. We are proud of our friendship, fraternal feelings and satisfactory cooperation. We shall persist in and defend our common principle and hope."

Half a month later, His Majesty King Hussein visited China. Before a banquet given by President Li Xiannian, King Hussein and his wife shook hands with CATIC President Sun Zhaoqing and said: "CATIC employees work very diligently in Jordan, quality of construction is very good too. They contributed to the cooperation and friendship between Jordan and China. For this, I, on behalf of Jordanian Government, express thanks to them."

On July 24th, 1984, Prime Minister, Vice Prime Minister, three ministers and five vice ministers of Jordanian Government, accompanied by Governor of Maan Province and the General Manager of Housing Company, visited CATIC construction site the second time. The Prime Minister once again praised consummate construction quality of CATIC, and wished friendship between the peoples of Jordan and China last forever.

After gaining reputation for its construction project in Jordan, CATIC developed contracting engineering work in Kuwait and UAE. In March 1984, CATIC signed a contract with a local company of Kuwait for providing labourers in the second stage C−3 project of Jahara housing construction, and signed a contract with local company of Abu Dhabi for providing labourers in the Military Academy construction. In 1985, contract for providing manual labour to Jahara Housing Center Project in Kuwait, and sub—contract for Small Sports Club Project in U.A.E. were signed. At the same time CATIC set up representative branches and offices one after another in Kuwait and U.A.E. and made full preparations to further develop contracting engineering work.

From 1980 to 1986, CATIC signed totally contracts of thirty five construction projects with building areas of 900,000 square metres. Ten thousand men—times of construction workers were sent abroad in succession. With the support of Ministry of Foreign Economic Relations and Trade and in close cooperation with the Ministry of Nuclear Industry and other departments, CATIC went through a process of learning, practice, and summing—up experience. It not only successfully fulfilled its tasks, but also was freed from losses occurred in the primary stage. It opened up a new prospect of gaining slight profit and earning foreign exchange for the State.

Section 5   Import and Export Organizations of Aviation Industry

CATIC was formed in January 1979. Under the leadership of the Ministry of Aviation Industry CATIC manages independently foreign trade and is responsible for export of aero products and nonaero products manufactured in factories and institutes subordinate to the Ministry of Aviation Industry, introduction of advanced technology, special—purpose equipment and accessory equipment, special raw materials and auxiliary materials as well as import of foreign funds. It is also in charge of technical exchange in the field of aviation industry between countries, and international contracting engineering. It is an attempt to reform the foreign trade system — to change foreign trade management from the import and export companies alone, which are directly under the Ministry of Foreign Economic Relations and Trade to collaboration of the professional import and export companies of the relevant ministries. The fact shows that this reform has brought great benefits, which mainly are: carry out the integrations of technology with trade, industry with trade and import with export; quick transmission of information both at home and abroad; quick solution to problems; direct dialog between suppliers and customers, which is helpful to arouse the enthusiasm of enterprises and institutions of the aviation industry; proper import of advanced technology from abroad and earning more foreign exchange through export. CATIC earned a considerable amount of foreign exchange the year it was formed. Three years from then on, earnings of foreign exchange increased sharply. Earnings of 1980 were 2.46 times that of 1979, while amount of export in 1986 was 5.5 times that in 1979. Through import and export trade, factories paid to the State a certain amount of tax and profits.

With the growth of import and export trade of China's aviation industry CATIC's structure and management are being perfected, and business scope is being expanded.

Employees increased from 80 people at its founding to 220. They manage the whole import and export trade of the aviation industry. Under CATIC there are China Aero Technical Service Company, CATIC Design and Construction Engineering Company, CATIC Civil Aircraft Sales Company and CATIC Nonaero Product Department. In addition, according to different countries and areas twenty branches were formed.

Fig. 112   Building Complex of CATIC Industry and Trade
Centre in Shenzhen Special Economic Zone

1. CATIC Domestic Branches, and Industry and Trade Centres

Industry and trade centres were set up respectively in three special economic zones of Shenzhen, Xiamen and Zhuhai. Taking advantage of favourable conditions for foreign trade in special economic zones, CATIC unfold foreign trade activities, attracted and utilized foreign investments and vigorously supported the development of special economic zones. With several years' efforts, CATIC Industry and Trade Centre in Shenzhen Special Economic Zone has already become one of the important foreign trade departments of this special economic zone.

In Shenzhen Industry and Trade Centre twenty nine export—orientation factories were established with an export rate of 80% of average annual output. Tian Ma Micro Electronics Company jointly run by the Industry and Trade Centre and Electronic Bureau of Beijing Municipality produced liquid—crystal display with annual output of twelve million chips of which 99% were exported.

CATIC formed its branches respectively in Shanghai, Fuzhou and Guangzhou as windows

—516—

for foreign trade. Either industry and trade centres or branches carried out industrial production and trade activities.

Each branch, industry and trade centre managed the export of nonaero products of surrounding aviation factories and enforced horizontal ties with local enterprises. For example, CATIC Shanghai Branch and Changshu, Jiangsu Province invested jointly in forming the Global Aluminium Base Materials Company to produce aluminium foil.

Up to 1986, all branches, industry and trade centres have been making every effort to establish joint venture enterprises with European and American companies, so as to introduce and utilize foreign funds and advanced technology and make full use of favourable conditions of coastal cities for foreign trade to set up bases for producing technical products of good quality and cheap price for export to the world market.

Each branch also undertook storage and transport tasks of import and export goods for the whole aviation industry. During the Sixth Five-year Plan period, Shanghai Branch stored and transported 22,000 tons, 177,000 cases of imported and exported goods. This was the main port for import and export. At the beginning owing to lack of experience, goods were kept too long in stock, but afterwards situation improved greatly, and the period of storage and transport was shortened to no more than 45 days. Import and export goods through Guangzhou Port were increasing daily, and during the Sixth Five-year Plan period, the amount of storage and transport was up to 11,000 tons, 32,000 cases.

2. Branches in Foreign Countries and Hong Kong Region

CATIC set up representative offices or branches in countries and regions where trade contacts were more frequent. By the end of 1986, overseas representative offices and branches have been formed in the following fourteen cities: London of U.K., New York and Los Angeles of U.S.A., Montreal of Canada, Hamburg of F.R.G., Paris and Marseilles of France, Tokyo of Japan, Amman of Jordan, Abu Dhabi of U.A.E., Kuwait, Cairo of Egypt, Islamabad of Pakistan and Mogadishu of Somalic etc.. In addition, an office was founded in Hong Kong.

The forms and tasks of all these overseas branches are:

a. To join the overseas trade centre set up by the Ministry of Foreign Economic Relations and Trade as a branch of CATIC. There are CATIC branches in the China Trade Centre in New York, U.S.A., and in the Western European China Trade Centre in F.R.G.. All these branches are commercial enterprises registered in locality and are corporate bodies with requisite qualification. They manage their business and accounting independently, and assume sole responsibility for their profits or losses. Their business scope includes: purchase materials, negotiation for cooperation, conduct compensation trade and sub-contracting production of civil aircraft parts and components for the head office of CATIC and factories, institutes of the aviation industry; help the head office of CATIC in technology import as well as act as a commission agent.

b. To act as representative offices. With the agreement of the local government representative offices were founded, and entrusted by CATIC head office to manage cooperation trade with the countries where they located. For example, Representative Office in London is in charge of implementation of the contract for introducting aircraft electronic equipment from U.K.; Representative Office in Paris is in charge of implementation of the contract for introducting Dauphin helicopter; Representative Office in Tokyo is responsible for implementing the contract for import of nonaero products. These representative offices are also responsible to recommand the head office of CATIC the advanced technology required to be imported, at the same time recommand CATIC products to relevant companies and firms of the country where they located. There are some other representative offices which are mainly in charge of sales of aircraft, product support and contracting construction project. These offices are mostly located in the countries of the third world.

With the further development of foreign trade of China's aviation industry, CATIC subsidiaries are being increased, and the turn over of import and export trade has been constantly raising too.

Section 6 New Development in International Cooperation

In recent years all Chinese aircraft and aeroengine companies have initiated and expanded their co-operation with some major foreign aircraft and aeroengine manufacturers in the fields of technology and subcontract production and encouraging success has already been achieved. The co-operation is beneficial to both sides and it is good to the advancement of technology and production of Chinese aviation industry. It is expected to further expand in the future.

1. Production and Technology Co-operation with Boeing Company of the United States in the subcontract production of aircraft parts and components

The CATIC of China signed a contract with Boeing in 1980 for subcontract production of machined parts of Boeing Model 747, which was performed by the Xi'an Aircraft Company. To carry out the contract the company studied Boeing's technical standards and quality control system, received a production approval from Boeing to its working process consisting a dozen or so work steps, and delivered qualified finished parts. More contracts were signed later for the production of service doors of Boeing Model 737, wing rib subassemblies of Boeing Model 747 and vertical fins of Boeing Model 737. The performance of contract for machined parts of Model 747 was completed in 1985 and the others are still being performed. The vertical fin of Model 737 is a large subassembly and, hence, more demanding to manufacturing and to management. The first finished vertical fin was delivered to Boeing in March, 1988 and its quality was in conformity with Boeing's standards. Therefore, the delivery of the vertical fin marked a new step forward in the subcontract production.

In addition to the Xi'an Aircraft Company, the Hongyuan Forging and Casting Factory and the Shenyang Aircraft Company of the MAI, and the Southwest Aluminum Factory of the Non−ferrous Metal Inc. also successively became Boeing's subcontractors. The first contract awarded to the Shenyang Aircraft Company was for the machined parts of Boeing Model 757. The purpose of the contract on the Chinese side was not so much for parts supply but rather for a pioneer production to learn and adapt itself to Boeing's requirements in technology, quality control and management. Through the performance of the contract the Shenyang Aircraft Company obtained from Boeing a production certificate for nonconventional machining and, therefore, it is allowed to process more complicated products. Hongyuan Forging and Casting Factory has obtained Boeing's several orders for titanium alloy forgings after the production certificate was issued by Boeing while the Southwest Aluminum Factory has begun its production of aluminum alloy forgings for Boeing.

There are following peculiarities in the aforementioned co−operation with Boeing:

a. A step by step approach has been adopted, by which the subcontract production has been proceeded from small and simple machined parts to large, complicated and difficult subassemblies. This approach was considered a bit slow by some people but it has been proved successful by the facts that the Chinese aircraft factories, among them are the Xi'an Aircraft Company and the Shenyang Aircraft Company, have adapted themselves to the subcontract production and that they are now preparing to process larger subassemblies and to cooperate even on a much more complicated product−− Chinese trunk−line airliner.

b. For both parties' long−term interest Boeing subcontract not only aircraft parts and subassemblies to Chinese aircraft factories but also aircraft forgings to Chinese material industry. In addition Boeing is also considering the possibility of Chinese raw material supply.

c. In the co−operation China has learned from Boeing western technical standards and quality control requirements, obtained production certificates and reduced the gap in technology with western countries. Besides, help has also been obtained from Boeing when the problems in management were found with the increase of the subcontract products and , therefore, these factories were pushed to improve their production management.

d. Beginning in 1985 and with Boeing's help all raw materials needed for the subcontract production have been successfully purchased abroad. The experience in purchasing foreign raw materials has been obtained and personnel have been trained.

2.　Co−operation in Production and Technology with McDonnell Douglas Corporation

a. Subcontract Production

The CATIC signed a contract in 1979 with McDonnell Douglas to manufacture and assemble main landing gear doors for the MD−80 airliners in the Shanghai Aircraft Factory. This was the first contract received by Chinese aviation industry in subcontract production of civil aircraft components for western countries. Due to the smooth performance of the first contract McDonnell Douglas awarded later more contracts to the Shanghai Aircraft Factory for production of MD-80 nose landing gear doors, avionics maintenance doors, service doors and freight doors. So far 440 main landing gear doors and 380 nose landing gear doors have been delivered. Two more contracts were obtained in 1988. One was for the production of MD-82 tailplanes by the Shanghai Aircraft Factory and the other for the production of MD-82 nose section by the Chengdu Aircraft Company.

b. Co-operation

When the subcontract production went into its fifth year,i.e. 1985, and China purchased some MD-82s the co-operation was developed into a bigger scale. The Shanghai Aircraft Factory would finally assemble, flight test, and deliver MD-82s with the parts and components supplied by McDonnell Douglas. A total of 25 MD-82s are to be produced in this phase.

What we can find in the co-operation with McDonnell Douglas are as follows:

i) McDonnell Douglas really is an aircraft manufacturer with reputation as one of a few biggest aircraft manufacturers in the world and it has also showed its boldness and courage in the co-operation with China. It was the first one who subcontract to China its main landing gear doors which were not too small products, when the potential capability of Chinese aircraft industry was far from being known to the west. After the co-operation with the Shanghai Aircraft Factory McDonnell Douglas further chose the Chengdu Aircraft Company as its subcontractor to manufacture MD-82 nose section which consists of several thousands of parts. This decision could not be made if McDonnell Douglas did not take a broad and long-term view and was not determined to bear risk.

ii) In the early 1980s the Shanghai Aircraft Factory had less experience in production than other Chinese aircraft factories. Therefore, more problems had to be solved in setting up qualified technical management system and quality control system. The joint efforts made by McDonnell Douglas and the Shanghai Aircraft Factory for the success of today are praiseworthy.

iii) With the help from McDonnell Douglas the Shanghai Aircraft Factory has been the first among Chinese aircraft factories to obtain FAA production certificates for both parts production and aircraft final assembly. This prepared the condition for manufacture of Chinese airliners to be designed according to the international airworthiness regulations.

3. Co-operation in Production and Technology with Lockheed Corporation

a. Co-operation in Technology

The Shaanxi Aircraft Company is cooperating with Lockheed in the modification of Chinese Y-8 medium transport. A contract for technical consultation for the improvement of Y-8 was signed in 1987. The co-operation has been carried out in the following three areas:

i) The assessment of the general design concepts of the pressurised cabin and the loading door and ramp at the rear of cabin, which are to be incorporated in the Y-8 improved version.

The original main freight door at the rear of cabin was redesigned into a loading door and ramp of C-130 type while the unpressurised cabin was changed into a pressurised one and the aerodynamic shape of the rear fuselage was kept unchanged. What were solved in these two designs of improvement were the computation of the external load distribution, fatigue resistance and fail—safe designs, controllability and stability, center of gravity control in airdropping, analyses of wing external fuel tanks flutter and the loading door buffet, design of airdropping freight trajectory in the air and design of clearance between the airdropping freight and the airplane at the moment when the airdropping freight just left the airplane. The solutions to these problems have resulted in a better general design.

ii) Lockheed assisted the Shaanxi Aircraft Company in some difficult flight test subjects of the Y—8 prototype airplane. Some valuable data were obtained, which would serve as the basis of the improvement in the longitudinal and lateral stabilities of the Y—8 airplane.

iii) Through the co—operation designers of the Shaanxi Aircraft Company began to understand and to be familiar with the military standards and FAA regulations of the USA. This will certainly lay a foundation for the future Chinese transport designs in accordance with international standards.

After the co—operation in the past year the Y—8 has come into its detailed design phase. The improved version of Y—8 is expected to make its first flight in 1990.

b. Subcontract Production

A subcontract for production of several assemblies of C—130 including tail cones was signed in 1986 between the Shenyang Aircraft Company and Lockheed Corporation. The Shenyang Aircraft Company began its delivery in 1988.

4. Co—operation with Airbus Industrie

Three main partners of Airbus Industrie, British Aerospace, MBB and Aerospatiale, respectively subcontract the production of machined parts of wing ribs of the A320, emergency exit doors of the A320 and service doors of the A300 / A310 to the Shenyang Aircraft Company and the Xi'an Aircraft Company. To comply with Airbus Industrie's standards these two Chinese companies made great efforts in improving heat treatment, surface treatment and nondestructive testing. So far the Shenyang Aircraft Company has delivered 30 sets of A320 wing ribs to British Aerospace. Delivery to the Aerospatiale has just begun. First delivery to MBB will take place in 1989.

Because the Airbus Industrie is a multi—nation consortium, the time period needed for making decisions on awarding subcontract production to Chinese aviation industry is longer than that needed by other companies. Therefore both parties thought the progress of the co—operation too slow. The success of Airbus Industrie in its several airliner development programs and the growth of CAAC's interest in Airbus have presaged the possible expansion of co—operation. A discussion about the subcontract production of A330 / A340 parts was held in 1987 and it is believed that the co—operation between the two parties will be further discussed in near future.

5. Co-operation with Aircraft Manufacturers of the United Kingdom

a. British Aerospace

In addition to subcontracts from Airbus Industrie, British Aerospace actively subcontract production of aircraft parts for its own aircraft BAe 146 and ATP to Chinese aircraft factories. Since 1981 British Aerospace has successively subcontracted the production of BAe 146 main landing gear doors, freight doors, service doors, avionics maintenance doors,etc., to the Harbin Aircraft Factory, and ATP rudder assemblies to the Shenyang Aircraft Company with the parts supplied by British Aerospace. Up to now BAe 146 main landing gear doors have been produced and delivered regularly for a couple of years. The delivery of ATP rudders began in 1988 and in 1989 will begin the deliveries of the others. The raw materials for the production of all BAe 146 doors are purchased abroad by China. The relationship of co-operation between the two parties is quite good.

b. Shorts

The production of cabin doors, freight doors and service doors of the SD3 series has been subcontracted to the Harbin Aircraft Factory of China since 1982. One hundred sets have already been delivered. In 1986 the Harbin Aircraft Factory began its production of central wing of the SD3-60, which is a big assembly and consists of more than 3,000 parts, and so far 20 sets have been delivered. The discussion about further expansion of co-operation has lasted a period of time and it is believed that the substantive negotiation will take place as soon as the problems related to the purchasing of raw materials by China are solved to lighten the burden on Shorts.

6. Co-operation with Aircraft Manufacturers of Canada

a. Canadair Limited

A subcontract signed in September, 1980 for production of 7 subassemblies of Canadair CL-215 airplane was the first among those obtained by the Xi'an Aircraft Company. No doubt the successful performance of the subcontract helped the company set up its reputation in subcontract production . All its later co-operation with Boeing, Aerospatiale and Aeritalia is the expansion and deepening of the subcontract signed with Canadair. Now the subcontract is still being well performed. The discussion about additional orders for aforementioned subassemblies and new subcontract production for the improved CL-215 was held not long ago.

b. De Havilland

De Havilland was an independent aircraft manufacturer when the negotiation for the subcontract production was held but it became a part of Boeing when the subcontract was signed. This subcontract specified that the production of Dash-8 freight doors would be undertaken by the Shenyang Aircraft Company. First delivery has taken place in 1988.

7, Cooperation with GE in Engine Technology and Parts Production

a. Cooperation in Engine Technology

In his meeting with Mr. Brian Rowe Senior Vice president of the General Electric Company (GE) in 1986, Vice Premier Li Peng asked the company to help us improve the performance of the WJ5A1 turboprop engine installed on Y−7 aircraft. GE accepted this task enthusiastically. An agreement was then achieved between CATIC and the Harbin Engine Company and GE Aircraft Engines Group that the cooperation should be carried out with emphasis on improvement in the specific fuel consumption and operating life of the engine. The turbine section of the engine would be redesigned by the Harbin Engine Company with the help of GE to reduce its specific fuel consumption and extend its operating life. In May 1987, a technical consulting contract was formally signed by both sides. In 1988 the cooperative preliminary design on the modification concept was accomplished by technical personnel from both sides at a factory of GE in Lynn, Massachusetts, U.S.A. and the results were satisfactory. Then the Harbin Aeroengine Factory began the detail design and a prototype of the modified engine was scheduled to be turned out in 1989.

b. Engine Parts Production

In the early 1980s, the Shenyang Engine Company began to produce the parts of CF−6 engine for GE.

According to their importance to the aircraft safety, the engine parts are divided by GE into three categories: i.e. normal, important and critical. Through several years' cooperation, now GE had confidence in the quality, cost and delivery time of these parts made by Chinese aeroengine factories under subcontracts. So the Shenyang Aeroengine Factory was certified to manufacture at first the normal parts of CF−6 engine such as seals and rings, and then some critical parts such as compressor disk, turbine disk and combustor inner and outer liners of CJ610 engine, rear shaft of high pressure turbine of CFM56 engine and a few parts of CT64 engine.

The subcontracted production business has been constantly growing. After 1984, GE awarded the Xian Engine Company a subcontract for manufacturing turbine disk of the LM2500 gas turbine engine. With a diameter of more than 1,000 mm, this engine has six turbine disks in diameters of 600−1,000 mm. The Xian Engine Company was initially assigned to produce engines with a diameter of more than 1,000 mm and so its equipment, technology and manufacturing process were well suited for manufacturing the parts of LM2500 engine. Through several years' cooperation, the mutual trust in each other was deepened. On the basis of its existing accurate equipment, the Xian Engine Company is now enlarging its capacity − setting up a production line of turbine disk for GE.

8. Cooperation with Aeritalia on Q−5M

A contract was signed in 1986 between CATIC, Nanchang Aircraft Company and Aeritalia to modify Q−5 attack aircraft designed and developed by Nanchang Aircraft Company. The modified aircraft will be named Q−5M. With the aircraft and its engine performance unaffected, the modification only involves the transplanting of the avionics and fire control system from the

AMX attack aircraft co–developed by Aeritalia and Brazil into Q–5 to improve its combat capability. There are eight items of avionics to be installed on Q–5 aircraft: digital central computer, dual data bus, Litton inertial navigation system, Agusta head up display, air data computer, weapons aiming computer, FIRR P–2500 radar, friend or foe identification system and VHF / UHF radio. Aeritalia is the main contractor of the whole system.

The programme will be carried out in two steps. First step: Aeritalia provides 4 sets of the above mentioned avionics equipment for use on two Q–5 aircraft; Second step: Nanchang Aircraft Company installs the avionics system into the aircraft and flight tests in Nanchang. The installation of the first aircraft was finished in August 1988 and its flight test is begun.

9. Cooperation with PW in Aeroengine Parts Production and Gas Turbine Engines

In 1981, the Pratt Whitney Aircraft (PW) of the United States began to order from CATIC aeroengine parts for its JT8D, JT9D and PW4000 engines. The ordered items included flame tube, gas collector, compressor case and stator shroud, and turbine exhaust case. Those factories that undertook the production of these parts, made much progress in production management and manufacturing technologies such as nondestructive inspection, welding, arc plasma spraying and NC machining.

In 1986, a contract on cooperative development and production of a new gas turbine engine was signed between CATIC and the Gas Turbine Powerplant Division of PW. This is an industrial or marine gas turbine engine derived from JT8D aeroengine. Designated as FT8, the engine is of 22,000 kW (30,000 hp) class. Now it is in development stage. In 1987, 58 Chinese engineers joined the engineering work in the United States and many American experts worked in the Chengdu Aeroengine Factory where parts for prototype engines are being manufactured. After the completion of the engine development, the Chinese side will be responsible for production of the power turbine section and some parts of the gas generator, with a work–sharing of about one third of the whole engine. The engine will be sold on the world market.

As a form of offset trade, PW offered the Chinese aviation community 5 scholarships for Master's degree every two years. In 1986, after examination, the first Chinese students were chosen and sent to the United States from organizations of MAI and CAAC.

10. Cooperation with the British Company Thorn–EMI

Recently CATIC and Thorn–EMI are discussing to cooperate in developing a Chinese early–warning aircraft.

Thorn–EMI has rich experience in airborne microwave radar systems which had been in operation with the military for many years. The newest of its development is an airborne reconnaissance system series named Skymaster. It is an airborne early–warning and shipborne reconnaissance radar series. Its main features are: multi–mode operation, software controlled, automatic tracking, TWT1(X) – band transmitter, stabilized antenna, 360 ° search, automatic sector–scan and narrow beam. This radar has been installed in the Royal Air Force Sea King helicopter and the Spanish Navy Sikorsky helicopter for early warning purpose.

CATIC and Thorn–EMI are jointly studying to install the Skymaster radar on the Chinese made Y–12 light transport and Y–8 medium transport aircraft, to convert them into early–warning aircraft.

Chapter XXIII   Chinese Society of Aeronautics and Astronautics

Chinese Society of Aeronautics and Astronautics (CSAA) is a national academic mass organization subordinate to the China Association for Science and Technology (CAST). It consists of those people who are engaged in aerospace scientific and technological work, and have reached a certain level in their profession and come together on a voluntary basis.

The main tasks of CSAA are: unfolding academic exchanges both at home and abroad, providing scientific and technological consultation, popularizing knowledge of aeronautical science, revitalizing academic thinking and promoting development of aeronautical science and technology.

Section 1   General Description

After the founding of new China, in order to develop academic exchange and promote development of aeronautical undertaking in China, vast number of scientific and technological personnel in aeronautical field germinated an idea to organize an academic society. At a meeting of all aeronautical departments of universities in China, held by the Ministry of Education in 1951, and in 1956 when the State organized the experts to make the national science and technology development plan, some people suggested to form a national academic organization in aeronautical engineering field.

In the early 1960s, a series of important scientific research institutions were established in aeronautical and astronautical industries and a contingent of scientific and technological personnel engaged in aeronautical and astronautical scientific research, production, operation and education also grew up, the objective conditions for setting up CSAA were gradually maturing. In June 1962,some professors of Beijing Institute of Aeronautics and Astronautics (BIAA) wrote a joint letter to CAST stating the concrete proposal for setting up the society. In November of the same year, Fan Changjiang, vice president of CAST voiced his support to it. In early 1963, with the vigorous help of Wu Guang, president of BIAA a number of well-known experts, professors, leading cadres and technical personnel in aeronautical and astronautical fields had an informal discussion and put forward a proposal for establishing CSAA. This proposal was approved by Vice Premier Nie Rongzhen very soon.

CSAA inaugural meeting was solemnly held in Beijing from February 20 to 28, 1964. Present at the meeting were 263 delegates from aeronautical and astronautical institutions, industrial departments, Air Force, Navy, CAAC and universities and colleges all over the country. More than 1,000 scientific and technological personnel from relevant departments in the capital attended the meeting as nonvoting delegates. Papers were read, topical reports were made and academic exchanges in groups were held at the meeting. This was the first grand meeting unprecedented in the Chinese aeronautical and astronautical fields. Zhang Aiping, Sun Zhiyuan, Chang Qiankun and Qian Xuesen spoke at the meeting, placing an ardent expectation on CSAA. They unanimously held that the founding of CSAA will play a great role in the growth and flourish of the Chinese aeronautical and astronautical undertaking.

Fig. 113   CSAA Inaugural Meeting

The meeting elected the first CSAA council which consisted of 104 members. Shen Yuan was elected president, Xu Lixing, Xu Changyu, Liang Shoupan, Guo Ronghuai and Wei Jian vice presidents, Wang Junkui secretary—general. The meeting discussed and approved the constitution of CSAA, decided to set up five technical committees, such as aerodynamics and flight mechanics, propulsion system, structural design and strength, manufacture and materials technologies, avionics and automatic control technical committees etc., and editorial board of publications, as well as recruited the first members into the Society. The administrative body of CSAA is affiliated to BIAA. In more than two years after the founding of CSAA, five national academic activities were organized in succession, and three delegations were dispatched to attend international academic conferences and to go abroad on visit and investigation. The academic publication "Acta Aeronautica et Astronautica Sinica" which reflects scientific and technological research results in aeronautical and astronautical fields of China came out. The popular science magazine "Aerospace Knowledge" for the youngsters was published too. In addition, popular courses on aviation knowledge were held in certain places. Regional societies of aeronautics and astronautics were set up or will be set up in five provinces and cities i.e. Beijing, Jiangsu, Liaoning, Shaanxi and Heilongjiang etc. and new members of the societies were recruited, so as to keep the scientific and technological personnel of aeronautical and astronautical fields in close contact with each other. The "cultural revolution" began just when the society had reaped its first fruits. At the end of 1966 CSAA administrative body and editorial department were compelled to disband.

In 1972, with the increase of technical exchanges between China and other countries there was an urgent need for CSAA to resume its activities. In March 1973, when the Ministry of Aviation Industry asked the State Council for restoring CSAA and resuming publication of "Aerospace Knowledge", it was approved by Ye Jianying and Li Xiannian very soon. This was the first national society officially approved to resume its activities in the "cultural revolution" period.

With the opening of the National Science Convention and the Third Plenary Session of the 11th Central Committee of the Party, China ushered in Spring of Science, and CSAA academic activities entered an unprecedentedly vigorous stage. In September 1979, the second national assembly of representatives of CSAA was held in Hangzhou. Present at the meeting were 340 delegates, the second CSAA council consisting of 163 members was elected. Shen Yuan was elected president, Xu Changyu, Tu Shoue, Liang Shoupan, Wu Zhonghua, Xu Lixing and Yao Jun vice presidents, and Wang Junkui secretary- general. Eleven technical committees restored and newly formed were as follows: committees of aerodynamics, flight mechanics and flight test, structural design and strength, propulsion system, avionics, automatic control, materials and manufacture technologies, human engineering, aerospace medicine and air rescue, air maintenance engineering and management science etc.. Meanwhile popular science working committee (concurrently editorial board of "Aerospace Knowledge") and editorial board of "Acta Aeronautica et Astronautica Sinica" were formed.

In March 1983, the third national assembly of representatives of CSAA was held in Xi'an. Present at the meeting were about 300 delegates, and the third CSAA council consisting of 150 members was elected. Ji Wenmei was elected CSAA president, Gao Zhenning, You Jiang, Yao Jun, Wang Wanlin, Li Ming, Zhuang Fengan, Cao Chuanjun and Zhang Azhou,vice presidents and Wang Nanshou secretary- general. The society also engaged Cao Lihuai, Mei Jiasheng and Shen Yuan as consultants. At the meeting aeronautical popular science committee was reorganized as popular science and education working committee, and the editorial board of "Aerospace Knowledge". At the same time the meeting decided that the administrative body of CSAA would be affiliated to the Ministry of Aviation Industry. After the third national assembly, the subordinate technical committees developed gradually from 11 to 16. Five new technical committees were: air weaponry and fire-control, composite material, instrumentation measurements, helicopter, light flight vehicle committees. Technical groups developed to 53. By the end of 1986, altogether 12 provinces and cities in China set up successively regional societies of aeronautics and astronautics such as Beijing, Shanghai, Heilongjiang, Liaoning, Jiangsu, Jiangxi, Shaanxi, Sichuan, Guizhou, Hunan, Hubei and Jilin etc.. Then CSAA members in the whole country amounted to 31,768 people. Regional societies formed their own technical committees and technical groups. They persisted in facing production, facing the grass—roots units and facing society, and extensively unfolded various activities in forms loved by the masses. They did a great deal in organizing academic exchanges, tackling difficult technical problems and popularizing sciences, consulting, discovering and cultivating personnel etc.. Besides, Sichuan and Jiangsu societies published magazines "Aeronautics and Astronautics" and "Jiangsu Aviation" respectively.

For more than 20 years since the founding of CSAA, it has always paid attention to coordination between national society and regional societies, enhancement of technical exchanges between China and other countries, sticked to the combination of scientific research with production and operation, the combination of professional activities with popular science activities and vigorously organized the mass of CSAA members, scientific and technical personnel to participate in academic activities. CSAA made great progress in the society work and contributed a great deal to promoting the development of aeronautical scientific and technological work of China.

Section 2   Academic Activities

CSAA academic activities have developed for more than 20 years, which can be divided into three periods: the initial period, restoration period and prosperous development period.

The initial period of the society was from 1964 to the beginning of the "cultural revolution" in 1966, during which five national academic conferences were arranged: the symposium on aerodynamics (jointly sponsored with the Chinese Society of Mechanics), the symposium on vehicle structural design and strength, the workshop on high—energy forming (jointly sponsored with New Technology Bureau of Academia Sinica) all held in 1965, a symposium on propulsion system held in 1966, etc..

Attending these symposia and workshop were about 1,000 delegates coming from 67 defence factories, 18 research institutes, 8 universities and colleges, 18 civil industrial and transportation units, as well as the Air Force, Navy, CAAC and Artillery etc.. Most of the delegates were middle—aged and young scientific and technical personnel, a few delegates were leading cadres and workers.

Academic exchange activities were not too often in this period, but they had three evident characteristics:

a.   Relating academic activities to production and practice. At the symposium on vehicle structural design and strength the delegates focused their discussions on aircraft design strength specifications and its production practice. Theses presented at the meeting were characterized with their close association with production. This symposium played an active part in the transition of China's aviation industry from licence production to design and development.

b. Paying attention to developing a democratic style of academic discussion. At the symposium on aerodynamics 75 pieces of theses were received and 45 pieces were read at group meetings. Among these theses 28 pieces reflected the results of experimental work covering the technical fields of low speed, transonic, supersonic and hypersonic wind tunnel design, instrumentation and test method. The delegates got—together and spoke out freely. On different academic questions they not only listened attentively to other's research results, but also raised doubts and aired their own views without hesitation. Vice Minister of Aviation Industry, Liu Ding and Vice Minister of Astronautic Industry, Qian Xuesen made reports at the symposium stating their own views on certain technical questions. All the delegates present at the symposium felt that they had learnt a great deal. For instance, they gained better results out of discussions or even hotly debating on supersonic wind tunnel air supply, safety problem of high pressure air supply and low pressure air supply.

c. Horizontal exchange and combination of military industry with civil industry. Before the founding of the Society, in general, people only exchanged their scientific research results within their own respective department and organization. There were few opportunities to exchange views beyond their own departments. However the Society is a mass organization consisting of different departments, industries and regions, which is convenient for horizontal exchange and connection. At the workshop on high—energy forming held in 1965 a total number of 200 and more people were present, they were from defence industries, civil industries and transportation departments, aeronautical and local universities and colleges, as well as related research institutes of Academia Sinica. They brought to the workshop technical information and results of 240 explosive forming tests. Through horizontal exchange, the delegates came to know that high—energy forming technique not only had been used increasingly in aircraft and rocket manufacture factories, but also was possible to be used in many civil industrial factories and mines. Finally the meeting put forward "Suggestions on Development of High—energy Forming" which had an active effect on the development and popularization of high—energy forming technique, and on transferring military industrial technique to civil applications.

CSAA restoration period is from 1974 to 1979 . During this period the Society was approved to resume its activities, but there was still a time of turmoil, regular academic exchange activities could not be carried out. In March 1977, the State Council approved the "Report on Restoration and Enhancement of Academic Societies' Work of Defence Industries." From then on the academic exchange activities of the Society revitalized gradually. Since early 1978, four lectures on operational research · and modernization of national defence were organized in succession in Beijing systematically introducing the significance of operational research and system analysis on modernization of national defence, basic method of operational research, general survey of management science and optimum parameter selection of weapon system etc.. Because of ten years' upheaval, research work on military operational research and system engineering was then in backwardness in China. However this discipline was developed rapidly in the world because of its important significance in science and technology, and military engineering. Therefore as soon as the Society first set forward this issue, it attracted the attention of the people from different fields. 2,000 people from departments of the armed services and its three headquarters (i.e. the Headquarters of the General Staff, the General Political Department and the General Logistics Department,) National Defence Science and Technology Commission, and National Defence Industry Office listened to these lectures. Delegates from 48 units attended the workshop on military operational research held in May of the same year. Vice Premier Wang Zhen approved the proposal put forward in the minutes of the workshop, and entrusted Zhang Aiping, Vice Chief of the General Staff to call the Headquarters of the General Staff, Academy of Military Sciences etc. to form a synthetic system analysis and system engineering group of operational research and to actively conduct research work on this subject. The suggestions made at the meeting on establishing system engineering society, starting publication of system engineering journal and forming system engineering research institute were accepted by the departments concerned and put into effect very soon. Afterwards in early 1979, a training course on system engineering / operational research was run. They spent three months to study systematically 14 courses. There were 150 people from more than 70 units in the country took the courses. These academic activities played a role in the development of the new discipline——system engineering / operational research in China.

After the CSAA second national assembly of representatives in 1979, with implementation of the spirit of the Third Plenary Session of the 11th Central Committee of CPC in depth, the policy of respecting knowledge, respecting qualified personnel was put into effect, the aeronautical academic activities entered a thriving period. For several years afterward, the depth and breadth of the content of academic exchanges, vigorous atmosphere of research and rich beneficial results were unprecedented since the founding of the Society. The obvious characteristics were as follows:

a. Items of academic exchanges have been increasing year after year. In 1979 there were 5, in 1980 10, in 1981 23, in 1982 39, in 1983 40, and in 1984 64. During the five years from 1980 to 1984, the Society organized 162 academic activities and received a total amount of 10,272 academic theses of which 7,095 pieces were read at symposia. Altogether 13,989 people took part in these academic activities.

b. Successfully organizing synthetic symposia. The forms used by the Society for academic exchange were mainly to hold middle and small scale workshop with definite topics. But after 1979 through organizing synthetic academic exchange, good results were achieved in reviewing achievements in multi-discipline science research and exchanging experiences. The annual meeting held in 1980 in Shanghai was a synthetic academic symposium which had great influences both at home and abroad. At the meeting 145 pieces (a total of 350 pieces received) of theses on aerodynamics, flight mechanics, structural design and strength, powerplant, avionics and automatic control etc. were exchanged. Present at the meeting were more than 300 delegates from 93 units of the country. Delegates from the American Institute of Aeronautics and Astronautics (AIAA) were also invited to attend the meeting. This activity was a general review and a great motivation of academic exchanges of the Society, and for the first time extended the influence of the Chinese aeronautical field to the outside world.

The symposium "China's Aviation in 2000" held in 1984 in Beijing was another synthetic academic exchange activity of profound significance after Shanghai annual meeting. At the symposium 18 synthetic research reports were exchanged, expounding the development status and the gap of aeronautical science and technology between China and the world in such different specialized disciplines as aerodynamics, structure and strength, powerplant, avionics, technology and materials, and in such different aero products as military aircraft, civil aircraft, helicopter and air to air missile. The symposium predicted the 2000's prospects of the aviation industry and aeronautical science and technology, and put forward direction, target, policy and suggestion for relevant science and technology development. The scope and coverage and the quantity of preparation work for this symposium were unprecedented in the history of aeronautical academic exchanges in China. It marked that CSAA had begun to devote much attention to policy−making study and was an important turning point of the direction for academic activities.

c. Attaching importance to research projects and subjects representing development trend. The first national early warning aircraft conference held in 1984 (150 people attended the meeting and 82 papers were received) was an advisory meeting, which guided in a sense the development of China's early warning aircraft. The academic exchange on composite materials was carried out earlier and more systematically. In 1980, CSAA convened the first national composite material symposium and formed the first technical committee of composites. Afterward CSAA together with the Chinese Society of Aerospace and the Chinese Society of Mechanics unfolded the academic activities in this respect. In recent years composite materials symposium or synthetic annual meeting were held and training courses were run every year. Foreign experts were invited to give lectures. These activities helped unite the relevant experts, scholars and scientific and technical personnel in the country to jointly push forward the development of China's composite science.

d. Paying great attention to contending, exploring and studying new academic ideas. At the symposium on separation flew and vortex movement held in 1984, through lively discussions, the orientation of research on separation flew and vortex movement was clarified. Emphasis should be put on turbulence module, especially on experimental research, and research on mechanism of the forming, developing and breaking of vortex. The symposium also maintained that on the basis of mechanism test and computer simulation research it was neccessary to attach importance to applied research and to solve as much as possible the practical problems for design. No doubt, these ideas were valuable to the relevant leading departments and scientific and technical personnel.

Moreover "illness of the aged aircraft" is a new concept which arose recently all over the world. CSAA convened a symposium specially on this subject in 1984, which probed into the origin, definition, characteristics and category of the "illness of the aged aircraft" on the basis of the actual conditions of Chinese—made aircraft in service. It was considered a pressing research subject both in production and operation and should be carried out as soon as possible.

e.   Emphasizing on the economic results in society. For example, the article "An Applied Research on the Substitution of Chemical Fibre for Cotton in Aeronautical Textile" delivered at the second aircraft safety and air rescue workshop summed up many years' experience in this respect, and concluded that in air rescue product, using polyvinyl fibre water—proof cloth instead of cotton cloth, using polyvinyl fibre rope instead of cotton rope will save 4 million Chinese Yuan. If this will be extentively used in every sector of the country, even more economic results will be gained.

The workshop on the development of civil aircraft held in 1986 was of important practical significance. This workshop was to probe into the policy for development of civil aircraft, in the light of vigorous growth of national economy, insufficiency of transportation means and great needs for CAAC airline, general aviation and civil aircraft. All the departments concerning scientific research, production, operation and foreign trade of civil aircraft in the whole country, as well as the State Science and Technology Commission, the State Planning Commission and the State Economic Commission all dispatched people to attend the workshop. There were 95 delegates representing 35 organizations. 58 papers were read. The meeting suggested to energetically develop the civil aviation as an important measure for speeding up the modernization of the nation's transportation system. It suggested that the Government should support the aviation industry in policy and funds, and set up administrative organ to coordinate the research, manufacture, operation, safety assurance and air traffic control of the national civil aviation.

Regional societies of aeronautics and astronautics in the whole country did a lot of work in helping local production and technical departments to tackle technical problems, propagate scientific and technological results and carry on scientific and technological consultations and services etc.. For example, Jiangsu Society of Aeronautics and Astronautics helped the Armed Forces to solve technical problems of using glass fiber rotors on remote—controlled helicopter; Liaoning Society of Aeronautics and Astronautics organized technical personnel to tackle difficult technical problems of mine explosive bomb, flame cutting, boiler soot cleaning agent; Shanghai Aeronautics and Astronautics Society organized the tackling of technical problems on circular NC tracer milling machine and automatic hydrautic elevator; Beijing Aerospace Society provided consultation service on electroplating without cyanide to factories; Jiangxi Society of Aeronautics and Astronautics arranged academic exchanges centralizing on development of new product. They all made good results in the above mentioned activities.

During this period, CSAA and some regional societies of aeronautics and astronautics also ran many kinds of short—term training classes and helped aeronautical scientific and technical personnel to gain new knowledge. Almost 1,000 people attended respectively 13 training classes on fracture mechanics, micro processor, modern cybernetics etc. run by Beijing Aerospace Society and 14 training classes on finite element and algorithmic language run by Jiangsu Society of Aeronautics and Astronautics. More practical study classes such as aeroengine life definition training class, composite material class for advanced studies and technical training class on satellite ground station etc. were all greatly appreciated.

In order to exchange academic research results and academic theses, CSAA created "Acta Aeronautica et Astronautica Sinica" in 1965, which was a quarterly for internal circulation at first, but later changed to bimonthly. CSAA stopped publication of the journal in the "cultural revolution". After resuming publication in 1977, according to practical needs of academic exchange, CSAA changed the journal to an unrestricted publication in 1979. In 1980, English abstracts and illustration titles were added, and the journal began to be circulated abroad. Professors Wang Derong, Lu Shijia and He Qingzhi were successively chief editor of this journal. "Acta Aeronautica et Astronautica Sinica" is a useful tool of academic activities in Chinese aeronautical field. By the end of 1986, 44 issues of the journal were edited and more than 600 pieces of theses and articles were published. Through this journal not only academic research results were timely exchanged, but also some outstanding talents were discovered and cultivated. In addition, to promote academic exchange, CSAA compiled and printed two annual documents i.e. "A Collection of the Thesis Titles" and "A Collection of the Thesis Abstracts" and proceedings of some theses of conferences and symposia.

Section 3 Popular Science Work

It is an important task for CSAA to popularize aeronautical knowledge to the vast masses, especially the youngsters. Since the founding of CSAA, varied activities have been unfolded in popular science, which were well received.

1. Vigorously Carrying Out Summer Camp Activities

CSAA paid much attention to popularizing aeronautical knowledge to the youngsters and fostering their love of China's aviation undertaking. As early as the mid 1960s, CSAA organized aeronautical summer camp activities for the youngsters in Beijing, Xi'an, Shenyang etc.. Being approved by the State in 1978, the national youngster aviation summer camp was sponsored jointly in Beijing by CAST, the Ministry of Education, the State Physical Culture and Sports Commission and the Preparatory Committee of the 10th National Congress of the Communist Youth League. This was an activity of great influence. Participating in this activity were 300 excellent middle school students from 23 nationalities in 29 provinces, municipalities and autonomous regions of the whole country, including those of Taiwan origin. Vice Premier Wang Zhen presented the camp flag at the opening ceremony of the summer camp. The camp arranged for the youngsters rich and varied activities including scientific lectures, visits, viewing and emulating aeronautical physical culture and sports, making model airplane, travelling over the capital by airplane and holding discussions with air force combat heroes and noted personages in aeronautical field. All these activities kindled the youngsters' enthusiasm for studying modern aeronautical science and technology and fostered the youngsters' fine style to love science, study science and use science. In 1984, CSAA ran the national youngsters' aeronautical summer camp of which the scale and the participant numbers were the largest since the founding of new China. 5,000 youngsters of 13 nationalities from 24 provinces, municipalities and autonomous regions took part in the camp activities, and there were about 400 activity counsellers. The camp was divided into Beijing, Shanghai, Jiangsu, Jiangxi, Liaoning, Shaanxi, Heilongjiang, Hunan, Guizhou and Sichuan etc. ten camp regions. The activities included: visiting aeronautical universities and colleges, factories and airports, holding popular science lectures with video tapes, movies and slides, making model planes and conducting competition of model plane demonstration, as well as travelling by plane and glider, and parachute jumping. In 1985 and 1986, CSAA also organized flight training summer camp for university students. All these activities produced good results in society. Each summer camp not only exerted an edifying influence of aeronautical science on the youngsters but also educated them in patriotism and socialism. Many campers said with feeling, "We cherish our aspirations to fly to the blue sky over our motherland. We want to be pioneers of a new generation to vitalize China's aviation cause."

2. Organizing Popular Science Lectures and Study Classes

In unfolding popular science, CSAA often helped cadres, workers and staff renew their knowledge through organizing lectures and study classes, popularizing and spreading new science and technology. Beginning from 1975, CSAA organized teachers and scientific and technological personnel of aeronautical universities and colleges to give lectures on popular aeronautical knowledge in Shaanxi, Jiangsu, Guizhou, Liaoning, Beijing and Sichuan etc. six provinces and municipalities. They went to more than 60 factories, offices, and units of armed forces to hold 260 lectures within two years. Cadres, workers and officers and men of the PLA attending the lectures amounted to 50,000 people. Topics of the lectures were: a. introduction of elementary knowledge of airplane, helicopter, aeroengine, rocket and missile; b. introduction of more than ten topics of new technology, new technical knowledge, such as numerical control technique, electrochemical machining, electro-spark technique, static pressure technique, new technologies of cyanogenless electroplating and machining, as well as elementary fracture mechanics etc. At the end of each lecture, technical discussions between the speaker and the audience were arranged. Meanwhile in connection with these lectures, technical films were shown more than 150 times with an audience of more than 170 thousand people.

After 1979, the Society's popular science work greatly developed. To meet the needs of the leading cadres and scientific and technical personnel at all levels for renewing their knowledge, CSAA and fraternal societies jointly ran a TV program of popular system engineering lecture,

Japanese Express Course and English Express Course for scientific and technical cadres, and micro—computer study class. About 1,000 and more scientific and technical personnel in the whole country participated in these activities. Most of them were scientific and technical backbones ranked higher than engineer and the leading cadres of factories and research institutes. Beginning from 1982, CSAA held nonperiodic scientific and technological lectures, the contents of which included system engineering, emulation technique, composite material and flight simulator and so on, and organized film week of popular aeronautical science many times. In addition, Sichuan and Heilongjiang societies of aeronautics and astronautics held friendly get—together of aeronautical and astronautical personnel, and scientific and technical summer camp providing good opportunities for the society members to exchange their experiences. All the above popular science activities had a strong appeal to the vast aeronautical, astronautical scientific and technical personnel as well as the youngsters.

3.   Putting On an Exhibition and Aerospace Knowledge Quiz

Aeronautical exhibition and quiz are popular science activities. In October 1981, CSAA put on in Beijing Children's Palace a model aircraft exhibition and model airplane and model warship materials fair, including simple paper models, micro models and wooden models the total of which were more than 300. More than 35,000 men—times visited the fair. 3 / 4 of the visitors were youngsters. CSAA and Beijing Aerospace Society jointly ran Beijing Xidan aeronautical popular science gallery. The popular aviation science gallery exhibited in 1982, with civil aviation serving "four modernizations" as its main theme gained the second place of the first class prize for excellent popular science work from Beijing Municipal Government. Both the popular aviation science gallery exhibited in 1983, with modern military airplane as its theme and the popular aviation science exhibition in 1984, with the ancient people's contributions to aeronautical technology won the first place of the top—grade prize for excellent popular science display from Beijing Municipal Government.

To celebrate the 35th anniversary of the founding of the People's Republic of China, the editorial board of "China Encyclopedia, Volume of Aeronautics and Astronautics," CSAA, Chinese Society of Aerospace jointly sponsored Chinese Aeronautical and Astronautical Picture Show which reproduced the arduous course of China's aviation industry from small to big, from licence production to design and development of aircraft. This was a big picture show which introduced to the public both at home and abroad Chinese aeronautical and astronautical undertakings for the first time since the founding of new China. This show brought many people's attention, and the number of visitors amounted to 60,000 men—times. These aero exhibits were also shown in Jiangsu, Shaanxi, Guizhou, and Northeastern regions.

In 1985, with the support of CAST, National Defense Science, Technology and Industry Commission, Ministry of Aviation Industry, the Air Force, Navy, CAAC, Ministry of Space Industry and BIAA, CSAA prepared to construct permanent CSAA Beijing Aerospace Hall which would be located in BIAA. Its basic task was to popularize aerospace science to society and, as a window of CSAA, to display the development of China's aerospace undertaking both at home and abroad, as well as to serve the teaching of BIAA. After finishing the first phase of construction two 600 square meters indoor exhibition halls and one 8,500 square meters outdoor exhibition area were built up. In October 1986, parts of the exhibition halls and area were formally opened to the public.

In order to popularize aerospace science and technology, train reserve forces for aeronautical and astronautical undertakings and celebrate the 35th anniversary of the founding of aviation industry and the 30th anniversary of the founding of space industry, CSAA and "Chinese Youth", "Aviation Times" and "Aerospace Knowledge" jointly sponsored the first national youth aerospace knowledge quiz in July 1986. About 56,000 pieces of test papers were received successively from provinces, municipalities and autonomous regions of the country and abroad. On December 27, 1986, the prize—giving ceremony was held in Beijing. The fact shows that knowledge quiz is a good form for propagation of popular science and extension of the influences of CSAA and its publications.

4. Popular Science Publications

"Aerospace Knowledge" is a monthly magazine of aerospace popular science, which started publication in 1958 and was compiled and published by BIAA before the founding of CSAA. Its content includes the basic knowledge of aeronautical and astronautical science and technology, the achievements in aeronautical and astronautical fields of China and the whole world, as well as introduction of flying sports and figures of aeronautical and astronautical fields. Total quantity of publication of the magazine amounted to 32 million copies. Before 1966 there was international exchange of aeronautical publications between China and Japan, U.K., G.D.R. etc., but CSAA was forced to stop publication of the magazine for seven years during the "cultural revolution." Beginning from 1978 the exchanges of aeronautical and popular science publications with foreign countries were resumed. Up to 1980, there were about ten thousand copies of the magazine sold in U.S., Japan, Southeast Asia, and Hong Kong and Macao regions besides the copies sold in China. In more than twenty years "Aerospace Knowledge" has made remarkable achievements in developing popular aeronautical science. It has become a bridge leading the vast youngsters readers to be interested in and love aerospace. Owing to reading this magazine for a long time many youngsters have been gradually fostered to love aerospace, then made their minds to devote themselves to China's aeronautical and astronautical undertakings. This magazine was praised in the national congresses of CAST, CSAA and Chinese Association of Popular Science Workers. Fang Yi, member of the Political Bureau of the Party's Central Committee autographed "With Soaring Aspirations" and presented it to the editorial board of the magazine, encouraging them to run their publications even better. In 1985, the first international aviation organization of the world — Federation Aeronautique Internationale (FAI) decided to award "Aerospace Knowledge" a prize of honor, commending the efforts made by the magazine to popularize aeronautical and astronautical knowledge to the masses. Prize–awarding ceremony was conducted at FAI Congress which was held in November of the same year in New Delhi, capital of India. Vice chief editor of the magazine, Xie Chu was invited to attend the congress and receive the prize. This was the first time for this international organization to award prize to China and it was also the first of Chinese popular science magazines to win the international prize.

In 1982, in order to meet the needs of the youngsters for model airplane activity, CSAA and Chinese Association of Flying Sports co–sponsored a new popular science magazine — "Model Airplane." This magazine is bimonthly published both at home and abroad.

In addition, CSAA worked out collection of aero slides "Airplanes of Every Description," recommended the Defense Industry Press to compile and publish popular science books such as "What Kind of Body Must a Pilot Have?" "Helicopter", and in cooperation with film studio compiled and produced "Wing Parachute", "Aerospace Summer Camp" and "Flying Out of the Earth" etc..

Section 4 International Association

To carry out academic exchanges between CSAA and foreign academic organizations and scientific and technical personnel is an effective way to promote mutual understanding between scientists of different countries and learn from each other.

1. Establishing Contact with Foreign Aeronautical Academic Organizations

Since 1979 CSAA has established contact with the societies of U.K., U.S.A. and Japan. ICAS is a united aeronautical academic organization of the largest scale in the world. In August 1982, CSAA sent a delegation headed by Wang Nanshou to attend the 13th ICAS conference and since then it became an official plenipotentiary member of ICAS. Wang Nanshou was a member of ICAS. In September 1984, CSAA delegation headed by Ji Wenmei attended an international conference held by ICAS in France. Ji Wenmei was nominated for a member of ICAS academic committee. After beginning contact with AIAA, CSAA sent three delegations in 1980, including scientific and technical leading cadres and scientists from the Ministry of Aviation Industry, Ministry of Space Industry, Air Force, CAAC and so on to attend respectively three U.S. academic conferences and visit 27 relevant agencies one after another. The delegations also extensively contacted American people in aeronautical field, thus furthered understanding of American aerospace scientific research, production and education. In September of the same year, CSAA invited AIAA 22–member delegation to attend Shanghai synthetic academic annual meeting. After the meeting the delegation visited in groups aeronautical factories, scientific research institutions and universities and colleges in the Southwest, the Northwest and the Northeast areas. The Chinese and American sides signed a memorandum on continuation of exchange between the two societies.

At the invitation of CSAA, a Delegation of Japanese Aerospace Society came to visit China in April 1980. They visited relevant Chinese scientific research and education units and held academic lectures and seminars in Beijing, Shenyang and Shanghai. The Chinese and Japanese sides also reached an agreement on the channel and form for the continuation of exchange between the two societies. In November 1982, CSAA delegation paid a return visit to Japan. Apart from this, CSAA also established contact with the Royal Aeronautical Society (RAS), and French and Italian aeronautical academic organizations.

2. Organizing International Academic Conferences

Under the sponsorship of CSAA and CSM an International Fracture Mechanics Symposium was held in Beijing in November 1983. Attending the symposium were 160 delegates among them 43 were respectively from Canada, F.R.G., France, Ireland, Holland, Poland, U.K., U.S.A., Japan, and Hong Kong region. Some well-known figures of international fracture mechanics circle were present at the symposium. Chinese and foreign delegates read 132 papers comprehensively expounding the research status and development trend of elastic and elastic-plastic fracture mechanics, engineering applications and test method of fracture mechanics, fatigue and fracture micro-mechanism and non metallic fracture etc.. The quality of Chinese papers and organizational work of the symposium were praised by foreign colleagues. Chinese delegates also commended this symposium for its beneficial results.

Fig. 114   Foreign expert lecturing in China

In September 1985, CSAA together with American Society of Mechanical Engineer (ASME) and CATIC sponsored Beijing International Gas Turbine Conference and Exposition. Attending the conference and displaying their products were about 600 scholars and firms from China, U.S.A., U.K., France, F.R.G., Japan, Canada, Switzerland, Sweden, Holland, Belgium, Denmark, Egypt, Pakistan, Singapore, Hong Kong etc. 16 countries and region. At the conference 154 pieces of papers were exchanged, of which 75 pieces were Chinese. Apart from foreign firms, 12 factories, institutes, universities and colleges of China's aviation industry exhibited their products which attracted attention of Chinese and foreign delegates.

3. Exchanging Visits of Scientific and Technical Personnel between China and Foreign Countries

Since its founding in the 1960s, CSAA positively sent scientific and technical specialists to go abroad to visit, attend international academic conferences, give lectures and investigate. After restoring external activities in 1973, CSAA in cooperation with departments of aviation and space, as well as the Air Force arranged scientific and technical personnel to go abroad for visit and technical investigation, and also organized many seminars and received foreign scientific and technical figures to visit China. During the "cultural revolution", when China was closed to the outside world, these activities opened a valuable window for aeronautical exchanges. After 1978, with the implementation of the open policy CSAA's international exchange developed even more vigorously. In 1979, CSAA invited in succession seven American scholars of Chinese origin to give lectures in China, and received an American Aero Transportation Delegation.

In February 1985, CSAA sent a delegation to attend the 4th international aircraft maintenance conference held in F.R.G.. At the conference a Chinese delegate read an article "Airplane Maintenance in China — A Way to Modernization" which was applauded by the audience. The chairman of the conference commented: "You have made an excellent report with all the information we want to know. It is the first time that rays of China illuminate the rostrum of international maintenance."

Since its founding, CSAA has met with difficulties and setbacks, but under the guidance of the policy of scientific and technical development of the Chinese Communist Party, and the leadership of CAST as well as with the supports of the relevant departments of aviation, space, the Air Force, Navy, CAAC and SPCSC etc., it has now a bright prospect. A celebration of the 20th anniversary of the founding of CSAA was held in February 1984.

Nie Rongzhen, member of the Political Bureau of the Party Central Committee and Vice Chairman of the Military Commission of CCCPC wrote a letter of congratulation saying: "On the occasion of the 20th anniversary of the founding of CSAA, I extend my heartfelt respects to CSAA experts, professors and other comrades concerned for their achievements made through 20 years' hard working, althrough I am not able to join you in the happy celebration. Aerospace undertaking is a very important part of the economic and defense construction of our country, so I hope all the experts and professors work hard together to achieve even more success in opening up a new prospect for our aerospace undertaking, in unfolding internal and external academic exchanges, and make even greater contributions to scientific research, production and operation of aeronautics and astronautics." On February 20th, 1984, CSAA hosted a tea party in Beijing to celebrate the 20th anniversary of the founding of CSAA with an attendance of more than 350 people. Fang Yi, member of the Political Bureau of the Party Central Committee and State Counsillor, Zhou Peiyuan, Vice Chairman of National Committee of Chinese People's Political Consultative Conference and President of CAST, Zhang Aiping, Vice Secretary—general of the Military Commission of CCCPC, State Councillor and Minister of National Defense were invited to be present at the party. At the party leaders and experts of the related departments made congratulatory speeches and wished CSAA even greater successes in promoting theoretical study of aeronautics and astronautics, unfolding internal and external academic exchanges, popularizing aerospace knowledge, and developing intelligence sources. Ji Wenmei, president of the council of CSAA expressed that CSAA will follow the policy of the Party Central Committee that science and technology should serve national economy and according to its characteristics of trans—industry and trans—department mass academic organization it will give full play to its numerous talents and concentrated knowledge to open up a new prospect of CSAA work, so as to serve national defense modernization and national economic construction and add to the prestige of aerospace undertaking of our country.

CONCLUTIONS

Thirty five years — from 1951 to 1986 have passed since the founding of new China's aviation industry. In the long process of history a period of thirty five years is only a twinkling of an eye. However, under the leadership of the Communist Party of China, it has added an unprecedented illustrious chapter to the history of the development of China's aviation industry.

Although the road is tortuous and it has taken double efforts and time to correct erroneous disruption of the Left and overcome the consequences of damages caused by the "cultural revolution", new China's aviation industry has been set up and grown up rapidly with few investment and on the basis of old China's broken industry. It has formed a system of considerable scale, with the combination of scientific research, production and education. It is basically complete with specialities. It has also developed and produced about ten thousand military and civil aircraft of various types which armed the Air Force and Navy, and partly satisfied the needs of internal general aviation and CAAC transportation, and also served as foreign aid to friendly countries. Some aircraft have been exported. The Chinese aviation industry has become an important force of defense and economic construction.

China is a great socialist country with a population of one billion, so she must establish her own independent and powerful aviation industry. As China is also a country with weak economic basis, it is impossible for her to follow exactly other countries, she must take her own paths. It is always an important subject for the founders of aviation industry to detect a way to develop aviation industry with Chinese characteristics. The detection was quite difficult, and cost too much. Lessons were learned, and valuable experience accumulated.

1. To Persist in Concentrating on Self-reliance and Vigorously Importing External Advanced Technology Is a Basic Experience for China to Develop Aviation Industry in Her Own Way

Self-reliance is a foothold of new China's aviation industry and herein lies the fundamental difference to old China's relying on foreign countries to do everything. Self-reliance is not to exclude foreign technology, they are supplementing each other and promoting each other. It was just because of the introduction of foreign advanced technology in the 1950s that China's aviation industry could be established very soon and jumped up and strode into the age of supersonic jet flight. And also just because the introduction of foreign technology was conducted under the guidance of self-reliance and from the very beginning it set up resolutely its own material and technical basis, trained its own technical personnel, raw material, element and parts were supplied mainly by domestic sources, China's aviation industry could withstand severe tests and continue to develop in the early 1960s when one foreign country unilaterally tore up the agreements all of a sudden. On the contrary, it overcame difficulties on its own, and grew up luxuriantly. The experience of history proved that centralizing on self-reliance is a basic policy which the existence and development of China's aviation industry lie on. It is neccessary to avoid two lopsided views so as to correctly carry through this policy: a. To set self—reliance against introduction of foreign technology and attempt to research everything by oneself from the beginning; b. To underestimate one's own capabilities, persist in introducing and copying blindly, but not to conduct one's own research and development, and not to digest and renew imported technology. Both of the two one—sided views were not helpful for raising the starting point of self—reliance and speeding up the development of the aviation industry.

In the contemporary era when aeronautical science and technology are developing with each passing day, competition of the world aviation products is getting acute day by day. To share responsibility for investment and risks through international cooperation in the field of aviation industry, and to share technologies and markets have become the world trend. After the late 1970s, with the implementation of the open policy China's aviation industry began to enter the international market, it met with serious challenges of international competition on the one hand, and on the other hand good conditions appeared for incorporating and using external technology. In this situation it was extremely important to correctly handle the relations between self—reliance and technology import and international cooperation. While vigorously strengthening scientific research, China's aviation industry has already started to develop multi—channel and multi—form technology import as well as scientific and technological cooperation. It began to achieve results of strengthening scientific research capability, improving performance of products and extending export of products. This is a new way for strengthening self—reliance capability, speeding up development of the aviation industry and entering into international market. This way should be followed unflinchingly.

2. To Work Out a Practical Development Plan and Strategy Is an Important Guarantee for Successful Development of the Aviation Industry

How could the aviation industry with high concentration of technologies be built up shortly after the founding of new China on the basis of very weak national economy and technology was to a great extent because of correct policy and stable programme of development. At that time according to an urgent need for strengthening national defense and supporting the Korean War and with the support of the Soviet Union, the State took the aviation industry as a key part of the national construction and defined the development policy of transition from aircraft repair to aircraft manufacture and then further to aircraft design and development, and on this basis a three to five years' development programme was worked out. Owing to the correct strategic plan and great support from other sectors it took only one Five—year Plan or more for the aviation industry to build a new enterprise which could fulfil trial production and mass production of trainers, fighters, transports and helicopters. These equipped the armed forces and laid a solid foundation for future development.

After entering the 1960s, the aviation industry began to shift from licence production to manufacture. Strengthening scientific research and development of new aircraft was put on the important agenda. Moreover in view of the need for enhancing territorial air defense a programme of "three steps" i.e. production, development and exploration for airplane development was arranged. However these important measures for strategic transformation was disrupted by the "cultural revolution". Only after the Third Plenary Session of the 11th Central Committee of the Party in 1978, through bringing order out of chaos, could the aviation industry take the correct path step by step and set an objective of "producing a generation, developing a generation and exploring a generation." But valuable funds and time were lost, thus causing the consequence of "when the new crop is still in the blade and the old stock is all consumed" —— temporary shortage of aero products.

The fact shows that correct development strategy and stable long-term plan are significant to the aviation industry which needs complicated technologies, heavier consumption of funds and longer period of product development. What the development strategy and long-term plan must solve is a question of macro policy decision, such as: position, function, objective of struggle, strategy for development, direction and measures of the adjustment of structure of production and product as well as definition of production policy etc. of the aviation industry in realization of the four modernizations. It is a prerequisite for instituting Five-year Plan and annual plan and micro invigorating of the economy. Any erroneous strategic decision and changeable development programme not only have a bearing on the success of a specific model of aircraft, but also delay the development of the whole aviation industry for several years, or more than ten years or even longer time. Therefore programme and strategy are matters of prime importance, which the decision maker of the aviation industry must exert every effort to consider and solve. After entering new development stage how to sum up the experience and lessons and institute the objective and programme for 2000 according to the development trend of the world aviation industry and the requirements of the internal socialist modernization and from actual condition is an important subject which should be further solved for flourishing aviation industry.

3. **To Persist in Seeking Truth from Facts and Expand Aviation Industry on the Basis of China's National Strength, i.e. Act According to One's Capability, and Cherish High Ambition Are Principles Which the Aviation Industry Must Follow**

From our experience in the past 30 years we can be assured that if we continue to do so, the aviation industry will successfully develop. Otherwise we will meet setbacks. At the initial stage of its development in the 1950s, the aviation industry strictly observed the principles formulated by the Central Government, concentrated its strength, guaranteed the key project, esteemed science and proceeded in an orderly way and step by step, so it developed rapidly and smoothly. In the period of readjustment of the 1960s, the excessive long front of capital construction and trial production was resolutly shortened, excellent quality of new type of aircraft and engineering development were ensured, so the situation regained the initiative very soon and the aviation industry reappeared thrivingly. At the new stage of development in the 1980s, the aviation industry stressed on " cutting short the battle front, making the key point stand out, vigorously promoting scientific research and updating quickly the products," it took on a new aspect. These three stages are better stages in the history of the aviation industry development. The advantages of these stages lie in practically and realistically handling the interrelations between the aeronautical industries development and the national economic development, taking care to unify needs and possibility, task and condition, advancing with steady steps and doing a job in a down-to-earth manner. On the contrary, during the " big leap forward" and the " cultural revolution" , under the influence of Left mistakes appeared enormous and impracticable plan, too much high target and arbitrary and unpractical directions. The quantity of production and technical requirements were too high beyond the national strength and capability of scientific and technological facilities. In the end, many types of products and projects already started were forced to stop, brought about a big leap and a sharp fall. This wasted both money and time, thus causing great losses. Experience proved that before the start or stop of an important production project or construction project full technical and economic study had to be conducted. Once the task is defined, technical target should be frozen. It is not allowed to go on "Non stop upgrading of the technical target." Only in so doing can the aviation industry advance.

4. To Uphold That Scientific Research Leads Other Things and to Speed Up Development of New Aircraft Are Key Points for the Aviation Industry to Keep Its Strong Vitality and Competitiveness

Immediately after implementing the transition from repair to manufacture in the mid 1950s, China's aviation industry started establishing scientific and technological institutions and began to design new airplane. In the early 1960s, the Chinese Aeronautical Establishment was formed, and new progress of engineering development of aircraft was continuously made. Just when production of the aviation industry had considerable scale, focal points of the work and investment shifted to scientific research, the aviation industry suffered much from the "cultural revolution" . Moreover at that time people lacked profound understanding of the law of aeronautical scientific research, and management system of scientific research and production changed many times. At the same time the third line (inland area) production bases construction was in full swing, making the production scale of the aviation industry extend still further, but scientific research was not strengthened as a key point, thus leading to weak scientific research capability and slow development of new products. This was a lesson of the development of aviation industry.

· Historical experience shows us that in handling relations between scientific research and production, it is necessary to uphold that scientific research starts before other things; When production has certain scale, it is necessary to shift promplty the focal point of work to strengthening scientific research. After the National Science Convention and the Third Plenary Session of the 11th Central Committee held in 1978, the aviation industry summed up its historical experience in this respect, put forward the policy of scientific research advancing before other things, and decided to shift the focal point of work from expanding production to enhancing scientific research and promoting development of new aircraft, the situation started to change for the better, and a new aspect appeared. People became aware that scientific research advancing before other things is an objective law of the development of the aviation industry and the principle which must be followed when the aviation industry proceeded from licence production to design.

In development of aeronautical scientific research it is also necessary to handle well the relations between advanced development and engineering development. Well advanced development and sufficient technical base are prerequisites for successful progress of engineering development. In the condition of insufficient technical base, if engineering development is forced to start, many technical problems will surely come up. This will certainly prolong development cycle. This has been proved by the experiences of numerous engineering development projects. Therefore after the transition from licence production to research and development, the aviation industry must give priority to vigorously strengthen advanced development. Meanwhile, advanced development must be oriented towards the target of the aviation industry, following the trend of development of the world aeronautical science and technology. The result of the advanced development should be applied to engineering development promptly, so as to effectively improve aircraft performance.

To put scientific research before other things requires a long—term programme of aeronautical research and development, suitable organizations of systems engineering management and sufficient research and test facilities. Furthermore, technical reformation of factories and research institutes must be done in a planned way. In a word, it is necessary to make scientific and technological progress a motive force for the development of the aviation industry. Only in this way can the strategic policy that economic development relys on science and technology and scientific and technological work caters to economic development be really carried through, scientific research be flourished and production be expanded.

5. To Improve Product Quality, Economic Benefits, Management and Capability of Enterprises Is the Basis for the Healthy Development of the Aviation Industry

Two fluctuations in quality of product have been experienced in the history of new China's aviation industry. People have become aware from this bitter experience that product quality is of exceptional importance to the aviation industry.

Through many year's efforts, quality control of the aviation industry developed greatly: from stressing on inspection of products to combining prevention with inspection and putting prevention first; from quality control mainly in the process of production to quality control in overall process of research and development, design, test, production, even product support; from quality control of product itself to examination and supervision of technical standards and production conditions, promotion of technical reformation and strict observation of relevant rules and regulations; from stressing on the final acceptance of the whole airplane to producing excellent products including airframe, engine, airborne equipment and armament system through coordinated activities of different departments and enterprises. In these developments quality legislation and quality supervision were gradually completed, quality responsibility was intensified and system of rewards and penalties became strict, so as to promote the development of total quality control.

On the basis of summing these experiences, to raise continuously quality control level by making use of good internal and external methods and sticking to high standards and strict demands, and to further carry out reformation and improve management and administration, thus making enterprises more commercial and with good quality of product and high economic benefits is an important task for the future of the aviation industry.

6. **To Stick to the Cooperation with Basic Industries for Developing Aircraft and Its Accessory Products As a Whole Is an Essential Requirement for Speeding Up the Development of the Aviation Industry**

Aircraft is a complicated system which assembles various kinds of scientific results and is an outcome of vigorous cooperation between the relevant departments of national economy. Soon after the founding of the aviation industry, the State arranged complete construction of aircraft and aeroengine, airborne equipment, armament, ground facilities, raw materials, elements and parts factories, at the same time organized basic industries, such as metallurgical, chemical, electronic, machine—building, building materials and textile etc. industries to support and cooperate with the aviation industry, thus forming gradually an industrial network for completion of aircraft. In the 1970s, to counter the problem of " incomplete provision of accessories" in research and development of new airplane, the State again put forward "five complete—set" demands, i.e. design as a complete set, trial production as a complete set, production as a complete set, product certification as a complete set and delivery as a complete set, thus promoting the technical progress of the accessory products and basic industries. After entering new stage of development the aviation industry enforced system engineering management in the development of new aircraft. In light of aircraft system, with the Ministry of Aviation Industry in the lead, unification and cooperation between industrial departments, regional scientific research and production organizations were organized, so that close interdependent and mutual assistance relations between aircraft manufacturers and accessory producers, and between the aviation industry and the basic industries were established. Just because superiorities of socialist system, coordinations of all the activities of the nation as in a chess game became possible and the relevant industries cooperated to overcome many difficulties, then the development of aircraft as a complete set could be realized. This is the important reason why China's aviation industry has actual strength.

Of course stressing on internal development as a complete set does not exclude necessary import from the international market. In the world of today, when science and technology expand extraordinarily rapidly, to purchase advanced accessory products from the international market to equipt aircraft is an important measure to increase performances of aircraft and one of the forms to promote internal technical progress. In the aircraft export in the 1980s, China already used this method and obtained good results. This should be taken as an important technical policy which will be applied to future development of new aircraft, in particular, development of civil aircraft. It is self—evident that while purchasing and importing foreign products, we must learn their technology and gradually make these products by ourselves.

7. To Persist in Combination of Aero Products with Nonaero Products and Facing Internal and External Markets Is the Policy Which Must Be Enforced for the Vitalization of the Aviation Industry

After the Third Plenary Session of the 11th Central Committee, the aviation industry underwent readjustment and reform, there were mainly two transforms: In guiding line of developmend, the transform from the combination of military products with civil products, with military products as the mainstay to the combination of military products with civil products, with civil products as the mainstay; In economic structure, the transform from product economy to planned commodity economy. This is a profound strategic transform. Through this transform the aviation industry will walk out of " the little world" of military industrial production and head for the "large battle field" of "four modernizations", and really set up new structure of combination of military with civil production. With its superiorities and specialities it not only serves the national defence construction, but also serves the development of civil aviation, the technical reform of the national economy, the light industry market and export. It takes time and a great deal of hard work to realize this transformation though there is a good beginning. It is mainly: to further readjust structure of product while ensuring development and production of military aircraft, to vigorously develop civil aircraft, nonaero products, transplant military technology to civil application, aero technology to nonaero application, to actually readjust scientific research and production capabilities, concentrate on forming new enterprise groups or research and development centres with capabilities of developing new products; to further restructure the management making enterprises economic entities and self managed etc.. After readjustment and reform, departments of the aviation industry should become not only a powerful backing of national defense construction, but also an equipment supplier for the development of civil aviation and technical reformation of national economy and a mainforce of earning foreign exchange through export. This is the objective of the development of the aviation industry.

8. To Vigorously Initiate Education and Foster All Kinds of Personnel for the Development of the Aviation Industry

At the very beginning of its construction, the aviation industry set up universities and colleges while building factories, trained personnel while expanding production, grasped both the training of senior specialists and the training of technical and professional workers and staff, and encouraged the enterprise to initiate education. With a series of these methods it trained a large quantity of various kinds of personnel forming a considerabe amount of workers and staff with a complete set of specialities to meet the requirements of the aviation industry development.

After entering the new stage of development, the aviation industry came up into a new situation, facing country's modernization drive, facing the world and facing the future, the importance and strategic position of education were even more conspicuous. The aviation industry needs all kinds of aeronautical universities and colleges to cultivate high qualified personnel. They should have both ability and political integrity, and be determined to devote themselves to China's aviation industry and do their jobs in a down—to—earth manner. In addition, to keep abreast of the rapidly renewal of knowledge requires running in—service education to constantly improve the quality of the masses of leading cadres, technical and managerial personnel, and skilled workers. Therefore, the development of the aviation industry must further rely on education, and aeronautical education must conform to this requirement to conduct readjustment and reformation.

9. **To Persist in Ideological and Political Work, So As to Constantly Enhance Socialist Initiative and Sense of Duty of the Workers and Staff and Foster Fine Style of Work Is a Basic Construction of the Aviation Industry**

The aviation industry of socialist China is not only for material production but also for educating people. Therefore the aviation industry always considers building up fine ways of thinking of the workers and staff an important task. Many years' practice has shown that in this work the following combinations must be taken care of: the combination of regular education of patriotism, collectivism, socialism and communism with the education of situation and task, principle and policy, democracy and legal system, and organization and discipline; combination of common ideological education with the education of professional ideal, professional morality, professional skill and professional discipline; combination of ideological and political work with the concrete work of scientific research, production and construction. It is especially important to foster the revolutionary ideal of devotion to aviation, the spirit of duty of serving the people, the self—consciousness of "quality first" and the strong will of building an enterprise through arduous effort and bravely climbing new heights of science and technology. Once the contingents of workers and staff have good ideological quality and become high—spirited, they will not be frightened when meeting with difficulties in scientific research, production and construction, but they can advance bravely to overcome the difficulties.

After entering the new stage of development under the new circumstances of socialist modernizations, and opening to the outside world and revitalizing the national economy many new problems have arisen in the cultivation of fine ideology and working style. At the important historical time, it is necessary to ensure the contigent to take over from the old generation and expand not only science and technology, but also their fine ideology and work style. The new generation should be not only specialists of all walks of life and skilled workers, but also creators who uphold the four cardinal principles and devote themselves to reform, the open policy and revitalizing economy. They should become well educated, self–disciplined citizens with high ideals and moral integrity, maintain political stability and unity and dedicate to the aviation cause and "four modernizations" of their motherland. In conformity with the new circumstances and demands, the importance of ideological and political work and its task are even more outstanding.

The thirty five years' career of the aviation industry is a mirror which refects progress and setbacks, exprience and lesson. People can see that the achievements made in aviation industry is enormous, but compared with the advanced world level, the aviation industry still has a long way to go. Recognition of this gap may be turned into the motive force of advance. New generation of the builders of the aviation industry is confident of creating a completely new future.

Under the leadership of the Communist Party of China the Chinese people are carrying out socialist modernization construction. The objective of struggle of the people is to triple the GNP of 1980 by the end of this century, thus enabling the people to lead a fairly well–to–do life and by the middle of the next century to reach the level of the moderately developed countries in terms of per capita GNP. At that time the Chinese people will be better–off and the modernization will be basically accomplished. This is a magnificent goal. The development of China's aviation industry should accord with and serve this general objective.

China is a country with a vast territory, where the aviation development has a broad prospect. Civil air transportation of new China has developed greatly, especially after opening to the outside world at the end of the 1970s. With the vigorous development of economy from the 1980s to the 1990s China's air transportation and general aviation for agriculture, forestry, animal husbandry, subsidiary occupations, industry and mining will increase speedily. The civil aircraft fleet needs to be increased and replaced in great quantity. At the same time modernization of national defense and development of foreign trade also need high performance aircraft. Before the year 2000, the gap between the supply and demands of aircraft in the country will become extremely obvious. To suit the circumstances,China's aviation industry will make full use of the favourable conditions brought up by the open policy, to vigorously strengthen scientific research and actively develop international cooperation, so as to further speed up the process of replacing the old aircraft with new ones. Development of civil aircraft will be placed on an important position with stress on trunk route aircraft of civil aviation and expanding accordingly commuter aircraft, general–aviation aircraft and helicopter to constantly provide CAAC with safe, economic and comfortable civil aircraft and make contributions to the development of traffic and transportation and promotion of the growth of economy. The aviation industry will also research and develop military aircraft of high performance step by step and in the order of importance and urgency to continuously provide the People's Liberation Army with good military equipment. In the meantime it will further bring its technical superiority and scientific research and productive capability into full play, take an active part in the study of national high technology and serve the development of national economy, foreign trade and export. In fulfilling these tasks China's aviation industry will be constantly expanding, strengthening and improving.

The aviation industry is charged with heary tasks for enhancing national defense and rejuvenation of economy. To support the development of the aviation industry is the consistent policy of the Communist Party of China and the People's Government. Under the guidance of the policy of reform, opening to outside world and revitalizing economy with the support of the people in the country and through the efforts made by all the workers and staff of the aviation industry, China's aviation industry will advance with firm steps, serve the four modernizations of the country with its great successes and contribute to the world aviation.

Prospects of China's aviation industry are magnificent!

POSTSCRIPT

To help more people abroad understand Chinese aviation industry and its achievements and capabilities, to promote technical and economical exchange and cooperation between China and foreign countries, the editorial board of the book " China Today: Aviation Industry" decided to publish an English version of the book.

Compared with the original Chinese text, the English version has very little alterations: a section of the new development in international cooperation of the Chinese aviation industry written by Gu Delin, Hua Runxi and Feng Shaozhou has been added, while some paragraphs and a few sections of little interest to our foreign readers have been omitted.

The translation and publishing of the English version have first won the support and commend from the minister of Aero—Space Industry, Mr. Lin Zongtang and vice ministers Jiang Xiesheng and He Wenzhi, and also assistance and cooperation from the Chinese Social Science Press and the Editorial Board of China Today Series. Their authorization made the publication possible.

Under the organization of the China Aero—Technology Translation Corporation, the translators finished the translation of the book in only three months in the hottest Summer time.

Four foreign friends Ms. Susan Bates from Rolls Royce, Ms. Anna Greenwood and Mr. Tim Glogan from British Aerospace, and Mr. Paul C.K. Sun from General Electric read some parts of the manuscript and their corrections and suggestions are especially valuable for the improvement of our translation. We express our heartfelt thanks to them for their help.

The translation and publishing of the English edition are sponsored by the Senior Technology Development & Consultancy Ltd. in Beijing with the cooperation and assistance from the China National Aero—Technology Import and Export Corp, The Bureau of International Cooperation and The Office of Information of the Ministry of Aero—Space Industry, The China Aero—Information Center and The Science Commission of the East City District of Beijing.

Here we acknowledge the contributions made directly or indirectly to the translation and publication of the book by all individuals or organizations.

We are sure that there is still much to improve in the translation which was done in such a short time, and what's more, our English is not what as we desired. We will be obliged for any criticism and suggestion as to the English translation.

Editorial Board
China Today : Aviation Industry
English Edition

December 1988

INDEX

AIRCRAFT

AEROENGINE

MISSILE

AIRBORNE EQUIPMENT

Gunsight

China Today :　Aviation Industry

English Edition

Published by the China Aviation Industry Press

Printed by Beijing Xinhua Printing House

first edition, 1989. (787 × 1092mm, 1 / 16)

Overseas Distribution : Senior Technology Development
&　Consultancy Ltd., STEDCO
(5 Liang Guo Chang Road, East City District, Beijing, China)
ISBN 7−80046−159−9 / V · 031